SQL Server Query Performance Tuning

Fourth Edition

Grant Fritchey

SQL Server Query Performance Tuning

ISBN-13 (pbk): 978-1-4302-6743-0

ISBN-13 (electronic): 978-1-4302-6742-3

Trademarked names, logos, and images may appear in this book. Rather than use a trademark symbol with every occurrence of a trademarked name, logo, or image we use the names, logos, and images only in an editorial fashion and to the benefit of the trademark owner, with no intention of infringement of the trademark.

The use in this publication of trade names, trademarks, service marks, and similar terms, even if they are not identified as such, is not to be taken as an expression of opinion as to whether or not they are subject to proprietary rights.

While the advice and information in this book are believed to be true and accurate at the date of publication, neither the authors nor the editors nor the publisher can accept any legal responsibility for any errors or omissions that may be made. The publisher makes no warranty, express or implied, with respect to the material contained herein.

Publisher: Heinz Weinheimer
Lead Editor: Jonathan Gennick
Technical Reviewer: Joseph Sack
Editorial Board: Steve Anglin, Mark Beckner, Ewan Buckingham, Gary Cornell, Louise Corrigan,
    Jim DeWolf, Jonathan Gennick, Robert Hutchinson, Michelle Lowman, James Markham,
    Matthew Moodie, Jeff Olson, Jeffrey Pepper, Douglas Pundick, Ben Renow-Clarke, Dominic Shakeshaft,
    Gwenan Spearing, Matt Wade, Steve Weiss
Coordinating Editor: Jill Balzano
Copy Editor: Kim Wimpsett
Compositor: SPi Global
Indexer: SPi Global
Artist: SPi Global
Cover Designer: Anna Ishchenko

Distributed to the book trade worldwide by Springer Science+Business Media New York, 233 Spring Street, 6th Floor, New York, NY 10013. Phone 1-800-SPRINGER, fax (201) 348-4505, e-mail orders-ny@springer-sbm.com, or visit www.springeronline.com.

For information on translations, please e-mail rights@apress.com, or visit www.apress.com.

Apress and friends of ED books may be purchased in bulk for academic, corporate, or promotional use. eBook versions and licenses are also available for most titles. For more information, reference our Special Bulk Sales–eBook Licensing web page at www.apress.com/bulk-sales.

Any source code or other supplementary materials referenced by the author in this text is available to readers at www.apress.com. For detailed information about how to locate your book's source code, go to www.apress.com/source-code/.

Contents at a Glance

Contents

About the Author

Grant Fritchey, SQL Server MVP, works for Red Gate Software, a market-leading software-tools vendor, as its product evangelist. He's done development of large-scale applications in languages such as VB, C#, and Java, and he has worked in SQL Server since version 6.0. In addition, he has worked in insurance, finance, and consulting, as well as for three failed dot coms. He is the author of *SQL Server Execution Plans* (Simple Talk Publishing, 2012) and *SQL Server 2012 Query Performance Tuning* (Apress, 2012). Grant is a coauthor of *Beginning SQL Server 2012 Administration* (Apress, 2012) and has one chapter in *SQL Server MVP Deep Dives Volume 2* (Manning, 2011) and *Pro SQL Server 2012 Practices* (Apress 2012). Grant travels and presents on various SQL Server topics at large conferences and small user groups around the world.

About the Technical Reviewer

Joseph Sack (SackHQ.com) is an independent consultant based in Minneapolis, Minnesota. With more than 17 years of experience in the industry, Joe is a consultant, author, speaker, SQL MVP, and SQL Server Microsoft Certified Master specializing in performance tuning, high availability, and disaster recovery. His latest publication is the Microsoft white paper "Optimizing Your Query Plans with the SQL Server 2014 Cardinality Estimator."

Acknowledgments

I realize I might be repeating myself, but certain things do bear repeating. Book writing, hard. Thank the gods I don't have to do this alone. Jonathan Gennick of Apress tried to convince me that the book needed an update, but I talked him out of it. Then we talked some more, and I realized he was right. Thanks for your patience and trust taking me down this path again, Jonathan. I found myself on my knees begging Joe Sack to be my tech editor again. This is as much his book as it is mine. Thanks for all your patient instruction, Joe. As before, anything that's wrong with this book is not from anything that you did. Thanks.

While I don't work there anymore, I learned so much at FM Global that I still need to give them credit for helping to build me, which helped to build this book.

Finally, thanks to the family for putting up with me going through this process again. Special thanks to my wife Michele for her help with some of the graphics.

—Grant Fritchey

Introduction

After all the years of work on SQL Server by Microsoft and all the work put in by talented data professionals, you'd think that fundamental performance problems would be a thing of the past, but they're not. Performance is frequently one of the last things on people's minds when they're developing a system. Unfortunately, that means it usually becomes the biggest problem after that system goes to production. You can't simply rely on getting a phone call that tells you that procedure X on database Y that runs on server Z is running *slow*. You need to have mechanisms in place to find this information for yourself. You also can't work off the general word slow. Slow compared to what? Last week? Last month? The way it ran in your development system? And once you've identified something as actually running slow, you need to identify why. Does it need an index? Does it have an index that it isn't using? Is it the CPU, the disk, the memory, the number of users, the amount of data? And now that you've identified what and why, you have to do something about it. How? Rewrite the query? Change the WHERE clause? The questions that will come your way when you start performance tuning are endless.

This book provides you with the tools you need to answer those questions. I'll show you how to set up mechanisms for collecting performance metrics on your server for the SQL Server instances and databases living there. I'll go over the more tactical methods of collecting data on individual T-SQL calls. Along the way, I'll be discussing index structure, choice, and maintenance; how best to write your T-SQL code; how to test that code; and a whole slew of other topics. One of my goals when writing this book was to deliver all these things using examples that resemble the types of queries you'll see in the real world. The tools and methods presented are mostly available with SQL Server Standard edition, although some are available only with SQL Server Enterprise edition. These are called out whenever you might encounter them. Almost all the tuning advice in the book is directly applicable to Microsoft Azure SQL Database (MASD), as well as to the more earthbound SQL Server 2014. Most of the tuning advice in the book is also immediately applicable to servers running within virtual machines (VMs). The primary differences for both MASD and VMs relate to what performance metrics you can collect and how much trust to put in them. The performance solutions that are code and structure related are immediately applicable to both these environments.

An argument can be made that a lot of the fundamentals for query tuning have not changed radically from SQL Server 2008 to 2012 to 2014. Therefore, the need for a new, updated version of this book may not be immediately clear. What has changed over those various releases of SQL Server is where queries run, what metrics are available to understand the system, and what tools you have available to tune your queries. The point of this latest update to the book, in addition to adding information about the new functionality available within SQL Server 2014, is to clarify the types of information and responses available on those other environments. I've taken the opportunity to completely restructure and rename the chapters. Several new chapters have been introduced, allowing me to both expand the scope of the material within the book and make it much easier to consume.

The main point is to learn how to answer all the various questions that are going to be presented to you. This book gives you the tools to do that and to answer those questions in a methodical manner that eliminates much of the guesswork that is so common in performance optimization today. Performance problems aren't something to be feared. With the right tools, you can tackle performance problems with a calmness and reliability that will earn the respect of your peers and your clients. That will contribute directly to your success and theirs.

Who This Book Is For

This book is for just about anyone responsible for the performance of the system. Database administrators, certainly, are targeted because they're responsible for setting up the systems, creating the infrastructure, and monitoring it over time. Developers are too, because who else is going to generate all the well-formed and highly performant T-SQL code? Database devel-opers, more than anyone, are the target audience, if only because that's what I do for work. Anyone who has the capability to write T-SQL, design tables, implement indexes, or manipulate server settings on the SQL Server system is going to need this information to one degree or another.

How This Book Is Structured

The purpose of this book was to use as many "real-looking" queries as possible. To do this, I needed a "real" database. I could have created one and forced everyone to track down the download. Instead, I chose to use the sample database created by Microsoft, called AdventureWorks2012. This is available through CodePlex (www.codeplex.com/ MSFTDBProdSamples). I suggest keeping a copy of the restore handy and resetting your sample database after you have read a couple of topics from the book. Microsoft updates these databases over time, so you might see different sets of data or different behavior with some of the queries than what is listed in this book. I chose AdventureWorks2012 not because it represents a perfect database design but because it suffers from a number of design flaws and data distribution issues that make it more accurately reflect the real world instead of some flawless test case.

To a degree, this book builds on the knowledge presented from previous chapters. However, most of the chapters present information unique within that topic, so it is possible for you to jump in and out of particular chapters. You will still receive the most benefit by a sequential reading of Chapter 1 through Chapter 26.

- Chapter 1, "SQL Query Performance Tuning," introduces the iterative process of performance tuning. You'll get a first glimpse at establishing a performance baseline, identifying bottlenecks, resolving the problems, and quantifying the improvements.

- Chapter 2, "Memory Performance Analysis," starts the process using Performance Monitor metrics and dynamic management objects as mechanisms for collecting information about memory on your systems.

- Chapter 3, "Disk Performance Analysis," continues exploring the system of bottlenecks with a chapter dedicated to understanding how to collect metrics on disk performance. You'll use Performance Monitor and dynamic management objects again as well as add a number of additional T-SQL queries.

- Chapter 4, "CPU Performance Analysis," concludes the system bottleneck discussions with CPU. I'll also cover some network monitoring, although that is a fairly rare issue within SQL Server, and there's little a DBA or developer can do about it usually. The tools used are the same as in the preceding chapters.

- Chapter 5, "Creating a Baseline," takes the information from all three of the preceding chapters and uses it to define a baseline. A baseline represents a known point in your system from which you can compare to understand how performance is changing over time within your system.

- Chapter 6, "Query Performance Metrics," defines the best ways to look "under the hood" and see what kinds of queries are being run on your system. It provides a detailed look at the new Extended Events tools. Several of the most useful dynamic management views and functions used to monitor queries are first identified in this chapter.

- Chapter 7, "Analyzing Query Performance," walks you through consuming the metrics gathered in the previous chapter and shows various methods available to analyze query performance. You're introduced for the first time to query execution plans as well as other utilities available within SQL Server for determining which queries are longest running, most frequently called, or in need of tuning.

- Chapter 8, "Index Architecture and Behavior," explains indexes and index architecture. It defines the differences between clustered and nonclustered indexes. It shows which types of indexes work best with different types of querying. Basic index maintenance is also introduced.

- Chapter 9, "Index Analysis," adds to the information from the preceding chapter and supplies more information about the use and functionality of indexes within SQL Server.

- Chapter 10, "Database Engine Tuning Advisor," covers the Microsoft tool Database Engine Tuning Advisor. The chapter goes over in detail how to use the Database Engine Tuning Advisor; you're introduced to the various mechanisms for calling the tool and shown how it works under real loads.

- Chapter 11, "Key Lookups and Solutions," takes on the classic performance problem, the key lookup, which is also known as the bookmark lookup. This chapter explores various solutions to the lookup operation.

- Chapter 12, "Statistics, Data Distribution, and Cardinality," introduces the concept of statistics. The optimizer uses statistics to make decisions regarding the execution of the query. Maintaining statistics, understanding how they're stored, learning how they work, and learning how they affect your queries are all topics covered within this chapter.

- Chapter 13, "Index Fragmentation," shows how indexes fragment over time. You'll learn how to identify when an index is fragmented. You'll also see what happens to your queries as indexes fragment, and you'll learn mechanisms to eliminate index fragmentation.

- Chapter 14, "Execution Plan Generation," presents the mechanisms that SQL Server uses to create execution plans. Plan reuse is an important concept within SQL Server. You'll learn how to identify whether plans are being reused. You'll get various mechanisms for looking at the cache. This chapter also introduces dynamic management views that allow excellent access to the cache.

- Chapter 15, "Execution Plan Cache Behavior," covers information about how plans move in and out of cache as well as other details about execution plan behaviors including query and plan hash and your ability to reuse execution plans in cache.

- Chapter 16, "Parameter Sniffing," explains the extremely helpful process running automatically within SQL Server called parameter sniffing. But, parameter sniffing can go bad and cause serious performance issues. The problem, and the solutions, all go back to system statistics.

- Chapter 17, "Query Recompilation," displays how and when SQL Server will recompile plans that were stored in cache. You'll learn how plan recompiles can hurt or help the performance of your system. You'll pick up mechanisms for forcing a recompile and for preventing one.

- Chapter 18, "Query Design Analysis," reveals how to write queries that perform well within your system. Common mistakes are explored, and solutions are provided. You'll learn several best practices to avoid common bottlenecks.

- Chapter 19, "Reduce Query Resource Use," demonstrates various methods to ensure you're using fewer resources such as CPU and I/O when running your queries. You'll learn about a number of antipatterns that you should avoid while writing your T-SQL.

- Chapter 20, "Blocking and Blocked Processes," teaches the best ways to recognize when various sessions on your server are in contention for resources. You'll learn how to monitor for blocking along with methods and techniques to avoid blocked sessions.

- Chapter 21, "Causes and Solutions for Deadlocks," shows how deadlocks occur on your system. You'll get methods for identifying sessions involved with deadlocks. The chapter also presents best practices for avoiding deadlocks or fixing your code if deadlocks are already occurring.

- Chapter 22, "Row-by-Row Processing," diagrams the inherent costs that cursors present to set-oriented T-SQL code. However, when cursors are unavoidable, you need to understand how they work, what they do, and how best to tune them within your environment if eliminating them outright is not an option.

- Chapter 23, "Memory-Optimized OLTP Tables and Procedures," introduces the new capabilities of in-memory data storage and retrieval. You'll also see how the in-memory stored procedure can radically change performance in a positive fashion. But, this technology isn't universally applicable, so I'll also go over some of the limitations and best practices for applicability.

- Chapter 24, "Database Performance Testing," provides you with mechanisms to replicate the performance of your production system onto test systems in order to help you validate that the changes you've introduced to your queries really are helpful. You'll be using the Distributed Replay utility, introduced in SQL Server 2012, along with all the other tools you've been using throughout the book.

- Chapter 25, "Database Workload Optimization," demonstrates how to take the information presented in all the previous chapters and put it to work on a real database workload. You'll identify the worst-performing procedures and put them through various tuning methods to arrive at better performance.

- Chapter 26, "SQL Server Optimization Checklist," summarizes all the preceding chapters into a set of checklists and best practices. The goal of the chapter is to enable you to have a place for quickly reviewing all you have learned from the rest of the book.

Downloading the Code

You can download the code examples used in this book from the Source Code section of the Apress web site (www.apress.com). Most of the code is straight T-SQL stored in .sql files, which can be opened and used in any SQL Server T-SQL editing tool. There are a couple of PowerShell scripts that will have to be run through a PowerShell command line.

Contacting the Author

You can contact the author, Grant Fritchey, at grant@scarydba.com. You can visit his blog at http://scarydba.com.

CHAPTER 1

■ ■ ■

SQL Query Performance Tuning

Query performance tuning remains an important part of today's database applications. Yes, hardware performance is constantly improving. Upgrades to SQL Server—especially to the optimizer, which helps determine how a query is executed, and the query engine, which executes the query—lead to better performance all on their own. At the same time, SQL Server instances are being put on virtual machines, either locally or in hosted environments, where the hardware behavior is not guaranteed. Databases are going to platform as a service systems such as Amazon RDS and Windows Azure SQL Database. You still have to deal with fundamental database design and code generation. In short, query performance tuning remains a vital mechanism for improving the performance of your database management systems. The beauty of query performance tuning is that, in many cases, a small change to an index or a SQL query can result in a far more efficient application at a very low cost. In those cases, the increase in performance can be orders of magnitude better than that offered by an incrementally faster CPU or a slightly better optimizer.

There are, however, many pitfalls for the unwary. As a result, a proven process is required to ensure that you correctly identify and resolve performance bottlenecks. To whet your appetite for the types of topics essential to honing your query optimization skills, the following is a quick list of the query optimization aspects I cover in this book:

- Identifying problematic SQL queries

- Analyzing a query execution plan

- Evaluating the effectiveness of the current indexes

- Avoiding bookmark lookups

- Evaluating the effectiveness of the current statistics

- Understanding parameter sniffing and fixing it when it breaks

- Analyzing and resolving fragmentation

- Optimizing execution plan caching

- Analyzing and avoiding statement recompilation

- Minimizing blocking and deadlocks

- Analyzing the effectiveness of cursor use

- Applying in-memory table storage and procedure execution

- Applying performance-tuning processes, tools, and optimization techniques to optimize SQL workloads

Before jumping straight into these topics, let's first examine why we go about performance tuning the way we do. In this chapter, I discuss the basic concepts of performance tuning for a SQL Server database system. It's important to have a process you follow in order to be able to find and identify performance problems, fix those problems, and document the improvements you've made. Without a well-structured process, you're going to be stabbing in the dark, hoping to hit a target. I detail the main performance bottlenecks and show just how important it is to design a database-friendly application, which is the consumer of the data, as well as how to optimize the database. Specifically, I cover the following topics:

- The performance tuning process
- Performance versus price
- The performance baseline
- Where to focus efforts in tuning
- The top 13 SQL Server performance killers

What I don't cover within these pages could fill a number of other books. The focus of this book is on T-SQL query performance tuning, as the title says. But, just so you're clear, there will be no coverage of the following:

- Hardware choices
- Application coding methodologies
- Server configuration (except where it impacts query tuning)
- SQL Server Integration Services
- SQL Server Analysis Services
- SQL Server Reporting Services
- PowerShell

The Performance Tuning Process

The performance tuning process consists of identifying performance bottlenecks, prioritizing the identified issues, troubleshooting their causes, applying different resolutions, and quantifying performance improvements—and then repeating the whole process again and again. It is necessary to be a little creative, since most of the time there is no one silver bullet to improve performance. The challenge is to narrow down the list of possible causes and evaluate the effects of different resolutions. You can even undo previous modifications as you iterate through the tuning process.

The Core Process

During the tuning process, you must examine various hardware and software factors that can affect the performance of a SQL Server–based application. You should be asking yourself the following general questions during the performance analysis:

- Is any other resource-intensive application running on the same server?
- Is the capacity of the hardware subsystem capable of withstanding the maximum workload?
- Is SQL Server configured properly?

- Does the shared environment, whether VM or platform, have adequate resources, or am I dealing with a configuration issue there or even resource contention from outside forces?

- Is the database connection between SQL Server and the database application efficient?

- Does the database design support the fastest data retrieval (and modification for an updatable database)?

- Is the user workload, consisting of SQL queries, optimized to reduce the load on SQL Server?

- What processes are causing the system to slow down as reflected in the measurement of various wait states, performance counters, and dynamic management objects?

- Does the workload support the required level of concurrency?

If any of these factors is not configured properly, then the overall system performance may suffer. Let's briefly examine these factors.

Having another resource-intensive application on the same server can limit the resources available to SQL Server. Even an application running as a service can consume a good part of the system resources and limit the resources available to SQL Server. For example, applications may be configured to work with the processor at a higher priority than SQL Server. *Priority* is the weight given to a resource that pushes the processor to give it greater preference when executing. To determine the priority of a process, follow these steps:

1. Launch Windows Task Manager.

2. Select View ➤ Select Columns.

3. Select the Base Priority check box.

4. Click the OK button.

These steps will add the Base Priority column to the list of processes. Subsequently, you will be able to determine that the SQL Server process (`sqlservr.exe`) by default runs at Normal priority, whereas the Windows Task Manager process (`taskmgr.exe`) runs at High priority. Therefore, to allow SQL Server to maximize the use of available resources, you should look for all the nonessential applications/services running on the SQL Server machine and ensure they are not acting as resource hogs.

Improperly configuring the hardware can prevent SQL Server from gaining the maximum benefit from the available resources. The main hardware resources to be considered are processor, memory, disk, and network. If the capacity of a particular hardware resource is small, then it can soon become a performance bottleneck for SQL Server. While I'm not covering hardware choices, as a part of tuning queries, you do need to understand how and where you may see performance bottlenecks because of the hardware you have. Chapters 2, 3, and 4 cover some of these hardware bottlenecks in detail.

You should also look at the configuration of SQL Server, since proper configuration is essential for an optimized application. There is a long list of SQL Server configurations that defines the generic behavior of a SQL Server installation. These configurations can be viewed and modified using a system stored procedure, sys.configurations. Many of these configurations can also be managed interactively through SQL Server Management Studio.

Since the SQL Server configurations are applicable for the complete SQL Server installation, a standard configuration is usually preferred. The good news is that, generally, you need not modify the majority of these configurations; the default settings work best for most situations. In fact, the general recommendation is to keep most SQL Server configurations at the default values. I discuss the configuration parameters in detail throughout this book and make a few recommendations for changing some. The same thing applies to database options. The default settings on the model database are adequate for most systems. You should probably adjust autogrowth settings from the defaults, but many of the other properties, such as autoclose or autoshrink, should be left off, while others, such as the automatic creation of statistics, should be left on in most circumstances.

If you're running inside of some hosted environment, you might be sharing a server with a number of other virtual machines or databases. In some cases, you can work with the vendor or your local administrators to adjust the settings of these virtual environments to help your SQL Server instance perform better. But, in many circumstance you'll have little to no control over the behavior of the systems at all. You'll need to work with the individual platform to determine when you're hitting limits on that platform that could also be causing performance issues.

Poor connectivity between SQL Server and the database application can hurt application performance. One of the questions you should ask yourself is, how good is the database connection? For example, the query executed by the application may be highly optimized, but the database connection used to submit this query may add considerable overhead to the query performance. Ensuring that you have an optimal network configuration with appropriate bandwidth will be a fundamental part of your system setup. This is especially true if you're hosting your environments on the cloud.

The design of the database should also be analyzed while troubleshooting performance. This helps you understand not only the entity-relationship model of the database but also why a query may be written in a certain way. Although it may not always be possible to modify an in-use database design because of wider implications on the database application, a good understanding of the database design helps you focus in the right direction and understand the impact of a resolution. This is especially true of the primary and foreign keys and the clustered indexes used in the tables.

The application may be slow because of poorly built queries, the queries might not be able to use the indexes, or perhaps even the indexes themselves are inefficient or missing. If any of the queries are not optimized sufficiently, they can seriously impact other queries' performance. I cover index optimization in depth in Chapters 8, 9, 11, 12 and 13. The next question at this stage should be, is a query slow because of its resource intensiveness or because of concurrency issues with other queries? You can find in-depth information on blocking analysis in Chapter 20.

When processes run on a server, even one with multiple processors, at times one process will be waiting on another to complete. You can get a fundamental understanding of the root cause of slowdowns by identifying what is waiting and what is causing it to wait. You can realize this through operating system counters that you access through dynamic management views within SQL Server and through Performance Monitor. I cover this information in Chapters 2–4 and in Chapter 20.

The challenge is to find out which factor is causing the performance bottleneck. For example, with slow-running SQL queries and high pressure on the hardware resources, you may find that both poor database design and a nonoptimized query workload are to blame. In such a case, you must diagnose the symptoms further and correlate the findings with possible causes. Because performance tuning can be time-consuming and costly, you should ideally take a preventive approach by designing the system for optimum performance from the outset.

To strengthen the preventive approach, every lesson that you learn during the optimization of poor performance should be considered an optimization guideline when implementing new database applications. There are also proven best practices that you should consider while implementing database applications. I present these best practices in detail throughout the book, and Chapter 26 is dedicated to outlining many of the optimization best practices.

Please ensure that you take the performance optimization techniques into consideration at the early stages of your database application development. Doing so will help you roll out your database projects without big surprises later.

Unfortunately, we rarely live up to this ideal and often find database applications needing performance tuning. Therefore, it is important to understand not only how to improve the performance of a SQL Server–based application but also how to diagnose the causes of poor performance.

Iterating the Process

Performance tuning is an iterative process where you identify major bottlenecks, attempt to resolve them, measure the impact of your changes, and return to the first step until performance is acceptable. When applying your solutions, you should follow the golden rule of making only one change at a time where possible. Any change usually affects other parts of the system, so you must reevaluate the effect of each change on the performance of the overall system.

As an example, adding an index may fix the performance of a specific query, but it could cause other queries to run more slowly, as explained in Chapters 8 and 9. Consequently, it is preferable to conduct a performance analysis in a test environment to shield users from your diagnosis attempts and intermediate optimization steps. In such a case, evaluating one change at a time also helps in prioritizing the implementation order of the changes on the production server based on their relative contributions. Chapter 24 explains how to automate testing your database and query performance.

You can keep on chipping away at the performance bottlenecks you've determined are the most painful and thus improve the system performance gradually. Initially, you will be able to resolve big performance bottlenecks and achieve significant performance improvements, but as you proceed through the iterations, your returns will gradually diminish. Therefore, to use your time efficiently, it is worthwhile to quantify the performance objectives first (for example, an 80 percent reduction in the time taken for a certain query, with no adverse effect anywhere else on the server) and then work toward them.

The performance of a SQL Server application is highly dependent on the amount and distribution of user activity (or workload) and data. Both the amount and distribution of workload and data usually change over time, and differing data can cause SQL Server to execute SQL queries differently. The performance resolution applicable for a certain workload and data may lose its effectiveness over a period of time. Therefore, to ensure an optimum system performance on a continuing basis, you need to analyze system and application performance at regular intervals. Performance tuning is a never-ending process, as shown in Figure 1-1.

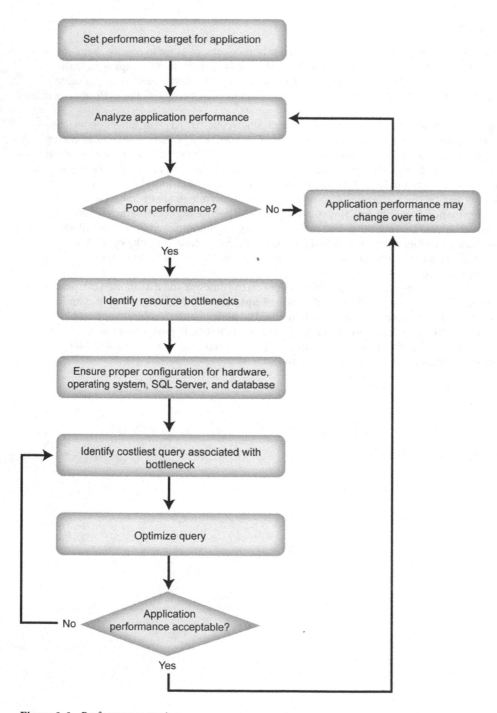

Figure 1-1. *Performance tuning process*

You can see that the steps to optimize the costliest query make for a complex process, which also requires multiple iterations to troubleshoot the performance issues within the query and apply one change at a time. Figure 1-2 shows the steps involved in the optimization of the costliest query.

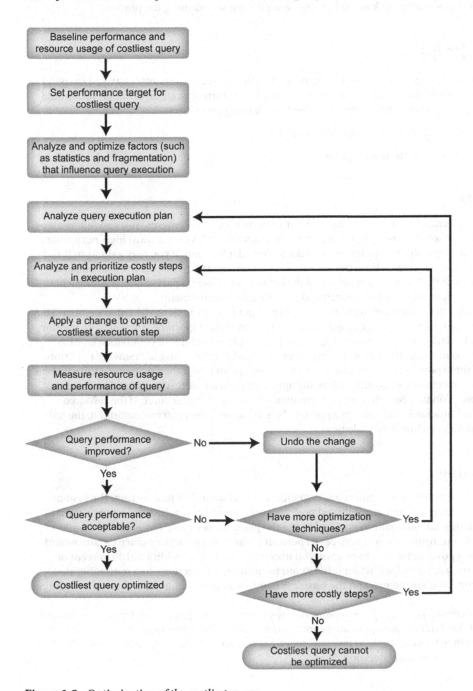

Figure 1-2. *Optimization of the costliest query*

As you can see from this process, there is quite a lot to do to ensure that you correctly tune the performance of a given query. It is important to use a solid process like this in performance tuning to focus on the main identified issues.

Having said this, it also helps to keep a broader perspective about the problem as a whole, since you may believe one aspect is causing the performance bottleneck when in reality something else is causing the problem.

Performance vs. Price

One of the points I touched on earlier is that to gain increasingly small performance increments, you need to spend increasingly large amounts of time and money. Therefore, to ensure the best return on your investment, you should be very objective while optimizing performance. Always consider the following two aspects:

- What is the acceptable performance for your application?
- Is the investment worth the performance gain?

Performance Targets

To derive maximum efficiency, you must realistically estimate your performance requirements. You can follow many best practices to improve performance. For example, you can have your database files on the most high-performance disk subsystem. However, before applying a best practice, you should consider how much you may gain from it and whether the gain will be worth the investment. Those performance requirements are usually set by someone else, either the application developers or the business consumers of the data. A fundamental part of query tuning will involve talking to these parties to determine a good enough and realistic set of requirements.

Sometimes it is really difficult to estimate the performance gain without actually making the enhancement. That makes properly identifying the source of your performance bottlenecks even more important. Are you CPU, memory, or disk bound? Is the cause code, data structure, or indexing, or are you simply at the limit of your hardware? Do you have a bad router, a poorly configured I/O path, or an improperly applied patch causing the network to perform slowly? Be sure you can make these possibly costly decisions from a known point rather than guessing. One practical approach is to increase a resource in increments and analyze the application's scalability with the added resource. A scalable application will proportionately benefit from an incremental increase of the resource, if the resource was truly causing the scalability bottleneck. If the results appear to be satisfactory, then you can commit to the full enhancement. Experience also plays an important role here.

"Good Enough" Tuning

Instead of tuning a system to the theoretical maximum performance, the goal should be to tune until the system performance is "good enough." This is a commonly adopted performance tuning approach. The cost investment after such a point usually increases exponentially in comparison to the performance gain. The 80:20 rule works very well: By investing 20 percent of your resources, you may get 80 percent of the possible performance enhancement, but for the remaining 20 percent possible performance gain, you may have to invest an additional 80 percent of resources. It is therefore important to be realistic when setting your performance objectives. Just remember that "good enough" is defined by you, your customers, and the business people you're working with. There is no standard to which everyone adheres.

A business benefits not by considering pure performance but by considering the price of performance. However, if the target is to find the scalability limit of your application (for various reasons, including marketing the product against its competitors), then it may be worthwhile to invest as much as you can. Even in such cases, using a third-party stress test lab may be a better investment decision.

Performance Baseline

One of the main objectives of performance analysis is to understand the underlying level of system use or pressure on different hardware and software subsystems. This knowledge helps you in the following ways:

- Allows you to analyze resource bottlenecks.

- Enables you to troubleshoot by comparing system utilization patterns with a preestablished baseline.

- Assists you in making accurate estimates in capacity planning and scheduling hardware upgrades.

- Aids you in identifying low-utilization periods when the database administrative activities can best be executed.

- Helps you estimate the nature of possible hardware downsizing or server consolidation. Why would a company downsize? Well, the company may have leased a very high-end system expecting strong growth, but because of poor growth, they now want to downsize their system setups. And consolidation? Companies sometimes buy too many servers or realize that the maintenance and licensing costs are too high. This would make using fewer servers very attractive.

- Some metrics make sense only when compared to previously recorded values. Without that previous measure you won't be able to make sense of the information.

Therefore, to better understand your application's resource requirements, you should create a baseline for your application's hardware and software usage. A *baseline* serves as a statistic of your system's current usage pattern and as a reference with which to compare future statistics. Baseline analysis helps you understand your application's behavior during a stable period, how hardware resources are used during such periods, and the characteristics of the software. With a baseline in place, you can do the following:

- Measure current performance and express your application's performance goals.

- Compare other hardware or software combinations against the baseline.

- Measure how the workload and/or data changes over time.

- Ensure that you understand what "normal" is on your server so that an arbitrary number isn't misinterpreted as an issue.

- Evaluate the peak and nonpeak usage pattern of the application. This information can be used to effectively distribute database administration activities, such as full database backup and database defragmentation during nonpeak hours.

You can use the Performance Monitor that is built into Windows to create a baseline for SQL Server's hardware and software resource utilization. You can also get snapshots of this information by using dynamic management views and dynamic management functions. Similarly, you may baseline the SQL Server query workload using Extended Events, which can help you understand the average resource utilization and execution time of SQL queries when conditions are stable. You will learn in detail how to use these tools and queries in Chapters 2-5.

Another option is to take advantage of one of the many tools that can generate an artificial load on a given server or database. Numerous third-party tools are available. Microsoft offers SQLIO (available at http://bit.ly/1eRBHiF), which measures the I/O capacity of your system. Microsoft also has SQLIOSim, a tool for generating SQL Server-specific calls and simulated loads (available at http://bit.ly/QtY9mf). These tools primarily focus on the disk subsystem and not on the queries you're running. To do that, you can use the performance testing tool added to SQL Server 2012, Distributed Replay, which is covered at length in Chapter 24.

Where to Focus Efforts

When you tune a particular system, pay special attention to the data access layer (the database queries and stored procedures executed by your code or through your object relational mapping engine or otherwise that are used to access the database). You will usually find that you can positively affect performance in the data access layer far more than if you spend an equal amount of time figuring out how to tune the hardware, operating system, or SQL Server configuration. Although a proper configuration of the hardware, operating system, and SQL Server instance is essential for the best performance of a database application, these fields have standardized so much that you usually need to spend only a limited amount of time configuring them properly for performance. Application design issues such as query design and indexing strategies, on the other hand, are unique to your code and data set. Consequently, there is usually more to optimize in the data access layer than in the hardware, operating system, or SQL Server configuration. Figure 1-3 shows the results of a survey of 346 data professionals (with permission from Paul Randal: http://bit.ly/1gRANRy).

What were the root causes of the last few SQL Server performance problems you debugged?
(Vote multiple times if you want!)

CPU power saving	2%	6
Other hardware or OS issue	2%	7
Virtualization	2%	7
SQL Server/database configuration	3%	10
Out-of-date/missing statistics	9%	31
Database/table structure/schema design	10%	38
Application code	12%	43
I/O subsystem problem	16%	60
Poor indexing strategy	19%	68
T-SQL code	26%	94
	Total: 364 responses	

Figure 1-3. *Root causes of performance problems*

As you can see, the first two issues are T-SQL code and poor indexing. Four of the top six issues are all directly related to the T-SQL, indexes, code, and data structure. My experience matches that of the other respondents. You can obtain the greatest improvement in database application performance by looking first at the area of data access, including logical/physical database design, query design, and index design.

Sure, if you concentrate on hardware configuration and upgrades, you may obtain a satisfactory performance gain. However, a bad SQL query sent by the application can consume all the hardware resources available, no matter how much you have. Therefore, a poor application design can make hardware upgrade requirements very high, even beyond your cost limits. In the presence of a heavy SQL workload, concentrating on hardware configurations and upgrades usually produces a poor return on investment.

You should analyze the stress created by an application on a SQL Server database at two levels:

- *High level*: Analyze how much stress the database application is creating on individual hardware resources and the overall behavior of the SQL Server installation. The best measures for this are the various wait states. This information can help you in two ways. First, it helps you identify the area to concentrate on within a SQL Server application where there is poor performance. Second, it helps you identify any lack of proper configuration at the higher levels. You can then decide which hardware resource may be upgraded if you are not able to tune the application using the Performance Monitor tool, as explained in Chapter 2.

- *Low level*: Identify the exact culprits within the application—in other words, the SQL queries that are creating most of the pressure visible at the overall higher level. This can be done using the Extended Events tool and various dynamic management views, as explained in Chapter 6.

SQL Server Performance Killers

Let's now consider the major problem areas that can degrade SQL Server performance. By being aware of the main performance killers in SQL Server in advance, you will be able to focus your tuning efforts on the likely causes.

Once you have optimized the hardware, operating system, and SQL Server settings, the main performance killers in SQL Server are as follows, in a rough order (with the worst appearing first):

- Insufficient indexing

- Inaccurate statistics

- Improper query design

- Poorly generated execution plans

- Excessive blocking and deadlocks

- Non-set-based operations, usually T-SQL cursors

- Inappropriate database design

- Excessive fragmentation

- Nonreusable execution plans

- Frequent recompilation of queries

- Improper use of cursors

- Improper configuration of the database transaction log

- Excessive use or improper configuration of `tempdb`

Let's take a quick look at each of these issues.

Insufficient Indexing

Insufficient indexing is usually one of the biggest performance killers in SQL Server. In the absence of proper indexing for a query, SQL Server has to retrieve and process much more data while executing the query. This causes high amounts of stress on the disk, memory, and CPU, increasing the query execution time significantly. Increased query execution time then can lead to excessive blocking and deadlocks in SQL Server. You will learn how to determine indexing strategies and resolve indexing problems in Chapters 8-12.

Generally, indexes are considered to be the responsibility of the database administrator (DBA). However, the DBA can't proactively define how to use the indexes, since the use of indexes is determined by the database queries and stored procedures written by the developers. Therefore, defining the indexes must be a shared responsibility since the developers usually have more knowledge of the data to be retrieved and the DBAs have a better understanding of how indexes work. Indexes created without the knowledge of the queries serve little purpose.

■ **Note**   Because indexes created without the knowledge of the queries serve little purpose, database developers need to understand indexes at least as well as they know T-SQL.

Inaccurate Statistics

SQL Server relies heavily on cost-based optimization, so accurate data distribution statistics are extremely important for the effective use of indexes. Without accurate statistics, SQL Server's built-in query optimizer can't accurately estimate the number of rows affected by a query. Because the amount of data to be retrieved from a table is highly important in deciding how to optimize the query execution, the query optimizer is much less effective if the data distribution statistics are not maintained accurately. Statistics can age without being updated. You can also see issues around data being distributed in a skewed fashion hurting statistics. Statistics on columns that auto-increment such as identity or date and time can be out of date as new data gets added. You will look at how to analyze statistics in Chapter 12.

Improper Query Design

The effectiveness of indexes depends in large part on the way you write SQL queries. Retrieving excessively large numbers of rows from a table or specifying a filter criterion that returns a larger result set from a table than is required renders the indexes ineffective. To improve performance, you must ensure that the SQL queries are written to make the best use of new or existing indexes. Failing to write cost-effective SQL queries may prevent SQL Server from choosing proper indexes, which increases query execution time and database blocking. Chapter 20 covers how to write effective queries.

Query design covers not only single queries but also sets of queries often used to implement database functionalities such as a queue management among queue readers and writers. Even when the performance of individual queries used in the design is fine, the overall performance of the database can be very poor. Resolving this kind of bottleneck requires a broad understanding of different characteristics of SQL Server, which can affect the performance of database functionalities. You will see how to design effective database functionality using SQL queries throughout the book.

Poorly Generated Execution Plans

The same mechanisms that allow SQL Server to establish an efficient stored procedure and reuse that procedure again and again instead of recompiling can, in some cases, work against you. A bad execution plan can be a real performance killer. Inaccurate and poorly performing plans are frequently caused when a process called *parameter sniffing* goes bad. Parameter sniffing is a process that comes from the mechanisms that the query optimizer uses to determine the best plan based on sampled or specific values from the statistics. It's important to understand how statistics and parameters combine to create execution plans and what you can do to control them. Statistics are covered in Chapter 12, and execution plan analysis is covered in Chapters 14 and 15. I've added Chapter 16 just to talk about bad parameter sniffing and how best to deal with it.

Excessive Blocking and Deadlocks

Because SQL Server is fully atomicity, consistency, isolation, and durability (ACID) compliant, the database engine ensures that modifications made by concurrent transactions are properly isolated from one another. By default, a transaction sees the data either in the state before another concurrent transaction modified the data or after the other transaction completed—it does not see an intermediate state.

Because of this isolation, when multiple transactions try to access a common resource concurrently in a noncompatible way, *blocking* occurs in the database. Two processes can't update the same piece of data the same time. Further, since all the updates within SQL Server are founded on a page of data, 8KB worth of rows, you can see blocking occurring even when two processes aren't updating the same row. Blocking is a good thing in terms of ensuring proper data storage and retrieval, but too much of it in the wrong place can slow you down.

Related to blocking, but actually a separate issue, a *deadlock* occurs when two resources attempt to escalate or expand locked resources and conflict with one another. The query engine determines which process is the least costly to roll back and chooses it as the *deadlock victim*. This requires that the database request be resubmitted for successful execution. Deadlocks are a fundamental performance problem even though many people think of them as a structural issue. The execution time of a query is adversely affected by the amount of blocking and deadlocks, if any, it faces.

For scalable performance of a multiuser database application, properly controlling the isolation levels and transaction scopes of the queries to minimize blocking and deadlocks is critical; otherwise, the execution time of the queries will increase significantly, even though the hardware resources may be highly underutilized. I cover this problem in depth in Chapters 20 and 21.

Non-Set-Based Operations

Transact-SQL is a set-based scripting language, which means it operates on sets of data. This forces you to think in terms of columns rather than in terms of rows. Non-set-based thinking leads to excessive use of cursors and loops rather than exploring more efficient joins and subqueries. The T-SQL language offers rich mechanisms for manipulating sets of data. For performance to shine, you need to take advantage of these mechanisms rather than force a row-by-row approach to your code, which will kill performance. Examples of how to do this are available throughout the book; also, I address T-SQL best practices in Chapter 18 and cursors in Chapter 22.

Inappropriate Database Design

A database should be adequately normalized to increase the performance of data retrieval and reduce blocking. For example, if you have an undernormalized database with customer and order information in the same table, then the customer information will be repeated in all the order rows of the customer. This repetition of information in every row will increase the number of page reads required to fetch all the orders placed by a customer. At the same time, a data writer working on a customer's order will reserve all the rows that include the customer information and thus could block all other data writers/data readers trying to access the customer profile.

Overnormalization of a database can be as bad as undernormalization. Overnormalization increases the number and complexity of joins required to retrieve data. An overnormalized database contains a large number of tables with a small number of columns. Overnormalization is not a problem I've run into a lot, but when I've seen it, it seriously impacts performance. It's much more common to be dealing with undernormalization or improper normalization of your structures.

Having too many joins in a query may also be because database entities have not been partitioned distinctly or the query is serving a complex set of requirements that could perhaps be better served by creating a new stored procedure.

Database design is a large subject. I will provide a few pointers in Chapter 18 and throughout the rest of the book. Because of the size of the topic, I won't be able to treat it in the complete manner it requires. However, if you want to read a book on database design with an emphasis on introducing the subject, I recommend reading *Pro SQL Server 2012 Relational Database Design and Implementation* by Louis Davidson et al. (Apress, 2012).

Excessive Fragmentation

While analyzing data retrieval operations, you can usually assume that the data is organized in an orderly way, as indicated by the index used by the data retrieval operation. However, if the pages containing the data are fragmented in a nonorderly fashion or if they contain a small amount of data because of frequent page splits, then the number of read operations required by the data retrieval operation will be much higher than might otherwise be required. The increase in the number of read operations caused by fragmentation hurts query performance. In Chapter 13, you will learn how to analyze and remove fragmentation.

Nonreusable Execution Plans

To execute a query in an efficient way, SQL Server's query optimizer spends a fair amount of CPU cycles creating a cost-effective execution plan. The good news is that the plan is cached in memory, so you can reuse it once created. However, if the plan is designed so that you can't plug parameter values into it, SQL Server creates a new execution plan every time the same query is resubmitted with different values. So, for better performance, it is extremely important to submit SQL queries in forms that help SQL Server cache and reuse the execution plans. I will also address topics such as plan freezing, forcing query plans, and using "optimize for ad hoc workloads." You will see in detail how to improve the reusability of execution plans in Chapter 15.

Frequent Recompilation of Queries

One of the standard ways of ensuring a reusable execution plan, independent of values used in a query, is to use a stored procedure or a parameterized query. Using a stored procedure to execute a set of SQL queries allows SQL Server to create a parameterized execution plan.

A *parameterized execution plan* is independent of the parameter values supplied during the execution of the stored procedure or parameterized query, and it is consequently highly reusable. Frequent recompilation of queries increases pressure on the CPU and the query execution time. I will discuss in detail the various causes and resolutions of stored procedure, and statement, recompilation in Chapter 15.

Improper Use of Cursors

By preferring a cursor-based (row-at-a-time) result set—or as Jeff Moden has so aptly termed it, Row By Agonizing Row (RBAR; pronounced "ree-bar")—instead of a regular set-based SQL query, you add a large amount of overhead to SQL Server. Use set-based queries whenever possible, but if you are forced to deal with cursors, be sure to use efficient cursor types such as fast-forward only. Excessive use of inefficient cursors increases stress on SQL Server resources, slowing down system performance. I discuss how to work with cursors properly, if you must, in Chapter 22.

Improper Configuration of the Database Transaction Log

By failing to follow the general recommendations in configuring a database transaction log, you can adversely affect the performance of an online transaction processing (OLTP)–based SQL Server database. For optimal performance, SQL Server heavily relies on accessing the database logs effectively. Chapter 3 covers some aspects of how to configure the database transaction log properly.

Excessive Use or Improper Configuration of tempdb

There is only one `tempdb` for any SQL Server instance. Since temporary storage (such as operations involving user objects such as temporary tables and table variables), system objects such as cursors or hash tables for joins), and operations including sorts and row versioning all use the `tempdb` database, `tempdb` can become quite a bottleneck. All these options and others lead to space, I/O, and contention issues within `tempdb`. I cover some configuration options to help with this in Chapter 3 and other options in other chapters appropriate to the issues addressed by that chapter.

Summary

In this introductory chapter, you have seen that SQL Server performance tuning is an iterative process, consisting of identifying performance bottlenecks, troubleshooting their cause, applying different resolutions, quantifying performance improvements, and then repeating these steps until your required performance level is reached. To assist in this process, you should create a system baseline to compare with your modifications. Throughout the performance tuning process, you need to be objective about the amount of tuning you want to perform—you can always make a query run a little bit faster, but is the effort worth the cost? Finally, since performance depends on the pattern of user activity and data, you must reevaluate the database server performance on a regular basis.

To derive the optimal performance from a SQL Server database system, it is extremely important that you understand the stresses on the server created by the database application. In the next two chapters, I discuss how to analyze these stresses, both at a higher system level and at a lower SQL Server activities level. Then I show how to combine the two.

In the rest of the book, you will examine in depth the biggest SQL Server performance killers, as mentioned earlier in the chapter. You will learn how these individual factors can affect performance if used incorrectly and how to resolve or avoid these traps.

CHAPTER 2

∎ ∎ ∎

Memory Performance Analysis

A system can directly impact SQL Server and the queries running on it in three primary places: memory, disk, and CPU. You're going to explore each of these in turn starting, in this chapter, with memory. Queries retrieving data in SQL Server must first load that data into memory. Any changes to data are first loaded into memory where the modifications are made, prior to writing them to disk. Many other operations take advantage of the speed of memory in the system, from sorting data due to an ORDER BY clause in a query to performing calculations to create hash tables for joining two tables. Because of all this work being done within the memory of the system, it's important that you understand how memory is being managed.

In this chapter I cover the following topics:

- The basics of the Performance Monitor tool

- Some of the dynamic management objects used to observe system behavior

- How and why hardware resources can be bottlenecks

- Methods of observing and measuring memory use within SQL Server and Windows

- Possible resolutions to memory bottlenecks

Performance Monitor Tool

Windows Server 2012 R2 provides a tool called Performance Monitor, which collects detailed information about the utilization of operating system resources. It allows you to track nearly every aspect of system performance, including memory, disk, processor, and the network. In addition, SQL Server 2014 provides extensions to the Performance Monitor tool that track a variety of functional areas within SQL Server.

Performance Monitor tracks resource behavior by capturing performance data generated by hardware and software components of the system, such as a processor, a process, a thread, and so on. The performance data generated by a system component is represented by a performance object. The performance object provides counters that represent specific aspects of a component, such as % Processor Time for a Processor object. Just remember, when running these counters within a virtual machine (VM), the performance measured for the counters in many instances, depending on the type of counter, is for the VM, not the physical server. That means some values collected on a VM are not going to accurately reflect physical reality.

There can be multiple instances of a system component. For instance, the Processor object in a computer with two processors will have two instances, represented as instances 0 and 1. Performance objects with multiple instances may also have an instance called Total to represent the total value for all the instances. For example, the processor usage of a computer with two processors can be determined using the following performance object, counter, and instance (as shown in Figure 2-1):

- *Performance object*: Processor

- *Counter*: % Processor Time

- *Instance*: _Total

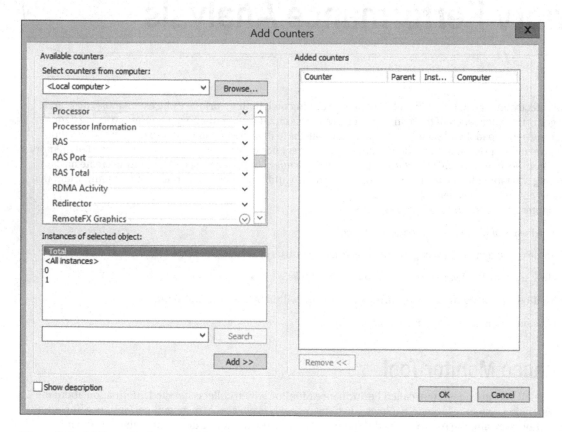

Figure 2-1. *Adding a Performance Monitor counter*

System behavior can be either tracked in real time in the form of graphs or captured as a file (called a *data collector set*) for offline analysis. The preferred mechanism on production servers is to use the file. You'll want to collect the information in a file in order to store it and transmit it as needed over time. Plus, writing the collection to a file takes up fewer resources than collecting it on the screen in active memory.

To run the Performance Monitor tool, execute perfmon from a command prompt, which will open the Performance Monitor suite. You can also right-click the Computer icon on the desktop or the Start menu, expand Diagnostics, and then expand the Performance Monitor. You can also go to the Start screen and start typing **Performance Monitor;** you'll see the icon for launching the application. Any of these methods will allow you to open the Performance Monitor utility.

You will learn how to set up the individual counters Chapter 5. Now that I've introduced the concept of the Performance Monitor, I'll introduce another metric gathering interface, dynamic management objects.

Dynamic Management Objects

To get an immediate snapshot of a large amount of data that was formerly available only in Performance Monitor, SQL Server offers some of the same data, plus a lot of different information, internally through a set of dynamic management views (DMVs) and dynamic management functions (DMFs) collectively referred to as *dynamic management objects* (DMOs). These are extremely useful mechanisms for capturing a snapshot of the current performance of your system. I'll introduce several DMOs throughout the book, but for now I'll focus on a few that are the most important for monitoring server performance and for establishing a baseline.

The sys.dm_os_performance_counters view displays the SQL Server counters within a query, allowing you to apply the full strength of T-SQL to the data immediately. For example, this simple query will return the current value for Logins/sec:

```
SELECT  dopc.cntr_value,
        dopc.cntr_type
FROM    sys.dm_os_performance_counters AS dopc
WHERE   dopc.object_name = 'SQLServer:General Statistics'
        AND dopc.counter_name = 'Logins/sec';
```

This returns the value of 200 for my test server. For your server, you'll need to substitute the appropriate server name in the object_name comparison if you have a named instance. Worth noting is the cntr_type column. This column tells you what type of counter you're reading (documented by Microsoft at http://bit.ly/1mmcRaN). For example, the previous counter returns the value 272696576, which means that this counter is an average value. There are values that are moments-in-time snapshots, accumulations since the server started, and others. Knowing what the measure represents is an important part of understanding these metrics.

There are a large number of DMOs that can be used to gather information about the server. I'll introduce one more here that you will find yourself accessing on a regular basis, sys.dm_os_wait_stats. This DMV shows an accumulated view of the threads within SQL Server that are waiting on various resources, collected since the last time SQL Server was started or the counters were reset. The wait times are recorded after the work is completed, so these numbers don't reflect any active threads. Identifying the types of waits that are occurring within your system is one of the easiest mechanisms to begin identifying the source of your bottlenecks. You can sort the data in various ways; this first example looks at the waits that have the longest current count using this simple query:

```
SELECT  TOP (10) dows.*
FROM    sys.dm_os_wait_stats AS dows
ORDER BY dows.wait_time_ms DESC;
```

Figure 2-2 displays the output.

	wait_type	waiting_tasks_count	wait_time_ms	max_wait_time_ms	signal_wait_time_ms
1	CLR_AUTO_EVENT	9	508535914	254266215	0
2	SLEEP_TASK	14984923	388244213	1140	126909
3	FT_IFTS_SCHEDULER_IDLE_WAIT	4382	265231915	600008	183
4	LOGMGR_QUEUE	1896835	258821422	339	6400
5	DIRTY_PAGE_POLL	2361462	258821409	587	8309
6	QDS_CLEANUP_STALE_QUERIES_TASK_MAIN_LOOP_SLEEP	4314	258820899	60080	121
7	SQLTRACE_INCREMENTAL_FLUSH_SLEEP	64585	258820850	4039	267
8	QDS_PERSIST_TASK_MAIN_LOOP_SLEEP	4314	258820020	60057	161
9	XE_TIMER_EVENT	58212	258815745	5050	258815745
10	REQUEST_FOR_DEADLOCK_SEARCH	51690	258807614	5080	258807614

Figure 2-2. *Output from sys.dm_os_wait_stats*

You can see not only the cumulative time that particular waits have accumulated but also a count of how often they have occurred and the maximum time that something had to wait. From here, you can identify the wait type and begin troubleshooting. One of the most common types of waits is I/O. If you see ASYNC_IO_COMPLETION, IO_COMPLETION, LOGMGR, WRITELOG, or PAGEIOLATCH in your top ten wait types, you may be experiencing I/O contention, and you now know where to start working. For a more detailed analysis of wait types and how to use them as a monitoring tool within SQL Server, read the Microsoft white paper "SQL Server 2005 Waits and Queues" (http://bit.ly/1e1I38f). Although it was written for SQL Server 2005, it is still largely applicable to newer versions of SQL Server. You can always find information about more obscure wait types by going directly to Microsoft through MSDN support (http://bit.ly/1hBzLrZ). Finally, when it comes to wait types, Bob Ward's repository (collected at http://bit.ly/1afzfjC) is a must-read even though it's not being maintained currently.

Hardware Resource Bottlenecks

Typically, SQL Server database performance is affected by stress on the following hardware resources:

- Memory
- Disk I/O
- Processor
- Network

Stress beyond the capacity of a hardware resource forms a bottleneck. To address the overall performance of a system, you need to identify these bottlenecks because they form the limit on overall system performance.

Identifying Bottlenecks

There is usually a relationship between resource bottlenecks. For example, a processor bottleneck may be a symptom of excessive paging (memory bottleneck) or a slow disk (disk bottleneck). If a system is low on memory, causing excessive paging, and has a slow disk, then one of the end results will be a processor with high utilization since the processor has to spend a significant number of CPU cycles to swap pages in and out of the memory and to manage the resultant high number of I/O requests. Replacing the processors with faster ones may help a little, but it is not the best overall solution. In a case like this, increasing memory is a more appropriate solution because it will decrease pressure on the disk and processor. In fact, upgrading the disk is probably a better solution than upgrading the processor. If you can, decreasing the workload could also help, and, of course, tuning the queries to ensure maximum efficiency is also an option.

One of the best ways of locating a bottleneck is to identify resources that are waiting for some other resource to complete its operation. You can use Performance Monitor counters or DMOs such as sys.dm_os_wait_stats to gather that information. The response time of a request served by a resource includes the time the request had to wait in the resource queue as well as the time taken to execute the request, so end user response time is directly proportional to the amount of queuing in a system.

Another way to identify a bottleneck is to reference the response time and capacity of the system. The amount of throughput, for example, to your disks should normally be something approaching what the vendor suggests the disk is capable of. So, measuring information such as disk sec/transfer will indicate when disks are slowing down because of excessive load.

Not all resources have specific counters that show queuing levels, but most resources have some counters that represent an overcommittal of that resource. For example, memory has no such counter, but a large number of hard page faults represents the overcommittal of physical memory (hard page faults are explained later in the chapter in the section "Pages/Sec and Page Faults/Sec"). Other resources, such as the processor and disk, have specific counters to indicate the level of queuing. For example, the counter Page Life Expectancy indicates how long a page will stay in the buffer pool without being referenced. This indicates how well SQL Server is able to manage its memory, since a longer life means that a piece of data in the buffer will be there, available, waiting for the next reference. However, a shorter life means that SQL Server is moving pages in and out of the buffer quickly, possibly suggesting a memory bottleneck.

You will see which counters to use in analyzing each type of bottleneck shortly.

Bottleneck Resolution

Once you have identified bottlenecks, you can resolve them in two ways.

- You can increase resource capacity.
- You can decrease the arrival rate of requests to the resource.

Increasing the capacity usually requires extra resources such as memory, disks, processors, or network adapters. You can decrease the arrival rate by being more selective about the requests to a resource. For example, when you have a disk subsystem bottleneck, you can either increase the capacity of the disk subsystem or decrease the number of I/O requests.

Increasing the capacity means adding more disks or upgrading to faster disks. Decreasing the arrival rate means identifying the cause of high I/O requests to the disk subsystem and applying resolutions to decrease their number. You may be able to decrease the I/O requests, for example, by adding appropriate indexes on a table to limit the amount of data accessed or by writing the T-SQL statement to include more or better filters in the WHERE clause.

Memory Bottleneck Analysis

Memory can be a problematic bottleneck because a bottleneck in memory will manifest on other resources, too. This is particularly true for a system running SQL Server. When SQL Server runs out of cache (or memory), a process within SQL Server (called *lazy writer*) has to work extensively to maintain enough free internal memory pages within SQL Server. This consumes extra CPU cycles and performs additional physical disk I/O to write memory pages back to disk.

SQL Server Memory Management

SQL Server manages memory for databases, including memory requirements for data and query execution plans, in a large pool of memory called the *buffer pool*. The memory pool used to consist of a collection of 8KB buffers to manage memory. Now there are multiple page allocations for data pages and plan cache pages, free pages, and so forth. The buffer pool is usually the largest portion of SQL Server memory. SQL Server manages memory by growing or shrinking its memory pool size dynamically.

You can configure SQL Server for dynamic memory management in SQL Server Management Studio (SSMS). Go to the Memory folder of the Server Properties dialog box, as shown in Figure 2-3.

21

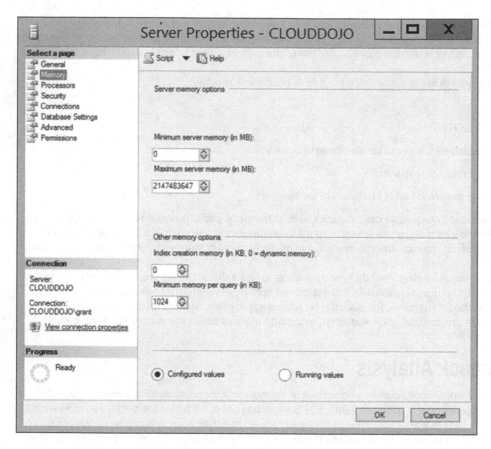

Figure 2-3. *SQL Server memory configuration*

The dynamic memory range is controlled through two configuration properties: Minimum(MB) and Maximum(MB).

- Minimum(MB), also known as min server memory, works as a floor value for the memory pool. Once the memory pool reaches the same size as the floor value, SQL Server can continue committing pages in the memory pool, but it can't be shrunk to less than the floor value. Note that SQL Server does not start with the min server memory configuration value but commits memory dynamically, as needed.

- Maximum(MB), also known as max server memory, serves as a ceiling value to limit the maximum growth of the memory pool. These configuration settings take effect immediately and do not require a restart. In SQL Server 2014 the lowest maximum memory is 64MB for a 32-bit system and 128MB for a 64-bit system.

Microsoft recommends that you use dynamic memory configuration for SQL Server, where min server memory is 0 and max server memory is set to allow some memory for the operating system, assuming a single instance on the machine. The amount of memory for the operating system depends on the system itself. For most systems with 8 GB –16GB of memory, you should leave about 2GB – 4GB for the OS. As the amount of memory in your server increases, you'll need to allocate more memory for the OS. A common recommendation is 4GB for every 16GB beyond 32GB of total system memory. You'll need to adjust this depending on your own system's needs and memory allocations. You should not run other memory-intensive applications on the same server as SQL Server, but if you must, I recommend you first get estimates on how much memory is needed by other applications and then configure SQL Server with a max server memory value set to prevent the other applications from starving SQL Server of memory. On a system where SQL Server is running on its own, I prefer to set the minimum server memory equal to the max value and simply dispatch with dynamic management. On a server with multiple SQL Server instances, you'll need to adjust these memory settings to ensure each instance has an adequate value. Just make sure you've left enough memory for the operating system and external processes.

Memory within SQL Server can be roughly divided into buffer pool memory, which represents data pages and free pages, and nonbuffer memory, which consists of threads, DLLs, linked servers, and others. Most of the memory used by SQL Server goes into the buffer pool. But you can get allocations beyond the buffer pool, known as private bytes, which can cause memory pressure not evident in the normal process of monitoring the buffer pool. Check Process: sqlservr: Private Bytes in comparison to SQL Server: Buffer Manager: Total pages if you suspect this issue on your system.

You can also manage the configuration values for min server memory and max server memory by using the sp_configure system stored procedure. To see the configuration values for these parameters, execute the sp_configure stored procedure as follows:

```
EXEC sp_configure 'show advanced options', 1;
GO
RECONFIGURE;
GO
EXEC sp_configure  'min server memory';
EXEC sp_configure  'max server memory';
```

Figure 2-4 shows the result of running these commands.

	name	minimum	maximum	config_value	run_value
1	min server memory (MB)	0	2147483647	0	16

	name	minimum	maximum	config_value	run_value
1	max server memory (MB)	128	2147483647	2147483647	2147483647

Figure 2-4. *SQL Server memory configuration properties*

Note that the default value for the min server memory setting is 0MB and for the max server memory setting is 2147483647MB.

You can also modify these configuration values using the sp_configure stored procedure. For example, to set max server memory to 10GB and min server memory to 5GB, execute the following set of statements (setmemory.sql in the download):

```
USE master;
EXEC sp_configure  'show advanced option',   1;
RECONFIGURE;
exec sp_configure  'min server memory (MB)',  5120;
exec sp_configure  'max server memory (MB)',  10240;
RECONFIGURE WITH OVERRIDE;
```

The min server memory and max server memory configurations are classified as advanced options. By default, the sp_configure stored procedure does not affect/display the advanced options. Setting show advanced option to 1 as shown previously enables the sp_configure stored procedure to affect/display the advanced options.

The RECONFIGURE statement updates the memory configuration values set by sp_configure. Since ad hoc updates to the system catalog containing the memory configuration values are not recommended, the OVERRIDE flag is used with the RECONFIGURE statement to force the memory configuration. If you do the memory configuration through Management Studio, Management Studio automatically executes the RECONFIGURE WITH OVERRIDE statement after the configuration setting.

Another way to see the settings but not to manipulate them is to use the sys.configurations system view. You can select from sys.configurations using standard T-SQL rather than having to execute a command.

You may need to allow for SQL Server sharing a system's memory. To elaborate, consider a computer with SQL Server and SharePoint running on it. Both servers are heavy users of memory and thus keep pushing each other for memory. The dynamic memory behavior of SQL Server allows it to release memory to SharePoint at one instance and grab it back as SharePoint releases it. You can avoid this dynamic memory management overhead by configuring SQL Server for a fixed memory size. However, please keep in mind that since SQL Server is an extremely resource-intensive process, it is highly recommended that you have a dedicated SQL Server production machine.

Now that you understand SQL Server memory management at a very high level, let's consider the performance counters you can use to analyze stress on memory, as shown in Table 2-1.

Table 2-1. *Performance Monitor Counters to Analyze Memory Pressure*

Object(Instance[,InstanceN])	Counter	Description	Values
Memory	Available Bytes	Free physical memory	System dependent
	Pages/sec	Rate of hard page faults	Average value < 50, but compare with baseline
	Page Faults/sec	Rate of total page faults	Compare with its baseline value for trend analysis
	Pages Input/sec	Rate of input page faults	
	Pages Output/sec	Rate of output page faults	
	Paging File %Usage Peak	Peak values in the memory paging file	
	Paging File: %Usage	Rate of usage of the memory paging file	
SQLServer:Buffer Manager	Buffer cache hit ratio	Percentage of requests served out of buffer cache	Compare with its baseline value for trend analysis
	Page Life Expectancy	Time page spends in buffer cache	Compare with its baseline value for trend analysis
	Checkpoint Pages/sec	Pages written to disk by checkpoint	Average value < 30, but compare with baseline
	Lazy writes/sec	Dirty aged pages flushed from buffer	Average value < 20, but compare with baseline
SQLServer:Memory Manager	Memory Grants Pending	Number of processes waiting for memory grant	Average value = 0
	Target Server Memory (KB)	Maximum physical memory SQL Server can have on the box	Close to size of physical memory
	Total Server Memory (KB)	Physical memory currently assigned to SQL	Close to target server memory (KB)
Process	Private Bytes	Size, in bytes, of memory that this process has allocated that can't be shared with other processes	

Memory and disk I/O are closely related. Even if you think you have a problem that is directly memory related, you should also gather I/O metrics in order to understand how the system is behaving between the two resources. I'll now walk you through these counters to get a better idea of possible uses.

Available Bytes

The Available Bytes counter represents free physical memory in the system. You can also look at Available Kbytes and Available Mbytes for the same data but with less granularity. For good performance, this counter value should not be too low. If SQL Server is configured for dynamic memory usage, then this value will be controlled by calls to a Windows API that determines when and how much memory to release. Extended periods of time with this value very low and SQL Server memory not changing indicates that the server is under severe memory stress.

Pages/Sec and Page Faults/Sec

To understand the importance of the Pages/sec and Page Faults/sec counters, you first need to learn about page faults. A *page fault* occurs when a process requires code or data that is not in its *working set* (its space in physical memory). It may lead to a soft page fault or a hard page fault. If the faulted page is found elsewhere in physical memory, then it is called a *soft page fault. A hard page fault* occurs when a process requires code or data that is not in its working set or elsewhere in physical memory and must be retrieved from disk.

The speed of a disk access is in the order of milliseconds for mechanical drives or as low as .1 milliseconds for a solid-state drive (SSD), whereas a memory access is in the order of nanoseconds. This huge difference in the speed between a disk access and a memory access makes the effect of hard page faults significant compared to that of soft page faults.

The Pages/sec counter represents the number of pages read from or written to disk per second to resolve hard page faults. The Page Faults/sec performance counter indicates the total page faults per second—soft page faults plus hard page faults—handled by the system. These are primarily measures of load and are not direct indicators of performance issues.

Hard page faults, indicated by Pages/sec, should not be consistently higher than normal. There are no hard-and-fast numbers for what indicates a problem because these numbers will vary widely between systems based on the amount and type of memory as well as the speed of disk access on the system.

If the Pages/sec counter is high, you can break it up into Pages Input/sec and Pages Output/sec.

- *Pages Input/sec*: An application will wait only on an input page, not on an output page.
- *Pages Output/sec*: Page output will stress the system, but an application usually does not see this stress. Pages output are usually represented by the application's dirty pages that need to be backed out to the disk. Pages Output/sec is an issue only when disk load become an issue.

Also, check Process:Page Faults/sec to find out which process is causing excessive paging in case of high Pages/sec. The Process object is the system component that provides performance data for the processes running on the system, which are individually represented by their corresponding instance name.

For example, the SQL Server process is represented by the sqlservr instance of the Process object. High numbers for this counter usually do not mean much unless Pages/sec is high. Page Faults/sec can range all over the spectrum with normal application behavior, with values from 0 to 1,000 per second being acceptable. This entire data set means a baseline is essential to determine the expected normal behavior.

Paging File %Usage and Page File %Usage

All memory in the Windows system is not the physical memory of the physical machine. Windows will swap memory that isn't immediately active in and out of the physical memory space to a paging file. These counters are used to understand how often this is occurring on your system. As a general measure of system performance, these counters are applicable only to the Windows OS and not to SQL Server. However, the impact of not enough virtual memory will affect SQL Server. These counters are collected in order to understand whether the memory pressures on SQL Server are internal or external. If they are external memory pressures, you will need to go into the Windows OS to determine what the problems might be.

Buffer Cache Hit Ratio

The *buffer cache* is the pool of buffer pages into which data pages are read, and it is often the biggest part of the SQL Server memory pool. This counter value should be as high as possible, especially for OLTP systems that should have fairly regimented data access, unlike a warehouse or reporting system. It is extremely common to find this counter value as 99 percent or more for most production servers. A low Buffer cache hit ratio value indicates that few requests could be served out of the buffer cache, with the rest of the requests being served from disk.

When this happens, either SQL Server is still warming up or the memory requirement of the buffer cache is more than the maximum memory available for its growth. If the cache hit ratio is consistently low, you might consider getting more memory for the system or reducing memory requirements through the use of good indexes and other query tuning mechanism, that is, unless you're dealing with reporting systems with lots of ad hoc queries. It's possible when working with reporting systems to consistently see the cache hit ratio become extremely low.

This makes the buffer cache hit ratio an interesting number for understanding aspects of system behavior, but it is not a value that would suggest, by itself, potential performance problems. While this number represents an interesting behavior within the system, it's not a great measure for precise problems but instead shows a type of behavior.

Page Life Expectancy

Page Life Expectancy indicates how long a page will stay in the buffer pool without being referenced. Generally, a low number for this counter means that pages are being removed from the buffer, lowering the efficiency of the cache and indicating the possibility of memory pressure. On reporting systems, as opposed to OLTP systems, this number may remain at a lower value since more data is accessed from reporting systems. It's also common to see Page Life Expectancy fall to very low levels during nightly loads. Since this is dependent on the amount of memory you have available and the types of queries running on your system, there are no hard-and-fast numbers that will satisfy a wide audience. Therefore, you will need to establish a baseline for your system and monitor it over time.

If you are on a machine with nonuniform memory access (NUMA), you need to know that the standard Page Life Expectancy counter is an average. To see specific measures, you'll need to use the Buffer Node:Page Life Expectancy counter.

Checkpoint Pages/Sec

The Checkpoint Pages/sec counter represents the number of pages that are moved to disk by a checkpoint operation. These numbers should be relatively low, for example, less than 30 per second for most systems. A higher number means more pages are being marked as dirty in the cache. A *dirty page* is one that is modified while in the buffer. When it's modified, it's marked as dirty and will get written back to the disk during the next checkpoint. Higher values on this counter indicate a larger number of writes occurring within the system, possibly indicative of I/O problems. But, if you are taking advantage of the new indirect checkpoints, which allow you to control when checkpoints occur in order to reduce recovery intervals, you might see different numbers here. Take that into account when monitoring databases with the indirect checkpoint configured.

Lazy Writes/Sec

The Lazy writes/sec counter records the number of buffers written each second by the buffer manager's lazy write process. This process is where the dirty, aged buffers are removed from the buffer by a system process that frees up the memory for other uses. A dirty, aged buffer is one that has changes and needs to be written to the disk. Higher values on this counter possibly indicate I/O issues or even memory problems. The Lazy writes/sec values should consistently be less than 20 for the average system. However, with as with all other counters, you must compare your values to a baseline measure.

Memory Grants Pending

The Memory Grants Pending counter represents the number of processes pending for a memory grant within SQL Server memory. If this counter value is high, then SQL Server is short of buffer memory. Under normal conditions, this counter value should consistently be 0 for most production servers.

Another way to retrieve this value, on the fly, is to run queries against the DMV sys.dm_ exec_query_memory_grants. A null value in the column grant_time indicates that the process is still waiting for a memory grant. This is one method you can use to troubleshoot query timeouts by identifying that a query (or queries) is waiting on memory in order to execute.

Target Server Memory (KB) and Total Server Memory (KB)

Target Server Memory (KB) indicates the total amount of dynamic memory SQL Server is willing to consume. Total Server Memory (KB) indicates the amount of memory currently assigned to SQL Server. The Total Server Memory (KB) counter value can be very high if the system is dedicated to SQL Server. If Total Server Memory (KB) is much less than Target Server Memory (KB), then either the SQL Server memory requirement is low, the max server memory configuration parameter of SQL Server is set at too low a value, or the system is in warm-up phase. The *warm-up phase* is the period after SQL Server is started when the database server is in the process of expanding its memory allocation dynamically as more data sets are accessed, bringing more data pages into memory.

You can confirm a low memory requirement from SQL Server by the presence of a large number of free pages, usually 5,000 or more. Also, you can directly check the status of memory by querying the DMO sys.dm_os_ring_buffers, which returns information about memory allocation within SQL Server. I cover sys.dm_os_ring_buffers in more detail in the following section.

Additional Memory Monitoring Tools

While you can get the basis for the behavior of memory within SQL Server from the Performance Monitor counters, once you know that you need to spend time looking at your memory usage, you'll need to take advantage of other tools and tool sets. The following are some of the commonly used reference points for identifying memory issues on a SQL Server system. A few of these tools are only of use for in-memory OLTP management. Some of these tools, while actively used by large numbers of the SQL Server community, are not documented within SQL Server Books Online. This means they are absolutely subject to change or removal.

DBCC MEMORYSTATUS

This command goes into the SQL Server memory and reads out the current allocations. It's a moment-in-time measurement, a snapshot. It gives you a set of measures of where memory is currently allocated. The results from running the command come back as two basic result sets, as you can see in Figure 2-5.

	Process/System Counts	Value
1	Available Physical Memory	6080708608
2	Available Virtual Memory	8779246280704
3	Available Paging File	6996623360
4	Working Set	231723008
5	Percent of Committed Memory in WS	100
6	Page Faults	4199150
7	System physical memory high	1
8	System physical memory low	0
9	Process physical memory low	0
10	Process virtual memory low	0

	Memory Manager	KB
1	VM Reserved	16048564
2	VM Committed	181924
3	Locked Pages Allocated	0
4	Large Pages Allocated	0
5	Emergency Memory	1024
6	Emergency Memory In Use	16
7	Target Committed	5733864
8	Current Committed	181928
9	Pages Allocated	118376
10	Pages Reserved	0
11	Pages Free	2680
12	Pages In Use	146488
13	Page Alloc Potential	6455960
14	NUMA Growth Phase	0
15	Last OOM Factor	0
16	Last OS Error	0

Figure 2-5. *Output of DBCC MEMORYSTATUS*

The first data set shows basic allocations of memory and counts of occurrences. For example, Available Physical Memory is a measure of the memory available on the system, whereas Page Faults is just a count of the number of page faults that have occurred.

The second data set shows different memory managers within SQL Server and the amount of memory they have consumed at the moment that the MEMORYSTATUS command was called.

Each of these can be used to understand where memory allocation is occurring within the system. For example, in most systems, most of the time the primary consumer of memory is the buffer pool. You can compare the Target Committed value to the Current Committed value to understand if you're seeing pressure on the buffer pool. When Target Committed is higher than Current Committed, you might be seeing buffer cache problems and need to figure out which process within your currently executing SQL Server processes is using the most memory. This can be done using a dynamic management object.

The remaining data sets are various memory managers, memory clerks, and other memory stores from the full dump of memory that DBCC MEMORYSTATUS produces. They're only going to be interesting in very narrow circumstances when dealing with particular aspects of SQL Server management, and they fall far outside the scope of this book to document them all. You can read more in the MSDN article "How to use the DBCC MEMORYSTATUS command" (http://bit.ly/1eJ2M2f).

Dynamic Management Objects

There are a large number of memory-related DMOs within SQL Server. Several of them have been updated with SQL Server 2014, and some new ones have been added. Reviewing all of them is outside the scope of this book. There are three that are the most frequently used when determining whether you have memory bottlenecks within SQL Server. There are also another two that are useful when you need to monitor your in-memory OLTP memory usage.

Sys.dm_os_memory_brokers

While most of the memory within SQL Server is allocated to the buffer cache, there are a number of processes within SQL Server that also can, and will, consume memory. These processes expose their memory allocations through this DMO. You can use this to see what processes might be taking resources away from the buffer cache in the event you have other indications of a memory bottleneck.

Sys.dm_os_memory_clerks

A memory clerk is the process that allocates memory within SQL Server. Looking at what these processes are up to allows you to understand whether there are internal memory allocation issues going on within SQL Server that might rob the procedure cache of needed memory. If the Performance Monitor counter for Private Bytes is high, you can determine which parts of the system are being consumed through the DMV.

If you have a database using in-memory OLTP storage, you can use sys.dm_db_xtp_table_memory_stats to look at the individual database objects. But if you want to look at the allocations of these objects across the entire instance, you'll need to use sys.dm_os_memory_clerks.

Sys.dm_os_ring_buffers

This DMV is not documented within Books Online, so it is subject to change or removal. It changed between SQL Server 2008R2 and SQL Server 2012. The queries I normally run against it still seem to work for SQL Server 2014, but you can't count on that. This DMV outputs as XML. You can usually read the output by eye, but you may need to implement XQuery to get really sophisticated reads from the ring buffers.

A ring buffer is nothing more than a recorded response to a notification. Ring buffers are kept within this DMV, and accessing sys.dm_os_ring_buffers allows you to see things changing within your memory. Table 2-2 describes the main ring buffers associated with memory.

Table 2-2. *Main Ring Buffers Associated with Memory*

Ring Buffer	Ring_buffer_type	Use
Resource Monitor	RING_BUFFER_ RESOURCE_MONITOR	As memory allocation changes, notifications of this change are recorded here. This information can be useful for identifying external memory pressure.
Out Of Memory	RING_BUFFER_OOM	When you get out-of-memory issues, they are recorded here so you can tell what kind of memory action failed.
Memory Broker	RING_BUFFER_ MEMORY_BROKER	As the memory internal to SQL Server drops, a low memory notification will force processes to release memory for the buffer. These notifications are recorded here, making this a useful measure for when internal memory pressure occurs.
Buffer Pool	RING_BUFFER_ BUFFER_POOL	Notifications of when the buffer pool itself is running out of memory are recorded here. This is just a general indication of memory pressure.

There are other ring buffers available, but they are not applicable to memory allocation issues.

Sys.dm_db_xtp_table_memory_stats

To see the memory in use by the tables and indexes that you created in-memory, you can query this DMV. The output measures the memory allocated and memory used for the tables and indexes. It outputs only the object_id, so you'll need to also query the system view sys.objects to get the names of tables or indexes. This DMV outputs for the database you are currently connected to when querying.

Sys.dm_xtp_system_memory_consumers

This DMV shows system structures that are used to manage the internals of the in-memory engine. It's not something you should normally have to deal with, but when troubleshooting memory issues, it's good to understand if you're dealing directly with something occurring within the system or just the amount of data that you've loaded into memory. The principal measures you'd be looking for here are the allocated and used bytes shown for each of the management structures.

Memory Bottleneck Resolutions

When there is high stress on memory, indicated by a large number of hard page faults, you can resolve a memory bottleneck using the flowchart shown in Figure 2-6.

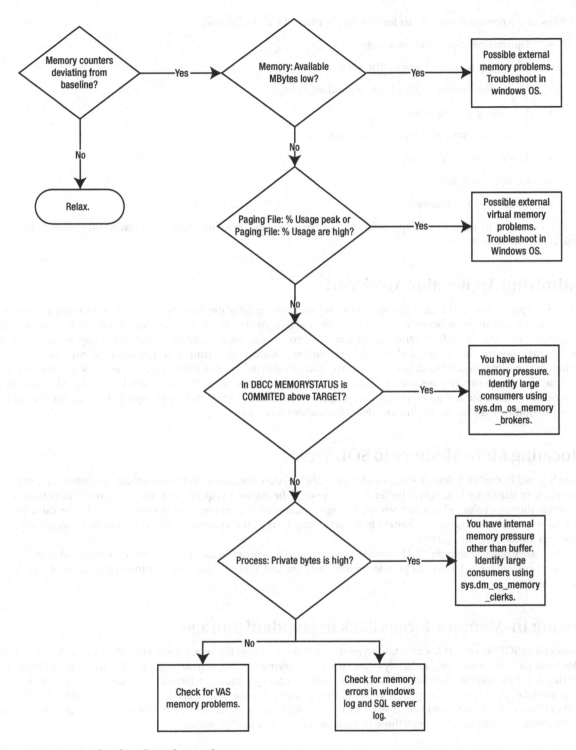

Figure 2-6. *Memory bottleneck resolution chart*

A few of the common resolutions for memory bottlenecks are as follows:

- Optimizing application workload

- Allocating more memory to SQL Server

- Moving in-memory tables back to standard storage

- Increasing system memory

- Changing from a 32-bit to a 64-bit processor

- Enabling 3GB of process space

- Compressing data

- Addressing fragmentation

And of course, fixing any of the query issues that can lead to excessive memory use is always an option. Let's take a look at each of these in turn.

Optimizing Application Workload

Optimizing application workload is the most effective resolution most of the time, but because of the complexity and challenges involved in this process, it is usually considered last. To identify the memory-intensive queries, capture all the SQL queries using Extended Events (which you will learn how to use in Chapter 3) and then group the trace output on the Reads column. The queries with the highest number of logical reads contribute most often to memory stress, but there is not a linear correlation between the two. You can also use sys.dm_exec_query_stats, a DMV that collects query metrics for queries that are actively in cache to identify the same thing. But, since this DMV is based on cache, it may not be as accurate as capturing metrics using Extended Events, although it will be quicker and easier. You will see how to optimize those queries in more detail throughout this book.

Allocating More Memory to SQL Server

As you learned in the "SQL Server Memory Management" section, the max server memory configuration can limit the maximum size of the SQL Server buffer memory pool. If the memory requirement of SQL Server is more than the max server memory value, which you can tell through the number of hard page faults, then increasing the value will allow the memory pool to grow. To benefit from increasing the max server memory value, ensure that enough physical memory is available in the system.

If you are using in-memory OLTP storage, you may need to adjust the memory percentages allocated to the resource pools you have defined for your in-memory objects. But, that will take memory from other parts of your SQL Server instance.

Moving In-Memory Tables Back to Standard Storage

Introduced in SQL Server 2014, a new table type was introduced called the *in-memory* table. This moves the storage of tables from the disk to memory, radically improving the performance. But, not all tables or all workloads will benefit from this new functionality. You need to keep an eye on your general query performance metrics for in-memory tables and take advantage of the specific DMVs that let you monitor the in-memory tables. I'll be covering all this in detail in Chapter 23. If your workload doesn't work well with in-memory tables or you just don't have enough memory in the system, you may need to move those in-memory tables back to disk storage.

Increasing System Memory

The memory requirement of SQL Server depends on the total amount of data processed by SQL activities. It is not directly correlated to the size of the database or the number of incoming SQL queries. For example, if a memory-intensive query performs a cross join between two small tables without any filter criteria to narrow down the result set, it can cause high stress on the system memory.

One of the easiest and quickest resolutions is to simply increase system memory by purchasing and installing more. However, it is still important to find out what is consuming the physical memory because if the application workload is extremely memory intensive, you could soon be limited by the maximum amount of memory a system can access. To identify which queries are using more memory, query the sys.dm_exec_query_memory_grants DMV and collect metrics on queries and their I/O use. Just be careful when running queries against this DMV using a JOIN or an ORDER BY statement; if your system is already under memory stress, these actions can lead to your query needing its own memory grant.

Changing from a 32-Bit to a 64-Bit Processor

Switching the physical server from a 32-bit processor to a 64-bit processor (and the attendant Windows Server software upgrade) radically changes the memory management capabilities of SQL Server. The limitations on SQL Server for memory go from 3GB to a limit of up to 8TB depending on the version of the operating system and the specific processor type.

Prior to SQL Server 2012, it was possible to add up to 64GB of data cache to a SQL Server instance through the use of Address Windowing Extensions. These were removed from SQL Server 2012, so a 32-bit instance of SQL Server is limited to accessing only 3GB of memory. Only small systems should be running 32-bit versions of SQL Server 2014 because of this limitation.

Compressing Data

Data compression has a number of excellent benefits for storing and retrieving information. It has an added benefit that many people aren't aware of: While compressed information is stored in memory, it remains compressed. This means more information can be moved while using less system memory, increasing your overall memory throughput. All this does come at some cost to the CPU, so you'll need to keep an eye on that to be sure you're not just transferring stress. Sometimes you may not see much compression because of the nature of your data.

Enabling 3GB of Process Address Space

Standard 32-bit addresses can map a maximum of 4GB of memory. The standard address spaces of 32-bit Windows operating system processes are therefore limited to 4GB. Out of this 4GB process space, by default the upper 2GB is reserved for the operating system, and the lower 2GB is made available to the application. If you specify a /3GB switch in the boot.ini file of the 32-bit OS, the operating system reserves only 1GB of the address space, and the application can access up to 3GB. This is also called *4-gig tuning* (4GT). No new APIs are required for this purpose.

Therefore, on a machine with 4GB of physical memory and the default Windows configuration, you will find available memory of about 2GB or more. To let SQL Server use up to 3GB of the available memory, you can add the **/3GB** switch in the boot.ini file as follows:

```
[boot loader]
timeout=30
default=multi(o)disk(o)rdisk(o)partition(1)\WINNT
[operating systems]
multi(o)disk(o)rdisk(o)partition(1)\WINNT=
"Microsoft Windows Server 2012 R2 Advanced Server"
/fastdetect /3GB
```

The **/3GB** switch should not be used for systems with more than 16GB of physical memory, as explained in the following section, or for systems that require a higher amount of kernel memory.

SQL Server 2014 on 64-bit systems can support up to 8TB on an x64 platform. It no longer makes much sense to put production systems, especially enterprise-level production systems, on 32-bit architecture.

Addressing Fragmentation

While fragmentation of storage may not sound like a performance issue, because of how SQL Server retrieves information from disk and into memory, a page of information is accessed. If you have a high level of fragmentation, that will translate itself straight to your memory management since you have to store the pages retrieved from disk in memory as they are, empty space and all. So, while fragmentation may affect storage, it also can affect memory. I address fragmentation in Chapter 17.

Summary

In this chapter, you were introduced to the Performance Monitor and DMOs. You explored different methods of gathering metrics on memory and memory behavior within SQL Server. Understanding how memory behaves will help you understand how your system is performing. You also saw a number of possible resolutions to memory issues, other than simply buying more memory. SQL Server will make use of as much memory as you can supply it, so manage this resource well.

In the next chapter, you will be introduced to the next system bottleneck, the disk and the disk subsystems.

CHAPTER 3

■ ■ ■

Disk Performance Analysis

The disks and the disk subsystem, which includes the controllers and connectors and management software, are one of the single slowest parts of any computing system. Over the years, memory has become faster and faster. The same can be said of CPUs. But disks, except for some of the radical improvements we've seen recently with technologies such as solid-state disks (SSDs), have not changed that much; disks are still one of the slowest parts of most systems. This means you're going to want to be able to monitor your disks to understand their behavior. In this chapter, you'll explore areas such as the following:

- Using system counters to gather disk performance metrics
- Using other mechanisms of gathering disk behavior
- Resolving disk performance issues

Disk Bottleneck Analysis

SQL Server can have demanding I/O requirements, and since disk speeds are comparatively much slower than memory and processor speeds, a contention in disk resources can significantly degrade SQL Server performance. Analysis and resolution of any disk resource bottleneck can improve SQL Server performance significantly.

Disk Counters

To analyze disk performance, you can use the counters shown in Table 3-1.

Table 3-1. Performance Monitor Counters to Analyze I/O Pressure

Object(Instance[,InstanceN])	Counter	Description	Value
PhysicalDisk(Data-disk, Log-disk)	% Disk Time	Percentage of time disk was busy	Average value < 85%, but compare to baseline
	Current Disk Queue Length	Number of outstanding disk requests at the time performance data is collected	Compare to baseline
	Avg. Disk Queue Length	Average number of queued disk requests during the sample interval	Compare to baseline

(*continued*)

Table 3-1. (*continued*)

Object(Instance[,InstanceN])	Counter	Description	Value
	Disk Transfers/sec	Rate of read/write operations on disk	Maximum value dependent on I/O subsystem
	Disk Bytes/sec	Amount of data transfer to/from per disk per second	Maximum value dependent on I/O subsystem
	Avg. Disk Sec/Read	Average time in ms to read from disk	Average value < 10 ms, but compare to baseline
	Avg. Disk Sec/Write	Average time in ms to write to disk	Average value < 10 ms, but compare to baseline

The PhysicalDisk counters represent the activities on a physical disk. LogicalDisk counters represent logical subunits (or partitions) created on a physical disk. If you create two partitions, say R: and S:, on a physical disk, then you can monitor the disk activities of the individual logical disks using logical disk counters. However, because a disk bottleneck ultimately occurs on the physical disk, not on the logical disk, it is usually preferable to use the PhysicalDisk counters.

Note that for a hardware redundant array of independent disks (RAID) subsystem (see the "Using a RAID Array" section for more on RAID), the counters treat the array as a single physical disk. For example, even if you have ten disks in a RAID configuration, they will all be represented as one physical disk to the operating system, and subsequently you will have only one set of PhysicalDisk counters for that RAID subsystem. The same point applies to storage area network (SAN) disks (see the "Using a SAN System" section for specifics). Because of this, some of the numbers represented in the previous table may be radically lower (or higher) than what your system can support.

Take all these numbers as general guidelines for monitoring your disks and adjust the numbers to account for the fact that technology is constantly shifting, and you may see different performance as the hardware improves. We're moving into more and more solid-state drives and even SSD arrays that make disk I/O operations orders of magnitude faster. Where we're not moving in SSD, we're taking advantage of iSCSI interfaces. As you work with these types of hardware, keep in mind that these numbers are more in line with platter-style disk drives and that those are fast becoming obsolete.

% Disk Time

The % Disk Time counter monitors the percentage of time the disk is busy with read/write activities. This is a good indicator of load but not a specific indicator of issues with performance. Record this information as part of the basic baseline in order to compare values to understand when disk access is radically changing.

Current Disk Queue Length

Current Disk Queue Length is the number of requests outstanding on the disk subsystem at the time the performance data is collected. It includes requests in service at the time of the snapshot. A disk subsystem will have only one disk queue. With modern systems including RAID, SAN, and other types of arrays, there can be a large number of disks and controllers facilitating the transfer of information to and from the disk. All this hardware makes measuring the disk queue length less important than it was previously, but this measure is still useful as an indicator of load on the system. You'll want to know when the queue length varies dramatically because it will be a possible sign of I/O issues. But, unlike the old days, there is no way to provide a value that you can compare your system against. Instead, you need to plan on capturing this information from your individual systems and using it as a comparison point over time.

Disk Transfers/Sec

Disk Transfers/sec monitors the rate of read and write operations on the disk. A typical hard disk drive today can do about 180 disk transfers per second for sequential I/O (IOPS) and 100 disk transfers per second for random I/O. In the case of random I/O, Disk Transfers/sec is lower because more disk arm and head movements are involved. OLTP workloads, which are workloads for doing mainly singleton operations, small operations, and random access, are typically constrained by disk transfers per second. So, in the case of an OLTP workload, you are more constrained by the fact that a disk can do only 100 disk transfers per second than by its throughput specification of 1000MB per second.

■ **Note**   An SSD can be anywhere from around 5,000 IOPS to as much as 500,000 IOPS for some over high-end SSD systems. Your monitoring of Disk Transfers/sec will need to scale accordingly.

Because of the inherent slowness of a disk, it is recommended that you keep disk transfers per second as low as possible.

Disk Bytes/Sec

The Disk Bytes/sec counter monitors the rate at which bytes are transferred to or from the disk during read or write operations. A typical disk spinning at 7200RPM can transfer about 1000MB per second. Generally, OLTP applications are not constrained by the disk transfer capacity of the disk subsystem since the OLTP applications access small amounts of data in individual database requests. If the amount of data transfer exceeds the capacity of the disk subsystem, then a backlog starts developing on the disk subsystem, as reflected by the Disk Queue Length counters.

Again, these numbers may be much higher for SSD access since it's largely limited by the latency caused by the drive to host interface.

Avg. Disk Sec/Read and Avg. Disk Sec/Write

Avg. Disk Sec/Read and Avg. Disk Sec/Write track the average amount of time it takes in milliseconds to read from or write to a disk. Having an understanding of just how well the disks are handling the writes and reads that they receive can be a strong indicator of where problems are. If it's taking more than about 10ms to move the data from or to your disk, you may need to take a look at the hardware and configuration to be sure everything is working correctly. You'll need to get even better response times for the transaction log to perform well.

Additional I/O Monitoring Tools

Just like with all the other tools, you'll need to supplement the information you gather from Performance Monitor with data available in other sources. The really good information for I/O and disk issues are all in DMOs.

Sys.dm_io_virtual_file_stats

This is a function that returns information about the files that make up a database. You call it something like the following:

```
SELECT  *
FROM    sys.dm_io_virtual_file_stats(DB_ID('AdventureWorks2012'), 2) AS divfs;
```

It returns several interesting columns of information about the file. The most interesting things are the stall data, which is the time that users are waiting on different I/O operations. First, io_stall_read_ms represents the amount of time in milliseconds that users are waiting for reads. Then there is io_stall_write_ms, which shows you the amount of time that write operations have had to wait on this file within the database. You can also look at the general number, io_stall, which represents all waits on I/O for the file. To make these numbers meaningful, you get one more value, sample_ms, which shows the amount of time measured. You can compare this value to the others to get a sense of the degree that I/O issues are holding up your system. Further, you can narrow this down to a particular file so you know what's slowing things down in the log or in a particular data file. This is an extremely useful measure for determining the existence of an I/O bottleneck. It doesn't help that much to identify the particular bottleneck.

Sys.dm_os_wait_stats

This is a generally useful DMO that shows aggregate information about waits on the system. To determine whether you have an I/O bottleneck, you can take advantage of this DMO by querying it like this:

```
SELECT  *
FROM    sys.dm_os_wait_stats AS dows
WHERE   wait_type LIKE 'PAGEIOLATCH%';
```

What you're looking at are the various I/O latch operations that are causing waits to occur. Like with sys.dm_io_virtual_status, you don't get a specific query from this DMO, but it does identify whether you have a bottleneck in I/O. Like many of the performance counters, you can't simply look for a value here. You need to compare the current values to a baseline value in order to arrive at your current situation.

The WHERE clause shown earlier uses PAGEIOLATCH%, but you should also look for waits related to other I/O processes such as WRITELOG, LOGBUFFER, and ASYNC_IO_COMPLETION.

When you run this query, you get a count of the waits that have occurred as well as an aggregation of the total wait time. You also get a max value for these waits so you know what the longest one was since it's possible that a single wait could have caused the majority of the wait time.

Disk Bottleneck Resolutions

A few of the common disk bottleneck resolutions are as follows:

- Optimizing application workload
- Using a faster I/O path
- Using a RAID array
- Using a SAN system
- Using Solid State Drives
- Aligning disks properly
- Using a battery-backed controller cache
- Adding system memory
- Creating multiple files and filegroups
- Moving the log files to a separate physical drive
- Using partitioned tables

I'll now walk you through each of these resolutions in turn.

Optimizing Application Workload

I cannot stress enough how important it is to optimize an application's workload in resolving a performance issue. The queries with the highest number of reads or writes will be the ones that cause a great deal of disk I/O. I'll cover the strategies for optimizing those queries in more detail throughout the rest of this book.

Using a Faster I/O Path

One of the most efficient resolutions, and one that you will adopt any time you can, is to use drives, controllers, and other architecture with faster disk transfers per second. However, you should not just upgrade disk drives without further investigation; you need to find out what is causing the stress on the disk.

Using a RAID Array

One way of obtaining disk I/O parallelism is to create a single pool of drives to serve all SQL Server database files, excluding transaction log files. The pool can be a single RAID array, which is represented in Windows Server 2012 R2 as a single physical disk drive. The effectiveness of a drive pool depends on the configuration of the RAID disks.

Out of all available RAID configurations, the most commonly used RAID configurations are the following (also shown in Figure 3-1):

- *RAID 0*: Striping with no fault tolerance

- *RAID 1*: Mirroring

- *RAID 5*: Striping with parity

- *RAID 1+0*: Striping with mirroring

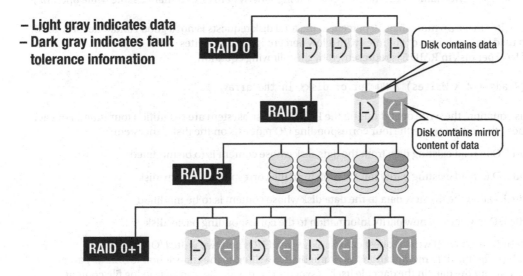

Figure 3-1. RAID configurations

RAID 0

Since this RAID configuration has no fault tolerance, you can use it only in situations where the reliability of data is not a concern. The failure of any disk in the array will cause complete data loss in the disk subsystem. Therefore, you shouldn't use it for any data file or transaction log file that constitutes a database, except, possibly, for the system temporary database called `tempdb`. The number of I/Os per disk in RAID 0 is represented by the following equation:

```
I/Os per disk = (Reads + Writes) / Number of disks in the array
```

In this equation, `Reads` is the number of read requests to the disk subsystem, and `Writes` is the number of write requests to the disk subsystem.

RAID 1

RAID 1 provides high fault tolerance for critical data by mirroring the data disk onto a separate disk. It can be used where the complete data can be accommodated in one disk only. Database transaction log files for user databases, operating system files, and SQL Server system databases (`master` and `msdb`) are usually small enough to use RAID 1.

The number of I/Os per disk in RAID 1 is represented by the following equation:

```
I/Os per disk =(Reads + 2 X Writes) / 2
```

RAID 5

RAID 5 is an acceptable option in many cases. It provides reasonable fault tolerance by effectively using only one extra disk to save the computed parity of the data in other disks, as shown in Figure 3-1. When there is a disk failure in RAID 5 configuration, I/O performance becomes terrible, although the system does remain usable while operating with the failed drive.

Any data where writes make up more than 10 percent of the total disk requests is not a good candidate for RAID 5. Thus, use RAID 5 on read-only volumes or volumes with a low percentage of disk writes.

The number of I/Os per disk in RAID 5 is represented by the following equation:

```
I/Os per disk = (Reads + 4 X Writes) / Number of disks in the array
```

As shown in this equation, the write operations on the RAID 5 disk subsystem are magnified four times. For each incoming write request, the following are the four corresponding I/O requests on the disk subsystem:

- One read I/O to read existing data from the data disk whose content is to be modified
- One read I/O to read existing parity information from the corresponding parity disk
- One write I/O to write the new data to the data disk whose content is to be modified
- One write I/O to write the new parity information to the corresponding parity disk

Therefore, the four I/Os for each write request consist of two read I/Os and two write I/Os.

In an OLTP database, all the data modifications are immediately written to the transaction log file as part of the database transaction, but the data in the data file itself is synchronized with the transaction log file content asynchronously in batch operations. This operation is managed by the internal process of SQL Server called the *checkpoint process*. The frequency of this operation can be controlled by using the recovery interval (min) configuration parameter of SQL Server. Just remember that the timing of checkpoints can be controlled through the use of indirect checkpoints introduced in SQL Server 2012.

Because of the continuous write operation in the transaction log file for a highly transactional OLTP database, placing transaction log files on a RAID 5 array will degrade the array's performance. Although, where possible, you should not place the transactional log files on a RAID 5 array, the data files may be placed on RAID 5 since the write operations to the data files are intermittent and batched together to improve the efficiency of the write operation.

RAID 6

RAID 6 is an added layer on top of RAID 5. An extra parity block is added to the storage of RAID 5. This doesn't negatively affect reads in any way. This means that, for reads, performance is the same as RAID 5. There is an added overhead for the additional write, but it's not that large. This extra parity block was added because RAID arrays are becoming so large these days that data loss is inevitable. The extra parity block acts as a check against this in order to better ensure that your data is safe.

RAID 1+0 (RAID 10)

RAID 1+0 (also referred to RAID 10) configuration offers a high degree of fault tolerance by mirroring every data disk in the array. It is a much more expensive solution than RAID 5, since double the number of data disks are required to provide fault tolerance. This RAID configuration should be used where a large volume is required to save data and more than 10 percent of disk requests are writes. Since RAID 1+0 supports *split seeks* (the ability to distribute the read operations onto the data disk and the mirror disk and then converge the two data streams), read performance is also very good. Thus, use RAID 1+0 wherever performance is critical.

The number of I/Os per disk in RAID 1+0 is represented by the following equation:

```
I/Os per disk = (Reads + 2 X Writes) / Number of disks in the array
```

Using a SAN System

SANs remain largely the domain of large-scale enterprise systems, although the cost has dropped. A SAN can be used to increase the performance of a storage subsystem by simply providing more spindles and disk drives to read from and write to. Because of their size, complexity, and cost, SANs are not necessarily a good solution in all cases. Also, depending on the amount of data, direct attached storage (DAS) can be configured to run faster. The principal strength of SAN systems is not reflected in performance but rather in the areas of scalability, availability, and maintenance.

Another area where SANs are growing are SAN devices that use Internet Small Computing System Interface (iSCSI) to connect a device to the network. Because of how the iSCSI interface works, you can make a network device appear to be locally attached storage. In fact, it can work nearly as fast as locally attached storage, but you get to consolidate your storage systems.

Conversely, you may achieve performance gains by going to local disks and getting rid of the SAN. SAN systems are extremely redundant by design. But, that redundancy adds a lot of overhead to disk operations, especially the type typically performed by SQL Server: lots of small writes done rapidly. While moving from a single local disk to a SAN can be an improvement, depending on your systems and the disk subsystem you put together, you could achieve even better performance outside the SAN.

Using Solid State Drives

Solid-state drives are taking the disk performance world by storm. These drives use memory instead of spinning disks to store information. They're quiet, lower power, and supremely fast. However, they're also quite expensive when compared to hard disk drives (HDD). At this writing, it costs approximately $.03/GB for a HDD and $.90/GB for an SSD. But that cost is offset by an increase in speed from approximately 100 operations per second to 5,000 operations per second and up. You can also put SSDs into arrays through a SAN or RAID, further increasing the performance benefits. There are a limited number of write operations possible on an SSD drive, but the failure rate is no higher than that from HDDs so far. There are also hybrid solutions with varying price points and performance metrics. For a hardware-only solution, implementing SSDs is probably the best operation you can do for a system that is I/O bound.

Aligning Disks Properly

Windows Server 2012 R2 aligns disks as part of the install process, so modern servers should not be running into this issue. However, if you have an older server, this can still be a concern. You'll also need to worry about this if you're moving volumes from a pre-Windows Server 2008 system. You will need to reformat these in order to get the alignment set appropriately. The way data is stored on a disk is in a series of *sectors* (also referred to as *blocks)* that are stored on tracks. A disk is out of alignment when the size of the track, determined by the vendor, consists of a number of sectors different from the default size that you're writing to. This means that one sector will be written correctly, but the next one will have to cross two tracks. This can more than double the amount of I/O required to write or read from the disk. The key is to align the partition so that you're storing the correct number of sectors for the track.

Adding System Memory

When physical memory is scarce, the system starts writing the contents of memory back to disk and reading smaller blocks of data more frequently, or reading large blocks, both of which cause a lot of paging. The less memory the system has, the more the disk subsystem is used. This can be resolved using the memory bottleneck resolutions enumerated in the previous section.

Creating Multiple Files and Filegroups

In SQL Server, each user database consists of one or more data files and usually one transaction log file. The data files belonging to a database can be grouped together in one or more filegroups for administrative and data allocation/placement purposes. For example, if a data file is placed in a separate filegroup, then write access to all the tables in the filegroup can be controlled collectively by making the filegroup read-only (transaction log files do not belong to any filegroup).

You can create a filegroup for a database from SQL Server Management Studio, as shown in Figure 3-2. The filegroups of a database are presented in the Filegroups pane of the Database Properties dialog box.

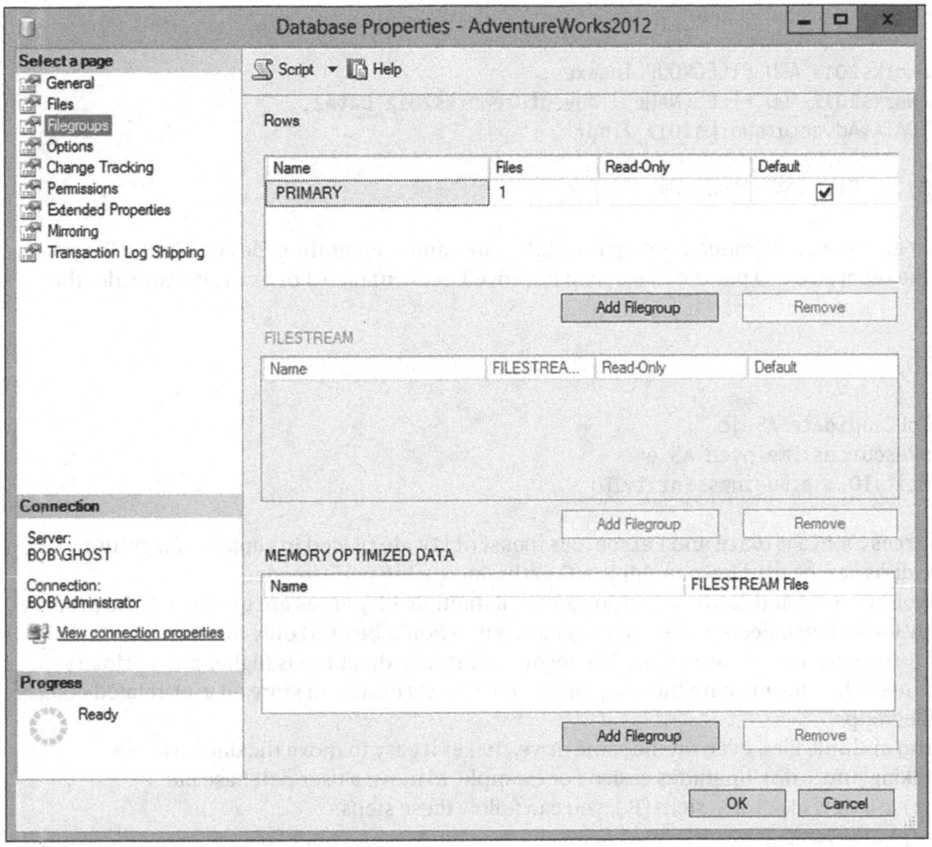

Figure 3-2. *Filegroups configuration*

In Figure 3-2, you can see that a single filegroup is created by default with AdventureWorks2012. You can add multiple files to multiple filegroups distributed across multiple I/O paths so that work can be done in parallel across the groups and distributed storage after you also move your database objects into those different groups, literally putting multiple spindles and multiple I/O paths to work. But, simply throwing lots of files, even on different disks, through a single disk controller may result in worse performance, not better.

You can add a data file to a filegroup in the Database Properties dialog box in the Files window by selecting from the drop-down list, as shown in Figure 3-3.

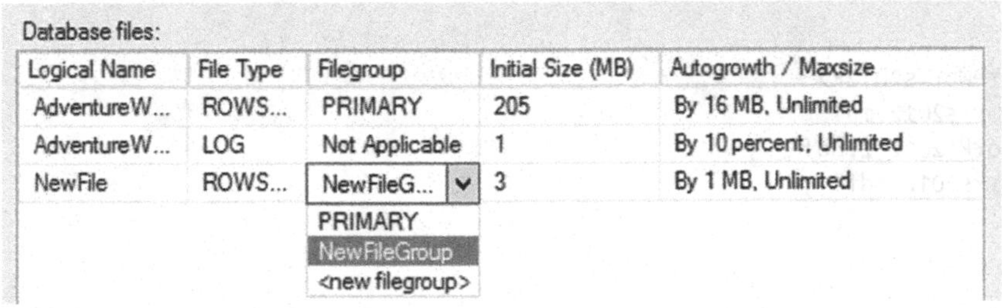

Figure 3-3. *Data files configuration*

43

You can also do this programmatically, as follows:

```
ALTER DATABASE AdventureWorks2012 ADD FILEGROUP Indexes;
ALTER DATABASE AdventureWorks2012 ADD FILE (NAME = AdventureWorks2012_Data2,
        FILENAME = 'S:\DATA\AdventureWorks2012_2.ndf',
        SIZE = 1mb,
        FILEGROWTH = 10%) TO FILEGROUP Indexes;
```

By separating tables that are frequently joined into separate filegroups and then putting files within the filegroups on separate disks or LUNS, the separated I/O paths can result in improved performance. For example, consider the following query:

```
SELECT  jc.JobCandidateID,
        e.ModifiedDate
FROM    HumanResources.JobCandidate AS jc
        INNER JOIN HumanResources.Employee AS e
        ON jc.BusinessEntityID = e.BusinessEntityID;
```

If the tables HumanResources.JobCandidate and Person.BusinessEntity are placed in separate filegroups containing one file each, the disks can be read from multiple I/O paths, increasing performance.

It is recommended for performance and recovery purposes that, if multiple filegroups are to be used, the primary filegroup should be used only for system objects and secondary filegroups should be used only for user objects. This approach improves the ability to recover from corruption. The recoverability of a database is higher if the primary data file and the log files are intact. Use the primary filegroup for system objects only, and store all user-related objects on one or more secondary filegroups.

Spreading a database into multiple files, even on the same drive, makes it easy to move the database files onto separate drives, making future disk upgrades easier. For example, to move a user database file (AdventureWorks2012_2.ndf) to a new disk subsystem (F:), you can follow these steps:

1. Detach the user database as follows:

   ```
   USE master;
   GO
   EXEC sp_detach_db 'AdventureWorks2012';
   GO
   ```

2. Copy the data file AdventureWorks2012_2.ndf to a folder F:\Data\ on the new disk subsystem.

3. Reattach the user database by referring files at appropriate locations, as shown here:

   ```
   USE master;
   GO
   sp_attach_db 'AdventureWorks2012R2'
   , 'R:\DATA\AdventureWorks2012.mdf'
   , 'F:\DATA\AdventureWorks2012_2.ndf'
   , 'S:\LOG\AdventureWorks2012.1df ';
   GO
   ```

4. To verify the files belonging to a database, execute the following commands:

```
USE AdventureWorks2012;
GO
SELECT * FROM sys.database_files;
GO
```

Moving the Log Files to a Separate Physical Disk

SQL Server transaction log files should always, when possible, be located on a separate hard disk drive from all other SQL Server database files. Transaction log activity primarily consists of sequential write I/O, unlike the nonsequential (or random) I/O required for the data files. Separating transaction log activity from other nonsequential disk I/O activity can result in I/O performance improvements because it allows the hard disk drives containing log files to concentrate on sequential I/O. But, remember, there are random transaction log reads and the data reads and writes can be sequential as much as the transaction log. There is just a strong tendency of transaction log writes to be sequential.

The major portion of time required to access data from a hard disk is spent on the physical movement of the disk spindle head to locate the data. Once the data is located, the data is read electronically, which is much faster than the physical movement of the head. With only sequential I/O operations on the log disk, the spindle head of the log disk can write to the log disk with a minimum of physical movement. If the same disk is used for data files, however, the spindle head has to move to the correct location before writing to the log file. This increases the time required to write to the log file and thereby hurts performance.

Even with an SSD disk, isolating the data from the transaction log means the work will be distributed to multiple locations, improving the performance.

Furthermore, for SQL Server with multiple OLTP databases, the transaction log files should be physically separated from each other on different physical drives to improve performance. An exception to this requirement is a read-only database or a database with few database changes. Since no online changes are made to the read-only database, no write operations are performed on the log file. Therefore, having the log file on a separate disk is not required for read-only databases.

As a general rule of thumb, you should try, where possible, to isolate files with the highest I/O from other files with high I/O. This will reduce contention on the disks and possibly improve performance. To identify those files using the most I/O, reference sys.dm_io_virtual_file_stats.

Using Partitioned Tables

In addition to simply adding files to filegroups and letting SQL Server distribute the data between them, it's possible to define a horizontal segmentation of data called a *partition* so that data is divided between multiple files by the partition. A filtered set of data is a segment; for example, if the partition is by month, the segment of data is any given month. Creating a partition moves the segment of data to a particular filegroup and only that filegroup. While partitioning is primarily a tool for making data management easier, you can see an increase in speed in some situations because when querying against well-defined partitions, only the files with the partitions of data you're interested in will be accessed during a given query through a process called *partition elimination*. If you assume for a moment that data is partitioned by month, then each month's data file can be set to read-only as each month ends. That read-only status means you'll recover the system faster and you can compress the storage resulting in some performance improvements. Just remember that partitions are primarily a manageability feature. While you can see some performance benefits from them in certain situations, it shouldn't be counted on as part of partitioning the data. SQL Server 2014 supports up to 15,000 partitions.

Summary

This chapter focused on gathering and interpreting metrics about the behavior of your disks. Just remember that every set of hardware can be fundamentally different, so applying any hard-and-fast set of metrics around behavior can be problematic. You now have the tools to gather disk performance metrics using Performance Monitor and some T-SQL commands. The resolutions for disk bottlenecks are varied but must be explored if you are dealing with bottlenecks related to disk behavior.

The next chapter completes the examination of system bottlenecks with a discussion of the CPU.

CHAPTER 4

■ ■ ■

CPU Performance Analysis

This chapter concludes the book's exploration of the system, with a discussion about CPU, network, and general SQL Server metrics. The CPU is the work engine of a system and keeps everything running. All the different calculations required for gathering and delivering data, maintaining the system, and ordering access are performed by the CPU. Getting bottlenecked on the CPU can be a difficult process to work out of. Unlike memory, which you can sometimes easily install more of, or disks, which you can sometimes easily add more or upgrade, CPUs are an integral part of the system you're running on and can frequently be upgraded only by buying newer machines. So, you'll want to keep an eye on CPU usage. Networks are seldom a major bottleneck for SQL Server, but it's good to keep an eye on them too. Finally, there are some SQL Server internal processes that you'll need to gather metrics on. This chapter covers the following topics:

- How to gather metrics on the processor
- Additional metrics available through T-SQL queries
- Methods for resolving processor bottlenecks

Processor Bottleneck Analysis

SQL Server makes heavy use of any processor resource available. You can use the Performance Monitor counters in Table 4-1 to analyze pressure on the processor resource.

Table 4-1. Performance Monitor Counters to Analyze CPU Pressure

Object(Instance[,InstanceN])	Counter	Description	Value
Processor(_Total)%	Processor Time	Percentage of time processor was busy	Average value < 80%, but compare to baseline
	% Privileged	Percentage of processor time spent in privileged mode	Average value < 10%, but compare to baseline
System	Processor Queue Length	Number of requests outstanding on the processor	Average value < 2, but compare to baseline
	Context Switches/sec	Rate at which processor is switched per processor from one thread to another	Average value < 5,000, but compare to baseline
SQL Server:SQL Statistics	Batch Requests/sec	SQL command batches received per second	Based on your standard workload
	SQL Compilations/sec	Number of times SQL is compiled	Based on your standard workload
	SQL Recompilations/sec	Number of recompiles	

Let's discuss these counters in more detail.

% Processor Time

% Processor Time should not be consistently high (greater than 80 percent). The effect of any sustained processor time greater than 90 percent is effectively the same as that of 100 percent. If % Processor Time is consistently high and disk and network counter values are low, your first priority must be to reduce the stress on the processor. Just remember that the numbers here are simply suggestions; people can disagree with these numbers for valid reasons. Use them as a starting point for evaluating your system, not as a specific recommendation.

For example, if % Processor Time is 85 percent and you are seeing excessive disk use by monitoring I/O counters, it is quite likely that a major part of the processor time is spent on managing the disk activities. This will be reflected in the % Privileged Time counter of the processor, as explained in the next section. In that case, it will be advantageous to optimize the disk bottleneck first. Further, remember that the disk bottleneck in turn can be because of a memory bottleneck, as explained earlier in the chapter.

You can track processor time as an aggregate of all the processors on the machine, or you can track the percentage utilization individually to particular processors. This allows you to segregate the data collection in the event that SQL Server runs on three processors of a four-processor machine. Remember, you might be seeing one processor maxed out while another processor has little load. The average value wouldn't reflect reality in that case. Use the average value as just an indicator and the individual values as more of a measure of actual load and processing on the system.

% Privileged Time

Processing on a Windows server is done in two modes: *user mode* and *privileged* (or *kernel*) mode. All system-level activities, including disk access, are done in privileged mode. If you find that % Privileged Time on a dedicated SQL Server system is 20 to 25 percent or more, then the system is probably doing a lot of external processing. It could be I/O, a filter driver such as encryption services, defective I/O components, or even out-of-date drivers. The % Privileged Time counter on a dedicated SQL Server system should be at most 5 to 10 percent, but use your baseline to establish what looks like normal behavior on your systems.

Processor Queue Length

Processor Queue Length is the number of threads in the processor queue. (There is a single processor queue, even on computers with multiple processors.) Unlike the disk counters, the Processor Queue Length counter does not read threads that are already running. On systems with lower CPU utilization, the Processor Queue Length counter is typically 0 or 1.

A sustained Processor Queue Length counter of greater than 2 generally indicates processor congestion. Because of multiple processors, you may need to take into account the number of schedulers dealing with the processor queue length. A processor queue length more than two times the number of schedulers (usually 1:1 with processors) can also indicate a processor bottleneck. Although a high % Processor Time counter indicates a busy processor, a sustained high Processor Queue Length counter is a more certain indicator. If the recommended value is exceeded, this generally indicates that there are more threads ready to run than the current number of processors can service in an optimal way.

Context Switches/Sec

The Context Switches/sec counter monitors the combined rate at which all processors on the computer are switched from one thread to another. A context switch occurs when a running thread voluntarily relinquishes the processor, is preempted by a higher-priority ready thread, or switches between user mode and privileged mode to use an executive or a subsystem service. It is the sum of Thread:Context Switches/sec for all threads running on all processors in the computer, and it is measured in numbers of switches.

A figure of 5,000 Context Switches/sec per processor is excellent to fair. High numbers are largely dictated by the speed of your CPUs, so measure performance over time and compare this number to your baseline to understand when you may be deviating.

Batch Requests/Sec

Batch Requests/sec gives you a good indicator of just how much load is being placed on the system, which has a direct correlation to how much load is being placed on the processor. Since you could see a lot of low-cost queries on your system or a few high-cost queries, you can't look at this number by itself but must reference the other counters defined in this section; 10,000 requests in a second would be considered a busy system. Greater values may be cause for concern, completely depending on what is normal for your system. The best way to know which value has meaning within your own systems is to establish a baseline and then monitor from there. Just remember that a high number here is not necessarily cause for concern. If all your other resources are in hand and you're sustaining a high number of batch requests/sec, it just means your server is busy.

SQL Compilations/Sec

The SQL Compilations/sec counter shows both batch compiles and statement recompiles as part of its aggregation. This number can be extremely high when a server is first turned on (or after a failover or any other startup type event), but it will stabilize over time. Once stable, significant or sustained spikes in compilations different from a baseline measure is cause for concern and will certainly manifest as problems in the processor since query compilation is an expensive operation. If you are working with some type of object-relational mapping engine, such as nHibernate or Entity Framework, a high number of compilations might be normal, though no less costly. Chapter 14 covers SQL compilation in detail.

SQL Recompilations/Sec

SQL Recompilations/sec is a measure of the recompiles of both batches and statements. A high number of recompiles can lead to processor stress. Because statement recompiles are part of this count, it can be much higher than in versions of SQL Server prior to 2005. Chapter 17 covers query recompilation in detail.

Other Tools for Measuring CPU Performance

You can use the DMOs to capture information about your CPU as well. The information in these DMOs will have to be captured by running the query and then keeping the information as part of your baseline measurement.

Sys.dm_os_wait_stats

Wait statistics are a good way to understand whether there are bottlenecks on the system. You can't simply say something greater than x is a bad number, though. You need to gather metrics over time in order to understand what represents normal on your system. The deviations from that are interesting. Queries against this DMO that look for signal wait time can indicate CPU bottlenecks.

Sys.dm_os_workers and Sys.dm_os_schedulers

These DMOs display the worker and scheduler threads within the Windows operating system. Running queries against these regularly will allow you to get counts of the number of processes that are in a runnable state. This is an excellent indication of processor load.

Processor Bottleneck Resolutions

A few of the common processor bottleneck resolutions are as follows:

- Optimizing application workload
- Eliminating or reducing excessive compiles/recompiles
- Using more or faster processors
- Not running unnecessary software

Let's consider each of these resolutions in turn.

Optimizing Application Workload

To identify the processor-intensive queries, capture all the SQL queries using Extended Events sessions (which I will discuss in the next chapter) and then group the output on the CPU column. The queries with the highest amount of CPU time contribute the most to the CPU stress. You should then analyze and optimize those queries to reduce stress on the CPU. Frequently, the cause for CPU stress is not extensive calculations within the queries but actually contention within logical I/O. Addressing I/O issues can often help you resolve CPU issues as well. You can also query directly against the sys.dm_exec_query_stats or sys.dm_exec_procedure_stats dynamic management view to see immediate issues in real time. Finally, using both a query hash and a query plan hash, you can identify and tune common queries or common execution plans (this is discussed in detail in Chapter 14). Most of the rest of the chapters in this book are concerned with optimizing application workload.

Eliminating Excessive Compiles/Recompiles

A certain number of query compiles and recompiles is simply to be expected, especially, as already noted, when working with ORM tools. It's when there is a large number of these over sustained periods that a problem exists. It's also worth noting the ratio between them. Having a high number of compiles and a low number of recompiles means that few queries are being reused within the system (query reuse is covered in detail in Chapter 9). A high number of recompiles will cause high processor use. Methods for addressing recompiles are covered in Chapter 17.

Using More or Faster Processors

One of the easiest resolutions, and one that you will adopt most of the time, is to increase system processing power. However, because of the high cost involved in a processor upgrade, you should first optimize CPU-intensive operations as much as possible.

The system's processing power can be increased by increasing the power of individual processors or by adding more processors. When you have a high % Processor Time counter and a low Processor Queue Length counter, it makes sense to increase the power of individual processors. In the case of both a high % Processor Time counter and a high Processor Queue Length counter, you should consider adding more processors. Increasing the number of processors allows the system to execute more requests simultaneously.

Not Running Unnecessary Software

Corporate policy frequently requires virus checking software be installed on the server. You can also have other products running on the server. When possible, no unnecessary software should be running on the same server as SQL Server. Exterior applications that have nothing to do with maintaining the Windows Server or SQL Server are best placed on a different machine.

Network Bottleneck Analysis

In SQL Server OLTP production environments, you will find few performance issues that are because of problems with the network. Most of the network issues you face in an OLTP environment are in fact hardware or driver limitations or issues with switches or routers. Most of these issues can be best diagnosed with the Network Monitor tool. However, Performance Monitor also provides objects that collect data on network activity, as shown in Table 4-2.

Table 4-2. *Performance Monitor Counters to Analyze Network Pressure*

Object(Instance[,InstanceN])	Counter	Description	Value
Network Interface(Network card)	Bytes Total/sec	Rate at which bytes are transferred on the NIC	Average value < 50% of NIC capacity, but compare with baseline
Network Segment	% Net Utilization	Percentage of network bandwidth in use on a network segment	Average value < 80% of network bandwidth, but compare with baseline

Bytes Total/Sec

You can use the Bytes Total/sec counter to determine how the network interface card (NIC) or network adapter is performing. The Bytes Total/sec counter should report high values to indicate a large number of successful transmissions. Compare this value with that reported by the Network Interface\Current Bandwidth performance counter, which reflects each adapter's bandwidth.

To allow headroom for spikes in traffic, you should usually average no more than 50 percent of capacity. If this number is close to the capacity of the connection and if processor and memory use are moderate, then the connection may well be a problem.

% Net Utilization

The % Net Utilization counter represents the percentage of network bandwidth in use on a network segment. The threshold for this counter depends on the type of network. For Ethernet networks, for example, 30 percent is the recommended threshold when SQL Server is on a shared network hub. For SQL Server on a dedicated full-duplex network, even though near 100 percent usage of the network is acceptable, it is advantageous to keep the network utilization below an acceptable threshold to keep room for the spikes in the load.

■ **Note** You must install the Network Monitor Driver to collect performance data using the Network Segment object counters.

In Windows Server 2012 R2, you can install the Network Monitor Driver from the local area connection properties for the network adapter. The Network Monitor Driver is available in the network protocol list of network components for the network adapter.

You can also look at the wait statistics in sys.dm_os_wait_stats for network-related waits. But, one that frequently comes up is ASYNC_NETWORK_IO. While this can be an indication of network-related waits, it's much more common to reflect waits caused by poor programming code that is not consuming a result set efficiently.

Network Bottleneck Resolutions

A few of the common network bottleneck resolutions are as follows:

- Optimizing application workload

- Adding network adapters

- Moderating and avoiding interruptions

Let's consider these resolutions in more detail.

Optimizing Application Workload

To optimize network traffic between a database application and a database server, make the following design changes in the application:

- Instead of sending a long SQL string, create a stored procedure for the SQL query. Then, you just need to send over the network the name of the stored procedure and its parameters.

- Group multiple database requests into one stored procedure. Then, only one database request is required across the network for the set of SQL queries implemented in the stored procedure.

- Request a small data set. Do not request table columns that are not used in the application logic.

- Move data-intensive business logic into the database as stored procedures or database triggers to reduce network round-trips.

- If data doesn't change frequently, try caching the information on the application instead of frequently calling the database for information that is going to be exactly the same as the last call.

- Minimize network calls, such as returning multiple result sets that are not consumed. A common issue is caused by a result set returned by SQL Server that includes each statement's row count. You can disable this by using SET NOCOUNT ON at the top of your query.

SQL Server Overall Performance

To analyze the overall performance of a SQL Server instance, besides examining hardware resource utilization, you should also examine some general aspects of SQL Server itself. You can use the performance counters presented in Table 4-3.

Table 4-3. Performance Monitor Counters to Analyze Generic SQL Pressure

Object(Instance[,InstanceN])	Counter
SQLServer:Access Methods	FreeSpace Scans/sec Full Scans/sec Table Lock Escalations/sec Worktables Created/sec
SQLServer:Latches	Total Latch Wait Time (ms)
SQLServer:Locks(_Total)	Lock Timeouts/sec Lock Wait Time (ms) Number of Deadlocks/sec
SQLServer:SQL Statistics	Batch Requests/sec SQL Re-Compilations/sec
SQLServer:General Statistics	Processes Blocked User Connections Temp Tables Creation Rate Temp Tables for Destruction

Let's break these down into different areas of concern in order to show the counters within the context where they would be more useful.

Missing Indexes

To analyze the possibility of missing indexes causing table scans or large data set retrievals, you can use the counter in Table 4-4.

Table 4-4. Performance Monitor Counter to Analyze Excessive Data Scans

Object(Instance[,InstanceN])	Counter
SQLServer:Access Methods	Full Scans/sec

Full Scans/Sec

This counter monitors the number of unrestricted full scans on base tables or indexes. Scans are not necessarily a bad thing. But they do represent a broader access of data, so they are likely to indicate a problem. A few of the main causes of a high Full Scans/sec value are as follows:

- Missing indexes
- Too many rows requested
- Not selective enough a predicate
- Improper T-SQL
- Data distribution or quantity doesn't support a seek

To further investigate queries producing these problems, use Extended Events to identify the queries (I will cover this tool in the next chapter). Queries with missing indexes, too many rows requested, or badly formed T-SQL will have a large number of logical reads, caused by scanning the entire table or entire index, and an increased CPU time.

Be aware that full scans may be performed for the temporary tables used in a stored procedure because most of the time you will not have indexes (or you will not need indexes) on temporary tables. Still, adding this counter to the baseline helps identify the possible increase in the use of temporary tables, which, when used inappropriately, can be bad for performance.

Dynamic Management Objects

Another way to check for missing indexes is to query the dynamic management view sys.dm_db_missing_index_details. This management view returns information that can suggest candidates for indexes based on the execution plans of the queries being run against the database. The view sys.dm_db_missing_index_details is part of a series of DMVs collectively referred to as the *missing indexes feature.* These DMVs are based on data generated from execution plans stored in the cache. You can query directly against this view to gather data to decide whether you want to build indexes based on the information available from within the view. Missing indexes will also be shown within the XML execution plan for a given query, but I'll cover that more in the next chapter. While these views are useful for suggesting possible indexes, since they can't be linked to a particular query, it can be unclear which of these indexes is most useful. You'll be better off using the techniques I show in the next chapter to associate a missing index with a particular query. For all the missing index suggestions, you must test them prior to implementing any suggestion on your systems.

The opposite problem to a missing index is one that is never used. The DMV sys.dm_db_index_usage_stats shows which indexes have been used, at least since the last restart of the SQL Server instance. Unfortunately, there are a number of ways that counters within this DMV get reset or removed, so you can't completely rely on it for a 100 percent accurate view of index use. You can also view the indexes in use with a lower-level DMV, sys.dm_db_index_operational_stats. It will help to show where indexes are slowing down because of contention or I/O. I'll cover these both in more detail in Chapter 20. You may also find that the suggestions from the Database Tuning Advisor (covered in Chapter 10) may be able to help you with specific indexes for specific queries.

Database Concurrency

To analyze the impact of database blocking on the performance of SQL Server, you can use the counters shown in Table 4-5.

Table 4-5. Performance Monitor Counters to Analyze SQL Server Locking

Object(Instance[,InstanceN])	Counter
SQLServer:Latches	Total Latch Wait Time (ms)
SQLServer:Locks(_Total)	Lock Timeouts/sec
	Lock Wait Time (ms)
	Number of Deadlocks/sec

Total Latch Wait Time (Ms)

Latches are used internally by SQL Server to protect the integrity of internal structures, such as a table row, and are not directly controlled by users. This counter monitors total latch wait time (in milliseconds) for latch requests that had to wait in the last second. A high value for this counter can indicate that SQL Server is spending too much time waiting on its internal synchronization mechanism.

Lock Timeouts/Sec and Lock Wait Time (Ms)

You should expect Lock Timeouts/sec to be 0 and Lock Wait Time (ms) to be very low. A nonzero value for Lock Timeouts/sec and a high value for Lock Wait Time (ms) indicate that excessive blocking is occurring in the database. Two approaches can be adopted in this case.

- You can identify the costly queries currently in cache using data from SQL Profiler or by querying sys. dm_exec_query_stats, and then you can optimize the queries appropriately.

- You can use blocking analysis to diagnose the cause of excessive blocking. It is usually advantageous to concentrate on optimizing the costly queries first because this, in turn, reduces blocking for others. In Chapter 20, you will learn how to analyze and resolve blocking.

- Extended Events supply a blocking event called blocked_process_report that you can enable and set a threshold in order to capture blocking information. Extended Events will be covered in Chapter 6, and blocked_process_report will be addressed in Chapter 20.

Just remember that some degree of locks are a necessary part of the system. You'll want to establish a baseline in order to track thoroughly whether a given value is cause for concern.

Number of Deadlocks/Sec

You should expect to see a 0 value for this counter. If you find a nonzero value, then you should identify the victimized request and either resubmit the database request automatically or suggest that the user do so. More importantly, an attempt should be made to troubleshoot and resolve the deadlock. Chapter 21 shows how to do this.

Nonreusable Execution Plans

Since generating an execution plan for a stored procedure query requires CPU cycles, you can reduce the stress on the CPU by reusing the execution plan. To analyze the number of stored procedures that are recompiling, you can look at the counter in Table 4-6.

Table 4-6. *Performance Monitor Counter to Analyze Execution Plan Reusability*

Object(Instance[,InstanceN])	Counter
SQLServer:SOL Statistics	SOL Re-Compilations/sec

Recompilations of stored procedures add overhead on the processor. You want to see a value as close to 0 as possible for the SOL Re-Compilations/sec counter, but you won't ever see that. If you consistently see values that deviate from your baseline measures or spike wildly, then you should use Extended Events to further investigate the stored procedures undergoing recompilations. Once you identify the relevant stored procedures, you should attempt to analyze and resolve the cause of recompilations. In Chapter 17, you will learn how to analyze and resolve various causes of recompilation.

General Behavior

SQL Server provides additional performance counters to track some general aspects of a SQL Server system. Table 4-7 lists a few of the most commonly used counters.

Table 4-7. *Performance Monitor Counters to Analyze Volume of Incoming Requests*

Object(Instance[,InstanceN])	Counter
SQLServer:General Statistics	User Connections
SQLServer:SQL Statistics	Batch Requests/sec

User Connections

Multiple read-only SQL Servers can work together in a load-balancing environment (where SQL Server is spread over several machines) to support a large number of database requests. In such cases, it is better to monitor the User Connections counter to evaluate the distribution of user connections across multiple SQL Server instances. User Connections can range all over the spectrum with normal application behavior. This is where a baseline is essential to determine the expected behavior. You will see how you can establish this baseline shortly.

Batch Requests/Sec

This counter is a good indicator of the load on SQL Server. Based on the level of system resource utilization and Batch Requests/sec, you can estimate the number of users SQL Server may be able to take without developing resource bottlenecks. This counter value, at different load cycles, helps you understand its relationship with the number of database connections. This also helps you understand SQL Server's relationship with Web Request/sec, that is, Active Server Pages.Requests/sec for web applications using Microsoft Internet Information Services (IIS) and Active Server Pages (ASP). All this analysis helps you better understand and predict system behavior as the user load changes.

The value of this counter can range over a wide spectrum with normal application behavior. A normal baseline is essential to determine the expected behavior.

Summary

In this chapter, you learned how to gather metrics on the CPU, network, and SQL Server in general. All this information feeds into your ability to understand what's happening on your system before you delve into attempting to tune queries. Remember that CPU is affected by the other resources since it's the thing that has to manage those resources, so some situations that can look like a CPU problem are better explained as a disk or memory issue. Networks are seldom a major bottleneck for SQL Server. You have a number of methods of observing SQL Server internals behavior through Performance Monitor counters, just like the other parts of the system. This concludes the discussion of the various system metrics. Next, you'll learn how to put all that together to create a baseline.

CHAPTER 5

■ ■ ■

Creating a Baseline

In the previous three chapters, you learned a lot about various possible system bottlenecks caused by memory, the disk, and the CPU. I also introduced a number of Performance Monitor metrics for gathering data on these parts of the system. Within the descriptions of most of the counters, I referred to comparing your metric to a baseline. This chapter will cover how to gather your metrics so that you have that baseline for later comparison. I'll go over how to configure an automated method gathering this information. A baseline is a fundamental part of understanding system behavior, so you should always have one available. This chapter covers the following topics:

- Considerations for monitoring virtual and hosted machines

- How to set up an automated collection of Performance Monitor metrics

- Considerations to avoid issues when using Performance Monitor

- Creating a baseline

Considerations for Monitoring Virtual and Hosted Machines

Before you start creating the baseline, I will talk about virtual machines (VMs). More and more SQL Server instances are running on VMs. When you are working with VMs or you are hosting VMs in remote environments such as Amazon or Microsoft Azure, many of the standard performance counters will no longer display meaningful information. If you monitor these counters within the VM, your numbers may not be helpful from a troubleshooting perspective. If you monitor these counters on the physical box, assuming you have access to it, which doubtless is shared by multiple different VMs, you will be unable to identify specific SQL Server instance resource bottlenecks. Because of this, additional information must be monitored when working with a VM. Most of the information that you can gather on disk and network performance are still applicable within a VM setting. And all query metric information will be accurate to those queries. It's the memory and CPU metrics that are completely different and quite unreliable.

This is because CPU and memory are shared between machines within a virtualized server environment. You may start a process on one CPU and finish it on another one entirely. Some virtual environments can actually change the memory allocated to a machine as that machine's demands for memory go up and down. With these kinds of changes, traditional monitoring just isn't applicable. The good news is that the major VM vendors provide you with guidance on how to monitor their systems and how to use SQL Server within their systems. You can largely rely on these third-party documents for the specifics of monitoring a VM. Taking the two most common hypervisors, VMware and HyperV, here is a document from each:

- VMware Monitoring Virtual Machine Performance (http://bit.ly/1f37tEh)

- Measuring Performance on HyperV (http://bit.ly/1aBHdxW)

The queues counters, such as processor queue length, are still applicable when monitoring within a VM. These indicate that the VM itself is starved for resources, starving your SQL Server instance so that it has to wait for access to the virtual CPU. The important thing to remember is that CPU and memory are going to be slower on a VM because the management of the VM is getting in the way of the system resources. You may also see slower I/O on a hosted VM because of the shared nature of hosted resources.

Creating a Baseline

Now that you have looked at a few of the main performance counters, let's see how to bring these counters together to create a system baseline. These are the steps you need to follow:

1. Create a reusable list of performance counters.

2. Create a counter log using your list of performance counters.

3. Minimize Performance Monitor overhead.

Creating a Reusable List of Performance Counters

Run the Performance Monitor tool on a Windows Server 2012 R2 machine connected to the same network as that of the SQL Server system. Add performance counters to the View Chart display of the Performance Monitor through the Properties ➤ Data ➤ Add Counters dialog box, as shown in Figure 5-1.

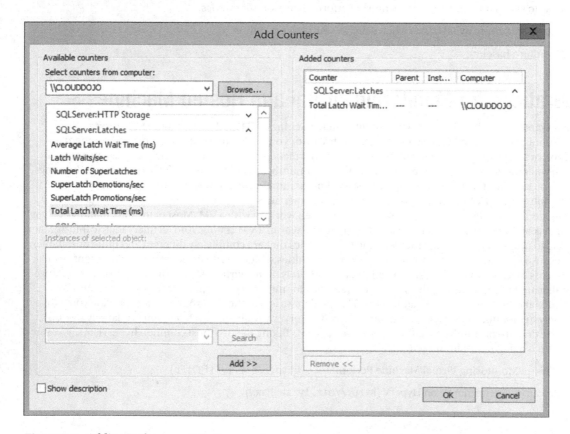

Figure 5-1. Adding Performance Monitor counters

For example, to add the performance counter SQLServer:Latches:Total Latch Wait Time(ms), follow these steps:

1. Select the option Select Counters from Computer and specify the computer name running SQL Server in the corresponding entry field.

2. Click the arrow next to the performance object SQLServer:Latches.

3. Choose the Total Latch Wait Time(ms) counter from the list of performance counters.

4. Click the Add button to add this performance counter to the list of counters to be added.

5. Continue as needed with other counters. When finished, click the OK button.

When creating a reusable list for your baseline, you can repeat the preceding steps to add all the performance counters listed in Table 5-1.

Table 5-1. *Performance Monitor Counters to Analyze SQL Server Performance*

Object(Instance[,InstanceN])	Counter
Memory	Available MBytes Pages/sec
PhysicalDisk(Data-disk, Log-disk)	% Disk Time Current Disk Queue Length Disk Transfers/sec Disk Bytes/sec
Processor(_Total)	% Processor Time % Privileged Time
System	Processor Queue Length Context Switches/sec
Network Interface(Network card)	Bytes Total/sec
Network Segment	% Net Utilization
SQLServer:Access Methods	FreeSpace Scans/sec Full Scans/sec
SQLServer:Buffer Manager	Buffer cache hit ratio
SQLServer:Latches	Total Latch Wait Time (ms)
SQLServer:Locks(_Total)	Lock Timeouts/sec Lock Wait Time (ms) Number of Deadlocks/sec
SQLServer:Memory Manager	Memory Grants Pending Target Server Memory (KB) Total Server Memory (KB)
SQLServer:SQL Statistics	Batch Requests/sec SQL Re-Compilations/sec
SQLServer:General Statistics	User Connections

Once you have added all the performance counters, close the Add Counters dialog box by clicking OK. To save the list of counters as an .htm file, right-click anywhere in the right frame of Performance Monitor and select the Save Settings As menu item.

The .htm file lists all the performance counters that can be used as a base set of counters to create a counter log or to view Performance Monitor graphs interactively for the same SQL Server machine. To use this list of counters for other SQL Server machines, open the .htm file in an editor such as Notepad and replace all instances of \\SQLServerMachineName with nothing, just a blank string) .

A shortcut to all this is outlined by Erin Stellato in the article "Customizing the Default Counters for Performance Monitor" (http://bit.ly/1brQKeZ).

You can also use this counter list file to view Performance Monitor graphs interactively in an Internet browser, as shown in Figure 5-2.

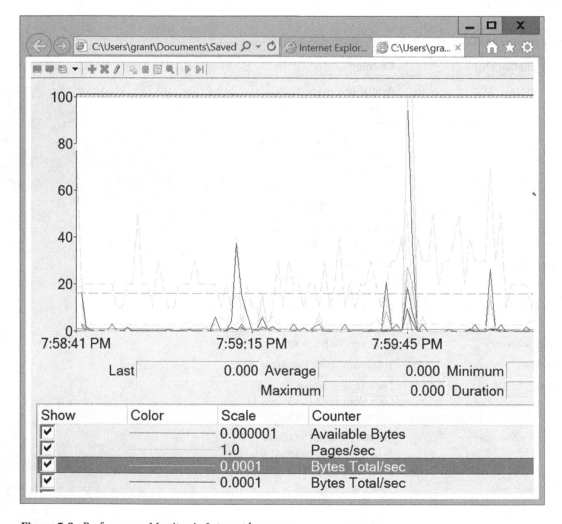

Figure 5-2. *Performance Monitor in Internet browser*

Creating a Counter Log Using the List of Performance Counters

Performance Monitor provides a counter log facility to save the performance data of multiple counters over a period of time. You can view the saved counter log using Performance Monitor to analyze the performance data. It is usually convenient to create a counter log from a defined list of performance counters. Simply collecting the data rather than viewing it through the GUI is the preferred method of automation to prepare for troubleshooting your server's performance or establishing a baseline.

Within Performance Monitor, expand Data Collector Sets ➤ User Defined. Right-click and select New ➤ Data Collector Set. Define the name of the set and make this a manual creation by clicking the appropriate radio button; then click Next just like I configured Figure 5-3:

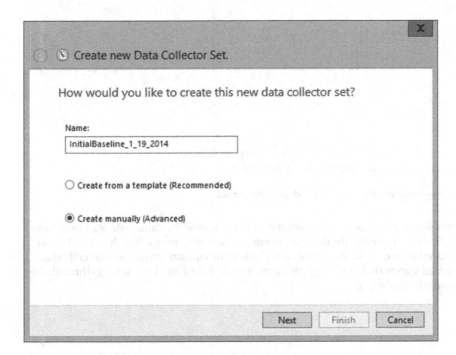

Figure 5-3. Naming the data collector set

You'll have to define what type of data you're collecting. In this case, select the check box Performance Counters under the Create Data Logs radio button and then click Next as shown in Figure 5-4:

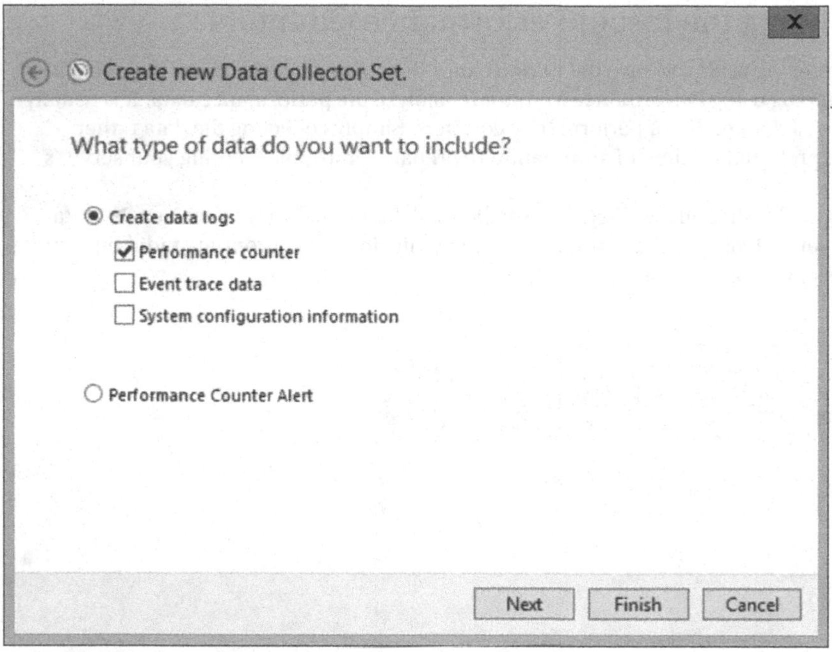

Figure 5-4. Selecting data logs and performance counters for the data collector set

Here you can define the performance objects you want to collect using the same Add Counters dialog box shown earlier in Figure 5-1. Clicking Next allows you to define the destination folder. Click Next, then select the radio button Open Properties for This Data Collector Set, and click Finish. You can schedule the counter log to automatically start at a specific time and stop after a certain time period or at a specific time. You can configure these settings through the Schedule pane. You can see an example in Figure 5-5:

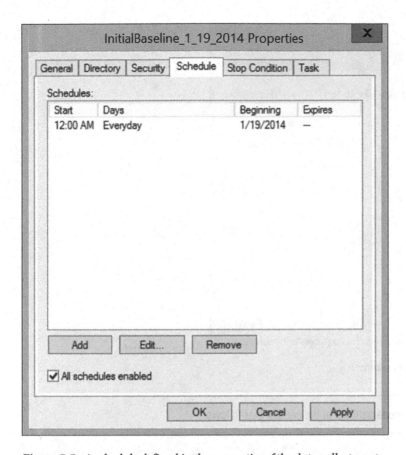

Figure 5-5. *A schedule defined in the properties of the data collector set*

Figure 5-6 summarizes which counters have been selected as well as the frequency with which the counters will be collected.

Figure 5-6. *Defining a Performance Monitor counter log*

■ **Note** I'll offer additional suggestions for these settings in the section that follows.

For additional information on how to create counter logs using Performance Monitor, please refer to the Microsoft Knowledge Base article "Performance Tuning Guidelines for Windows Server 2012 R2" (http://bit.ly/1icVvgn).

Performance Monitor Considerations

The Performance Monitor tool is designed to add as little overhead as possible, if used correctly. To minimize the impact of using this tool on a system, consider the following suggestions:

- Limit the number of counters, specifically performance objects.

- Use counter logs instead of viewing Performance Monitor graphs interactively.

- Run Performance Monitor remotely while viewing graphs interactively.

- Save the counter log file to a different local disk.

- Increase the sampling interval.

Let's consider each of these points in more detail.

Limit the Number of Counters

Monitoring large numbers of performance counters with small sampling intervals could incur some amount of overhead on the system. The bulk of this overhead comes from the number of performance objects you are monitoring, so selecting them wisely is important. The number of counters for the selected performance objects does not add much overhead because it gives only an attribute of the object itself. Therefore, it is important to know what objects you want to monitor and why.

Prefer Counter Logs

Use counter logs instead of viewing a Performance Monitor graph interactively because Performance Monitor graphing is more costly in terms of overhead. Monitoring current activities should be limited to short-term viewing of data, troubleshooting, and diagnosis. Performance data reported via a counter log is *sampled*, meaning that data is collected periodically rather than traced, whereas the Performance Monitor graph is updated in real time as events occur. Using counter logs will reduce that overhead.

View Performance Monitor Graphs Remotely

Since viewing the live performance data using Performance Monitor graphs creates a fair amount of overhead on the system, run the tool remotely on a different machine and connect to the SQL Server system through the tool. To remotely connect to the SQL Server machine, run the Performance Monitor tool on a machine connected to the network to which the SQL Server machine is also connected.

As shown in Figure 5-1, type the computer name (or IP address) of the SQL Server machine in the Select Counters from Computer box. Be aware that if you connect to the production server through a Windows Server 2012 R2 terminal service session, the major part of the tool will still run on the server.

However, I still encourage you to avoid using the Monitor Graphs for viewing live data. You can use the graphs to look at the files collected through counter logs and should have a bias toward using those logs.

Save Counter Log Locally

Collecting the performance data for the counter log does not incur the overhead of displaying any graph. So, while using counter log mode, it is more efficient to log counter values locally on the SQL Server system instead of transferring the performance data across the network. Put the counter log file on a local disk other than the ones that are monitored, meaning your SQL Server data and log files.

Then, after you collect the data, copy that counter log to your local machine to analyze it. That way, you're working only on a copy, and you're not adding I/O overhead to your storage location.

Increase the Sampling Interval

Because you are mainly interested in the resource utilization pattern during baseline monitoring, you can easily increase the performance data sampling interval to 60 seconds or more to decrease the log file size and reduce demand on disk I/Os. You can use a short sampling interval to detect and diagnose timing issues. Even while viewing Performance Monitor graphs interactively, increase the sampling interval from the default value of one second per sample. Just remember, changing the sampling size up or down can affect the granularity of the data as well as the quantity. You have to weigh these choices carefully.

System Behavior Analysis Against Baseline

The default behavior of a database application changes over time because of various factors such as the following:

- Data volume and distribution changes

- Increased user base

- Change in usage pattern of the application

- Additions to or changes in the application's behavior

- Installation of new service packs or software upgrades

- Changes to hardware

Because of these changes, the baseline created for the database server slowly loses its significance. It may not always be accurate to compare the current behavior of the system with an old baseline. Therefore, it is important to keep the baseline current by creating a new baseline at regular time intervals. It is also beneficial to archive the previous baseline logs so that they can be referred to later, if required. So while, yes, older baselines are not applicable to day-to-day operations, they do help you in establishing patterns and long-term trends.

The counter log for the baseline or the current behavior of the system can be analyzed using the Performance Monitor tool by following these steps:

1. Open the counter log. Use Performance Monitor's toolbar item View Log File Data and select the log file's name.

2. Add all the performance counters to analyze the performance data. Note that only the performance objects, counters, and instances selected during the counter log creation are shown in the selection lists.

3. Analyze the system behavior at different parts of the day by adjusting the time range accordingly, as shown in Figure 5-7.

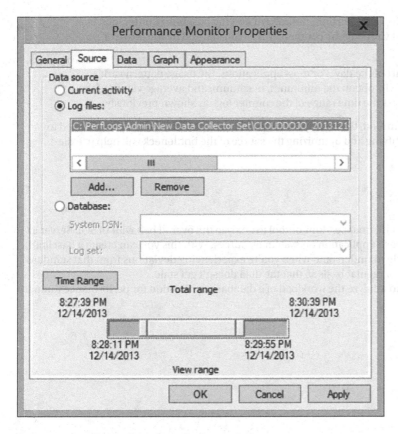

Figure 5-7. Defining time range for log analysis

During a performance review, you can analyze the system-level behavior of the database by comparing the current value of performance counters with the latest baseline. Take the following considerations into account while comparing the performance data:

- Use the same set of performance counters in both cases.

- Compare the minimum, maximum, and average values of the counters as applicable for the individual counters. I explained the specific values for the counters earlier.

- Some counters have an absolute good/bad value, as mentioned previously. The current value of these counters need not be compared with the baseline values. For example, if the current average value of the Deadlocks/min counter is 10, it indicates that the system is suffering from a large number of deadlocks. Even though it does not require a comparison with the baseline, it is still advantageous to review the corresponding baseline value because your deadlock issues might have existed for a long time. Having the archived baseline logs helps detect the evolving occurrence of the deadlock.

- Some counters do not have a definitive good/bad value. Because their value depends on the application, a relative comparison with the corresponding baseline counters is a must. For example, the current value of the User Connections counter for SQL Server does not signify anything good or bad with the application. But comparing it with the corresponding baseline value may reveal a big increase in the number of user connections, indicating an increase in the workload.

- Compare a range of values for the counters from the current and the baseline counter logs. The fluctuation in the individual values of the counters will be normalized by the range of values.

- Compare logs from the same part of the day. For most applications, the usage pattern varies during different parts of the day. To obtain the minimum, maximum, and average values of the counters for a specific time, adjust the time range of the counter logs as shown previously.

Once the system-level bottleneck is identified, the internal behavior of the application should be analyzed to determine the cause of the bottleneck. Identifying and optimizing the source of the bottleneck will help use the system resources efficiently.

Summary

In this chapter, you learned how to use the Performance Monitor tool to analyze the overall behavior of SQL Server as well as the effect of a slow-performing database application on system resources. With this you can create a baseline for your system behavior so that you'll be able to understand when you're experiencing deviations from that standard behavior. You'll want to collect a baseline on a regular basis so that the data doesn't get stale.

In the next chapter, you will learn how to analyze the workload of a database application for performance tuning.

CHAPTER 6

■ ■ ■

Query Performance Metrics

A common cause of slow SQL Server performance is a heavy database application workload—the nature and quantity of the queries themselves. Thus, to analyze the cause of a system bottleneck, it is important to examine the database application workload and identify the SQL queries causing the most stress on system resources. To do this, you can use Extended Events and other Management Studio tools.

In this chapter, I cover the following topics:

- The basics of Extended Events
- How to analyze SQL Server workload and identify costly SQL queries using Extended Events
- How to track query performance through dynamic management objects

Extended Events

Extended Events was introduced in SQL Server 2008, but with no GUI in place and a reasonably complex set of code to set it up, Extended Events wasn't used much to capture performance metrics. With SQL Server 2012, a GUI for managing Extended Events was introduced, taking away the final issue preventing Extended Events from becoming the preferred mechanism for gathering query performance metrics as well as other metrics and measures. SQL Profiler, previously the best mechanism for gathering these metrics, is in deprecation and will, within a release or two, be completely removed from the product. Trace events, also good, are still available but on their way out along with Profiler. As a result, most examples in the book will be using Extended Events.

Extended Events allows you to do the following:

- Graphically monitor SQL Server queries
- Collect query information in the background
- Analyze performance
- Diagnose problems such as deadlocks
- Debug a Transact-SQL (T-SQL) statement

You can also use Extended Events to capture other sorts of activities performed on a SQL Server instance. You can set up Extended Events from the graphical front end or through direct calls to the procedures. The most efficient way to define an Extended Events session is through the T-SQL commands, but a good place to start learning about sessions is through the GUI.

Extended Events Sessions

You will find the Extended Events infrastructure in the Management Studio GUI. You can navigate using the Object Explorer to the Management folder on a given instance to find the Extended Events folder. From there you can look at sessions that have already been built on the system. To start setting up your own sessions, just right-click the Sessions folder and select New Session. There is a wizard available for setting up sessions, but it doesn't do anything the regular GUI doesn't do, and the regular GUI is easy to use. A window opens to the first page, called General, as shown in Figure 6-1.

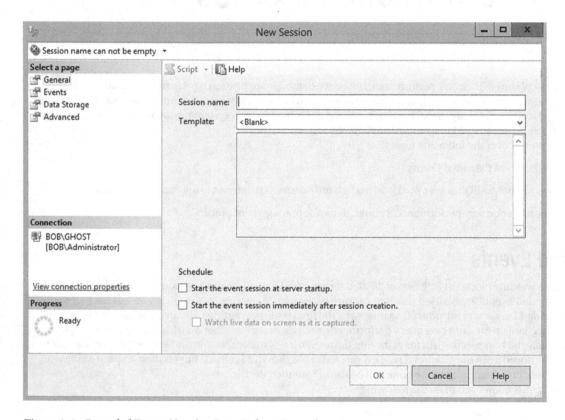

Figure 6-1. *Extended Events New Session window, General page*

You will have to supply a session name. I strongly suggest giving it a clear name so you know what the session is doing when you check it later. You also have the choice of using a template. Templates are predefined sessions that you can put to work with minimal effort. There are five templates immediately associated with query tuning.

- *Query Batch Sampling*: This template will capture queries and procedure calls for 20 percent of all active sessions on the server.

- *Query Batch Tracking*: This template captures all queries and procedures for all sessions on the server.

- *Query Detail Sampling*: This template contains a set of events that will capture every statement in queries and procedures for 20 percent of all active sessions on the server.

- *Query Detail Tracking*: This template is the same as Query Batch Tracking, but for every single statement in the system as well. This generates a large amount of data.

- *Query Wait Statistic*: This template captures wait statistics for each statement of every query and procedure for 20 percent of all active sessions.

For the example here, you'll skip the templates and set up your own events so you can see how it's done.

■ **Note**   Nothing is free or without risk. Extended Events is a much more efficient mechanism for gathering information about the system than the old trace events. Extended Events is not without cost and risk. Depending on the events you define and, even more, on some of the global fields that I discuss in more detail later in the chapter, you can see an impact on your system by implementing Extended Events. Exercise caution when using these events on your production system to ensure you don't implement a negative impact.

You must decide whether you want the session to start when the server starts. Collecting performance metrics over a long period of time generates lots of data that you'll have to deal with. You can also decide whether you'd like to start this session immediately after you create it and whether you want to watch live data. As you can see, the New Session window is actually pretty close to already being a wizard. It just lacks a Next button. Once you've provided a name and made the other choices here, click the next page, Events, as shown in Figure 6-2.

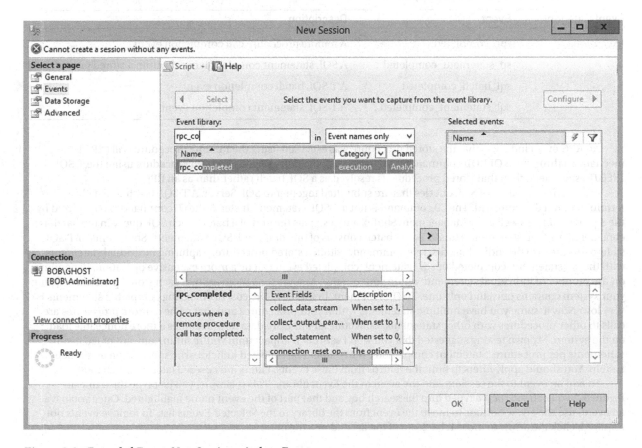

Figure 6-2. Extended Events New Session window, Events page

An *event* represents various activities performed in SQL Server and, in some cases, the underlying operating system. There's an entire architecture around event targets, event packages, and event sessions, but the use of the GUI means you don't have to worry about all those details. I will cover some of the architecture when showing how to script a session later in this chapter.

For performance analysis, you are mainly interested in the events that help you judge levels of resource stress for various activities performed on SQL Server. By *resource stress,* I mean things such as the following:

- What kind of CPU utilization was involved for the SQL activity?

- How much memory was used?

- How much I/O was involved?

- How long did the SQL activity take to execute?

- How frequently was a particular query executed?

- What kind of errors and warnings were faced by the queries?

You can calculate the resource stress of a SQL activity after the completion of an event, so the main events you use for performance analysis are those that represent the completion of a SQL activity. Table 6-1 describes these events.

Table 6-1. *Events to Monitor Query Completion*

Event Category	Event	Description
Execution	rpc_completed	A remote procedure call completion event
	sp_statement_completed	A SQL statement completion event within a stored procedure
	sql_batch_completed	A T-SQL batch completion event
	sql_statement_completed	A T-SQL statement completion event

An RPC event indicates that the stored procedure was executed using the Remote Procedure Call (RPC) mechanism through an OLEDB command. If a database application executes a stored procedure using the T-SQL EXECUTE statement, then that stored procedure is resolved as a SQL batch rather than as an RPC.

A *T-SQL batch* is a set of SQL queries that are submitted together to SQL Server. A T-SQL batch is usually terminated by a GO command. The GO command is not a T-SQL statement. Instead, the GO command is recognized by the sqlcmd utility, as well as by Management Studio, and it signals the end of a batch. Each SQL query in the batch is considered a T-SQL statement. Thus, a T-SQL batch consists of one or more T-SQL statements. Statements or T-SQL statements are also the individual, discrete commands within a stored procedure. Capturing individual statements with the sp_statement_completed or sql_statement_completed event can be a more expensive operation, depending on the number of individual statements within your queries. Assume for a moment that each stored procedure within your system contains one, and only one, T-SQL statement. In this case, the cost of collecting completed statements is very low. Now assume you have multiple statements within your procedures and that some of those procedures are calls to other procedures with other statements. Collecting all this extra data now becomes a more noticeable load on the system. My own testing suggested that you won't see much impact until you're hitting upward of ten distinct statements per procedure. Statement completion events should be collected judiciously, especially on a production system. You should apply filters to limit the returns from these events. Filters are covered later in this chapter.

To add an event to the session, find the event in the Event library. This is simple; you just type the name. In Figure 6-2 you can see *rpc_co* typed into the search box and that part of the event name highlighted. Once you have an event, use the arrow buttons to move the event from the library to the Selected Events list. To remove events not required, click the arrow to move it back out of the list and into the library.

Although the events listed in Table 6-1 represent the most common events used for determining query performance, you can sometimes use a number of additional events to diagnose the same thing. For example, as mentioned in Chapter 1, repeated recompilation of a stored procedure adds processing overhead, which hurts the performance of the database request. The execution category in the Event library includes an event, sql_statement_recompile, to indicate the recompilation of a statement (this event is explained in depth in Chapter 11). The Event library contains additional events to indicate other performance-related issues with a database workload. Table 6-2 shows a few of these events.

Table 6-2. *Events for Query Performance*

Event Category	Event	Description
Session	login logout	Keeps track of database connections when users connect to and disconnect from SQL Server.
	existing_connection	Represents all the users connected to SQL Server before the session was started.
errors	attention	Represents the intermediate termination of a request caused by actions such as query cancellation by a client or a broken database connection including timeouts.
	error_reported	Occurs when an error is reported.
	execution_warning	Indicates the occurrence of any warning during the execution of a query or a stored procedure.
	hash_warning	Indicates the occurrence of an error in a hashing operation.
warnings	missing_column_statistics	Indicates that the statistics of a column, which are statistics required by the optimizer to decide a processing strategy, are missing.
	missing_join_predicate	Indicates that a query is executed with no joining predicate between two tables.
	sort_warnings	Indicates that a sort operation performed in a query such as SELECT did not fit into memory.
lock	lock_deadlock	Occurs when a process is chosen as a deadlock victim.
	lock_deadlock_chain	Shows a trace of the chain of queries creating the deadlock.
	lock_timeout	Signifies that the lock has exceeded the timeout parameter, which is set by SET LOCK_TIMEOUT timeout_period(ms).
execution	sql_statement_recompile	Indicates that an execution plan for a query statement had to be recompiled because one did not exist, a recompilation was forced, or the existing execution plan could not be reused.
	rpc_starting	Represents the starting of a stored procedure. They are useful to identify procedures that started but could not finish because of an operation that caused an Attention event.
	Query_post_compilation_showplan	Shows the execution plan after a SQL statement has been compiled.
	Query_post_execution_showplan	Shows the execution plan after the SQL statement has been executed that includes execution statistics. Note, this event can be quite costly, so use it extremely sparingly and for short periods of time with good filters in place.
transactions	sql_transaction	Provides information about a database transaction, including information such as when a transaction starts, completes, and rolls back.

Global Fields

Once you've selected the events that are of interest in Events, you may need to configure some settings, such as global fields. On the Events screen, click the Configure button. This will change the view of the Events screen, as shown in Figure 6-3.

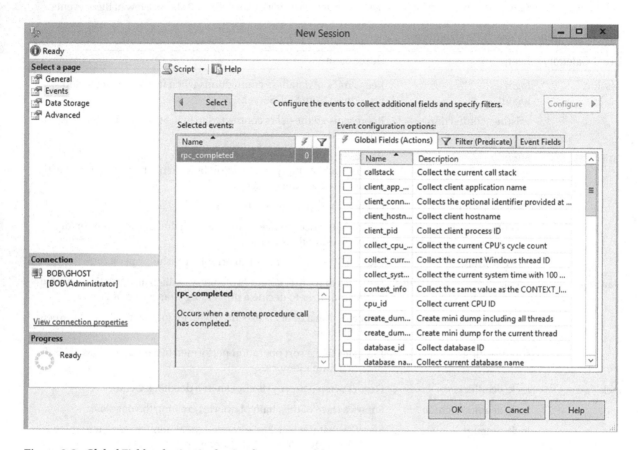

Figure 6-3. *Global Fields selection in the Configure part of the Events page*

The global fields, called *actions* in T-SQL, represent different attributes of an event, such as the user involved with the event, the execution plan for the event, some additional resource costs of the event, and the source of the event. These are additional pieces of information that can be collected with an event. They add overhead to the collection of the event. Each event has a set of data it collects, which I'll talk about later in the chapter, but this is your chance to add more. Most of the time, when I can, I avoid this overhead for most data collection. But sometimes, there is information here you'll want to collect.

To add an action, just click the check box in the list provided on the Global Fields page shown in Figure 6-6. You can use additional data columns from time to time to diagnose the cause of poor performance. For example, in the case of a stored procedure recompilation, the event indicates the cause of the recompile through the recompile_cause event field. (This field is explained in depth in Chapter 17.) A few of the commonly used additional actions are as follows:

- plan_handle
- query_hash
- query_plan_hash
- database_id
- client_app_name
- transaction_id
- session_id

Other information is available as part of the event fields. For example, the binary_data and integer_data event fields provide specific information about a given SQL Server activity. For instance, in the case of a cursor, they specify the type of cursor requested and the type of cursor created. Although the names of these additional fields indicate their purpose to a great extent, I will explain the usefulness of these global fields in later chapters as you use them.

Event Filters

In addition to defining events and actions for an Extended Events session, you can also define various filter criteria. These help keep the session output small, which is usually a good idea. You can add filters for event fields or global fields. You also get to choose whether you want each filter to be an OR or an AND to further control the methods of filtering. You also get to decide on the operator, such as less than, equal to, and so on. Finally, you set a value for the comparison. All this will act to filter the events captured, reducing the amount of data you're dealing with and, possibly, the load on your system. Table 6-3 describes the filter criteria that you may commonly use during performance analysis.

Table 6-3. SQL Trace Filters

Events	Filter Criteria Example	Use
sqlserver.username	= <some value>	This captures events only for a single user or login.
sqlserver.database_id	= <ID of the database to monitor>	This filters out events generated by other databases. You can determine the ID of a database from its name as follows: SELECT DB_ID('AdventureWorks20012').
duration	>=200	For performance analysis, you will often capture a trace for a large workload. In a large trace, there will be many event logs with a duration that is less than what you're interested in. Filter out these event logs because there is hardly any scope for optimizing these SQL activities.
physical_reads	>=2	This is similar to the criterion on the duration filter.
sqlserver.session_id	= <Database users to monitor>	This troubleshoots queries sent by a specific server session.

Figure 6-4 shows a snippet of the preceding filter criteria selection in the Session window.

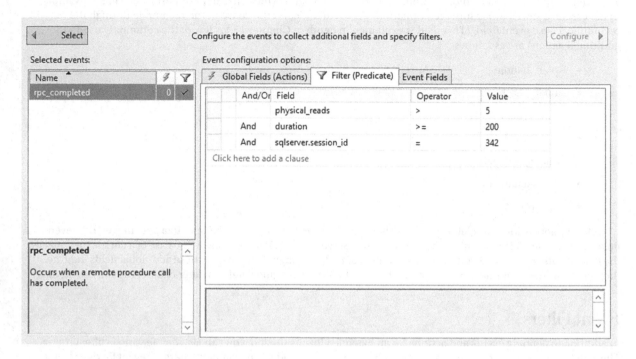

Figure 6-4. *Filters applied in the Session window*

If you look at the Field value in Figure 6-4, you'll note that it says sqlserver.session_id. This is because different sets of data are available to you, and they are qualified by the type of data being referenced. In this case, I'm talking specifically about a sqlserver.session_id. But I could be referring to something from sqlos or even the Extended Events package itself.

Event Fields

The standard event fields are included automatically with the event type. Table 6-4 shows some of the common actions that you use for performance analysis.

Table 6-4. Actions Command for Query Analysis

Data Column	Description
Statement	The SQL text from the rpc_completed event.
Batch_text	The SQL text from the sql_batch_completed event.
cpu_time	The CPU cost of an event in microseconds (mc). For example, CPU = 100 for a SELECT statement indicates that the statement took 100 mc to execute.
logical_reads	The number of logical reads performed for an event. For example, logical_reads = 800 for a SELECT statement indicates that the statement required a total of 800 page reads.
Physical_reads	The number of physical reads performed for an event. This can differ from the logical_reads value because of access to the disk subsystem.
writes	The number of logical writes performed for an event.
duration	The execution time of an event in ms.

Each logical read and write consists of an 8KB page activity in memory, which may require zero or more physical I/O operations. You can see the fields for any given event by clicking the Event Fields tab on display in Figure 6-5.

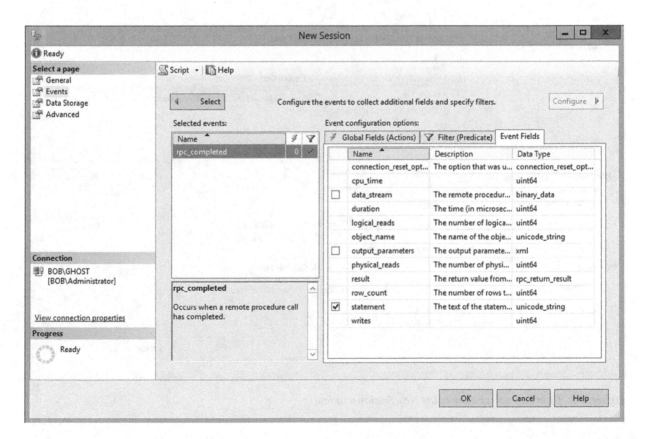

Figure 6-5. New Session window with the Event Fields tab in Configure on display

Some of the event fields are optional, but most of them are automatically included with the event. You can decide whether you want to include the optional fields. In Figure 6-5 you could include the output_parameters field by clicking the check box next to it.

Data Storage

The next page in the new Session window, Data Storage in the "Select a page" pane, is for determining how you're going to deal with the data generated by the session. The output mechanism is referred to as the *target*. You have two basic choices: output the information to a file or simply use the buffer to capture the events. You should use only small data sets with the buffer because it will consume memory. Because it works with memory within the system, the buffer is built so that, rather than overwhelm the system memory, it will drop events, so you're more likely to lose information using the buffer. In most circumstances for monitoring query performance, you should capture the output of the session to a file.

You have to select your target as shown in Figure 6-6.

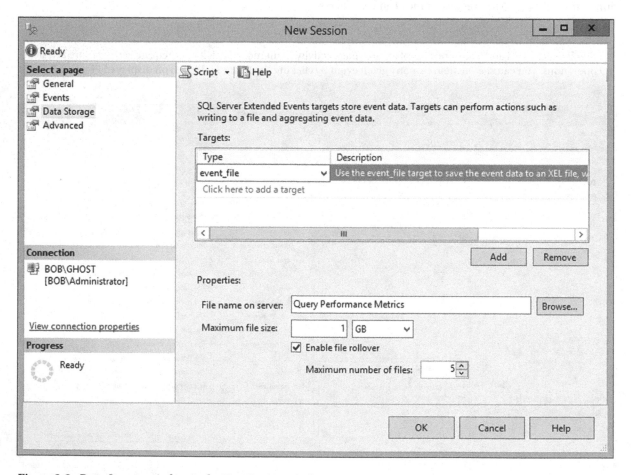

Figure 6-6. *Data Storage window in the New Session window*

As you can see, it defaulted to local storage on my server. You can specify an appropriate location on your system. You can also decide whether you're using more than one file, how many, and whether those files roll over. All of those are management decisions that you'll have to deal with as part of working with your environment and your SQL query monitoring. You can run this 24/7, but you have to be prepared to deal with large amounts of data depending on how stringent the filters you've created are.

In addition to the buffer or the file, you have other output options, but they're usually reserved for special types of monitoring and not usually necessary for query performance tuning.

Finishing the Session

Once you've defined the storage, you've set everything needed for the session. There is an Advanced page as well, but you really shouldn't need to modify this from the defaults on most systems. If you click OK, the session will get created. If you set up the session to start on the first tab, it will start immediately, but whether it starts or not, it will be stored on the server. One of the beauties of Extended Events sessions is that they're stored on the server, so you can turn them on and off as needed.

Assuming you either didn't automatically start the session or selected the option to watch the data live, you can do both to the session you just created. Right-click the session, and you'll see a menu of actions including Start Session, Stop Session, and Watch Live Data. If you start the session and you chose to observe the output, you should see a new window appear in Management Studio showing the events you're capturing. These events are coming off the same buffer as the one that is writing out to disk, so you can watch events in real time. Take a look at Figure 6-7 to see this in action.

BOB\GHOST - Query...Metrics: Live Data ✕

Displaying 20254 Events

name	timestamp
rpc_completed	2013-12-16 18:18:46.4221157
rpc_completed	2013-12-16 18:18:46.4229718
rpc_completed	2013-12-16 18:18:46.4241845
rpc_completed	2013-12-16 18:18:46.4254485
rpc_completed	2013-12-16 18:18:46.4268150
rpc_completed	2013-12-16 18:18:46.4276845

Event: rpc_completed (2013-12-16 18:18:46.4241845)

Details

Field	Value
connection_reset_...	None
cpu_time	0
data_stream	0x
duration	1116
logical_reads	81
object_name	sp_executesql
output_parameters	
physical_reads	0
result	OK
row_count	3
statement	exec sp_executesql N'dbo.uspGetEmployeeManagers @Busines...
writes	0

Figure 6-7. *Live output of the Extended Events session created by the wizard*

You can see the events at the top of the window showing the type of event and the date and time of the event. Clicking the event at the top will open the fields that were captured with the event on the bottom of the screen. As you can see, all the information I've been talking about is available to you. Also, if you're unhappy with having a divided output, you can right-click a column and select Show Column in Table from the context menu. This will move it up into the top part of the screen, displaying all the information in a single location, as shown in Figure 6-8.

name	timestamp	statement
rpc_completed	2013-12-16 18:18:46.4207855	exec sp_reset_c...
rpc_completed	2013-12-16 18:18:46.4221157	exec sp_execute...
rpc_completed	2013-12-16 18:18:46.4229718	exec sp_reset_c...
rpc_completed	2013-12-16 18:18:46.4241845	exec sp_execute...
rpc_completed	2013-12-16 18:18:46.4254485	exec sp_reset_c...
rpc_completed	2013-12-16 18:18:46.4268150	exec sp_execute...

Displaying 20254 Events

BOB\GHOST - Query...Metrics: Live Data

Figure 6-8. *The statement column has been added to the table*

You can also open the files you've collected through this interface and use it to browse the data. You can search within a column on the collected data, sort by them, and group by fields. One of the great ways to see an aggregate of all calls to a particular query is to use query_hash, a global field that you can add to your data collection. The GUI offers a lot of ways to manipulate the information you've collected.

Watching this information through the GUI and browsing through files is fine, but you're going to want to automate the creation of these sessions. That's what the next section covers.

Extended Events Automation

The ability to use the GUI to build a session and define the events you want to capture does make things simple, but, unfortunately, it's not a model that will scale. If you need to manage multiple servers where you're going to create sessions for capturing key query performance metrics, you're not going to want to connect to each one and go through the GUI to select the events, the output, and so on. This is especially true if you take into account the chance of a mistake. Instead, it's much better to learn how to work with sessions directly from T-SQL. This will enable you to build a session that can be run on a number of servers in your system. Even better, you're going to find that building sessions directly is easier in some ways than using the GUI, and you're going to be much more knowledgeable about how these processes work.

Creating a Session Script Using the GUI

You can create a scripted trace in one of two ways, manually or with the GUI. Until you get comfortable with all the requirements of the scripts, the easy way is to use the Extended Events tool GUI. These are the steps you'll need to perform:

1. Define a session.

2. Right-click the session, and select Script Sessions As, CREATE To, and File to output straight to a file. Or, use the Script button at the top of the New Session window to create a T-SQL command in the Query window.

These steps will generate the script that you need to create a session and output it to a file.

To manually create this new trace, use Management Studio as follows:

1. Open the script file or navigate to the Query window.

2. Modify the path and file location for the server you're creating this session on.

3. Execute the script.

Once the session is created, you can use the following command to start it:

```
ALTER EVENT SESSION [Query Performance Metrics]
ON SERVER
STATE = START;
```

You may want to automate the execution of the last step through the SQL Agent, or you can even run the script from the command line using the sqlcmd.exe utility. Whatever method you use, the final step will start the session. To stop the session, just run the same script with the STATE set to stop. I'll show how to do that in the next section.

Defining a Session Using T-SQL

If you look at the script defined in the previous section, you will see a single command that was used to define the session, CREATE EVENT SESSION.

Once the session has been defined, you can activate it using ALTER EVENT.

Once a session is started on the server, you don't have to keep Management Studio open any more. You can identify the active sessions by using the dynamic management view sys.dm_xe_sessions, as shown in the following query:

```
SELECT  dxs.name,
        dxs.create_time
FROM    sys.dm_xe_sessions AS dxs;
```

Figure 6-9 shows the output of the view.

	name	create_time
1	system_health	2013-12-14 19:56:07.163
2	sp_server_diagnostics session	2013-12-14 19:56:07.847
3	Query Performance Metrics	2013-12-17 02:25:44.900

Figure 6-9. *Output of sys.dm_xe_sessions*

The number of rows returned indicates the number of sessions active on SQL Server. I have two other sessions running in addition to the one I created in this chapter. You can stop a specific session by executing the stored procedure ALTER EVENT SESSION.

```
ALTER EVENT SESSION [Query Performance Metrics]
ON SERVER
STATE = STOP;
```

To verify that the session is stopped successfully, reexecute the query against the catalog view sys.dm_xe_sessions, and ensure that the output of the view doesn't contain the named session.

Using a script to create your sessions allows you to automate across a large number of servers. Using the scripts to start and stop the sessions means you can control them through scheduled events such as through SQL Agent. In Chapter 18, you will learn how to control the schedule of a session while capturing the activities of a SQL workload over an extended period of time.

■ **Note**   The time captured through a session defined as illustrated in this section is stored in microseconds, not milliseconds. This difference between units can cause confusion if not taken into account. You must filter based on microseconds.

Extended Events Recommendations

Extended Events is such a game-changer in the way that information is collected that many of the problematic areas that used to come up when using trace events have been largely eliminated. You have a much reduced need to worry as much about severely limiting the number of events collected or the number of fields returned. But, as was noted earlier, you can still negatively impact the system by overloading the events being collected. There are still a few specific areas you need to watch out for.

- Set max file size appropriately.
- Avoid debug events.
- Avoid use of No_Event_Loss.

I'll go over these in a little more detail in the following sections.

Set Max File Size Appropriately

The default value for files is 1GB. That's actually very small when you consider the amount of information that can be gathered with Extended Events. It's a good idea to set this number much higher, somewhere in the 50GB to100GB range to ensure you have adequate space to capture information and you're not waiting on the file subsystem to create files for you while your buffer fills. This can lead to event loss. But, it does depend on your system. If you have a good grasp of the level of output you can expect, set the file size more appropriate to your individual environment.

Avoid Debug Events

Not only does Extended Events provide you with a mechanism for observing the behavior of SQL Server and its internals in a way that far exceeds what was possible under trace events, but Microsoft uses the same functionality as part of troubleshooting SQL Server. A number of events are related to debugging SQL Server. These are not available by default through the wizard, but you do have access to them through the T-SQL command, and there's a way to enable them through the channel selection in the Session editor window.

Without direct guidance from Microsoft, do not use them. They are subject to change and are meant for Microsoft internal use only. If you do feel the need to experiment, you need to pay close attention to any of the events that include a break action. This means that should the event fire, it will stop SQL Server at the exact line of code that caused the event to fire. This means your server will be completely offline and in an unknown state. This could lead to a major outage if you were to do it in a production system. It could lead to loss of data and corruption of your database.

Avoid Use of No_Event_Loss

Extended Events is set up such that some events will be lost. It's extremely likely, by design. But, you can use a setting, No_Event_Loss, when configuring your session. If you do this on systems that are already under load, you may see a significant additional load placed on the system since you're effectively telling it to retain information in the buffer regardless of consequences. For small and focused sessions that are targeting a particular behavior, this approach can be acceptable.

Other Methods for Query Performance Metrics

Setting up an Extended Event session allows you to collect a lot of data for later use, but the collection can be a little bit expensive. In addition, you have to wait on the results, and then you have a lot of data to deal with. If you need to immediately capture performance metrics about your system, especially as they pertain to query performance, then the dynamic management views sys.dm_exec_query_stats for queries and sys.dm_exec_procedure_stats for stored procedures are what you need. If you still need a historical tracking of when queries were run and their individual costs, an Extended Events session is still the best tool. But if you just need to know, at this moment, the longest-running queries or the most physical reads, then you can get that information from these two dynamic management objects. But, the data in these objects are dependent on the query plan remaining in the cache. If the plan ages out of cache, this data just goes away. The sys.dm_exec_query_stats DMO will return results for all queries, including stored procedures, but the sys.dm_exec_procedure_stats will return information only for stored procedures.

Since both these DMOs are just views, you can simply query against them and get information about the statistics of queries in the plan cache on the server. Table 6-5 shows some of the data returned from the sys.dm_exec_query_stats DMO.

Table 6-5. *sys.dm_exec_query_stats Output*

Column	Description
Plan_handle	Pointer that refers to the execution plan
Creation_time	Time that the plan was created
Last_execution time	Last time the plan was used by a query
Execution_count	Number of times the plan has been used
Total_worker_time	Total CPU time used by the plan since it was created
Total_logical_reads	Total number of reads used since the plan was created
Total_logical_writes	Total number of writes used since the plan was created
Query_hash	A binary hash that can be used to identify queries with similar logic
Query_plan_hash	A binary hash that can be used to identify plans with similar logic

Table 6-5 is just a sampling. For complete details, see Books Online.

To filter the information returned from sys.dm_exec_query_stats, you'll need to join it with other dynamic management functions such as sys.dm_exec_sql_text, which shows the query text associated with the plan, or sys. dm_query_plan, which has the execution plan for the query. Once joined to these other DMOs, you can filter on the database or procedure that you want to see. These other DMOs are covered in detail in other chapters of the book. I'll show examples of using sys.dm_exec_query_stats and the others, in combination, throughout the rest of the book. Just remember that these queries are cache dependent. As a given execution plan ages out of the cache, this information will be lost.

Summary

In this chapter, you saw that you can use Extended Events to identify the queries causing a high amount of stress on the system resources in a SQL workload. Collecting the session data can, and should be, automated using system stored procedures. For immediate access to statistics about running queries, use the DMV sys.dm_exec_query_stats.

Now that you have a mechanism for gathering metrics on queries that have been running against your system, in the next chapter you'll explore how to gather information about a query as it runs so that you don't have to resort to these measurement tools each time you run a query.

CHAPTER 7

■ ■ ■

Analyzing Query Performance

The previous chapter showed how to gather query performance metrics. This chapter will show how to consume those metrics to identify long-running or frequently called queries. Then I'll go over the tools built right into Management Studio so you can understand how a given query is performing. I'll also spend a lot of time talking about using execution plans, which are your best view into the decisions made by the query optimizer.

In this chapter, I cover the following topics:

- How to analyze the processing strategy of a costly SQL query using Management Studio
- How to analyze methods used by the query optimizer for a SQL query
- How to measure the cost of a SQL query using SQL utilities

Costly Queries

Now that you have seen two different ways of collecting query performance metrics, let's look at what the data represents: the costly queries themselves. When the performance of SQL Server goes bad, a few things are most likely happening.

- First, certain queries create high stress on system resources. These queries affect the performance of the overall system because the server becomes incapable of serving other SQL queries fast enough.

- Additionally, the costly queries block all other queries requesting the same database resources, further degrading the performance of those queries. Optimizing the costly queries improves not only their own performance but also the performance of other queries by reducing database blocking and pressure on SQL Server resources.

- Finally, a query that by itself is not terribly costly could be called thousands of times a minute, which, by the simple accumulation of less than optimal code, can lead to major resource bottlenecks.

To begin to determine which queries you need to spend time working with, you're going to use the resources that I've talked about so far. For example, assuming the queries are in cache, you will be able to use the DMOs to pull together meaningful data to determine the most costly queries. Alternatively, because you've captured the queries using Extended Events, you can access that data as a means to identify the costliest queries.

One small note on the Extended Events data: if it's going to be collected to a file, you'll then need to load the data into a table or just query it directly. You can read directly from the Extended Events fileby querying it using this system function:

```
SELECT  *
FROM    sys.fn_xe_file_target_read_file('C:\Sessions\QueryPerformanceMetrics*.xel',
                                        NULL, NULL, NULL);
```

The query returns each event as a single row. The data about the event is stored in an XML column, event_data. You'll need to use XQuery to read the data directly, but once you do, you can search, sort, and aggregate the data captured. I'll walk you through a full example of this mechanism in the next section.

Identifying Costly Queries

The goal of SQL Server is to return result sets to the user in the shortest time. To do this, SQL Server has a built-in, cost-based optimizer called the *query optimizer,* which generates a cost-effective strategy called a *query execution plan.* The query optimizer weighs many factors, including (but not limited to) the usage of CPU, memory, and disk I/O required to execute a query, all derived from the various sources such as statistics about the data maintained by indexes or generated on the fly, constraints on the data, and some knowledge of the system the queries are running such as the number of CPUs and the amount of memory. From all that the optimizer creates a cost-effective execution plan.

In the data returned from a session, the cpu_time and logical_reads or physical_reads fields also show where a query costs you. The cpu_time field represents the CPU time used to execute the query. The two reads fields represent the number of pages (8KB in size) a query operated on and thereby indicates the amount of memory or I/O stress caused by the query. It also indicates disk stress since memory pages have to be backed up in the case of action queries, populated during first-time data access, and displaced to disk during memory bottlenecks. The higher the number of logical reads for a query, the higher the possible stress on the disk could be. An excessive number of logical pages also increases load on the CPU in managing those pages. This is not an automatic correlation. You can't always count on the query with the highest number of reads being the poorest performer. But it is a general metric and a good starting point. Although minimizing the number of I/Os is not a requirement for a cost-effective plan, you will often find that the least costly plan generally has the fewest I/Os because I/O operations are expensive.

The queries that cause a large number of logical reads usually acquire locks on a correspondingly large set of data. Even reading (as opposed to writing) may require shared locks on all the data, depending on the isolation level. These queries block all other queries requesting this data (or part of the data) for the purposes of modifying it, not for reading it. Since these queries are inherently costly and require a long time to execute, they block other queries for an extended period of time. The blocked queries then cause blocks on further queries, introducing a chain of blocking in the database. (Chapter 13 covers lock modes.)

As a result, it makes sense to identify the costly queries and optimize them first, thereby doing the following:

- Improving the performance of the costly queries themselves

- Reducing the overall stress on system resources

- Reducing database blocking

The costly queries can be categorized into the following two types:

- *Single execution*: An individual execution of the query is costly.

- *Multiple executions*: A query itself may not be costly, but the repeated execution of the query causes pressure on the system resources.

You can identify these two types of costly queries using different approaches, as explained in the following sections.

Costly Queries with a Single Execution

You can identify the costly queries by analyzing a session output file or by querying sys.dm_exec_query_stats. For this example, we'll start with identifying queries that perform a large number of logical reads, so you should sort the session output on the logical_reads data column. You can change that around to sort on duration or CPU, or even combine them in interesting ways. You can access the session information by following these steps:

1. Capture a session that contains a typical workload.

2. Save the session output to a file.

3. Open the file by using File ➤ Open and select a .xel file to use the data browser window. Sort the information there.

4. Alternatively, you can query the trace file for analysis sorting by the logical_reads field.

```
WITH    xEvents
        AS (SELECT      object_name AS xEventName,
                        CAST (event_data AS XML) AS xEventData
            FROM        sys.fn_xe_file_target_read_file('C:\Sessions\QueryPerformanceMetrics*.xel',
                                            NULL, NULL, NULL)
            )
    SELECT  xEventName,
            xEventData.value('(/event/data[@name=''duration'']/value)[1]',
                            'bigint') Duration,
            xEventData.value('(/event/data[@name=''physical_reads'']/value)[1]',
                            'bigint') PhysicalReads,
            xEventData.value('(/event/data[@name=''logical_reads'']/value)[1]',
                            'bigint') LogicalReads,
            xEventData.value('(/event/data[@name=''cpu_time'']/value)[1]',
                            'bigint') CpuTime,
            CASE xEventName
              WHEN 'sql_batch_completed'
              THEN xEventData.value('(/event/data[@name=''batch_text'']/value)[1]',
                                    'varchar(max)')
              WHEN 'rpc_completed'
              THEN xEventData.value('(/event/data[@name=''statement'']/value)[1]',
                                    'varchar(max)')
              END AS SQLText,
            xEventData.value('(/event/data[@name=''query_hash'']/value)[1]',
                            'binary(8)') QueryHash
    INTO    Session_Table
    FROM    xEvents;

SELECT  st.xEventName,
        st.Duration,
        st.PhysicalReads,
        st.LogicalReads,
        st.CpuTime,
        st.SQLText,
        st.QueryHash
FROM    Session_Table AS st
ORDER BY st.LogicalReads DESC;
```

Let's break down this query a little. First, I'm creating a common table expression (CTE) called xEvents. I'm doing that just because it makes the code a little easier to read. It doesn't fundamentally change any behavior. I prefer it when I have to both read from a file and convert the data type. Then my XML queries in the following statement make a little more sense. Note that I'm using a wildcard when reading from the file, QueryPerformanceMetrics*.xel. This makes it possible for me to read in all rollover files created by the Extended Events session (for more details, see Chapter 6).

Depending on the amount of data collected and the size of your files, running queries directly against the files you've collected from Extended Events may be excessively slow. In that case, use the same basic function, sys.fn_xe_file_target_read_file, to load the data into a table instead of querying it directly. Once that's done, you can apply indexing to the table in order to speed up the queries. I used the previous script to put the data into a table and then queried that table for my output. This will work fine for testing, but for a more permanent solution you'd want to have a database dedicated to storing this type of data with tables having the appropriate structures rather than using a shortcut like INTO as I did here.

In some cases, you may have identified a large stress on the CPU from the System Monitor output. The pressure on the CPU may be because of a large number of CPU-intensive operations, such as stored procedure recompilations, aggregate functions, data sorting, hash joins, and so on. In such cases, you should sort the session output on the cpu_time field to identify the queries taking up a large number of processor cycles.

Costly Queries with Multiple Executions

As I mentioned earlier, sometimes a query may not be costly by itself, but the cumulative effect of multiple executions of the same query might put pressure on the system resources. In this situation, sorting on the logical_reads field won't help you identify this type of costly query. You instead want to know the total number of reads, total CPU time, or just the accumulated duration performed by multiple executions of the query.

- Query the session output and group on some of the values you're interested in.

- Access the sys.dm_exec_query_stats DMO to retrieve the information from the production server. This assumes that you're dealing with an issue that is either recent or not dependent on a known history because this data is only what is currently in the procedure cache.

But if you're looking for an accurate historical view of the data, you can go to the metrics you've collected with extended events. Once the session data is imported into a database table, execute a SELECT statement to find the total number of reads performed by the multiple executions of the same query as follows:

```
SELECT COUNT(*) AS TotalExecutions,
    st.xEventName,
    st.SQLText,
    SUM(st.Duration) AS DurationTotal,
    SUM(st.CpuTime) AS CpuTotal,
    SUM(st.LogicalReads) AS LogicalReadTotal,
    SUM(st.PhysicalReads) AS PhysicalReadTotal
FROM Session_Table AS st
GROUP BY st.xEventName, st.SQLText
ORDER BY LogicalReadTotal DESC;
```

The TotalExecutions column in the preceding script indicates the number of times a query was executed. The LogicalReadTotal column indicates the total number of logical reads performed by the multiple executions of the query.

The costly queries identified by this approach are a better indication of load than the costly queries with single execution identified by a session. For example, a query that requires 50 reads might be executed 1,000 times. The query itself may be considered cheap enough, but the total number of reads performed by the query turns out to be 50,000 (=50 x 1,000), which cannot be considered cheap. Optimizing this query to reduce the reads by even 10 for individual execution reduces the total number of reads by 10,000 (=10 x 1,000), which can be more beneficial than optimizing a single query with 5,000 reads.

The problem with this approach is that most queries will have a varying set of criteria in the WHERE clause or that procedure calls will have different values passed in. That makes the simple grouping by the query or procedure with parameters just impossible. You can take care of this problem with a number of approaches. Because you have Extended Events, you can actually put it to work for you. For example, the rpc_completed event captures the procedure name as a field. You can simply group on that field. For batches, you can add the query_hash field and then group on that. Another way is to clean the data, removing the parameter values, as outlined on the Microsoft Developers Network at http://bit.ly/1e1I38f. Although it was written originally for SQL Server 2005, the concepts will work fine with SQL Server 2014.

Getting the same information out of the sys.dm_exec_query_stats view simply requires a query against the DMV.

```
SELECT  s.totalexecutioncount,
        t.text,
        s.TotalExecutionCount,
        s.TotalElapsedTime,
        s.TotalLogicalReads,
        s.TotalPhysicalReads
FROM    (SELECT deqs.plan_handle,
                SUM(deqs.execution_count) AS TotalExecutionCount,
                SUM(deqs.total_elapsed_time) AS TotalElapsedTime,
                SUM(deqs.total_logical_reads) AS TotalLogicalReads,
                SUM(deqs.total_physical_reads) AS TotalPhysicalReads
         FROM   sys.dm_exec_query_stats AS deqs
         GROUP BY deqs.plan_handle
        ) AS s
        CROSS APPLY sys.dm_exec_sql_text(s.plan_handle) AS t
ORDER BY s.TotalLogicalReads DESC ;
```

Another way to take advantage of the data available from the execution DMOs is to use query_hash and query_plan_hash as aggregation mechanisms. While a given stored procedure or parameterized query might have different values passed to it, changing query_hash and query_plan_hash for these will be identical (most of the time). This means you can aggregate against the hash values to identify common plans or common query patterns that you wouldn't be able to see otherwise. The following is just a slight modification from the previous query:

```
SELECT  s.TotalExecutionCount,
        t.text,
        s.TotalExecutionCount,
        s.TotalElapsedTime,
        s.TotalLogicalReads,
        s.TotalPhysicalReads
FROM    (SELECT deqs.query_plan_hash,
                SUM(deqs.execution_count) AS TotalExecutionCount,
                SUM(deqs.total_elapsed_time) AS TotalElapsedTime,
                SUM(deqs.total_logical_reads) AS TotalLogicalReads,
                SUM(deqs.total_physical_reads) AS TotalPhysicalReads
```

```
       FROM    sys.dm_exec_query_stats AS deqs
       GROUP BY deqs.query_plan_hash
    ) AS s
    CROSS APPLY (SELECT plan_handle
                    FROM    sys.dm_exec_query_stats AS deqs
                    WHERE   s.query_plan_hash = deqs.query_plan_hash
                ) AS p
    CROSS APPLY sys.dm_exec_sql_text(p.plan_handle) AS t
ORDER BY TotalLogicalReads DESC;
```

This is so much easier than all the work required to gather session data that it makes you wonder why you would ever use Extended Events at all. The main reason is precision. The sys.dm_exec_ query_stats view is a running aggregate for the time that a given plan has been in memory. An Extended Events session, on the other hand, is a historical track for whatever time frame you ran it in. You can even add session results to a database. With a list of data that you can generate totals about the events in a more precise manner rather than simply relying on a given moment in time. But understand that a lot of troubleshooting of performance problems is focused on what has happened recently on the server, and since sys.dm_exec_query_stats is based in the cache, the DMV usually represents a recent picture of the system, so sys.dm_exec_query_stats is extremely important. But, if you're dealing with that much more tactical situation of what the heck is running slow right now, you would use sys.dm_exec_requests.

Identifying Slow-Running Queries

Because a user's experience is highly influenced by the response time of their requests, you should regularly monitor the execution time of incoming SQL queries and find out the response time of slow-running queries, creating a query performance baseline. If the response time (or duration) of slow-running queries becomes unacceptable, then you should analyze the cause of performance degradation. Not every slow-performing query is caused by resource issues, though. Other concerns such as blocking can also lead to slow query performance. Blocking is covered in detail in Chapter 12.

To identify slow-running queries, just change the queries against your session data to change what you're ordering by, like this:

```
WITH xEvents AS
(SELECT object_name AS xEventName,
    CAST (event_data AS xml) AS xEventData
FROM sys.fn_xe_file_target_read_file
('C:\Sessions\QueryPerformanceMetrics*.xel', NULL, NULL, NULL)
)
SELECT
    xEventName,
    xEventData.value('(/event/data[@name=''duration'']/value)[1]','bigint') Duration,
    xEventData.value('(/event/data[@name=''physical_reads'']/value)[1]','bigint') PhysicalReads,
    xEventData.value('(/event/data[@name=''logical_reads'']/value)[1]','bigint') LogicalReads,
    xEventData.value('(/event/data[@name=''cpu_time'']/value)[1]','bigint') CpuTime,
    xEventData.value('(/event/data[@name=''batch_text'']/value)[1]','varchar(max)') BatchText,
    xEventData.value('(/event/data[@name=''statement'']/value)[1]','varchar(max)') StatementText,
    xEventData.value('(/event/data[@name=''query_plan_hash'']/value)[1]','binary(8)') QueryPlanHash
FROM xEvents
ORDER BY Duration DESC;
```

For a slow-running system, you should note the duration of slow-running queries before and after the optimization process. After you apply optimization techniques, you should then work out the overall effect on the system. It is possible that your optimization steps may have adversely affected other queries, making them slower.

Execution Plans

Once you have identified a costly query, you need to find out *why* it is so costly. You can identify the costly procedure from Extended Events or sys.dm_exec_procedure_stats, rerun it in Management Studio, and look at the execution plan used by the query optimizer. An execution plan shows the processing strategy (including multiple intermediate steps) used by the query optimizer to execute a query.

To create an execution plan, the query optimizer evaluates various permutations of indexes and join strategies. Because of the possibility of a large number of potential plans, this optimization process may take a long time to generate the most cost-effective execution plan. To prevent the overoptimization of an execution plan, the optimization process is broken into multiple phases. Each phase is a set of transformation rules that evaluate various permutations of indexes and join strategies ultimately attempting to find a good enough plan, not a perfect plan. It's that difference between good enough and perfect that can lead to poor performance because of inadequately optimized execution plans. The query optimizer will attempt only a limited number of optimizations before it simply goes with the least costly plan it has currently.

After going through a phase, the query optimizer examines the estimated cost of the resulting plan. If the query optimizer determines that the plan is cheap enough, it will use the plan without going through the remaining optimization phases. However, if the plan is not cheap enough, the optimizer will go through the next optimization phase. I will cover execution plan generation in more depth in Chapter 9.

SQL Server displays a query execution plan in various forms and from two different types. The most commonly used forms in SQL Server 2012 are the graphical execution plan and the XML execution plan. Actually, the graphical execution plan is simply an XML execution plan parsed for the screen. The two types of execution plan are the estimated plan and the actual plan. The *estimated* plan represents the results coming from the query optimizer, and the *actual* plan is that same plan plus some runtime metrics. The beauty of the estimated plan is that it doesn't require the query to be executed. The plans generated by these types can differ, but only if a statement-level recompile occurs during execution. Most of the time the two types of plans will be the same. The primary difference is the inclusion of some execution statistics in the actual plan that are not present in the estimated plan.

The graphical execution plan uses icons to represent the processing strategy of a query. To obtain a graphical estimated execution plan, select Query -> Display Estimated Execution Plan. An XML execution plan contains the same data available through the graphical plan but in a more programmatically accessible format. Further, with the XQuery capabilities of SQL Server, XML execution plans can be queried as if they were tables. An XML execution plan is produced by the statement SET SHOWPLAN_XML for an estimated plan and by the statement SET STATISTICS XML for the actual execution plan. You can also right-click a graphical execution plan and select Showplan XML. You can also pull plans directly out of the plan cache using a DMO, sys.dm_exec_query_plan. The plans stored in cache have no runtime information, so they are technically estimated plans.

■ **Note**   You should make sure your database is set to Compatibility Mode 120 so that it accurately reflects updates to SQL Server 2014.

You can obtain the estimated XML execution plan for the costliest query identified previously using the SET SHOWPLAN_XML command as follows:

```
USE AdventureWorks2012;
GO
SET SHOWPLAN_XML ON;
GO
```

```
SELECT  soh.AccountNumber,
        sod.LineTotal,
        sod.OrderQty,
        sod.UnitPrice,
        p.Name
FROM    Sales.SalesOrderHeader soh
JOIN    Sales.SalesOrderDetail sod
        ON soh.SalesOrderID = sod.SalesOrderID
JOIN    Production.Product p
        ON sod.ProductID = p.ProductID
WHERE   sod.LineTotal > 20000;

GO
SET SHOWPLAN_XML OFF;
GO
```

Running this query results in a link to an execution plan, not an execution plan or any data. Clicking the link will open an execution plan. Although the plan will be displayed as a graphical plan, right-clicking the plan and selecting Show Execution Plan XML will display the XML data. Figure 7-1 shows a portion of the XML execution plan output.

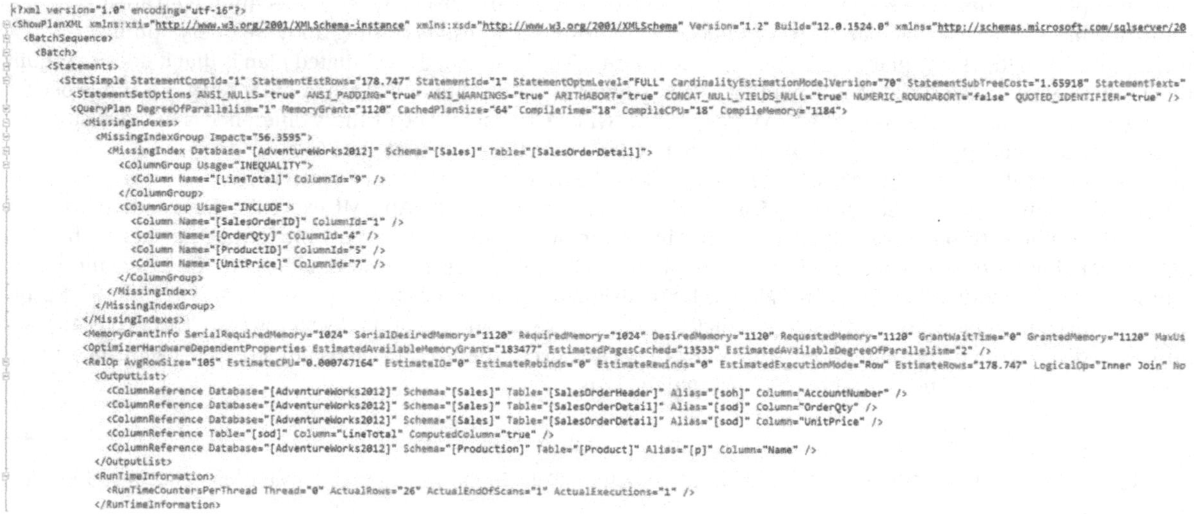


```xml
<?xml version="1.0" encoding="utf-16"?>
<ShowPlanXML xmlns:xsi="http://www.w3.org/2001/XMLSchema-instance" xmlns:xsd="http://www.w3.org/2001/XMLSchema" Version="1.2" Build="12.0.1524.0" xmlns="http://schemas.microsoft.com/sqlserver/20
  <BatchSequence>
    <Batch>
      <Statements>
        <StmtSimple StatementCompId="1" StatementEstRows="178.747" StatementId="1" StatementOptmLevel="FULL" CardinalityEstimationModelVersion="70" StatementSubTreeCost="1.65918" StatementText="
          <StatementSetOptions ANSI_NULLS="true" ANSI_PADDING="true" ANSI_WARNINGS="true" ARITHABORT="true" CONCAT_NULL_YIELDS_NULL="true" NUMERIC_ROUNDABORT="false" QUOTED_IDENTIFIER="true" />
          <QueryPlan DegreeOfParallelism="1" MemoryGrant="1120" CachedPlanSize="64" CompileTime="18" CompileCPU="18" CompileMemory="1184">
            <MissingIndexes>
              <MissingIndexGroup Impact="56.3595">
                <MissingIndex Database="[AdventureWorks2012]" Schema="[Sales]" Table="[SalesOrderDetail]">
                  <ColumnGroup Usage="INEQUALITY">
                    <Column Name="[LineTotal]" ColumnId="9" />
                  </ColumnGroup>
                  <ColumnGroup Usage="INCLUDE">
                    <Column Name="[SalesOrderID]" ColumnId="1" />
                    <Column Name="[OrderQty]" ColumnId="4" />
                    <Column Name="[ProductID]" ColumnId="5" />
                    <Column Name="[UnitPrice]" ColumnId="7" />
                  </ColumnGroup>
                </MissingIndex>
              </MissingIndexGroup>
            </MissingIndexes>
            <MemoryGrantInfo SerialRequiredMemory="1024" SerialDesiredMemory="1120" RequiredMemory="1024" DesiredMemory="1120" RequestedMemory="1120" GrantWaitTime="0" GrantedMemory="1120" MaxUs
            <OptimizerHardwareDependentProperties EstimatedAvailableMemoryGrant="183477" EstimatedPagesCached="13533" EstimatedAvailableDegreeOfParallelism="2" />
            <RelOp AvgRowSize="105" EstimateCPU="0.000747164" EstimateIO="0" EstimateRebinds="0" EstimateRewinds="0" EstimatedExecutionMode="Row" EstimateRows="178.747" LogicalOp="Inner Join" No
              <OutputList>
                <ColumnReference Database="[AdventureWorks2012]" Schema="[Sales]" Table="[SalesOrderHeader]" Alias="[soh]" Column="AccountNumber" />
                <ColumnReference Database="[AdventureWorks2012]" Schema="[Sales]" Table="[SalesOrderDetail]" Alias="[sod]" Column="OrderQty" />
                <ColumnReference Database="[AdventureWorks2012]" Schema="[Sales]" Table="[SalesOrderDetail]" Alias="[sod]" Column="UnitPrice" />
                <ColumnReference Table="[sod]" Column="LineTotal" ComputedColumn="true" />
                <ColumnReference Database="[AdventureWorks2012]" Schema="[Production]" Table="[Product]" Alias="[p]" Column="Name" />
              </OutputList>
              <RunTimeInformation>
                <RunTimeCountersPerThread Thread="0" ActualRows="26" ActualEndOfScans="1" ActualExecutions="1" />
              </RunTimeInformation>
```


Figure 7-1. *XML execution plan output*

Analyzing a Query Execution Plan

Let's start with the costly query identified in the previous query. Copy it (minus the `SET SHOWPLAN_XML` statements) into Management Studio, and turn on Include Actual Execution Plan. Now, on executing this query, you'll see the execution plan in Figure 7-2.

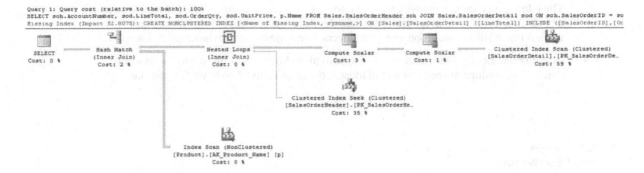

Figure 7-2. *Query execution plan*

Execution plans show two different flows of information. Reading from the left side, you can see the logical flow, starting with the SELECT operator and proceeding through each of the execution steps. Starting from the right side and reading the other way is the physical flow of information, pulling data from the Clustered Index Scan operator first and then proceeding to each subsequent step. Most of the time, reading in the direction of the physical flow of data is more applicable to understanding what's happening with the execution plan, but not always. Sometimes the only way to understand what is happening in an execution plan is to read it in the logical processing order, left to right. Each step represents an operation performed to get the final output of the query. Some of the aspects of a query execution represented by an execution plan are as follows:

- If a query consists of a batch of multiple queries, the execution plan for each query will be displayed in the order of execution. Each execution plan in the batch will have a relative estimated cost, with the total cost of the whole batch being 100 percent.

- Every icon in an execution plan represents an operator. They will each have a relative estimated cost, with the total cost of all the nodes in an execution plan being 100 percent (although inaccuracies in statistics, or even bugs in SQL Server, can lead to situations where you see costs more than 100 percent, but these are uncommon).

- Usually the first physical operator in an execution represents a data retrieval mechanism from a database object (a table or an index). For example, in the execution plan in Figure 7-2, the three starting points represent retrievals from the SalesOrderHeader, SalesOrderDetail, and Product tables.

- Data retrieval will usually be either a table operation or an index operation. For example, in the execution plan in Figure 7-2, all three data retrieval steps are index operations.

- Data retrieval on an index will be either an index scan or an index seek. For example, you can see a clustered index scan, a clustered index seek, and an index scan in Figure 7-2.

- The naming convention for a data retrieval operation on an index is [Table Name].[Index Name].

- The logical flow of the plan is from left to right, just like reading a book in English. The data flows from right to left between operators and is indicated by a connecting arrow between the operators.

- The thickness of a connecting arrow between operators represents a graphical representation of the number of rows transferred.

- The joining mechanism between two operators in the same column will be a nested loop join, a hash match join, or a merge join. For example, in the execution plan shown in Figure 7-2, there is one hash and one loop join. (Join mechanisms are covered in more detail later.)

- Running the mouse over a node in an execution plan shows a pop-up window with some details. The tooltips are not very useful most of the time. Figure 7-3 shows an example.

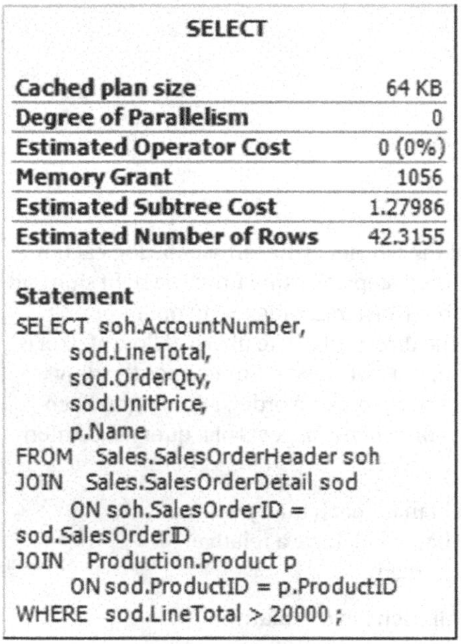

SELECT	
Cached plan size	64 KB
Degree of Parallelism	0
Estimated Operator Cost	0 (0%)
Memory Grant	1056
Estimated Subtree Cost	1.27986
Estimated Number of Rows	42.3155

```
Statement
SELECT  soh.AccountNumber,
        sod.LineTotal,
        sod.OrderQty,
        sod.UnitPrice,
        p.Name
FROM    Sales.SalesOrderHeader soh
JOIN    Sales.SalesOrderDetail sod
        ON soh.SalesOrderID =
sod.SalesOrderID
JOIN    Production.Product p
        ON sod.ProductID = p.ProductID
WHERE   sod.LineTotal > 20000 ;
```

Figure 7-3. *Tooltip sheet from an execution plan operator*

- A complete set of details about an operator is available in the Properties window, as shown in Figure 7-4, which you can open by right-clicking the operator and selecting Properties.

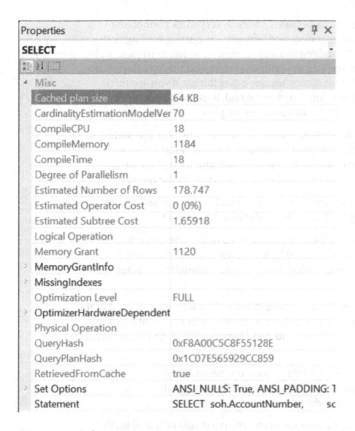

Figure 7-4. *Select operator properties*

- An operator detail shows both physical and logical operation types at the top. Physical operations represent those actually used by the storage engine, while the logical operations are the constructs used by the optimizer to build the estimated execution plan. If logical and physical operations are the same, then only the physical operation is shown. It also displays other useful information, such as row count, I/O cost, CPU cost, and so on.

- Reading through the properties on many of the operators can be necessary to understand how a query is being executed within SQL Server in order to better know how to tune that query.

Identifying the Costly Steps in an Execution Plan

The most immediate approach in the execution plan is to find out which steps are relatively costly. These steps are the starting point for your query optimization. You can choose the starting steps by adopting the following techniques:

- Each node in an execution plan shows its relative estimated cost in the complete execution plan, with the total cost of the whole plan being 100 percent. Therefore, focus attention on the nodes with the highest relative cost. For example, the execution plan in Figure 7-2 has one step with 59 percent estimated cost.

- An execution plan may be from a batch of statements, so you may also need to find the most costly estimated statement. In Figure 7-2 you can see at the top of the plan the text "Query 1." In a batch situation, there will be multiple plans, and they will be numbered in the order they occurred within the batch.

- Observe the thickness of the connecting arrows between nodes. A very thick connecting arrow indicates a large number of rows being transferred between the corresponding nodes. Analyze the node to the left of the arrow to understand why it requires so many rows. Check the properties of the arrows too. You may see that the estimated rows and the actual rows are different. This can be caused by out-of-date statistics, among other things. If you see thick arrows through much of the plan and then a thin arrow at the end, it might be possible to modify the query or indexes to get the filtering done earlier in the plan.

- Look for hash join operations. For small result sets, a nested loop join is usually the preferred join technique. You will learn more about hash joins compared to nested loop joins later in this chapter. Just remember that hash joins are not necessarily bad, and loop joins are not necessarily good. It does depend on the amounts of data being returned by the query.

- Look for key lookup operations. A lookup operation for a large result set can cause a large number of random reads. I will cover key lookups in more detail in Chapter 11.

- There may be warnings, indicated by an exclamation point on one of the operators, which are areas of immediate concern. These can be caused by a variety of issues, including a join without join criteria or an index or a table with missing statistics. Usually resolving the warning situation will help performance.

- Look for steps performing a sort operation. This indicates that the data was not retrieved in the correct sort order. Again, this may not be an issue, but it is an indicator of potential problems, possibly a missing or incorrect index. This assumes you don't have an ORDER BY clause, which could be the cause of the sort operation.

- Watch for extra operators that may be placing additional load on the system such as table spools. They may be necessary for the operation of the query, or they may indicate an improperly written query or badly designed indexes.

- The default cost threshold for parallel query execution is an estimated cost of 5, and that's very low. Watch for parallel operations where they are not warranted. Just remember that the estimated costs are numbers assigned by the query optimizer representing a mathematical model of CPU and I/O but are not actual measures.

Analyzing Index Effectiveness

To examine a costly step in an execution plan further, you should analyze the data retrieval mechanism for the relevant table or index. First, you should check whether an index operation is a seek or a scan. Usually, for best performance, you should retrieve as few rows as possible from a table, and an index *seek* is usually the most efficient way of accessing a small number of rows. A *scan* operation usually indicates that a larger number of rows have been accessed. Therefore, it is generally preferable to seek rather than scan.

Next, you want to ensure that the indexing mechanism is properly set up. The query optimizer evaluates the available indexes to discover which index will retrieve data from the table in the most efficient way. If a desired index is not available, the optimizer uses the next best index. For best performance, you should always ensure that the best index is used in a data retrieval operation. You can judge the index effectiveness (whether the best index is used or not) by analyzing the Argument section of a node detail for the following:

- A data retrieval operation

- A join operation

Let's look at the data retrieval mechanism for the SalesOrderHeader table in the previous execution plan (Figure 7-2). Figure 7-5 shows the operator properties.

⊿ Misc	
▷ Defined Values	[AdventureWorks2012].[Sales].[SalesOrderHeader].AccountNumber
Description	Scanning a particular range of rows from a clustered index.
Estimated CPU Cost	0.0001581
Estimated Execution Mode	Row
Estimated I/O Cost	0.003125
Estimated Number of Executions	218.91096
Estimated Number of Rows	1
Estimated Operator Cost	0.614244 (35%)
Estimated Rebinds	216.149
Estimated Rewinds	1.76196
Estimated Row Size	26 B
Estimated Subtree Cost	0.614244
Forced Index	False
ForceScan	False
ForceSeek	False
Logical Operation	Clustered Index Seek
Node ID	12
NoExpandHint	False
▷ Object	[AdventureWorks2012].[Sales].[SalesOrderHeader].[PK_SalesOrderHeader_SalesOrderID] [soh]
Ordered	True
▷ Output List	[AdventureWorks2012].[Sales].[SalesOrderHeader].AccountNumber
Parallel	False
Physical Operation	Clustered Index Seek
Scan Direction	FORWARD
▷ Seek Predicates	Seek Keys[1]: Prefix: [AdventureWorks2012].[Sales].[SalesOrderHeader].SalesOrderID = Scalar O|
Storage	RowStore
TableCardinality	31465

Figure 7-5. *Data retrieval mechanism for the SalesOrderHeader table*

In the operator properties for the SalesOrderHeader table, the Object property specifies the index used, PK_SalesOrderHeader_SalesOrderID. It uses the following naming convention: [Database]. [Owner].[Table Name]. [Index Name]. The Seek Predicates property specifies the column, or columns, used to find keys in the index. The SalesOrderHeader table is joined with the SalesOrderDetail table on the SalesOrderId column. The SEEK works on the fact that the join criteria, SalesOrderId, is the leading edge of the clustered index and primary key, PK_SalesOrderHeader.

Sometimes you may have a different data retrieval mechanism. Instead of the Seek Predicates property you saw in Figure 7-5, Figure 7-6 shows a simple predicate, indicating a totally different mechanism for retrieving the data.

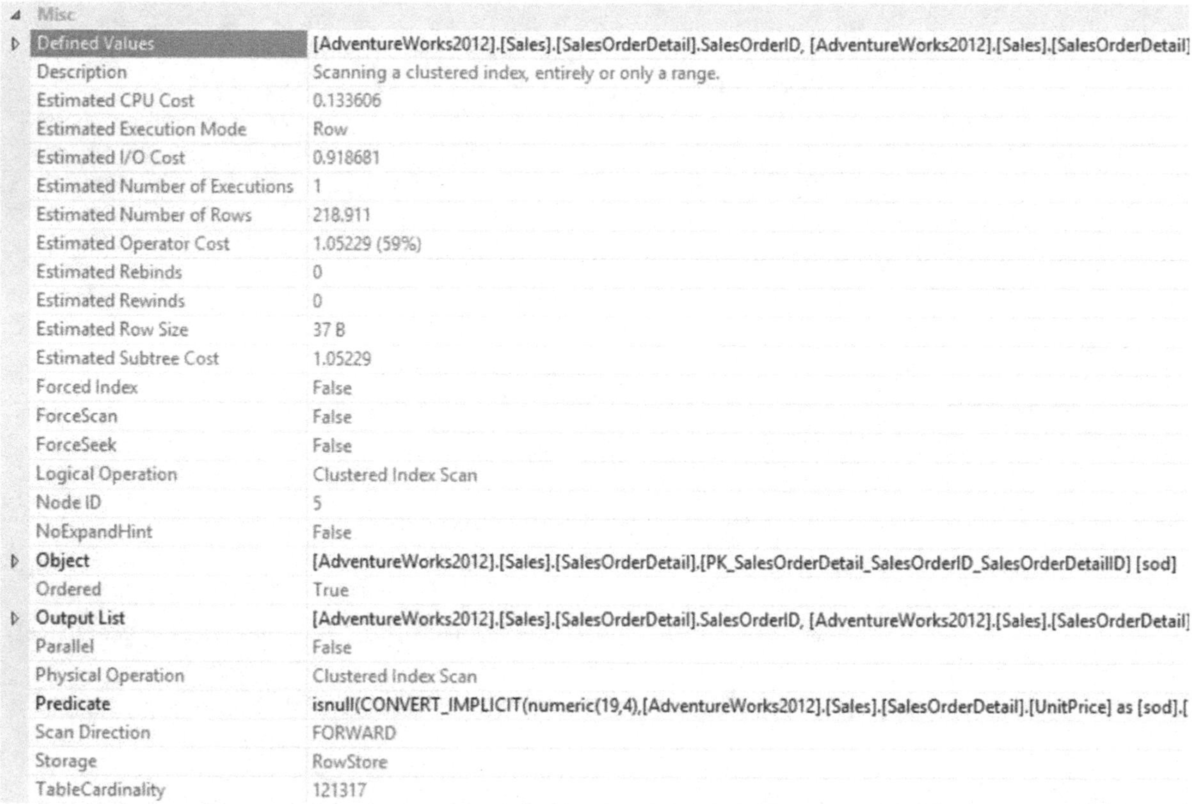

◢ Misc	
▷ Defined Values	[AdventureWorks2012].[Sales].[SalesOrderDetail].SalesOrderID, [AdventureWorks2012].[Sales].[SalesOrderDetail]
Description	Scanning a clustered index, entirely or only a range.
Estimated CPU Cost	0.133606
Estimated Execution Mode	Row
Estimated I/O Cost	0.918681
Estimated Number of Executions	1
Estimated Number of Rows	218.911
Estimated Operator Cost	1.05229 (59%)
Estimated Rebinds	0
Estimated Rewinds	0
Estimated Row Size	37 B
Estimated Subtree Cost	1.05229
Forced Index	False
ForceScan	False
ForceSeek	False
Logical Operation	Clustered Index Scan
Node ID	5
NoExpandHint	False
▷ Object	[AdventureWorks2012].[Sales].[SalesOrderDetail].[PK_SalesOrderDetail_SalesOrderID_SalesOrderDetailID] [sod]
Ordered	True
▷ Output List	[AdventureWorks2012].[Sales].[SalesOrderDetail].SalesOrderID, [AdventureWorks2012].[Sales].[SalesOrderDetail]
Parallel	False
Physical Operation	Clustered Index Scan
Predicate	isnull(CONVERT_IMPLICIT(numeric(19,4),[AdventureWorks2012].[Sales].[SalesOrderDetail].[UnitPrice] as [sod].[
Scan Direction	FORWARD
Storage	RowStore
TableCardinality	121317

Figure 7-6. *A variation of the data retrieval mechanism, a scan*

In the properties in Figure 7-6, there is no seek predicate. Because of the function being performed on the column, the ISNULL and the CONVERT_IMPLICIT, the entire table must be checked for the existence of the Predicate value.

```
isnull(CONVERT_IMPLICIT(numeric(19,4),[AdventureWorks2012].[Sales].[SalesOrderDetail].
[UnitPrice] as [sod].[UnitPrice],0)*((1.0)-CONVERT_IMPLICIT(numeric(19,4),[AdventureWorks2012].
[Sales].[SalesOrderDetail].[UnitPriceDiscount] as [sod].[UnitPriceDiscount],0))*CONVERT_I
MPLICIT(numeric(5,0),[AdventureWorks2012].[Sales].[SalesOrderDetail].[OrderQty] as [sod].
[OrderQty],0),(0.000000))>(20000.000000)
```

Because a calculation is being performed on the data, the index doesn't store the results of the calculation, so instead of simply looking information up on the index, you have to scan the data, perform the calculation, and then check that the data is correct.

Analyzing Join Effectiveness

In addition to analyzing the indexes used, you should examine the effectiveness of join strategies decided by the optimizer. SQL Server uses three types of joins.

- Hash joins

- Merge joins

- Nested loop joins

In many simple queries affecting a small set of rows, nested loop joins are far superior to both hash and merge joins. As joins get more complicated, the other join types are used where appropriate. None of the join types is by definition bad or wrong. You're primarily looking for places where the optimizer may have chosen a type not compatible with the data in hand. This is usually caused by discrepancies in the statistics available to the optimizer when it's deciding which of the types to use.

Hash Join

To understand SQL Server's hash join strategy, consider the following simple query:

```
SELECT  p.*
FROM    Production.Product p
        JOIN Production.ProductCategory pc
        ON p.ProductSubcategoryID = pc.ProductCategoryID;
```

Table 7-1 shows the two tables' indexes and number of rows.

Table 7-1. *Indexes and Number of Rows of the Products and ProductCategory Tables*

Table	Indexes	Number of Rows
Product	Clustered index on ProductID	504
ProductCategory	Clustered index on ProductCategoryld	4

Figure 7-7 shows the execution plan for the preceding query.

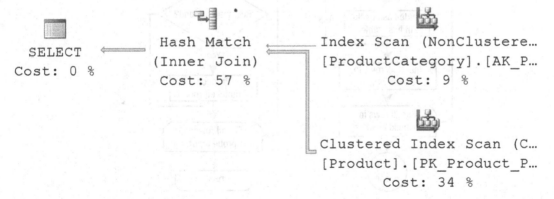

Figure 7-7. *Execution plan with a hash join*

You can see that the optimizer used a hash join between the two tables.

A hash join uses the two join inputs as a *build input* and a *probe input*. The build input is shown as the top input in the execution plan, and the probe input is shown as the bottom input. Usually the smaller of the two inputs serves as the build input because it's going to be stored on the system, so the optimizer attempts to minimize the memory used.

The hash join performs its operation in two phases: the *build phase* and the *probe phase*. In the most commonly used form of hash join, the *in-memory hash join,* the entire build input is scanned or computed, and then a hash table is built in memory. Each row from the outer input is inserted into a hash bucket depending on the hash value computed for the *hash key* (the set of columns in the equality predicate). A hash is just a mathematical construct run against the values in question and used for comparison purposes.

This build phase is followed by the probe phase. The entire probe input is scanned or computed one row at a time, and for each probe row, a hash key value is computed. The corresponding hash bucket is scanned for the hash key value from the probe input, and the matches are produced. Figure 7-8 illustrates the process of an in-memory hash join.

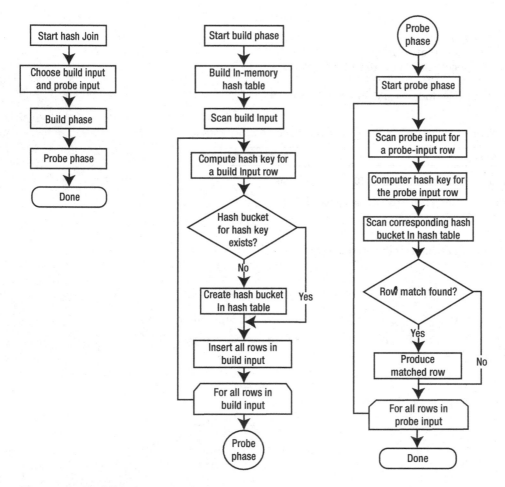

Figure 7-8. *Workflow for an in-memory hash join*

The query optimizer uses hash joins to process large, unsorted, nonindexed inputs efficiently. Let's now look at the next type of join: the merge join.

Merge Join

In the previous case, input from the Product table is larger, and the table is not indexed on the joining column (ProductCategoryID). Using the following simple query, you can see different behavior:

```
SELECT   pm.*
FROM     Production.ProductModel pm
JOIN     Production.ProductModelProductDescriptionCulture pmpd
         ON pm.ProductModelID = pmpd.ProductModelID ;
```

Figure 7-9 shows the resultant execution plan for this query.

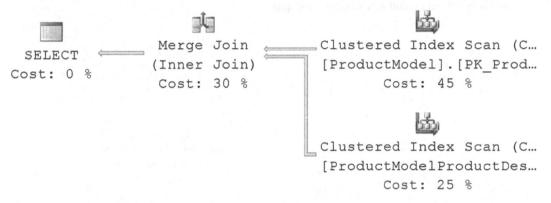

Figure 7-9. *Execution plan with a merge join*

For this query, the optimizer used a merge join between the two tables. A merge join requires both join inputs to be sorted on the merge columns, as defined by the join criterion. If indexes are available on both joining columns, then the join inputs are sorted by the index. Since each join input is sorted, the merge join gets a row from each input and compares them for equality. A matching row is produced if they are equal. This process is repeated until all rows are processed.

In situations where the data is ordered by an index, a merge join can be one of the fastest join operations, but if the data is not ordered and the optimizer still chooses to perform a merge join, then the data has to be ordered by an extra operation, a sort. This can make the merge join slower and more costly in terms of memory and I/O resources.

In this case, the query optimizer found that the join inputs were both sorted (or indexed) on their joining columns. You can see this in the properties of the Index Scan operators, as shown in Figure 7-10.

Number of Executions	1
Object	[AdventureWork
Ordered	True
Output List	[AdventureWork
Parallel	False

Figure 7-10. *Properties of Clustered Index Scan showing that the data is Ordered*

As a result of the data being ordered by the indexes in use, the merge join was chosen as a faster join strategy than any other join in this situation.

Nested Loop Join

The final type of join I'll cover here is the nested loop join. For better performance, you should always strive to access a limited number of rows from individual tables. To understand the effect of using a smaller result set, decrease the join inputs in your query as follows:

```
SELECT  pm.*
FROM    Production.ProductModel pm
JOIN    Production.ProductModelProductDescriptionCulture pmpd
        ON pm.ProductModelID = pmpd.ProductModelID
        WHERE pm.Name = 'HL Mountain Front Wheel';
```

Figure 7-11 shows the resultant execution plan of the new query.

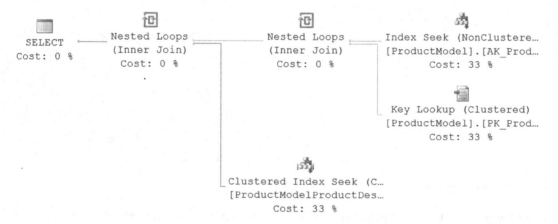

Figure 7-11. *Execution plan with a nested loop join*

As you can see, the optimizer used a nested loop join between the two tables. It also added another nested loop to perform the Key Lookup operation (I'll talk more about that in Chapter 6).

A nested loop join uses one join input as the outer input table and the other as the inner input table. The outer input table is shown as the top input in the execution plan, and the inner input table is shown as the bottom input table. The outer loop consumes the outer input table row by row. The inner loop, executed for each outer row, searches for matching rows in the inner input table.

Nested loop joins are highly effective if the outer input is quite small and the inner input is larger but indexed. In many simple queries affecting a small set of rows, nested loop joins are far superior to both hash and merge joins. Joins operate by gaining speed through other sacrifices. A loop join can be fast because it uses memory to take a small set of data and compare it quickly to a second set of data. A merge join similarly uses memory and a bit of tempdb to do its ordered comparisons. A hash join uses memory and tempdb to build out the hash tables for the join. Although a loop join can be faster at small data sets, it can slow down as the data sets get larger or there aren't indexes to support the retrieval of the data. That's why SQL Server has different join mechanisms.

Even for small join inputs, such as in the previous query, it's important to have an index on the joining columns. As you saw in the preceding execution plan, for a small set of rows, indexes on joining columns allow the query optimizer to consider a nested loop join strategy. A missing index on the joining column of an input will force the query optimizer to use a hash join instead.

Table 7-2 summarizes the use of the three join types.

Table 7-2. *Characteristics of the Three Join Types*

Join Type	Index on Joining Columns	Usual Size of Joining Tables	Presorted	Join Clause
Hash	Inner table: Not indexed Outer table: Optional Optimal condition: Small outer table, large inner table	Any	No	Equi-join
Merge	Both tables: Must Optimal condition: Clustered or covering index on both	Large	Yes	Equi-join
Nested loop	Inner table: Must Outer table: Preferable	Small	Optional	All

■ **Note** The outer table is usually the smaller of the two joining tables in the hash and loop joins.

I will cover index types, including clustered and covering indexes, in Chapter 8.

Actual vs. Estimated Execution Plans

There are estimated and actual execution plans. To a degree, these are interchangeable. But, the actual plan carries with it information from the execution of the query, specifically the row counts affected and some other information, that is not available in the estimated plans. This information can be extremely useful, especially when trying to understand statistic estimations. For that reason, actual execution plans are preferred when tuning queries.

Unfortunately, you won't always be able to access them. You may not be able to execute a query, say in a production environment. You may have access only to the plan from cache, which contains no runtime information. So, there are situations where the estimated plan is what you will have to work with.

However, there are other situations where the estimated plans will not work at all. Consider the following stored procedure:

```
IF (SELECT  OBJECT_ID('p1')
    ) IS NOT NULL
    DROP PROC p1
GO
CREATE PROC p1
AS
    CREATE TABLE t1 (c1 INT);
    INSERT  INTO t1
            SELECT  ProductID
            FROM    Production.Product;
    SELECT  *
    FROM    t1;
    DROP TABLE t1;
GO
```

You may try to use SHOWPLAN_XML to obtain the estimated XML execution plan for the query as follows:

```
SET SHOWPLAN_XML ON;
GO
EXEC p1 ;
GO
SET SHOWPLAN_XML OFF;
GO
```

But this fails with the following error:

```
Msg 208, Level 16, State 1, Procedure p1, Line 360
Invalid object name 't1'.
```

Since SHOWPLAN_XML doesn't actually execute the query, the query optimizer can't generate an execution plan for INSERT and SELECT statements on the table (t1) because it doesn't exist until the query is executed. Instead, you can use STATISTICS XML as follows:

```
SET STATISTICS XML ON;
GO
EXEC p1;
GO
SET STATISTICS XML OFF;
GO
```

Since STATISTICS XML executes the query, the table is created and accessed within the query, which is all captured by the execution plan. Figure 7-12 shows the results of the query and the two plans for the two statements within the procedure provided by STATISTICS XML.

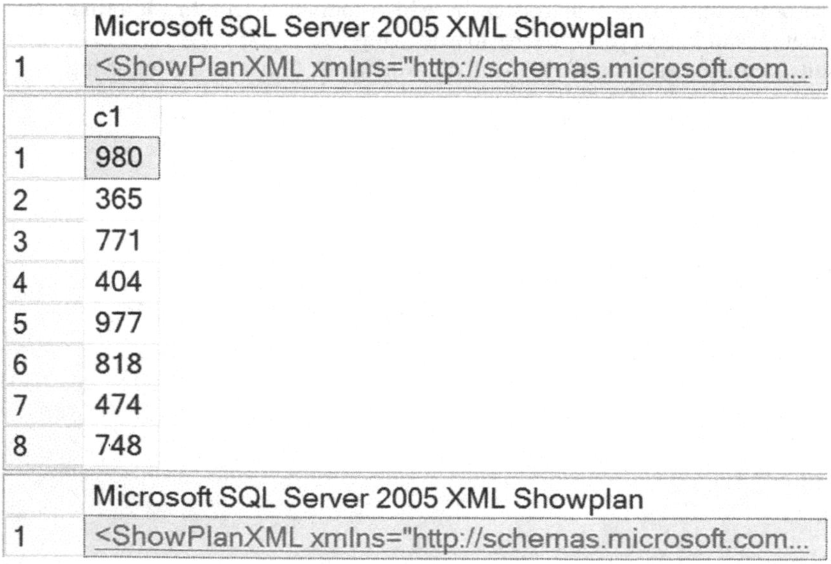

	Microsoft SQL Server 2005 XML Showplan
1	<ShowPlanXML xmlns="http://schemas.microsoft.com...

	c1
1	980
2	365
3	771
4	404
5	977
6	818
7	474
8	748

	Microsoft SQL Server 2005 XML Showplan
1	<ShowPlanXML xmlns="http://schemas.microsoft.com...

Figure 7-12. *STATISTICS PROFILE output*

■ **Tip** Remember to switch Query ➤ Show Execution Plan off in Management Studio, or you will see the graphical, rather than textual, execution plan.

Plan Cache

One final place to access execution plans is to read them directly from the memory space where they are stored, the plan cache. Dynamic management views and functions are provided from SQL Server to access this data. To see a listing of execution plans in cache, run the following query:

```
SELECT  p.query_plan,
        t.text
FROM    sys.dm_exec_cached_plans r
        CROSS APPLY sys.dm_exec_query_plan(r.plan_handle) p
        CROSS APPLY sys.dm_exec_sql_text(r.plan_handle) t;
```

The query returns a list of XML execution plan links. Opening any of them will show the execution plan. These execution plans are the compiled plans, but they contain no execution metrics. Working further with columns available through the dynamic management views will allow you to search for specific procedures or execution plans.

While not having the runtime data is somewhat limiting, having access to execution plans, even as the query is executing, is an invaluable resource for someone working on performance tuning. As mentioned earlier, you might not be able to execute a query in a production environment, so getting any plan at all is useful.

Query Resource Cost

Even though the execution plan for a query provides a detailed processing strategy and the estimated relative costs of the individual steps involved, it doesn't provide the actual cost of the query in terms of CPU usage, reads/writes to disk, or query duration. While optimizing a query, you may add an index to reduce the relative cost of a step. This may adversely affect a dependent step in the execution plan, or sometimes it may even modify the execution plan itself. Thus, if you look only at the execution plan, you can't be sure that your query optimization benefits the query as a whole, as opposed to that one step in the execution plan. You can analyze the overall cost of a query in different ways.

You should monitor the overall cost of a query while optimizing it. As explained previously, you can use Extended Events to monitor the duration, cpu, reads and writes information for the query. Extended Events is an extremely efficient mechanism for gathering metrics. You should plan on taking advantage of this fact and use this mechanism to gather your query performance metrics. Just understand that collecting this information leads to large amounts of data that you will have to find a place to maintain within your system.

There are other ways to collect performance data that are more immediate than Extended Events.

Client Statistics

Client statistics capture execution information from the perspective of your machine as a client of the server. This means that any times recorded include the time it takes to transfer data across the network, not merely the time involved on the SQL Server machine itself. To use them, simply click Query ➤ Include Client Statistics. Now, each time you run a query, a limited set of data is collected including the execution time, the number of rows affected, the round-trips to the server, and more. Further, each execution of the query is displayed separately on the Client

Statistics tab, and a column aggregating the multiple executions shows the averages for the data collected. The statistics will also show whether a time or count has changed from one run to the next, showing up as arrows, as shown in Figure 7-13. For example, consider this query:

```
SELECT TOP 100
       p.*
FROM   Production.Product p;
```

The client statistics information for the query should look something like that shown in Figure 7-13.

	Trial 2	Trial 1	Average
Client Execution Time	01:55:21	01:55:13	
Query Profile Statistics			
Number of INSERT, DELETE and UPDATE statements	0	→ 0	→ 0.0000
Rows affected by INSERT, DELETE, or UPDATE statem...	0	→ 0	→ 0.0000
Number of SELECT statements	1	→ 1	→ 1.0000
Rows returned by SELECT statements	100	→ 100	→ 100.0000
Number of transactions	0	→ 0	→ 0.0000
Network Statistics			
Number of server roundtrips	1	→ 1	→ 1.0000
TDS packets sent from client	1	→ 1	→ 1.0000
TDS packets received from server	4	→ 4	→ 4.0000
Bytes sent from client	146	→ 146	→ 146.0000
Bytes received from server	12533	→ 12533	→ 12533.0000
Time Statistics			
Client processing time	31	↑ 0	→ 15.5000
Total execution time	31	↑ 0	→ 15.5000
Wait time on server replies	0	→ 0	→ 0.0000

Figure 7-13. *Client statistics*

Although capturing client statistics can be a useful way to gather data, it's a limited set of data, and there is no way to show how one execution is different from another. You could even run a completely different query, and its data would be mixed in with the others, making the averages useless. If you need to, you can reset the client statistics. Select the Query menu and then the Reset Client Statistics menu item.

Execution Time

Both Duration and CPU represent the time factor of a query. To obtain detailed information on the amount of time (in milliseconds) required to parse, compile, and execute a query, use SET STATISTICS TIME as follows:

```
SET STATISTICS TIME ON
GO
SELECT  soh.AccountNumber,
        sod.LineTotal,
        sod.OrderQty,
        sod.UnitPrice,
        p.Name
```

```
FROM    Sales.SalesOrderHeader soh
        JOIN Sales.SalesOrderDetail sod
        ON soh.SalesOrderID = sod.SalesOrderID
        JOIN Production.Product p
        ON sod.ProductID = p.ProductID
WHERE   sod.LineTotal > 1000;
GO
SET STATISTICS TIME OFF
GO
```

The output of STATISTICS TIME for the preceding SELECT statement is as follows:

```
SQL Server parse and compile time:
   CPU time = 0 ms, elapsed time = 0 ms.

(32101 row(s) affected)

 SQL Server Execution Times:
   CPU time = 328 ms,  elapsed time = 643 ms.
SQL Server parse and compile time:
   CPU time = 0 ms, elapsed time = 0 ms.
```

The CPU time = 328 ms part of the execution times represents the CPU value provided by the Profiler tool and the Server Trace option. Similarly, the corresponding Elapsed time = 643 ms represents the Duration value provided by the other mechanisms.

A 0 ms parse and compile time signifies that the optimizer reused the existing execution plan for this query and therefore didn't have to spend any time parsing and compiling the query again. If the query is executed for the first time, then the optimizer has to parse the query first for syntax and then compile it to produce the execution plan. This can be easily verified by clearing out the cache using the system call DBCC FREEPROCCACHE and then rerunning the query.

```
SQL Server parse and compile time:
   CPU time = 32 ms, elapsed time = 33 ms.

(32101 row(s) affected)

 SQL Server Execution Times:
   CPU time = 187 ms,  elapsed time = 678 ms.
SQL Server parse and compile time:
   CPU time = 0 ms, elapsed time = 0 ms.
```

This time, SQL Server spent 32 ms of CPU time and a total of 33 ms parsing and compiling the query.

■ **Note**   You should not run DBCC FREEPROCCACHE on your production systems unless you are prepared to incur the not insignificant cost of recompiling every query on the system. In some ways, this will be as costly to your system as a reboot or a SQL Server instance restart.

STATISTICS IO

As discussed in the "Identifying Costly Queries" section earlier in the chapter, the number of reads in the Reads column is frequently the most significant cost factor among duration, cpu, reads, and writes. The total number of reads performed by a query consists of the sum of the number of reads performed on all tables involved in the query. The reads performed on the individual tables may vary significantly, depending on the size of the result set requested from the individual table and the indexes available.

To reduce the total number of reads, it will be useful to find all the tables accessed in the query and their corresponding number of reads. This detailed information helps you concentrate on optimizing data access on the tables with a large number of reads. The number of reads per table also helps you evaluate the impact of the optimization step (implemented for one table) on the other tables referred to in the query.

In a simple query, you determine the individual tables accessed by taking a close look at the query. This becomes increasingly difficult the more complex the query becomes. In the case of stored procedures, database views, or functions, it becomes more difficult to identify all the tables actually accessed by the optimizer. You can use STATISTICS IO to get this information, irrespective of query complexity.

To turn STATISTICS IO on, navigate to Query ➤ Query Options ➤ Advanced ➤ Set Statistics IO in Management Studio. You may also get this information programmatically as follows:

```
SET STATISTICS IO ON;
GO
SELECT  soh.AccountNumber,
        sod.LineTotal,
        sod.OrderQty,
        sod.UnitPrice,
        p.Name
FROM    Sales.SalesOrderHeader soh
        JOIN Sales.SalesOrderDetail sod
        ON soh.SalesOrderID = sod.SalesOrderID
        JOIN Production.Product p
        ON sod.ProductID = p.ProductID
WHERE   sod.SalesOrderID = 71856;
GO
SET STATISTICS IO OFF;
GO
```

If you run this query and look at the execution plan, it consists of three clustered index seeks with two loop joins. If you remove the WHERE clause and run the query again, you get a set of scans and some hash joins. That's an interesting fact—but you don't know how it affects the query I/O usage! You can use SET STATISTICS IO as shown previously to compare the cost of the query (in terms of logical reads) between the two processing strategies used by the optimizer.

You get following STATISTICS IO output when the query uses the hash join:

```
(121317 row(s) affected)
Table 'Workfile'. Scan count 0, logical reads 0...
Table 'Worktable'. Scan count 0, logical reads 0...
Table 'SalesOrderDetail'. Scan count 1, logical reads 1246...
Table 'SalesOrderHeader'. Scan count 1, logical reads 689...
Table 'Product'. Scan count 1, logical reads 6...

(1 row(s) affected)
```

Now when you add back in the WHERE clause to appropriately filter the data, the resultant STATISTICS IO output turns out to be this:

```
(2 row(s) affected)
Table 'Product'. Scan count 0, logical reads 4...
Table 'SalesOrderDetail'. Scan count 1, logical reads 3...
Table 'SalesOrderHeader'. Scan count 0, logical reads 3...

(1 row(s) affected)
```

Logical reads for the SalesOrderDetail table have been cut from 1,246 to 3 because of the index seek and the loop join. It also hasn't significantly affected the data retrieval cost of the Product table.

While interpreting the output of STATISTICS IO, you mostly refer to the number of logical reads. The number of physical reads and read-ahead reads will be nonzero when the data is not found in the memory, but once the data is populated in memory, the physical reads and read-ahead reads will tend to be zero.

There is another advantage to knowing all the tables used and their corresponding reads for a query. Both the duration and CPU values may fluctuate significantly when reexecuting the same query with no change in table schema (including indexes) or data because the essential services and background applications running on the SQL Server machine can affect the processing time of the query under observation. But, don't forget that logical reads are not always the most accurate measure. Duration and CPU are absolutely useful and an important part of any query tuning.

During optimization steps, you need a nonfluctuating cost figure as a reference. The reads (or logical reads) don't vary between multiple executions of a query with a fixed table schema and data. For example, if you execute the previous SELECT statement ten times, you will probably get ten different figures for duration and CPU, but Reads will remain the same each time. Therefore, during optimization, you can refer to the number of reads for an individual table to ensure that you really have reduced the data access cost of the table. Just never assume that is your only measure or even the primary one. It's just a constant measure and therefore useful.

Even though the number of logical reads can also be obtained from the Extended Events, you get another benefit when using STATISTICS IO. The number of logical reads for a query shown by Profiler or the Server Trace option increases as you use different SET statements (mentioned previously) along with the query. But the number of logical reads shown by STATISTICS IO doesn't include the additional pages that are accessed as SET statements are used with a query. Thus, STATISTICS IO provides a consistent figure for the number of logical reads.

Summary

In this chapter, you saw that you can use Extended Events to identify the queries causing a high amount of stress on the system resources in a SQL workload. Collecting the session data can, and should be, automated using system stored procedures. For immediate access to statistics about running queries, use the DMV sys.dm_exec_query_stats. You can further analyze these queries with Management Studio to find the costly steps in the processing strategy of the query. For better performance, it is important to consider both the index and join mechanisms used in an execution plan while analyzing a query. The number of data retrievals (or reads) for the individual tables provided by SET STATISTICS IO helps concentrate on the data access mechanism of the tables with most number of reads. You also should focus on the CPU cost and overall time of the most costly queries.

Once you identify a costly query and finish the initial analysis, the next step should be to optimize the query for performance. Because indexing is one of the most commonly used performance-tuning techniques, in the next chapter I will discuss in depth the various indexing mechanisms available in SQL Server.

CHAPTER 8

■ ■ ■

Index Architecture and Behavior

The right index on the right column, or columns, is the basis on which query tuning begins. A missing index or an index placed on the wrong column, or columns, can be the basis for all performance problems starting with basic data access, continuing through joins, and ending in filtering clauses. For these reasons, it is extremely important for everyone—not just a DBA—to understand the different indexing techniques that can be used to optimize the database design.

In this chapter, I cover the following topics:

- What an index is

- The benefits and overhead of an index

- General recommendations for index design

- Clustered and nonclustered index behavior and comparisons

- Recommendations for clustered and nonclustered indexes

What Is an Index?

One of the best ways to reduce disk I/O is to use an index. An index allows SQL Server to find data in a table without scanning the entire table. An index in a database is analogous to an index in a book. Say, for example, that you wanted to look up the phrase *table scan* in this book. In the paper version, without the index at the back of the book, you would have to peruse the entire book to find the text you needed. With the index, you know exactly where the information you want is stored.

While tuning a database for performance, you create indexes on the different columns used in a query to help SQL Server find data quickly. For example, the following query against the Production.Product table results in the data shown in Figure 8-1 (the first 10 of 500+ rows):

```
SELECT TOP 10
        p.ProductID,
        p.[Name],
        p.StandardCost,
        p.[Weight],
        ROW_NUMBER() OVER (ORDER BY p.Name DESC) AS RowNumber
FROM Production.Product p
ORDER BY p.Name DESC;
```

	ProductID	Name	StandardCost	Weight	RowNumber
1	852	Women's Tights, S	30.9334	NULL	1
2	853	Women's Tights, M	30.9334	NULL	2
3	854	Women's Tights, L	30.9334	NULL	3
4	867	Women's Mountain Shorts, S	26.1763	NULL	4
5	868	Women's Mountain Shorts, M	26.1763	NULL	5
6	869	Women's Mountain Shorts, L	26.1763	NULL	6
7	870	Water Bottle - 30 oz.	1.8663	NULL	7
8	842	Touring-Panniers, Large	51.5625	NULL	8
9	965	Touring-3000 Yellow, 62	461.4448	30.00	9
10	964	Touring-3000 Yellow, 58	461.4448	29.79	10

Figure 8-1. *Sample Production.Product table*

The preceding query scanned the entire table since there was no WHERE clause. If you need to add a filter through the WHERE clause to retrieve all the products where StandardCost is greater than 150, without an index the table will still have to be scanned, checking the value of StandardCost at each row to determine which rows contain a value greater than 150. An index on the StandardCost column could speed up this process by providing a mechanism that allows a structured search against the data rather than a row-by-row check. You can take two different, and fundamental, approaches for creating this index.

- *Like a dictionary*: A dictionary is a distinct listing of words in alphabetical order. An index can be stored in a similar fashion. The data is ordered, although it will still have duplicates. The first ten rows, ordered by StandardCost DESC instead of by Name, would look like the data shown in Figure 8-2. Notice the RowNumber column shows the original placement of the row when ordering by Name.

	ProductID	Name	StandardCost	Weight	RowNumber
1	749	Road-150 Red, 62	2171.2942	15.00	125
2	753	Road-150 Red, 56	2171.2942	14.68	126
3	752	Road-150 Red, 52	2171.2942	14.42	127
4	751	Road-150 Red, 48	2171.2942	14.13	128
5	750	Road-150 Red, 44	2171.2942	13.77	129
6	774	Mountain-100 Silver, 48	1912.1544	21.42	170
7	773	Mountain-100 Silver, 44	1912.1544	21.13	171
8	772	Mountain-100 Silver, 42	1912.1544	20.77	172
9	771	Mountain-100 Silver, 38	1912.1544	20.35	173
10	778	Mountain-100 Black, 48	1898.0944	21.42	174

Figure 8-2. *Product table sorted on StandardCost*

So, now if you wanted to find all the data in the rows where StandardCost is greater than 150, the index would allow you to find them immediately by moving down to the first value greater than 150. An index that applies order to the data stored based on the index key order is known as a *clustered index*. Because of how SQL Server stores data, this is one of the most important indexes in your database design. I explain this in detail later in the chapter.

- *Like a book's Index architecture*: An ordered list can be created without altering the layout of the table, similar to the way the index of a book is created. Just like the keyword index of a book lists the keywords in a separate section with a page number to refer to the main content of the book, the list of StandardCost values is created as a separate structure and refers to the corresponding row in the Product table through a pointer. For the example, I'll use RowNumber as the pointer. Table 8-1 shows the structure of the manufacturer index.

Table 8-1. *Structure of the Manufacturer Index*

StandardCost	RowNumber
2171.2942	125
2171.2942	126
2171.2942	127
2171.2942	128
2171.2942	129
1912.1544	170

SQL Server can scan the manufacturer index to find rows where StandardCost is greater than 150. Since the StandardCost values are arranged in a sorted order, SQL Server can stop scanning as soon as it encounters the row with a value of 150 or less. This type of index is called a *nonclustered index*, and I explain it in detail later in the chapter.

In either case, SQL Server will be able to find all the products where StandardCost is greater than 150 more quickly than without an index under most circumstances.

You can create indexes on either a single column (as described previously) or a combination of columns in a table. SQL Server automatically creates indexes for certain types of constraints (for example, PRIMARY KEY and UNIQUE constraints).

The Benefit of Indexes

SQL Server has to be able to find data, even when no index is present on a table. When no clustered index is present to establish a storage order for the data, the storage engine will simply read through the entire table to find what it needs. A table without a clustered index is called a *heap table*. A heap is just an unordered stack of data with a row identifier as a pointer to the storage location. This data is not ordered or searchable except by walking through the data, row by row, in a process called a *scan*. When a clustered index is placed on a table, the key values of the index establish an order for the data. Further, with a clustered index, the data is stored with the index so that the data itself is now ordered. When a clustered index is present, the pointer on the nonclustered index consists of the values that define the clustered index key. This is a big part of what makes clustered indexes so important.

Data within SQL Server is stored on a page, which is 8KB in size. A page is the minimum amount of information that moves off the disk and into memory, so how much you can store on a page becomes important. Since a page has a limited amount of space, it can store a larger number of rows if the rows contain a fewer number of columns or the columns are of smaller size. The nonclustered index usually doesn't (and shouldn't) contain all the columns of the table; it usually contains only a limited number of the columns. Therefore, a page will be able to store more rows of a nonclustered index than rows of the table itself, which contains all the columns. Consequently, SQL Server will be able to read more values for a column from a page representing a nonclustered index on the column than from a page representing the table that contains the column.

Another benefit of a nonclustered index is that because it is in a separate structure from the data table, it can be put in a different filegroup, with a different I/O path, as explained in Chapter 3. This means that SQL Server can access the index and table concurrently, making searches even faster.

Indexes store their information in a balanced tree, referred to as a *B-tree*, structure, so the number of reads required to find a particular row is minimized. The following example shows the benefit of a B-tree structure.

Consider a single-column table with 27 rows in a random order and only 3 rows per leaf page. Suppose the layout of the rows in the pages is as shown in Figure 8-3.

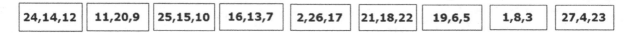

Figure 8-3. *Initial layout of 27 rows*

To search the row (or rows) for the column value of 5, SQL Server has to scan all the rows and the pages, since even the last row in the last page may have the value 5. Because the number of reads depends on the number of pages accessed, nine read operations (retrieving pages from the disk and transferring them to memory) have to be performed without an index on the column. This content can be ordered by creating an index on the column, with the resultant layout of the rows and pages shown in Figure 8-4.

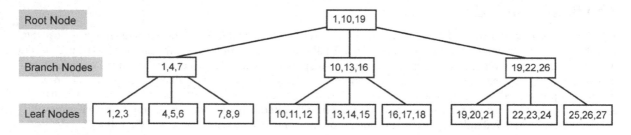

Figure 8-4. *Ordered layout of 27 rows*

Indexing the column arranges the content in a sorted fashion. This allows SQL Server to determine the possible value for a row position in the column with respect to the value of another row position in the column. For example, in Figure 8-4, when SQL Server finds the first row with the column value 6, it can be sure that there are no more rows with the column value 5. Thus, only two read operations are required to fetch the rows with the value 5 when the content is indexed. However, what happens if you want to search for the column value 25? This will require nine read operations! This problem is solved by implementing indexes using the B-tree structure (as in Figure 8-5).

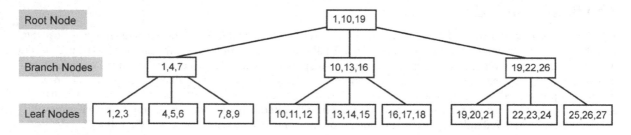

Figure 8-5. *B-tree layout of 27 rows*

A B-tree consists of a starting node (or page) called a *root node* with *branch nodes* (or pages) growing out of it (or linked to it). All keys are stored in the leaves. Contained in each interior node (above the leaf nodes) are pointers to its branch nodes and values representing the smallest value found in the branch node. Keys are kept in sorted order within each node. B-trees use a balanced tree structure for efficient record retrieval—a B-tree is balanced when the leaf nodes are all at the same level from the root node. For example, creating an index on the preceding content will generate the balanced B-tree structure shown in Figure 8-5. At the bottom level, all the leaf nodes are connected to each other through a doubly linked list, meaning each page points to the page that follows it, and the page that follows it points back to the preceding page. This prevents having to go back up the chain when pages are traversed beyond the definitions of the intermediate pages.

The B-tree algorithm minimizes the number of pages to be accessed to locate a desired key, thereby speeding up the data access process. For example, in Figure 8-5, the search for the key value 5 starts at the top root node. Since the key value is between 1 and 10, the search process follows the left branch to the next node. As the key value 5 falls between the values 4 and 7, the search process follows the middle branch to the next node with the starting key value of 4. The search process retrieves the key value 5 from this leaf page. If the key value 5 doesn't exist in this page, the search process will stop since it's the leaf page. Similarly, the key value 25 can also be searched using the same number of reads.

Index Overhead

The performance benefit of indexes does come at a cost. Tables with indexes require more storage and memory space for the index pages in addition to the data pages of the table. Data manipulation queries (INSERT, UPDATE, and DELETE statements, or the CUD part of Create, Read, Update, Delete [CRUD]) can take longer, and more processing time is required to maintain the indexes of constantly changing tables. This is because, unlike a SELECT statement, data manipulation queries modify the data content of a table. If an INSERT statement adds a row to the table, then it also has to add a row in the index structure. If the index is a clustered index, the overhead is greater still because the row has to be added to the data pages themselves in the right order, which may require other data rows to be repositioned below the entry position of the new row. The UPDATE and DELETE data manipulation queries change the index pages in a similar manner.

When designing indexes, you'll be operating from two different points of view: the existing system, already in production, where you need to measure the overall impact of an index, and the tactical approach where all you worry about is the immediate benefits of an index, usually when initially designing a system. When you have to deal with the existing system, you should ensure that the performance benefits of an index outweigh the extra cost in processing resources. You can do this by using Extended Events (explained in Chapter 3) to do an overall workload optimization (explained in Chapter 25). When you're focused exclusively on the immediate benefits of an index, SQL Server supplies a series of dynamic management views that provide detailed information about the performance of indexes, sys.dm_db_index_operational_stats or sys.dm_db_index_usage_stats. The view sys.dm_db_index_operational_stats shows the low-level activity, such as locks and I/O, on an index that is in use. The view sys.dm_db_index_usage_stats returns statistical counts of the various index operations that have occurred to an index over time. Both of these will be used more extensively in Chapter 20 when I discuss blocking.

■ **Note** Throughout the book, I use the STATISTICS IO and STATISTICS TIME measurements against the queries that I'm running. You can add SET commands to the code, or you can change the connection settings for the query window. I suggest just changing the connection settings.

To understand the overhead cost of an index on data manipulation queries, consider the following example. First, create a test table with 10,000 rows.

```
IF (SELECT  OBJECT_ID('Test1')
   ) IS NOT NULL
     DROP TABLE dbo.Test1;
GO
CREATE TABLE dbo.Test1
     (
      C1 INT,
      C2 INT,
      C3 VARCHAR(50)
     );
```

```
WITH    Nums
          AS (SELECT TOP (10000)
                          ROW_NUMBER() OVER (ORDER BY (SELECT 1
                                                       )) AS n
              FROM      master.sys.all_columns ac1
                        CROSS JOIN master.sys.all_columns ac2
              )
   INSERT  INTO dbo.Test1
          (C1, C2, C3)
          SELECT  n,
                  n,
                  'C3'
          FROM    Nums;
```

Run an UPDATE statement, like so:

```
UPDATE  dbo.Test1
SET     C1 = 1,
        C2 = 1
WHERE   C2 = 1;
```

Then the number of logical reads reported by SET STATISTICS IO is as follows:
Table 'Test1'. Scan count 1, logical reads 29
Add an index on column c1, like so:

```
CREATE CLUSTERED INDEX iTest
ON dbo.Test1(C1);
```

Then the resultant number of logical reads for the same UPDATE statement increases from 29 to 42 but also has added a worktable with an additional 5 reads for a total of 47:

```
Table 'Test1'. Scan count 1, logical reads 42
Table 'Worktable'. Scan count 1, logical reads 5
```

The number of reads goes up because it was necessary to rearrange the data in order to store it in the correct order within the clustered index, increasing the number of reads beyond what was necessary for a heap table to just add the data to the end of the existing storage.

Even though it is true that the amount of overhead required to maintain indexes increases for data manipulation queries, be aware that SQL Server must first find a row before it can update or delete it; therefore, indexes can be helpful for UPDATE and DELETE statements with necessary WHERE clauses. The increased efficiency in using the index to locate a row usually offsets the extra overhead needed to update the indexes, unless the table has a lot of indexes. Further, the vast majority of systems are read heavy, meaning they have a lot more data being retrieved than is being inserted or modified.

To understand how an index can benefit even data modification queries, let's build on the example. Create another index on table t1. This time, create the index on column c2 referred to in the WHERE clause of the UPDATE statement.

```
CREATE INDEX iTest2
ON dbo.Test1(C2);
```

After adding this new index, run the UPDATE command again.

```
UPDATE  dbo.Test1
SET     C1 = 1,
        C2 = 1
WHERE   C2 = 1;
```

The total number of logical reads for this UPDATE statement decreases from 47 to 20 (=15 + 5).

```
Table 'Test1'. Scan count 1, logical reads 15
Table 'Worktable'. Scan count 1, logical reads 5
```

■ **Note**   A *worktable* is a temporary table used internally by SQL Server to process the intermediate results of a query. Worktables are created in the tempdb database and are dropped automatically after query execution.

The examples in this section have demonstrated that although having an index adds some overhead cost to action queries, the overall result is a decrease in cost because of the beneficial effect of indexes on searching, even during updates.

Index Design Recommendations

The main recommendations for index design are as follows:

- Examine the WHERE clause and JOIN criteria columns.
- Use narrow indexes.
- Examine column uniqueness.
- Examine the column data type.
- Consider column order.
- Consider the type of index (clustered versus nonclustered).

Let's consider each of these recommendations in turn.

Examine the WHERE Clause and JOIN Criteria Columns

When a query is submitted to SQL Server, the query optimizer tries to find the best data access mechanism for every table referred to in the query. Here is how it does this:

1. The optimizer identifies the columns included in the WHERE clause and the JOIN criteria.

2. The optimizer then examines indexes on those columns.

3. The optimizer assesses the usefulness of each index by determining the selectivity of the clause (that is, how many rows will be returned) from statistics maintained on the index.

4. Constraints such as primary keys and foreign keys are also assessed and used by the optimizer to determine selectivity of the objects in use in the query.

5. Finally, the optimizer estimates the least costly method of retrieving the qualifying rows, based on the information gathered in the previous steps.

■ **Note** Chapter 12 covers statistics in more depth.

To understand the significance of a WHERE clause column in a query, let's consider an example. Let's return to the original code listing that helped you understand what an index is; the query consisted of a SELECT statement without any WHERE clause, as follows:

```
SELECT  p.ProductID,
        p.Name,
        p.StandardCost,
        p.Weight
FROM    Production.Product p;
```

The query optimizer performs a clustered index scan, the equivalent of a table scan against a heap on a table that has a clustered index, to read the rows as shown in Figure 8-6 (switch on the Include Actual Execution Plan option by using Ctrl+M inside a query window, as well as the Set Statistics IO option by right-clicking and selecting Query Options and then selecting the appropriate check box in the Advanced tab).

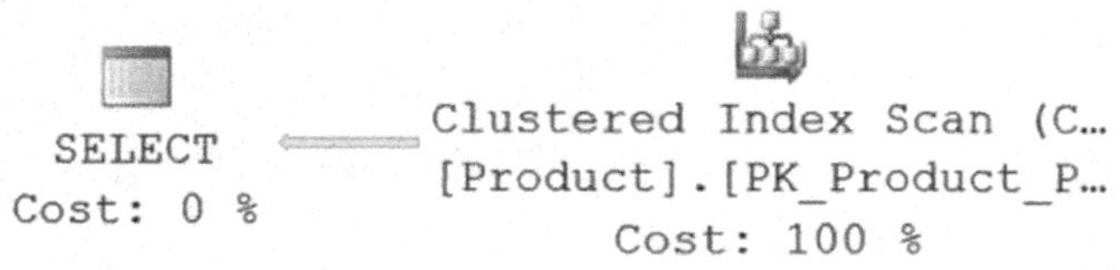

Figure 8-6. *Execution plan with no WHERE clause*

The number of logical reads reported by SET STATISTICS IO for the SELECT statement is as follows:

Table 'Product'. Scan count 1, logical reads **15**

To understand the effect of a WHERE clause column on the query optimizer's decisions, let's add a WHERE clause to retrieve a single row.

```
SELECT  p.ProductID,
        p.Name,
        p.StandardCost,
        p.Weight
FROM    Production.Product AS p
WHERE   p.ProductID = 738 ;
```

With the WHERE clause in place, the query optimizer examines the WHERE clause column ProductID, identifies the availability of the index PK_Product_ProductId on column ProductId, assesses a high selectivity (that is, only one row will be returned) for the WHERE clause from the statistics on index PK_Product_ProductId, and decides to use that index to retrieve the data, as shown in Figure 8-7.

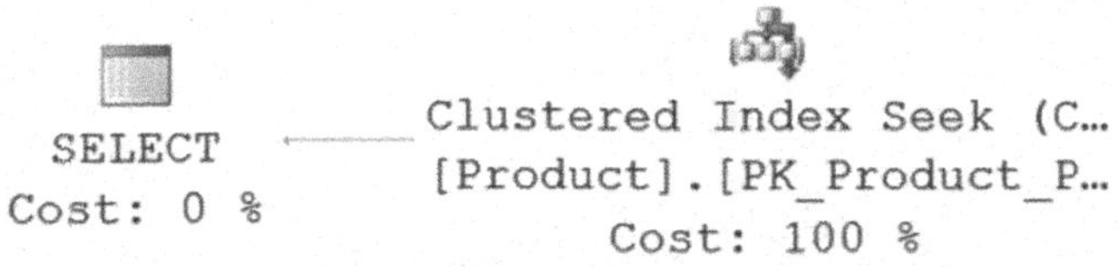

```
                                    ᛗ᛫ᛈ
   ▦                    Clustered Index Seek (C...
 SELECT   ————————      [Product].[PK_Product_P...
Cost: 0 %                      Cost: 100 %
```

Figure 8-7. *Execution plan with a WHERE clause*

The resultant number of logical reads is as follows:

```
Table 'Product'. Scan count 0, logical reads 2
```

The behavior of the query optimizer shows that the WHERE clause column helps the optimizer choose an optimal indexing operation for a query. This is also applicable for a column used in the JOIN criteria between two tables. The optimizer looks for the indexes on the WHERE clause column or the JOIN criterion column and, if available, considers using the index to retrieve the rows from the table. The query optimizer considers indexes on the WHERE clause columns and the JOIN criteria columns while executing a query. Therefore, having indexes on the frequently used columns in the WHERE clause, the HAVING clause, and the JOIN criteria of a SQL query helps the optimizer avoid scanning a base table.

When the amount of data inside a table is so small that it fits onto a single page (8KB), a table scan may work better than an index seek. If you have a good index in place but you're still getting a scan, consider this issue.

Use Narrow Indexes

For best performance, you should use as narrow a data type as is practical when creating indexes. Narrow in this context means as small a data type as you realistically can. You should also avoid very wide data type columns in an index. Columns with string data types (CHAR, VARCHAR, NCHAR, and NVARCHAR) sometimes can be quite wide, as can binary and globally unique identifiers (GUIDs). Unless they are absolutely necessary, minimize the use of wide data type columns with large sizes in an index. You can create indexes on a combination of columns in a table. For the best performance, use as few columns in an index as necessary. But, use the columns you need to use to define a useful key for the index.

A narrow index can accommodate more rows in an 8KB index page than a wide index. This has the following effects:

- Reduces I/O (by having to read fewer 8KB pages)

- Makes database caching more effective because SQL Server can cache fewer index pages, consequently reducing the logical reads required for the index pages in the memory

- Reduces the storage space for the database

To understand how a narrow index can reduce the number of logical reads, create a test table with 20 rows and an index.

```
IF (SELECT  OBJECT_ID('Test1')
   ) IS NOT NULL
   DROP TABLE dbo.Test1;
GO
CREATE TABLE dbo.Test1 (C1 INT, C2 INT);
```

```
WITH    Nums
            AS (SELECT      1 AS n
                UNION ALL
                SELECT     n + 1
                FROM       Nums
                WHERE      n < 20
                )
    INSERT  INTO dbo.Test1
            (C1, C2)
            SELECT  n,
                    2
            FROM    Nums;

CREATE INDEX iTest ON dbo.Test1(C1);
```

Since the indexed column is narrow (the INT data type is 4 bytes), all the index rows can be accommodated in one 8KB index page. As shown in Figure 8-8, you can confirm this in the dynamic management views associated with indexes.

	Name	type_desc	page_count	record_count	index_level
1	NULL	HEAP	1	20	0
2	iTest	NONCLUSTERED	1	20	0

Figure 8-8. *Number of pages for a narrow, nonclustered index*

```
SELECT  i.Name,
        i.type_desc,
        ddips.page_count,
        ddips.record_count,
        ddips.index_level
FROM    sys.indexes i
        JOIN sys.dm_db_index_physical_stats(DB_ID(N'AdventureWorks2012'),
                                    OBJECT_ID(N'dbo.Test1'), NULL,
                                    NULL, 'DETAILED') AS ddips
        ON i.index_id = ddips.index_id
WHERE   i.object_id = OBJECT_ID(N'dbo.Test1');
```

The sys.indexes system table is stored in each database and contains the basic information on every index in the database. The dynamic management function, sys.dm_db_index_physical_stats, contains the more detailed information about the statistics on the index (you'll learn more about this DMF in Chapter 13). To understand the disadvantage of a wide index key, modify the data type of the indexed column c1 from INT to CHAR(500) (narrow_ alter.sql in the download).

```
DROP INDEX dbo.Test1.iTest;
ALTER TABLE dbo.Test1 ALTER COLUMN C1 CHAR(500);
CREATE INDEX iTest ON dbo.Test1(C1);
```

The width of a column with the INT data type is 4 bytes, and the width of a column with the CHAR(500) data type is 500 bytes. Because of the large width of the indexed column, two index pages are required to contain all 20 index rows. You can confirm this in the sys.dm_db_index_physical_stats dynamic management function by running the query against it again (see Figure 8-9).

	Name	type_desc	page_count	record_count	index_level
1	NULL	HEAP	2	25	0
2	iTest	NONCLUSTERED	2	20	0
3	iTest	NONCLUSTERED	1	2	1

Figure 8-9. *Number of pages for a wide, nonclustered index*

A large index key size increases the number of index pages, thereby increasing the amount of memory and disk activities required for the index. It is always recommended that the index key size be as narrow as you can make it.

Drop the test table before continuing.

```
DROP TABLE dbo.Test1;
```

Examine Column Uniqueness

Creating an index on columns with a very low range of possible unique values (such as MaritalStatus) will not benefit performance because the query optimizer will not be able to use the index to effectively narrow down the rows to be returned. Consider a MaritalStatus column with only two unique values: M and S. When you execute a query with the MaritalStatus column in the WHERE clause, you end up with a large number of rows from the table (assuming the distribution of M and S is relatively even), resulting in a costly table or clustered index scan. It is always preferable to have columns in the WHERE clause with lots of unique rows (or *high selectivity*) to limit the number of rows accessed. You should create an index on those columns to help the optimizer access a small result set.

Furthermore, while creating an index on multiple columns, which is also referred to as a *composite index*, column order matters. In many cases, using the most selective column first will help filter the index rows more efficiently.

■ **Note** The importance of column order in a composite index is explained later in the chapter in the "Consider Column Order" section.

From this, you can see that it is important to know the selectivity of a column before creating an index on it. You can find this by executing a query like this one; just substitute the table and column name:

```
SELECT  COUNT(DISTINCT e.MaritalStatus) AS DistinctColValues,
        COUNT(e.MaritalStatus) AS NumberOfRows,
        (CAST(COUNT(DISTINCT e.MaritalStatus) AS DECIMAL)
         / CAST(COUNT(e.MaritalStatus) AS DECIMAL)) AS Selectivity,
                (1.0/(COUNT(DISTINCT e.MaritalStatus))) AS Density
FROM    HumanResources.Employee AS e;
```

The column with the highest number of unique values (or selectivity) can be the best candidate for indexing when referred to in a WHERE clause or a join criterion. You may also have the exceptional data where you have hundreds of rows of common data with only a few that are unique. The few will also benefit from an index. You can make this even more beneficial by using filtered indexes (discussed in more detail later).

To understand how the selectivity of an index key column affects the use of the index, take a look at the MaritalStatus column in the HumanResources.Employee table. If you run the previous query, you'll see that it contains only two distinct values in 290 rows, which is a selectivity of .0069 and a density of .5. A query to look only for a MaritalStatus of M would look like this:

```
SELECT   e.*
FROM     HumanResources.Employee AS e
WHERE    e.MaritalStatus = 'M'
         AND e.BirthDate = '1984-12-05'
         AND e.Gender = 'M';
```

This results in the execution plan in Figure 8-10 and the following I/O and elapsed time:

```
Table 'Employee'. Scan count 1, logical reads 9
CPU time = 0 ms, elapsed time = 49 ms.
```

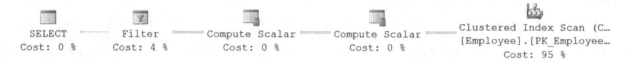

Figure 8-10. *Execution plan with no index*

The data is returned by scanning the clustered index (where the data is stored) to find the appropriate values where MaritalStatus = 'M'. (The other operators will be covered in Chapters 14 and 15.) If you were to place an index on the column, like so, and run the query again, the execution plan remains the same.

```
CREATE INDEX IX_Employee_Test ON HumanResources.Employee (Gender);
```

The data is just not selective enough for the index to be used, let alone be useful. If instead you use a composite index that looks like this:

```
CREATE INDEX IX_Employee_Test ON
HumanResources.Employee (BirthDate,  Gender,  MaritalStatus)
WITH  (DROP_EXISTING = ON) ;
```

and then rerun the query to see the execution plan in Figure 8-11 and the performance results, you get this:

```
Table 'Employee'. Scan count 1, logical reads 4
CPU time = 0 ms, elapsed time = 38 ms.
```

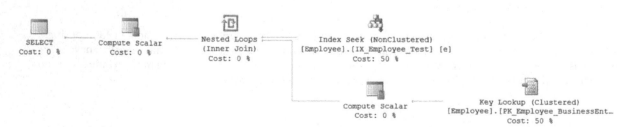

Figure 8-11. *Execution plan with a composite index*

Now you're doing better than you were with the clustered index scan. A nice clean Index Seek operation takes less than half the time to gather the data. The rest is spent in the Key Lookup operation. A Key Lookup operation used to be referred to as a *bookmark lookup*.

■ **Note**   You will learn more about key lookups in Chapter 11.

Although none of the columns in question would probably be selective enough on their own to make a decent index, except possibly the birthdate column, together they provide enough selectivity for the optimizer to take advantage of the index offered.

It is possible to attempt to force the query to use the first test index you created. If you drop the compound index, create the original again, and then modify the query as follows by using a query hint to force the use of the original Index architecture:

```
SELECT  e.*
FROM    HumanResources.Employee AS e WITH (INDEX (IX_Employee_Test))
WHERE   e.BirthDate = '1984-12-05'
        AND e.Gender = 'F'
        AND e.MaritalStatus = 'M';
```

then the results and execution plan shown in Figure 8-12, while similar, are not the same.

```
Table 'Employee'. Scan count 1, logical reads 414
CPU time = 0 ms, elapsed time = 103 ms.
```

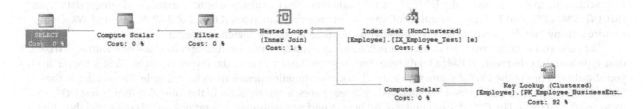

Figure 8-12. *Execution plan when the index is chosen with a query hint*

You see the same index seek, but the number of reads has more than doubled, and the estimated costs within the execution plan have changed. Although forcing the optimizer to choose an index is possible, it clearly isn't always an optimal approach.

Another way to force a different behavior since SQL Server 2012 is the FORCESEEK query hint. FORCESEEK makes it so the optimizer will choose only Index Seek operations. If the query were rewritten like this:

```
SELECT  e.*
FROM    HumanResources.Employee AS e WITH (FORCESEEK)
WHERE   e.BirthDate = '1984-12-05'
        AND e.Gender = 'F'
        AND e.MaritalStatus = 'M';
```

which changes the I/O, execution time, and execution plan results yet again (Figure 8-13), you end up with these results:

```
Table 'Employee'. Scan count 1, logical reads 414
CPU time = 0 ms, elapsed time = 90 ms.
```

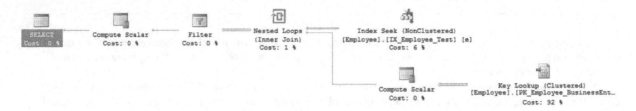

Figure 8-13. *Forcing a Seek operation using FORCESEEK query hint*

Limiting the options of the optimizer and forcing behaviors can in some situations help, but frequently, as shown with the results here, an increase in execution time and the number of reads is not helpful.

Before moving on, be sure to drop the test index from the table.

```
DROP INDEX HumanResources.Employee.IX_Employee_Test;
```

Examine the Column Data Type

The data type of an index matters. For example, an index search on integer keys is fast because of the small size and easy arithmetic manipulation of the INTEGER (or INT) data type. You can also use other variations of integer data types (BIGINT, SMALLINT, and TINYINT) for index columns, whereas string data types (CHAR, VARCHAR, NCHAR, and NVARCHAR) require a string match operation, which is usually costlier than an integer match operation.

Suppose you want to create an index on one column and you have two candidate columns—one with an INTEGER data type and the other with a CHAR(4) data type. Even though the size of both data types is 4 bytes in SQL Server 2014, you should still prefer the INTEGER data type index. Look at arithmetic operations as an example. The value 1 in the CHAR(4) data type is actually stored as 1 followed by three spaces, a combination of the following four bytes: 0x35, 0x20, 0x20, and 0x20. The CPU doesn't understand how to perform arithmetic operations on this data, and therefore it converts to an integer data type before the arithmetic operations, whereas the value 1 in an integer data type is saved as 0x00000001. The CPU can easily perform arithmetic operations on this data.

Of course, most of the time, you won't have the simple choice between identically sized data types, allowing you to choose the more optimal type. Keep this information in mind when designing and building your indexes.

Consider Column Order

An index key is sorted on the first column of the index and then subsorted on the next column within each value of the previous column. The first column in a compound index is frequently referred to as the *leading edge* of the index. For example, consider Table 8-2.

Table 8-2. *Sample Table*

c1	c2
1	1
2	1
3	1
1	2
2	2
3	2

If a composite index is created on the columns (c1, c2), then the index will be ordered as shown in Table 8-3.

Table 8-3. *Composite Index on Columns (c1, c2)*

c1	c2
1	1
1	2
2	1
2	2
3	1
3	2

As shown in Table 8-3, the data is sorted on the first column (c1) in the composite index. Within each value of the first column, the data is further sorted on the second column (c2).

Therefore, the column order in a composite index is an important factor in the effectiveness of the index. You can see this by considering the following:

- Column uniqueness
- Column width
- Column data type

For example, suppose most of your queries on table t1 are similar to the following:

```
SELECT * FROM t1 WHERE c2=12 ;
SELECT * FROM t1 WHERE c2=12 AND c1=11 ;
```

An index on (c2, c1) will benefit both the queries. But an index on (c1, c2) will not be helpful to both queries because it will sort the data initially on column c1, whereas the first SELECT statement needs the data to be sorted on column c2.

To understand the importance of column ordering in an index, consider the following example. In the Person.Address table, there is a column for City and another for PostalCode. Create an index on the table like this:

```
CREATE INDEX IX_Test ON Person.Address (City, PostalCode);
```

A simple SELECT statement run against the table that will use this new index will look something like this:

```
SELECT   a.*
FROM     Person.Address AS a
WHERE    a.City = 'Dresden';
```

The I/O and execution time for the query is as follows:

```
Table 'Address'. Scan count 1, logical reads 74
CPU time = 0 ms, elapsed time = 209 ms.
```

And the execution plan in Figure 8-14 shows the use of the index.

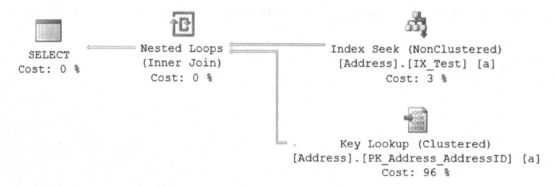

Figure 8-14. *Execution plan for query against leading edge of index*

So, this query is taking advantage of the leading edge of the index to perform a Seek operation to retrieve the data. If, instead of querying using the leading edge, you use another column in the index like the following query:

```
SELECT   *
FROM     Person.Address AS a
WHERE    a.PostalCode = 'WA3 7BH';
```

the results are as follows:

```
Table 'Address'. Scan count 1, logical reads 211
CPU time = 16 ms, elapsed time = 267 ms.
```

And the execution plan is clearly different, as you can see in Figure 8-15.

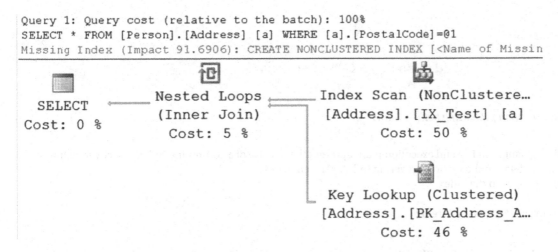

```
Query 1: Query cost (relative to the batch): 100%
SELECT * FROM [Person].[Address] [a] WHERE [a].[PostalCode]=@1
Missing Index (Impact 91.6906): CREATE NONCLUSTERED INDEX [<Name of Missin
```

Figure 8-15. *Execution plan for query against inner columns*

Both queries return 31 rows from the same table, but the number of reads jumped from 74 to 180. You begin to see the difference between the Index Seek operation in Figure 8-14 and the Index Scan operation in Figure 8-15. Also note that because it had to perform a scan, the optimizer indicated that there might be a possible index to help improve the performance of the query.

Missing index information is useful as a pointer to the potential for a new or better index on a table, but don't assume it's always correct. You can right-click the place where the missing index information is and select Missing Index Details from the context menu. That will open a new query window with the details of the index laid out, ready for creation. If you do decide to test that index, make sure you rename it from the default name.

Finally, to see the order of the index really shine, change the query to this:

```
SELECT   a.AddressID,
         a.City,
         a.PostalCode
FROM     Person.Address AS a
WHERE    a.City = 'Gloucestershire'
         AND a.PostalCode = 'GL7 1RY';
```

Executing this query will return the same number of rows as the previous queries, resulting in the following:

```
Table 'Address'. Scan count 1, logical reads 2
CPU time = 15 ms, elapsed time = 0 ms.
```

The execution plan is visible in Figure 8-16.

Figure 8-16. *Execution plan using both columns*

The radical changes in I/O and execution plan represent the real use of a compound index, the covering index. This is covered in detail in the section "Covering Indexes" in chapter 9.

When finished, drop the index.

```
DROP INDEX Person.Address.IX_Test;
```

Consider the Type of Index

In SQL Server, from all the different types of indexes available to you, most of the time you'll be working with the two main index types: *clustered* and *nonclustered*. Both types have a B-tree structure. The main difference between the two types is that the leaf pages in a clustered index are the data pages of the table and are therefore in the same order as the data to which they point. This means the clustered index is the table. As you proceed, you will see that the difference at the leaf level between the two index types becomes important when determining the type of index to use.

Clustered Indexes

The leaf pages of a clustered index and the data pages of the table the index is on are one and the same. Because of this, table rows are physically sorted on the clustered index column, and since there can be only one physical order of the table data, a table can have only one clustered index.

■ **Tip** When you create a primary key constraint, SQL Server automatically creates it as a unique clustered index on the primary key if one does not already exist and if it is not explicitly specified that the index should be a unique nonclustered index. This is not a requirement; it's just default behavior. You can change the definition of the primary key prior to creating it on the table.

Heap Tables

As mentioned earlier in the chapter, a table with no clustered index is called a *heap table*. The data rows of a heap table are not stored in any particular order or linked to the adjacent pages in the table. This unorganized structure of the heap table usually increases the overhead of accessing a large heap table when compared to accessing a large nonheap table (a table with a clustered index).

Relationship with Nonclustered Indexes

There is an interesting relationship between a clustered index and the nonclustered indexes in SQL Server. An index row of a nonclustered index contains a pointer to the corresponding data row of the table. This pointer is called a *row locator*. The value of the row locator depends on whether the data pages are stored in a heap or on a clustered index. For a nonclustered index, the row locator is a pointer to the row identifier (RID) for the data row in a heap. For a table with a clustered index, the row locator is the clustered index key value.

For example, say you have a heap table with no clustered index, as shown in Table 8-4.

Table 8-4. *Data Page for a Sample Table*

RowID (Not a Real Column)	c1	c2	c3
1	A1	A2	A3
2	B1	B2	B3

A nonclustered index on column c1 in a heap will cause the row locator for the index rows to contain a pointer to the corresponding data row in the database table, as shown in Table 8-5.

Table 8-5. *Nonclustered Index Page with No Clustered Index*

c1	Row Locator
A1	Pointer to RID = 1
B1	Pointer to RID = 2

On creating a clustered index on column c2, the row locator values of the nonclustered index rows are changed. The new value of the row locator will contain the clustered index key value, as shown in Table 8-6.

Table 8-6. *Nonclustered Index Page with a Clustered Index on c2*

c1	Row Locator
A1	A2
B1	B2

To verify this dependency between a clustered and a nonclustered index, let's consider an example. In the AdventureWorks2012 database, the table dbo.DatabaseLog contains no clustered index, just a nonclustered primary key. If a query is run against it like the following, then the execution will look like Figure 8-17.

```
SELECT  dl.DatabaseLogID,
        dl.PostTime
FROM    dbo.DatabaseLog AS dl
WHERE   dl.DatabaseLogID = 115;
```

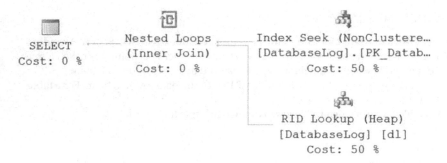

Figure 8-17. *Execution plan against a heap*

As you can see, the index was used in a Seek operation. But because the data is stored separately from the nonclustered index, an additional operation, the RID Lookup operation, is required in order to retrieve the data, which is then joined back to the information from the Index Seek operation through a Nested Loop operation. This is a classic example of what is known as a *lookup*, in this case an RID lookup, which is explained in more detail in the "Defining the Lookup" section. A similar query run against a table with a clustered index in place will look like this:

```
SELECT  d.DepartmentID,
        d.ModifiedDate
FROM    HumanResources.Department AS d
WHERE   d.DepartmentID = 10 ;
```

Figure 8-18 shows this execution plan returned.

```
    ▣                        ⟋ⓢ⟍
 SELECT  ──────── Clustered Index Seek  (C...
Cost: 0 %        [Department].[PK_Depart...
                      Cost: 100 %
```

Figure 8-18. *Execution plan with a clustered index*

Although the primary key is used in the same way as the previous query, this time it's against a clustered index. As you now know, this means the data is stored with the index, so the additional column doesn't require a lookup operation to get the data. Everything is returned by the simple clustered Index Seek operation.

To navigate from a nonclustered index row to a data row, this relationship between the two index types requires an additional indirection for navigating the B-tree structure of the clustered index. Without the clustered index, the row locator of the nonclustered index would be able to navigate directly from the nonclustered index row to the data row in the base table. The presence of the clustered index causes the navigation from the nonclustered index row to the data row to go through the B-tree structure of the clustered index, since the new row locator value points to the clustered index key.

On the other hand, consider inserting an intermediate row in the clustered index key order or expanding the content of an intermediate row. For example, imagine a clustered index table containing four rows per page, with clustered index column values of 1, 2, 4, and 5. Adding a new row in the table with the clustered index value 3 will require space in the page between values 2 and 4. If enough space is not available in that position, a page split will occur on the data page (or clustered index leaf page). Even though the data page split will cause relocation of the data rows, the nonclustered index row locator values need not be updated. These row locators continue to point to the same logical key values of the clustered index key, even though the data rows have physically moved to a different location. In the case of a data page split, the row locators of the nonclustered indexes need not be updated. This is an important point since tables often have a large number of nonclustered indexes.

Things don't work the same way for heap tables. While page splits in a heap are not a common occurence, and when heaps do split, they don't rearrange locations in the same way as clustered indexes, you can have rows move in a heap, usually due to updates causing the heap to not fit on it's current page. Anything that causes the location of rows to be moved in a heap results in a forwarding record being placed into the original location pointing to that new location, necessitating even more I/O activity.

■ **Note**   Page splits and their effect on performance are explained in more detail in Chapter 13.

Clustered Index Recommendations

The relationship between a clustered index and a nonclustered index imposes some considerations on the clustered index, which are explained in the sections that follow.

Create the Clustered Index First

Since all nonclustered indexes hold clustered index keys within their index rows, the order of nonclustered and clustered index creation is important. For example, if the nonclustered indexes are built before the clustered index is created, then the nonclustered index row locator will contain a pointer to the corresponding RID of the table. Creating the clustered index later will modify all the nonclustered indexes to contain clustered index keys as the new row locator value. This effectively rebuilds all the nonclustered indexes.

For the best performance, I recommend you create the clustered index *before* you create any nonclustered index. This allows the nonclustered indexes to have their row locator set to the clustered index keys at the time of creation. This does not have any effect on the final performance, but rebuilding the indexes may be quite a large job.

As part of creating the clustered index first, I also suggest you design the tables in your database around the clustered index. It should be the first index created because you should be storing your data as a clustered index by default.

Keep Clustered Indexes Narrow

Since all nonclustered indexes hold the clustered keys as their row locator, for the best performance keep the overall byte size of the clustered index as small as possible. If you create a wide clustered index, say CHAR(500), in addition to having fewer rows per page in the cluster, this will add 500 bytes to every nonclustered index. Thus, keep the number of columns in the clustered index to a minimum, and carefully consider the byte size of each column to be included in the clustered index. A column of the integer data type often makes a good candidate for a clustered index, whereas a string data type column will be a less-than-optimal choice.

To understand the effect of a wide clustered index on a nonclustered index, consider this example. Create a small test table with a clustered index and a nonclustered index.

```
IF (SELECT  OBJECT_ID('Test1')
    ) IS NOT NULL
    DROP TABLE dbo.Test1;
GO
CREATE TABLE dbo.Test1 (C1 INT, C2 INT);
```

```
WITH    Nums
          AS (SELECT TOP (20)
                       ROW_NUMBER() OVER (ORDER BY (SELECT 1
                                                    )) AS n
              FROM       master.sys.all_columns ac1
                         CROSS JOIN master.sys.all_columns ac2
             )
   INSERT INTO dbo.Test1
          (C1, C2)
          SELECT  n,
                  n + 1
          FROM    Nums;

CREATE CLUSTERED INDEX iClustered
ON dbo.Test1  (C2);

CREATE NONCLUSTERED INDEX iNonClustered
ON dbo.Test1  (C1);
```

Since the table has a clustered index, the row locator of the nonclustered index contains the clustered index key value. Therefore:

- Width of the nonclustered index row = width of the nonclustered index column + width of the clustered index column = size of INT data type + size of INT data type

  ```
  = 4 bytes + 4 bytes = 8 bytes
  ```

With this small size of a nonclustered index row, all the rows can be stored in one index page. You can confirm this by querying against the index statistics, as shown in Figure 8-19.

	name	type_desc	page_count	record_count	index_level
1	iClustered	CLUSTERED	1	20	0
2	iNonClustered	NONCLUSTERED	1	20	0

Figure 8-19. *Number of index pages for a narrow index*

```
SELECT  i.name,
        i.type_desc,
        s.page_count,
        s.record_count,
        s.index_level
FROM    sys.indexes i
        JOIN sys.dm_db_index_physical_stats(DB_ID(N'AdventureWorks2012'),
                                            OBJECT_ID(N'dbo.Test1'), NULL,
                                            NULL, 'DETAILED') AS s
        ON i.index_id = s.index_id
WHERE   i.object_id = OBJECT_ID(N'dbo.Test1');
```

To understand the effect of a wide clustered index on a nonclustered index, modify the data type of the clustered indexed column c2 from INT to CHAR(500).

```
DROP INDEX dbo.Test1.iClustered;
ALTER TABLE dbo.Test1 ALTER COLUMN C2 CHAR(500);
CREATE CLUSTERED INDEX iClustered ON dbo.Test1(C2);
```

Running the query against sys.dm_db_index_physical_stats again returns the result in Figure 8-20.

	name	type_desc	page_count	record_count	index_level
1	iClustered	CLUSTERED	2	20	0
2	iClustered	CLUSTERED	1	2	1
3	iNonClustered	NONCLUSTERED	2	20	0
4	iNonClustered	NONCLUSTERED	1	2	1

Figure 8-20. *Number of index pages for a wide index*

You can see that a wide clustered index increases the width of the nonclustered index row size. Because of the large width of the nonclustered index row, one 8KB index page can't accommodate all the index rows. Instead, two index pages will be required to store all 20 index rows. In the case of a large table, an expansion in the size of the nonclustered indexes because of a large clustered index key size can significantly increase the number of pages of the nonclustered indexes.

Therefore, a large clustered index key size not only affects its own width but also widens all nonclustered indexes on the table. This increases the number of index pages for all the indexes on the table, increasing the logical reads and disk I/Os required for the indexes.

Rebuild the Clustered Index in a Single Step

Because of the dependency of nonclustered indexes on the clustered index, rebuilding the clustered index as separate DROP INDEX and CREATE INDEX statements causes all the nonclustered indexes to be rebuilt twice. To avoid this, use the DROP_EXISTING clause of the CREATE INDEX statement to rebuild the clustered index in a single atomic step. Similarly, you can also use the DROP_EXISTING clause with a nonclustered index.

It's worth noting that in SQL Server 2005 and newer, when you perform a straight rebuild of a clustered index, you won't see the nonclustered indexes rebuilt as well.

Where Possible, Make the Clustered Index Unique

Because the clustered index is used to store the data, you must be able to find each row. While the clustered index doesn't have to be unique purely in terms of its definition and storage, if the key values are not unique, SQL Server would be unable to find the rows unless there was a way to make the cluster uniquely identify the location of each discrete row of data. So, SQL Server will add a value to a nonunique clustered index to make it unique. This value is called a *uniqueifier*. It adds to the size of your clustered index as well as all nonclustered indexes, as noted earlier. It also means a little bit of added processing to get the unique value as each row gets inserted. For all these reasons, it makes sense to make the clustered index unique where you can. This is a big reason why the default behavior for primary keys is to make them a clustered index.

You don't have to make the clustered index unique. But you do need to take the uniqifier into account when you're defining your storage and indexes.

When to Use a Clustered Index

In certain situations, using a clustered index is helpful. I discuss these situations in the sections that follow.

Accessing the Data Directly

With all the data stored on the leaf pages of a clustered index, any time you access the cluster, the data is immediately available. One use for a clustered index is to support the most commonly used access path to the data. Any access of the clustered index does not require any additional reads to retrieve the data, which means seeks or scans against the clustered index do not require any additional reads to retrieve that data. This is another likely reason that Microsoft has made the primary key a clustered index by default. Since the primary key is frequently the most likely means of accessing data in a table, it serves well as a clustered index.

Just remember that the primary key being the clustered index is a default behavior but not necessarily the most common access path to the data. This could be through foreign key constraints, alternate keys in the table, or other columns. Plan and design the cluster with storage and access in mind, and you should be fine.

The clustered index works well as the primary path to the data only if you're accessing a considerable portion of the data within a table. If, on the other hand, you're accessing small subsets of the data, you might be better off with a nonclustered covering index. Also, you have to take into account the number and types of columns that define the access path to the data. Since the key of a clustered index becomes the pointer for nonclustered indexes, excessively wide clustered keys can seriously impact performance and storage for nonclustered indexes.

Retrieving Presorted Data

Clustered indexes are particularly efficient when the data retrieval needs to be sorted (a covering nonclustered index is also useful for this). If you create a clustered index on the column or columns that you may need to sort by, then the rows will be physically stored in that order, eliminating the overhead of sorting the data after it is retrieved.

Let's see this in action. Create a test table as follows:

```
IF (SELECT  OBJECT_ID('od')
    ) IS NOT NULL
    DROP TABLE dbo.od ;
 GO
SELECT  pod.*
INTO    dbo.od
FROM    Purchasing.PurchaseOrderDetail AS pod;
```

The new table od is created with data only. It doesn't have any indexes. You can verify the indexes on the table by executing the following, which returns nothing:

```
EXEC sp_helpindex 'dbo.od';
```

To understand the use of a clustered index, fetch a large range of rows ordered on a certain column.

```
SELECT  od.*
FROM    dbo.od
WHERE   od.ProductID BETWEEN 500 AND 510
ORDER BY od.ProductID;
```

You can obtain the cost of executing this query (without any indexes) from the STATISTICS IO output.

```
Table 'od'. Scan count 1, logical reads 78
CPU time = 15 ms, elapsed time = 388 ms.
```

To improve the performance of this query, you should create an index on the WHERE clause column. This query requires both a range of rows and a sorted output. The result set requirement of this query meets the recommendations for a clustered index. Therefore, create a clustered index as follows and reexamine the cost of the query.

```
CREATE CLUSTERED INDEX i1 ON od(ProductID);
```

When you run the query again, the resultant cost of the query (with a clustered index) is as follows:

```
Table 'od'.  Scan count 1,  logical reads 8
CPU time = 16 ms, elapsed time = 373 ms.
```

Creating the clustered index reduced the number of logical reads and therefore should contribute to the query performance improvement.

On the other hand, if you create a nonclustered index (instead of a clustered index) on the candidate column, then the query performance may be affected adversely. Let's verify the effect of a nonclustered index in this case.

```
DROP INDEX od.i1;
CREATE NONCLUSTERED INDEX i1 on dbo.od(ProductID);
```

The resultant cost of the query (with a nonclustered index) is as follows:

```
Table 'od'. Scan count 1, logical reads 78
CPU time = 0 ms, elapsed time = 434 ms.
```

The nonclustered index isn't even used directly in the resulting execution plan. Instead, you get a table scan, but the estimated costs for sorting the data in this new plan are different from the original table scan because of the added selectivity that the index provides the optimizer to estimate costs, even though the index isn't used. Drop the test table when you're done.

```
DROP TABLE dbo.od;
```

Poor Design Practices for a Clustered Index

In certain situations, you are better off not using a clustered index. I discuss these in the sections that follow.

Frequently Updatable Columns

If the clustered index columns are frequently updated, this will cause the row locator of all the nonclustered indexes to be updated accordingly, significantly increasing the cost of the relevant action queries. This also affects database concurrency by blocking all other queries referring to the same part of the table and the nonclustered indexes during that period. Therefore, avoid creating a clustered index on columns that are highly updatable.

■ **Note**   Chapter 20 covers blocking in more depth.

To understand how the cost of an UPDATE statement that modifies only a clustered key column is increased by the presence of nonclustered indexes on the table, consider the following example. The Sales.SpecialOfferProduct table has a composite clustered index on the primary key, which is also the foreign key from two different tables; this is a classic many-to-many join. In this example, I update one of the two columns using the following statement (note the use of the transaction to keep the test data intact):

```
BEGIN TRAN
SET STATISTICS IO ON;
UPDATE  Sales.SpecialOfferProduct
SET     ProductID = 345
WHERE   SpecialOfferID = 1
        AND  ProductID = 720;
SET STATISTICS IO OFF;
ROLLBACK TRAN
```

The STATISTICS IO output shows the reads necessary.

```
Table 'Product'. Scan count 0, logical reads 2
Table 'SalesOrderDetail'. Scan count 1, logical reads 1246
Table 'SpecialOfferProduct'. Scan count 0, logical reads 15
```

If you added a nonclustered index to the table, you would see the reads increase, as shown here:

```
CREATE NONCLUSTERED INDEX ixTest
ON Sales.SpecialOfferProduct (ModifiedDate);
```

When you run the same query again, the output of STATISTICS IO changes for the SpecialOfferProduct table.

```
Table 'Product'. Scan count 0, logical reads 2
Table 'SalesOrderDetail'. Scan count 1, logical reads 1246
Table 'SpecialOfferProduct'. Scan count 0, logical reads 19
```

The number of reads caused by the update of the clustered index is increased with the addition of the nonclustered index. Be sure to drop the index.

```
DROP INDEX Sales.SpecialOfferProduct.ixTest;
```

Wide Keys

Since all nonclustered indexes hold the clustered keys as their row locator, for performance reasons you should avoid creating a clustered index on a very wide column (or columns) or on too many columns. As explained in the preceding section, a clustered index must be as narrow as possible.

Nonclustered Indexes

A nonclustered index does not affect the order of the data in the table pages because the leaf pages of a nonclustered index and the data pages of the table are separate. A pointer (the row locator) is required to navigate from an index row in the nonclustered index to the data row, whether stored on a cluster or in a heap. As you learned in the earlier "Clustered Indexes" section, the structure of the row locator depends on whether the data pages are stored in a heap or a clustered index. For a heap, the row locator is a pointer to the RID for the data row; for a table with a clustered index, the row locator is the clustered index key.

Nonclustered Index Maintenance

The row locator value of the nonclustered indexes continues to have the same clustered index value, even when the clustered index rows are physically relocated.

In a table that is a heap, where there is no clustered index, to optimize this maintenance cost, SQL Server adds a pointer to the old data page to point to the new data page after a page split, instead of updating the row locator of all the relevant nonclustered indexes. Although this reduces the maintenance cost of the nonclustered indexes, it increases the navigation cost from the nonclustered index row to the data row within the heap, since an extra link is added between the old data page and the new data page. Therefore, having a clustered index as the row locator decreases this overhead associated with the nonclustered index.

Defining the Lookup Operation

When a query requests columns that are not part of the nonclustered index chosen by the optimizer, a lookup is required. This may be a key lookup when going against a clustered index or an RID lookup when performed against a heap. In the past, the common term for these lookups came from the old definition name, *bookmark lookup*. That term is being used less and less since people haven't seen that phrase in execution plans since SQL Server 2000. Now you just refer to it as a lookup and then define the type, key, or RID. The lookup fetches the corresponding data row from the table by following the row locator value from the index row, requiring a logical read on the data page besides the logical read on the index page and a join operation to put the data together in a common output. However, if all the columns required by the query are available in the index itself, then access to the data page is not required. This is known as a *covering index*.

These lookups are the reason that large result sets are better served with a clustered index. A clustered index doesn't require a lookup, since the leaf pages and data pages for a clustered index are the same.

■ **Note** Chapter 11 covers lookup operations in more detail.

Nonclustered Index Recommendations

Since a table can have only one clustered index, you can use the flexibility of multiple nonclustered indexes to help improve performance. I explain the factors that decide the use of a nonclustered index in the following sections.

When to Use a Nonclustered Index

A nonclustered index is most useful when all you want to do is retrieve a small number of rows and columns from a large table. As the number of columns to be retrieved increases, the ability to have a covering index decreases. Then, if you're also retrieving a large number of rows, the overhead cost of any lookup rises proportionately. To retrieve a small number of rows from a table, the indexed column should have a high selectivity.

Furthermore, there will be indexing requirements that won't be suitable for a clustered index, as explained in the "Clustered Indexes" section.

- Frequently updatable columns
- Wide keys

In these cases, you can use a nonclustered index since, unlike a clustered index, it doesn't affect other indexes in the table. A nonclustered index on a frequently updatable column isn't as costly as having a clustered index on that column. The UPDATE operation on a nonclustered index is limited to the base table and the nonclustered index. It doesn't affect any other nonclustered indexes on the table. Similarly, a nonclustered index on a wide column (or set of columns) doesn't increase the size of any other index, unlike that with a clustered index. However, remain cautious, even while creating a nonclustered index on a highly updatable column or a wide column (or set of columns), since this can increase the cost of action queries, as explained earlier in the chapter.

■ **Tip**   A nonclustered index can also help resolve blocking and deadlock issues. I cover this in more depth in Chapters 20 and 21.

When Not to Use a Nonclustered Index

Nonclustered indexes are not suitable for queries that retrieve a large number of rows. Such queries are better served with a clustered index, which doesn't require a separate lookup to retrieve a data row. Since a lookup requires additional logical reads to get to the data page besides the logical read on the nonclustered index page, the cost of a query using a nonclustered index increases significantly for a large number of rows, such as when in a loop join that requires one lookup after another. The SQL Server query optimizer takes this cost into effect and accordingly can discard the nonclustered index when retrieving a large result set.

If your requirement is to retrieve a large result set from a table, then having a nonclustered index on the filter criterion (or the join criterion) column will probably not be useful unless you use a special type of nonclustered index called a *covering index*. I describe this index type in detail in Chapter 9.

Clustered vs. Nonclustered Indexes

The main considerations in choosing between a clustered and a nonclustered index are as follows:

- Number of rows to be retrieved
- Data-ordering requirement
- Index key width
- Column update frequency
- Lookup cost
- Any disk hot spots

Benefits of a Clustered Index over a Nonclustered Index

When deciding upon a type of index on a table with no indexes, the clustered index is usually the preferred choice. Because the index page and the data pages are the same, the clustered index doesn't have to jump from the index row to the base row as is required in the case of a noncovering nonclustered index.

To understand how a clustered index can outperform a nonclustered index in these circumstances, even in retrieving a small number of rows, create a test table with a high selectivity for one column.

```
IF (SELECT  OBJECT_ID('dbo.Test1')
    ) IS NOT NULL
    DROP TABLE dbo.Test1;
GO
CREATE TABLE dbo.Test1 (C1 INT,C2 INT);

WITH    Nums
        AS (SELECT TOP (10000)
                        ROW_NUMBER() OVER (ORDER BY (SELECT 1
                                            )) AS n
            FROM        master.sys.all_columns AS ac1
                        CROSS JOIN master.sys.all_columns AS ac2
            )
    INSERT  INTO dbo.Test1
            (C1,C2)
            SELECT  n,
                    2
            FROM    Nums;
```

The following SELECT statement fetches only 1 out of 10,000 rows from the table:

```
SELECT  t.C1,
        t. C2
FROM    dbo.Test1 AS t
WHERE   C1 = 1000;
```

This will be with the graphical execution plan shown in Figure 8-21 and the output of SET STATISTICS IO and STATISTICS TIME as follows:

```
Table 'Test1'. Scan count 1, logical reads 39
CPU time = 0 ms, elapsed time = 1 ms.
```

Figure 8-21. *Execution plan with no index*

Considering the small size of the result set retrieved by the preceding SELECT statement, a nonclustered column on c1 can be a good choice.

```
CREATE NONCLUSTERED INDEX incl ON dbo.Test1(C1);
```

You can run the same SELECT command again. Since retrieving a small number of rows through a nonclustered index is more economical than a table scan, the optimizer used the nonclustered index on column c1, as shown in Figure 8-22. The number of logical reads reported by STATISTICS IO is as follows:

```
Table 'Test1'. Scan count 1, logical reads 3
CPU time = 0 ms, elapsed time = 0 ms.
```

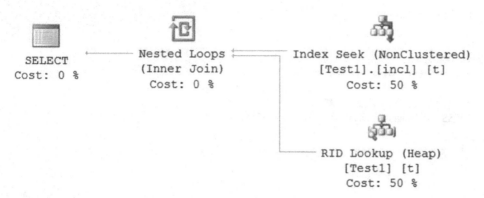

Figure 8-22. *Execution plan with a nonclustered index*

Even though retrieving a small result set using a column with high selectivity is a good pointer toward creating a nonclustered index on the column, a clustered index on the same column can be equally beneficial or even better. To evaluate how the clustered index can be more beneficial than the nonclustered index, create a clustered index on the same column.

```
CREATE CLUSTERED INDEX icl ON dbo.Test1(C1);
```

Run the same SELECT command again. From the resultant execution plan (see Figure 8-22) of the preceding SELECT statement, you can see that the optimizer used the clustered index (instead of the nonclustered index) even for a small result set. The number of logical reads for the SELECT statement decreased from three to two (Figure 8-23).

```
Table  't1'.  Scan count 1,  logical reads 2
CPU time = 0 ms, elapsed time = 0 ms.
```

Figure 8-23. *Execution plan with a clustered index*

■ **Note** Because a table can have only one clustered index and that index is where the data is stored, I would generally reserve the clustered index for the most frequently used access path to the data.

Benefits of a Nonclustered Index over a Clustered Index

As you learned in the previous section, a nonclustered index is preferred over a clustered index in the following situations:

- When the index key size is large.

- To avoid the overhead cost associated with a clustered index since rebuilding the clustered index rebuilds all the nonclustered indexes of the table.

- To resolve blocking by having a database reader work on the pages of a nonclustered index, while a database writer modifies other columns (not included in the nonclustered index) in the data page; in this case, the writer working on the data page won't block a reader that can get all the required column values from the nonclustered index without hitting the base table. I'll explain this in detail in Chapter 13.

- When all the columns (from a table) referred to by a query can be safely accommodated in the nonclustered index itself, as explained in this section.

As already established, the data-retrieval performance when using a nonclustered index is generally poorer than that when using a clustered index because of the cost associated with jumping from the nonclustered index rows to the data rows in the base table. In cases where the jump to the data rows is not required, the performance of a nonclustered index should be just as good as—or even better than—a clustered index. This is possible if the nonclustered index, the key plus any included columns at the page level, includes all the columns required from the table.

To understand the situation in which a nonclustered index can outperform a clustered index, consider the following example. Assume for these purposes that you need to examine the credit cards that are expiring between the months of June 2008 and September 2008. You may have a query that returns a large number of rows and looks like this:

```
SELECT  cc.CreditCardID,
        cc.CardNumber,
        cc.ExpMonth,
        cc.ExpYear
FROM    Sales.CreditCard cc
WHERE   cc.ExpMonth BETWEEN 6 AND 9
        AND cc.ExpYear = 2008
ORDER BY cc.ExpMonth;
```

The following are the I/O and time results. Figure 8-24 shows the execution plan.

```
Table 'CreditCard'. Scan count 1, logical reads 189
CPU time = 16 ms, elapsed time = 240 ms.
```

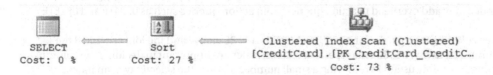

Figure 8-24. *Execution plan scanning the clustered index*

The clustered index is on the primary key, and although most access against the table may be through that key, making the index useful, the clustered index in this instance is just not performing in the way you need. Although you could expand the definition of the index to include all the other columns in the query, they're not really needed to make the clustered index function, and they would interfere with the operation of the primary key. Instead, you can use the INCLUDE operation to store the columns defined within it at the leaf level of the index. They don't affect the key structure of the index in any way but provide the ability, through the sacrifice of some additional disk space, to make a nonclustered index covering (covered in more detail later). In this instance, creating a different index is in order.

```
CREATE NONCLUSTERED INDEX ixTest
ON Sales.CreditCard (ExpMonth, ExpYear)
INCLUDE (CardNumber);
```

Now when the query is run again, this is the result:

```
Table 'CreditCard'. Scan count 1, logical reads 32
CPU time = 0 ms, elapsed time = 166 ms.
```

Figure 8-25 shows the corresponding execution plan.

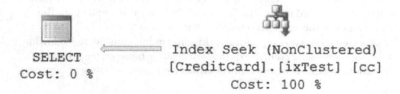

Figure 8-25. *Execution plan with a nonclustered index*

In this case, the SELECT statement doesn't include any column that requires a jump from the nonclustered index page to the data page of the table, which is what usually makes a nonclustered index costlier than a clustered index for a large result set and/or sorted output. This kind of nonclustered index is called a *covering index*.

Clean up the index after the testing is done.

```
DROP INDEX Sales.CreditCard.ixTest;
```

Summary

In this chapter, you learned that indexing is an effective method for reducing the number of logical reads and disk I/O for a query. Although an index may add overhead to action queries, even action queries such as UPDATE and DELETE can benefit from an index.

To decide the index key columns for a particular query, evaluate the WHERE clause and the join criteria of the query. Factors such as column selectivity, width, data type, and column order are important in deciding the columns in an index key. Since an index is mainly useful in retrieving a small number of rows, the selectivity of an indexed column should be very high. It is important to note that nonclustered indexes contain the value of a clustered index key as their row locator because this behavior greatly influences the selection of an index type.

In the next chapter, you will learn more about other functionality and other types of indexes available to help you tune your queries.

■ ■ ■

## CHAPTER 9

Index Analysis

In the previous chapter I introduced the concepts surrounding indexes. This chapter takes that information and adds more functionality. There's a lot of interesting interaction between indexes that you can take advantage of. There are also a number of settings that affect the behavior of indexes that I didn't address in the preceding chapter. I'll show you methods to squeeze even more performance out of your system.

In this chapter, I cover the following topics:

- Advanced indexing techniques

- Special index types

- Additional characteristics of indexes

Advanced Indexing Techniques

Here are a few of the more advanced indexing techniques that you can consider:

- *Covering indexes*: These were introduced in Chapter 8.

- *Index intersections*: Use multiple nonclustered indexes to satisfy all the column requirements (from a table) for a query.

- *Index joins*: Use the index intersection and covering index techniques to avoid hitting the base table.

- *Filtered indexes*: To be able to index fields with odd data distributions or sparse columns, you can apply a filter to an index so that it indexes only some data.

- *Indexed views*: These materialize the output of a view on disk.

- *Index compression*: The storage of indexes can be compressed through SQL Server, putting more rows of data on a page and improving performance.

- *Columnstore indexes*: Instead of grouping and storing data for a row, like traditional indexes, these indexes group and store based on columns.

I cover these topics in more detail in the following sections.

Covering Indexes

A *covering index* is a nonclustered index built upon all the columns required to satisfy a SQL query without going to the heap or the clustered index. If a query encounters an index and does not need to refer to the underlying structures at all, then the index can be considered a covering index.

For example, in the following SELECT statement, irrespective of where the columns are used within the statement, all the columns (StateProvinceId and PostalCode) should be included in the nonclustered index to cover the query fully:

```
SELECT   a.PostalCode
FROM     Person.Address AS a
WHERE    a.StateProvinceID = 42;
```

Then all the required data for the query can be obtained from the nonclustered index page, without accessing the data page. This helps SQL Server save logical and physical reads. If you run the query, you'll get the following I/O and execution time as well as the execution plan in Figure 9-1.

```
Table 'Address'. Scan count 1, logical reads 19
CPU time = 0 ms,  elapsed time = 17 ms.
```

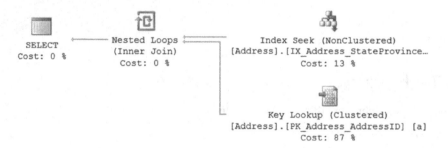

Figure 9-1. *Query without a covering index*

Here you have a classic lookup with the Key Lookup operator pulling the PostalCode data from the clustered index and joining it with the Index Seek operator against the IX_Address_StateProvinceId index.

Although you can re-create the index with both key columns, another way to make an index a covering index is to use the new INCLUDE operator. This stores data with the index without changing the structure of the index itself. Use the following to re-create the index:

```
CREATE NONCLUSTERED INDEX [IX_Address_StateProvinceID]
ON [Person].[Address]  ([StateProvinceID] ASC)
INCLUDE  (PostalCode)
WITH (
DROP_EXISTING = ON);
```

If you rerun the query, the execution plan (Figure 9-2), I/O, and execution time change.

```
Table 'Address'. Scan count 1, logical reads 2
CPU time = 0 ms,  elapsed time = 14 ms.
```

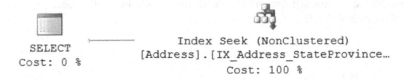

Figure 9-2. *Query with a covering index*

The reads have dropped from 19 to 2, and the execution plan is just about as simple as possible; it's a single Index Seek operation against the new and improved index, which is now covering. A covering index is a useful technique for reducing the number of logical reads of a query. Adding columns using the INCLUDE statement makes this functionality easier to achieve without adding to the number of columns in an index or the size of the index key since the included columns are stored only at the leaf level of the index.

The INCLUDE is best used in the following cases:

- You don't want to increase the size of the index keys, but you still want to make the index a covering index.

- You have a data type that cannot be an index key column but can be added to the nonclustered index through the INCLUDE command.

- You've already exceeded the maximum number of key columns for an index (although this is a problem best avoided).

A Pseudoclustered Index

The covering index physically organizes the data of all the indexed columns in a sequential order. Thus, from a disk I/O perspective, a covering index that doesn't use included columns becomes a clustered index for all queries satisfied completely by the columns in the covering index. If the result set of a query requires a sorted output, then the covering index can be used to physically maintain the column data in the same order as required by the result set—it can then be used in the same way as a clustered index for sorted output. As shown in the previous example, covering indexes can give better performance than clustered indexes for queries requesting a range of rows and/or sorted output. The included columns are not part of the key and therefore wouldn't offer the same benefits for ordering as the key columns of the index.

Recommendations

To take advantage of covering indexes, be careful with the column list in SELECT statements to move only the data you need to. It's also a good idea to use as few columns as possible to keep the index key size small for the covering indexes. Add columns using the INCLUDE statement in places where it makes sense. Since a covering index includes all the columns used in a query, it has a tendency to be very wide, increasing the maintenance cost of the covering indexes. You must balance the maintenance cost with the performance gain that the covering index brings. If the number of bytes from all the columns in the index is small compared to the number of bytes in a single data row of that table and you are certain the query taking advantage of the covered index will be executed frequently, then it may be beneficial to use a covering index.

■ **Tip**   Covering indexes can also help resolve blocking and deadlocks, as you will see in Chapters 19 and 20.

Before building a lot of covering indexes, consider how SQL Server can effectively and automatically create covering indexes for queries on the fly using index intersection.

Index Intersections

If a table has multiple indexes, then SQL Server can use multiple indexes to execute a query. SQL Server can take advantage of multiple indexes, selecting small subsets of data based on each index and then performing an intersection of the two subsets (that is, returning only those rows that meet all the criteria). SQL Server can exploit multiple indexes on a table and then employ a join algorithm to obtain the *index intersection* between the two subsets.

In the following SELECT statement, for the WHERE clause columns, the table has a nonclustered index on the SalesPersonID column, but it has no index on the OrderDate column:

```
--SELECT * is intentionally used in this query
SELECT  soh.*
FROM    Sales.SalesOrderHeader AS soh
WHERE   soh.SalesPersonID = 276
        AND soh.OrderDate BETWEEN '4/1/2005' AND '7/1/2005';
```

Figure 9-3 shows the execution plan for this query.

Figure 9-3. *Execution plan with no index on the OrderDate column*

As you can see, the optimizer didn't use the nonclustered index on the SalesPersonID column. Since the value of the OrderDate column is also required, the optimizer chose the clustered index to fetch the value of all the referred columns. The I/O for retrieving this data was as follows:

```
Table 'SalesOrderHeader'. Scan count 1, logical reads 689
CPU time = 16 ms,  elapsed time = 47 ms.
```

To improve the performance of the query, the OrderDate column can be added to the nonclustered index on the SalesPersonId column or defined as an included column on the same index. But in this real-world scenario, you may have to consider the following while modifying an existing index:

- It may not be permissible to modify an existing index for various reasons.

- The existing nonclustered index key may be already quite wide.

- The cost of other queries using the existing index will be affected by the modification.

In such cases, you can create a new nonclustered index on the OrderDate column.

```
CREATE NONCLUSTERED INDEX IX_Test
ON Sales.SalesOrderHeader (OrderDate);
```

Run your SELECT command again.
Figure 9-4 shows the resultant execution plan of the SELECT statement.

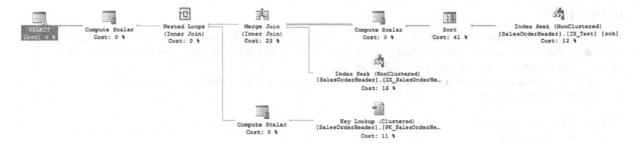

Figure 9-4. *Execution plan with an index on the OrderDate column*

As you can see, SQL Server exploited both the nonclustered indexes as index seeks (rather than scans) and then employed an intersection algorithm to obtain the index intersection of the two subsets. It then did a Key Lookup from the resulting dataset to retrieve the rest of the data not included in the indexes. But, the complexity of the plan suggests that performance might be worse. Checking the statistics I/O and time, you can see that in fact you did get a good performance improvement:

```
Table 'SalesOrderHeader'. Scan count 2, logical reads 10
CPU time = 0 ms,  elapsed time = 31 ms.
```

The reads dropped from 689 to 10 even though the plan used three different access points within the table. The execution time also dropped. You can also see there are additional operations occurring within the plan, such as the Sort and the Key Lookup, that you might be able to eliminate with further adjustments to the indexes. However, it's worth noting, since you're returning all the columns through the SELECT * command, that you can't eliminate the Key Lookup by using INCLUDE columns, so you may also need to adjust the query.

To improve the performance of a query, SQL Server can use multiple indexes on a table. Therefore, instead of creating wide index keys, consider creating multiple narrow indexes. SQL Server will be able to use them together where required, and when not required, queries benefit from narrow indexes. While creating a covering index, determine whether the width of the index will be acceptable and whether using include columns will get the job done. If not, then identify the existing nonclustered indexes that include most of the columns required by the covering index. You may already have two existing nonclustered indexes that jointly serve all the columns required by the covering index. If it is possible, rearrange the column order of the existing nonclustered indexes appropriately, allowing the optimizer to consider an index intersection between the two nonclustered indexes.

At times, it is possible that you may have to create a separate nonclustered index for the following reasons:

- Reordering the columns in one of the existing indexes is not allowed.

- Some of the columns required by the covering index may not be included in the existing nonclustered indexes.

- The total number of columns in the two existing nonclustered indexes may be more than the number of columns required by the covering index.

In such cases, you can create a nonclustered index on the remaining columns. If the combined column order of the new index and an existing nonclustered index meets the requirement of the covering index, the optimizer will be able to use index intersection. While identifying the columns and their order for the new index, try to maximize their benefit by keeping an eye on other queries, too.

Drop the index that was created for the tests.

```
DROP INDEX Sales.SalesOrderHeader.IX_Test;
```

Index Joins

The *index join* is a variation of index intersection, where the covering index technique is applied to the index intersection. If no single index covers a query but multiple indexes together can cover the query, SQL Server can use an index join to satisfy the query fully without going to the base table.

Let's look at this indexing technique at work. Make a slight modification to the query from the "Index Intersections" section like this:

```
SELECT   soh.SalesPersonID,
         soh.OrderDate
FROM     Sales.SalesOrderHeader AS soh
WHERE    soh.SalesPersonID = 276
         AND soh.OrderDate BETWEEN '4/1/2005' AND '7/1/2005';
```

The execution plan for this query is shown in Figure 9-5, and the reads are as follows:

```
Table 'SalesOrderHeader'.  Scan count 1,  logical reads 689
CPU time = 0 ms,  elapsed time = 55 ms.
```

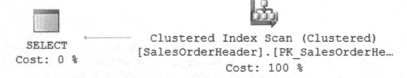

Figure 9-5. *Execution plan with no index join*

As shown in Figure 9-5, the optimizer didn't use the existing nonclustered index on the SalesPersonID column. Since the query requires the value of the OrderDate column also, the optimizer selected the clustered index to retrieve values for all the columns referred to in the query. If an index is created on the OrderDate column like this:

```
CREATE NONCLUSTERED INDEX IX_Test
ON Sales.SalesOrderHeader (OrderDate ASC);
```

and the query is rerun, then Figure 9-6 shows the result, and you can see the reads here:

```
Table 'SalesOrderHeader'. Scan count 2, logical reads 4
CPU time = 0 ms,  elapsed time = 35 ms.
```

Figure 9-6. *Execution plan with an index join*

The combination of the two indexes acts like a covering index reducing the reads against the table from 689 to 4 because it's using two Index Seek operations joined together instead of a clustered index scan.

But what if the WHERE clause didn't result in both indexes being used? Instead, you know that both indexes exist and that a seek against each would work like the previous query, so you choose to use an index hint.

```
SELECT  soh.SalesPersonID,
        soh.OrderDate
FROM    Sales.SalesOrderHeader AS soh WITH
           (INDEX (IX_Test,
                      IX_SalesOrderHeader_SalesPersonID))
WHERE   soh.OrderDate BETWEEN '4/1/2002' AND '7/1/2002';
```

The results of this new query are shown in Figure 9-7, and the I/O is as follows:

```
Table 'Workfile'. Scan count 0, logical reads 0
Table 'Worktable'. Scan count 0, logical reads 0
Table 'SalesOrderHeader'. Scan count 2, logical reads 59
CPU time = 16 ms,  elapsed time = 144 ms.
```

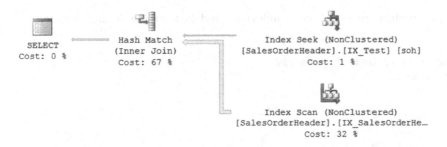

Figure 9-7. *Execution plan with index join through a hint*

The reads have clearly increased, and you have work tables and work files that use tempdb to store data during the processing. Most of the time, the optimizer makes good choices when it comes to indexes and execution plans. Although query hints are available to allow you to take control from the optimizer, this control can cause as many problems as it solves. In attempting to force an index join as a performance benefit, instead the forced selection of indexes slowed down the execution of the query.

Remove the test index before continuing.

```
DROP INDEX Sales.SalesOrderHeader.IX_Test;
```

■ **Note** While generating a query execution plan, the SQL Server optimizer goes through the optimization phases not only to determine the type of index and join strategy to be used but also to evaluate the advanced indexing techniques such as index intersection and index join. Therefore, in some cases, instead of creating wide covering indexes, consider creating multiple narrow indexes. SQL Server can use them together to serve as a covering index yet use them separately where required. But you will need to test to be sure which works better in your situation—wider indexes or index intersections and joins.

Filtered Indexes

A filtered index is a nonclustered index that uses a filter, basically a WHERE clause, to create a highly selective set of keys against a column or columns that may not have good selectivity otherwise. For example, a column with a large number of NULL values may be stored as a sparse column to reduce the overhead of those NULL values. Adding a filtered index to the column will allow you to have an index available on the data that is not NULL. The best way to understand this is to see it in action.

The Sales.SalesOrderHeader table has more than 30,000 rows. Of those rows, 27,000+ have a null value in the PurchaseOrderNumber column and the SalesPersonId column. If you wanted to get a simple list of purchase order numbers, the query might look like this:

```
SELECT   soh.PurchaseOrderNumber,
         soh.OrderDate,
         soh.ShipDate,
         soh.SalesPersonID
FROM     Sales.SalesOrderHeader AS soh
WHERE    PurchaseOrderNumber LIKE 'PO5%'
         AND soh.SalesPersonID IS NOT NULL;
;
```

Running the query results in, as you might expect, a clustered index scan, and the following I/O and execution time, as shown in Figure 9-8:

```
Table 'SalesOrderHeader'. Scan count 1, logical reads 689
CPU time = 0 ms,  elapsed time = 87 ms.
```

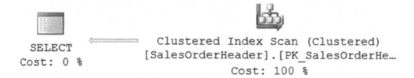

Figure 9-8. *Execution plan without an index*

To fix this, it is possible to create an index and include some of the columns from the query to make this a covering index (as shown in Figure 9-9).

```
CREATE NONCLUSTERED INDEX IX_Test
ON Sales.SalesOrderHeader(PurchaseOrderNumber,SalesPersonID)
INCLUDE  (OrderDate,ShipDate);
```

Figure 9-9. *Execution plan with a covering index*

When you rerun the query, the performance improvement is fairly radical (see Figure 9-33 and the I/O and time in the following result).

```
Table 'SalesOrderHeader'. Scan count 1, logical reads 5
CPU time = 0 ms,  elapsed time = 69 ms.
```

As you can see, the covering index dropped the reads from 689 to 5 and the time from 87 ms to 69 ms. Normally, this would be enough. Assume for a moment that this query has to be called frequently. Now, every bit of speed you can wring from it will pay dividends. Knowing that so much of the data in the indexed columns is null, you can adjust the index so that it filters out the null values, which aren't used by the index anyway, reducing the size of the tree and therefore the amount of searching required.

```
CREATE NONCLUSTERED INDEX IX_Test
ON Sales.SalesOrderHeader(PurchaseOrderNumber,SalesPersonID)
INCLUDE (OrderDate,ShipDate)
WHERE PurchaseOrderNumber IS NOT NULL AND SalesPersonID IS NOT NULL
WITH (DROP_EXISTING = ON);
```

The final run of the query is visible in the following result and in Figure 9-10.

```
Table 'SalesOrderHeader'.  Scan count 1,  logical reads 4
CPU time = 0 ms,   elapsed time = 55 ms.
```

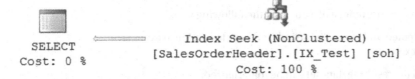

Figure 9-10. Execution plan with a filtered index

Although in terms of sheer numbers reducing the reads from 5 to 4 isn't much, it is a 20 percent reduction in the I/O cost of the query, and if this query were running hundreds or even thousands of times in a minute, like some queries do, that 20 percent reduction would be a great payoff indeed. Another visible evidence of the payoff is in the execution time, which dropped again from 69 ms to 55 ms.

Filtered indexes improve performance in many ways.

- Improving the efficiency of queries by reducing the size of the index

- Reducing storage costs by making smaller indexes

- Cutting down on the costs of index maintenance because of the reduced size

But, everything does come with a cost. You may see issues with parameterized queries not matching the filtered index, therefore preventing its use. Statistics are not updated based on the filtering criteria, but rather on the entire table just like a regular index. Like with any of the suggestions in this book, test in your environment to ensure that filtered indexes are helpful.

One of the first places suggested for their use is just like the previous example, eliminating NULL values from the index. You can also isolate frequently accessed sets of data with a special index so that the queries against that data perform much faster. You can use the WHERE clause to filter data in a fashion similar to creating an indexed view (covered in more detail in the "Indexed Views" section) without the data maintenance headaches associated with indexed views by creating a filtered index that is a covering index, just like the earlier example.

Filtered indexes require a specific set of ANSI settings when they are accessed or created.

- ON: ANSI_NULLS, ANSI_PADDING, ANSI_WARNINGS, ARITHABORT, CONCAT_NULL_YIELDS_NULL, QUOTED_IDENTIFIER

- OFF: NUMERIC_ROUNDABORT

When completed, drop the testing index.

```
DROP INDEX Sales.SalesOrderHeader.IX_Test;
```

Indexed Views

A database view in SQL Server is similar to a virtual table but is just the output of a SELECT statement. You create a view using the CREATE VIEW statement, and you can write queries against it exactly as if it were a table. A view doesn't store any data—only the SELECT statement associated with it. Every time a view is queried, the SELECT statement that defines the view is sent to the optimizer.

A database view can be materialized on the disk by creating a unique clustered index on the view. Such a view is referred to as an *indexed view* or a *materialized view.* After a unique clustered index is created on the view, the view's result set is materialized immediately and persisted in physical storage in the database, saving the overhead of performing costly operations during query execution. After the view is materialized, multiple nonclustered indexes can be created on the indexed view. Effectively, this turns a view (again, just a query) into a real table with defined storage.

Benefit

You can use an indexed view to increase the performance of a query in the following ways:

- Aggregations can be precomputed and stored in the indexed view to minimize expensive computations during query execution.

- Tables can be prejoined, and the resulting data set can be materialized.

- Combinations of joins or aggregations can be materialized.

Overhead

Indexed views can produce major overhead on an OLTP database. Some of the overheads of indexed views are as follows:

- Any change in the base tables has to be reflected in the indexed view by executing the view's SELECT statement.

- Any changes to a base table on which an indexed view is defined may initiate one or more changes in the nonclustered indexes of the indexed view. The clustered index will also have to be changed if the clustering key is updated.

- The indexed view adds to the ongoing maintenance overhead of the database.

- Additional storage is required in the database.

The restrictions on creating an indexed view include the following:

- The first index on the view must be a unique clustered index.

- Nonclustered indexes on an indexed view can be created only after the unique clustered index is created.

- The view definition must be *deterministic*—that is, it is able to return only one possible result for a given query. (A list of deterministic and nondeterministic functions is provided in SQL Server Books Online.)

- The indexed view must reference only base tables in the same database, not other views.

- The indexed view may contain float columns. However, such columns cannot be included in the clustered index key.

- The indexed view must be schema bound to the tables referred to in the view to prevent modifications of the table schema (frequently a major problem).

- There are several restrictions on the syntax of the view definition. (A list of the syntax limitations on the view definition is provided in SQL Server Books Online.)

- The list of SET options that must be fixed are as follows:

  - ON: ARITHABORT, CONCAT_NULL_YIELDS_NULL, QUOTED_IDENTIFIER, ANSI_NULLS, ANSI_PADDING, and ANSI_WARNING

  - OFF: NUMERIC_ROUNDABORT

■ **Note** If the query connection settings don't match these ANSI standard settings, you may see errors on the insert/update/delete of tables that are used within the indexed view.

Usage Scenarios

Reporting systems benefit the most from indexed views. OLTP systems with frequent writes may not be able to take advantage of the indexed views because of the increased maintenance cost associated with updating both the view and the underlying base tables. The net performance improvement provided by an indexed view is the difference between the total query execution savings offered by the view and the cost of storing and maintaining the view.

If you are using the Enterprise edition of SQL Server, an indexed view need not be referenced in the query for the query optimizer to use it during query execution. This allows existing applications to benefit from the newly created indexed views without changing those applications. Otherwise, you would need to directly reference it within your T-SQL code on editions of SQL Server other than Enterprise. The query optimizer considers indexed views only for queries with nontrivial cost. You may also find that the new columnstore index will work better for you than indexed views, especially when you're preaggregating data. I'll cover the columnstore index in a section later in this chapter.

Let's see how indexed views work with the following example. Consider the following three queries:

```
SELECT  p.[Name] AS ProductName,
        SUM(pod.OrderQty) AS OrderQty,
        SUM(pod.ReceivedQty) AS ReceivedQty,
        SUM(pod.RejectedQty) AS RejectedQty
FROM    Purchasing.PurchaseOrderDetail AS pod
        JOIN Production.Product AS p
        ON p.ProductID = pod.ProductID
GROUP BY p.[Name];

SELECT  p.[Name] AS ProductName,
        SUM(pod.OrderQty) AS OrderQty,
        SUM(pod.ReceivedQty) AS ReceivedQty,
        SUM(pod.RejectedQty) AS RejectedQty
```

```
FROM    Purchasing.PurchaseOrderDetail AS pod
        JOIN Production.Product AS p
        ON p.ProductID = pod.ProductID
GROUP BY p.[Name]
HAVING  (SUM(pod.RejectedQty) / SUM(pod.ReceivedQty)) > .08;


SELECT  p.[Name] AS ProductName,
        SUM(pod.OrderQty) AS OrderQty,
        SUM(pod.ReceivedQty) AS ReceivedQty,
        SUM(pod.RejectedQty) AS RejectedQty
FROM    Purchasing.PurchaseOrderDetail AS pod
        JOIN Production.Product AS p
        ON p.ProductID = pod.ProductID
WHERE   p.[Name] LIKE 'Chain%'
GROUP BY p.[Name];
```

All three queries use the aggregation function SUM on columns of the PurchaseOrderDetail table. Therefore, you can create an indexed view to precompute these aggregations and minimize the cost of these complex computations during query execution.

Here are the number of logical reads performed by these queries to access the appropriate tables:

```
Table 'Workfile'. Scan count 0, logical reads 0
Table 'Worktable'. Scan count 0, logical reads 0
Table 'Product'. Scan count 1, logical reads 6
Table 'PurchaseOrderDetail'. Scan count 1, logical reads 66
CPU time = 0 ms,  elapsed time = 128 ms.

Table 'Workfile'. Scan count 0, logical reads 0
Table 'Worktable'. Scan count 0, logical reads 0
Table 'Product'. Scan count 1, logical reads 6
Table 'PurchaseOrderDetail'. Scan count 1, logical reads 66
CPU time = 0 ms,  elapsed time = 158 ms.

Table 'PurchaseOrderDetail'. Scan count 5, logical reads 894
Table 'Product'. Scan count 1, logical reads 2, physical rea
CPU time = 0 ms,  elapsed time = 139 ms.
```

I'll use the following script to create an indexed view to precompute the costly computations and join the tables:

```
IF EXISTS ( SELECT  *
            FROM    sys.views
            WHERE   object_id = OBJECT_ID(N'[Purchasing].[IndexedView]') )
    DROP VIEW [Purchasing].[IndexedView];
GO
CREATE VIEW Purchasing.IndexedView
WITH SCHEMABINDING
AS
SELECT  pod.ProductID,
        SUM(pod.OrderQty) AS OrderQty,
        SUM(pod.ReceivedQty) AS ReceivedQty,
        SUM(pod.RejectedQty) AS RejectedQty,
        COUNT_BIG(*) AS [Count]
```

```
FROM    Purchasing.PurchaseOrderDetail AS pod
GROUP BY pod.ProductID;
GO
CREATE UNIQUE CLUSTERED INDEX iv
ON Purchasing.IndexedView (ProductID);
GO
```

Certain constructs such as AVG are disallowed. (For the complete list of disallowed constructs, refer to SQL Server Books Online.) If aggregates are included in the view, like in this one, you must include COUNT_BIG by default.

The indexed view materializes the output of the aggregate functions on the disk. This eliminates the need for computing the aggregate functions during the execution of a query interested in the aggregate outputs. For example, the third query requests the sum of ReceivedQty and RejectedQty for certain products from the PurchaseOrderDetail table. Because these values are materialized in the indexed view for every product in the PurchaseOrderDetail table, you can fetch these preaggregated values using the following SELECT statement on the indexed view:

```
SELECT  iv.ProductID,
        iv.ReceivedQty,
        iv.RejectedQty
FROM    Purchasing.IndexedView AS iv;
```

As shown in the execution plan in Figure 9-11, the SELECT statement retrieves the values directly from the indexed view without accessing the base table (PurchaseOrderDetail).

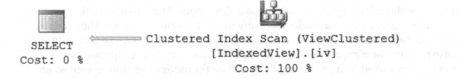

```
SELECT          <========= Clustered Index Scan (ViewClustered)
Cost: 0 %                      [IndexedView].[iv]
                              Cost: 100 %
```

Figure 9-11. *Execution plan with an indexed view*

The indexed view benefits not only the queries based on the view directly but also other queries that may be interested in the materialized data. For example, with the indexed view in place, the three queries on PurchaseOrderDetail benefit without being rewritten (see the execution plan in Figure 9-12 for the execution plan from the first query), and the number of logical reads decreases, as shown here:

```
Table 'Product'. Scan count 1, logical reads 13
Table 'IndexedView'. Scan count 1, logical reads 4
CPU time = 0 ms,  elapsed time = 88 ms.

Table 'Product'. Scan count 1, logical reads 13
Table 'IndexedView'. Scan count 1, logical reads 4
CPU time = 0 ms,  elapsed time = 0 ms.

Table 'IndexedView'. Scan count 0, logical reads 10
Table 'Product'. Scan count 1, logical reads 2
CPU time = 0 ms,  elapsed time = 41 ms.
```

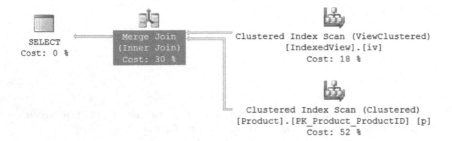

Figure 9-12. Execution plan with the indexed view automatically used

Even though the queries are not modified to refer to the new indexed view, the optimizer still uses the indexed view to improve performance. Thus, even existing queries in the database application can benefit from new indexed views without any modifications to the queries. If you do need different aggregations than what the indexed view offers, you'll be out of luck. Here again the columnstore index shines.

Make sure to clean up.

```
DROP VIEW Purchasing.IndexedView;
```

Index Compression

Data and index compression were introduced in SQL Server 2008 (available in the Enterprise and Developer editions). *Compressing* an index means getting more key information onto a single page. This can lead to significant performance improvements because fewer pages and fewer index levels are needed to store the index. There will be overhead in the CPU as the key values in the index are compressed and decompressed, so this may not be a solution for all indexes. Memory benefits also because the compressed pages are stored in memory in a compressed state.

By default, an index will be not be compressed. You have to explicitly call for the index to be compressed when you create the index. There are two types of compression: row- and page-level compression. *Row-level compression* identifies columns that can be compressed (for details, look in Books Online) and compresses the storage of that column and does this for every row. *Page-level compression* is actually using row-level compression and then adding additional compression on top to reduce storage size for the nonrow elements stored on a page. Nonleaf pages in an index receive no compression under the page type. To see index compression in action, consider the following index:

```
CREATE NONCLUSTERED INDEX IX_Test
ON Person.Address(City ASC, PostalCode ASC);
```

This index was created earlier in the chapter. If you were to re-create it as defined here, this creates a row type of compression on an index with the same two columns as the first test index IX_Test.

```
CREATE NONCLUSTERED INDEX IX_Comp_Test
ON Person.Address (City,PostalCode)
WITH (DATA_COMPRESSION = ROW);
```

Create one more index.

```
CREATE NONCLUSTERED INDEX IX_Comp_Page_Test
ON Person.Address  (City,PostalCode)
WITH (DATA_COMPRESSION = PAGE);
```

To examine the indexes being stored, modify the original query against sys.dm_db_index_ physical_stats to add another column, compressed_page_count.

```
SELECT   i.Name,
         i.type_desc,
         s.page_count,
         s.record_count,
         s.index_level,
         compressed_page_count
FROM     sys.indexes i
         JOIN sys.dm_db_index_physical_stats(DB_ID(N'AdventureWorks2012'),
                                    OBJECT_ID(N'Person.Address'),NULL,
                                    NULL,'DETAILED') AS s
         ON i.index_id = s.index_id
WHERE    i.OBJECT_ID = OBJECT_ID(N'Person.Address');
```

Running the query, you get the results in Figure 9-13.

	Name	type_desc	page_count	record_count	index_level	compressed_page_count
12	IX_Test	NONCLUSTERED	106	19614	0	0
13	IX_Test	NONCLUSTERED	1	106	1	0
14	IX_Comp_Test	NONCLUSTERED	63	19614	0	0
15	IX_Comp_Test	NONCLUSTERED	1	63	1	0
16	IX_Comp_Page_Test	NONCLUSTERED	25	19614	0	25
17	IX_Comp_Page_Test	NONCLUSTERED	1	25	1	0

Figure 9-13. sys.dm_db_index_physical_stats output about compressed indexes

For this index, you can see that the page compression was able to move the index from 106 pages to 25, of which 25 were compressed. The row type compression in this instance made a difference in the number of pages in the index but was not nearly as dramatic as that of the page compression.

To see that compression works for you without any modification to code, run the following query:

```
SELECT   a.City,
         a.PostalCode
FROM     Person.Address AS a
WHERE    a.City = 'Newton'
         AND a.PostalCode = 'V2M1N7';
```

The optimizer chose, on my system, to use the IXCompPageTest index. Even if I forced it to use the IXTest index thusly, the performance was identical, although one extra page was read in the second query:

```
SELECT   a.City,
         a.PostalCode
FROM     Person.Address AS a WITH (INDEX = IX_Test)
WHERE    a.City = 'Newton'
         AND a.PostalCode = 'V2M1N7';
```

So, although one index is taking up radically less room on approximately one-quarter as many pages, it's done at no cost in performance.

Compression has a series of impacts on other processes within SQL Server, so further understanding of the possible impacts as well as the possible benefits should be explored thoroughly prior to implementation. In most cases, the cost to the CPU is completely outweighed by the benefits everywhere else, but you should test and monitor your system.

Clean up the indexes after you finish testing.

```
DROP INDEX Person.Address.IX_Test;
DROP INDEX Person.Address.IX_Comp_Test;
DROP INDEX Person.Address.IX_Comp_Page_Test;
```

Columnstore Indexes

Introduced in SQL Server 2012, the columnstore index is used to index information by columns rather than by rows. This is especially useful when working within data warehousing systems where large amounts of data have to be aggregated and accessed quickly. The information stored within a columnstore index is grouped on each column, and these groupings are stored individually. This makes aggregations on different sets of columns extremely fast since the columnstore index can be accessed rather than accessing large numbers of rows in order to aggregate the information. Further, you get more speed because the storage is column oriented, so you'll be touching storage only for the columns you're interested in, not the entire row of columns. Finally, you'll see some performance enhancements from columnstore because the columnar data is stored compressed. The columnstore comes in two types, similar to regular indexes: a clustered columnstore and a nonclustered columnstore. The nonclustered column store cannot be updated. You must drop it and then re-create it (or, if you're using partitioning, you can switch in and out different partitions). A clustered column store was introduced in SQL Server 2014 and is available there and only in the Enterprise version for production machines. There are a number of limits on using columnstore indexes.

- You can't use certain data types such as binary, text, varchar(max), uniqueidentifier (in SQL Server 2012, this data type works in SQL Server 2014), clr data types, xml, or decimal with a precision greater than 18.

- You can't create a columnstore index on a sparse column.

- When creating a clustered columnstore, it can be the only index on the table.

- A table on which you want to create a clustered columnstore can't have any constraints including primary key or foreign key constraints.

For the complete list of restrictions, refer to Books Online.

Columnstores are primarily meant for use within data warehouses and therefore work best when dealing with the associated styles of storage such as star schemas. In the AdventureWorks2012 database, the Production.TransactionHistoryArchive table is a structure that is more likely to be used for aggregate queries than many of the other structures. Since it's an archive table, the load of it is also controlled so that a columnstore index could be used successfully here. Take this query as an example:

```
SELECT  tha.ProductID,
        COUNT(tha.ProductID) AS CountProductID,
        SUM(tha.Quantity) AS SumQuantity,
        AVG(tha.ActualCost) AS AvgActualCost
FROM    Production.TransactionHistoryArchive AS tha
GROUP BY tha.ProductID;
```

If you run this query against the table as it is currently configured, you'll see an execution plan that looks like Figure 9-14.

Figure 9-14. A clustered index scan and hash match aggregate for a GROUP BY query

The reads and execution time for the query are as follows:

```
Table 'Worktable'. Scan count 0, logical reads 0, physical reads 0
Table 'Workfile'. Scan count 0, logical reads 0, physical reads 0,
Table 'TransactionHistoryArchive'. Scan count 1, logical reads 628
CPU time = 16 ms, elapsed time = 126 ms.
```

There are a large number of reads, and this query uses quite a bit of CPU and is not terribly fast to execute. We have two types of columnstore indexes to choose from. If you want to just add a nonclustered columnstore index to an existing table, it's possible.

```
CREATE NONCLUSTERED COLUMNSTORE INDEX ix_csTest
ON Production.TransactionHistoryArchive
(ProductID,
Quantity,
ActualCost);
```

With the nonclustered columnstore index in place, the optimizer now has the option of using that index to satisfy the foregoing query. Just like all other indexes available to the optimizer, costs are associated with the columnstore index, so it may or may not be chosen to satisfy the requirements for any given query against the table. In this case, if you rerun the original aggregate query, you can see that the optimizer determined that the costs associated with using the columnstore index were beneficial to the query. The execution plan now looks like Figure 9-15.

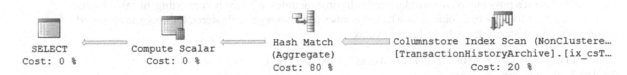

Figure 9-15. The columnstore index is used instead of the clustered index

As you can see, the basic operations of the query are the same, but the columnstore index is scanned instead of the clustered index. The real differences are seen in the reads and execution times for the query.

```
Table 'Worktable'. Scan count 0, logical reads 0
Table 'TransactionHistoryArchive'. Scan count 1, logical reads 48
CPU time = 0 ms,  elapsed time = 122 ms.
```

The radical reduction in the number of reads required to retrieve the data and the marginal increase in speed are all the result of being able to reference information that is indexed by column instead of by row. The foregoing query ran in what's called *row mode*. A columnstore index has two operations: batch mode and row mode. Of the two, batch mode is much faster. It takes advantage of a special method of accessing the data that allows for pulling large sets of data, in batches, so that decompression isn't necessary. The batch mode processing also has extra benefits when working with multiprocessor machines and modern processors with big caches. To see whether a columnstore ran in batch or row mode, you just have to check the properties of the columnstore operation. For example, in the query in question, Figure 9-16 shows the property sheet from the columnstore scan operator.

Figure 9-16. Actual execution mode

There is a limited set of operations, documented in Books Online, that result in batch mode processing, but when working with those operations on a system with enough processors, you will see yet another substantial performance enhancement.

Columnstore indexes don't require you to have the columns in a particular order, unlike clustered and nonclustered indexes. Also, unlike these other indexes, you should place multiple columns within a columnstore index so that you get benefits across those columns. Put another way, if you anticipate that you'll need to query the column at some point, add it proactively to the columnstore index definition. But if you're retrieving large numbers of columns from a columnstore index, you might see some performance degradation.

You can see a clustered columnstore index in action too. Since you can't have constraints, you'll simply re-create the table with this script:

```
SELECT  *
INTO    dbo.TransactionHistoryArchive
FROM    Production.TransactionHistoryArchive;

CREATE INDEX ClusteredColumnstoreTest
ON dbo.TransactionHistoryArchive
(TransactionID);
```

From there, it's possible to create a clustered columnstore index, effectively converting the table from a traditional clustered table to a columnstore table because, like with regular clustered indexes, the clustered columnstore index stores the data. Here's the syntax:

```
CREATE CLUSTERED COLUMNSTORE INDEX ClusteredColumnstoreTest
ON dbo.TransactionHistoryArchive
WITH (DROP_EXISTING = ON);
```

This results in a table that is now stored as a clustered columnstore. If you modify the aggregate query from earlier to run against this new table and you point your queries at this table, you'll see the same execution plan and performance as you saw against the nonclustered columnstore index. But, this new structure can be updated, unlike the index you created previously.

While the limitations for the use of the columnstore index are somewhat stringent, especially with the nonclustered columnstore index, the benefits for structures that can operate within those limitations are clear.

Be sure to clean up any of the remaining objects.

```
DROP TABLE dbo.TransactionHistoryArchive;
DROP INDEX Production.TransactionHistoryArchive.ix_csTest;
```

Special Index Types

As special data types and storage mechanisms are introduced to SQL Server by Microsoft, methods for indexing these special storage types are also developed. Explaining all the details possible for each of these special index types is outside the scope of the book. In the following sections, I introduce the basic concepts of each index type in order to facilitate the possibility of their use in tuning your queries.

Full-Text

You can store large amounts of text in SQL Server by using the MAX value in the VARCHAR, NVARCHAR, CHAR, and NCHAR fields. A normal clustered or nonclustered index against these large fields would be unsupportable because a single value can far exceed the page size within an index. So, a different mechanism of indexing text is to use the full-text engine, which must be running to work with full-text indexes. You can also build a full-text index on VARBINARY data.

You need to have one column on the table that is unique. The best candidates for performance are integers: INT or BIGINT. This column is then used along with the word to identify which row within the table it belongs to, as well as its location within the field. SQL Server allows for incremental changes, either change tracking or time-based, to the full-text indexes as well as complete rebuilds.

SQL Server 2012 introduces another method for working with text called Semantic Search. It uses phrases from documents to identify relationships between different sets of text stored within the database.

Spatial

Introduced in SQL Server 2008 is the ability to store spatial data. This data can be either a geometry type or the very complex geographical type, literally identifying a point on the earth. To say the least, indexing this type of data is complicated. SQL Server stores these indexes in a flat B-tree, similar to regular indexes, except that it is also a hierarchy of four grids linked together. Each of the grids can be given a density of low, medium, or high, outlining how big each grid is. There are mechanisms to support indexing of the spatial data types so that different types of queries, such as finding when one object is within the boundaries or near another object, can benefit from performance increases inherent in indexing.

A spatial index can be created only against a column of type geometry or geography. It has to be on a base table, it must have no indexed views, and the table must have a primary key. You can create up to 249 spatial indexes on any given column on a table. Different indexes are used to define different types of index behavior. More information is available in the book *Beginning Spatial with SQL Server 2008* by Alastair Aitchison (Apress, 2009).

XML

Introduced as a data type in SQL Server 2005, XML can be stored not as text but as well-formed XML data within SQL Server. This data can be queried using the XQuery language as supported by SQL Server. To enhance the performance capabilities, a special set of indexes has been defined. An XML column can have one primary and several secondary indexes. The primary XML shreds the properties, attributes, and elements of the XML data and stores it as an internal table. There must be a primary key on the table, and that primary key must be clustered in order to create an XML index. After the XML index is created, the secondary indexes can be created. These indexes have types Path, Value, and Property, depending on how you query the XML. For more details, check out *Pro SQL Server 2008 XML* by Michael Coles (Apress, 2008).

Additional Characteristics of Indexes

Other index properties can affect performance, positively and negatively. A few of these behaviors are explored here.

Different Column Sort Order

SQL Server supports creating a composite index with a different sort order for the different columns of the index. Suppose you want an index with the first column sorted in ascending order and the second column sorted in descending order to eliminate a sort operation, which can be quite costly. You could achieve this as follows:

```
CREATE NONCLUSTERED INDEX i1 ON t1(c1 ASC, c2 DESC);
```

Index on Computed Columns

You can create an index on a computed column, as long as the expression defined for the computed column meets certain restrictions, such as that it references columns only from the table containing the computed column and it is deterministic.

Index on BIT Data Type Columns

SQL Server allows you to create an index on columns with the BIT data type. The ability to create an index on a BIT data type column by itself is not a big advantage since such a column can have only two unique values, except for the rare circumstance where the vast majority of the data is one value and only a few rows are the other. As mentioned previously, columns with such low selectivity (number of unique values) are not usually good candidates for indexing. However, this feature comes into its own when you consider covering indexes. Because covering indexes require including all the columns in the index, the ability to add the BIT data type column to an index key allows covering indexes to have such a column, if required (outside of the columns that would be part of the INCLUDE operator).

CREATE INDEX Statement Processed As a Query

The CREATE INDEX operation is integrated into the query processor. The optimizer can use existing indexes to reduce scan cost and sort while creating an index.

Take, for example, the Person.Address table. A nonclustered index exists on a number of columns: AddressLine1, AddressLine2, City, StateProvinceId, and PostalCode. If you needed to run queries against the City column with the existing index, you'll get a scan of that index. Now create a new index like this:

```
CREATE INDEX IX_Test
ON Person.Address(City);
```

You can see in Figure 9-17 that, instead of scanning the table, the optimizer chose to scan the index in order to create the new index because the column needed for the new index was contained within the other nonclustered index.

Figure 9-17. Execution plan for CREATE INDEX

Parallel Index Creation

SQL Server supports parallel plans for a CREATE INDEX statement, as supported in other SQL queries. On a multiprocessor machine, index creation won't be restricted to a single processor but will benefit from the multiple processors. You can control the number of processors to be used in a CREATE INDEX statement with the max degree of parallelism configuration parameter of SQL Server. The default value for this parameter is 0, as you can see by executing the sp_configure stored procedure.

```
EXEC sp_configure
    'max degree of parallelism' ;
```

The default value of 0 means that SQL Server can use all the available CPUs in the system for the parallel execution of a T-SQL statement. On a system with four processors, the maximum degree of parallelism can be set to 2 by executing spconfigure.

```
EXEC sp_configure
    'max degree of parallelism',
    2 ;
RECONFIGURE WITH OVERRIDE ;
```

This allows SQL Server to use up to two CPUs for the parallel execution of a T-SQL statement. This configuration setting takes effect immediately, without a server restart.

The query hint MAXDOP can be used for the CREATE INDEX statement. Also, be aware that the parallel CREATE INDEX feature is available only in SQL Server Enterprise editions.

Online Index Creation

The default creation of an index is done as an offline operation. This means exclusive locks are placed on the table, restricting user access while the index is created. It is possible to create the indexes as an online operation. This allows users to continue to access the data while the index is being created. This comes at the cost of increasing the amount of time and resources it takes to create the index. Introduced in SQL Server 2012, indexes with varchar(MAX), nvarchar(MAX), and nbinary(MAX) can actually be rebuilt online. Online index operations are available only in SQL Server Enterprise editions.

Considering the Database Engine Tuning Advisor

A simple approach to indexing is to use the Database Engine Tuning Advisor tool provided by SQL Server. This tool is a usage-based tool that looks at a particular workload and works with the query optimizer to determine the costs associated with various index combinations. Based on the tool's analysis, you can add or drop indexes as appropriate.

■ **Note** I will cover the Database Engine Tuning Advisor tool in more depth in Chapter 5.

Summary

In this chapter, you learned that there are a number of additional functions in and around indexes that expand on the behavior defined the preceding chapter.

In the next chapter, you will learn more about the Database Engine Tuning Advisor, the SQL Server–provided tool that can help you determine the correct indexes in a database for a given SQL workload.

CHAPTER 10

■ ■ ■

Database Engine Tuning Advisor

SQL Server's performance frequently depends upon having the proper indexes on the database tables. However, as the workload and data change over time, the existing indexes may not be entirely appropriate, and new indexes may be required. The task of deciding upon the correct indexes is complicated by the fact that an index change that benefits one set of queries may be detrimental to another set of queries.

To help you through this process, SQL Server provides a tool called the Database Engine Tuning Advisor. This tool can help identify an optimal set of indexes and statistics for a given workload without requiring an expert understanding of the database schema, workload, or SQL Server internals. It can also recommend tuning options for a small set of problem queries. In addition to the tool's benefits, I cover its limitations in this chapter, because it is a tool that can cause more harm than good if used without deliberate intent.

In this chapter, I cover the following topics:

- How the Database Engine Tuning Advisor works

- How to use the Database Engine Tuning Advisor on a set of problematic queries for index recommendations, including how to define traces

- The limitations of the Database Engine Tuning Advisor

Database Engine Tuning Advisor Mechanisms

You can run the Database Engine Tuning Advisor directly by selecting Microsoft SQL Server 2012 ➤ Performance Tools ➤ Database Engine Tuning Advisor. You can also run it from the command prompt (dta.exe), from SQL Profiler (Tools ➤ Database Engine Tuning Advisor), from a query in Management Studio (highlight the required query, and select Query ➤ Analyze Query in the Database Engine Tuning Advisor), or from Management Studio (select Tools ➤ Database Engine Tuning Advisor). Once the tool is open and you're connected to a server, you should see a window like the one in Figure 10-1. I'll run through the options to define and run an analysis in this section and then follow up in the next session with some detailed examples.

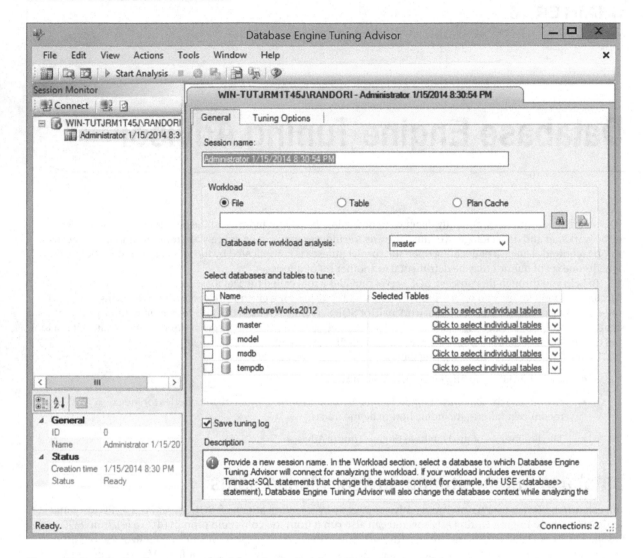

Figure 10-1. *Selecting the server and database in the Database Engine Tuning Advisor*

The Database Engine Tuning Advisor is already connected to a server. From here, you begin to outline the workload and the objects you want to tune. Creating a session name is necessary to label the session for documentation purposes. Then you need to pick a workload. The workload can come from a trace file or a table, or, introduced in SQL Server 2012, you can use the queries that exist in the plan cache. Finally, you need to browse to the appropriate location. The workload is defined depending on how you launched the Database Engine Tuning Advisor. If you launched it from a query window, you would see a Query radio button, and the File and Table radio buttons would be disabled. You also have to define the Database for Workload Analysis setting and finally select a database to tune.

■ **Tip** The Database Engine Tuning Advisor recommends indexed views only for platforms that support them. SQL Server 2014 Enterprise edition does, but Standard edition doesn't.

When you select a database, you can also select individual tables to be tuned by clicking the drop-down box on the right side of the screen; you'll see a list of tables like those in Figure 10-2.

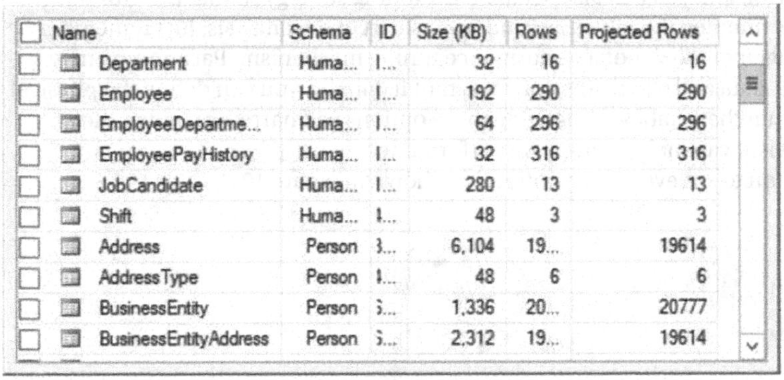

	Name	Schema	ID	Size (KB)	Rows	Projected Rows	
☐	Department	Huma...	I...	32	16	16	
☐	Employee	Huma...	I...	192	290	290	
☐	EmployeeDepartme...	Huma...	I...	64	296	296	
☐	EmployeePayHistory	Huma...	I...	32	316	316	
☐	JobCandidate	Huma...	I...	280	13	13	
☐	Shift	Huma...	I...	48	3	3	
☐	Address	Person	3...	6,104	19...	19614	
☐	AddressType	Person	I...	48	6	6	
☐	BusinessEntity	Person	5...	1,336	20...	20777	
☐	BusinessEntityAddress	Person	3...	2,312	19...	19614	

Figure 10-2. *Clicking the boxes defines individual tables for tuning in the Database Engine Tuning Advisor*

Once you define the workload, you need to select the Tuning Options tab, which is shown in Figure 10-3.

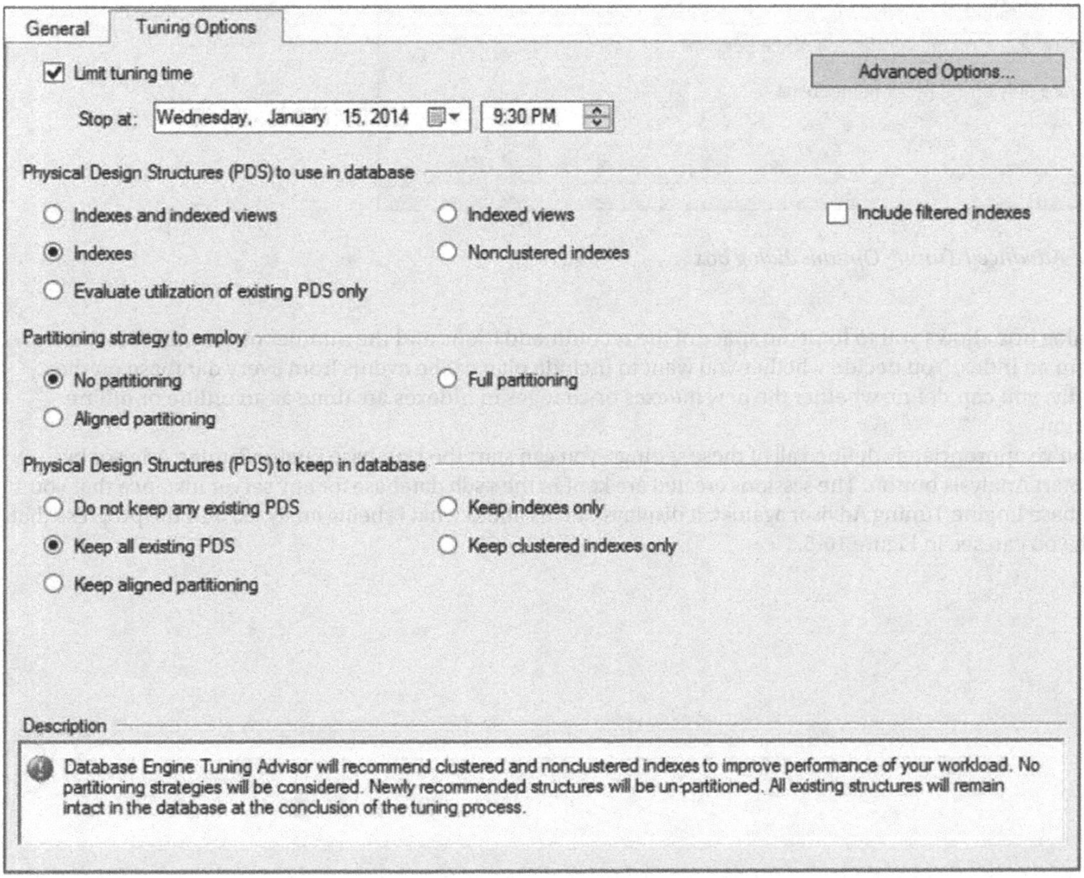

Figure 10-3. *Defining options in the Database Engine Tuning Advisor*

You define the length of time you want the Database Engine Tuning Advisor to run by selecting Limit Tuning Time and then defining a date and time for the tuning to stop. The longer the Database Engine Tuning Advisor runs, the better recommendations it should make. You pick the type of physical design structures to be considered for creation by the Database Engine Tuning Advisor, and you can also set the partitioning strategy so that the Tuning Advisor knows whether it should consider partitioning the tables and indexes as part of the analysis. Just remember, partitioning is first and foremost a data management tool, not a performance tuning mechanism. Partitioning may not necessarily be a desirable outcome if your data and structures don't warrant it. Finally, you can define the physical design structures that you want left alone within the database. Changing these options will narrow or widen the choices that the Database Engine Tuning Advisor can make to improve performance.

You can click the Advanced Options button to see even more options, as shown in Figure 10-4.

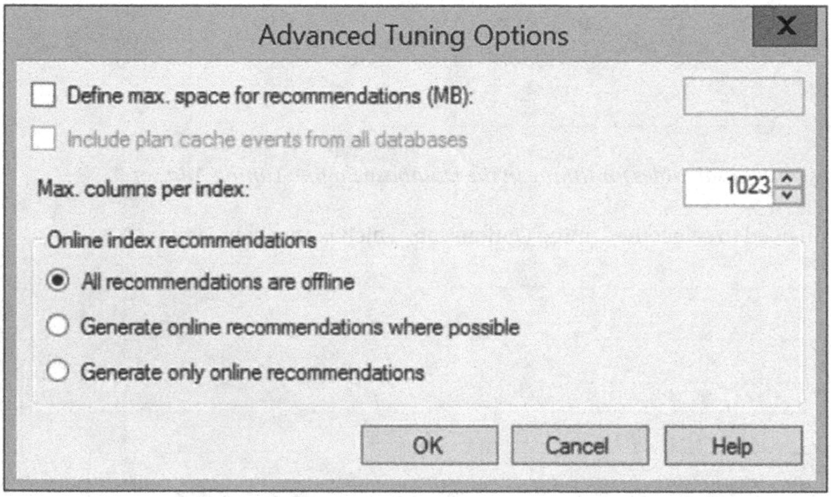

Figure 10-4. *Advanced Tuning Options dialog box*

This dialog box allows you to limit the space of the recommendations and the number of columns that can be included in an index. You decide whether you want to include plan cache events from every database on the system. Finally, you can define whether the new indexes or changes in indexes are done as an online or offline index operation.

Once you've appropriately defined all of these settings, you can start the Database Engine Tuning Advisor by clicking the Start Analysis button. The sessions created are kept in the msdb database for any server instance that you run the Database Engine Tuning Advisor against. It displays details about what is being analyzed and the progress that made, which you can see in Figure 10-5.

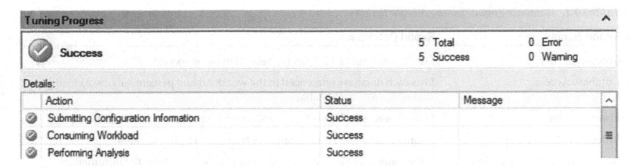

Figure 10-5. *Tuning progress*

You'll see more detailed examples of the progress displayed in the example analysis in the next session.

After the analysis completes, you'll get a list of recommendations (visible in Figure 10-6), and a number of reports become available. Table 10-1 describes the reports.

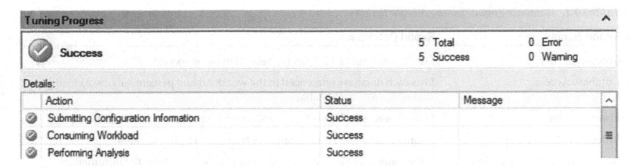

Figure 10-6. *Query tuning general settings*

Table 10-1. *Database Engine Tuning Advisor Reports*

Report Name	Report Description
Column Access	Lists the columns and tables referenced in the workload
Database Access	Lists each database referenced in the workload and percentage of workload statements for each database
Event Frequency	Lists all events in the workload ordered by frequency of occurrence
Index Detail (Current)	Defines indexes and their properties referenced by the workload
Index Detail (Recommended)	Is the same as the Index Detail (Current) report but shows the information about the indexes recommended by the Database Engine Tuning Advisor
Index Usage (Current)	Lists the indexes and the percentage of their use referenced by the workload
Index Usage (Recommended)	Is the same as the Index Usage (Current) report but from the recommended indexes
Statement Cost	Lists the performance improvements for each statement if the recommendations are implemented
Statement Cost Range	Breaks down the cost improvements by percentiles to show how much benefit you can achieve for any given set of changes; these costs are estimated values provided by the optimizer
Statement Detail	Lists the statements in the workload, their cost, and the reduced cost if the recommendations are implemented
Statement-to-Index Relationship	Lists the indexes referenced by individual statements; current and recommended versions of the report are available
Table Access	Lists the tables referenced by the workload
View-to-Table Relationship	Lists the tables referenced by materialized views
Workload Analysis	Gives details about the workload, including the number of statements, the number of statements whose cost is decreased, and the number where the cost remains the same

Database Engine Tuning Advisor Examples

The best way to learn how to use the Database Engine Tuning Advisor is to use it. It's not a terribly difficult tool to master, so I recommend opening it and getting started.

Tuning a Query

You can use the Database Engine Tuning Advisor to recommend indexes for a complete database by using a workload that fairly represents all SQL activities. You can also use it to recommend indexes for a set of problematic queries.

To learn how you can use the Database Engine Tuning Advisor to get index recommendations on a set of problematic queries, say you have a simple query that is called rather frequently. Because of the frequency, you want a quick turnaround for some tuning. This is the query:

```
SELECT  soh.DueDate,
        soh.CustomerID,
        soh.Status
FROM    Sales.SalesOrderHeader AS soh
WHERE   soh.DueDate BETWEEN '1/1/2008' AND '2/1/2008';
```

To analyze the query, right-click it in the query window and select Analyze Query in the Database Engine Tuning Advisor. The advisor opens with a window where you can change the session name to something meaningful. In this case, I chose Report Query Round 1 – 1/16/2014. The database and tables don't need to be edited. The first tab, General, will look like Figure 10-6 when you're done.

Because this query is important and tuning it is extremely critical to the business, I'm going to change some settings on the Tuning Options tab to try to maximize the possible suggestions. For the purposes of the example, I'm going to let the Database Engine Tuning Advisor run for the default of one hour, but for bigger loads or more complex queries, you might want to consider giving the system more time. I'm going to select the Include Filtered Indexes check box so that if a filtered index will help, it can be considered. I'm also going to switch the Partitioning Strategy to Employ setting from No Partitioning to Full Partitioning. Finally, I'm going to allow the Database Engine Tuning Advisor to come up with structural changes if it can find any that will help by switching from Keep All Existing PDS to Do Not Keep Any Existing PDS. Once completed, the Tuning Options tab will look like Figure 10-7.

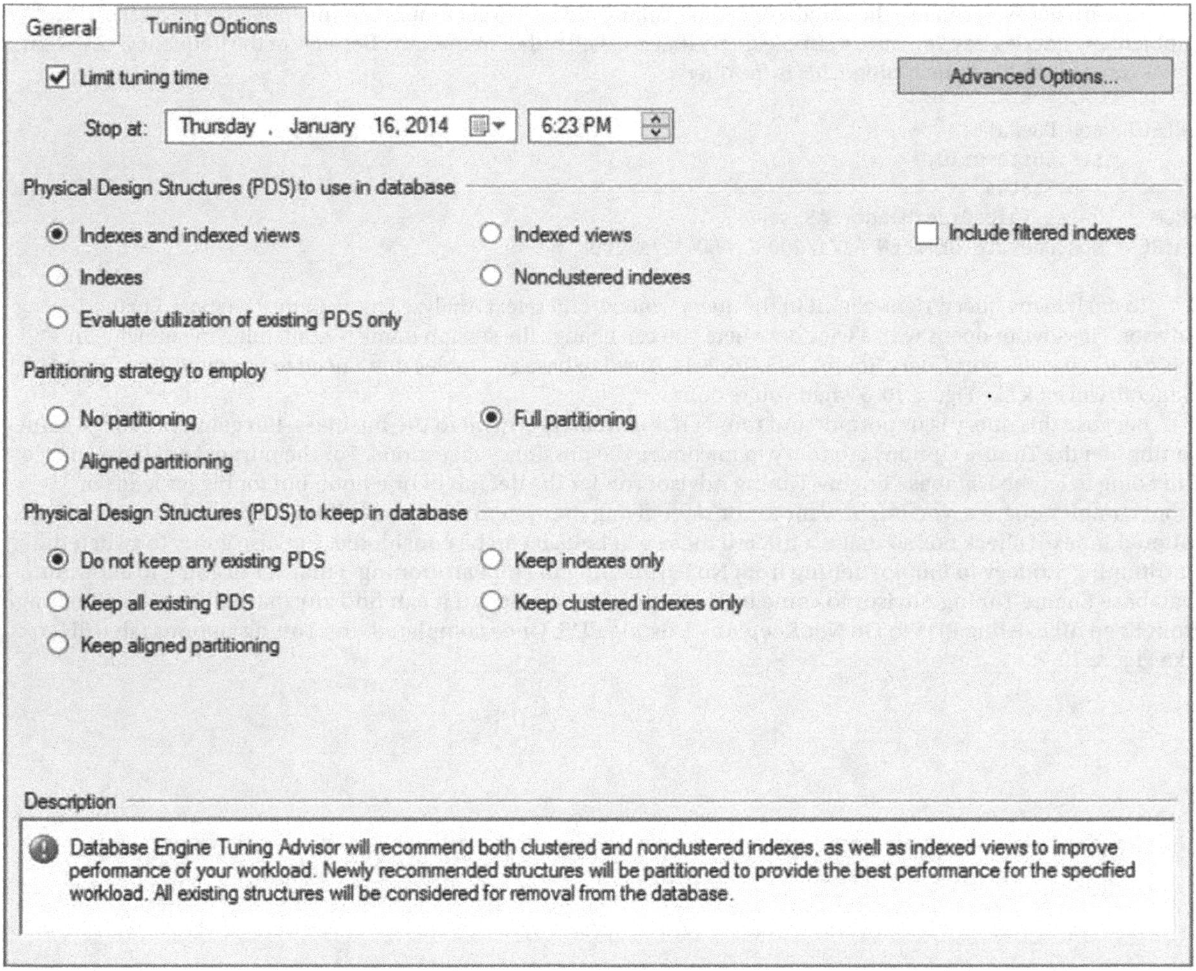

Figure 10-7. *Tuning Options tab adjusted*

Notice that the description at the bottom of the screen changes as you change the definitions in the selections made above. After starting the analysis, the progress screen should appear. Although the settings were for one hour of evaluations, it took only about a minute for the DTA to evaluate this query. The initial recommendations were not a good set of choices. As you can see in Figure 10-8, the Database Engine Tuning Advisor has recommended dropping a huge swath of indexes in the database. This is not the type of recommendation you want when running the tool.

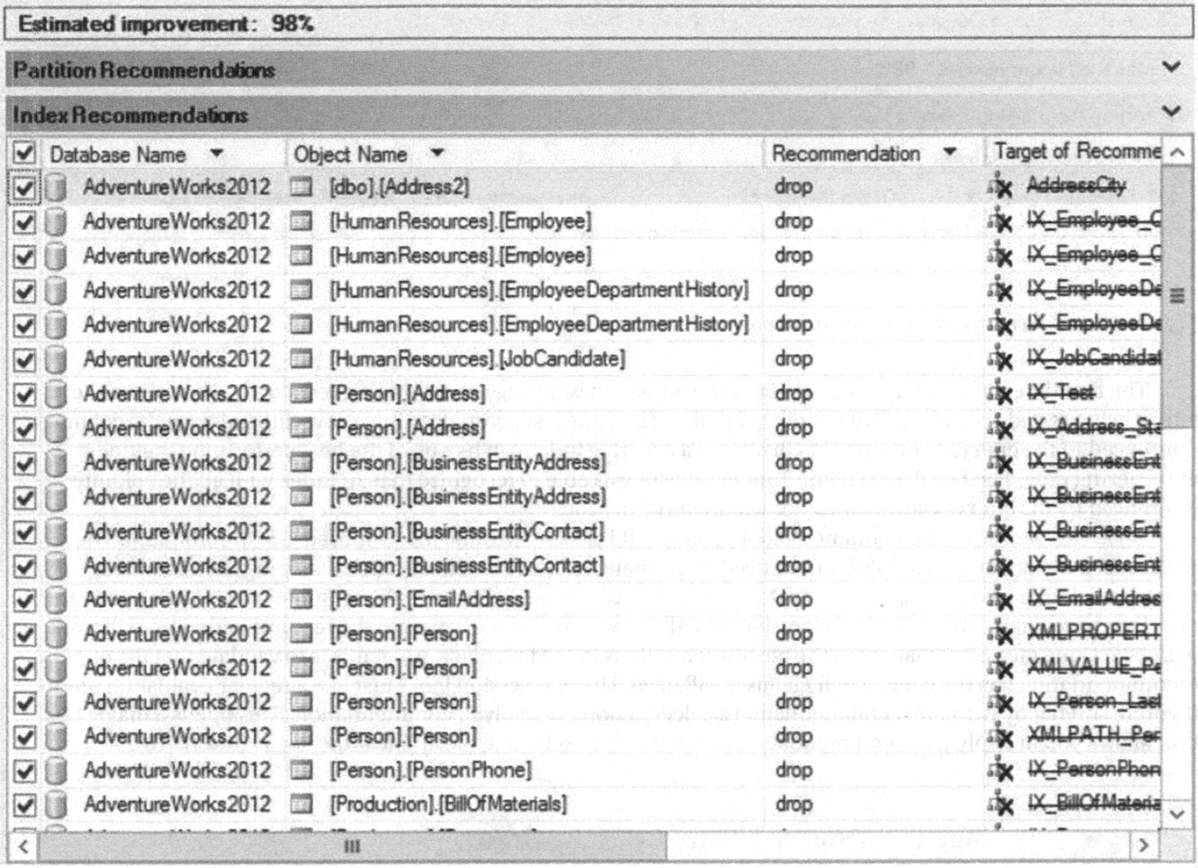

	Database Name ▼		Object Name ▼		Recommendation ▼		Target of Recomme ∧
☑	AdventureWorks2012		[dbo].[Address2]		drop		AddressCity
☑	AdventureWorks2012		[HumanResources].[Employee]		drop		IX_Employee_C
☑	AdventureWorks2012		[HumanResources].[Employee]		drop		IX_Employee_C
☑	AdventureWorks2012		[HumanResources].[EmployeeDepartmentHistory]		drop		IX_EmployeeDe
☑	AdventureWorks2012		[HumanResources].[EmployeeDepartmentHistory]		drop		IX_EmployeeDe
☑	AdventureWorks2012		[HumanResources].[JobCandidate]		drop		IX_JobCandidat
☑	AdventureWorks2012		[Person].[Address]		drop		IX_Test
☑	AdventureWorks2012		[Person].[Address]		drop		IX_Address_Sta
☑	AdventureWorks2012		[Person].[BusinessEntityAddress]		drop		IX_BusinessEnt
☑	AdventureWorks2012		[Person].[BusinessEntityAddress]		drop		IX_BusinessEnt
☑	AdventureWorks2012		[Person].[BusinessEntityContact]		drop		IX_BusinessEnt
☑	AdventureWorks2012		[Person].[BusinessEntityContact]		drop		IX_BusinessEnt
☑	AdventureWorks2012		[Person].[EmailAddress]		drop		IX_EmailAddres
☑	AdventureWorks2012		[Person].[Person]		drop		XMLPROPERT
☑	AdventureWorks2012		[Person].[Person]		drop		XMLVALUE_Pe
☑	AdventureWorks2012		[Person].[Person]		drop		IX_Person_Last
☑	AdventureWorks2012		[Person].[Person]		drop		XMLPATH_Per
☑	AdventureWorks2012		[Person].[PersonPhone]		drop		IX_PersonPhon
☑	AdventureWorks2012		[Production].[BillOfMaterials]		drop		IX_BillOfMateria

Estimated improvement: 98%

Partition Recommendations

Index Recommendations

Figure 10-8. *Query tuning initial recommendations*

This is because the Database Engine Tuning Advisor assumes that the load being tested is the full load of the database. If there are indexes not being used, then they should be removed. This is a best practice and one that should be implemented on any database. However, in this case, this is a single query, not a full load of the system. To see whether the advisor can come up with a more meaningful set of recommendations, you must start a new session.

This time, I'll adjust the options so that the Database Engine Tuning Advisor will not be able to drop any of the existing structure. This is set on the Tuning Options tab (shown earlier in Figure 10-7). There I'll change the Physical Design Structure (PDS) to Keep in Database setting from Do Not Keep Any Existing PDS to Keep All Existing PDS. I'll keep the running time the same because the evaluation worked well within the time frame. After running the Database Engine Tuning Advisor again, it finishes in less than a minute and displays the recommendations shown in Figure 10-9.

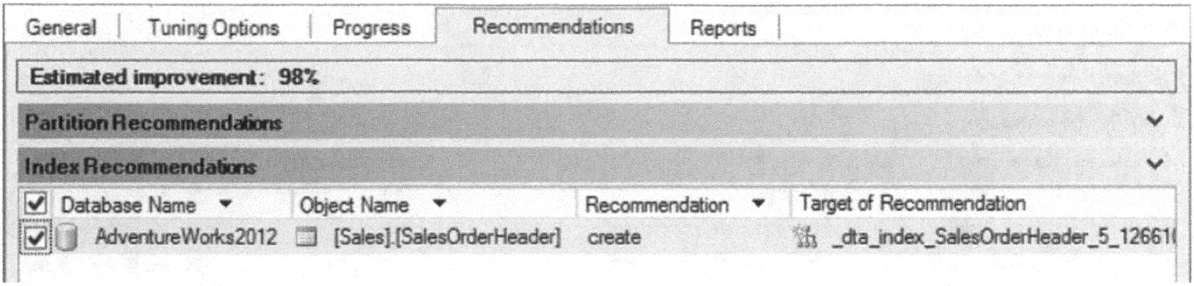

Figure 10-9. *Query tuning recommendations*

The first time through, the Database Engine Tuning Advisor suggested dropping most of the indexes on the tables being tested and a bunch of the related tables. This time it suggests creating a covering index on the columns referenced in the query. As outlined in Chapter 4, a covering index can be one of the best performing methods of retrieving data. The Database Engine Tuning Advisor was able to recognize that an index with all the columns referenced by the query, a covering index, would perform best.

Once you've received a recommendation, you should closely examine the proposed T-SQL command. The suggestions are not always helpful, so you need to evaluate and test them to be sure. Assuming the examined recommendation looks good, you'll want to apply it. Select Actions ⊕ Evaluate Recommendations. This opens a new Database Engine Tuning Advisor session and allows you to evaluate whether the recommendations will work using the same measures that made the recommendations in the first place. All of this is to validate that the original recommendation has the effect that it claims it will have. The new session looks just like a regular evaluation report. If you're still happy with the recommendations, select Actions ⊕ Apply Recommendation. This opens a dialog box that allows you to apply the recommendation immediately or schedule the application (see Figure 10-10).

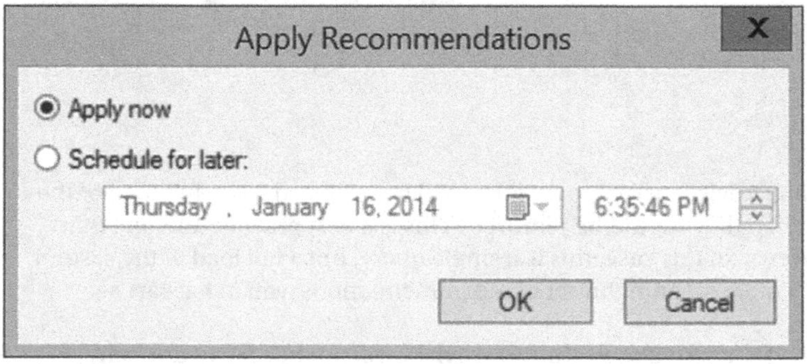

Figure 10-10. *Apply Recommendations dialog box*

If you click the OK button, the Database Engine Tuning Advisor will apply the index to the database where you've been testing queries (see Figure 10-11).

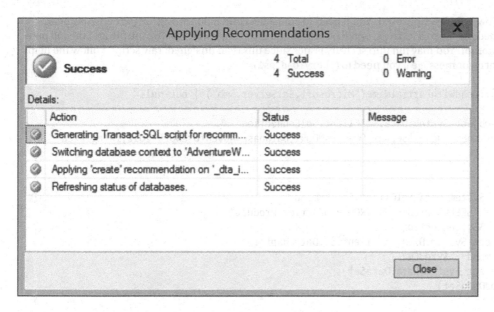

Figure 10-11. *A successful tuning session applied*

After you generate recommendations, you may want to, instead of applying them on the spot, save the T-SQL statements to a file and accumulate a series of changes for release to your production environment during scheduled deployment windows. Also, just taking the defaults, you'll end up with a lot of indexes named something like this: _dta_index_SalesOrderHeader_5_1266103551__K4_6_11. That's not terribly clear, so saving the changes to T-SQL will also allow you to make your changes more human readable. Remember that applying indexes to tables, especially large tables, can cause a performance impact to processes actively running on the system while the index is being created.

Although getting index suggestions one at a time is nice, it would be better to be able to get large swaths of the database checked all at once. That's where tuning a trace workload comes in.

Tuning a Trace Workload

Capturing a trace from the real-world queries that are running against a production server is a way to feed meaningful data to the Database Engine Tuning Advisor. (Capturing traces will be covered in Chapter 17.) The easiest way to define a trace for use in the Database Engine Tuning Advisor is to implement the trace using the Tuning template. Start the trace on the system you need to tune. I generated an artificial load by running queries in a loop from the PowerShell sqlps.exe command prompt. This is the PowerShell command prompt with the SQL Server configuration settings. It gets installed with SQL Server.

To find something interesting, I'm going to create one stored procedure with an obvious tuning issue.

```
CREATE PROCEDURE dbo.uspProductSize
AS
SELECT  p.ProductID,
        p.Size
FROM    Production.Product AS p
WHERE   p.Size = '62';
```

Here is the simple PowerShell script I used. You'll need to adjust the connection string for your environment. After you have downloaded the file to a location, you'll be able to run it by simply referencing the file and the full path through the command prompt. You may run into security issues since this is an unsigned, raw script. Follow the help guidance provided in that error message if you need to (queryload.ps1).

```
[reflection.assembly]::LoadWithPartialName("Microsoft.SqlServer.Smo") | out-null
# Get the connection
$SqlConnection = New-Object System.Data.SqlClient.SqlConnection
$SqlConnection.ConnectionString = "Server=DOJO\RANDORI;Database=AdventureWorks2012;Integrated
Security=True"

# Load Product data
$ProdCmd = New-Object System.Data.SqlClient.SqlCommand
$ProdCmd.CommandText = "SELECT ProductID FROM Production.Product"
$ProdCmd.Connection = $SqlConnection
$SqlAdapter = New-Object System.Data.SqlClient.SqlDataAdapter
$SqlAdapter.SelectCommand = $ProdCmd
$ProdDataSet = New-Object System.Data.DataSet
$SqlAdapter.Fill($ProdDataSet)

# Load the Employee data
$EmpCmd = New-Object System.Data.SqlClient.SqlCommand
$EmpCmd.CommandText = "SELECT BusinessEntityID FROM HumanResources.Employee"
$EmpCmd.Connection = $SqlConnection
$SqlAdapter.SelectCommand = $EmpCmd
$EmpDataSet = New-Object System.Data.DataSet
$SqlAdapter.Fill($EmpDataSet)

# Set up the procedure to be run
$WhereCmd = New-Object System.Data.SqlClient.SqlCommand
$WhereCmd.CommandText = "dbo.uspGetWhereUsedProductID @StartProductID = @ProductId, @CheckDate=NULL"
$WhereCmd.Parameters.Add("@ProductID",[System.Data.SqlDbType]"Int")
$WhereCmd.Connection = $SqlConnection

# And another one
$BomCmd = New-Object System.Data.SqlClient.SqlCommand
$BomCmd.CommandText = "dbo.uspGetBillOfMaterials @StartProductID = @ProductId, @CheckDate=NULL"
$BomCmd.Parameters.Add("@ProductID",[System.Data.SqlDbType]"Int")
$BomCmd.Connection = $SqlConnection

# And one more
$ManCmd = New-Object System.Data.SqlClient.SqlCommand
$ManCmd.CommandText = "dbo.uspGetEmployeeManagers @BusinessEntityID =@EmpId"
$ManCmd.Parameters.Add("@EmpId",[System.Data.SqlDbType]"Int")
$ManCmd.Connection = $SqlConnection

# And the special
$SpecCmd = New-Object System.Data.SqlClient.SqlCommand
$SpecCmd.CommandText = "dbo.uspProductSize"
$SpecCmd.Connection = $SqlConnection
```

```
# Loop forever
while(1 -ne 0)
{
    foreach($row in $ProdDataSet.Tables[0])
    {
        $SqlConnection.Open()
        $ProductId = $row[0]
        $WhereCmd.Parameters["@ProductID"].Value = $ProductId
        $WhereCmd.ExecuteNonQuery() | Out-Null
        $SqlConnection.Close()

        foreach($row in $EmpDataSet.Tables[0])
        {
            $SqlConnection.Open()
            $EmpId = $row[0]
            $ManCmd.Parameters["@EmpID"].Value = $EmpId
            $ManCmd.ExecuteNonQuery() | Out-Null
            $SqlConnection.Close()
        }

        $SqlConnection.Open()
        $BomCmd.Parameters["@ProductID"].Value = $ProductId
        $BomCmd.ExecuteNonQuery() | Out-Null
                    $SpecCmd.ExecuteNonQuery() | Out-Null
        $SqlConnection.Close()
    }
}
```

■ **Note**   For more information on PowerShell, check out *Windows PowerShell* by Don Jones and Jeffrey Hicks (Sapien, 2010).

Once you've created the trace file, open the Database Engine Tuning Advisor. It defaults to a file type, so you'll only have to browse to the trace file location. As before, you'll want to select the AdventureWorks2012 database as the database for workload analysis from the drop-down list. To limit the suggestions, also select AdventureWorks2012 from the list of databases at the bottom of the screen. Set the appropriate tuning options and start the analysis. This time, it will take more than a minute to run (see Figure 10-12).

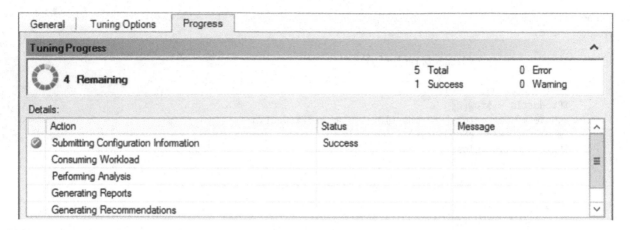

Figure 10-12. Database tuning engine in progress

The processing runs for about 15 minutes on my machine. Then it generates output, shown in Figure 10-13.

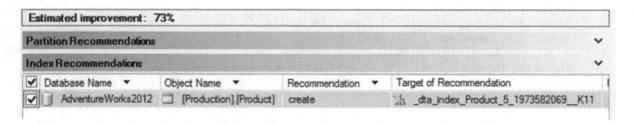

Figure 10-13. Recommendation for a manual statistic

After running all the queries through the Database Engine Tuning Advisor, the advisor came up with a suggestion for a new index for the Product table that would improve the performance the query. Now I just need to save that to a T-SQL file so that I can edit the name prior to applying it to my database.

Tuning from the Procedure Cache

Introduced in SQL Server 2012 is the ability to use the query plans that are stored in the cache as a source for tuning recommendations. The process is simple. There's just one more choice on the General page that lets you choose the plan cache as a source for the tuning effort, as shown in Figure 10-14.

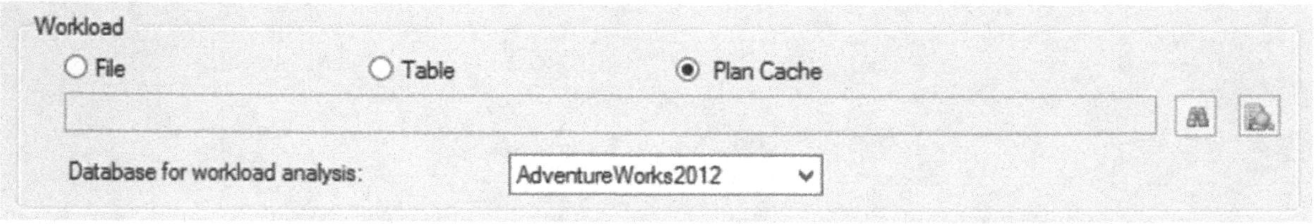

Figure 10-14. Selecting Plan Cache as the source for the DTA

All other options behave exactly the same way as previously outlined in this chapter. The processing time is radically less than when the advisor processes a workload. It has only the queries in cache to process, so, depending on the amount of memory in your system, this can be a short list. The results from processing my cache suggested one index on the Person table. This is estimated to enhance performance by about 45 percent, as you can see in Figure 10-15.

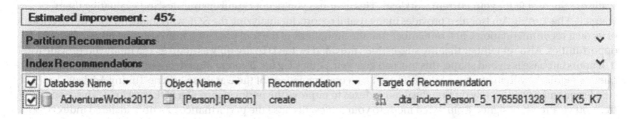

Figure 10-15. *Recommendations from the plan cache*

This gives you one more mechanism to try to tune your system in an automated fashion. But it is limited to the queries that are currently in cache. Depending on the volatility of your cache (the speed at which plans age out or are replaced by new plans), this may or may not prove useful.

Database Engine Tuning Advisor Limitations

The Database Engine Tuning Advisor recommendations are based on the input workload. If the input workload is not a true representation of the actual workload, then the recommended indexes may sometimes have a *negative* effect on some queries that are missing in the workload. But most importantly, in many cases, the Database Engine Tuning Advisor may not recognize possible tuning opportunities. It has a sophisticated testing engine, but in some scenarios, its capabilities are limited.

For a production server, you should ensure that the SQL trace includes a complete representation of the database workload. For most database applications, capturing a trace for a complete day usually includes most of the queries executed on the database, although there are exceptions to this such as weekly, monthly, or year-end processing. Be sure you understand your load and what's needed to capture it appropriately. A few of the other considerations/limitations with the Database Engine Tuning Advisor are as follows:

- *Trace input using the* SQL:BatchCompleted *event*: As mentioned earlier, the SQL trace input to the Database Engine Tuning Advisor must include the SOL:BatchCompleted event; otherwise, the wizard won't be able to identify the queries in the workload.

- *Query distribution in the workload*: In a workload, a query may be executed multiple times with the same parameter value. Even a small performance improvement to the most common query can make a bigger contribution to the performance of the overall workload, compared to a large improvement in the performance of a query that is executed only once.

- *Index hints*: Index hints in a SQL query can prevent the Database Engine Tuning Advisor from choosing a better execution plan. The wizard includes all index hints used in a SQL query as part of its recommendations. Because these indexes may not be optimal for the table, remove all index hints from queries before submitting the workload to the wizard, bearing in mind that you need to add them back in to see whether they do actually improve performance.

Summary

As you learned in this chapter, the Database Engine Tuning Advisor can be a useful tool for analyzing the effectiveness of existing indexes and recommending new indexes for a SQL workload. As the SQL workload changes over time, you can use this tool to determine which existing indexes are no longer in use and which new indexes are required to improve performance. It can be a good idea to run the wizard occasionally just to check that your existing indexes really are the best fit for your current workload. This assumes you're not capturing metrics and evaluating them yourself. The Tuning Advisor also provides many useful reports for analyzing the SQL workload and the effectiveness of its own recommendations. Just remember that the limitations of the tool prevent it from spotting all tuning opportunities. Also remember that the suggestions provided by the DTA are only as good as the input you provide to it. If your database is in bad shape, this tool can give you a quick leg up. If you're already monitoring and tuning your queries regularly, you may see no benefit from the recommendations of the Database Engine Tuning Advisor.

Frequently, you will rely on nonclustered indexes to improve the performance of a SQL workload. This assumes that you've already assigned a clustered index to your tables. Because the performance of a nonclustered index is highly dependent on the cost of the bookmark lookup associated with the nonclustered index, you will see in the next chapter how to analyze and resolve a lookup.

CHAPTER 11

■ ■ ■

Key Lookups and Solutions

To maximize the benefit from nonclustered indexes, you must minimize the cost of the data retrieval as much as possible. A major overhead associated with nonclustered indexes is the cost of excessive lookups, formerly known as *bookmark lookups*, which are a mechanism to navigate from a nonclustered index row to the corresponding data row in the clustered index or the heap. Therefore, it makes sense to look at the cause of lookups and to evaluate how to avoid this cost.

In this chapter, I cover the following topics:

- The purpose of lookups

- The drawbacks of using lookups

- Analysis of the cause of lookups

- Techniques to resolve lookups

Purpose of Lookups

When a SQL query requests information through a query, the optimizer can use a nonclustered index, if available, on the columns in the WHERE or JOIN clause to retrieve the data. If the query refers to columns that are not part of the nonclustered index being used to retrieve the data, then navigation is required from the index row to the corresponding data row in the table to access these remaining columns.

For example, in the following SELECT statement, if the nonclustered index used by the optimizer doesn't include all the columns, navigation will be required from a nonclustered index row to the data row in the clustered index or heap to retrieve the value of those columns:

```
SELECT  p.[Name],
        AVG(sod.LineTotal)
FROM    Sales.SalesOrderDetail AS sod
        JOIN Production.Product p
        ON sod.ProductID = p.ProductID
WHERE   sod.ProductID = 776
GROUP BY sod.CarrierTrackingNumber,
        p.[Name]
HAVING  MAX(sod.OrderQty) > 1
ORDER BY MIN(sod.LineTotal);
```

The SalesOrderDetail table has a nonclustered index on the ProductID column. The optimizer can use the index to filter the rows from the table. The table has a clustered index on SalesOrderID and SalesOrderDetailID, so they would be included in the nonclustered index. But since they're not referenced in the query, they won't help the query at all. The other columns (LineTotal, CarrierTrackingNumber, OrderQty, and LineTotal) referred to by the query are not available in the nonclustered index. To fetch the values for those columns, navigation from the nonclustered index row to the corresponding data row through the clustered index is required, and this operation is a key lookup. You can see this in action in Figure 11-1.

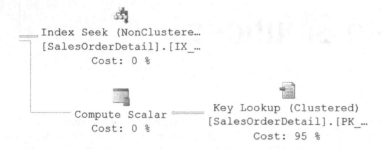

Figure 11-1. Key lookup in part of a more complicated execution plan

To better understand how a nonclustered index can cause a lookup, consider the following SELECT statement, which requests only a few rows but all columns because of the wildcard * from the SalesOrderDetail table by using a filter criterion on column ProductID:

```
SELECT  *
FROM    Sales.SalesOrderDetail AS sod
WHERE   sod.ProductID = 776 ;
```

The optimizer evaluates the WHERE clause and finds that the column ProductID included in the WHERE clause has a nonclustered index on it that filters the number of rows down. Since only a few rows, 228, are requested, retrieving the data through the nonclustered index will be cheaper than scanning the clustered index (containing more than 120,000 rows) to identify the matching rows. The nonclustered index on the column ProductID will help identify the matching rows quickly. The nonclustered index includes the column ProductID and the clustered index columns SalesOrderID and SalesOrderDetailID; all the other columns being requested are not included. Therefore, as you may have guessed, to retrieve the rest of the columns while using the nonclustered index, you require a lookup.

This is shown in the following metrics and in the execution plan in Figure 11-2 (you can turn on STATISTICS IO using the Query ➤ Query Options menu). Look for the Key Lookup (Clustered) operator. That is the lookup in action.

```
Table 'SalesOrderDetail'. Scan count 1, logical reads 710
CPU time = 0 ms,  elapsed time = 104 ms.
```

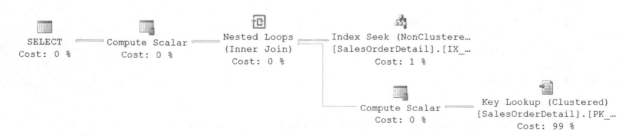

Figure 11-2. Execution plan with a bookmark lookup

Drawbacks of Lookups

A lookup requires data page access in addition to index page access. Accessing two sets of pages increases the number of logical reads for the query. Additionally, if the pages are not available in memory, a lookup will probably require a random (or nonsequential) I/O operation on the disk to jump from the index page to the data page as well as requiring the necessary CPU power to marshal this data and perform the necessary operations. This is because, for a large table, the index page and the corresponding data page usually won't be directly next to each other on the disk.

The increased logical reads and costly physical reads (if required) make the data retrieval operation of the lookup quite costly. In addition, you'll have processing for combining the data retrieved from the index with the data retrieved through the lookup operation, usually through one of the JOIN operators. This cost factor is the reason that nonclustered indexes are better suited for queries that return a small set of rows from the table. As the number of rows retrieved by a query increases, the overhead cost of a lookup becomes unacceptable.

To understand how a lookup makes a nonclustered index ineffective as the number of rows retrieved increases, let's look at a different example. The query that produced the execution plan in Figure 11-2 returned just a few rows from the SalesOrderDetail table. Leaving the query the same but changing the filter to a different value will, of course, change the number of rows returned. If you change the parameter value to look like this:

```
SELECT  *
FROM    Sales.SalesOrderDetail AS sod
WHERE   sod.ProductID = 793;
```

then running the query returns more than 700 rows, with different performance metrics and a completely different execution plan (Figure 11-3).

```
Table 'SalesOrderDetail'. Scan count 1, logical reads 1246
CPU time = 15 ms,  elapsed time = 137 ms.
```

Figure 11-3. *A different execution plan for a query returning more rows*

To determine how costly it will be to use the nonclustered index, consider the number of logical reads (1,246) performed by the query during the table scan. If you force the optimizer to use the nonclustered index by using an index hint, like this:

```
SELECT  *
FROM    Sales.SalesOrderDetail AS sod WITH (INDEX (IX_SalesOrderDetail_ProductID))
WHERE   sod.ProductID = 793 ;
```

then the number of logical reads increases from 1,246 to 2,173:

```
Table 'SalesOrderDetail'. Scan count 1, logical reads 2173
CPU time = 31 ms,  elapsed time = 319 ms.
```

Figure 11-4 shows the corresponding execution plan.

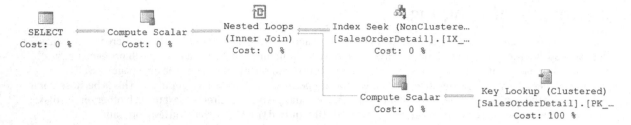

Figure 11-4. *Execution plan for fetching more rows with an index hint*

To benefit from nonclustered indexes, queries should request a relatively well-defined set of data. Application design plays an important role for the requirements that handle large result sets. For example, search engines on the Web mostly return a limited number of articles at a time, even if the search criterion returns thousands of matching articles. If the queries request a large number of rows, then the increased overhead cost of a lookup can make the nonclustered index unsuitable; subsequently, you have to consider the possibilities of avoiding the lookup operation.

Analyzing the Cause of a Lookup

Since a lookup can be a costly operation, you should analyze what causes a query plan to choose a lookup step in an execution plan. You may find that you are able to avoid the lookup by including the missing columns in the nonclustered index key or as INCLUDE columns at the index page level and thereby avoid the cost overhead associated with the lookup.

To learn how to identify the columns not included in the nonclustered index, consider the following query, which pulls information from the HumanResources.Employee table based on NationalIDNumber:

```
SELECT  NationalIDNumber,
        JobTitle,
        HireDate
FROM    HumanResources.Employee AS e
WHERE   e.NationalIDNumber = '693168613' ;
```

This produces the following performance metrics and execution plan (see Figure 11-5):

```
Table 'Employee'. Scan count 0, logical reads 4
CPU time = 0 ms, elapsed time = 53 ms
```

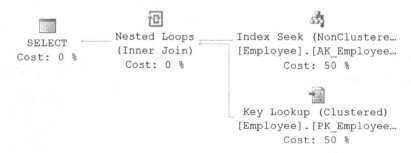

Figure 11-5. *Execution plan with a lookup*

As shown in the execution plan, you have a key lookup. The SELECT statement refers to columns NationalIDNumber, JobTitle, and HireDate. The nonclustered index on column NationalIDNumber doesn't provide values for columns JobTitle and HireDate, so a lookup operation was required to retrieve those columns from the data storage location. It's a Key Lookup because it's retrieving the data through the use of the clustered key stored with the nonclustered index. If the table were a heap, it would be an RID lookup. However, in the real world, it usually won't be this easy to identify all the columns used by a query. Remember that a lookup operation will be caused if all the columns referred to in any part of the query (not just the selection list) aren't part of the nonclustered index used.

In the case of a complex query based on views and user-defined functions, it may be too difficult to find all the columns referred to by the query. As a result, you need a standard mechanism to find the columns returned by the lookup that are not included in the nonclustered index.

If you look at the properties on the Key Lookup (Clustered) operation, you can see the output list for the operation. This shows you the columns being output by the lookup. To get the list of output columns quickly and easily and be able to copy them, right-click the operator, which in this case is Key Lookup (Clustered). Then select the Properties menu item. Scroll down to the Output List property in the Properties window that opens (Figure 11-6). This property has an expansion arrow, which allows you to expand the column list, and has further expansion arrows next to each column, which allow you to expand the properties of the column.

▲ Output List	[AdventureWorks2012].[HumanResources].[Employee].JobTitle, [Adv
◢ [1]	[AdventureWorks2012].[HumanResources].[Employee].JobTitle
Alias	[e]
Column	JobTitle
Database	[AdventureWorks2012]
Schema	[HumanResources]
Table	[Employee]
▷ [2]	[AdventureWorks2012].[HumanResources].[Employee].HireDate

Figure 11-6. *Key lookup Properties window*

To get the list of columns directly from the Properties window, click the ellipsis on the right side of the Output List property. This opens the output list in a text window from which you can copy the data for use when modifying your index (Figure 11-7).

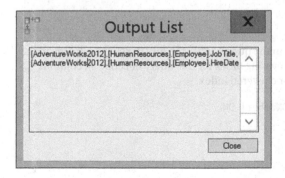

Figure 11-7. *The required columns that were not available in the nonclustered index*

Resolving Lookups

Since the relative cost of a lookup can be high, you should, wherever possible, try to get rid of lookup operations. In the preceding section, you needed to obtain the values of columns JobTitle and HireDate without navigating from the index row to the data row. You can do this in three different ways, as explained in the following sections.

Using a Clustered Index

For a clustered index, the leaf page of the index is the same as the data page of the table. Therefore, when reading the values of the clustered index key columns, the database engine can also read the values of other columns without any navigation from the index row. In the previous example, if you convert the nonclustered index to a clustered index for a particular row, SQL Server can retrieve values of all the columns from the same page.

Simply saying that you want to convert the nonclustered index to a clustered index is easy to do. However, in this case, and in most cases you're likely to encounter, it isn't possible to do so since the table already has a clustered index in place. The clustered index on this table also happens to be the primary key. You would have to drop all foreign key constraints, drop and re-create the primary key as a nonclustered index, and then re-create the index against NationalIDNumber. Not only do you need to take into account the work involved, but you may seriously affect other queries that are dependent on the existing clustered index.

■ **Note**   Remember that a table can have only one clustered index.

Using a Covering Index

In Chapter 8, you learned that a covering index is like a pseudoclustered index for the queries since it can return results without recourse to the table data. So, you can also use a covering index to avoid a lookup.

To understand how you can use a covering index to avoid a lookup, examine the query against the HumanResources.Employee table again.

```
SELECT  NationalIDNumber,
        JobTitle,
        HireDate
FROM    HumanResources.Employee AS e
WHERE   e.NationalIDNumber = '693168613';
```

To avoid this bookmark, you can add the columns referred to in the query, JobTitle and HireDate, directly to the nonclustered index key. This will make the nonclustered index a covering index for this query because all columns can be retrieved from the index without having to go to the heap or clustered index.

```
CREATE UNIQUE NONCLUSTERED INDEX [AK_Employee_NationalIDNumber] ON
[HumanResources].[Employee]
(NationalIDNumber ASC,
JobTitle ASC,
HireDate ASC )
WITH DROP_EXISTING;
```

Now when the query gets run, you'll see the following metrics and a different execution plan (Figure 11-8):

```
Table 'Employee'. Scan count 0, logical reads 2
CPU time = 0 ms, elapsed time = 0 ms.
```

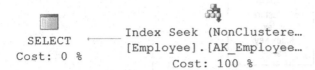

Figure 11-8. Execution plan with a covering index

There are a couple of caveats to creating a covering index by changing the key, however. If you add too many columns to a nonclustered index, it becomes wider. The index maintenance cost associated with the action queries can increase, as discussed in Chapter 8. Therefore, evaluate closely whether adding a key value will provide benefits to the general use of the index. If a key value is not going to be used for searches within the index, then it doesn't make sense to add it to the key. Also evaluate the number of columns (for size and data type) to be added to the nonclustered index key. If the total width of the additional columns is not too large (best determined through testing and measuring the resultant index size), then those columns can be added in the nonclustered index key to be used as a covering index. Also, if you add columns to the index key, depending on the index, of course, you may be affecting other queries in a negative fashion. They may have expected to see the index key columns in a particular order or may not refer to some of the columns in the key, causing the index to not be used by the optimizer. Only modify the index by adding keys if it makes sense based on these evaluations, especially because you have an alternative to modifying the key.

Another way to arrive at the covering index, without reshaping the index by adding key columns, is to use the INCLUDE columns. Change the index to look like this:

```
CREATE UNIQUE NONCLUSTERED INDEX [AK_Employee_NationalIDNumber]
ON [HumanResources].[Employee]
(NationalIDNumber ASC)
INCLUDE  (JobTitle,HireDate)
WITH DROP_EXISTING ;
```

Now when the query is run, you get the following metrics and execution plan (Figure 11-9):

```
Table 'Employee'. Scan count 1, logical reads 2
CPU time = 0 ms, elapsed time = 0 ms.
```

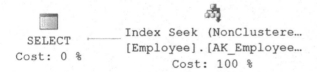

Figure 11-9. Execution plan with INCLUDE columns

The index is still covering, exactly as it was in the execution plan displayed in Figure 11-8. Because the data is stored at the leaf level of the index, when the index is used to retrieve the key values, the rest of the columns in the INCLUDE statement are available for use, almost like they were part of the key. Refer to Figure 11-10.

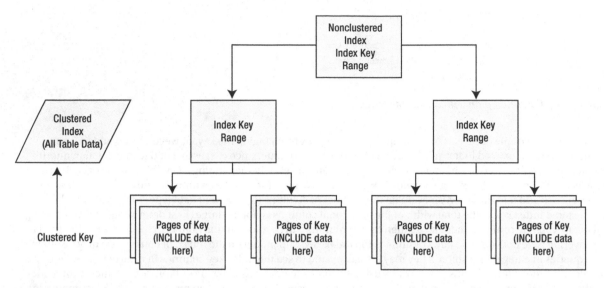

Figure 11-10. *Index storage using the INCLUDE keyword*

Another way to get a covering index is to take advantage of the structures within SQL Server. If the previous query were modified slightly to retrieve a different set of data instead of a particular NationalIDNumber and its associated JobTitle and HireDate, this time the query would retrieve the NationalIDNumber as an alternate key and the BusinessEntityID, the primary key for the table, over a range of values.

```
SELECT  NationalIDNumber,
        BusinessEntityID
FROM    HumanResources.Employee AS e
WHERE   e.NationalIDNumber BETWEEN '693168613'
                        AND       '7000000000';
```

The original index on the table doesn't reference the BusinessEntityID column in any way.

```
CREATE UNIQUE NONCLUSTERED INDEX [AK_Employee_NationalIDNumber]
ON [HumanResources].[Employee]
(
[NationalIDNumber] ASC
)WITH DROP_EXISTING ;
```

When the query is run against the table, you can see the results shown in Figure 11-11.

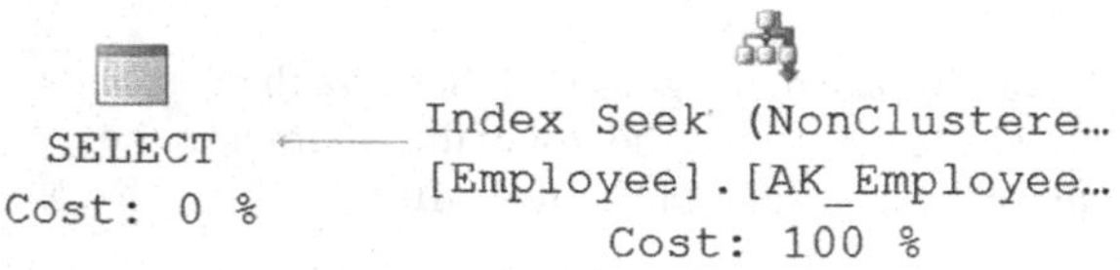

```
  SELECT     ←——————   Index Seek (NonClustere...
  Cost: 0 %             [Employee].[AK_Employee...
                              Cost: 100 %
```

Figure 11-11. *Unexpected covering index*

How did the optimizer arrive at a covering index for this query based on the index provided? It's aware that on a table with a clustered index, the clustered index key, in this case the BusinessEntityID column, is stored as a pointer to the data with the nonclustered index. That means any query that incorporates a clustered index and a set of columns from a nonclustered index as part of the filtering mechanisms of the query, the WHERE clause, or the join criteria can take advantage of the covering index.

To see how these three different indexes are reflected in storage, you can look at the statistics of the indexes themselves using DBCC SHOWSTATISTICS. When you run the following query against the index, you can see the output in Figure 11-12:

```
DBCC SHOW_STATISTICS('HumanResources.Employee',
AK_Employee_NationalIDNumber);
```

	Name	Updated	Rows	Rows Sampled	Steps	Density	Average key length	String Index	Filter Expression	Unfiltered Rows
1	AK_Employee_NationalIDNumber	Jan 27 2014 2:01PM	290	290	177	1	21.66207	YES	NULL	290

	All density	Average Length	Columns
1	0.003448276	17.66207	NationalIDNumber
2	0.003448276	21.66207	NationalIDNumber, BusinessEntityID

	RANGE_HI_KEY	RANGE_ROWS	EQ_ROWS	DISTINCT_RANGE_ROWS	AVG_RANGE_ROWS
1	10708100	0	1	0	1
2	112457891	2	1	2	1

Figure 11-12. *DBCC SHOW_STATISTICS output for original index*

As you can see, the NationalIDNumber is listed first, but the primary key for the table is included as part of the index, so a second row that includes the BusinessEntityID column is there. It makes the average length of the key about 22 bytes. This is how indexes that refer to the primary key values as well as the index key values can function as covering indexes.

If you run the same DBCC SHOW_STATISTICS on the first alternate index you tried, with all three columns included in the key, like so, you will see a different set of statistics (Figure 11-13):

```
CREATE UNIQUE NONCLUSTERED INDEX [AK_Employee_NationalIDNumber] ON
[HumanResources].[Employee]
(NationalIDNumber ASC,
JobTitle ASC,
HireDate ASC )
WITH DROP_EXISTING ;
```

	Name	Updated	Rows	Rows Sampled	Steps	Density	Average key length	String Index	Filter Expression	Unfiltered Rows
1	AK_Employee_NationalIDNumber	Jan 27 2014 2:06PM	290	290	177	1	74.48276	YES	NULL	290

	All density	Average Length	Columns
1	0.003448276	17.66207	NationalIDNumber
2	0.003448276	67.48276	NationalIDNumber, JobTitle
3	0.003448276	70.48276	NationalIDNumber, JobTitle, HireDate
4	0.003448276	74.48276	NationalIDNumber, JobTitle, HireDate, BusinessE...

	RANGE_HI_KEY	RANGE_ROWS	EQ_ROWS	DISTINCT_RANGE_ROWS	AVG_RANGE_ROWS
1	10708100	0	1	0	1
2	112457891	2	1	2	1

Figure 11-13. *DBCC SHOW_STATISTICS output for a wide key covering index*

You now see the columns added up, all three of the index key columns, and finally the primary key added on. Instead of a width of 22 bytes, it's grown to 74. That reflects the addition of the JobTitle column, a VARCHAR(50) as well as the 6-byte-wide datetime field.

Finally, looking at the statistics for the second alternate index, with the included columns you'll see the output in Figure 11-14.

```
CREATE UNIQUE NONCLUSTERED INDEX [AK_Employee_NationalIDNumber]
ON [HumanResources].[Employee]
(NationalIDNumber ASC )
INCLUDE  (JobTitle,HireDate)
WITH DROP_EXISTING ;
```

	Name	Updated	Rows	Rows Sampled	Steps	Density	Average key length	String Index	Filter Expression	Unfiltered Rows
1	AK_Employee_NationalIDNumber	Jan 27 2014 2:08PM	290	290	177	1	21.66207	YES	NULL	290

	All density	Average Length	Columns
1	0.003448276	17.66207	NationalIDNumber
2	0.003448276	21.66207	NationalIDNumber, BusinessEntityID

	RANGE_HI_KEY	RANGE_ROWS	EQ_ROWS	DISTINCT_RANGE_ROWS	AVG_RANGE_ROWS
1	10708100	0	1	0	1
2	112457891	2	1	2	1

Figure 11-14. DBCC SHOW_STATISTICS output for a covering index using INCLUDE

Now the key width is back to the original size because the columns in the INCLUDE statement are stored not with the key but at the leaf level of the index.

There is more interesting information to be gleaned from the data stored about statistics, but I'll cover that in Chapter 12.

Using an Index Join

If the covering index becomes very wide, then you might consider an index join technique. As explained in Chapter 9, the index join technique uses an index intersection between two or more indexes to cover a query fully. Since the index join technique requires access to more than one index, it has to perform logical reads on all the indexes used in the index join. Consequently, it requires a higher number of logical reads than the covering index. But since the multiple narrow indexes used for the index join can serve more queries than a wide covering index (as explained in Chapter 9), you can certainly consider the index join as a technique to avoid lookups.

To better understand how an index join can be used to avoid lookups, run the following query against the PurchaseOrderHeader table in order to retrieve a PurchaseOrderID for a particular vendor on a particular date:

```
SELECT  poh.PurchaseOrderID,
        poh.VendorID,
        poh.OrderDate
FROM    Purchasing.PurchaseOrderHeader AS poh
WHERE   VendorID = 1636
        AND poh.OrderDate = '12/5/2007' ;
```

When run, this query results in a Key Lookup operation (Figure 11-15) and the following I/O:

```
Table 'Employee'. Scan count 1, logical reads 10
CPU time = 15 ms,  elapsed time = 19 ms.
```

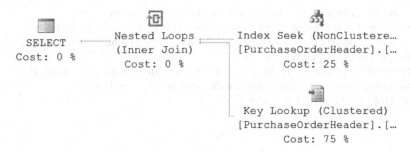

Figure 11-15. *A Key Lookup operation*

The lookup is caused since all the columns referred to by the SELECT statement and WHERE clause are not included in the nonclustered index on column VendorID. Using the nonclustered index is still better than not using it, since that would require a scan on the table (in this case, a clustered index scan) with a larger number of logical reads.

To avoid the lookup, you can consider a covering index on the column OrderDate, as explained in the previous section. But in addition to the covering index solution, you can consider an index join. As you learned, an index join requires narrower indexes than the covering index and thereby provides the following two benefits.

- Multiple narrow indexes can serve a larger number of queries than the wide covering index.

- Narrow indexes require less maintenance overhead than the wide covering index.

To avoid the lookup using an index join, create a narrow nonclustered index on column OrderDate that is not included in the existing nonclustered index.

```
CREATE NONCLUSTERED INDEX Ix_TEST
ON Purchasing.PurchaseOrderHeader(OrderDate);
```

If you run the SELECT statement again, the following output and the execution plan shown in Figure 11-16 are returned:

```
Table 'PurchaseOrderHeader'. Scan count 2, logical reads 4
CPU time = 0 ms,  elapsed time = 28 ms.
```

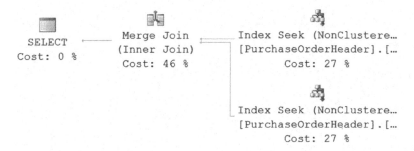

Figure 11-16. *Execution plan without a lookup*

From the preceding execution plan, you can see that the optimizer used the nonclustered index, IX_PurchaseOrder_VendorID, on column VendorID and the new nonclustered index, IxTEST, on column OrderID to serve the query fully without hitting the storage location of the rest of the data. This index join operation avoided the lookup and consequently decreased the number of logical reads from 10 to 4.

It is true that a covering index on columns VendorID and OrderID (c1, c2) could reduce the number of logical reads further. But it may not always be possible to use covering indexes, since they can be wide and have their associated overhead. In such cases, an index join can be a good alternative.

Summary

As demonstrated in this chapter, the lookup step associated with a nonclustered index can make data retrieval through a nonclustered index very costly. The SQL Server optimizer takes this into account when generating an execution plan, and if it finds the overhead cost of using a nonclustered index to be high, it discards the index and performs a table scan (or a clustered index scan if the table is stored as a clustered index). Therefore, to improve the effectiveness of a nonclustered index, it makes sense to analyze the cause of a lookup and consider whether you can avoid it completely by adding fields to the index key or to the INCLUDE column (or index join) and creating a covering index.

Up to this point, you have concentrated on indexing techniques and presumed that the SQL Server optimizer would be able to determine the effectiveness of an index for a query. In the next chapter, you will see the importance of statistics in helping the optimizer determine the effectiveness of an index.

CHAPTER 12

■■■

Statistics, Data Distribution, and Cardinality

By now, you should have a good understanding of the importance of indexes. But, the index alone is not what the optimizer uses to determine how it's going to access data. The optimizer must have information about the data that defines an index or a column. That information is referred to as a *statistic*. Statistics define both the distribution of data and the uniqueness or selectivity of the data. Statistics are maintained both on indexes and on columns within the system. You can even define statistics manually yourself.

In this chapter, you'll learn the importance of statistics in query optimization. Specifically, I will cover the following topics:

- The role of statistics in query optimization

- The importance of statistics on columns with indexes

- The importance of statistics on nonindexed columns used in join and filter criteria

- Analysis of single-column and multicolumn statistics, including the computation of selectivity of a column for indexing

- Statistics maintenance

- Effective evaluation of statistics used in a query execution

The Role of Statistics in Query Optimization

SQL Server's query optimizer is a cost-based optimizer; it decides on the best data access mechanism and join strategy by identifying the selectivity, how unique the data is, and which columns are used in filtering the data (meaning via the WHERE or JOIN clause). Statistics exist with an index, but they also exist on columns without an index that are used as part of a predicate. As you learned in Chapter 7, a nonclustered index is a great way to retrieve data that is covered by the index, whereas with queries that need columns outside the key, a clustered index can work better. With a large result set, going to the clustered index or table directly is usually more beneficial.

Up-to-date information on data distribution in the columns referenced as predicates helps the optimizer determine the query strategy to use. In SQL Server, this information is maintained in the form of statistics, which are essential for the cost-based optimizer to create an effective query execution plan. Through the statistics, the optimizer can make reasonably accurate estimates about how long it will take to return a result set or an intermediate result set and therefore determine the most effective operations to use to efficiently retrieve or modify the data as defined by the T-SQL statement. As long as you ensure that the default statistical settings for the database are set, the optimizer will be able to do its best to determine effective processing strategies dynamically. Also, as a safety measure while troubleshooting performance, you should ensure that the automatic statistics maintenance routine is doing its job

193

as desired. Where necessary, you may even have to take manual control over the creation and/or maintenance of statistics. (I cover this in the "Manual Maintenance" section, and I cover the precise nature of the functions and shape of statistics in the "Analyzing Statistics" section.) In the following section, I show you why statistics are important to indexed columns and nonindexed columns functioning as predicates.

Statistics on an Indexed Column

The usefulness of an index is largely dependent on the statistics of the indexed columns; without statistics, SQL Server's cost-based query optimizer can't decide upon the most effective way of using an index. To meet this requirement, SQL Server automatically creates the statistics of an index key whenever the index is created. It isn't possible to turn this feature off.

As data changes, the data retrieval mechanism required to keep the cost of a query low may also change. For example, if a table has only one matching row for a certain column value, then it makes sense to retrieve the matching rows from the table by going through the nonclustered index on the column. But if the data in the table changes so that a large number of rows are added with the same column value, then using the nonclustered index may no longer make sense. To be able to have SQL Server decide this change in processing strategy as the data changes over time, it is vital to have up-to-date statistics.

SQL Server can keep the statistics on an index updated as the contents of the indexed column are modified. By default, this feature is turned on and is configurable through the Properties ➤ Options ➤ Auto Update Statistics setting of a database. Updating statistics consumes extra CPU cycles and associated I/O. To optimize the update process, SQL Server uses an efficient algorithm to decide when to execute the update statistics procedure, based on factors such as the number of modifications and the size of the table.

- When a table with no rows gets a row

- When a table has fewer than 500 rows and is increased by 500 or more rows

- When a table has more than 500 rows and is increased by 500 rows + 20 percent of the number of rows

This built-in intelligence keeps the CPU utilization by each process low. It's also possible to update the statistics asynchronously. This means when a query would normally cause statistics to be updated, instead that query proceeds with the old statistics, and the statistics are updated offline. This can speed up the response time of some queries, such as when the database is large or when you have a short timeout period.

When you have large data sets, usually measured in millions of rows or better, you can modify how often statistics are updated. Instead of a fixed 20 percent for updates, you can get a sliding scale that uses an ever smaller percentage of changes for an ever greater number of rows. This ensures that you see more frequent statistics updates on large-scale systems. This functionality requires the modification of the database at a low level using a trace flag. The command looks like this:

```
DBCC TRACEON(2371,-1);
```

Turning on trace flag 2371 will modify the statistics updates from the default described earlier to the sliding approach.

You can manually disable (or enable) the auto update statistics and the auto update statistics asynchronously features by using the ALTER DATABASE command. By default, the auto update statistics feature is enabled, and it is strongly recommended that you keep it enabled. The auto update statistics asynchronously feature is disabled by default. Turn this feature on only if you've determined it will help with timeouts on your database.

■ **Note** I explain ALTER DATABASE later in this chapter in the "Manual Maintenance" section.

Benefits of Updated Statistics

The benefits of performing an auto update usually outweigh its cost on the system resources. If you have large tables and I mean hundreds of gigabytes for a single table, you may be in a situation where letting the statistics update automatically is less beneficial. In this case, you may want to try using the sliding scale, or you may be in a situation where automatic statistics maintenance doesn't work well. But this is an edge case, and even here, you may find that an auto update of the statistics doesn't negatively impact your system.

To more directly control the behavior of the data, instead of using the tables in AdventureWorks2012, for this set of examples, you will create one manually. Specifically, create a test table with only three rows and a nonclustered index.

```
IF (SELECT  OBJECT_ID('Test1')
    ) IS NOT NULL
    DROP TABLE dbo.Test1;
GO
CREATE TABLE dbo.Test1 (C1 INT, C2 INT IDENTITY);

SELECT TOP 1500
        IDENTITY( INT,1,1 ) AS n
INTO    #Nums
FROM    Master.dbo.SysColumns sC1,
        Master.dbo.SysColumns sC2;

INSERT  INTO dbo.Test1
        (C1)
        SELECT  n
        FROM    #Nums;

DROP TABLE #Nums;

CREATE NONCLUSTERED INDEX i1 ON dbo.Test1 (C1) ;
```

If you execute a SELECT statement with a selective filter criterion on the indexed column to retrieve only one row, as shown in the following line of code, then the optimizer uses a nonclustered index seek, as shown in the execution plan in Figure 12-1.

```
SELECT  *
FROM    dbo.Test1
WHERE   C1 = 2;
```

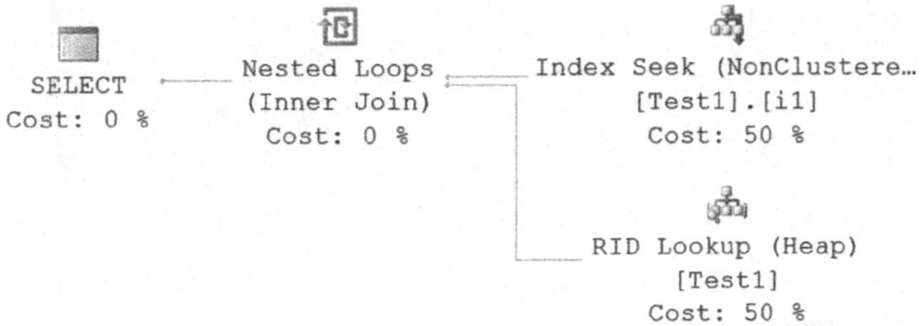

Figure 12-1. *Execution plan for a small result set*

To understand the effect of small data modifications on a statistics update, create a session using Extended Events. In the session, add the event auto_stats, which captures statistics update and create events, and add sql_batch_completed. Here's the script to create an Extended Events session:

```
CREATE EVENT SESSION [Statistics] ON SERVER
ADD EVENT sqlserver.auto_stats(
    ACTION(sqlserver.sql_text)),
ADD EVENT sqlserver.missing_column_statistics(SET collect_column_list=(1)
    ACTION(sqlserver.sql_text)
    WHERE ([sqlserver].[database_name]=N'AdventureWorks2012'))
WITH (MAX_MEMORY=4096 KB,EVENT_RETENTION_MODE=ALLOW_SINGLE_EVENT_LOSS,MAX_DISPATCH_LATENCY=30
SECONDS,MAX_EVENT_SIZE=0 KB,MEMORY_PARTITION_MODE=NONE,TRACK_CAUSALITY=ON,STARTUP_STATE=OFF)
GO
```

Add only one row to the table.

```
INSERT   INTO dbo.Test1
         (C1)
VALUES   (2);
```

When you reexecute the preceding SELECT statement, you get the same execution plan as shown in Figure 12-1. Figure 12-2 shows the events generated by the SELECT query.

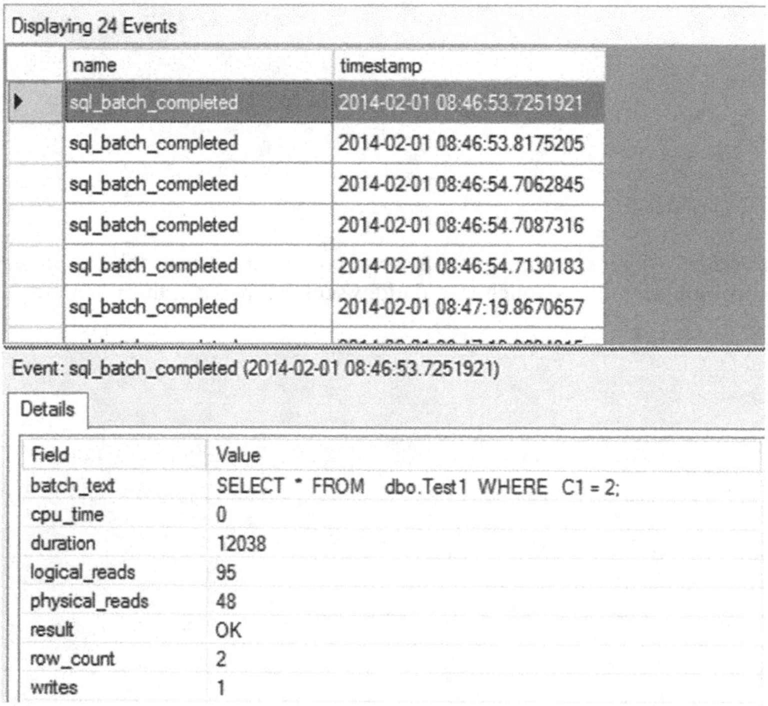

Figure 12-2. *Session output on the addition of a small number of rows*

The session output doesn't contain any SQL activity representing a statistics update because the number of changes fell below the threshold where any table that has more than 500 rows must have an increase of 500 rows plus 20 percent of the number of rows.

To understand the effect of large data modification on statistics update, add 1,500 rows to the table.

```
SELECT TOP 1500
        IDENTITY( INT,1,1 ) AS n
INTO    #Nums
FROM    Master.dbo.SysColumns sc1,
        Master.dbo.SysColumns sC2;
INSERT  INTO dbo.Test1
        (C1)
        SELECT  2
        FROM    #Nums;
DROP TABLE #Nums;
```

Now, if you reexecute the SELECT statement, like so, a large result set (1,502 rows out of 3,001 rows) will be retrieved:

```
SELECT  *
FROM    dbo.Test1
WHERE   C1 = 2;
```

Since a large result set is requested, scanning the base table directly is preferable to going through the nonclustered index to the base table 1,502 times. Accessing the base table directly will prevent the overhead cost of bookmark lookups associated with the nonclustered index. This is represented in the resultant execution plan (see Figure 12-3).

Figure 12-3. *Execution plan for a large result set*

Figure 12-4 shows the resultant session output.

name	timestamp
▶ auto_stats	2014-02-01 08:50:06.4158968
auto_stats	2014-02-01 08:50:06.4301300
sql_batch_completed	2014-02-01 08:50:06.4828968
sql_batch_completed	2014-02-01 08:50:06.4934048
sql_batch_completed	2014-02-01 08:50:07.4309800
sql_batch_completed	2014-02-01 08:50:07.4332431

Event: auto_stats (2014-02-01 08:50:06.4158968)

Details

Field	Value
count	1
database_id	5
database_name	
duration	0
index_id	2
job_id	0
job_type	StatsUpdate
last_error	0
object_id	1255675521
retries	0
statistics_list	Loading and updating: dbo.Test1.i1
status	Loading and updating stats
success	True

Figure 12-4. *Session output on the addition of a large number of rows*

The session output includes multiple auto_stats events since the threshold was exceeded by the large-scale update this time. You can tell what each of the events is doing by looking at the details. Figure 12-4 shows the job_type value, in this case StatsUpdate. You'll also see the statistics that are being updated listed in the statistics_list column. Another point of interest is the Status column, which can tell you more about what part of the statistics update process is occurring, in this case "Loading and update stats." These SQL activities consume some extra CPU cycles. However, by doing this, the optimizer determines a better data-processing strategy and keeps the overall cost of the query low. After the statistics update completes, the query then runs using the up-to-date statistics to arrive at the execution plan shown in Figure 12-3.

Drawbacks of Outdated Statistics

As explained in the preceding section, the auto update statistics feature allows the optimizer to decide on an efficient processing strategy for a query as the data changes. If the statistics become outdated, however, then the processing strategies decided on by the optimizer may not be applicable for the current data set and thereby will degrade performance.

To understand the detrimental effect of having outdated statistics, follow these steps:

1. Re-create the preceding test table with 1,500 rows only and the corresponding nonclustered index.

2. Prevent SQL Server from updating statistics automatically as the data changes. To do so, disable the auto update statistics feature by executing the following SQL statement:

```
ALTER DATABASE AdventureWorks2012 SET AUTO_UPDATE_STATISTICS OFF;
```

3. Add 1,500 rows to the table like before.

Now, reexecute the SELECT statement to understand the effect of the outdated statistics on the query optimizer. The query is repeated here for clarity:

```
SELECT *
FROM dbo.Test1
WHERE C1 = 2;
```

Figure 12-5 and Figure 12-6 show the resultant execution plan and the session output for this query, respectively.

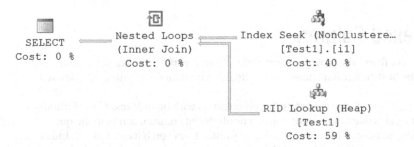

Figure 12-5. *Execution plan with AUTO_UPDATE_STATISTICS OFF*

Field	Value
batch_text	SELECT * FROM dbo.Test1 WHERE C1 = 2;
cpu_time	16000
duration	96120
logical_reads	1514
physical_reads	0
result	OK
row_count	1501
writes	0

Figure 12-6. *Session output details with AUTO_UPDATE_STATISTICS OFF*

With the auto update statistics feature switched off, the query optimizer has selected a different execution plan from the one it selected with this feature on. Based on the outdated statistics, which have only one row for the filter criterion (C1 = 2), the optimizer decided to use a nonclustered index seek. The optimizer couldn't make its decision based on the current data distribution in the column. For performance reasons, it would have been better to hit the base table directly instead of going through the nonclustered index, since a large result set (1,501 rows out of 3,000 rows) is requested.

You can see that turning off the auto update statistics feature has a negative effect on performance by comparing the cost of this query with and without updated statistics. Table 12-1 shows the difference in the cost of this query.

Table 12-1. *Cost of the Query With and Without Updated Statistics*

Statistics Update Status	Figure	Cost	
		CPU (ms)	Number of Reads
Updated	Figure 12-4	63	34
Not updated	Figure 12-6	96	1514

The number of logical reads and the CPU utilization are significantly higher when the statistics are out-of-date, even though the data returned is identical and the query was precisely the same. Therefore, it is recommended that you keep the auto update statistics feature on. The benefits of keeping statistics updated outweigh the costs of performing the update. Before you leave this section, turn AUTO_UPDATE_STATISTICS back on (although you can also manually update statistics if you choose).

```
ALTER DATABASE AdventureWorks2012 SET AUTO_UPDATE_STATISTICS ON;
```

Statistics on a Nonindexed Column

Sometimes you may have columns in join or filter criteria without any index. Even for such nonindexed columns, the query optimizer is more likely to make the best choice if it knows the cardinality and data distribution, also known as the *statistics*, of those columns.

In addition to statistics on indexes, SQL Server can build statistics on columns with no indexes. The information on data distribution, or the likelihood of a particular value occurring in a nonindexed column, can help the query optimizer determine an optimal processing strategy. This benefits the query optimizer even if it can't use an index to actually locate the values. SQL Server automatically builds statistics on nonindexed columns if it deems this information valuable in creating a better plan, usually when the columns are used in a predicate. By default, this feature is turned on, and it's configurable through the Properties ➤ Options ➤ Auto Create Statistics setting of a database. You can override this setting programmatically by using the ALTER DATABASE command. However, for better performance, it is strongly recommended that you keep this feature on.

In general, you should not disable the automatic creation of statistics on nonindexed columns. One of the scenarios in which you may consider disabling this feature is while executing a series of ad hoc SQL activities that you will not execute again. Even in such a case, you should test whether you're better off paying the cost of automatic statistics creation to get a better plan in this one case as compared to affecting the performance of other SQL Server activities. So, for most systems, you should keep this feature on and not be concerned about it.

Benefits of Statistics on a Nonindexed Column

To understand the benefit of having statistics on a column with no index, create two test tables with disproportionate data distributions, as shown in the following code. Both tables contain 10,001 rows. Table Test1 contains only one row for a value of the second column (Test1_C2) equal to 1, and the remaining 10,000 rows contain this column value as 2. Table Test2 contains exactly the opposite data distribution.

```
IF (SELECT  OBJECT_ID('dbo.Test1')
    ) IS NOT NULL
      DROP TABLE dbo.Test1;
GO

CREATE TABLE dbo.Test1
    (Test1_C1 INT IDENTITY,
     Test1_C2 INT
    );

INSERT  INTO dbo.Test1
        (Test1_C2)
VALUES  (1);

SELECT TOP 10000
        IDENTITY( INT,1,1 ) AS n
INTO    #Nums
FROM    Master.dbo.SysColumns scl,
        Master.dbo.SysColumns sC2 ;

INSERT  INTO dbo.Test1
        (Test1_C2)
        SELECT  2
        FROM    #Nums
GO

CREATE CLUSTERED INDEX i1 ON dbo.Test1(Test1_C1)

--Create second table with 10001 rows, -- but opposite data distribution IF(SELECT
OBJECT_ID('dbo.Test2')) IS NOT NULL
IF (SELECT  OBJECT_ID('dbo.Test2')
    ) IS NOT NULL
      DROP TABLE dbo.Test2;
GO

CREATE TABLE dbo.Test2
    (Test2_C1 INT IDENTITY,
     Test2_C2 INT
    );

INSERT  INTO dbo.Test2
        (Test2_C2)
VALUES  (2);

INSERT  INTO dbo.Test2
        (Test2_C2)
        SELECT  1
        FROM    #Nums;
DROP TABLE #Nums;
GO

CREATE CLUSTERED INDEX il ON dbo.Test2(Test2_C1);
```

Table 12-2 illustrates how the tables will look.

Table 12-2. *Sample Tables*

	Table Test1		**Table Test2**	
Column	Test1_c1	Test1_C2	Test2_c1	Test2_C2
Row1	1	1	1	2
Row2	2	2	2	1
RowN	N	2	N	1
Row10001	10001	2	10001	1

To understand the importance of statistics on a nonindexed column, use the default setting for the auto create statistics feature. By default, this feature is on. You can verify this using the DATABASEPROPERTYEX function (although you can also query the sys.databases view).

```
SELECT  DATABASEPROPERTYEX('AdventureWorks2012',
'IsAutoCreateStatistics');
```

■ **Note**   You can find a detailed description of configuring the auto create statistics feature later in this chapter.

Use the following SELECT statement to access a large result set from table Test1 and a small result set from table Test2. Table Test1 has 10,000 rows for the column value of Test1_C2 = 2, and table Test2 has 1 row for Test2_C2 = 2. Note that these columns used in the join and filter criteria have no index on either table.

```
SELECT  Test1.Test1_C2,
        Test2.Test2_C2
FROM    dbo.Test1
JOIN    dbo.Test2
        ON Test1.Test1_C2 = Test2.Test2_C2
WHERE   Test1.Test1_C2 = 2 ;
```

Figure 12-7 shows the execution plan for this query.

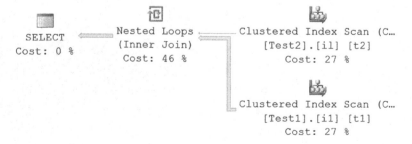

Figure 12-7. *Execution plan with AUTO_CREATE_STATISTICS ON*

Figure 12-8 shows the session output with all completed events and the auto_stats events for this query. You can use this to evaluate some of the added costs for a given query.

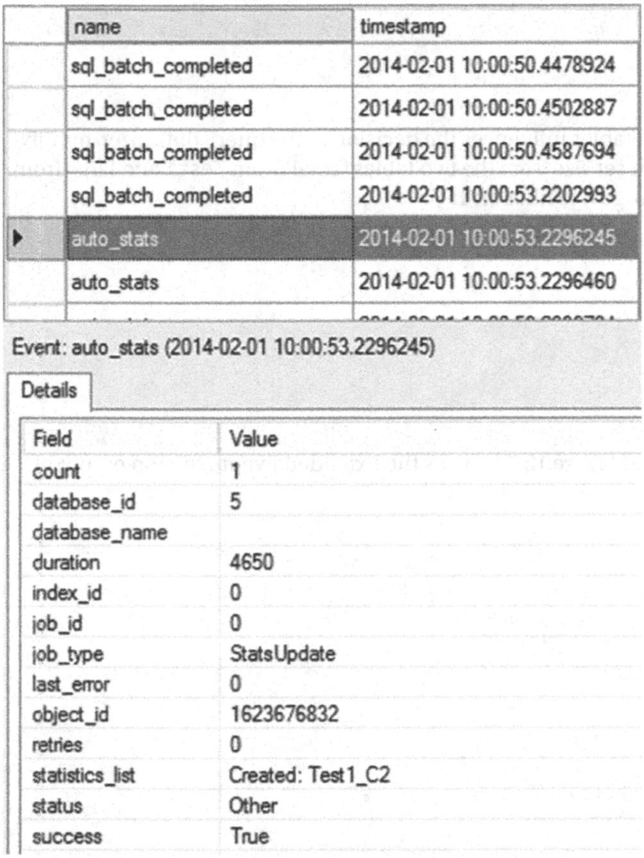

name	timestamp
sql_batch_completed	2014-02-01 10:00:50.4478924
sql_batch_completed	2014-02-01 10:00:50.4502887
sql_batch_completed	2014-02-01 10:00:50.4587694
sql_batch_completed	2014-02-01 10:00:53.2202993
auto_stats	2014-02-01 10:00:53.2296245
auto_stats	2014-02-01 10:00:53.2296460

Event: auto_stats (2014-02-01 10:00:53.2296245)

Details

Field	Value
count	1
database_id	5
database_name	
duration	4650
index_id	0
job_id	0
job_type	StatsUpdate
last_error	0
object_id	1623676832
retries	0
statistics_list	Created: Test1_C2
status	Other
success	True

Figure 12-8. *Extended Events session output with AUTO_CREATE_STATISTICS ON*

The session output shown in Figure 12-8 includes two auto_stats events creating statistics on the nonindexed columns referred to in the JOIN and WHERE clauses, Test2_C2 and Test1_C2. This activity consumes a few extra CPU cycles (since none could be detected) and took about 10,000 microseconds, or 10ms. However, by consuming these extra CPU cycles, the optimizer decides upon a better processing strategy for keeping the overall cost of the query low.

To verify the statistics automatically created by SQL Server on the nonindexed columns of each table, run this SELECT statement against the sys.stats table:

```
SELECT  s.name,
        s.auto_created,
        s.user_created
FROM    sys.stats AS s
WHERE   object_id = OBJECT_ID('Test1');
```

Figure 12-9 shows the automatic statistics created for table Test1.

	name	auto_created	user_created
1	i1	0	0
2	_WA_Sys_00000002_60C757A0	1	0

Figure 12-9. *Automatic statistics for table Test1*

To verify how a different result set size from the two tables influences the decision of the query optimizer, modify the filter criteria of the query to access an opposite result set size from the two tables (small from Test1 and large from Test2). Instead of filtering on Test1.Test1_C2 = 2, change it to filter on 1:

```
SELECT  t1.Test1_C2,
        t2.Test2_C2
FROM    dbo.Test1 AS t1
JOIN    dbo.Test2 AS t2
        ON t1.Test1_C2 = t2.Test2_C2
WHERE   t1.Test1_C2 = 1;
```

Figure 12-10 shows the resultant execution plan, and Figure 12-11 shows the Extended Events session output of this query.

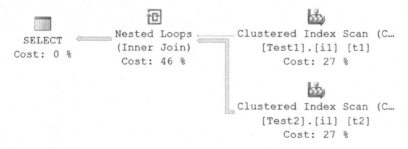

Figure 12-10. *Execution plan for a different result set*

Field	Value
batch_text	SELECT t1.Test1_C2, t2.Test2...
cpu_time	16000
duration	62016
logical_reads	56
physical_reads	0
result	OK
row_count	10000
writes	0

Figure 12-11. *Trace output for a different result set*

The resultant session output doesn't perform any additional SQL activities to manage statistics. The statistics on the nonindexed columns (Test1.Test1_C2 and Test2.Test2_C2) had already been created when the indexes themselves were created and updated as the data changed.

For effective cost optimization, in each case the query optimizer selected different processing strategies, depending upon the statistics on the nonindexed columns (Test1.Test1_C2 and Test2.Test2_C2). You can see this from the previous two execution plans. In the first, table Test1Test1 is the outer table for the nested loop join, whereas in the latest one, table Test2 is the outer table. By having statistics on the nonindexed columns (Test1.Test1_C2 and Test2.Test2_C2), the query optimizer can create a cost-effective plan suitable for each case.

An even better solution would be to have an index on the column. This would not only create the statistics on the column but also allow fast data retrieval through an Index Seek operation, while retrieving a small result set. However, in the case of a database application with queries referring to nonindexed columns in the WHERE clause, keeping the auto create statistics feature on still allows the optimizer to determine the best processing strategy for the existing data distribution in the column.

If you need to know which column or columns might be covered by a given statistic, you need to look into the sys.stats_columns system table. You can query it in the same way as you did the sys.stats table.

```
SELECT  *
FROM    sys.stats_columns
WHERE   object_id = OBJECT_ID('Test1');
```

This will show the column being referenced by the automatically created statistics. You can use this information to help you if you decide you need to create an index to replace the statistics because you will need to know which columns to create the index on. The column listed here is the ordinal position of the column within the table. To see the column name, you'd need to modify the query.

```
SELECT  c.name,
        sc.object_id,
        sc.stats_column_id,
        sc.stats_id
FROM    sys.stats_columns AS sc
JOIN sys.columns AS c
        ON c.object_id = sc.object_id
           AND c.column_id = sc.column_id
WHERE   sc.object_id = OBJECT_ID('Test1');
```

Drawback of Missing Statistics on a Nonindexed Column

To understand the detrimental effect of not having statistics on nonindexed columns, drop the statistics automatically created by SQL Server and prevent SQL Server from automatically creating statistics on columns with no index by following these steps:

1. Drop the automatic statistics created on column Test1.Test1_C2 through the Manage Statistics dialog box, as shown in the section "Benefits of Statistics on a Nonindexed Column," or use the following SQL command, substituting the system name automatically given the statistics for the phrase StatisticsName:

    ```
    DROP STATISTICS [Test1].StatisticsName;
    ```

2. Similarly, drop the corresponding statistics on column Test2.Test2_C2.

3. Disable the auto create statistics feature by deselecting the Auto Create Statistics check box
    for the corresponding database or by executing the following SQL command:

```
ALTER DATABASE AdventureWorks2012 SET AUTO_CREATE_STATISTICS OFF;
```

Now reexecute the SELECT statement --nonindexed_select.

```
SELECT  Test1.Test1_C2,
        Test2.Test2_C2
FROM    dbo.Test1
        JOIN dbo.Test2
        ON Test1.Test1_C2 = Test2.Test2_C2
WHERE   Test1.Test1_C2 = 2;
```

Figure 12-12 and Figure 12-13 show the resultant execution plan and Extended Events output, respectively.

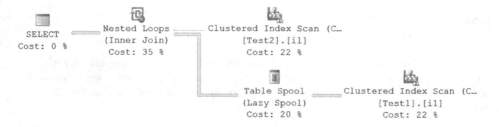

Figure 12-12. *Execution plan with AUTO_CREATE_STATISTICS OFF*

Event: sql_batch_completed (2014-06-15 09:12:46.3346463)

Details

Field	Value
batch_text	SELECT Test1.Test1_C2, Test2.Test2_C2 FROM dbo....
cpu_time	16000
duration	139682
logical_reads	20229
physical_reads	0
result	OK
row_count	10000
writes	19

Figure 12-13. *Trace output with AUTO_CREATE_STATISTICS OFF*

With the auto create statistics feature off, the query optimizer selected a different execution plan compared to the one it selected with the auto create statistics feature on. On not finding statistics on the relevant columns, the optimizer chose the first table (Test1) in the FROM clause as the outer table of the nested loop join operation. The optimizer couldn't make its decision based on the actual data distribution in the column. You can see the warning, an exclamation point, in the execution plan, indicating the missing statistics information on the data access operators, the clustered index scans. If you modify the query to reference table Test2 as the first table in the FROM clause, then the optimizer selects table Test2 as the outer table of the nested loop join operation. Figure 12-14 shows the execution plan.

```
SELECT  Test1.Test1_C2,
        Test2.Test2_C2
FROM    dbo.Test2
JOIN    dbo.Test1
        ON Test1.Test1_C2 = Test2.Test2_C2
WHERE   Test1.Test1_C2 = 2;
```

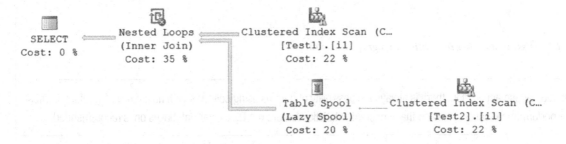

Figure 12-14. *Execution plan with AUTO_CREATE_STATISTICS OFF (a variation)*

You can see that turning off the auto create statistics feature has a negative effect on performance by comparing the cost of this query with and without statistics on a nonindexed column. Table 12-3 shows the difference in the cost of this query.

Table 12-3. *Cost Comparison of a Query With and Without Statistics on a Nonindexed Column*

Statistics on Nonindexed Column	Figure	Cost	
		Duration (ms)	Number of Reads
With statistics	Figure 12-11	98	48
Without statistics	Figure 12-13	262	20273

The number of logical reads and the CPU utilization are higher with no statistics on the nonindexed columns. Without these statistics, the optimizer can't create a cost-effective plan because it effectively has to guess at the selectivity through a set of built-in heuristic calculations.

A query execution plan highlights the missing statistics by placing an exclamation point on the operator that would have used the statistics. You can see this in the clustered index scan operators in the previous execution plans (Figures 12-12 and 12-14), as well as in the detailed description in the Warnings section in the properties of a node in a graphical execution plan, as shown in Figure 12-15 for table Test1.

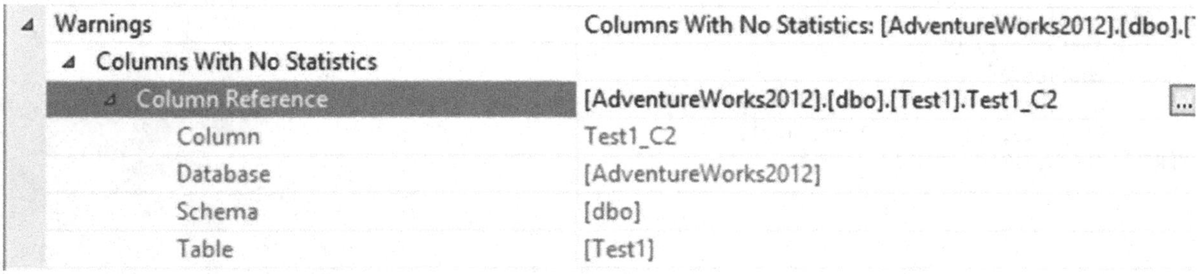

⊿ Warnings	Columns With No Statistics: [AdventureWorks2012].[dbo].[
⊿ **Columns With No Statistics**	
⊿ Column Reference	[AdventureWorks2012].[dbo].[Test1].Test1_C2 ...
Column	Test1_C2
Database	[AdventureWorks2012]
Schema	[dbo]
Table	[Test1]

Figure 12-15. *Missing statistics indication in a graphical plan*

■ **Note**   In a database application, there is always the possibility of queries using columns with no indexes. Therefore, in most systems, for performance reasons, leaving the auto create statistics feature of SQL Server databases on is recommended.

You can query the plans in cache to identify those plans that may have missing statistics.

```
SELECT  dest.text AS query,
        deqs.execution_count,
        deqp.query_plan
FROM    sys.dm_exec_query_stats AS deqs
        CROSS APPLY sys.dm_exec_text_query_plan(deqs.plan_handle,
                                        deqs.statement_start_offset,
                                        deqs.statement_end_offset) AS detqp
        CROSS APPLY sys.dm_exec_query_plan(deqs.plan_handle) AS deqp
        CROSS APPLY sys.dm_exec_sql_text(deqs.sql_handle) AS dest
WHERE   detqp.query_plan LIKE '%ColumnsWithNoStatistics%';
```

This query cheats just a little bit. I'm using a wildcard on both sides of a variable with the LIKE operator, which is actually a common code issue (addressed in more detail in Chapter 18), but the alternative in this case is to run an XQuery, which requires loading the XML parser. Depending on the amount of memory available to your system, this approach, the wildcard search, can work a lot faster than querying the XML of the execution plan directly. Query tuning isn't just about using a single method but understanding how they all fit together.

If you are in a situation where you need to disable the automatic creation of statistics, you may still want to track where statistics may have been useful to your queries. You can use the Extended Events missing_column_statistics to capture that information. For the previous examples, you can see an example of the output of this event in Figure 12-16.

Field	Value
attach_activity_id.g...	7CF1EEF6-80F9-40C1-96ED-988AB61F8B5F
attach_activity_id.s...	1
attach_activity_id_...	6770E97F-1000-4FC2-815C-D4CD79FD281F
attach_activity_id_...	0
column_list	NO STATS:([AdventureWorks2012].[dbo].[Test2].[Test2_C2], [A...
sql_text	SELECT Test1.Test1_C2, Test2.Test2_C2 FROM dbo....

Figure 12-16. *Output from missing_column_statistics Extended Events event*

The `column_list` will show which columns did not have statistics, and the `sql_text` event field will show which query it is applicable to. You can then decide whether you want to create your own statistics to benefit the query in question.

Before proceeding, be sure to turn the automatic creation of statistics back on.

```
ALTER DATABASE AdventureWorks2012 SET AUTO_CREATE_STATISTICS ON;
```

Analyzing Statistics

Statistics are collections of information defined within three sets of data: the header, the density graph, and the histograms. One of the most commonly used of these data sets is the histogram. A *histogram* is a statistical construct that shows how often data falls into varying categories called *steps*. The histogram stored by SQL Server consists of a sampling of data distribution for a column or an index key (or the first column of a multicolumn index key) of up to 200 rows. The information on the range of index key values between two consecutive samples is one step. These steps consist of varying size intervals between the 200 values stored. A step provides the following information:

- The top value of a given step (RANGE_HI_KEY)

- The number of rows equal to RANGE_HI_KEY (EQ_ROWS)

- The number of rows between the previous top value and the current top value, without counting either of these boundary points (RANGE_ROWS)

- The number of distinct values in the range (DISTINCT_RANGE_ROWS); if all values in the range are unique, then RANGE_ROWS equals DISTINCT_RANGE_ROWS

- The average number of rows equal to any potential key value within a range (AVG_RANGE_ROWS)

For example, when referencing an index, the value of AVG_RANGE_ROWS for a key value within a step in the histogram helps the optimizer decide how (and whether) to use the index when the indexed column is referred to in a WHERE clause. Because the optimizer can perform a SEEK or SCAN operation to retrieve rows from a table, the optimizer can decide which operation to perform based on the number of potential matching rows for the index key value. This can be even more precise when referencing the RANGE_HI_KEY since the optimizer can know that it should find a fairly precise number of rows from that value (assuming the statistics are up-to-date).

To understand how the optimizer's data retrieval strategy depends on the number of matching rows, create a test table with different data distributions on an indexed column.

```
IF (SELECT  OBJECT_ID('dbo.Test1')
   ) IS NOT NULL
     DROP TABLE dbo.Test1 ;
GO

CREATE TABLE dbo.Test1 (C1 INT, C2 INT IDENTITY) ;

INSERT  INTO dbo.Test1
        (C1)
VALUES  (1) ;

SELECT TOP 10000
        IDENTITY( INT,1,1 ) AS n
INTO    #Nums
FROM    Master.dbo.SysColumns sc1,
        Master.dbo.SysColumns sc2 ;

INSERT  INTO dbo.Test1
        (C1)
        SELECT  2
        FROM    #Nums ;

DROP TABLE #Nums;

CREATE NONCLUSTERED INDEX FirstIndex ON dbo.Test1 (C1) ;
```

When the preceding nonclustered index is created, SQL Server automatically creates statistics on the index key. You can obtain statistics for this nonclustered index (FirstIndex) by executing the DBCC SHOW_STATISTICS command.

```
DBCC SHOW_STATISTICS(Test1, FirstIndex);
```

Figure 12-17 shows the statistics output.

	Name	Updated	Rows	Rows Sampled	Steps	Density	Average key length	String Index	Filter Expression	Unfiltered Rows
1	FirstIndex	Jun 15 2014 9:23AM	10001	10001	2	0	4	NO	NULL	10001

	All density	Average Length	Columns
1	0.5	4	C1

	RANGE_HI_KEY	RANGE_ROWS	EQ_ROWS	DISTINCT_RANGE_ROWS	AVG_RANGE_ROWS
1	1	0	1	0	1
2	2	0	10000	0	1

Figure 12-17. *Statistics on index iFirstIndex*

Now, to understand how effectively the optimizer decides upon different data retrieval strategies based on statistics, execute the following two queries requesting different numbers of rows:

```
--Retrieve 1 row;
SELECT  *
FROM    dbo.Test1
WHERE   C1 = 1;
```

```
--Retrieve 10000 rows;
SELECT  *
FROM    dbo.Test1
WHERE   C1 = 2;
```

Figure 12-18 shows execution plans of these queries.

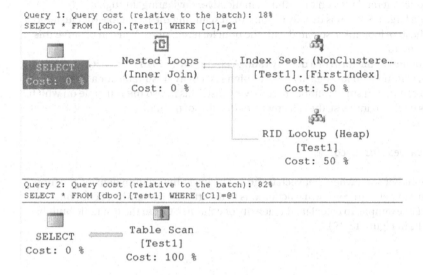

Figure 12-18. *Execution plans of small and large result set queries*

From the statistics, the optimizer can find the number of rows needed for the preceding two queries. Understanding that there is only one row to be retrieved for the first query, the optimizer chose an Index Seek operation, followed by the necessary RID Lookup to retrieve the data not stored with the clustered index. For the second query, the optimizer knows that a large number of rows (10,000 rows) will be affected and therefore avoided the index to attempt to improve performance. (Chapter 6 explains indexing strategies in detail.)

Besides the information contained in the histogram, the header has other useful information including the following:

- The time statistics were last updated

- The number of rows in the table

- The average index key length

- The number of rows sampled for the histogram

- Densities for combinations of columns

Information on the time of the last update can help you decide whether you should manually update the statistics. The average key length represents the average size of the data in the index key columns. It helps you understand the width of the index key, which is an important measure in determining the effectiveness of the index. As explained in Chapter 6, a wide index might be costly to maintain and requires more disk space and memory pages but, as explained in the next section, can make an index extremely selective.

Density

When creating an execution plan, the query optimizer analyzes the statistics of the columns used in the filter and JOIN clauses. A filter criterion with high selectivity limits the number of rows from a table to a small result set and helps the optimizer keep the query cost low. A column with a unique index will have a high selectivity since it can limit the number of matching rows to one.

On the other hand, a filter criterion with low selectivity will return a large result set from the table. A filter criterion with low selectivity makes a nonclustered index on the column ineffective. Navigating through a nonclustered index to the base table for a large result set is usually costlier than scanning the base table (or clustered index) directly because of the cost overhead of lookups associated with the nonclustered index. You can observe this behavior in the execution plan in Figure 12-18.

Statistics track the selectivity of a column in the form of a density ratio. A column with high selectivity (or uniqueness) will have low density. A column with low density (that is, high selectivity) is suitable for a filtering criteria because it can help the optimizer retrieve a small number of rows very fast. This is also the principle on which filtered indexes operate since the filter's goal is to increase the selectivity, or density, of the index.

Density can be expressed as follows:

```
Density = 1 / Number of distinct values for a column
```

Density will always come out as a number somewhere between 0 and 1. The lower the column density, the more suitable it is for use as an index key. You can perform your own calculations to determine the density of columns within your own indexes and statistics. For example, to calculate the density of column c1 from the test table built by create_t3.sql, use the following (results in Figure 12-19):

```
SELECT  1.0 / COUNT(DISTINCT C1)
FROM    dbo.Test1;
```

	(No column name)
1	0.500000000000

Figure 12-19. Results of density calculation for column C1

You can see this as actual data in the All density column in the output from DBCC SHOW_ STATISTICS. This high-density value for the column makes it a less suitable candidate for an index, even a filtered index. However, the statistics of the index key values maintained in the steps help the query optimizer use the index for the predicate C1 = 1, as shown in the previous execution plan.

Statistics on a Multicolumn Index

In the case of an index with one column, statistics consist of a histogram and a density value for that column. Statistics for a composite index with multiple columns consist of one histogram for the first column only and multiple density values. This is one reason why it's generally a good practice to put the more selective column, the one with the lowest density, first when building a compound index or compound statistics. The density values include the density for the first column and for each prefix combination of the index key columns. Multiple density values help the optimizer find the selectivity of the composite index when multiple columns are referred to by predicates in the WHERE and JOIN clauses. Although the first column can help determine the histogram, the final density of the column itself would be the same regardless of column order.

Multicolumn density graphs can come through multiple columns in the key of an index or from manually created statistics. But, you'll never see a multicolumn density graph created by the automatic statistics creation process. Let's look at a quick example. Here's a query that could easily generate a set of statistics with two columns:

```
SELECT    p.Name,
          p.Class
FROM      Production.Product AS p
WHERE     p.Color = 'Red' AND
          p.DaysToManufacture > 15;
```

An index on the columns p.Color and p.DaysToManufacture would have a multicolumn density value. Before running this, here's a query that will let you just look at the basic construction of statistics on a given table:

```
SELECT    s.name,
          s.auto_created,
          s.user_created,
          s.filter_definition,
          sc.column_id,
          c.name AS ColumnName
FROM      sys.stats AS s
          JOIN sys.stats_columns AS sc ON sc.stats_id = s.stats_id
AND sc.object_id = s.object_id
          JOIN sys.columns AS c ON c.column_id = sc.column_id
AND c.object_id = s.object_id
WHERE     s.object_id = OBJECT_ID('Production.Product');
```

Running this query against the Production.Product table results in Figure 12-20.

	name	auto_created	user_created	filter_definition	column_id	ColumnName
1	PK_Product_ProductID	0	0	NULL	1	ProductID
2	AK_Product_ProductNumber	0	0	NULL	3	ProductNumber
3	AK_Product_Name	0	0	NULL	2	Name
4	AK_Product_rowguid	0	0	NULL	24	rowguid

Figure 12-20. *List of statistics for the Product table*

You can see the indexes on the table, and each one consists of a single column. Now I'll run the query that could generate a multicolumn density graph. But, rather than trying to track down the statistics information through SHOWSTATISTICS, I'll just query the system tables again. The results are in Figure 12-21.

	name	auto_created	user_created	filter_definition	column_id	ColumnName
1	PK_Product_ProductID	0	0	NULL	1	ProductID
2	AK_Product_ProductNumber	0	0	NULL	3	ProductNumber
3	AK_Product_Name	0	0	NULL	2	Name
4	AK_Product_rowguid	0	0	NULL	24	rowguid
5	_WA_Sys_00000006_75A278F5	1	0	NULL	6	Color
6	_WA_Sys_0000000F_75A278F5	1	0	NULL	15	DaysToManufacture

Figure 12-21. *Two new statistics have been added to the Product table*

213

As you can see, instead of adding a single statistic with multiple columns, two new statistics were created. You will get a multicolumn statistic only in a multicolumn index key or with manually created statistics.

To better understand the density values maintained for a multicolumn index, you can modify the nonclustered index used earlier to include two columns.

```
CREATE NONCLUSTERED INDEX FirstIndex
ON dbo.Test1(C1,C2) WITH DROP_EXISTING = ON;
```

Figure 12-22 shows the resultant statistics provided by DBCC SHOWSTATISTICS.

	Name	Updated	Rows	Rows Sampled	Steps	Density	Average key length	String Index	Filter Expression	Unfiltered Rows
1	FirstIndex	Nov 28 2011 4:42PM	10001	10001	2	0	8	NO	NULL	10001

	All density	Average Length	Columns
1	0.5	4	C1
2	9.999E-05	8	C1, C2

	RANGE_HI_KEY	RANGE_ROWS	EQ_ROWS	DISTINCT_RANGE_ROWS	AVG_RANGE_ROWS
1	1	0	1	0	1
2	2	0	10000	0	1

Figure 12-22. *Statistics on the multicolumn index FirstIndex*

As you can see, there are two density values under the All density column.

- The density of the first column

- The density of the (first + second) columns

For a multicolumn index with three columns, the statistics for the index would also contain the density value of the (first + second + third) columns. The histogram won't contain a selectivity values for any other combination of columns. Therefore, this index (FirstIndex) won't be very useful for filtering rows only on the second column (C2), because that value of the second column (C2) alone isn't maintained in the histogram.

You can compute the second density value (0.000099990000) shown in Figure 12-19 through the following steps. This is the number of distinct values for a column combination of (C1, C2).

```
SELECT  1.0 / COUNT(*)
FROM    (SELECT DISTINCT
                C1,
                C2
        FROM    dbo.Test1
        ) DistinctRows;
```

Statistics on a Filtered Index

The purpose of a filtered index is to limit the data that makes up the index and therefore change the density and histogram to make the index perform better. Instead of a test table, this example will use a table from the AdventureWorks2012 database. Create an index on the Sales.PurchaseOrderHeader table on the PurchaseOrderNumber column.

```
CREATE INDEX IX_Test
ON Sales.SalesOrderHeader (PurchaseOrderNumber);
```

Figure 12-23 shows the header and the density of the output from DBCC SHOWSTATISTICS run against this new index.

```
DBCC SHOW_STATISTICS('Sales.SalesOrderHeader',IX_Test);
```

Name	Updated	Rows	Rows Sampled	Steps	Density	Average key length	String Index	Filter Expression	Unfiltered Rows
1	IX_Test	Feb 12 2014 8:02PM	31465	31465	152	1	7.01516	YES	NULL	31465

	All density	Average Length	Columns
1	0.000262674	3.01516	PurchaseOrderNumber
2	3.178134E-05	7.01516	PurchaseOrderNumber, SalesOrderID

	RANGE_HI_KEY	RANGE_ROWS	EQ_ROWS	DISTINCT_RANGE_ROWS	AVG_RANGE_ROWS
1	NULL	0	27659	0	1
2	PO10005144378	0	1	0	1
	PO1...				
150	PO8903194371	127	1	127	1
151	PO9280166971	63	1	63	1
152	PO9976195169	149	1	149	1

Figure 12-23. *Statistics header of an unfiltered index*

If the same index is re-created to deal with values of the column that are not null, it would look something like this:

```
CREATE INDEX IX_Test
ON Sales.SalesOrderHeader (PurchaseOrderNumber)
WHERE PurchaseOrderNumber IS NOT NULL
WITH DROP_EXISTING = ON;
```

And now, in Figure 12-24, take a look at the statistics information.

Name	Updated	Rows	Rows Sampled	Steps	Density	Average key length	String Index	Filter Expression	Unfiltered Rows
1	IX_Test	Feb 12 2014 8:00PM	3806	3806	151	1	28.92696	YES	([PurchaseOrderNumber] IS NOT NULL)	31465

	All density	Average Length	Columns
1	0.000262743	24.92696	PurchaseOrderNumber
2	0.000262743	28.92696	PurchaseOrderNumber, SalesOrderID

	RANGE_HI_KEY	RANGE_ROWS	EQ_ROWS	DISTINCT_RANGE_ROWS	AVG_RANGE_ROWS
1	PO10005144378	0	1	0	1
2	...10092...				
149	PO8903194371	127	1	127	1
150	PO9280166971	63	1	63	1
151	PO9976195169	149	1	149	1

Figure 12-24. *Statistics header for a filtered index*

First you can see that the number of rows that compose the statistics has radically dropped in the filtered index because there is a filter in place, from 31465 to 3806. Notice also that the average key length has increased since you're no longer dealing with zero-length strings. A filter expression has been defined rather than the NULL value visible in Figure 12-21. But the unfiltered rows of both sets of data are the same.

The density measurements are interesting. Notice that the density is close to the same for both values, but the filtered density is slightly lower, meaning fewer unique values. This is because the filtered data, while marginally less selective, is actually more accurate, eliminating all the empty values that won't contribute to a search. And the density of the second value, which represents the clustered index pointer, is identical with the value of the density of the PurchaseOrderNumber alone because each represents the same amount of unique data. The density of the additional clustered index in the previous column is a much smaller number because of all the unique values of SalesOrderId that are not included in the filtered data because of the elimination of the null values. You can also see the first column of the histogram shows a NULL value in Figure 12-23 but has a value in Figure 12-24.

One other option open to you is to create filtered statistics. This allows you to create even more fine-tuned histograms. This can be especially useful on partitioned tables. This is necessary because statistics are not automatically created on partitioned tables and you can't create your own using CREATE STATISTICS. You can create filtered indexes by partition and get statistics or create filtered statistics specifically by partition.

Before going on, clean the indexes created, if any.

```
DROP INDEX Sales.SalesOrderHeader.IX_Test;
```

Cardinality

The statistics, consisting of the histogram and density, are used by the query optimizer to calculate how many rows are to be expected by each process (called *operations*) within the execution of the query. This calculation to determine the number of rows returned is called the *cardinality estimate*. Cardinality represents the number of rows in a set of data, which means it's directly related to the density measures in SQL Server. Starting in SQL Server 2014, a new cardinality estimator is at work. This is the first change to the core cardinality estimation process since SQL Server 7.0. The changes to some areas of the estimator means that the optimizer reads from the statistics in the same way as previously, but the optimizer makes different kinds of calculations to determine the number of rows that are going to go through each operation in the execution plan depending on the cardinality calculations that have been modified.

Most of the time this data is pulled from the histogram. In the case of a single predicate, the values simply use the selectivity defined by the histogram. But, when multiple columns are used for filtering, the cardinality calculation has to take into account the potential selectivity of each column. Prior to SQL Server 2014, there were a couple of simple calculations used to determine cardinality. For an AND combination, the calculation was based on multiplying the selectivity of the first column by the selectivity of the second, something like this:

```
Selectivity1 * Selectivity2 * Selectivity3 ...
```

An OR calculation between two columns was more complex. The new calculation looks like this:

```
Selectivity1 * Power(Selectivity2,1/2) * Power(Selectivity3,1/4) ...
```

In short, instead of simply multiplying the selectivity to make more and more selective data, a softer calculation is supplied going from the least selective to the most selective data, but arriving at a softer, less skewed estimate by getting the power of 1/2 the selectivity, and then 1/4, and then 1/8, and so on, depending on how many columns of data are involved. It won't change all execution plans generated, but the more accurate estimates could change them in some locations.

In SQL Server 2014, several sets of new calculations are taking place. This means that for most queries, on average, you may see performance enhancements if your statistics are up-to-date because more accurate cardinality calculations means the optimizer will make better choices. But, you may also see performance degradation with some queries because of the changes in the way cardinality is calculated. This is to be expected because of the wide variety of workloads, schemas, and data distributions that you may encounter.

Another new cardinality estimation was introduced with SQL Server 2014. In SQL Server 2012 and earlier, when a value in an index that consisted of an increasing or decreasing increment, such as an identity column or a datetime value, introduced a new row that fell outside the existing histogram, the optimizer would fall back on its default estimate for data without statistics, which was one row. This could lead to seriously inaccurate query plans, causing poor performance. Now, there are all new calculations.

First, if you have created statistics using a FULLSCAN, explained in detail in the "Statistics Maintenance" section, and there have been no modifications to the data, then the cardinality estimation works the same as it did before. But, if the statistics have been created with a default sampling or data has been modified, then the cardinality estimator works off the average number of rows returned within that set of statistics and assumes that instead of a single row. This can make for much more accurate execution plans, but assuming only a reasonably consistent distribution of data. An uneven distribution, referred to as *skewed data*, can lead to bad cardinality estimations that can result in behavior similar to bad parameter sniffing, covered in detail in Chapter 16.

You can now observe cardinality estimations in action using Extended Events using the event query_optimizer_estimate_cardinality. I won't go into all the details of every possible output from the events, but I do want to show how you can observe optimizer behavior and correlate it between execution plans and the cardinality estimations. For the vast majority of query tuning, this won't be all that helpful, but if you're unsure of how the optimizer is making the estimates that it does, or if those estimates seem inaccurate, you can use this method to further investigate the information.

First, you should set up an Extended Events session with the query_optimizer_estimate_cardinality event. I've created an example including the auto_stats event. Then, I ran a query.

```
SELECT   so.Description,
         p.Name AS ProductName,
         p.ListPrice,
         p.Size,
         pv.AverageLeadTime,
         pv.MaxOrderQty,
         v.Name AS VendorName
FROM     Sales.SpecialOffer AS so
JOIN     Sales.SpecialOfferProduct AS sop
ON       sop.SpecialOfferID = so.SpecialOfferID
JOIN     Production.Product AS p
ON       p.ProductID = sop.ProductID
JOIN     Purchasing.ProductVendor AS pv
ON       pv.ProductID = p.ProductID
JOIN     Purchasing.Vendor AS v
ON       v.BusinessEntityID = pv.BusinessEntityID
WHERE so.DiscountPct > .15;
```

I chose a query that's a little complex so that there are plenty of operators in the execution plan. When I run the query, I can then see the output of the Extended Events session, as shown in Figure 12-25.

| | auto_stats | 2014-06-15 09:55:47.6338978 | Loading without updating: Purchasing.Vendor.PK_Vendor_BusinessEntityID |
| ▶ | query_optimizer_estimate_car... | 2014-06-15 09:55:47.6340754 | NULL |

Event: query_optimizer_estimate_cardinality (2014-06-15 09:55:47.6340754)

Details

Field	Value
attach_activity_id.g...	04EEA60E-ADBA-4218-B272-25862722EAFB
attach_activity_id.s...	13
calculator	<CalculatorList><JoinCalculator CalculatorName="CSelCalcExpre...
creation_time	2014-06-15 09:55:47.6300000
input_relation	<Operator Name="LogOp_Join" ClassNo="14"><StatsCollection ...
query_hash	15027420434628505523
sql_text	SELECT so.Description, p.Name AS ProductName, ...
stats_collection	<StatsCollection Name="CStCollJoin" Id="10" Card="100.32"><...
stats_collection_id	10

Figure 12-25. *Session showing output from query_optimizer_estimate_cardinality event*

The first event visible in Figure 12-25 shows the auto_stats event firing where it loaded the statistics for an index, Purchasing.ProductVendor.IX_ProductVendor_BusinessEntityID. This means the statistics were readied prior to the cardinality estimation firing. There were a number of these events, including one for the PK_ProductID column. Then, the information on the Details tab is the output from the cardinality estimation calculation. The detailed information is contained as XML in the calculator field and the input_relation field. These will show the types of calculations and the values used in those calculations.

If you also capture the execution plan for the query, you get additional information in the plan to help you correlate the cardinality estimations to the operations within the plan. If you look at the properties for the Seek Operator for the PK_ProductID column, you get a value as shown in Figure 12-26.

Seek Predicates	Seek Keys[1]: Pref
StatsCollectionId	28
Storage	RowStore
TableCardinality	504

Figure 12-26. *The properties of the clustered index seek operator*

The value of the StatsCollectionId directly corresponds the event shown in Figure 12-25 and the stats_collection_id field there. This allows you to match the statistics collection events to specific operators within the execution plans.

Enabling and Disabling the Cardinality Estimator

If you create a database in SQL Server 2014, it's going to automatically come with the compatibility level set to 120, which is the correct version for SQL Server 2014. But, if you restore or attach a database from a previous version of SQL Server, the compatibility level will be set to that version, 110 or before. That database will then use the SQL Server 7 cardinality estimator. You can tell this by looking at the execution plan in the first operator (SELECT/INSERT/UPDATE/DELETE) at the properties for the CardinalityEstimationModelVersion, as shown in Figure 12-27.

CardinalityEstimationModelVersion	70

Figure 12-27. *Property in the first operator showing the cardinality estimator in use*

The value shown for SQL Server 2014 will correspond to the version, 120. That's how you can tell what version of the cardinality estimator is in use. This is important because, since the estimates can lead to changes in execution plans, it's really important that you understand how to troubleshoot the issues in the event that you get a degradation in performance caused by the new cardinality estimations.

If you suspect that you are experiencing problems from the upgrade, you should absolutely compare your actual rows returned to the estimated rows returned in the operations within the execution plan. That's always a great way to determine whether statistics or cardinality estimations are causing you issues. You have the option of disabling the entire upgrade by setting the compatibility level to 110, but that also disables other SQL Server 2014 functionality, so it might not be a good choice. You can run a trace flag against the restore of the database using OPTION (QUERYTRACEON 9481), you'll target just the cardinality estimator for that database. If you determine in a given query that you're having issues with the new cardinality estimator, you can take advantage of trace flags in the query in the same way.

```
SELECT   p.Name,
         p.Class
FROM     Production.Product AS p
WHERE    p.Color = 'Red' AND
         p.DaysToManufacture > 15
         OPTION(QUERYTRACEON 9481);
```

Conversely, if you have turned off the cardinality estimator using the trace flag or compatibility level, you can selectively turn it on for a given query using the same functionality as earlier but substituting 2312 for the trace flag value.

Statistics Maintenance

SQL Server allows a user to manually override the maintenance of statistics in an individual database. The four main configurations controlling the automatic statistics maintenance behavior of SQL Server are as follows:

- New statistics on columns with no index (auto create statistics)

- Updating existing statistics (auto update statistics)

- The degree of sampling used to generate statistics

- Asynchronous updating of existing statistics (auto update statistics async)

You can control the preceding configurations at the levels of a database (all indexes and statistics on all tables) or on a case-by-case basis on individual indexes or statistics. The auto create statistics setting is applicable for nonindexed columns only, because SQL Server always creates statistics for an index key when the index is created. The auto update statistics setting, and the asynchronous version, is applicable for statistics on both indexes and WHERE clause columns with no index.

Automatic Maintenance

By default, SQL Server automatically takes care of statistics. Both the auto create statistics and auto update statistics settings are on by default. As explained previously, it is usually better to keep these settings on. The auto update statistics async setting is off by default.

Auto Create Statistics

The auto create statistics feature automatically creates statistics on nonindexed columns when referred to in the WHERE clause of a query. For example, when this SELECT statement is run against the Sales.SalesOrderHeader table on a column with no index, statistics for the column are created.

```
SELECT  cc.CardNumber,
        cc.ExpMonth,
        cc.ExpYear
FROM    Sales.CreditCard AS cc
WHERE   cc.CardType = 'Vista';
```

Then the auto create statistics feature (make sure it is turned back on if you have turned it off) automatically creates statistics on column CardType. You can see this in the Extended Events session output in Figure 12-28.

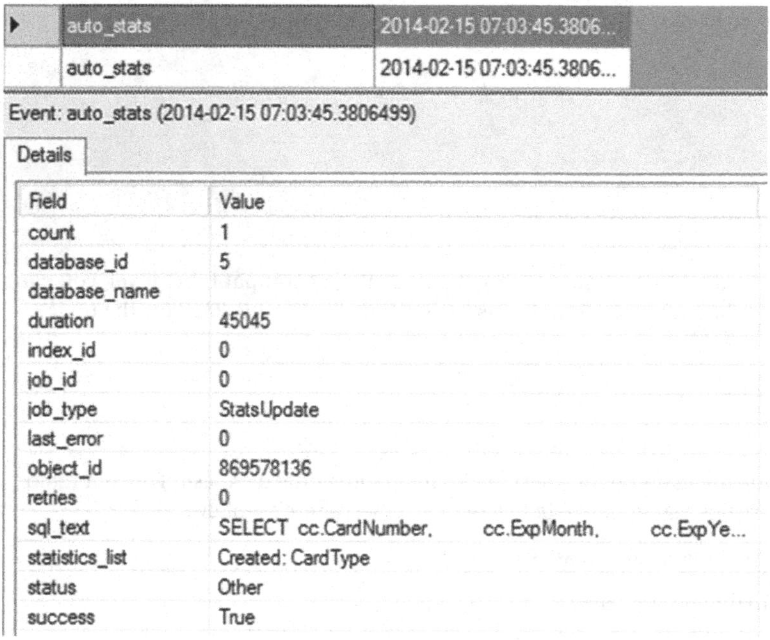

Figure 12-28. Session output with AUTO_CREATE_STATISTICS ON

The auto_stats event fires to create the new set of statistics. You can see the details of what is happening in the statistics_list field: "Created: CardType."

Auto Update Statistics

The auto update statistics feature automatically updates existing statistics on the indexes and columns of a permanent table when the table is referred to in a query, provided the statistics have been marked as out-of-date. The types of changes are action statements, such as INSERT, UPDATE, and DELETE. The default threshold for the number of changes depends on the number of rows in the table, as shown in Table 12-4.

Table 12-4. *Update Statistics Threshold for Number of Changes*

Number of Rows	Threshold for Number of Changes
0	> 1 insert
<500	> 500 changes
>500	500 + 20 percent of row changes

Row changes are counted as the number of inserts, updates, or deletes in the table.

Using a threshold reduces the frequency of the automatic update of statistics. For example, consider the following table (--autoupdates in the download):

```
IF (SELECT  OBJECT_ID('dbo.Test1')
    ) IS NOT NULL
     DROP TABLE dbo.Test1;

CREATE TABLE dbo.Test1 (C1 INT);

CREATE INDEX ixl ON dbo.Test1(C1);

INSERT  INTO dbo.Test1
        (C1)
VALUES  (0);
```

After the nonclustered index is created, a single row is added to the table. This outdates the existing statistics on the nonclustered index. If the following SELECT statement is executed with a reference to the indexed column in the WHERE clause, like so, then the auto update statistics feature automatically updates statistics on the nonclustered index, as shown in the session output in Figure 12-29.

```
SELECT  C1
FROM    dbo.Test1
WHERE   C1 = 0;
```

►	auto_stats	2014-02-16 08:23:07.6030...

Event: auto_stats (2014-02-16 08:23:07.6030355)

Details

Field	Value
count	1
database_id	5
database_name	
duration	1004
index_id	2
job_id	0
job_type	StatsUpdate
last_error	0
object_id	2007678200
retries	0
sql_text	SELECT C1 FROM dbo.Test1 WHERE C1 = 0;
statistics_list	Updated: dbo.Test1.ixd
status	Other
success	True

Figure 12-29. *Session output with AUTO_UPDATE_STATISTICS ON*

Once the statistics are updated, the change-tracking mechanisms for the corresponding tables are set to 0. This way, SQL Server keeps track of the number of changes to the tables and manages the frequency of automatic updates of statistics.

For large tables, you may find that you need more frequent updates on the statistics. As was mentioned previously, you can use trace flag 2371 to modify the default behaviour of the automatic update of statistics. With the trace flag enabled, a sliding scale is used to update statistics more frequently as the amount of data within the system increases.

Auto Update Statistics Asynchronously

If auto update statistics asynchronously is set to on, the basic behavior of statistics in SQL Server isn't changed radically. When a set of statistics is marked as out-of-date and a query is then run against those statistics, the statistics update does not interrupt the execution of the query, like normally happens. Instead, the query finishes execution using the older set of statistics. Once the query completes, the statistics are updated. The reason this may be attractive is that when statistics are updated, query plans in the procedure cache are removed, and the query being run must be recompiled. So, rather than make a query wait for both the update of the statistics and a recompile of the procedure, the query completes its run. The next time the same query is called, it will have updated statistics waiting for it, and it will have to recompile only.

Although this functionality does make recompiles somewhat faster, it can also cause queries that could benefit from updated statistics and a new execution plan to work with the old execution plan. Careful testing is required before turning this functionality on to ensure it doesn't cause more harm than good.

■ **Note** If you are attempting to update statistics asynchronously, you must also have `AUTO_UPDATE_STATISTICS` set to ON.

Manual Maintenance

The following are situations in which you need to interfere with or assist the automatic maintenance of statistics:

- *When experimenting with statistics*: Just a friendly suggestion—please spare your production servers from experiments such as the ones you are doing in this book.

- *After upgrading from a previous version to SQL Server 2014*: Since the statistics maintenance of SQL Server 2014 has been upgraded and modified, you should manually update the statistics of the complete database immediately after the upgrade instead of waiting for SQL Server to update it over time with the help of automatic statistics. Further, I suggest you use a `FULLSCAN` for this statistics update to ensure they are as accurate as possible. The only versions that I know this does not apply to are the ones from SQL Server 2008 to SQL Server 2008 R2. There is some debate over whether this is necessary, but, in most situations, it's a safe and prudent thing to do.

- *While executing a series of ad hoc SQL activities that you won't execute again*: In such cases, you must decide whether you want to pay the cost of automatic statistics maintenance to get a better plan for that one case while affecting the performance of other SQL Server activities. So, in general, you might not need to be concerned with such one-timers. This is mainly applicable to larger databases, but you can test it in your environment if you think it may apply.

- *When you come upon an issue with the automatic statistics maintenance and the only workaround for the time being is to keep the automatic statistics maintenance feature off*: Even in these cases, you can turn the feature off for the specific database table that faces the problem instead of disabling it for the complete database. Issues like this can be found in large data sets where the data is updated a lot but not enough to trigger the threshold update. Also, it can be used in cases where the sampling level of the automatic updates are not adequate for some data distributions.

- *While analyzing the performance of a query, you realize that the statistics are missing for a few of the database objects referred to by the query*: This can be evaluated from the graphical and XML execution plans, as explained earlier in the chapter.

- *While analyzing the effectiveness of statistics, you realize that they are inaccurate*: This can be determined when poor execution plans are being created from what should be good sets of statistics.

SQL Server allows a user to control many of its automatic statistics maintenance features. You can enable (or disable) the automatic statistics creation and update features by using the auto create statistics and auto update statistics settings, respectively, and then you can get your hands dirty.

Manage Statistics Settings

You can control the auto create statistics setting at a database level. To disable this setting, use the ALTER DATABASE command:

```
ALTER DATABASE AdventureWorks2012 SET AUTO_CREATE_STATISTICS OFF;
```

You can control the auto update statistics setting at different levels of a database, including all indexes and statistics on a table, or at the individual index or statistics level. To disable auto update statistics at the database level, use the ALTER DATABASE command.

```
ALTER DATABASE AdventureWorks2012 SET AUTO_UPDATE_STATISTICS OFF;
```

Disabling this setting at the database level overrides individual settings at lower levels. Auto update statistics asynchronously requires that the auto update statistics be on first. Then you can enable the asynchronous update.

```
ALTER DATABASE AdventureWorks2012 SET AUTO_UPDATE_STATISTICS_ASYNC ON;
```

To configure auto update statistics for all indexes and statistics on a table in the current database, use the sp_autostats system stored procedure.

```
USE AdventureWorks2012;
EXEC sp_autostats
    'HumanResources.Department',
    'OFF';
```

You can also use the same stored procedure to configure this setting for individual indexes or statistics. To disable this setting for the AK_Department_Name index on AdventureWorks2012.HumanResources.Department, execute the following statements:

```
EXEC sp_autostats
    'HumanResources.Department',
    'OFF',
    AK_Department_Name;
```

You can also use the UPDATE STATISTICS command's WITH NORECOMPUTE option to disable this setting for all or individual indexes and statistics on a table in the current database. The sp_createstats stored procedure also has the NORECOMPUTE option. The NORECOMPUTE option will not disable automatic update of statistics for the database, but it will for a given set of statistics.

Avoid disabling the automatic statistics features, unless you have confirmed through testing that this brings a performance benefit. If the automatic statistics features are disabled, then you are responsible for manually identifying and creating missing statistics on the columns that are not indexed and then keeping the existing statistics up-to-date. In general, you're only going to want to disable the automatic statistics features for very large tables.

If you want to check the status of whether a table has its automatic statistics turned off, you can use this:

```
EXEC sp_autostats 'HumanResources.Department';
```

Reset the automatic maintenance of the index so that it is on where it has been turned off.

```
EXEC sp_autostats
    'HumanResources.Department',
    'ON';
EXEC sp_autostats
    'HumanResources.Department',
    'ON',
    AK_Department_Name;
```

Generate Statistics

To create statistics manually, use one of the following options:

- CREATE STATISTICS: You can use this option to create statistics on single or multiple columns of a table or an indexed view. Unlike the CREATE INDEX command, CREATE STATISTICS uses sampling by default.

- sys.sp_createstats: Use this stored procedure to create single-column statistics for all eligible columns for all user tables in the current database. This includes all columns except computed columns; columns with the NTEXT, TEXT, GEOMETRY, GEOGRAPHY, or IMAGE data type; sparse columns; and columns that already have statistics or are the first column of an index. This is mainly meant for backward compatibility, and I don't recommend using it.

Similarly, to update statistics manually, use one of the following options:

- UPDATE STATISTICS: You can use this option to update the statistics of individual or all index keys and nonindexed columns of a table or an indexed view.

- sys.sp_updatestats: Use this stored procedure to update statistics of all user tables in the current database.

You may find that allowing the automatic updating of statistics is not quite adequate for your system. Scheduling UPDATE STATISTICS for the database during off-hours is an acceptable way to deal with this issue. UPDATE STATISTICS is the preferred mechanism because it offers a greater degree of flexibility and control. It's possible, because of the types of data inserted, that the sampling method for gathering the statistics, used because it's faster, may not gather the appropriate data. In these cases, you can force a FULLSCAN so that all the data is used to update the statistics just like what happens when the statistics are initially created. This can be a costly operation, so it's best to be selective about which indexes receive this treatment and when it is run.

___

■ **Note**   In general, you should always use the default settings for automatic statistics. Consider modifying these settings only after identifying that the default settings appear to detract from performance.

___

Statistics Maintenance Status

You can verify the current settings for the autostats feature using the following:

- sys.databases
- DATABASEPROPERTYEX
- sp_autostats

Status of Auto Create Statistics

You can verify the current setting for auto create statistics by running a query against the sys.databases system table.

```
SELECT  is_auto_create_stats_on
FROM    sys.databases
WHERE   [name] = 'AdventureWorks2012';
```

A return value of 1 means enabled, and a value of 0 means disabled.

You can also verify the status of specific indexes using the sp_autostats system stored procedure, as shown in the following code. Supplying any table name to the stored procedure will provide the configuration value of auto create statistics for the current database under the Output section of the global statistics settings.

```
USE AdventureWorks2012;
EXEC sys.sp_autostats
    'HumanResources.Department';
```

Figure 12-30 shows an excerpt of the preceding sp_autostats statement's output.

	Index Name	AUTOSTATS	Last Updated
1	[PK_Department_DepartmentID]	ON	2012-03-14 13:14:41.373
2	[AK_Department_Name]	ON	2012-03-14 13:14:44.550

Figure 12-30. *sp_autostats output*

A return value of ON means enabled, and a value of OFF means disabled. This stored procedure is more useful when verifying the status of auto update statistics, as explained earlier in this chapter.

Status of Auto Update Statistics

You can verify the current setting for auto update statistics, and auto update statistics asynchronously, in a similar manner to auto create statistics. Here's how to do it using the function DATABASEPROPERTYEX:

```
SELECT  DATABASEPROPERTYEX('AdventureWorks2012', 'IsAutoUpdateStatistics');
```

Here's how to do it using sp_autostats.

```
USE AdventureWorks2012;
EXEC sp_autostats
    'Sales.SalesOrderDetail';
```

Analyzing the Effectiveness of Statistics for a Query

For performance reasons, it is extremely important to maintain proper statistics on your database objects. Issues with statistics can be fairly common. You need to keep your eyes open to the possibility of problems with statistics while analyzing the performance of a query. If an issue with statistics does arise, then it can really take you for a ride. In fact, checking that the statistics are up-to-date at the beginning of a query-tuning session eliminates an easily fixed problem. In this section, you'll see what you can do should you find statistics to be missing or out-of-date.

While analyzing an execution plan for a query, look for the following points to ensure a cost-effective processing strategy:

- Indexes are available on the columns referred to in the filter and join criteria.

- In the case of a missing index, statistics should be available on the columns with no index. It is preferable to have the index itself.

- Since outdated statistics are of no use and can even be misleading, it is important that the estimates used by the optimizer from the statistics are up-to-date.

You analyzed the use of a proper index in Chapter 6. In this section, you will analyze the effectiveness of statistics for a query.

Resolving a Missing Statistics Issue

To see how to identify and resolve a missing statistics issue, consider the following example. To more directly control the data, I'll use a test table instead of one of the AdventureWorks2012 tables. First disable both auto create statistics and auto update statistics using the ALTER DATABASE command.

```
ALTER DATABASE AdventureWorks2012 SET AUTO_CREATE_STATISTICS OFF;
ALTER DATABASE AdventureWorks2012 SET AUTO_UPDATE_STATISTICS OFF;
```

Create a test table with a large number of rows and a nonclustered index.

```
IF EXISTS ( SELECT  *
            FROM    sys.objects
            WHERE   object_id = OBJECT_ID(N'dbo.Test1') )
    DROP TABLE  [dbo].[Test1] ;
        GO

CREATE TABLE dbo.Test1 (C1 INT, C2 INT, C3 CHAR(50)) ;
INSERT   INTO dbo.Test1
        (C1, C2, C3)
VALUES   (51, 1, 'C3') ,
        (52, 1, 'C3') ;

CREATE NONCLUSTERED INDEX iFirstIndex ON dbo.Test1 (C1, C2) ;

SELECT TOP 10000
        IDENTITY( INT,1,1 ) AS n
INTO    #Nums
FROM    Master.dbo.SysColumns scl,
        Master.dbo.SysColumns sC2 ;

INSERT   INTO dbo.Test1
        (C1, C2, C3)
        SELECT  n % 50,
                n,
                'C3'
        FROM    #Nums ;
DROP TABLE #Nums ;
```

Since the index is created on (C1, C2), the statistics on the index contain a histogram for the first column, C1, and density values for the prefixed column combinations (C1 and C1 * C2). There are no histograms or density values alone for column C2.

To understand how to identify missing statistics on a column with no index, execute the following SELECT statement. Since the auto create statistics feature is off, the optimizer won't be able to find the data distribution for the column C2 used in the WHERE clause. Before executing the query, ensure you have enabled "Include Actual Execution Plan" by clicking the query toolbar or hitting CTRL+M.

```
SELECT  *
FROM    dbo.Test1
WHERE   C2 = 1;
```

If you right-click the execution plan, you can take a look at the XML data behind it. As shown in Figure 12-31, the XML execution plan indicates missing statistics for a particular execution step under its Warnings element. This shows that the statistics on column Test1.C2 are missing.

```
<ColumnsWithNoStatistics>
  <ColumnReference Database="[AdventureWorks2012]" Schema="[dbo]" Table="[Test1]" Column="C2" />
</ColumnsWithNoStatistics>
```

Figure 12-31. Missing statistics indication in an XML plan

The information on missing statistics is also provided by the graphical execution plan, as shown in Figure 12-32.

Figure 12-32. Missing statistics indication in a graphical plan

The graphical execution plan shows an operator with the yellow exclamation point. This indicates some problem with the operator in question. You can obtain a detailed description of the warning by right-clicking the Table Scan operator and then selecting Properties from the context menu. There's a warning section in the properties page that you can drill into, as shown in Figure 12-33.

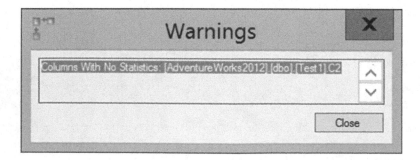

Figure 12-33. Property values from the warning in the Index Scan operator

Figure 12-33 shows that the statistics for the column are missing. This may prevent the optimizer from selecting the best processing strategy. The current cost of this query, as shown by SET STATISTICS IO and SET STATISTICS TIME, is as follows:

```
Table 'Test1'. Scan count 1, logical reads 84
SQL Server Execution Times: CPU time = 0 ms, elapsed time = 22 ms.
```

To resolve this missing statistics issue, you can create the statistics on column Test1.C2 by using the CREATE STATISTICS statement.

```
CREATE STATISTICS Stats1 ON Test1(C2);
```

Before rerunning the query, be sure to clean out the procedure cache because this query will benefit from simple parameterization.

```
DBCC FREEPROCCACHE();
```

■ **Caution** This should not be run on a production system because it will cause all plans stored in cache to be removed, causing massive recompiles on all queries, which could cause a serious negative impact on performance.

Figure 12-34 shows the resultant execution plan with statistics created on column C2.

```
Table 'Test1'. Scan count 1, logical reads 34
SQL Server Execution Times:CPU time = 0 ms, elapsed time = 17 ms.
```

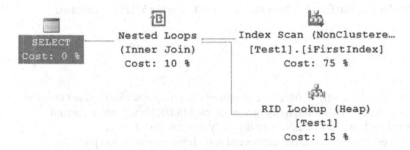

Figure 12-34. Execution plan with statistics in place

The query optimizer uses statistics on a noninitial column in a composite index to determine whether scanning the leaf level of the composite index to obtain the RID lookup information will be a more efficient processing strategy than scanning the whole table. In this case, creating statistics on column C2 allows the optimizer to determine that instead of scanning the base table, it will be less costly to scan the composite index on (C1, C2) and bookmark lookup to the base table for the few matching rows. Consequently, the number of logical reads has decreased from 84 to 34, but the elapsed time has decreased only slightly.

Resolving an Outdated Statistics Issue

Sometimes outdated or incorrect statistics can be more damaging than missing statistics. Based on old statistics or a partial scan of changed data, the optimizer may decide upon a particular indexing strategy, which may be highly inappropriate for the current data distribution. Unfortunately, the execution plans don't show the same glaring warnings for outdated or incorrect statistics as they do for missing statistics. However, there is an event called `inaccurate_cardinality_estimate`. This is a debug event, which means its use could be somewhat problematic on a production system. I strongly caution you in its use, only when properly filtered and only for short periods of time, but I want to point it out.

The more traditional, and safer, approach to identify outdated statistics is to examine how close the optimizer's estimation of the number of rows affected is to the actual number of rows affected.

The following example shows you how to identify and resolve an outdated statistics issue. Figure 12-35 shows the statistics on the nonclustered index key on column C1 provided by `DBCC SHOW_STATISTICS`.

```
DBCC SHOW_STATISTICS (Test1, iFirstIndex);
```

	Name	Updated	Rows	Rows Sampled	Steps	Density	Average key length	String Index	Filter Expression	Unfiltered Rows
1	iFirstIndex	Feb 16 2014 9:09AM	2	2	2	0	8	NO	NULL	2

	All density	Average Length	Columns
1	0.5	4	C1
2	0.5	8	C1, C2

	RANGE_HI_KEY	RANGE_ROWS	EQ_ROWS	DISTINCT_RANGE_ROWS	AVG_RANGE_ROWS
1	51	0	1	0	1
2	52	0	1	0	1

Figure 12-35. Statistics on index FirstIndex

These results say that the density value for column C1 is 0.5. Now consider the following SELECT statement:

```
SELECT  *
FROM    dbo.Test1
WHERE   C1 = 51;
```

Since the total number of rows in the table is currently 10,002, the number of matching rows for the filter criteria C1 = 51 can be estimated to be 5,001 (=0.5 x 10,002). This estimated number of rows (5,001) is way off the actual number of matching rows for this column value. The table actually contains only one row for C1 = 51.

You can get the information on both the estimated and actual number of rows from the execution plan. An estimated plan refers to and uses the statistics only, not the actual data. This means it can be wildly different from the real data, as you're seeing now. The actual execution plan, on the other hand, has both the estimated and actual numbers of rows available.

Executing the query results in this execution plan (Figure 12-36) and performance:

```
Table 'Test1'. Scan count 1, logical reads 84
SQL Server Execution Times:CPU time = 0 ms, elapsed time = 16 ms.
```

Figure 12-36. *Execution plan with outdated statistics*

To see the estimated and actual rows, you can view the properties of the Table Scan operator (Figure 12-37).

Properties	
Table Scan	
⚙ ↓ □	
⊿ Misc	
Actual Execution Mode	Row
Actual Number of Batches	0
Actual Number of Rows	1
Actual Rebinds	0
Actual Rewinds	0
Defined Values	[AdventureWorks20'
Description	Scan rows from a tab
Estimated CPU Cost	0.0111592
Estimated Execution Mode	Row
Estimated I/O Cost	0.0646065
Estimated Number of Executions	1
Estimated Number of Rows	5001
Estimated Operator Cost	0.0757657 (100%)

Figure 12-37. *Properties showing row count discrepancy*

From the estimated rows value vs. the actual rows value, it's clear that the optimizer made an incorrect estimation based on out-of-date statistics. If the difference between the estimated rows and actual rows is more than a factor of 10, then it's quite possible that the processing strategy chosen may not be very cost-effective for the current data distribution. An inaccurate estimation may misguide the optimizer in deciding the processing strategy. Statistics can be off for a number of reasons. Table variables and multistatement user-defined functions don't have statistics at all, so all estimates for these objects assume a single row, without regard to how many rows are actually involved with the objects.

To help the optimizer make an accurate estimation, you should update the statistics on the nonclustered index key on column C1 (alternatively, of course, you can just leave the auto update statistics feature on).

```
UPDATE STATISTICS Test1 iFirstIndex WITH FULLSCAN;
```

A FULLSCAN might not be needed here. The sampled method of statistics creation is usually fairly accurate and is much faster. But, on systems that aren't experiencing stress, or during off-hours, I tend to favor using FULLSCAN because of the improved accuracy. Either approach is valid as long as you're getting the statistics you need.

If you run the query again, you'll get the following statistics, and the resultant output is as shown in Figure 12-38:

```
Table 'Test1'. Scan count 1, logical reads 4
SQL Server Execution Times:
    CPU time = 0 ms, elapsed time = 0 ms.
```

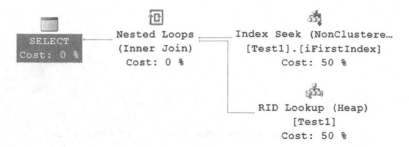

Figure 12-38. *Actual and estimated number of rows with up-to-date statistics*

The optimizer accurately estimated the number of rows using updated statistics and consequently was able to come up with a more efficient plan. Since the estimated number of rows is 1, it makes sense to retrieve the row through the nonclustered index on C1 instead of scanning the base table.

Updated, accurate statistics on the index key column help the optimizer come to a better decision on the processing strategy and thereby reduce the number of logical reads from 84 to 4 and reduce the execution time from 16ms to -0ms (there is a -4ms lag time).

Before continuing, turn the statistics back on for the database.

```
ALTER DATABASE AdventureWorks2012 SET AUTO_CREATE_STATISTICS ON;
ALTER DATABASE AdventureWorks2012 SET AUTO_UPDATE_STATISTICS ON;
```

Recommendations

Throughout this chapter, I covered various recommendations for statistics. For easy reference, I've consolidated and expanded upon these recommendations in the sections that follow.

Backward Compatibility of Statistics

Statistical information in SQL Server 2014 can be generated differently from that in previous versions of SQL Server. However, SQL Server 2014 transfers the statistics during upgrade and, by default, automatically updates these statistics over time as the data changes. For the best performance, however, I suggest manually update the statistics immediately after an upgrade, preferably, where possible, using FULLSCAN.

Auto Create Statistics

This feature should usually be left on. With the default setting, during the creation of an execution plan, SQL Server determines whether statistics on a nonindexed column will be useful. If this is deemed beneficial, SQL Server creates statistics on the nonindexed column. However, if you plan to create statistics on nonindexed columns manually, then you have to identify exactly for which nonindexed columns statistics will be beneficial.

Auto Update Statistics

This feature should usually be left on, allowing SQL Server to decide on the appropriate execution plan as the data distribution changes over time. Usually the performance benefit provided by this feature outweighs the cost overhead. You will seldom need to interfere with the automatic maintenance of statistics, and such requirements are usually identified while troubleshooting or analyzing performance. To ensure that you aren't facing surprises from the automatic statistics features, it's important to analyze the effectiveness of statistics while diagnosing SQL Server issues.

Unfortunately, if you come across an issue with the auto update statistics feature and have to turn it off, make sure to create a SQL Server job to update the statistics and schedule it to run at regular intervals. For performance reasons, where possible, ensure that the SQL job is scheduled to run during off-peak hours.

You can create a SQL Server job to update the statistics from SQL Server Management Studio by following these simple steps:

1. Select ServerName ➤ SQL Server Agent ➤ Jobs, right-click, and select New Job.

2. On the General page of the New Job dialog box, enter the job name and other details, as shown in Figure 12-39.

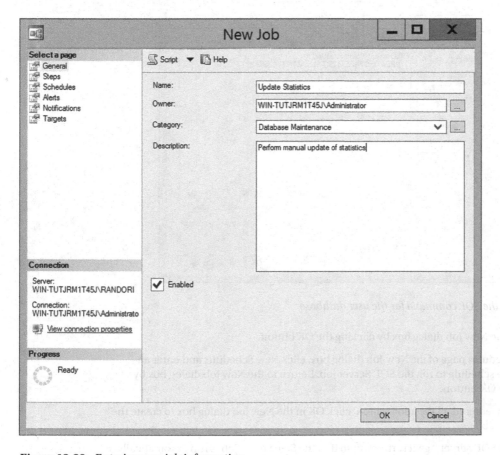

Figure 12-39. Entering new job information

3. Choose the Steps page, click New, and enter the SQL command for the user database, as shown in Figure 12-40. This is a short method for ensuring all statistics are updated across all tables in a database. It's not very precise, and it could create a large load depending on the size of your system, so be sure this is what you need on your system before running it.

```
EXEC sys.sp_MSforeachtable
    'UPDATE STATISTICS ? ALL WITH FULLSCAN';
```

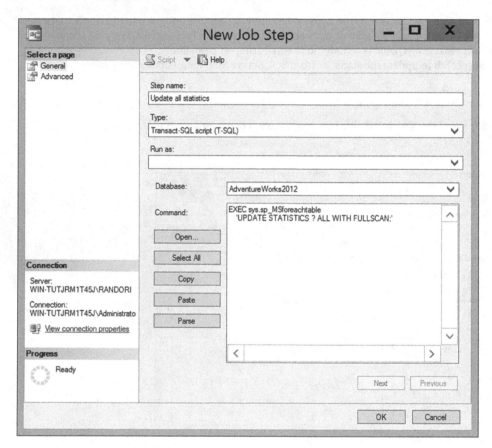

Figure 12-40. *Entering the SQL command for the user database*

4. Return to the New Job dialog box by clicking the OK button.

5. On the Schedules page of the New Job dialog box, click New Schedule, and enter an appropriate schedule to run the SQL Server job. Return to the New Job dialog box by clicking the OK button.

6. Once you've entered all the information, click OK in the New Job dialog box to create the SQL Server job.

7. Ensure that SQL Server Agent is running so that the SQL Server job is run automatically at the set schedule.

Another approach to statistics maintenance would be run one of the scripts developed and maintained by Ola Holengren (http://bit.ly/JijaNI).

Automatic Update Statistics Asynchronously

Waiting for statistics to be updated before plan generation, which is the default behavior, will be just fine in most cases. In the rare circumstances where the statistics update or the execution plan recompiles resulting from that update are expensive (more expensive than the cost of out-of-date statistics), then you can turn on the asynchronous update of statistics. Just understand that it may mean that procedures that would benefit from more up-to-date statistics will suffer until the next time they are run. Don't forget—you do need automatic update of statistics enabled in order to enable the asynchronous updates.

Amount of Sampling to Collect Statistics

It is generally recommended that you use the default sampling rate. This rate is decided by an efficient algorithm based on the data size and number of modifications. Although the default sampling rate turns out to be best in most cases, if for a particular query you find that the statistics are not very accurate, then you can manually update them with FULLSCAN. You also have the option of setting a specific sample percentage using the SAMPLE number. The number can be either a percentage or a set number of rows.

If this is required repeatedly, then you can add a SQL Server job to take care of it. For performance reasons, ensure that the SQL job is scheduled to run during off-peak hours. To identify cases in which the default sampling rate doesn't turn out to be the best, analyze the statistics effectiveness for costly queries while troubleshooting the database performance. Remember that FULLSCAN is expensive, so you should run it only on those tables or indexes that you've determined will really benefit from it.

Summary

As discussed in this chapter, SQL Server's cost-based optimizer requires accurate statistics on columns used in filter and join criteria to determine an efficient processing strategy. Statistics on an index key are always created during the creation of the index, and, by default, SQL Server also keeps the statistics on indexed and nonindexed columns updated as the data changes. This enables it to determine the best processing strategies applicable to the current data distribution.

Even though you can disable both the auto create statistics and auto update statistics features, it is recommended that you leave these features *on,* since their benefit to the optimizer is almost always more than their overhead cost. For a costly query, analyze the statistics to ensure that the automatic statistics maintenance lives up to its promise. The best news is that you can rest easy with a little vigilance since automatic statistics do their job well most of the time. If manual statistics maintenance procedures are used, then you can use SQL Server jobs to automate these procedures.

Even with proper indexes and statistics in place, a heavily fragmented database will incur an increased data retrieval cost. In the next chapter, you will see how fragmentation in an index can affect query performance, and you'll learn how to analyze and resolve fragmentation.

CHAPTER 13

∎∎∎

Index Fragmentation

As explained in Chapter 8, index column values are stored in the leaf pages of an index's B-tree structure. When you create an index (clustered or nonclustered) on a table, the cost of data retrieval is reduced by properly ordering the leaf pages of the index and the rows within the leaf pages. In an OLTP database, data changes continually, causing fragmentation of the indexes. As a result, the number of reads required to return the same number of rows increases over time.

In this chapter, I cover the following topics:

- The causes of index fragmentation, including an analysis of page splits caused by INSERT and UPDATE statements

- The overhead costs associated with fragmentation

- How to analyze the amount of fragmentation

- Techniques used to resolve fragmentation

- The significance of the fill factor in helping to control fragmentation

- How to automate the fragmentation analysis process

Causes of Fragmentation

Fragmentation occurs when data is modified in a table. When you insert or update data in a table (via INSERT or UPDATE), the table's corresponding clustered indexes and the affected nonclustered indexes are modified. This can cause an index leaf page split if the modification to an index can't be accommodated in the same page. A new leaf page will then be added that contains part of the original page and maintains the logical order of the rows in the index key. Although the new leaf page maintains the *logical* order of the data rows in the original page, this new page usually won't be *physically* adjacent to the original page on the disk. Or, put a slightly different way, the logical key order of the index doesn't match the physical order within the file.

For example, suppose an index has nine key values (or index rows) and the average size of the index rows allows a maximum of four index rows in a leaf page. As explained in Chapter 8, the 8KB leaf pages are connected to the previous and next leaf pages to maintain the logical order of the index. Figure 13-1 illustrates the layout of the leaf pages for the index.

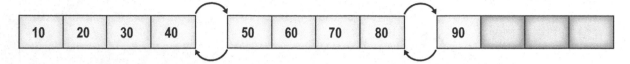

Figure 13-1. *Leaf pages layoutx*

Since the index key values in the leaf pages are always sorted, a new index row with a key value of 25 has to occupy a place between the existing key values 20 and 30. Because the leaf page containing these existing index key values is full with the four index rows, the new index row will cause the corresponding leaf page to split. A new leaf page will be assigned to the index, and part of the first leaf page will be moved to this new leaf page so that the new index key can be inserted in the correct logical order. The links between the index pages will also be updated so that the pages are logically connected in the order of the index. As shown in Figure 13-2, the new leaf page, even though linked to the other pages in the correct logical order, can be physically out of order.

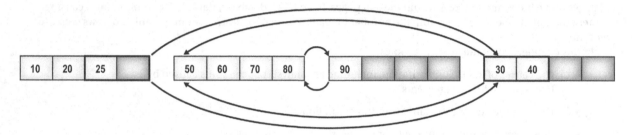

Figure 13-2. *Out-of-order leaf pages*

The pages are grouped together in bigger units called *extents*, which can contain eight pages. SQL Server uses an extent as a physical unit of allocation on the disk. Ideally, the physical order of the extents containing the leaf pages of an index should be the same as the logical order of the index. This reduces the number of switches required between extents when retrieving a range of index rows. However, page splits can physically disorder the pages within the extents, and they can also physically disorder the extents themselves. For example, suppose the first two leaf pages of the index are in extent 1, and say the third leaf page is in extent 2. If extent 2 contains free space, then the new leaf page allocated to the index because of the page split will be in extent 2, as shown in Figure 13-3.

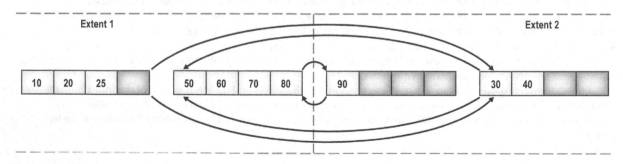

Figure 13-3. *Out-of-order leaf pages distributed across extents*

With the leaf pages distributed between two extents, ideally you expect to read a range of index rows with a maximum of one switch between the two extents. However, the disorganization of pages between the extents can cause more than one extent switch while retrieving a range of index rows. For example, to retrieve a range of index rows between 25 and 90, you will need three extent switches between the two extents, as follows:

- First extent switch to retrieve the key value 30 after the key value 25

- Second extent switch to retrieve the key value 50 after the key value 40

- Third extent switch to retrieve the key value 90 after the key value 80

This type of fragmentation is called *external fragmentation*. External fragmentation is always undesirable.

Fragmentation can also happen within an index page. If an INSERT or UPDATE operation creates a page split, then free space will be left behind in the original leaf page. Free space can also be caused by a DELETE operation. The net effect is to reduce the number of rows included in a leaf page. For example, in Figure 13-3, the page split caused by the INSERT operation has created an empty space within the first leaf page. This is known as *internal fragmentation*.

For a highly transactional database, it is desirable to deliberately leave some free space within your leaf pages so that you can add new rows, or change the size of existing rows, without causing a page split. In Figure 13-3, the free space within the first leaf page allows an index key value of 26 to be added to the leaf page without causing a page split.

■ **Note** Note that this index fragmentation is different from disk fragmentation. The index fragmentation cannot be fixed simply by running the disk defragmentation tool because the order of pages within a SQL Server file is understood only by SQL Server, not by the operating system.

Heap pages can become fragmented in the same way. Unfortunately, because of how heaps are stored and how any nonclustered indexes use the physical data location for retrieving data from the heap, defragmenting heaps is quite problematic. You can use the REBUILD command of ALTER TABLE to perform a heap rebuild, but understand that you will force a rebuild of any nonclustered indexes associated with that table.

SQL Server 2014 exposes the leaf and nonleaf pages and other data through a dynamic management view called sys.dm_db_index_physical_stats. It stores both the index size and the fragmentation. I'll cover it in more detail in the next section. The DMV is much easier to work with than the old DBCC SHOWCONTIG.

Let's now take a look at the mechanics of fragmentation.

Page Split by an UPDATE Statement

To show what happens when a page split is caused by an UPDATE statement, I'll use a constructed table. This small test table will have a clustered index, which orders the rows within one leaf (or data) page as follows:

```
USE AdventureWorks2012;
GO
IF (SELECT  OBJECT_ID('Test1')
    ) IS NOT NULL
    DROP TABLE dbo.Test1;
GO
CREATE TABLE dbo.Test1
    (C1 INT,
     C2 CHAR(999),
     C3 VARCHAR(10)
     )
```

```
INSERT  INTO dbo.Test1
VALUES  (100, 'C2', ''),
        (200, 'C2', ''),
        (300, 'C2', ''),
        (400, 'C2', ''),
        (500, 'C2', ''),
        (600, 'C2', ''),
        (700, 'C2', ''),
        (800, 'C2', '');

CREATE CLUSTERED INDEX iClust
ON dbo.Test1(C1);
```

The average size of a row in the clustered index leaf page (excluding internal overhead) is not just the sum of the average size of the clustered index columns; it's the sum of the average size of all the columns in the table, since the leaf page of the clustered index and the data page of the table are the same. Therefore, the average size of a row in the clustered index based on the foregoing sample data is as follows:

```
= (Average size of [C1]) + (Average size of [C2]) + (Average size of [C3]) bytes = (Size of INT) +
(Size of CHAR(999)) + (Average size of data in [C3]) bytes
= 4 + 999 + 0 = 1,003 bytes
```

The maximum size of a row in SQL Server is 8,060 bytes. Therefore, if the internal overhead is not very high, all eight rows can be accommodated in a single 8KB page.

To determine the number of leaf pages assigned to the iClust clustered index, execute the SELECT statement against sys.dm_db_index_physical_stats.

```
SELECT  ddips.avg_fragmentation_in_percent,
        ddips.fragment_count,
        ddips.page_count,
        ddips.avg_page_space_used_in_percent,
        ddips.record_count,
        ddips.avg_record_size_in_bytes
FROM    sys.dm_db_index_physical_stats(DB_ID('AdventureWorks2012'),
                                OBJECT_ID(N'dbo.Test1'), NULL,
                                NULL,'Sampled') AS ddips ;
```

You can see the results of this query in Figure 13-4.

	avg_fragmentation_in_percent	fragment_count	page_count	avg_page_space_used_in_percent	record_count	avg_record_size_in_bytes
1	0	1	1	100	8	1010

Figure 13-4. *Physical layout of index iClust*

From the page_count column in this output, you can see that the number of pages assigned to the clustered index is 1. You can also see the average space used, 100, in the avg_ page_space_used_in_percent column. From this you can infer that the page has no free space left to expand the content of C3, which is of type VARCHAR(10) and is currently empty.

> ■ **Note** I'll analyze more of the information provided by `sys.dm_db_index_physical_stats` in the "Analyzing the Amount of Fragmentation" section later in this chapter.

Therefore, if you attempt to expand the content of column C3 for one of the rows as follows, it should cause a page split:

```
UPDATE  dbo.Test1
SET     C3 = 'Add data'
WHERE   C1 = 200;
```

Selecting the data from `sys.dm_db_index_physical_stats` results in the information in Figure 13-5.

	avg_fragmentation_in_percent	fragment_count	page_count	avg_page_space_used_in_percent	record_count	avg_record_size_in_bytes
1	50	2	2	50.0741289844329	8	1011.75

Figure 13-5. *i1 index after a data update*

From the output in Figure 13-5, you can see that SQL Server has added a new page to the index. On a page split, SQL Server generally moves half the total number of rows in the original page to the new page. Therefore, the rows in the two pages are distributed as shown in Figure 13-6.

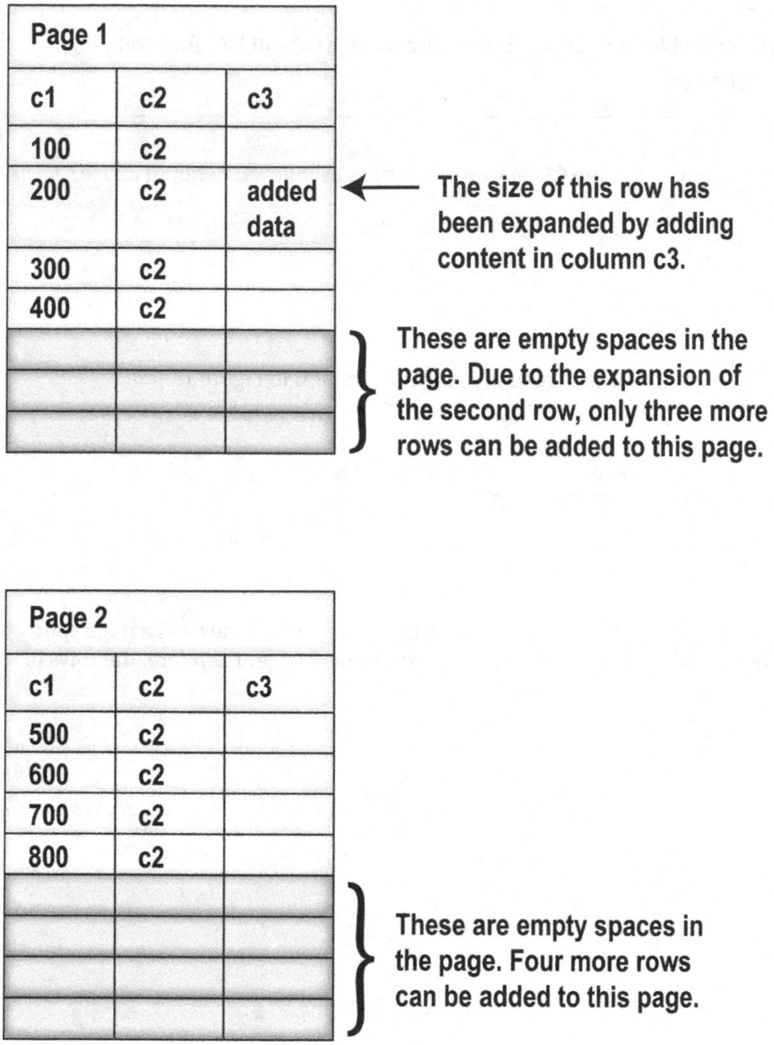

Page 1		
c1	c2	c3
100	c2	
200	c2	added data
300	c2	
400	c2	

← The size of this row has been expanded by adding content in column c3.

} These are empty spaces in the page. Due to the expansion of the second row, only three more rows can be added to this page.

Page 2		
c1	c2	c3
500	c2	
600	c2	
700	c2	
800	c2	

} These are empty spaces in the page. Four more rows can be added to this page.

Figure 13-6. Page split caused by an UPDATE statement

From the preceding tables, you can see that the page split caused by the UPDATE statement results in an internal fragmentation of data in the leaf pages. If the new leaf page can't be written physically next to the original leaf page, there will be external fragmentation as well. For a large table with a high amount of fragmentation, a larger number of leaf pages will be required to hold all the index rows.

Another way to look at the distribution of pages is to use some less thoroughly documented DBCC commands. First up, you can look at the pages in the table using DBCC IND.

```
DBCC IND(AdventureWorks2012,'dbo.Test1',-1)
```

This command lists the pages that make up a table. You get an output like Figure 13-7.

	PageFID	PagePID	IAMFID	IAMPID	ObjectID	IndexID	PartitionNumber	PartitionID	iam_chain_type	PageType
1	1	24257	NULL	NULL	68195293	1	1	72057594066567168	In-row data	10
2	1	24256	1	24257	68195293	1	1	72057594066567168	In-row data	1
3	1	24258	1	24257	68195293	1	1	72057594066567168	In-row data	2
4	1	24259	1	24257	68195293	1	1	72057594066567168	In-row data	1

Figure 13-7. Output from DBCC IND showing two pages

If you focus on the PageType, you can see that there are now two pages of PageType = 1, which is a data page. There are other columns in the output that also show how the pages are linked together.

To show the resultant distribution of rows shown in the previous pages, you can add a trailing row to each page:

```
INSERT  INTO dbo.Test1
VALUES  (410, 'C4', ''),
        (900, 'C4', '');
```

These new rows are accommodated in the existing two leaf pages without causing a page split. You can confirm this by querying the other mechanism for looking at page information, DBCC PAGE. To call this, you'll need to get the PagePID from the output of DBCC IND. This will enable you to pull back a full dump of everything on a page.

```
DBCC TRACEON(3604);
DBCC PAGE('AdventureWorks2012',1,24256,3);
```

The output from this is involved to interpret, but if you scroll down to the bottom, you can see the output, as shown in Figure 13-8.

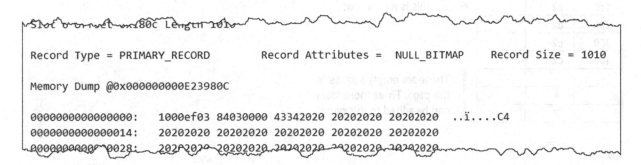

```
Slot 0 Offset 0x80C Length 1010

Record Type = PRIMARY_RECORD          Record Attributes = NULL_BITMAP      Record Size = 1010

Memory Dump @0x000000000E23980C

0000000000000000:    1000ef03 84030000 43342020 20202020 20202020  ..ï....C4
0000000000000014:    20202020 20202020 20202020 20202020 20202020
0000000000000028:    20202020 20202020 20202020 20202020 20202020
```

Figure 13-8. Pages after adding more rows

On the right side of the screen, you can see the output from the memory dump, a value, "C4." That was added by the foregoing data. Both rows were added to one page in my tests. Getting into a full explanation of all possible permutations of these two DBCC calls is far beyond the scope of this chapter. Know that you can determine which page data is stored on for any given table.

Page Split by an INSERT Statement

To understand how a page split can be caused by an INSERT statement, create the same test table as you did previously, with the eight initial rows and the clustered index. Since the single index leaf page is completely filled, any attempt to add an intermediate row as follows should cause a page split in the leaf page.

```
INSERT  INTO Test1
VALUES  (110, 'C2', '');
```

You can verify this by examining the output of sys.dm_db_index_physical_stats (Figure 13-9).

	avg_fragmentation_in_percent	fragment_count	page_count	avg_page_space_used_in_percent	record_count	avg_record_size_in_bytes
1	50	2	2	56.2391895231035	9	1010

Figure 13-9. *Pages after insert*

As explained previously, half the rows from the original leaf page are moved to the new page. Once space is cleared in the original leaf page, the new row is added in the appropriate order to the original leaf page. Be aware that a row is associated with only one page; it cannot span multiple pages. Figure 13-10 shows the resultant distribution of rows in the two pages.

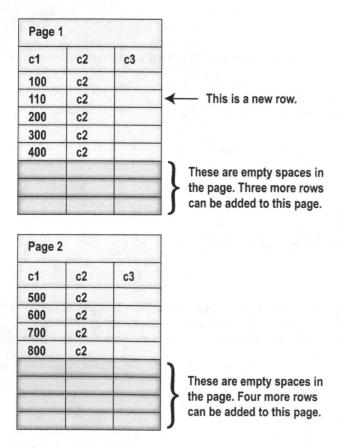

Figure 13-10. *Page split caused by an INSERT statement*

From the previous index pages, you can see that the page split caused by the INSERT statement spreads the rows sparsely across the leaf pages, causing internal fragmentation. It often causes external fragmentation also, since the new leaf page may not be physically adjacent to the original page. For a large table with a high amount of fragmentation, the page splits caused by the INSERT statement will require a larger number of leaf pages to accommodate all the index rows.

To demonstrate the row distribution shown in the index pages, you can run the script to create dbo.Test1 again, adding more rows to the pages:

```
INSERT  INTO dbo.Test1
VALUES  (410, 'C4', ''),
        (900, 'C4', '');
```

The result is the same as for the previous example: These new rows can be accommodated in the two existing leaf pages without causing any page split. You can validate that by calling DBCC IND and DBCC PAGE. Note that in the first page, new rows are added in between the other rows in the page. This won't cause a page split since free space is available in the page.

What about when you have to add rows to the trailing end of an index? In this case, even if a new page is required, it won't split any existing page. For example, adding a new row with C1 equal to 1,300 will require a new page, but it won't cause a page split since the row isn't added in an intermediate position. Therefore, if new rows are added in the order of the clustered index, then the index rows will be always added at the trailing end of the index, preventing the page splits otherwise caused by the INSERT statements.

Fragmentation caused by page splits hurts data retrieval performance, as you will see next.

Fragmentation Overhead

Both internal and external fragmentations adversely affect data retrieval performance. External fragmentation causes a noncontiguous sequence of index pages on the disk, with new leaf pages far from the original leaf pages and with their physical ordering different from their logical ordering. Consequently, a range scan on an index will need more switches between the corresponding extents than ideally required, as explained earlier in the chapter. Also, a range scan on an index will be unable to benefit from read-ahead operations performed on the disk. If the pages are arranged contiguously, then a read-ahead operation can read pages in advance without much head movement.

For better performance, it is preferable to use sequential I/O, since this can read a whole extent (eight 8KB pages together) in a single disk I/O operation. By contrast, a noncontiguous layout of pages requires nonsequential or random I/O operations to retrieve the index pages from the disk, and a random I/O operation can read only 8KB of data in a single disk operation (this may be acceptable, however, if you are retrieving only one row). The increasing speed of hard drives, especially SSDs, has reduced the impact of this issue, but it's still there.

In the case of internal fragmentation, rows are distributed sparsely across a large number of pages, increasing the number of disk I/O operations required to read the index pages into memory and increasing the number of logical reads required to retrieve multiple index rows from memory. As mentioned earlier, even though it increases the cost of data retrieval, a little internal fragmentation can be beneficial because it allows you to perform INSERT and UPDATE queries without causing page splits. For queries that don't have to traverse a series of pages to retrieve the data, fragmentation can have minimal impact. Put another way, retrieving a single value from the index won't be impacted by the fragmentation; or, at most, it might have an additional level in the B-Tree that it has to travel down.

To understand how fragmentation affects the cost of a query, create a test table with a clustered index and insert a highly fragmented data set in the table. Since an INSERT operation in between an ordered data set can cause a page split, you can easily create the fragmented data set by adding rows in the following order:

```
IF (SELECT  OBJECT_ID('Test1')
    ) IS NOT NULL
    DROP TABLE dbo.Test1;
GO
```

```
CREATE TABLE dbo.Test1
    (
    C1 INT,
    C2 INT,
    C3 INT,
    c4 CHAR(2000)
    );

CREATE CLUSTERED INDEX i1 ON dbo.Test1 (C1);

WITH    Nums
        AS (SELECT TOP (10000)
                    ROW_NUMBER() OVER (ORDER BY (SELECT 1
                                                )) AS n
            FROM        master.sys.All_Columns ac1
                        CROSS JOIN master.sys.All_Columns ac2
            )
    INSERT  INTO dbo.Test1
            (C1, C2, C3, c4)
            SELECT  n,
                    n,
                    n,
                    'a'
            FROM    Nums;

WITH    Nums
        AS (SELECT      1 AS n
            UNION ALL
            SELECT      n + 1
            FROM        Nums
            WHERE       n < 100
            )
    INSERT  INTO dbo.Test1
            (C1, C2, C3, c4)
            SELECT  41 - n,
                    n,
                    n,
                    'a'
            FROM    Nums;
```

To determine the number of logical reads required to retrieve a small result set and a large result set from this fragmented table, execute the two SELECT statements with STATISTICS IO and TIME set to ON:

```
--Reads 6 rows
SELECT  *
FROM    dbo.Test1
WHERE   C1 BETWEEN 21 AND 23;

--Reads all rows
SELECT  *
FROM    dbo.Test1
WHERE   C1 BETWEEN 1 AND 10000;
```

The number of logical reads performed by the individual queries is, respectively, as follows:

```
Table 'Test1'. Scan count 1, logical reads 8
CPU time = 0 ms,    elapsed time = 19 ms.
Table 'Test1'. Scan count 1, logical reads 2542
CPU time = 0 ms,    elapsed time = 317 ms.
```

To evaluate how the fragmented data set affects the number of logical reads, rearrange the index leaf pages physically by rebuilding the clustered index.

```
ALTER INDEX i1 ON dbo.Test1 REBUILD;
```

With the index leaf pages rearranged in the proper order, rerun --fragmentstats. The number of logical reads required by the preceding two SELECT statements reduces to 5 and 13, respectively.

```
Table 'Test1'. Scan count 1, logical reads 6
CPU time = 0 ms,    elapsed time = 15 ms.
Table 'Test1'. Scan count 1, logical reads 2536
CPU time = 0 ms,    elapsed time = 297 ms.
```

Performance improved for the smaller data set but didn't change much for the larger data set because just dropping a couple of pages isn't likely to have that big of an impact. The cost overhead because of fragmentation usually increases in line with the number of rows retrieved because this involves reading a greater number of out-of-order pages. For *point queries* (queries retrieving only one row), fragmentation doesn't usually matter, since the row is retrieved from one leaf page only, but this isn't always the case. Because of the internal structure of the index, fragmentation may increase the cost of even a point query.

■ **Note**   The lesson from this section is that, for better query performance, it is important to analyze the amount of fragmentation in an index and rearrange it if required.

Analyzing the Amount of Fragmentation

You can analyze the fragmentation ratio of an index by using the sys.dm_db_index_physical_ stats dynamic management function. For a table with a clustered index, the fragmentation of the clustered index is congruous with the fragmentation of the data pages since the leaf pages of the clustered index and data pages are the same. sys.dm_db_index_physical_stats also indicates the amount of fragmentation in a heap table (or a table with no clustered index). Since a heap table doesn't require any row ordering, the logical order of the pages isn't relevant for the heap table.

The output of sys.dm_db_index_physical_stats shows information on the pages and extents of an index (or a table). A row is returned for each level of the B-tree in the index. A single row for each allocation unit in a heap is returned. As explained earlier, in SQL Server, eight contiguous 8KB pages are grouped together in an extent that is 64KB in size. For small tables (much less than 64KB), the pages in an extent can belong to more than one index or table—these are called *mixed extents*. If there are lots of small tables in the database, mixed extents help SQL Server conserve disk space.

As a table (or an index) grows and requests more than eight pages, SQL Server creates an extent dedicated to the table (or index) and assigns the pages from this extent. Such an extent is called a *uniform extent,* and it serves up to eight page requests for the same table (or index). Uniform extents help SQL Server lay out the pages of a table (or an index) contiguously. They also reduce the number of page creation requests by an eighth, since a set of eight pages is created in the form of an extent. Information stored in a uniform extent can still be fragmented, but accessing an allocation of pages is going to be much more efficient. If you have mixed extents, you have pages shared between multiple objects, and you have fragmentation within those extents, accessing the information becomes even more problematic. But there is no defragmenting done on mixed extents.

To analyze the fragmentation of an index, let's re-create the table with the fragmented data set used in the "Fragmentation Overhead" section. You can obtain the fragmentation detail of the clustered index (Figure 13-11) by executing the query against the sys.dm_db_index_physical_stats dynamic view used earlier.

	avg_fragmentation_in_percent	fragment_count	page_count	avg_page_space_used_in_percent	record_count	avg_record_size_in_bytes
1	76.9230769230769	11	13	80.6599456387447	42	2019.38

Figure 13-11. *Fragmented statistics*

```
SELECT  ddips.avg_fragmentation_in_percent,
        ddips.fragment_count,
        ddips.page_count,
        ddips.avg_page_space_used_in_percent,
        ddips.record_count,
        ddips.avg_record_size_in_bytes
FROM    sys.dm_db_index_physical_stats(DB_ID('AdventureWorks2012'),
                                OBJECT_ID(N'dbo.Test1'),NULL,
                        NULL,'Sampled') AS ddips;
```

The dynamic management function sys.dm_db_index_physical_stats scans the pages of an index to return the data. You can control the level of the scan, which affects the speed and the accuracy of the scan. To quickly check the fragmentation of an index, use the Limited option. You can obtain an increased accuracy with only a moderate decrease in speed by using the Sample option, as in the previous example, which scans 1 percent of the pages. For the most accuracy, use the Detailed scan, which hits all the pages in an index. Just understand that the Detailed scan can have a major performance impact depending on the size of the table and index in question. If the index has fewer than 10,000 pages and you select the Sample mode, then the Detailed mode is used instead. This means that despite the choice made in the earlier query, the Detailed scan mode was used. The default mode is Limited.

By defining the different parameters, you can get fragmentation information on different sets of data. By removing the OBJECTID function in the earlier query and supplying a NULL value, the query would return information on all indexes within the database. Don't get surprised by this and accidentally run a Detailed scan on all indexes. You can also specify the index you want information on or even the partition with a partitioned index.

The output from sys.dm_db_index_physical_stats includes 21 different columns. I selected the basic set of columns used to determine the fragmentation and size of an index. This output represents the following:

- avg_fragmentation_in_percent: This number represents the logical average fragmentation for indexes and heaps as a percentage. If the table is a heap and the mode is Sampled, then this value will be NULL. If average fragmentation is less than 10 to 20 percent and the table isn't massive, fragmentation is unlikely to be an issue. If the index is between 20 and 40 percent, fragmentation might be an issue, but it can generally be helped by defragmenting the index through an index reorganization (more information on index reorganization and index rebuild is available in the "Fragmentation Resolutions" section). Large-scale fragmentation, usually greater than 40 percent, may require an index rebuild. Your system may have different requirements than these general numbers.

- fragment_count: This number represents the number of fragments, or separated groups of pages, that make up the index. It's a useful number to understand how the index is distributed, especially when compared to the pagecount value. fragmentcount is NULL when the sampling mode is Sampled. A large fragment count is an additional indication of storage fragmentation.

- page_count: This number is a literal count of the number of index or data pages that make up the statistic. This number is a measure of size but can also help indicate fragmentation. If you know the size of the data or index, you can calculate how many rows can fit on a page. If you then correlate this to the number of rows in the table, you should get a number close to the pagecount value. If the pagecount value is considerably higher, you may be looking at a fragmentation issue. Refer to the avg_fragmentation_in_percent value for a precise measure.

- avg_page_space_used_in_percent: To get an idea of the amount of space allocated within the pages of the index, use this number. This value is NULL when the sampling mode is Limited.

- recordcount: Simply put, this is the number of records represented by the statistics. For indexes, this is the number of records within the current level of the B-tree as represented from the scanning mode. (Detailed scans will show all levels of the B-tree, not simply the leaf level.) For heaps, this number represents the records present, but this number may not correlate precisely to the number of rows in the table since a heap may have two records after an update and a page split.

- avg_record_size_in_bytes: This number simply represents a useful measure for the amount of data stored within the index or heap record.

Running sys.dm_db_index_physical_stats with a Detailed scan will return multiple rows for a given index. That is, multiple rows are displayed if that index spans more than one level. Multiple levels exist in an index when that index spans more than a single page. To see what this looks like and to observe some of the other columns of data present in the dynamic management function, run the query this way:

```
SELECT  ddips.*
FROM    sys.dm_db_index_physical_stats(DB_ID('AdventureWorks2012'),
                                OBJECT_ID(N'dbo.Test1'),NULL,
                    NULL,'Detailed') AS ddips;
```

To make the data readable, I've broken down the resulting data table into three pieces in a single graphic; see Figure 13-12.

	database_id	object_id	index_id	partition_number	index_type_desc	alloc_unit_type_desc
1	5	212195806	1	1	CLUSTERED INDEX	IN_ROW_DATA
2	5	212195806	1	1	CLUSTERED INDEX	IN_ROW_DATA

index_depth	index_level	avg_fragmentation_in_percent	fragment_count	avg_fragment_size_in_pages	page_count
2	0	76.9230769230769	11	1.18181818181818	13
2	1	0	1	1	1

avg_page_space_used_in_percent	record_count	ghost_record_count	version_ghost_record_count	min_record_size_in_bytes
80.6599456387447	42	0	0	2019
2.50803063998023	13	0	0	11

max_record_size_in_bytes	avg_record_size_in_bytes	forwarded_record_count	compressed_page_count
2027	2019.38	NULL	0
14	13.769	NULL	0

Figure 13-12. *Detailed scan of fragmented index*

As you can see, two rows were returned, representing the leaf level of the index (index_ level = 0) and representing the first level of the B-tree (index_level = 1), which is the second row. You can see the additional information offered by sys.dm_db_index_physical_stats that can provide more detailed analysis of your indexes. For example, you can see the minimum and maximum record sizes, as well as the index depth (the number of levels in the B-tree) and how many records are on each level. A lot of this information will be less useful for basic fragmentation analysis, which is why I chose to limit the number of columns in the samples as well as use the Sampled scan mode.

Analyzing the Fragmentation of a Small Table

Don't be overly concerned with the output of sys.dm_db_index_physical_stats for small tables. For a small table or index with fewer than eight pages, SQL Server uses mixed extents for the pages. For example, if a table (SmallTable1 or its clustered index) contains only two pages, then SQL Server allocates the two pages from a mixed extent instead of dedicating an extent to the table. The mixed extent may contain pages of other small tables/indexes also, as shown in Figure 13-13.

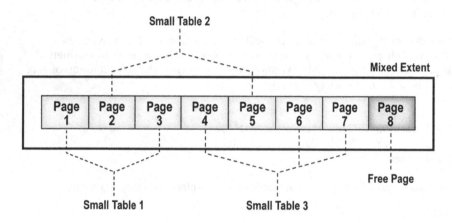

Figure 13-13. *Mixed extent*

The distribution of pages across multiple mixed extents may lead you to believe that there is a high amount of external fragmentation in the table or the index, when in fact this is by design in SQL Server and is therefore perfectly acceptable.

To understand how the fragmentation information of a small table or index may look, create a small table with a clustered index.

```
IF (SELECT  OBJECT_ID('dbo.Test1')
    ) IS NOT NULL
    DROP TABLE dbo.Test1;
GO

CREATE TABLE dbo.Test1
    (C1 INT,
     C2 INT,
     C3 INT,
     C4 CHAR(2000)
    );
```

```
DECLARE @n INT = 1;

WHILE @n <= 28
    BEGIN
        INSERT  INTO dbo.Test1
        VALUES  (@n, @n, @n, 'a');
        SET @n = @n + 1;
    END

CREATE CLUSTERED INDEX FirstIndex ON dbo.Test1(C1);
```

In the preceding table, with each INT taking 4 bytes, the average row size is 2,012 (=4 + 4 + 4 + 2,000) bytes. Therefore, a default 8KB page can contain up to four rows. After all 28 rows are added to the table, a clustered index is created to physically arrange the rows and reduce fragmentation to a minimum. With the minimum internal fragmentation, seven (=28 / 4) pages are required for the clustered index (or the base table). Since the number of pages is not more than eight, SQL Server uses pages from mixed extents for the clustered index (or the base table). If the mixed extents used for the clustered index are not side by side, then the output of sys.dm_db_index_physical_stats may express a high amount of external fragmentation. But as a SQL user, you can't reduce the resultant external fragmentation. Figure 13-14 shows the output of sys.dm_db_index_physical_stats.

	avg_fragmentation_in_percent	fragment_count	page_count	avg_page_space_used_in_percent	record_count	avg_record_size_in_bytes
1	42.8571428571429	5	7	99.8517420311342	28	2019

Figure 13-14. Fragmentation of a small clustered index

From the output of sys.dm_db_index_physical_stats, you can analyze the fragmentation of the small clustered index (or the table) as follows:

- avg_fragmentation_in_percent: Although this index may cross to multiple extents, the fragmentation shown here is not an indication of external fragmentation because this index is being stored on mixed extents.

- Avg_page_space_used_in_percent: This shows that all or most of the data is stored well within the seven pages displayed in the pagecount field. This eliminates the possibility of logical fragmentation.

- Fragment_count: This shows that the data is fragmented and stored on more than one extent, but since it's less than eight pages long, SQL Server doesn't have much choice about where it stores the data.

In spite of the preceding misleading values, a small table (or index) with fewer than eight pages is simply unlikely to benefit from efforts to remove the fragmentation because it will be stored on mixed extents.

Once you determine that fragmentation in an index (or a table) needs to be dealt with, you need to decide which defragmentation technique to use. The factors affecting this decision, and the different techniques, are explained in the following section.

Fragmentation Resolutions

You can resolve fragmentation in an index by rearranging the index rows and pages so that their physical and logical orders match. To reduce external fragmentation, you can physically reorder the leaf pages of the index to follow the logical order of the index. You achieve this through the following techniques:

- Dropping and re-creating the index
- Re-creating the index with the DROP_EXISTING = ON clause
- Executing the ALTER INDEX REBUILD statement on the index
- Executing the ALTER INDEX REORGANIZE statement on the index

Dropping and Re-creating the Index

One of the apparently easiest ways to remove fragmentation in an index is to drop the index and then re-create it. Dropping and re-creating the index reduces fragmentation the most since it allows SQL Server to use completely new pages for the index and populate them appropriately with the existing data. This avoids both internal and external fragmentation. Unfortunately, this method has a large number of serious shortcomings.

- *Blocking*: This technique of defragmentation adds a high amount of overhead on the system, and it causes blocking. Dropping and re-creating the index blocks all other requests on the table (or on any other index on the table). It can also be blocked by other requests against the table.

- *Missing index*: With the index dropped, and possibly being blocked and waiting to be re-created, queries against the table will not have the index available for use. This can lead to the poor performance that the index was intended to remedy.

- *Nonclustered indexes*: If the index being dropped is a clustered index, then all the nonclustered indexes on the table have to be rebuilt after the cluster is dropped. They then have to be rebuilt again after the cluster is re-created. This leads to further blocking and other problems such as statement recompiles (covered in detail in Chapter 17).

- *Unique constraints*: Indexes that are used to define a primary key or a unique constraint cannot be removed using the DROP INDEX statement. Also, both unique constraints and primary keys can be referred to by foreign key constraints. Prior to dropping the primary key, all foreign keys that reference the primary key would have to be removed first. Although this is possible, this is a risky and time-consuming method for defragmenting an index.

It is possible to use the ONLINE option for dropping a clustered index, which means the index is still readable while it is being dropped, but that saves you only from the foregoing blocking issue. For all these reasons, dropping and re-creating the index is not a recommended technique for a production database, especially at anything outside off-peak times.

Re-creating the Index with the DROP_EXISTING Clause

To avoid the overhead of rebuilding the nonclustered indexes twice while rebuilding a clustered index, use the DROPEXISTING clause of the CREATE INDEX statement. This re-creates the clustered index in one atomic step, avoiding re-creating the nonclustered indexes since the clustered index key values used by the row locators remain the same. To rebuild a clustered key in one atomic step using the DROP_EXISTING clause, execute the CREATE INDEX statement as follows:

```
CREATE UNIQUE CLUSTERED INDEX FirstIndex
ON dbo.Test1(C1)
WITH (DROP_EXISTING = ON);
```

You can use the DROP_EXISTING clause for both clustered and nonclustered indexes, and even to convert a nonclustered index to a clustered index. However, you can't use it to convert a clustered index to a nonclustered index. The drawbacks of this defragmentation technique are as follows:

- *Blocking*: Similar to the DROP and CREATE methods, this technique also causes and faces blocking from other queries accessing the table (or any index on the table).

- *Index with constraints*: Unlike the first method, the CREATE INDEX statement with DROP_EXISTING can be used to re-create indexes with constraints. If the constraint is a primary key or the unique constraint is associated with a foreign key, then failing to include the UNIQUE keyword in the CREATE statement will result in an error like this:

■ **Note**   Msg 1907, Level 16, State 1, Line 1 Cannot recreate index 'PK_Name'. The new index definition does not match the constraint being enforced by the existing index.

- *Table with multiple fragmented indexes*: As table data fragments, the indexes often become fragmented as well. If this defragmentation technique is used, then all the indexes on the table have to be identified and rebuilt individually.

You can avoid the last two limitations associated with this technique by using ALTER INDEX REBUILD, as explained next.

Executing the ALTER INDEX REBUILD Statement

ALTER INDEX REBUILD rebuilds an index in one atomic step, just like CREATE INDEX with the DROP_EXISTING clause. Since ALTER INDEX REBUILD also rebuilds the index physically, it allows SQL Server to assign fresh pages to reduce both internal and external fragmentation to a minimum. But unlike CREATE INDEX with the DROP_EXISTING clause, it allows an index (supporting either the PRIMARY KEY or UNIQUE constraint) to be rebuilt dynamically without dropping and re-creating the constraints.

To understand the use of ALTER INDEX REBUILD to defragment an index, consider the fragmented table used in the "Fragmentation Overhead" and "Analyzing the Amount of Fragmentation" sections. This table is repeated here:

```
IF (SELECT  OBJECT_ID('Test1')
    ) IS NOT NULL
    DROP TABLE dbo.Test1 ;
GO
CREATE TABLE dbo.Test1
    (C1 INT,
     C2 INT,
     C3 INT,
     c4 CHAR(2000)
    ) ;

CREATE CLUSTERED INDEX i1 ON dbo.Test1 (C1) ;

WITH    Nums
        AS (SELECT      1 AS n
            UNION ALL
            SELECT      n + 1
```

```
            FROM      Nums
            WHERE     n < 21
            )
INSERT  INTO dbo.Test1
        (C1, C2, C3, c4)
        SELECT  n,
                n,
                n,
                'a'
        FROM    Nums ;

WITH    Nums
        AS (SELECT     1 AS n
            UNION ALL
            SELECT    n + 1
            FROM      Nums
            WHERE     n < 21
            )
INSERT  INTO dbo.Test1
        (C1, C2, C3, c4)
        SELECT  41 - n,
                n,
                n,
                'a'
        FROM    Nums;
```

If you take a look at the current fragmentation, you can see that it is both internally and externally fragmented (Figure 13-15).

	avg_fragmentation_in_percent	fragment_count	page_count	avg_page_space_used_in_percent	record_count	avg_record_size_in_bytes
1	76.9230769230769	11	13	80.6599456387447	42	2019.38

Figure 13-15. *Internal and external fragmentation*

You can defragment the clustered index (or the table) by using the ALTER INDEX REBUILD statement.

```
ALTER INDEX i1 ON dbo.Test1 REBUILD;
```

Figure 13-16 shows the resultant output of the standard SELECT statement against sys.dm_db_index_physical_stats.

	avg_fragmentation_in_percent	fragment_count	page_count	avg_page_space_used_in_percent	record_count	avg_record_size_in_bytes
1	36.3636363636364	6	11	95.3298739807265	42	2019.38

Figure 13-16. *Fragmentation resolved by ALTER INDEX REBUILD*

Compare the preceding results of the query in Figure 13-16 with the earlier results in Figure 13-15. You can see that both internal and external fragmentation have been reduced efficiently. Here's an analysis of the output:

- *Internal fragmentation*: The table has 42 rows with an average row size (2,019.38 bytes) that allows a maximum of four rows per page. If the rows are highly defragmented to reduce the internal fragmentation to a minimum, then there should be 11 data pages in the table (or leaf pages in the clustered index). You can observe the following in the preceding output:

  - *Number of leaf (or data) pages*: pagecount = 11

  - *Amount of information in a page*: avg_page_space_used_in_percent = 95.33 percent

- *External fragmentation*: A minimum of two extents is required to hold the 11 pages. For a minimum of external fragmentation, there should not be any gap between the two extents, and all pages should be physically arranged in the logical order of the index. The preceding output illustrates the number of out-of-order pages = avg_ fragmentation_in_percent = 36.6 percent. Although this may not be a perfect level of fragmentation, being greater than 20 percent, this is adequate considering the size of the index. With fewer extents, aligned with each other, access will be faster.

Rebuilding an index in SQL Server 2005 and greater will also compact the large object (LOB) pages. You can choose not to by setting a value LOB_COMPACTION = OFF. If you aren't worried about storage but you are concerned about how long your index reorganization is taking, this might be advisable to turn off.

When you use the PAD_INDEX setting while creating an index, it determines how much free space to leave on the index intermediate pages, which can help you deal with page splits. This is taken into account during the index rebuild, and the new pages will be set back to the original values you determined at the index creation unless you specify otherwise. I've almost never seen this make a major difference on most systems. You'll need to test on your system to determine whether it can help.

If you don't specify otherwise, the default behavior is to defragment all indexes across all partitions. If you want to control the process, you just need to specify which partition you want to rebuild when.

As shown previously, the ALTER INDEX REBUILD technique effectively reduces fragmentation. You can also use it to rebuild *all* the indexes of a table in one statement.

```
ALTER INDEX ALL ON dbo.Test1 REBUILD;
```

Although this is the most effective defragmentation technique, it does have some overhead and limitations:

- *Blocking*: Similar to the previous two index-rebuilding techniques, ALTER INDEX REBUILD introduces blocking in the system. It blocks all other queries trying to access the table (or any index on the table). It can also be blocked by those queries.

- *Transaction rollback*: Since ALTER INDEX REBUILD is fully atomic in action, if it is stopped before completion, then all the defragmentation actions performed up to that time are lost. You can run ALTER INDEX REBUILD using the ONLINE keyword, which will reduce the locking mechanisms, but it will increase the time involved in rebuilding the index.

Executing the ALTER INDEX REORGANIZE Statement

ALTER INDEX REORGANIZE reduces the fragmentation of an index without rebuilding the index. It reduces external fragmentation by rearranging the existing leaf pages of the index in the logical order of the index key. It compacts the rows within the pages, reducing internal fragmentation, and discards the resultant empty pages. This technique doesn't use any new pages for defragmentation.

To avoid the blocking overhead associated with ALTER INDEX REBUILD, this technique uses a nonatomic online approach. As it proceeds through its steps, it requests a small number of locks for a short period. Once each step is done, it releases the locks and proceeds to the next step. While trying to access a page, if it finds that the page is being used, it skips that page and never returns to the page again. This allows other queries to run on the table along with the `ALTER INDEX REORGANIZE` operation. Also, if this operation is stopped intermediately, then all the defragmentation steps performed up to then are preserved.

Since `ALTER INDEX REORGANIZE` doesn't use any new pages to reorder the index and it skips the locked pages, the amount of defragmentation provided by this approach is usually less than that of `ALTER INDEX REBUILD`. To observe the relative effectiveness of `ALTER INDEX REORGANIZE` compared to `ALTER INDEX REBUILD`, rebuild the test table used in the previous section on `ALTER INDEX REBUILD`.

Now, to reduce the fragmentation of the clustered index, use `ALTER INDEX REORGANIZE` as follows:

```
ALTER INDEX i1 ON dbo.Test1 REORGANIZE;
```

Figure 13-17 shows the resultant output from `sys.dm_db_index_physical_stats`.

	avg_fragmentation_in_percent	fragment_count	page_count	avg_page_space_used_in_percent	record_count	avg_record_size_in_bytes
1	45.4545454545455	7	11	95.3298739807265	42	2019.38

Figure 13-17. *Results of ALTER INDEX REORGANIZE*

From the output, you can see that `ALTER INDEX REORGANIZE` doesn't reduce fragmentation as effectively as `ALTER INDEX REBUILD`, as shown in the previous section. For a highly fragmented index, the `ALTER INDEX REORGANIZE` operation can take much longer than rebuilding the index. Also, if an index spans multiple files, `ALTER INDEX REORGANIZE` doesn't migrate pages between the files. However, the main benefit of using `ALTER INDEX REORGANIZE` is that it allows other queries to access the table (or the indexes) simultaneously.

Table 13-1 summarizes the characteristics of these four defragmentation techniques.

Table 13-1. *Characteristics of Defragmentation Techniques*

Characteristics/Issues	Drop and Create Index	Create Index with DROP_ EXISTING	ALTER INDEX REBUILD	ALTER INDEX REORGANIZE
Rebuild nonclustered indexes on clustered index fragmentation	Twice	No	No	No
Missing indexes	Yes	No	No	No
Defragment index with constraints	Highly complex	Moderately complex	Easy	Easy
Defragment multiple indexes together	No	No	Yes	Yes
Concurrency with others	Low	Low	Medium, depending on concurrent user activity	High
Intermediate cancellation	Dangerous with no transaction	Progress lost	Progress lost	Progress preserved
Degree of defragmentation	High	High	High	Moderate to low
Apply new fill factor	Yes	Yes	Yes	No
Statistics are updated	Yes	Yes	Yes	No

You can also reduce internal fragmentation by compressing more rows within a page, reducing free spaces within the pages. The maximum amount of compression that can be done within the leaf pages of an index is controlled by the fill factor, as you will see next.

When dealing with large databases and the indexes associated, it may become necessary to split up the tables and the indexes across disks using partitioning. Indexes on partitions can also become fragmented as the data within the partition changes. When dealing with a portioned index, you will need to determine whether you want to either REORGANIZE or REBUILD one, some, or all partitions as part of the ALTER INDEX command. Partitioned indexes cannot be rebuilt online. Keep in mind that doing anything that affects all partitions is likely to be a costly operation.

If compression is specified on an index, even on a partitioned index, you must be sure to set the compression while performing the ALTER INDEX operation to what it was before; if you don't, it will be lost, and you'll have to rebuild the index again. This is especially important for nonclustered indexes, which will not inherit the compression setting from the table.

Defragmentation and Partitions

If you have massive databases, a standard mechanism for effectively managing the data is to break it up into partitions. While partitions can, in some rare cases, help with performance, they are first and foremost for managing data. But, one of the issues with indexes and partitions is that if you rebuild the index, it's unavailable during the rebuild. This means that with partitions, which are on massive indexes, you can expect to have a major portion of your data offline during the rebuild. SQL Server 2012 introduced the ability to do an online rebuild. If you had a partitioned index, it would look like this:

```
ALTER INDEX i1 ON dbo.Test1
REBUILD PARTITION = ALL
WITH (ONLINE = ON);
```

This can rebuild the entire partition and do it as an online operation, meaning it keeps the index largely available while it does the rebuild. But, for some partitions, this is a massive undertaking that will probably result in excessive load on the server and the need for a lot more tempdb storage. SQL Server 2014 introduced new functionality that lets you designate individual partitions.

```
ALTER INDEX i1 ON dbo.Test1
REBUILD PARTITION = 1
WITH (ONLINE = ON);
```

This reduces the overhead of the rebuild operation while still keeping the index mostly available during the rebuild. I do emphasize that it is "mostly" online because there is still some degree of locking and contention that will occur during the rebuild. It's not a completely free operation. It's just radically improved over the alternative.

Talking about the locking involved with index rebuild operations in partitions, you also have one other new piece of functionality introduced in SQL Server 2014. You can now modify the lock priority used during the rebuild operation by again adjusting the REBUILD command.

```
ALTER INDEX i1 ON dbo.Test1
REBUILD P ARTITION = 1
WITH (ONLINE = ON(WAIT_AT_LOW_PRIORITY(MAXDURATION=20,ABORT_AFTER_WAIT=SELF)));
```

What this does is set the duration that the rebuild operation is willing to wait, in minutes. Then, it allows you to determine which processes get aborted in order to clear the system for the index rebuild. You can have it stop itself or the blocking process. The most interesting thing is that the waiting process is set to low priority, so it's not using a lot of system resources, and any transactions that come in won't be blocked by this process.

Between these two new pieces of functionality, the management of indexes in partitions is much easier with SQL Server 2014.

Significance of the Fill Factor

The internal fragmentation of an index is reduced by getting more rows per leaf page in an index. Getting more rows within a leaf page reduces the total number of pages required for the index and in turn decreases disk I/O and the logical reads required to retrieve a range of index rows. On the other hand, if the index key values are highly transactional, then having fully used index pages will cause page splits. Therefore, for a transactional table, a good balance between maximizing the number of rows in a page and avoiding page splits is required.

SQL Server allows you to control the amount of free space within the leaf pages of the index by using the *fill factor*. If you know that there will be enough INSERT queries on the table or UPDATE queries on the index key columns, then you can pre-add free space to the index leaf page using the fill factor to minimize page splits. If the table is read-only, you can create the index with a high fill factor to reduce the number of index pages.

The default fill factor is 0, which means the leaf pages are packed to 100 percent, although some free space is left in the branch nodes of the B-tree structure. The fill factor for an index is applied only when the index is created. As keys are inserted and updated, the density of rows in the index eventually stabilizes within a narrow range. As you saw in the previous chapter's sections on page splits caused by UPDATE and INSERT, when a page split occurs, generally half the original page is moved to a new page, which happens irrespective of the fill factor used during the index creation.

To understand the significance of the fill factor, let's use a small test table with 24 rows.

```
IF (SELECT  OBJECT_ID('dbo.Test1')
    ) IS NOT NULL
    DROP TABLE dbo.Test1;
GO
CREATE TABLE dbo.Test1 (C1 INT, C2 CHAR(999)) ;

WITH    Nums
        AS (SELECT    1 AS n
            UNION ALL
            SELECT    n + 1
            FROM      Nums
            WHERE     n < 24
            )
    INSERT  INTO dbo.Test1
            (C1, C2)
            SELECT  n * 100,
                    'a'
            FROM    Nums ;
```

Increase the maximum number of rows in the leaf (or data) page by creating a clustered index with the default fill factor.

```
CREATE CLUSTERED INDEX FillIndex ON Test1(C1);
```

Since the average row size is 1,010 bytes, a clustered index leaf page (or table data page) can contain a maximum of eight rows. Therefore, at least three leaf pages are required for the 24 rows. You can confirm this in the sys.dm_db_index_physical_stats output shown in Figure 13-18.

	avg_fragmentation_in_percent	fragment_count	page_count	avg_page_space_used_in_percent	record_count	avg_record_size_in_bytes
1	66.6666666666667	3	3	100	24	1010

Figure 13-18. *Fill factor set to default value of 0*

Note that `avg_page_space_used_in_percent` is 100 percent, since the default fill factor allows the maximum number of rows to be compressed in a page. Since a page cannot contain a part row to fill the page fully, `avg_page_space_used_in_percent` will be often a little less than 100 percent, even with the default fill factor.

To reduce the initial frequency of page splits caused by INSERT and UPDATE operations, create some free space within the leaf (or data) pages by re-creating the clustered index with a fill factor as follows:

```
ALTER INDEX FillIndex ON dbo.Test1 REBUILD
WITH  (FILLFACTOR= 75);
```

Because each page has a total space for eight rows, a fill factor of 75 percent will allow six rows per page. Thus, for 24 rows, the number of leaf pages should increase to four, as in the `sys.dm_db_index_physical_stats` output shown in Figure 13-19.

	avg_fragmentation_in_percent	fragment_count	page_count	avg_page_space_used_in_percent	record_count	avg_record_size_in_bytes
1	50	3	4	74.9938225846306	24	1010

Figure 13-19. Fill factor set to 75

Note that `avg_page_space_used_in_percent` is about 75 percent, as set by the fill factor. This allows two more rows to be inserted in each page without causing a page split. You can confirm this by adding two rows to the first set of six rows (C1 = 100 - 600, contained in the first page).

```
INSERT  INTO dbo.Test1
VALUES  (110, 'a'),  --25th row
        (120, 'a') ;  --26th row
```

Figure 13-20 shows the current fragmentation.

	avg_fragmentation_in_percent	fragment_count	page_count	avg_page_space_used_in_percent	record_count	avg_record_size_in_bytes
1	50	3	4	81.2453669384729	26	1010

Figure 13-20. Fragmentation after new records

From the output, you can see that the addition of the two rows has not added any pages to the index. Accordingly, `avg_page_space_used_in_percent` increased from 74.99 percent to 81.25 percent. With the addition of two rows to the set of the first six rows, the first page should be completely full (eight rows). Any further addition of rows within the range of the first eight rows should cause a page split and thereby increase the number of index pages to five.

```
INSERT  INTO dbo.Test1
VALUES  (130, 'a') ;  --27th row
```

Now `sys.dm_db_index_physical_stats` displays the difference in Figure 13-21.

	avg_fragmentation_in_percent	fragment_count	page_count	avg_page_space_used_in_percent	record_count	avg_record_size_in_bytes
1	60	4	5	67.4919693600198	27	1010

Figure 13-21. Number of pages goes up

Note that even though the fill factor for the index is 75 percent, `Avg. Page Density (full)` has decreased to 67.49 percent, which can be computed as follows:

```
Avg. Page Density (full)
= Average rows per page / Maximum rows per page
= (27 / 5) / 8
= 67.5%
```

From the preceding example, you can see that the fill factor is applied when the index is created. But later, as the data is modified, it has no significance. Irrespective of the fill factor, whenever a page splits, the rows of the original page are distributed between two pages, and `avg_page_space_used_in_percent` settles accordingly. Therefore, if you use a nondefault fill factor, you should ensure that the fill factor is reapplied regularly to maintain its effect.

You can reapply a fill factor by re-creating the index or by using `ALTER INDEX REORGANIZE` or `ALTER INDEX REBUILD`, as was shown. `ALTER INDEX REORGANIZE` takes the fill factor specified during the index creation into account. `ALTER INDEX REBUILD` also takes the original fill factor into account, but it allows a new fill factor to be specified, if required.

Without periodic maintenance of the fill factor, for both default and nondefault fill factor settings, `avg_page_space_used_in_percent` for an index (or a table) eventually settles within a narrow range. Therefore, in most cases, without manual maintenance of the fill factor, the default fill factor is generally good enough.

You should also consider one final aspect when deciding upon the fill factor. Even for a heavy OLTP application, the number of database reads typically outnumbers writes by a factor of 5 to 10. Specifying a fill factor other than the default can degrade read performance by an amount inversely proportional to the fill factor setting, since it spreads keys over a wider area. Before setting the fill factor at a database-wide level, use Performance Monitor to compare the `SOL Server:Buffer Manager:Page reads/sec` counter to the `SOL Server:Buffer Manager:Page writes/sec` counter, and use the fill factor option only if writes are a substantial fraction of reads (greater than 30 percent). Further, the optimizer takes the number of pages into account in the choices it makes when constructing the execution plan. If you have a larger number of pages, you may see some poor choices in plans causing some bad performance.

Automatic Maintenance

In a database with a great deal of transactions, tables and indexes become fragmented over time. Thus, to improve performance, you should check the fragmentation of the tables and indexes regularly, and you should defragment the ones with a high amount of fragmentation. You also may need to take into account the workload and defragment indexes as dictated by the load as well as the fragmentation level of the index. You can do this analysis for a database by following these steps:

1. Identify all user tables in the current database to analyze fragmentation.

2. Determine fragmentation of every user table and index.

3. Determine user tables and indexes that require defragmentation by taking into account the following considerations:

   - A high level of fragmentation where `avg_fragmentation_in_percent` is greater than 20 percent

   - Not a very small table/index—that is, `pagecount` is greater than 8

4. Defragment tables and indexes with high fragmentation.

A sample SQL stored procedure is included here for easy reference. This script will perform the basic actions, and I include it here for educational purposes. But for a fully functional script that includes a large degree of capability, I strongly recommend using the script from Michelle Ufford located here: `http://bit.ly/1cjmzXv`. Another set of scripts that are popular are Ola Hollengren's scripts at `http://bit.ly/JijaNI`.

My script performs the following actions:

- Walks all databases on the system and identifies indexes on user tables in each database that meets the fragmentation criteria and saves them in a temporary table

- Based on the level of fragmentation, reorganizes lightly fragmented indexes and rebuilds those that are highly fragmented

Here's how to analyze and resolve database fragmentation (store this where appropriate on your system; I have a designated database for enterprise-level scripts):

```
CREATE PROCEDURE IndexDefrag
AS
DECLARE @DBName NVARCHAR(255),
    @TableName NVARCHAR(255),
    @SchemaName NVARCHAR(255),
    @IndexName NVARCHAR(255),
    @PctFrag DECIMAL,
    @Defrag NVARCHAR(MAX)

IF EXISTS ( SELECT   *
            FROM     sys.objects
            WHERE    object_id = OBJECT_ID(N'#Frag') )
    DROP TABLE #Frag;
CREATE TABLE #Frag (
DBName NVARCHAR(255),
TableName NVARCHAR(255),
SchemaName NVARCHAR(255),
IndexName NVARCHAR(255),
AvgFragment DECIMAL)
EXEC sys.sp_MSforeachdb 'INSERT INTO #Frag ( DBName, TableName, SchemaName, IndexName, AvgFragment )
SELECT    ''?''  AS DBName ,t.Name AS TableName ,sc.Name AS SchemaName ,i.name AS IndexName ,s.avg_
fragmentation_in_percent FROM          ?.sys.dm_db_index_physical_stats(DB_ID(''?''), NULL, NULL,
NULL,   ''Sampled'') AS s JOIN ?.sys.indexes i ON s.Object_Id = i.Object_id
AND s.Index_id = i.Index_id JOIN ?.sys.tables t ON i.Object_id = t.Object_Id JOIN ?.sys.schemas sc
ON t.schema_id = sc.SCHEMA_ID

WHERE s.avg_fragmentation_in_percent > 20
AND t.TYPE = ''U''
AND s.page_count > 8
ORDER BY TableName,IndexName';

DECLARE cList CURSOR
FOR
SELECT  *
FROM    #Frag

OPEN cList;
FETCH NEXT FROM cList
INTO @DBName,@TableName,@SchemaName,@IndexName,@PctFrag;
```

```
WHILE @@FETCH_STATUS = 0
    BEGIN
        IF @PctFrag BETWEEN 20.0 AND 40.0
            BEGIN
                SET @Defrag = N'ALTER INDEX ' + @IndexName + ' ON ' + @DBName
                    + '.' + @SchemaName + '.' + @TableName + ' REORGANIZE';
                EXEC sp_executesql @Defrag;
                PRINT 'Reorganize index: ' + @DBName + '.' + @SchemaName + '.'
                    + @TableName + '.' + @IndexName;
            END
        ELSE
            IF @PctFrag > 40.0
                BEGIN
                    SET @Defrag = N'ALTER INDEX ' + @IndexName + ' ON '
                        + @DBName + '.' + @SchemaName + '.' + @TableName
                        + ' REBUILD';
                    EXEC sp_executesql @Defrag;
                    PRINT 'Rebuild index: ' + @DBName + '.' + @SchemaName
                        + '.' + @TableName + '.' + @IndexName;
                END
        FETCH NEXT FROM cList
INTO @DBName,@TableName,@SchemaName,@IndexName,@PctFrag;
    END
CLOSE cList;
DEALLOCATE cList;
DROP TABLE #Frag;
GO
```

To automate the fragmentation analysis process, you can create a SQL Server job from SQL Server Enterprise Manager by following these simple steps:

1. Open Management Studio, right-click the SQL Server Agent icon, and select New ➤ Job.

2. On the General page of the New Job dialog box, enter the job name and other details, as shown in Figure 13-22.

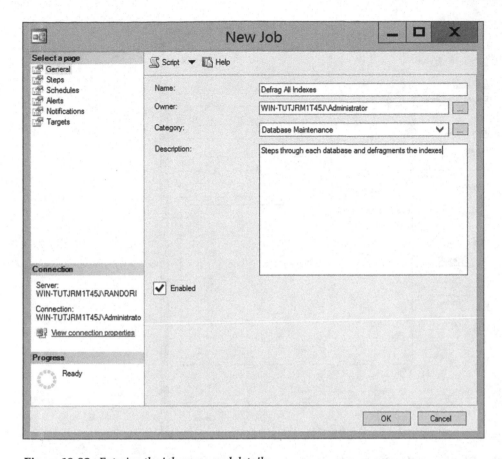

Figure 13-22. *Entering the job name and details*

3. On the Steps page of the New Job dialog box, click New, and enter the SQL command for the user database, as shown in Figure 13-23.

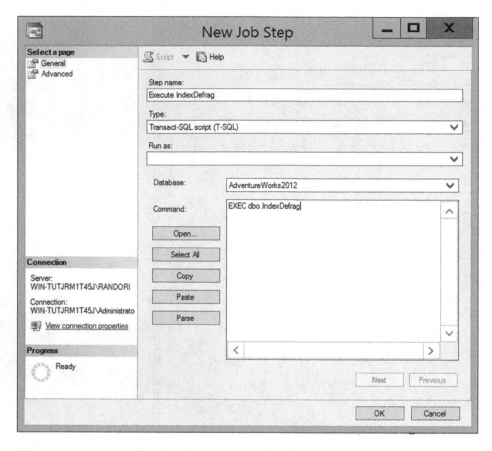

Figure 13-23. *Entering the SQL command for the user database*

4. On the Advanced page of the New Job Step dialog box, enter an output file name to report the fragmentation analysis outcome, as shown in Figure 13-24.

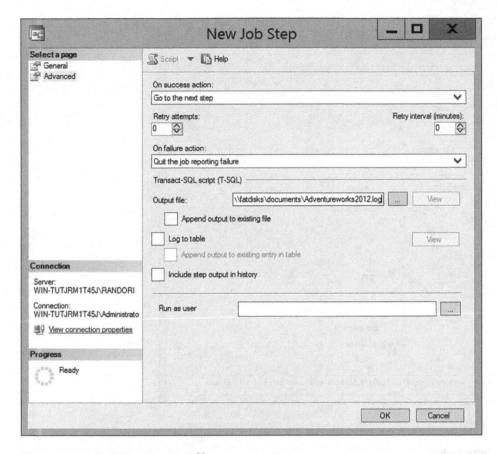

Figure 13-24. *Entering an output file name*

5. Return to the New Job dialog box by clicking OK.

6. On the Schedules page of the New Job dialog box, click New Schedule, and enter an appropriate schedule to run the SQL Server job, as shown in Figure 13-25.

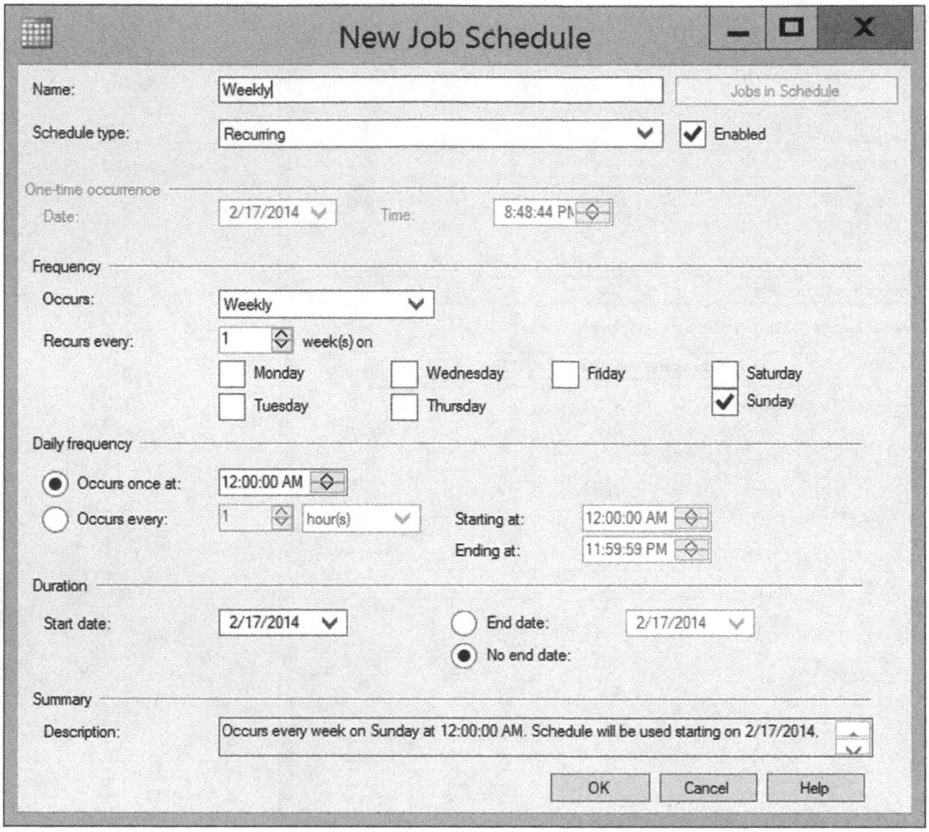

Figure 13-25. *Entering a job schedule*

Schedule this stored procedure to execute during nonpeak hours. To be certain about the usage pattern of your database, log the SQLServer:SOL Statistics\Batch Requests/ sec performance counter for a complete day. It will show you the fluctuation in load on the database. (I explain this performance counter in detail in Chapter 2.)

7. Return to the New Job dialog box by clicking the OK button.

8. Once you've entered all the information, click OK in the New Job dialog box to create the SQL Server job. A SQL Server job is created that schedules the spIndexDefrag stored procedure to run at a regular (weekly) time interval.

9. Ensure that SQL Server Agent is running so that the SQL Server job will run automatically according to the set schedule.

The SQL job will automatically analyze and defragment the fragmentation of each database every Sunday at 1 a.m. Figure 13-26 shows the corresponding output of the FragmentationOutput.txt file.

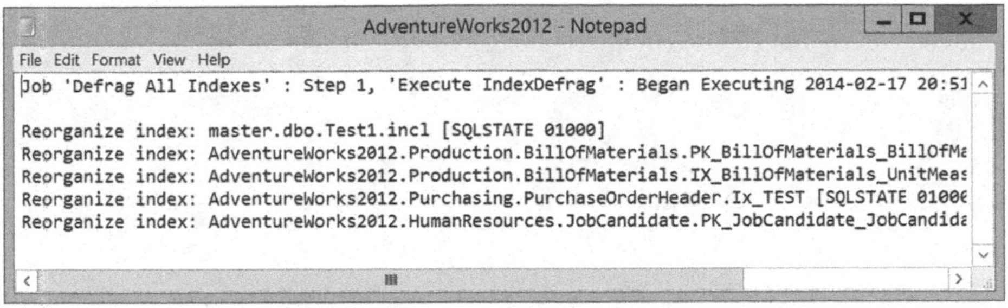

Figure 13-26. FragmentationOutput.txt file output

The output shows that the job analyzed the fragmentation of the database and identified a series of indexes for defragmentation, specifically for reorganization. Subsequently, it defragments the index. The stored procedure defragmented only the database object that was highly fragmented. Thus, the next run of the SQL job generally won't identify these same indexes for defragmentation.

In addition to this script, Michelle's script, or Ola's scripts, you can use the maintenance plans built into SQL Server. However, I don't recommend them because you surrender a lot of control for a little bit of ease of use. You'll be much happier with the results you get from one of the sets of scripts recommended earlier.

Summary

As you learned in this chapter, in a highly transactional database, page splits caused by INSERT and UPDATE statements fragment the tables and indexes, increasing the cost of data retrieval. You can avoid these page splits by maintaining free spaces within the pages using the fill factor. Since the fill factor is applied only during index creation, you should reapply it at regular intervals to maintain its effectiveness. You can determine the amount of fragmentation in an index (or a table) using sys.dm_db_index_physical_stats. Upon determining a high amount of fragmentation, you can use either ALTER INDEX REBUILD or ALTER INDEX REORGANIZE, depending on the required amount of defragmentation and database concurrency.

Defragmentation rearranges the data so that its physical order on the disk matches its logical order in the table/index, thus improving the performance of queries. However, unless the optimizer decides upon an effective execution plan for the query, query performance even after defragmentation can remain poor. Therefore, it is important to have the optimizer use efficient techniques to generate cost-effective execution plans.

In the next chapter, I explain execution plan generation and the techniques the optimizer uses to decide upon an effective execution plan.

CHAPTER 14

■ ■ ■

Execution Plan Generation

The performance of any query depends on the effectiveness of the execution plan decided upon by the optimizer, as you learned in previous chapters. Because the overall time required to execute a query is the sum of the time required to generate the execution plan plus the time required to execute the query based on this execution plan, it is important that the cost of generating the execution plan itself is low. The cost incurred when generating the execution plan depends on the process of generating the execution plan, the process of caching the plan, and the reusability of the plan from the plan cache. In this chapter, you will learn how an execution plan is generated.

In this chapter, I cover the following topics:

- Execution plan generation and caching

- The SQL Server components used to generate an execution plan

- Strategies to optimize the cost of execution plan generation

- Factors affecting parallel plan generation

Execution Plan Generation

SQL Server uses a cost-based optimization technique to determine the processing strategy of a query. The optimizer considers both the metadata of the database objects, such as unique constraints or index size, and the current distribution statistics of the columns referred to in the query when deciding which index and join strategies should be used.

The cost-based optimization allows a database developer to concentrate on implementing a business rule, rather than on the exact syntax of the query. At the same time, the process of determining the query-processing strategy remains quite complex and can consume a fair amount of resources. SQL Server uses a number of techniques to optimize resource consumption.

- Syntax-based optimization of the query

- Trivial plan match to avoid in-depth query optimization for simple queries

- Index and join strategies based on current distribution statistics

- Query optimization in stepped phases to control the cost of optimization

- Execution plan caching to avoid the regeneration of query plans

The following techniques are performed in order, as shown in Figure 14-1.

- Parsing

- Binding

- Query optimization

- Execution plan generation, caching, and hash plan generation

- Query execution

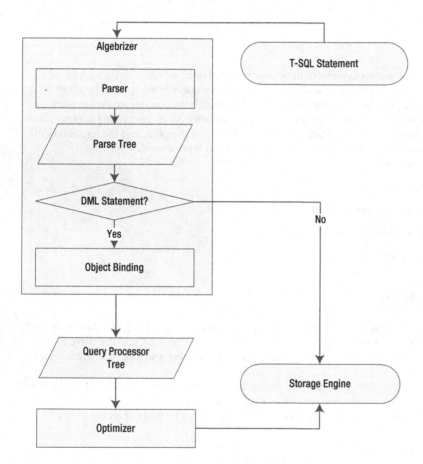

Figure 14-1. *SQL Server techniques to optimize query execution*

Let's take a look at these steps in more detail.

Parser

When a query is submitted, SQL Server passes it to the algebrizer within the *relational engine*. (This relational engine is one of the two main parts of SQL Server data retrieval and manipulation, with the other being the *storage engine*, which is responsible for data access, modifications, and caching.) The relational engine takes care of parsing, name and type resolution, and optimization. It also executes a query as per the query execution plan and requests data from the storage engine.

The first part of the algebrizer process is the parser. The parser checks an incoming query, validating it for the correct syntax. The query is terminated if a syntax error is detected. If multiple queries are submitted together as a batch as follows (note the error in syntax), then the parser checks the complete batch together for syntax and cancels the complete batch when it detects a syntax error. (Note that more than one syntax error may appear in a batch, but the parser goes no further than the first one.)

```
CREATE TABLE dbo.Test1 (c1 INT);
INSERT  INTO dbo.Test1
VALUES  (1);
CEILEKT * FROM dbo.t1; --Error:  I meant,  SELECT * FROM t1
```

On validating a query for correct syntax, the parser generates an internal data structure called a *parse tree* for the algebrizer. The parser and algebrizer taken together are called *query compilation*.

Binding

The parse tree generated by the parser is passed to the next part of the algebrizer for processing. The algebrizer now resolves all the names of the different objects, meaning the tables, the columns, and so on, that are being referenced in the T-SQL in a process called *binding*. It also identifies all the various data types being processed. It even checks for the location of aggregates (such as GROUP BY and MAX). The output of all these verifications and resolutions is a binary set of data called a *query processor tree*.

To see this part of the algebrizer in action, if the following batch query is submitted, then the first three statements before the error statement are executed, and the errant statement and the one after it are cancelled.

```
IF (SELECT  OBJECT_ID('dbo.Test1')
    ) IS NOT NULL
      DROP TABLE dbo.Test1;
GO
CREATE TABLE dbo.Test1 (c1 INT) ;
INSERT  INTO dbo.Test1
VALUES  (1);
SELECT  'Before Error',
        c1
FROM    dbo.Test1 AS t;
SELECT  'error',
        c1
FROM    dbo.no_Test1;
  --Error:  Table doesn't exist
SELECT  'after error' c1
FROM    dbo.Test1 AS t;
```

If a query contains an implicit data conversion, then the normalization process adds an appropriate step to the query tree. The process also performs some syntax-based optimization. For example, if the following query is submitted, then the syntax-based optimization transforms the syntax of the query, as shown in the T-SQL in Figure 14-2 taken from the SELECT operator properties in the execution plan, where BETWEEN becomes >= and <=.

```
SELECT   soh.AccountNumber,
         soh.OrderDate,
         soh.PurchaseOrderNumber,
         soh.SalesOrderNumber
FROM     Sales.SalesOrderHeader AS soh
WHERE    soh.SalesOrderID BETWEEN 62500 AND 62550;
```

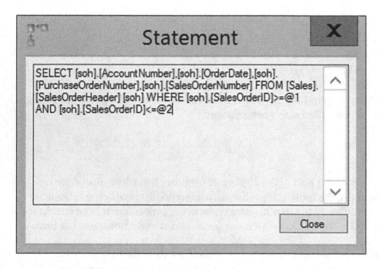

Figure 14-2. *Syntax-based optimization*

You can also see some evidence of parameterization, discussed in more detail later in this chapter. The execution plan generated from the query looks like Figure 14-3.

Figure 14-3. *Execution plan with a warning*

You should also note the warning indicator on the SELECT operator. Looking at the properties for this operator, you can see that SalesOrderID is actually getting converted as part of the process and the optimizer is warning you.

```
Type conversion in expression (CONVERT(nvarchar(23),[soh].[SalesOrderID],0)) may affect
"CardinalityEstimate" in query plan choice
```

I left this example in, with the warning, to illustrate a couple of points. First, warnings can be unclear. In this case, the warning is coming from the calculated column, SalesOrderNumber. It's doing a conversion of the SalesOrderID to a string and adding a value to it. In the way it does it, the optimizer recognizes that this could be problematic, so it gives you a warning. But, you're not referencing the column in any kind of filtering fashion such as the WHERE clause, JOINS, or HAVING. Because of that, you can safely ignore the warning. I also left it in because it illustrates just fine that AdventureWorks is a good example database because it has the same types of poor choices that are sometimes in databases in the real world too.

For most Data Definition Language (DDL) statements (such as CREATE TABLE, CREATE PROC, and so on), after passing through the algebrizer, the query is compiled directly for execution, since the optimizer need not choose among multiple processing strategies. For one DDL statement in particular, CREATE INDEX, the optimizer can determine an efficient processing strategy based on other existing indexes on the table, as explained in Chapter 8.

For this reason, you will never see any reference to CREATE TABLE in an execution plan, although you will see reference to CREATE INDEX. If the normalized query is a Data Manipulation Language (DML) statement (such as SELECT, INSERT, UPDATE, or DELETE), then the query processor tree is passed to the optimizer to decide the processing strategy for the query.

Optimization

Based on the complexity of a query, including the number of tables referred to and the indexes available, there may be several ways to execute the query contained in the query processor tree. Exhaustively comparing the cost of all the ways of executing a query can take a considerable amount of time, which may sometimes override the benefit of finding the most optimized query. Figure 14-4 shows that to avoid a high optimization overhead compared to the actual execution cost of the query, the optimizer adopts different techniques, namely, the following:

- Simplification
- Trivial plan match
- Multiple optimization phases
- Parallel plan optimization

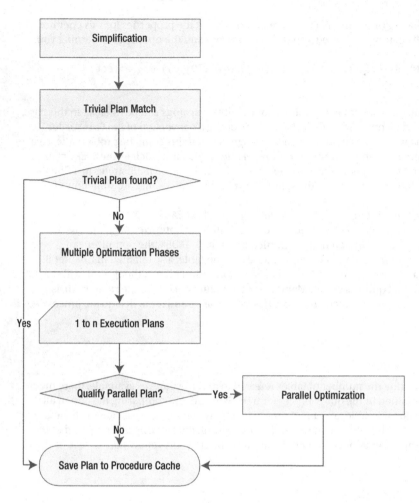

Figure 14-4. *Query optimization steps*

Simplification

Before the optimizer begins to process your query, the logical engine has already identified all the objects referenced in your database. When the optimizer begins to construct your execution plan, it first ensures that all objects being referenced are actually used and necessary to return your data accurately. If you were to write a query with a three-table join but only two of the tables were actually referenced by either the SELECT criteria or the WHERE clauses, the optimizer may choose to leave the other table out of the processing. This is known as the *simplification* step. It's actually part of a larger set of processing that gathers statistics and starts the process of estimating the cardinality of the data involved in your query. The optimizer also gathers the necessary information about your constraints, especially the foreign key constraints, that will help it make decisions about the join order, which it can rearrange as needed in order to arrive at a good enough plan.

Trivial Plan Match

Sometimes there might be only one way to execute a query. For example, a heap table with no indexes can be accessed in only one way: via a table scan. To avoid the runtime overhead of optimizing such queries, SQL Server maintains a list of patterns that define a trivial plan. If the optimizer finds a match, then a similar plan is generated for the query without any optimization. The generated plans are then stored in the procedure cache. Eliminating the optimization phase means that the cost for generating a trivial plan is very low. This is not to imply that trivial plans are desired or preferable to more complex plans. Trivial plans are available only for extremely simple queries. Once the complexity of the query rises, it must go through optimization.

Multiple Optimization Phases

For a nontrivial query, the number of alternative processing strategies to be analyzed can be high, and it may take a long time to evaluate each option. Therefore, the optimizer goes through three different levels of optimizations. These are referred to as search 0, search 1, and search 2. But it's easier to think of them as *transaction*, *quick plan*, and *full optimization*. Depending on the size and complexity of the query, these different optimizations may be tried one at a time, or the optimizer might skip straight to full optimization. Each of the optimizations takes into account using different join techniques and different ways of accessing the data through scans, seeks, and other operations.

The index variations consider different indexing aspects, such as single-column index, composite index, index column order, column density, and so forth. Similarly, the join variations consider the different join techniques available in SQL Server: nested loop join, merge join, and hash join. (Chapter 4 covers these join techniques in detail.) Constraints such as unique values and foreign key constraints are also part of the optimization decision-making process.

The optimizer considers the statistics of the columns referred to in the WHERE clause to evaluate the effectiveness of the index and the join strategies. Based on the current statistics, it evaluates the cost of the configurations in multiple optimization phases. The cost includes many factors, including (but not limited to) usage of CPU, memory, and disk I/O (including random versus sequential I/O estimation) required to execute the query. After each optimization phase, the optimizer evaluates the cost of the processing strategy. This cost is an estimation only, not an actual measure or prediction of behavior; it's a mathematical construct based on the statistics and the processes under consideration. If the cost is found to be cheap enough, then the optimizer stops further iteration through the optimization phases and quits the optimization process. Otherwise, it keeps iterating through the optimization phases to determine a cost-effective processing strategy.

Sometimes a query can be so complex that the optimizer needs to extensively iterate through the optimization phases. While optimizing the query, if it finds that the cost of the processing strategy is more than the cost threshold for parallelism, then it evaluates the cost of processing the query using multiple CPUs. Otherwise, the optimizer proceeds with the serial plan.

You can find out some detail of what occurred during the multiple optimization phases via two sources. Take, for example, this query:

```
SELECT  soh.SalesOrderNumber,
        sod.OrderQty,
        sod.LineTotal,
        sod.UnitPrice,
        sod.UnitPriceDiscount,
        p.[Name] AS ProductName,
        p.ProductNumber,
        ps.[Name] AS ProductSubCategoryName,
        pc.[Name] AS ProductCategoryName
FROM    Sales.SalesOrderHeader AS soh
JOIN    Sales.SalesOrderDetail AS sod
        ON soh.SalesOrderID = sod.SalesOrderID
```

```
JOIN    Production.Product AS p
        ON sod.ProductID = p.ProductID
JOIN    Production.ProductModel AS pm
        ON p.ProductModelID = pm.ProductModelID
JOIN    Production.ProductSubcategory AS ps
        ON p.ProductSubcategoryID = ps.ProductSubcategoryID
JOIN    Production.ProductCategory AS pc
        ON ps.ProductCategoryID = pc.ProductCategoryID
WHERE   soh.CustomerID = 29658;
```

When this query is run, the execution plan in Figure 14-5, a nontrivial plan for sure, is returned.

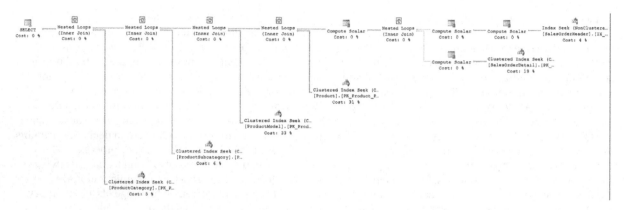

Figure 14-5. *Nontrivial execution plan*

I realize that this execution plan is hard to read, but don't try to read it. The important point to take away is that it involves quite a few tables, each with indexes and statistics that all had to be taken into account to arrive at this execution plan. The first place you can go to look for information about the optimizer's work on this execution plan is the property sheet of the first operator, in this case the T-SQL SELECT operator, at the far left of the execution plan. Figure 14-6 shows the property sheet.

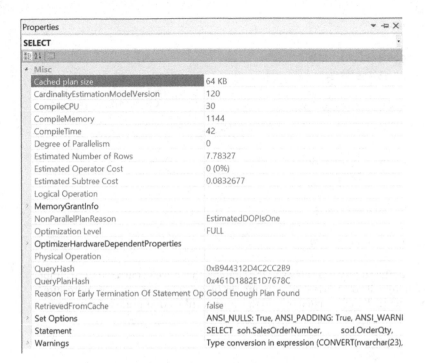

Figure 14-6. *SELECT operator property sheet*

Starting at the top, you can see information directly related to the creation and optimization of this execution plan.

- The size of the cached plan, which is 64 bytes
- The number of CPU cycles used to compile the plan, which is 30ms
- The amount of memory used, which is 1144KB
- The compile time, which is 42ms

The Optimization Level property (`StatementOptmLevel` in the XML plan) shows what type of processing occurred within the optimizer. In this case, FULL means that the optimizer did a full optimization. This is further displayed in the property Reason for Early Termination of Statement, which is Good Enough Plan Found. So, the optimizer took 42ms to track down a plan that it deemed good enough in this situation. You can also see the `QueryPlanHash` value, also known as the *fingerprint*, for the execution plan (you can find more details on this in the section "Query Plan Hash and Query Hash"). The properties of the SELECT (and the INSERT, UPDATE, and DELETE) operators are an important first stopping point when evaluating any execution plan because of this information.

The second source for optimizer information is the dynamic management view `sys.Dm_exec_query_optimizer_info`. This DMV is an aggregation of the optimization events over time. It won't show the individual optimizations for a given query, but it will track the optimizations performed. This isn't as immediately handy for tuning an individual query, but if you are working on reducing the costs of a workload over time, being able to track this information can help you determine whether your query tuning is making a positive difference, at least in terms of optimization time. Some of the data returned is for internal SQL Server use only. Figure 14-7 shows a truncated example of the useful data returned in the results from the following query:

```
SELECT  deqoi.counter,
        deqoi.occurrence,
        deqoi.value
FROM    sys.dm_exec_query_optimizer_info AS deqoi;
```

	counter	occurrence	value
1	optimizations	95	1
2	elapsed time	95	0.00768421052631579
3	final cost	95	0.0495308886615486
4	trivial plan	25	1
5	tasks	70	707.514285714286
6	no plan	0	NULL
7	search 0	28	1
8	search 0 time	28	0.00503571428571429
9	search 0 tasks	28	1164.39285714286
10	search 1	42	1
11	search 1 time	42	0.0014047619047619

Figure 14-7. Output from sys.dm_exec_query_optimizer_info

Running this query before and after another query can show you the changes that have occurred in the number and type of optimizations completed. Although, if you can isolate your queries on a test box, you can be more sure that you get before and after differences that are directly related only to the query you're attempting to measure.

Parallel Plan Optimization

The optimizer considers various factors while evaluating the cost of processing a query using a parallel plan. Some of these factors are as follows:

- Number of CPUs available to SQL Server
- SQL Server edition
- Available memory
- Cost threshold for parallelism
- Type of query being executed
- Number of rows to be processed in a given stream
- Number of active concurrent connections

If only one CPU is available to SQL Server, then the optimizer won't consider a parallel plan. The number of CPUs available to SQL Server can be restricted using the *affinity* setting of the SQL Server configuration. The affinity value is set to either specific CPUs, or, to specific NUMA nodes. You can also set it to ranges. For example, to allow SQL Server to use only CPU0 to CPU3 in an eight-way box, execute these statements:

```
USE master;
EXEC sp_configure 'show advanced option','1';
RECONFIGURE;
ALTER SERVER CONFIGURATION SET PROCESS AFFINITY CPU = 0 TO 3;
GO
```

This configuration takes effect immediately. affinity is a special setting, and I recommend you use it only in instances where taking control away from SQL Server makes sense, such as when you have multiple instances of SQL Server running on the same machine and you want to isolate them from each other. You can also bind I/O to a specific set of processors using the affinity I/O option in the same way.

Even if multiple CPUs are available to SQL Server, if an individual query is not allowed to use more than one CPU for execution, then the optimizer discards the parallel plan option. The maximum number of CPUs that can be used for a parallel query is governed by the max degree of parallelism setting of the SQL Server configuration. The default value is 0, which allows all the CPUs (availed by the affinity mask setting) to be used for a parallel query. You can also control parallelism through the Resource Governor. If you want to allow parallel queries to use no more than two CPUs out of CPU0 to CPU3, limited by the preceding affinity mask setting, execute the following statements:

```
USE master;
EXEC sp_configure 'show advanced option','1';
RECONFIGURE;
EXEC sp_configure 'max degree of parallelism',2;
RECONFIGURE;
```

This change takes effect immediately, without any restart. The max degree of parallelism setting can also be controlled at a query level using the MAXDOP query hint.

```
SELECT  *
FROM    dbo.t1
WHERE   C1 = 1
OPTION  (MAXDOP 2);
```

Changing the max degree of parallelism setting is best determined by the needs of your application and the workloads on it. I will usually leave the max degree of parallelism set to the default value unless indications arise that suggest a change is necessary. I will usually adjust the cost threshold for parallelism up from its default value of 5.

Since parallel queries require more memory, the optimizer determines the amount of memory available before choosing a parallel plan. The amount of memory required increases with the degree of parallelism. If the memory requirement of the parallel plan for a given degree of parallelism cannot be satisfied, then SQL Server decreases the degree of parallelism automatically or completely abandons the parallel plan for the query in the given workload context. You can see this part of the evaluation in the SELECT properties of Figure 14-6.

Queries with a very high CPU overhead are the best candidates for a parallel plan. Examples include joining large tables, performing substantial aggregations, and sorting large result sets, all common operations on reporting systems (less so on OLTP systems). For simple queries usually found in transaction-processing applications, the additional coordination required to initialize, synchronize, and terminate a parallel plan outweighs the potential performance benefit.

Whether a query is simple is determined by comparing the estimated execution time of the query with a cost threshold. This cost threshold is controlled by the cost threshold for parallelism setting of the SQL Server configuration. By default, this setting's value is 5, which means that if the estimated execution time of the serial plan is more than 5 seconds, then the optimizer considers a parallel plan for the query. For example, to modify the cost threshold to 35 seconds, execute the following statements:

```
USE master;
EXEC sp_configure 'show advanced option','1';
RECONFIGURE;
EXEC sp_configure 'cost threshold for parallelism',35;
RECONFIGURE;
```

This change takes effect immediately, without any restart. If only one CPU is available to SQL Server, then this setting is ignored. I've found that OLTP systems suffer when the cost threshold for parallelism is set this low. Usually increasing the value to somewhere between 30 and 50 will be beneficial. Be sure to test this suggestion against your system to ensure it works well for you.

Another option is to simply look at the plans in your cache and then make an estimate, based on the queries there and the type of workload they represent to arrive at a specific number. You can separate your OLTP queries from your reporting queries and then focus on the reporting queries most likely to benefit from parallel execution. Take an average of those costs and set your cost threshold to that number.

■ **Note**   While I do refer to these values as being measured in seconds, that is just a construct used by the optimizer. They are not literal measures.

The DML action queries (INSERT, UPDATE, and DELETE) are executed serially. However, the SELECT portion of an INSERT statement and the WHERE clause of an UPDATE or a DELETE statement can be executed in parallel. The actual data changes are applied serially to the database. Also, if the optimizer determines that the estimated cost is too low, it does not introduce parallel operators.

Note that, even at execution time, SQL Server determines whether the current system workload and configuration information allow for parallel query execution. If parallel query execution is allowed, SQL Server determines the optimal number of threads and spreads the execution of the query across those threads. When a query starts a parallel execution, it uses the same number of threads until completion. SQL Server reexamines the optimal number of threads before executing the parallel query the next time.

Once the processing strategy is finalized by using either a serial plan or a parallel plan, the optimizer generates the execution plan for the query. The execution plan contains the detailed processing strategy decided by the optimizer to execute the query. This includes steps such as data retrieval, result set joins, result set ordering, and so on. A detailed explanation of how to analyze the processing steps included in an execution plan is presented in Chapter 4. The execution plan generated for the query is saved in the plan cache for future reuse.

Execution Plan Caching

The execution plan of a query generated by the optimizer is saved in a special part of SQL Server's memory pool called the *plan cache* or *procedure cache*. (The procedure cache is part of the SQL Server buffer cache and is explained in Chapter 2.) Saving the plan in a cache allows SQL Server to avoid running through the whole query optimization process again when the same query is resubmitted. SQL Server supports different techniques such as *plan cache aging* and *plan cache types* to increase the reusability of the cached plans. It also stores two binary values called the *query hash* and the *query plan hash*.

■ **Note**   I discuss the techniques supported by SQL Server for improving the effectiveness of execution plan reuse in this Chapter 15.

Components of the Execution Plan

The execution plan generated by the optimizer contains two components.

- *Query plan*: This represents the commands that specify all the physical operations required to execute a query.

- *Execution context*: This maintains the variable parts of a query within the context of a given user.

I will cover these components in more detail in the next sections.

Query Plan

The query plan is a reentrant, read-only data structure, with commands that specify all the physical operations required to execute the query. The reentrant property allows the query plan to be accessed concurrently by multiple connections. The physical operations include specifications on which tables and indexes to access, how and in what order they should be accessed, the type of join operations to be performed between multiple tables, and so forth. No user context is stored in the query plan.

Execution Context

The execution context is another data structure that maintains the variable part of the query. Although the server keeps track of the execution plans in the procedure cache, these plans are context neutral. Therefore, each user executing the query will have a separate execution context that holds data specific to their execution, such as parameter values and connection details.

Aging of the Execution Plan

The procedure cache is part of SQL Server's buffer cache, which also holds data pages. As new execution plans are added to the procedure cache, the size of the procedure cache keeps growing, affecting the retention of useful data pages in memory. To avoid this, SQL Server dynamically controls the retention of the execution plans in the procedure cache, retaining the frequently used execution plans and discarding plans that are not used for a certain period of time.

SQL Server keeps track of the frequency of an execution plan's reuse by associating an age field to it. When an execution plan is generated, the age field is populated with the cost of generating the plan. A complex query requiring extensive optimization will have an age field value higher than that for a simpler query.

At regular intervals, the current cost of all the execution plans in the procedure cache is examined by SQL Server's lazy writer process (which manages most of the background processes in SQL Server). If an execution plan is not reused for a long time, then the current cost will eventually be reduced to 0. The cheaper the execution plan was to generate, the sooner its cost will be reduced to 0. Once an execution plan's cost reaches 0, the plan becomes a candidate for removal from memory. SQL Server removes all plans with a cost of 0 from the procedure cache when memory pressure increases to such an extent that there is no longer enough free memory to serve new requests. However, if a system has enough memory and free memory pages are available to serve new requests, execution plans with a cost of 0 can remain in the procedure cache for a long time so that they can be reused later, if required.

As well as changing the costs downward, execution plans can also find their costs increased to the max cost of generating the plan every time the plan is reused (or to the current cost of the plan for ad hoc plans). For example, suppose you have two execution plans with generation costs equal to 100 and 10. Their starting cost values will therefore be 100 and 10, respectively. If both execution plans are reused immediately, their age fields will be set back to that maximum cost. With these cost values, the lazy writer will bring down the cost of the second plan to 0 much earlier than that of the first one, unless the second plan is reused more often. Therefore, even if a costly plan is reused less frequently than a cheaper plan, because of the effect of the initial cost, the costly plan can remain at a nonzero cost value for a longer period of time.

Summary

SQL Server's cost-based query optimizer decides upon an effective execution plan based not on the exact syntax of the query but by evaluating the cost of executing the query using different processing strategies. The cost evaluation of using different processing strategies is done in multiple optimization phases to avoid spending too much time optimizing a query. Then, the execution plans are cached to save the cost of execution plan generation when the same queries are reexecuted.

In the next chapter, I will discuss how the plans get reused from the cache in different ways depending on how they're called.

## CHAPTER 15

Execution Plan Cache Behavior

Once all the processing necessary to generate an execution plan has been completed, it would be crazy for SQL Server to throw away that work and do it all again each time a query gets called. Instead, it saves the plans created in a memory space on the server called the *plan cache*. This chapter is going to walk through how you can monitor the plan cache in order to see how SQL Server reuses execution plans.

In this chapter, I cover the following topics:

- How to analyze execution plan caching

- Query plan hash and query hash as mechanisms for identifying queries to tune

- Execution plans gone wrong and parameter sniffing

- Ways to improve the reusability of execution plan caching

Analyzing the Execution Plan Cache

You can obtain a lot of information about the execution plans in the procedure cache by accessing various dynamic management objects. The initial DMO for working with execution plans is sys.dm_exec_cached_plans.

```
SELECT  *
FROM    sys.dm_exec_cached_plans;
```

Table 15-1 shows some of the useful information provided by sys.dmexeccachedplans (this is easier to read in Grid view).

Table 15-1. *sys.dm_exec_cached_plans*

Column Name	Description
refcounts	This represents the number of other objects in the cache referencing this plan.
usecounts	This is the number of times this object has been used since it was added to the cache.
size_in_bytes	This is the size of the plan stored in the cache.
cacheobjtype	This specifies what type of plan this is; there are several, but of particular interest are these:
	Compiled plan: A completed execution plan
	Compiled plan stub: A marker used for ad hoc queries (you can find more details in the "Ad Hoc Workload" section of this chapter)
	Parse tree: A plan stored for accessing a view
Objtype	This is the type of object that generated the plan. Again, there are several, but these are of particular interest:
	Proc Prepared Ad hoc View
Parent_plan_handle	This is the identifier for this plan in memory; it is used to retrieve query text and execution plans.

Using the DMV sys.dm_exec_cached_plans all by itself gets you only a small part of the information. DMOs are best used in combination with other DMOs and other system views. For example, using the dynamic management function sys.dm_exec_query_plan(plan_handle) in combination with sys.dm_exec_cached_plans will also bring back the XML execution plan itself so that you can display it and work with it. If you then bring in sys.dm_exec_sql_text(plan_handle), you can also retrieve the original query text. This may not seem useful while you're running known queries for the examples here, but when you go to your production system and begin to pull in execution plans from the cache, it might be handy to have the original query. To get aggregate performance metrics about the cached plan, you can use sys.dm_exec_query_stats to return that data. Among other pieces of data, the query hash and query plan hash are stored in this DMF. Finally, to see execution plans for queries that are currently executing, you can use sys.dm_exec_requests.

In the following sections, I'll explore how the plan cache works with actual queries of these DMOs.

Execution Plan Reuse

When a query is submitted, SQL Server checks the procedure cache for a matching execution plan. If one is not found, then SQL Server performs the query compilation and optimization to generate a new execution plan. However, if the plan exists in the procedure cache, it is reused with the private execution context. This saves the CPU cycles that otherwise would have been spent on the plan generation.

Queries are submitted to SQL Server with filter criteria to limit the size of the result set. The same queries are often resubmitted with different values for the filter criteria. For example, consider the following query:

```
SELECT  soh.SalesOrderNumber,
        soh.OrderDate,
        sod.OrderQty,
        sod.LineTotal
```

```
FROM    Sales.SalesOrderHeader AS soh
JOIN    Sales.SalesOrderDetail AS sod
        ON soh.SalesOrderID = sod.SalesOrderID
WHERE   soh.CustomerID = 29690
        AND sod.ProductID = 711;
```

When this query is submitted, the optimizer creates an execution plan and saves it in the procedure cache to reuse in the future. If this query is resubmitted with a different filter criterion value—for example, soh.CustomerlD = 29500—it will be beneficial to reuse the existing execution plan for the previously supplied filter criterion value. But whether the execution plan created for one filter criterion value can be reused for another filter criterion value depends on how the query is submitted to SQL Server.

The queries (or workload) submitted to SQL Server can be broadly classified into two categories that determine whether the execution plan will be reusable as the value of the variable parts of the query changes.

- Ad hoc
- Prepared

■ **Tip** To test the output of sys.dm_exec_cached_plans for this chapter, it will be necessary to remove the plans from cache on occasion by executing DBCC FREEPROCCACHE. Do not run this on your production server since flushing the cache will require all execution plans to be rebuilt as they are executed, placing a serious strain on your production system for no good reason. You can use DBCC FREEPROCCACHE(plan_handle) to target specific plans. Retrieve the plan_handle using the DMOs I've already talked about.

Ad Hoc Workload

Queries can be submitted to SQL Server without explicitly isolating the variables from the query. These types of queries executed without explicitly converting the variable parts of the query into parameters are referred to as *ad hoc workloads* (or queries). Most of the examples in the book so far are ad hoc queries. For further example, consider this query:

```
SELECT  soh.SalesOrderNumber,
        soh.OrderDate,
        sod.OrderQty,
        sod.LineTotal
FROM    Sales.SalesOrderHeader AS soh
JOIN    Sales.SalesOrderDetail AS sod
        ON soh.SalesOrderlD = sod.SalesOrderlD
WHERE   soh.CustomerlD = 29690
        AND sod.productid = 711;
```

If the query is submitted as is, without explicitly converting either of the hard-coded values to a parameter (that can be supplied to the query when executed), then the query is an ad hoc query. Setting the values to local variables using the DECLARE statement is not the same as parameters.

In this query, the filter criterion value is embedded in the query itself and is not explicitly parameterized to isolate it from the query. This means you cannot reuse the execution plan for this query unless you use the same values and all the spacing and carriage returns are identical. However, the places where values are used in the queries can be explicitly parameterized in three different ways that are jointly categorized as a prepared workload.

Prepared Workload

Prepared workloads (or queries) explicitly parameterize the variable parts of the query so that the query plan isn't tied to the value of the variable parts. In SQL Server, queries can be submitted as prepared workloads using the following three methods:

- *Stored procedures*: Allows saving a collection of SQL statements that can accept and return user-supplied parameters

- *Sp_executesql*: Allows executing a SQL statement or a SQL batch that may contain user-supplied parameters, without saving the SQL statement or batch

- *Prepare/execute model*: Allows a SQL client to request the generation of a query plan that can be reused during subsequent executions of the query with different parameter values, without saving the SQL statements in SQL Server

For example, the SELECT statement shown previously can be explicitly parameterized using a stored procedure as follows:

```
IF (SELECT  OBJECT_ID('dbo.BasicSalesInfo')
    ) IS NOT NULL
    DROP PROC dbo.BasicSalesInfo;
GO
CREATE PROC dbo.BasicSalesInfo
    @ProductID INT,
    @CustomerID INT
AS
SELECT  soh.SalesOrderNumber,
        soh.OrderDate,
        sod.OrderQty,
        sod.LineTotal
FROM    Sales.SalesOrderHeader AS soh
JOIN    Sales.SalesOrderDetail AS sod
        ON soh.SalesOrderID = sod.SalesOrderID
WHERE   soh.CustomerID = @CustomerID
        AND sod.ProductID = @ProductID;
```

The plan of the SELECT statement included within the stored procedure will embed the parameters (@ProductID and @CustomerId), not variable values. I will cover these methods in more detail shortly.

Plan Reusability of an Ad Hoc Workload

When a query is submitted as an ad hoc workload, SQL Server generates an execution plan and stores that plan in the cache, where it can be reused if the same ad hoc query is resubmitted. Since there are no parameters, the hard-coded values are stored as part of the plan. For a plan to be reused from the cache, the T-SQL must match exactly. This includes all spaces and carriage returns plus any values supplied with the plan. If any of these change, the plan cannot be reused.

To understand this, consider the ad hoc query you've used before:

```
SELECT  soh.SalesOrderNumber,
        soh.OrderDate,
        sod.OrderQty,
        sod.LineTotal
```

```
FROM    Sales.SalesOrderHeader AS soh
JOIN    Sales.SalesOrderDetail AS sod
        ON soh.SalesOrderID = sod.SalesOrderID
WHERE   soh.CustomerID = 29690
        AND sod.ProductID = 711;
```

The execution plan generated for this ad hoc query is based on the exact text of the query, which includes comments, case, trailing spaces, and hard returns. You'll have to use the exact text to pull the information out of sys.dm_exec_cached_plans.

```
SELECT    c.usecounts
    ,c.cacheobjtype
    ,c.objtype
FROM        sys.dm_exec_cached_plans c
    CROSS APPLY sys.dm_exec_sql_text(c.plan_handle) t
WHERE       t.text = 'SELECT  soh.SalesOrderNumber,
        soh.OrderDate,
        sod.OrderQty,
        sod.LineTotal
FROM    Sales.SalesOrderHeader AS soh
JOIN    Sales.SalesOrderDetail AS sod
        ON soh.SalesOrderID = sod.SalesOrderID
WHERE   soh.CustomerID = 29690
        AND sod.ProductID = 711;';
```

Figure 15-1 shows the output of sys.dm_exec_cached_plans.

	usecounts	cacheobjtype	objtype
1	1	Compiled Plan Stub	Adhoc

Figure 15-1. *sys.dm_exec_cached_plans output*

You can see from Figure 15-1 that a compiled plan is generated and saved in the procedure cache for the preceding ad hoc query. To find the specific query, I used the query itself in the WHERE clause. You can see that this plan has been used once up until now (usecounts = 1). If this ad hoc query is reexecuted, SQL Server reuses the existing executable plan from the procedure cache, as shown in Figure 15-2.

	usecounts	cacheobjtype	objtype
1	2	Compiled Plan	Adhoc

Figure 15-2. *Reusing the executable plan from the procedure cache*

In Figure 15-2, you can see that the usecounts value for the preceding query's executable plan has increased to 2, confirming that the existing plan for this query has been reused. If this query is executed repeatedly, the existing plan will be reused every time.

Since the plan generated for the preceding query includes the filter criterion value, the reusability of the plan is limited to the use of the same filter criterion value. Reexecute the query, but change son.CustomerID to 29500.

```
SELECT   soh.SalesOrderNumber,
         soh.OrderDate,
         sod.OrderQty,
         sod.LineTotal
FROM     Sales.SalesOrderHeader AS soh
JOIN     Sales.SalesOrderDetail AS sod
         ON soh.SalesOrderID = sod.SalesOrderID
WHERE    soh.CustomerID = 29500
         AND sod.ProductID = 711;
```

The existing plan can't be reused, and if the sys.dm_exec_cached_plans is rerun as is, you'll see that the execution count hasn't increased (Figure 15-3).

	usecounts	cacheobjtype	objtype
1	2	Compiled Plan	Adhoc

Figure 15-3. *sys.dm_exec_cached_plans shows that the existing plan is not reused*

Instead, I'll adjust the query against sys.dm_exec_cached_plans.

```
SELECT   c.usecounts,
         c.cacheobjtype,
         c.objtype,
         t.text,
         c.plan_handle
FROM     sys.dm_exec_cached_plans c
CROSS APPLY sys.dm_exec_sql_text(c.plan_handle) t
WHERE    t.text LIKE 'SELECT  soh.SalesOrderNumber,
         soh.OrderDate,
         sod.OrderQty,
         sod.LineTotal
FROM     Sales.SalesOrderHeader AS soh
JOIN     Sales.SalesOrderDetail AS sod
         ON soh.SalesOrderID = sod.SalesOrderID%';
```

You can see the output from this query in Figure 15-4.

	usecounts	cacheobjtype	objtype	text		plan_handle
1	1	Compiled Plan	Adhoc	SELECT soh.SalesOrderNumber,	soh.Order...	0x06000500FE3F7918600F25730200000001000000000000...
2	2	Compiled Plan	Adhoc	SELECT soh.SalesOrderNumber,	soh.Order...	0x060005003176D518401F25730200000001000000000000...

Figure 15-4. *sys.dm_exec_cached_plans showing that the existing plan can't be reused*

From the sys.dm_exec_cached_plans output in Figure 15-4, you can see that the previous plan for the query hasn't been reused; the corresponding usecounts value remained at the old value of 2. Instead of reusing the existing plan, a new plan is generated for the query and is saved in the procedure cache with a new plan_handle. If this ad hoc query is reexecuted repeatedly with different filter criterion values, a new execution plan will be generated every time. The inefficient reuse of the execution plan for this ad hoc query increases the load on the CPU by consuming additional CPU cycles to regenerate the plan.

To summarize, ad hoc plan caching uses statement-level caching and is limited to an exact textual match. If an ad hoc query is not complex, SQL Server can implicitly parameterize the query to increase plan reusability by using a feature called *simple parameterization*. The definition of a simple query for simple parameterization is limited to fairly simple cases such as ad hoc queries with only one table. As shown in the previous example, most queries requiring a join operation cannot be autoparameterized.

Optimize for an Ad Hoc Workload

If your server is going to primarily support ad hoc queries, it is possible to achieve a degree of performance improvement. One server option is called optimize for ad hoc workloads. Enabling this for the server changes the way the engine deals with ad hoc queries. Instead of saving a full compiled plan for the query the first time it's called, a compiled plan stub is stored. The stub does not have a full execution plan associated, saving the storage space required for it and the time saving it to the cache. This option can be enabled without rebooting the server.

```
EXEC sp_configure
    'optimize for ad hoc workloads',
    1;
GO
RECONFIGURE;
```

After changing the option, flush the cache and then rerun the ad hoc query. Modify the query against sys.dm_exec_cached_plans so that you include the size_in_bytes column; then run it to see the results in Figure 15-5.

	usecounts	cacheobjtype	objtype	text		size_in_bytes
1	1	Compiled Plan Stub	Adhoc	SELECT soh.SalesOrderNumber.	soh.Order...	352

Figure 15-5. *sys.dm_exec_cached_plans showing a compiled plan stub*

Figure 15-5 shows in the cacheobjtype column that the new object in the cache is a compiled plan stub. Stubs can be created for lots more queries with less impact on the server than full compiled plans. But the next time an ad hoc query is executed, a fully compiled plan is created. To see this in action, run the query one more time and check the results in sys.dm_exec_ cachedplans, as shown in Figure 15-6.

	usecounts	cacheobjtype	objtype	text		size_in_bytes
1	1	Compiled Plan	Adhoc	SELECT soh.SalesOrderNumber.	soh.Order...	65536

Figure 15-6. *The compiled plan stub has become a compiled plan*

Check the `cacheobjtype` value. It has changed from Compiled Plan Stub to Compiled Plan. Finally, to see the real difference between a stub and a full plan, check the `sizeinbytes` column in Figure 15-5 and Figure 15-6. The size changed from 352 in the stub to 65536 in the full plan. This shows precisely the savings available when working with lots of ad hoc queries. Before proceeding, be sure to disable `optimize for ad hoc workloads`.

```
EXEC sp_configure
    'optimize for ad hoc workloads',
    0;
GO
RECONFIGURE;
```

Personally, I see little downside to implementing this on just about any system. Like with all recommendations, you should test it to ensure your system isn't exceptional. However, the cost of writing the plan into memory when it's called a second time is extremely trivial to the savings in memory overall that you see by not storing plans that are only ever going to be used once. In all my testing and experience, this is a pure benefit with little downside.

Simple Parameterization

When an ad hoc query is submitted, SQL Server analyzes the query to determine which parts of the incoming text might be parameters. It looks at the variable parts of the ad hoc query to determine whether it will be safe to parameterize them automatically and use the parameters (instead of the variable parts) in the query so that the query plan can be independent of the variable values. This feature of automatically converting the variable part of a query into a parameter, even though not parameterized explicitly (using a prepared workload technique), is called *simple parameterization*.

During simple parameterization, SQL Server ensures that if the ad hoc query is converted to a parameterized template, the changes in the parameter values won't widely change the plan requirement. On determining the simple parameterization to be safe, SQL Server creates a parameterized template for the ad hoc query and saves the parameterized plan in the procedure cache.

The parameterized plan is not based on the dynamic values used in the query. Since the plan is generated for a parameterized template, it can be reused when the ad hoc query is reexecuted with different values for the variable parts.

To understand the simple parameterization feature of SQL Server, consider the following query:

```
SELECT  a.*
FROM    Person.Address AS a
WHERE   a.AddressID = 42;
```

When this ad hoc query is submitted, SQL Server can treat this query as it is for plan creation. However, before the query is executed, SQL Server tries to determine whether it can be safely parameterized. On determining that the variable part of the query can be parameterized without affecting the basic structure of the query, SQL Server parameterizes the query and generates a plan for the parameterized query. You can observe this from the `sys.dm_exec_ cached_plans` output shown in Figure 15-7.

	usecounts	cacheobjtype	objtype	text
1	1	Compiled Plan	Adhoc	SELECT c.usecounts, c.cacheobjtype, c.objtype...
2	1	Compiled Plan	Adhoc	SELECT a.* FROM Person.Address AS a WHERE a.Ad...
3	1	Compiled Plan	Prepared	(@1 tinyint)SELECT [a].* FROM [Person].[Address] [a] WHE...

Figure 15-7. sys.dm_exec_cached_plans output showing an autoparameterized plan

The usecounts of the executable plan for the parameterized query appropriately represents the number of reuses as 1. Also, note that the objtype for the autoparameterized executable plan is no longer Adhoc; it reflects the fact that the plan is for a parameterized query, Prepared.

The original ad hoc query, even though not executed, gets compiled to create the query tree required for the simple parameterization of the query. The compiled plan for the ad hoc query will be saved in the plan cache. But before creating the executable plan for the ad hoc query, SQL Server figured out that it was safe to autoparameterize and thus autoparameterized the query for further processing. This is visible as the highlighted line in Figure 15-7.

Since this ad hoc query has been autoparameterized, SQL Server will reuse the existing execution plan if you reexecute simpleparameterization.sql with a different value for the variable part.

```
SELECT.*
FROM        Person.Address AS a
WHERE       a.[AddressID] = 52; --previous value was 42
```

Figure 15-8 shows the output of sys.dm_exec_cached_plans.

	usecounts	cacheobjtype	objtype	text
1	1	Compiled Plan	Adhoc	SELECT a.* FROM Person.Address AS a WHERE ...
2	1	Compiled Plan	Adhoc	SELECT a.* FROM Person.Address AS a WHERE a.Ad...
3	2	Compiled Plan	Prepared	(@1 tinyint)SELECT [a].* FROM [Person].[Address] [a] WHE...

Figure 15-8. *sys.dm_exec_cached_plans output showing reuse of the autoparameterized plan*

From Figure 15-8, you can see that although a new plan has been generated for this ad hoc query, the ad hoc one using an AddressId value of 52, the existing prepared plan is reused as indicated by the increase in the corresponding usecounts value to 2. The ad hoc query can be reexecuted repeatedly with different filter criterion values, reusing the existing execution plan—all this despite that the original text of the two queries does not match. The parameterized query for both would be the same, so it was reused.

There is one more aspect to note in the parameterized query for which the execution plan is cached. In Figure 15-7, observe that the body of the parameterized query doesn't exactly match with that of the ad hoc query submitted. For instance, in the ad hoc query, there are no square brackets on any of the objects.

On realizing that the ad hoc query can be safely autoparameterized, SQL Server picks a template that can be used instead of the exact text of the query.

To understand the significance of this, consider the following query:

```
SELECT  a.*
FROM    Person.Address AS a
WHERE   a.AddressID BETWEEN 40 AND 60;
```

Figure 15-9 shows the output of sys.dm_exec_cached_plans.

	usecounts	cacheobjtype	objtype	text
1	1	Compiled Plan	Adhoc	SELECT a.* FROM Person.Address AS a WHERE a.AddressID BETWEEN 40 AND 60;
2	1	Compiled Plan	Prepared	(@1 tinyint,@2 tinyint)SELECT [a].* FROM [Person].[Address] [a] WHERE [a].[AddressID]>=@1 AND [a].[AddressID]<=@2

Figure 15-9. *sys.dm_exec_cached_plans output showing plan simple parameterization using a template*

From Figure 15-9, you can see that SQL Server put the query through the simplification process and substituted a pair of >= and <= operators, which are equivalent to the BETWEEN operator. Then the parameterization step modified the query again. That means instead of resubmitting the preceding ad hoc query using the BETWEEN clause, if a similar query using a pair of >= and <= is submitted, SQL Server will be able to reuse the existing execution plan. To confirm this behavior, let's modify the ad hoc query as follows:

```
SELECT   a.*
FROM     Person.Address AS a
WHERE    a.AddressID >= 40
         AND a.AddressID <= 60;
```

Figure 15-10 shows the output of sys.dm_exec_cached_plans.

	usecounts	cacheobjtype	objtype	text
1	1	Compiled Plan	Adhoc	SELECT a.* FROM Person.Address AS a WHERE a.AddressID >= 40 AND a.AddressID <= 60;
2	1	Compiled Plan	Adhoc	SELECT a.* FROM Person.Address AS a WHERE a.AddressID BETWEEN 40 AND 60;
3	2	Compiled Plan	Prepared	(@1 tinyint,@2 tinyint)SELECT [a].* FROM [Person].[Address] [a] WHERE [a].[AddressID]>=@1 AND [a].[AddressID]<=@2

Figure 15-10. *sys.dm_exec_cached_plans output showing reuse of the autoparameterized plan*

From Figure 15-10, you can see that the existing plan is reused, even though the query is syntactically different from the query executed earlier. The autoparameterized plan generated by SQL Server allows the existing plan to be reused not only when the query is resubmitted with different variable values but also for queries with the same template form.

Simple Parameterization Limits

SQL Server is highly conservative during simple parameterization because the cost of a bad plan can far outweigh the cost of generating a new plan. The conservative approach prevents SQL Server from creating an unsafe autoparameterized plan. Thus, simple parameterization is limited to fairly simple cases, such as ad hoc queries with only one table. An ad hoc query with a join operation between two (or more) tables (as shown in the early part of the "Plan Reusability of an Ad Hoc Workload" section) is not considered safe for simple parameterization.

In a scalable system, do not rely on simple parameterization for plan reusability. The simple parameterization feature of SQL Server makes an educated guess as to which variables and constants can be parameterized. Instead of relying on SQL Server for simple parameterization, you should actually specify it programmatically while building your application.

Forced Parameterization

If the system you're working on consists of primarily ad hoc queries, you may want to attempt to increase the number of queries that accept parameterization. You can modify a database to attempt to force, within certain restrictions, all queries to be parameterized just like in simple parameterization.

To do this, you have to change the database option PARAMETERIZATION to FORCED using ALTER DATABASE like this:

```
ALTER DATABASE AdventureWorks2012 SET PARAMETERIZATION FORCED;
```

But, if you have a query that is in any way complicated, you won't get simple parameterization.

```
SELECT  ea.EmailAddress,
        e.BirthDate,
        a.City
FROM    Person.Person AS p
JOIN    HumanResources.Employee AS e
    ON p.BusinessEntityID = e.BusinessEntityID
JOIN    Person.BusinessEntityAddress AS bea
    ON e.BusinessEntityID = bea.BusinessEntityID
JOIN    Person.Address AS a
    ON bea.AddressID = a.AddressID
JOIN    Person.StateProvince AS sp
    ON a.StateProvinceID = sp.StateProvinceID
JOIN    Person.EmailAddress AS ea
    ON p.BusinessEntityID = ea.BusinessEntityID
WHERE   ea.EmailAddress LIKE 'david%'
    AND sp.StateProvinceCode = 'WA';
```

When you run this query, simple parameterization is not applied, as you can see in Figure 15-11.

	usecounts	cacheobjtype	objtype	text
1	1	Compiled Plan	Adhoc	SELECT c.usecounts, c.cacheobjtype, c.objtype, t.text FROM sys.dm_exec_cached_plans c CROSS AP...
2	1	Compiled Plan	Adhoc	SELECT ea.EmailAddress, e.BirthDate, a.City FROM Person.Person AS p JOIN HumanResources.Employee AS e ...

Figure 15-11. *A more complicated query doesn't get parameterized*

No prepared plans are visible in the output from sys.dm_exec_cached_plans. But if you use the previous script to set PARAMETERIZATION to FORCED, clear the cache, and rerun the query, the output from sys.dmexeccachedplans changes so that the output looks different, as shown in Figure 15-12.

	usecounts	cacheobjtype	objtype	text
1	1	Compiled Plan	Adhoc	SELECT c.usecounts, c.cacheobjtype, c.objtype, t.text FR...
2	1	Compiled Plan	Adhoc	SELECT ea.EmailAddress, e.BirthDate, a.City FROM Person.Person A...
3	1	Compiled Plan	Prepared	(@0 varchar(8000))select ea . EmailAddress , e . BirthDate , a . City from Perso...

Figure 15-12. *Forced parameterization changes the plan*

Now a prepared plan is visible in the third row. However, only a single parameter was supplied, @0 varchar(8000). If you get the full text of the prepared plan out of sys.dm_exec_ querytext and format it, it looks like this:

```
(@0 varchar(8000))
SELECT  ea.EmailAddress,
        e.BirthDate,
        a.City
FROM    Person.Person AS p
JOIN    HumanResources.Employee AS e
        ON p.BusinessEntityID = e.BusinessEntityID
```

```
JOIN    Person.BusinessEntityAddress AS bea
        ON e.BusinessEntityID = bea.BusinessEntityID
JOIN    Person.Address AS a
        ON bea.AddressID = a.AddressID
JOIN    Person.StateProvince AS sp
        ON a.StateProvinceID = sp.StateProvinceID
JOIN    Person.EmailAddress AS ea
        ON p.BusinessEntityID = ea.BusinessEntityID
WHERE   ea.EmailAddress LIKE 'david%'
        AND sp.StateProvinceCode = @0
```

Because of its restrictions, forced parameterization was unable to substitute anything for the string 'david%', but it was able to for the string 'WA'. Worth noting is that the variable was declared as a full 8,000-length VARCHAR instead of the three-character NCHAR like the actual column in the Person.StateProvince table. Although you have a parameter, it might lead to implicit data conversions that could prevent the use of an index.

Before you start using forced parameterization, the following list of restrictions may give you information to help you decide whether forced parameterization will work in your database. (This is a partial list; for the complete list, please consult Books Online.)

- INSERT ... EXECUTE queries

- Statements inside procedures, triggers, and user-defined functions since they already have execution plans

- Client-side prepared statements (you'll find more detail on these later in this chapter)

- Queries with the query hint RECOMPILE

- Pattern and escape clause arguments used in a LIKE statement (as shown earlier)

This gives you an idea of the types of restrictions placed on forced parameterization. Forced parameterization is really going to be potentially helpful only if you are suffering from large amounts of compiles and recompiles because of ad hoc queries. Any other load won't benefit from the use of forced parameterization.

Before continuing, change the database back to SIMPLE PARAMETERIZATION.

```
ALTER DATABASE AdventureWorks2012 SET PARAMETERIZATION SIMPLE;
```

Plan Reusability of a Prepared Workload

Defining queries as a prepared workload allows the variable parts of the queries to be explicitly parameterized. This enables SQL Server to generate a query plan that is not tied to the variable parts of the query, and it keeps the variable parts separate in an execution context. As you saw in the previous section, SQL Server supports three techniques to submit a prepared workload.

- Stored procedures

- sp_executesql

- Prepare/execute model

In the sections that follow, I cover each of these techniques in more depth and point out where it's possible for parameterized execution plans to cause problems.

Stored Procedures

Using stored procedures is a standard technique for improving the effectiveness of plan caching. When the stored procedure is compiled at execution time (this is different for native compiled procedures, which are covered in Chapter 22), a plan is generated for each of the SQL statements within the stored procedure. The execution plan generated for the stored procedure can be reused whenever the stored procedure is reexecuted with different parameter values.

In addition to checking sys.dm_exec_cached_plans, you can track the execution plan caching for stored procedures using the Extended Events tool. Extended Events provides the events listed in Table 15-2 to track the plan caching for stored procedures.

Table 15-2. *Events to Analyze Plan Caching for the Stored Procedures Event Class*

Event	Description
sp_cache_hit	The plan is found in the cache.
sp_cache_miss	The plan is not found in the cache.
sp_cache_insert	The event fires when a plan is added to cache.
sp_cache_remove	The event fires when a plan gets removed from cache.

To track the stored procedure plan caching using trace events, you can use these events along with the other stored procedure events and data columns shown in Table 15-3.

Table 15-3. *Data Columns to Analyze Plan Caching for Stored Procedures Event Class*

Event	Data Column
SP:CacheHit	EventClass
SP:CacheMiss	TextData
SP:Completed	LoginName
SP:ExecContextHit	SPID
SP:Starting	StartTime
SP:StmtCompleted	

To understand how stored procedures can improve plan caching, reexamine the procedure created earlier called BasicSalesInfo. The procedure is repeated here for clarity:

```
IF (SELECT   OBJECT_ID('BasicSalesInfo')
    ) IS NOT NULL
    DROP PROC dbo.BasicSalesInfo ;
GO
CREATE PROC dbo.BasicSalesInfo
    @ProductID INT,
    @CustomerID INT
```

```
AS
SELECT    soh.SalesOrderNumber,
          soh.OrderDate,
          sod.OrderQty,
          sod.LineTotal
FROM      Sales.SalesOrderHeader AS soh
JOIN      Sales.SalesOrderDetail AS sod
          ON soh.SalesOrderID = sod.SalesOrderID
WHERE     soh.CustomerID = @CustomerID
          AND sod.ProductID = @ProductID;
```

To retrieve a result set for soh.CustomerId = 29690 and sod.ProductId=711, you can execute the stored procedure like this:

```
EXEC dbo.BasicSalesInfo
    @CustomerID = 29690,
    @ProductID = 711;
```

Figure 15-13 shows the output of sys.dm_exec_cached_plans.

	usecounts	cacheobjtype	objtype	text
1	1	Compiled Plan	Proc	CREATE PROC dbo.BasicSalesInfo @ProductID INT, ...

Figure 15-13. sys.dm_exec_cached_plans output showing stored procedure plan caching

From Figure 15-13, you can see that a compiled plan of type Proc is generated and cached for the stored procedure. The usecounts value of the executable plan is 1 since the stored procedure is executed only once.

Figure 15-14 shows the Extended Events output for this stored procedure execution.

sp_cache_miss	2014-02-25 19:20:30.7314035
sp_cache_insert	2014-02-25 19:20:30.7367904
sql_batch_completed	2014-02-25 19:20:30.8292183

Event: sp_cache_miss (2014-02-25 19:20:30.7314035)

Details

Field	Value
cached_text	EXEC dbo.BasicSalesInfo @CustomerID = 29690, @Prod...
database_id	5
database_name	AdventureWorks2012
object_id	598388816
object_name	
object_type	ADHOC

Figure 15-14. Extended Events output showing that the stored procedure plan isn't easily found in the cache

From the Extended Events output, you can see that the plan for the stored procedure is not found in the cache. When the stored procedure is executed the first time, SQL Server looks in the procedure cache and fails to find any cache entry for the procedure BasicSalesInfo, causing an sp_cache_miss event. On not finding a cached plan, SQL Server makes arrangements to compile the stored procedure. Subsequently, SQL Server generates and saves the plan and proceeds with the execution of the stored procedure. You can see this in the sp_cache_insert event. Figure 15-15 shows the details.

Field	Value
cached_text	
database_id	5
database_name	AdventureWorks2012
object_id	436196604
object_name	BasicSalesInfo
object_type	PROC
plan_handle	0xF0000000000000008521438FA7F0000A01F0000000000000...

Figure 15-15. *Details of the sp_cache_hit extended event*

If this stored procedure is reexecuted to retrieve a result set for @ProductId = 777, then the existing plan is reused, as shown in the sys.dm_exec_cached_plans output in Figure 15-16.

	usecounts	cacheobjtype	objtype	text
2	2	Compiled Plan	Proc	CREATE PROC dbo.BasicSalesInfo @ProductID INT. ...

Figure 15-16. *sys.dm_exec_cached_plans output showing reuse of the stored procedure plan*

```
EXEC dbo.BasicSalesInfo
    @CustomerID = 29690,
    @ProductID = 777;
```

You can also confirm the reuse of the execution plan from the Extended Events output, as shown in Figure 15-17.

▶	sp_cache_hit	2014-02-25 19:21:44.2242339

Event: sp_cache_hit (2014-02-25 19:21:44.2242339)

Details

Field	Value
cached_text	
database_id	5
database_name	AdventureWorks2012
object_id	436196604
object_name	BasicSalesInfo
object_type	PROC
plan_handle	0x00B71F6F00000000FEFFFFFFFFFFFFFFF08455C46FA7F0000...

Figure 15-17. *Profiler trace output showing reuse of the stored procedure plan*

From the Extended Events output, you can see that the existing plan is found in the procedure cache. On searching the cache, SQL Server finds the executable plan for the stored procedure BasicSalesInfo causing an sp_cache_hit event. Once the existing execution plan is found, SQL reuses the plan to execute the stored procedure. One interesting note: The sp_cache_miss event just prior is for the SQL batch calling the procedure. Because of the change to the parameter value, that statement was not found in the cache, but the procedure's execution plan was. This apparently "extra" cache miss event can cause confusion.

These other aspects of stored procedures are worth considering:

- Stored procedures are compiled on first execution.
- Stored procedures have other performance benefits, such as reducing network traffic.
- Stored procedures have additional benefits, such as the isolation of the data.

Stored Procedures Are Compiled on First Execution

The execution plan of a stored procedure is generated when it is executed the first time. When the stored procedure is created, it is only parsed and saved in the database. No normalization and optimization processes are performed during the stored procedure creation. This allows a stored procedure to be created before creating all the objects accessed by the stored procedure. For example, you can create the following stored procedure, even when table NotHere referred to in the stored procedure does not exist:

```
IF (SELECT  OBJECT_ID('dbo.MyNewProc')
    ) IS NOT NULL
    DROP PROCEDURE dbo.MyNewProc
GO
CREATE PROCEDURE dbo.MyNewProc
AS
SELECT  MyID
FROM    dbo.NotHere; --Table no_tl doesn't exist
```

The stored procedure will be created successfully since the normalization process to bind the referred object to the query tree (generated by the command parser during the stored procedure execution) is not performed during the stored procedure creation. The stored procedure will report the error when it is first executed (if table NotHere is not created by then) since the stored procedure is compiled the first time it is executed.

Other Performance Benefits of Stored Procedures

Besides improving the performance through execution plan reusability, stored procedures provide the following performance benefits:

- *Business logic is close to the data*: The parts of the business logic that perform extensive operations on data stored in the database should be put in stored procedures since SQL Server's engine is extremely powerful for relational and set theory operations.
- *Network traffic is reduced*: The database application, across the network, sends just the name of the stored procedure and the parameter values. Only the processed result set is returned to the application. The intermediate data doesn't need to be passed back and forth between the application and the database.

Additional Benefits of Stored Procedures

Some of the other benefits provided by stored procedures are as follows:

- *The application is isolated from data structure changes*: If all critical data access is made through stored procedures, then when the database schema changes, the stored procedures can be re-created without affecting the application code that accesses the data through the stored procedures. In fact, the application accessing the database need not even be stopped.

- *There is a single point of administration*: All the business logic implemented in stored procedures is maintained as part of the database and can be managed centrally on the database itself. Of course, this benefit is highly relative, depending on whom you ask. To get a different opinion, ask a non-DBA!

- *Security can be increased*: User privileges on database tables can be restricted and can be allowed only through the standard business logic implemented in the stored procedure. For example, if you want user UserOne to be restricted from physically deleting rows from table RestrictedAccess and to be allowed to mark only the rows virtually deleted through stored procedure MarkDeleted by setting the rows' status as 'Deleted', then you can execute the DENY and GRANT commands as follows:

```
IF (SELECT  OBJECT_ID('dbo.RestrictedAccess')
    ) IS NOT NULL
    DROP TABLE dbo.RestrictedAccess;
GO
CREATE TABLE dbo.RestrictedAccess (ID INT,Status VARCHAR(7));
INSERT  INTO t1
VALUES  (1,'New');
GO
IF (SELECT  OBJECT_ID('dbo.MarkDeleted')
    ) IS NOT NULL
    DROP PROCEDURE dbo.MarkDeleted;
GO
CREATE PROCEDURE dbo.MarkDeleted @ID INT
AS
UPDATE  dbo.RestrictedAccess
SET     Status = 'Deleted'
WHERE   ID = @ID;
GO

--Prevent user u1 from deleting rows
DENY DELETE ON dbo.RestrictedAccess TO UserOne;

--Allow user u1 to mark a row as 'deleted'
GRANT EXECUTE ON dbo.MarkDeleted TO UserOne;
```

This assumes the existence of user UserOne. Note that if the query within the stored procedure MarkDeleted is built dynamically as a string (@sql) as follows, then granting permission to the stored procedure won't grant any permission to the query, since the dynamic query isn't treated as part of the stored procedure:

```
CREATE PROCEDURE dbo.MarkDeleted @ID INT
AS
DECLARE @SQL NVARCHAR(MAX);
```

```
SET @SQL = 'UPDATE   dbo.RestrictedAccess
SET      Status = ''Deleted''
WHERE    ID = ' + @ID;

EXEC sys.sp_executesql @SQL;
GO

GRANT EXECUTE ON dbo.MarkDeleted TO UserOne;
```

Consequently, user UserOne won't be able to mark the row as 'Deleted' using the stored procedure MarkDeleted. (I cover the aspects of using a dynamic query in the stored procedure in the next chapter.)

Since stored procedures are saved as database objects, they add maintenance overhead to the database administration. Many times, you may need to execute just one or a few queries from the application. If these singleton queries are executed frequently, you should aim to reuse their execution plans to improve performance. But creating stored procedures for these individual singleton queries adds a large number of stored procedures to the database, increasing the database administrative overhead significantly. To avoid the maintenance overhead of using stored procedures and yet derive the benefit of plan reuse, submit the singleton queries as a prepared workload using the sp_executesql system stored procedure.

sp_executesql

sp_executesql is a system stored procedure that provides a mechanism to submit one or more queries as a prepared workload. It allows the variable parts of the query to be explicitly parameterized, and it can therefore provide execution plan reusability as effective as a stored procedure. The SELECT statement from BasicSalesInfo can be submitted through sp_ executesql as follows:

```
DECLARE @query NVARCHAR(MAX),
    @paramlist NVARCHAR(MAX);

SET @query = N'SELECT     soh.SalesOrderNumber ,soh.OrderDate ,sod.OrderQty ,sod.LineTotal FROM
    Sales.SalesOrderHeader AS soh
JOIN Sales.SalesOrderDetail AS sod ON soh.SalesOrderID = sod.SalesOrderID WHERE
    soh.CustomerID = @CustomerID
AND sod.ProductID = @ProductID';

SET @paramlist = N'@CustomerID INT, @ProductID INT';

EXEC sp_executesql @query,@paramlist,@CustomerID = 29690,@ProductID = 711;
```

Note that the strings passed to the sp_executesql stored procedure are declared as NVARCHAR and that they are built with a prefix of N. This is required since sp_executesql uses Unicode strings as the input parameters.

The output of sys.dm_exec_cached_plans is shown next (see Figure 15-18).

```
SELECT  c.usecounts,
        c.cacheobjtype,
        c.objtype,
        t.text
FROM    sys.dm_exec_cached_plans c
CROSS APPLY sys.dm_exec_sql_text(c.plan_handle) t
WHERE text LIKE '(@CustomerID%';
```

	usecounts	cacheobjtype	objtype	text
1	1	Compiled Plan	Prepared	(@CustomerID INT, @ProductID INT)SELECT soh.S...

Figure 15-18. *sys.dm_exec_cached_plans output showing a parameterized plan generated using sp_executesql*

In Figure 15-18, you can see that the plan is generated for the parameterized part of the query submitted through sp_executesql. Since the plan is not tied to the variable part of the query, the existing execution plan can be reused if this query is resubmitted with a different value for one of the parameters (d.ProductID=777), as follows:

```
EXEC sp_executesql @query,@paramlist,@CustomerID = 29690,@ProductID = 777;
```

Figure 15-19 shows the output of sys.dm_exec_cached_plans.

	usecounts	cacheobjtype	objtype	text
1	2	Compiled Plan	Prepared	(@CustomerID INT, @ProductID INT)SELECT soh.S...

Figure 15-19. *sys.dm_exec_cached_plans output showing reuse of the parameterized plan generated using sp_executesql*

From Figure 15-19, you can see that the existing plan is reused (usecounts is 2 on the plan on line 2) when the query is resubmitted with a different variable value. If this query is resubmitted many times with different values for the variable part, the existing execution plan can be reused without regenerating new execution plans.

The query for which the plan is created (the text column) matches the exact textual string of the parameterized query submitted through sp_executesql. Therefore, if the same query is submitted from different parts of the application, ensure that the same textual string is used in all places. For example, if the same query is resubmitted with a minor modification in the query string (say in lowercase instead of uppercase letters), then the existing plan is not reused, and instead a new plan is created, as shown in the sys. dm_exec_cached_plans output in Figure 15-20.

```
SET @query = N'SELECT    soh.SalesOrderNumber ,soh.OrderDate ,sod.OrderQty ,sod.LineTotal FROM
Sales.SalesOrderHeader AS soh JOIN Sales.SalesOrderDetail AS sod ON soh.SalesOrderID = sod.
SalesOrderID where     soh.CustomerID = @CustomerID AND sod.ProductID = @ProductID' ;
```

	usecounts	cacheobjtype	objtype	text
1	1	Compiled Plan	Prepared	(@CustomerID INT, @ProductID INT)SELECT soh.S...
2	2	Compiled Plan	Prepared	(@CustomerID INT, @ProductID INT)SELECT soh.S...

Figure 15-20. *sys.dm_exec_cached_plans output showing sensitivity of the plan generated using sp_executesql*

Another way to see that there are two different plans created in cache is to use additional dynamic management objects to see the properties of the plans in cache.

```
SELECT  decp.usecounts,
        decp.cacheobjtype,
        decp.objtype,
        dest.text,
        deqs.creation_time,
        deqs.execution_count,
```

```
        deqs.query_hash,
        deqs.query_plan_hash
FROM    sys.dm_exec_cached_plans AS decp
CROSS APPLY sys.dm_exec_sql_text(decp.plan_handle) AS dest
JOIN    sys.dm_exec_query_stats AS deqs
        ON decp.plan_handle = deqs.plan_handle
WHERE   dest.text LIKE '(@CustomerID INT, @ProductID INT)%' ;
```

Figure 15-21 shows the results from this query.

	usecounts	cacheobjtype	objtype	text	creation_time	execution_count	query_hash	query_plan_hash
1	1	Compiled Plan	Prepared	(@CustomerID INT, @ProductID INT)SELECT soh.S...	2014-02-25 19:47:47.387	1	0x8C19421B146C824D	0xA1905031A71C112A
2	2	Compiled Plan	Prepared	(@CustomerID INT, @ProductID INT)SELECT soh.S...	2014-02-25 19:41:25.510	2	0x8C19421B146C824D	0xA1905031A71C112A

Figure 15-21. *Additional output from sys.dm_exec_query_stats*

The output from sys.dm_exec_query_stats shows that the two versions of the query have different creation_time values. More interestingly, they have identical query_hashs but different query_plan_hashs (more on the hash values in that section later). All this shows that changing the case resulted in differing execution plans being stored in cache.

In general, use sp_executesql to explicitly parameterize queries to make their execution plans reusable when the queries are resubmitted with different values for the variable parts. This provides the performance benefit of reusable plans without the overhead of managing any persistent object as required for stored procedures. This feature is exposed by both ODBC and OLEDB through SOLExecDirect and ICommandWithParameters, respectively. Like .NET developers or users of ADO.NET (ADO 2.7 or newer), you can submit the preceding SELECT statement using ADO Command and Parameters. If you set the ADO Command Prepared property to FALSE and use ADO Command ('SELECT * FROM "Order Details" d, Orders o WHERE d.OrderID=o.OrderID and d.ProductID=?') with ADO Parameters, ADO.NET will send the SELECT statement using sp_executesql. Most object-to-relational mapping tools, such as nHibernate or Entity Framework, also have mechanisms to allow for preparing statements and using parameters.

Along with the parameters, sp_executesql sends the entire query string across the network every time the query is reexecuted. You can avoid this by using the prepare/execute model of ODBC and OLEDB (or OLEDB .NET).

Prepare/Execute Model

ODBC and OLEDB provide a prepare/execute model to submit queries as a prepared workload. Like sp_executesql, this model allows the variable parts of the queries to be parameterized explicitly. The prepare phase allows SQL Server to generate the execution plan for the query and return a handle of the execution plan to the application. This execution plan handle is used by the execute phase to execute the query with different parameter values. This model can be used only to submit queries through ODBC or OLEDB, and it can't be used within SQL Server itself—queries within stored procedures can't be executed using this model.

The SQL Server ODBC driver provides the SOLPrepare and SOLExecute APIs to support the prepare/execute model. The SQL Server OLEDB provider exposes this model through the ICommandPrepare interface. The OLEDB .NET provider of ADO.NET behaves similarly.

■ **Note**   For a detailed description of how to use the prepare/execute model in a database application, please refer to the MSDN article "Preparing SQL Statements" (http://bit.ly/MskJcG).

Query Plan Hash and Query Hash

With SQL Server 2008, new functionality around execution plans and the cache was introduced called the *query plan hash* and the *query hash*. These are binary objects using an algorithm against the query or the query plan to generate the binary hash value. These are useful for a common practice in developing known as *copy and paste*. You will find that common patterns and practices will be repeated throughout your code. Under the best circumstances, this is a good thing because you will see the best types of queries, joins, set-based operations, and so on, copied from one procedure to another as needed. But sometimes, you will see the worst possible practices repeated over and over again in your code. This is where the query hash and the query plan hash come into play to help you out.

You can retrieve the query plan hash and the query hash from sys.dm_exec_query_stats or sys.dm_exec_requests. Although this is a mechanism for identifying queries and their plans, the hash values are not unique. Dissimilar plans can arrive at the same hash, so you can't rely on this as an alternate primary key.

To see the hash values in action, create two queries.

```
SELECT  *
FROM    Production.Product AS p
JOIN    Production.ProductSubcategory AS ps
        ON p.ProductSubcategoryID = ps.ProductSubcategoryID
JOIN    Production.ProductCategory AS pc
        ON ps.ProductCategoryID = pc.ProductCategoryID
WHERE   pc.[Name] = 'Bikes'
        AND ps.[Name] = 'Touring Bikes';


SELECT  *
FROM    Production.Product AS p
JOIN    Production.ProductSubcategory AS ps
        ON p.ProductSubcategoryID = ps.ProductSubcategoryID
JOIN    Production.ProductCategory AS pc
        ON ps.ProductCategoryID = pc.ProductCategoryID
where   pc.[Name] = 'Bikes'
        and ps.[Name] = 'Road Bikes';
```

Note that the only substantial difference between the two queries is that ProductSubcategory.Name is different, with Touring Bikes in one and Road Bikes in the other. However, also note that the WHERE and AND keywords in the second query are lowercase. After you execute each of these queries, you can see the results of these format changes from sys.dm_exec_query_stats in Figure 15-22 from the following query:

```
SELECT  deqs.execution_count,
        deqs.query_hash,
        deqs.query_plan_hash,
        dest.text
FROM    sys.dm_exec_query_stats AS deqs
CROSS APPLY sys.dm_exec_sql_text(deqs.plan_handle) dest
WHERE   dest.text LIKE 'SELECT  *
FROM    Production.Product AS p%';
```

	execution_count	query_hash	query_plan_hash	text
1	1	0xD82929ADC1184DCF	0xEE1B9433EDB9EE01	SELECT * FROM Production.Product AS p JOI...
2	1	0xD82929ADC1184DCF	0xEE1B9433EDB9EE01	SELECT * FROM Production.Product AS p JOI...

Figure 15-22. *sys.dm_exec_query_stats showing the plan hash values*

Two different plans were created because these are not parameterized queries; they are too complex to be considered for simple parameterization, and forced parameterization is off. These two plans have identical hash values because they varied only in terms of the values passed. The differences in case did not matter to the query hash or the query plan hash value. If, however, you changed the SELECT criteria in queryhash, then the values would be retrieved from sys.dm_exec_query_stats, as shown in Figure 15-23, and the query would have changes.

```
SELECT   p.ProductID
FROM     Production.Product AS p
JOIN     Production.ProductSubcategory AS ps
         ON p.ProductSubcategoryID = ps.ProductSubcategoryID
JOIN     Production.ProductCategory AS pc
         ON ps.ProductCategoryID = pc.ProductCategoryID
WHERE    pc.[Name] = 'Bikes'
         AND ps.[Name] = 'Touring Bikes';
```

	execution_count	query_hash	query_plan_hash	text
1	1	0xD82929ADC1184DCF	0xEE1B9433EDB9EE01	SELECT * FROM Production.Product AS p JOIN ...
2	1	0xD82929ADC1184DCF	0xEE1B9433EDB9EE01	SELECT * FROM Production.Product AS p JOIN ...
3	1	0x5D1D4E36885B5BF9	0xB93D77ECE9843096	SELECT p.ProductID FROM Production.Product ...

Figure 15-23. sys.dm_exec_query_stats showing a different hash

Although the basic structure of the query is the same, the change in the columns returned was enough to change the query hash value and the query plan hash value.

Because differences in data distribution and indexes can cause the same query to come up with two different plans, the query_hash can be the same, and the query_plan_hash can be different. To illustrate this, execute two new queries.

```
SELECT   p.[Name],
         tha.TransactionDate,
         tha.TransactionType,
         tha.Quantity,
         tha.ActualCost
FROM     Production.TransactionHistoryArchive tha
JOIN     Production.Product p
         ON tha.ProductID = p.ProductID
WHERE    p.ProductID = 461;

SELECT   p.[Name],
         tha.TransactionDate,
         tha.TransactionType,
         tha.Quantity,
         tha.ActualCost
FROM     Production.TransactionHistoryArchive tha
JOIN     Production.Product p
         ON tha.ProductID = p.ProductID
WHERE    p.ProductID = 712;
```

Like the original queries used earlier, these queries vary only by the values passed to the ProductID column. When both queries are run, you can select data from sys.dm_exec_query_ stats to see the hash values (Figure 15-24).

	execution_count	query_hash	query_plan_hash	text	
1	1	0xD4FA47AE35195F89	0x12375C8B908754AB	SELECT p.[Name],	tha.TransactionDate, ...
2	1	0xD4FA47AE35195F89	0xECA99937BF5E3180	SELECT p.[Name],	tha.TransactionDate, ...

Figure 15-24. *Differences in the query_plan_hash*

You can see the queryhash values are identical, but the query_plan_hash values are different. This is because the execution plans created, based on the statistics for the values passed in, are radically different, as you can see in Figure 15-25.

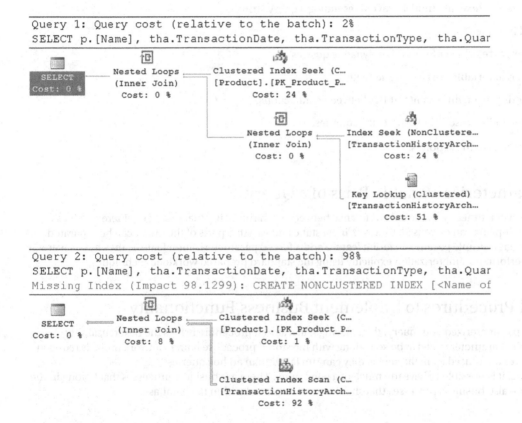

Figure 15-25. *Different parameters result in radically different plans*

The query plan hash and the query hash values can be useful tools for tracking down common issues between disparate queries, but as you've seen, they're not going to retrieve an accurate set of information in every possibility. They do add yet another useful tool in identifying other places where query performance could be poor. They can also be used to track execution plans over time. You can capture the query_plan_hash for a query after deploying it to production and then watch it over time to see whether it changes because of data changes. With this you can also keep track of aggregated query stats by plan, referencing sys.dm_exec_ querystats, although remember that the aggregated data is reset when the server is restarted or the plan cache is cleared in any way. Keep these tools in mind while tuning your queries.

Execution Plan Cache Recommendations

The basic purpose of the plan cache is to improve performance by reusing execution plans. Thus, it is important to ensure that your execution plans actually are reusable. Since the plan reusability of ad hoc queries is inefficient, it is generally recommended that you rely on prepared workload techniques as much as possible. To ensure efficient use of the plan cache, follow these recommendations:

- Explicitly parameterize variable parts of a query.
- Use stored procedures to implement business functionality.
- Use sp_executesql to avoid stored procedure maintenance.
- Use the prepare/execute model to avoid resending a query string.
- Avoid ad hoc queries.
- Use sp_executesql over EXECUTE for dynamic queries.
- Parameterize variable parts of queries with care.
- Avoid modifying environment settings between connections.
- Avoid the implicit resolution of objects in queries.

Let's take a closer look at these points.

Explicitly Parameterize Variable Parts of a Query

A query is often run several times, with the only difference between each run being that there are different values for the variable parts. Their plans can be reused, however, if the static and variable parts of the query can be separated. Although SQL Server has a simple parameterization feature and a forced parameterization feature, they have severe limitations. Always perform parameterization explicitly using the standard prepared workload techniques.

Create Stored Procedures to Implement Business Functionality

If you have explicitly parameterized your query, then placing it in a stored procedure brings the best reusability possible. Since only the parameters need to be sent along with the stored procedure name, network traffic is reduced. Since stored procedures are reused from the cache, they can run faster than ad hoc queries.

Like anything else, it is possible to have too much of a good thing. There are business processes that belong in the database, but there are also business processes that should never be placed within the database.

Code with sp_executesql to Avoid Stored Procedure Maintenance

If the object maintenance required for the stored procedures becomes a consideration or you are using queries generated on the client side, then use sp_executesql to submit the queries as prepared workloads. Unlike the stored procedure model, sp_executesql doesn't create any persistent objects in the database. sp_executesql is suited to execute a singleton query or a small batch query.

The complete business logic implemented in a stored procedure can also be submitted with sp_executesql as a large query string. However, as the complexity of the business logic increases, it becomes difficult to create and maintain a query string for the complete logic.

Also, using sp sp_executesql and stored procedures with appropriate parameters prevents SQL injection attacks on the server.

Implement the Prepare/Execute Model to Avoid Resending a Query String

sp_executesql requires the query string to be sent across the network every time the query is reexecuted. It also requires the cost of a query string match at the server to identify the corresponding execution plan in the procedure cache. In the case of an ODBC or OLEDB (or OLEDB .NET) application, you can use the prepare/execute model to avoid resending the query string during multiple executions, since only the plan handle and parameters need to be submitted. In the prepare/execute model, since a plan handle is returned to the application, the plan can be reused by other user connections; it is not limited to the user who created the plan.

Avoid Ad Hoc Queries

Do not design new applications using ad hoc queries! The execution plan created for an ad hoc query cannot be reused when the query is resubmitted with a different value for the variable parts. Even though SQL Server has the simple parameterization and forced parameterization features to isolate the variable parts of the query, because of the strict conservativeness of SQL Server in parameterization, the feature is limited to simple queries only. For better plan reusability, submit the queries as prepared workloads.

There are systems built upon the concept of nothing but ad hoc queries. This is functional and can work within SQL Server, but, as you've seen, it carries with it large amounts of additional overhead that you'll need to plan for. Also, ad hoc queries are generally how SQL injection gets introduced to a system.

Prefer sp_executesql Over EXECUTE for Dynamic Queries

SQL query strings generated dynamically within stored procedures or a database application should be executed using spexecutesql instead of the EXECUTE command. The EXECUTE command doesn't allow the variable parts of the query to be explicitly parameterized.

To understand the preceding comparison between sp_executesql and EXECUTE, consider the dynamic SQL query string used to execute the SELECT statement in adhocsproc.

```
DECLARE @n VARCHAR(3) = '776',
    @sql VARCHAR(MAX);

SET @sql = 'SELECT * FROM Sales.SalesOrderDetail sod  '
    + 'JOIN Sales.SalesOrderHeader soh  '
    + 'ON sod.SalesOrderID=soh.SalesOrderID ' + 'WHERE    sod.ProductID='''
    + @n + '''';

--Execute the dynamic query using EXECUTE statement
EXECUTE (@sql);
```

The EXECUTE statement submits the query along with the value of d.ProductID as an ad hoc query and thereby may or may not result in simple parameterization. Check the output yourself by looking at the cache.

```
SELECT  deqs.execution_count,
        deqs.query_hash,
        deqs.query_plan_hash,
        dest.text,
        deqp.query_plan
FROM    sys.dm_exec_query_stats AS deqs
CROSS APPLY sys.dm_exec_sql_text(deqs.plan_handle) dest
CROSS APPLY sys.dm_exec_query_plan(deqs.plan_handle) AS deqp;
```

For improved plan cache reusability, execute the dynamic SQL string as a parameterized query using
sp_executesql.

```
DECLARE @n NVARCHAR(3) = '776',
    @sql NVARCHAR(MAX),
    @paramdef NVARCHAR(6);

SET @sql = 'SELECT * FROM Sales.SalesOrderDetail sod  '
    + 'JOIN Sales.SalesOrderHeader soh  '
    + 'ON sod.SalesOrderID=soh.SalesOrderID ' + 'WHERE    sod.ProductID=@1' ;
SET @paramdef = N'@1 INT';

--Execute the dynamic query using sp_executesql system stored procedure
EXECUTE sp_executesql
    @sql,
    @paramdef,
    @1 = @n;
```

Executing the query as an explicitly parameterized query using sp_executesql generates a parameterized plan
for the query and thereby increases the execution plan reusability.

Parameterize Variable Parts of Queries with Care

Be careful while converting variable parts of a query into parameters. The range of values for some variables may vary
so drastically that the execution plan for a certain range of values may not be suitable for the other values. This can
lead to bad parameter sniffing (covered in Chapter 16).

Do Not Allow Implicit Resolution of Objects in Queries

SQL Server allows multiple database objects with the same name to be created under different schemas. For example,
table t1 can be created using two different schemas (u1 and u2) under their individual ownership. The default owner
in most systems is dbo (database owner). If user u1 executes the following query, then SQL Server first tries to find
whether table t1 exists for user u1's default schema.

```
SELECT * FROM t1 WHERE c1 = 1;
```

If not, then it tries to find whether table t1 exists for the dbo user. This implicit resolution allows user u1 to create
another instance of table t1 under a different schema and access it temporarily (using the same application code)
without affecting other users.

On a production database, I recommend using the schema owner and avoiding implicit resolution. If not, using
implicit resolution adds the following overhead on a production server:

- It requires more time to identify the objects.

- It decreases the effectiveness of plan cache reusability.

Summary

SQL Server's cost-based query optimizer decides upon an effective execution plan not based on the exact syntax of the query but by evaluating the cost of executing the query using different processing strategies. The cost evaluation of using different processing strategies is done in multiple optimization phases to avoid spending too much time optimizing a query. Then, the execution plans are cached to save the cost of execution plan generation when the same queries are reexecuted. To improve the reusability of cached plans, SQL Server supports different techniques for execution plan reuse when the queries are rerun with different values for the variable parts.

Using stored procedures is usually the best technique to improve execution plan reusability. SQL Server generates a parameterized execution plan for the stored procedures so that the existing plan can be reused when the stored procedure is rerun with the same or different parameter values. However, if the existing execution plan for a stored procedure is invalidated, the plan can't be reused without a recompilation, decreasing the effectiveness of plan cache reusability.

In the next chapter, I will discuss how to troubleshoot and resolve bad parameter sniffing.

CHAPTER 16

■ ■ ■

Parameter Sniffing

In the previous chapter, I discussed how to get execution plans into cache and how to get them reused. It's a laudable goal and one of the many ways to improve the overall performance of the system. One of the best mechanisms for ensuring plan reuse is to parameterize the query, through either stored procedures, prepared statements, or sp_executesql. All these mechanisms create a parameter that is used instead of a hard-coded value when creating the plan. These parameters can be sampled, or sniffed, by the optimizer to use the values contained within when creating the execution plan. When this works well, as it does most of the time, you benefit from more accurate plans. But when it goes wrong and becomes bad parameter sniffing, you can see serious performance issues.

In this chapter, I cover the following topics:

- The helpful mechanisms behind parameter sniffing
- How parameter sniffing can turn bad
- Mechanisms for dealing with bad parameter sniffing

Parameter Sniffing

When a parameterized query is sent to the optimizer and there is no existing plan in cache, the optimizer will perform its function to create an execution plan for manipulating the data as requested by the T-SQL statement. When this parameterized query is called, the values of the parameters are set, either through your program or through defaults in the parameter definitions. Either way, there is a value there. The optimizer knows this. So, it takes advantage of that fact and reads the value of the parameters. This is the "sniffing" aspect of the process known as *parameter sniffing*. With these values available, the optimizer will then use those specific values to look at the statistics of the data to which the parameters refer. With specific values and a set of accurate statistics, you'll get a better execution plan. This beneficial process of parameter sniffing is running all the time, automatically, for all your parameterized queries, regardless of where they come from.

You can also get sniffing of local variables. Before proceeding with that, though, let's delineate between a local variable and a parameter since, within a T-SQL statement, they can look the same. This example shows both a local variable and a parameter:

```
CREATE PROCEDURE dbo.ProductDetails
(@ProductID INT)
AS
DECLARE @CurrentDate DATETIME = GETDATE();

SELECT  p.Name,
        p.Color,
        p.DaysToManufacture,
        pm.CatalogDescription
```

```
FROM    Production.Product AS p
JOIN    Production.ProductModel AS pm
        ON pm.ProductModelID = p.ProductModelID
WHERE   p.ProductID = @ProductID
        AND pm.ModifiedDate < @CurrentDate;
GO
```

The parameter in the previous query is @ProductID. The local variable is @CurrentDate. It's important to differentiate these since when you get down to the WHERE clause, they look exactly the same.

If you get a recompile of any statement that is using local variables, those variables can be sniffed by the optimizer the same way it sniffs parameters. Just be aware of this. Other than this unique situation with the recompile, local variables are unknown quantities to the optimizer when it goes to compile a plan. Normally only parameters can be sniffed.

To see parameter sniffing in action and to show that it's useful, let's start with a different procedure.

```
IF (SELECT  OBJECT_ID('dbo.AddressByCity')
    ) IS NOT NULL
    DROP PROC dbo.AddressByCity;
GO
CREATE PROC dbo.AddressByCity @City NVARCHAR(30)
AS
SELECT  a.AddressID,
        a.AddressLine1,
        AddressLine2,
        a.City,
        sp.[Name] AS StateProvinceName,
        a.PostalCode
FROM    Person.Address AS a
JOIN    Person.StateProvince AS sp
        ON a.StateProvinceID = sp.StateProvinceID
WHERE   a.City = @City;
```

After creating the procedure, run it with this parameter:

```
EXEC dbo.AddressByCity @City = N'London';
```

This will result in the following I/O and execution times as well as the query plan in Figure 16-1.

```
Table 'Address'. Scan count 1, logical reads 216
Table 'StateProvince'. Scan count 1, logical reads 3
CPU time = 0 ms,     elapsed time = 124 ms.
```

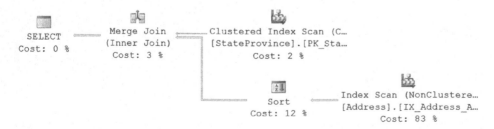

Figure 16-1. Execution plan of AddressByCity

The optimizer sniffed the value London and arrived at a plan based on the data distribution that the city of London represented within the statistics on the Address table. There may be other tuning opportunities in that query or with the indexes on the table, but the plan is optimal for London. You can write an identical query using a local variable just like this:

```
DECLARE @City NVARCHAR(30) = N'London';

SELECT  a.AddressID,
        a.AddressLine1,
        AddressLine2,
        a.City,
        sp.[Name] AS StateProvinceName,
        a.PostalCode
FROM    Person.Address AS a
JOIN    Person.StateProvince AS sp
        ON a.StateProvinceID = sp.StateProvinceID
WHERE   a.City = @City;
```

When this query gets executed, the results of the I/O and execution times are different.

```
Table 'StateProvince'. Scan count 0, logical reads 868
Table 'Address'. Scan count 1, logical reads 216
CPU time = 0 ms,  elapsed time = 212 ms.
```

The execution time has gone up, and you've moved from 219 reads total to 1084. This somewhat explained by taking a look at the new execution plan shown in Figure 16-2.

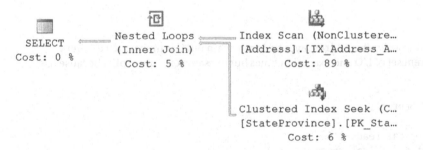

Figure 16-2. *An execution plan created using a local variable*

What has happened is that the optimizer was unable to sample, or sniff, the value for the local variable and therefore had to use an average number of rows from the statistics. You can see this by looking at the estimated number of rows in the properties of the Index Scan operator. It shows 34.113. Yet, if you look at the data returned, there are actually 434 rows for the value London. In short, if the optimizer thinks it needs to retrieve 434 rows, it creates a plan using the merge join and only 219 reads. But, if it thinks it's returning only about 34 rows, it uses the plan with a nested loop join, which, by the nature of the nested loop that seeks in the lower value once for each value in the upper set of data, results in 1,084 reads and slower performance.

That is parameter sniffing in action resulting in improved performance. Now, let's see what happens when parameter sniffing goes bad.

Bad Parameter Sniffing

Parameter sniffing creates problems when you have issues with your statistics. The values passed in the parameter may be representative of your data and the data distribution within the statistics. In this case, you'll see a good execution plan. But what happens when the parameter passed is not representative of the rest of the data in the table? This situation can arise because your data is just distributed in a nonaverage way. For example, most values in the statistics will return only a few rows, say six, but some values will return hundreds of rows. The same thing works the other way, with a common distribution of large amounts of data and an uncommon set of small values. In this case, an execution plan is created, based on the nonrepresentative data, but it's not useful to most of the queries. This situation most frequently exposes itself through a sudden, and sometimes quite severe, drop in performance. It can even, seemingly randomly, fix itself when a recompile event allows a better representative data value to be passed in a parameter.

You can also see this occur when the statistics are out of date or are inaccurate because of being sampled instead of scanned (for more details on statistics in general, see Chapter 12). Regardless, the situation creates a plan that is less than useful and stores it in cache. For example, take the following stored procedure:

```
CREATE PROC dbo.AddressByCity @City NVARCHAR(30)
AS
SELECT  a.AddressID,
        a.AddressLine1,
        AddressLine2,
        a.City,
        sp.[Name] AS StateProvinceName,
        a.PostalCode
FROM    Person.Address AS a
JOIN    Person.StateProvince AS sp
        ON a.StateProvinceID = sp.StateProvinceID
WHERE   a.City = @City;
GO
```

If the stored procedure created previously, dbo.AddressByCity, is run again but this time with a different parameter, then it returns with a different set of I/O and execution times but the same execution plan because it is reused from cache.

```
EXEC dbo.AddressByCity @City = N'Mentor';

Table 'Address'. Scan count 1, logical reads 216
Table 'StateProvince'. Scan count 1, logical reads 3
CPU time = 15 ms,    elapsed time = 84 ms.
```

The I/O is the same since the same execution plan is reused. The execution time is faster because fewer rows are being returned. You can verify that the plan was reused by taking a look at the output from sys.dm_exec_query_stats (in Figure 16-3).

```
SELECT  dest.text,
        deqs.execution_count,
        deqs.creation_time
FROM    sys.dm_exec_query_stats AS deqs
CROSS APPLY sys.dm_exec_sql_text(deqs.sql_handle) AS dest
WHERE   dest.text LIKE 'CREATE PROC dbo.AddressByCity%';
```

	text	execution_count	creation_time
1	CREATE PROC dbo.AddressByCity @City NVARCHAR(3...	2	2014-03-05 19:16:47.600

Figure 16-3. Output from sys.dm_exec_query_stats verifies procedure reuse

To show how bad parameter sniffing can occur, you can reverse the order of the execution of the procedures. First flush the buffer cache by running DBCC FREEPROCCACHE, which should not be run against a production machine. Then rerun the queries in reverse order. The first query, using the parameter value Mentor, results in the following I/O and execution plan (Figure 16-4):

```
Table  'StateProvince'.  Scan count 0,  logical reads 2
Table  'Address'.  Scan count 1,  logical reads 216
CPU time = 0 ms,    elapsed time = 78 ms
```

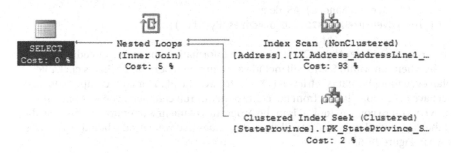

Figure 16-4. The execution plan changes

Figure 16-4 is not the same execution plan as that shown in Figure 16-2. The number of reads drops slightly, but the execution time stays roughly the same. The second execution, using London as the value for the parameter, results in the following I/O and execution times:

```
Table  'StateProvince'.  Scan count 0,  logical reads 868
Table  'Address'.  Scan count 1,  logical reads 216
CPU time = 0 ms,    elapsed time = 283 ms.
```

This time the reads are radically higher, up to what they were when using the local variable, and the execution time was increased. The plan created in the first execution of the procedure with the parameter London created a plan best suited to retrieve the 434 rows that match those criteria in the database. Then the next execution of the procedure using the parameter value Mentor did well enough using the same plan generated by the first execution. When the order is reversed, a new execution plan was created for the value Mentor that did not work at all well for the value London.

In these examples, I've actually cheated just a little. If you were to look at the distribution of the data in the statistics in question, you'd find that the average number of rows returned is around 34, while London's 434 is an outlier. The slightly better performance you saw when the procedure was compiled for London reflects the fact that a different plan was needed. However, the performance for values like Mentor was slightly reduced with the plan for London. Yet, the improved plan for Mentor was absolutely disastrous for a value like London. Now comes the hard part.

You have to determine which of your plans is correct for your system's load. One plan is slightly worse for the average values, while another plan is better for average values but seriously hurts the outliers. The question is, is it better to have somewhat slower performance for all possible data sets and support the outliers' better performance or let the outliers suffer in order to support a larger cross section of the data because it may be called more frequently? You'll have to figure this out on your own system.

Identifying Bad Parameter Sniffing

This will be an intermittent problem. You'll sometimes get one plan that works well enough and no one complains, and you'll sometimes get another, and suddenly the phone is ringing off the hook with complaints about the speed of the system. Therefore, the problem is difficult to track down. The trick is in identifying that you are getting two (or sometimes more) execution plans for a given parameterized query. When you start getting these intermittent changes in performance, you must capture the query plans involved. One method for doing this would be pull the estimated plans directly out of cache using the sys.dm_exec_query_plan DMO like this:

```
SELECT  deps.execution_count,
        deps.total_elapsed_time,
        deps.total_logical_reads,
        deps.total_logical_writes,
        deqp.query_plan
FROM    sys.dm_exec_procedure_stats AS deps
CROSS APPLY sys.dm_exec_query_plan(deps.plan_handle) AS deqp
WHERE   deps.object_id = OBJECT_ID('AdventureWorks2012.dbo.AddressByCity');
```

This query is using the sys.dm_exec_procedure_stats DMO to retrieve information about the procedure in cache and the query plan. The results when run within SSMS will include a column for query_plan that is clickable. Clicking it will open a graphical plan even though what is retrieved is XML. To save the plan for later comparison, just right-click the plan itself and select Save Execution Plan As from the context menu. You can then keep this plan in order to compare it to a later plan. What you're going to look at is in the properties of the first operator, in this case the SELECT operator. There you'll find the Parameter List item that will show the values that were used when the plan was compiled by the optimizer, as shown in Figure 16-5.

Parameter List	@City
Column	@City
Parameter Compiled Value	N'London'

Figure 16-5. *Parameter values used to compile the query plan*

You can then use this value to look at your statistics to understand why you're seeing a plan that is different from what you expected. In this case, if I run the following query, I can check out the histogram to see where values like London would likely be stored and how many rows I can expect:

```
DBCC SHOW_STATISTICS('Person.Address','_WA_Sys_00000004_164452B1');
```

Figure 16-6 shows the applicable part of the histogram.

	RANGE_HI_KEY	RANGE_ROWS	EQ_ROWS	DISTINCT_RANGE_ROWS	AVG_RANGE_ROWS
85	Lavender Bay	5	85	3	1.666667
86	Lebanon	0	111	0	1
87	Leeds	0	55	0	1
88	Lemon Grove	32	109	2	16
89	Les Ulis	0	94	0	1
90	Lille	32	56	2	16
91	Lincoln Acres	0	102	0	1
92	London	32	434	2	16
93	Long Beach	0	97	0	1
94	Los Angeles	2	93	2	1
95	Lynnwood	2	101	1	2
96	Malabar	32	81	2	16

Figure 16-6. *Part of the histogram showing how many rows you can expect*

You can see that the value of London returns a lot more rows than any of the average rows displayed in AVG_RANGE_ROWS, and it's higher than many of the other steps RANG_HI_KEY counts that are stored in EQ_ROWS. In short, the value for London is skewed from the rest of the data. That's why the plan there is different from others.

You'll have to go through the same sort of evaluation of the statistics and compile-time parameter values in order to understand where bad parameter sniffing is coming from.

But, if you have a parameterized query that is suffering from bad parameter sniffing, you can take control in several different ways to attempt to reduce the problem.

Mitigating Bad Parameter Sniffing

Once you've identified that you're experiencing bad parameter sniffing in one case, you don't just have to suffer with it. You can do something about it, but you have to make a decision. You have several choices for mitigating the behavior of bad parameter sniffing.

- You can force a recompile of the plan at the time of execution by running sp_ recompile against the procedure prior to executing.

- Another way to force the recompile is to use EXEC <procedure name> WITH RECOMPILE.

- Yet another mechanism for forcing recompiles on each execution would be to create the procedure using WITH RECOMPILE as part of the procedure definition.

- You can also use OPTION (RECOMPILE) on individual statements to have only those statements instead of the entire procedure recompile. This is frequently the best approach if you're going to force recompiles.

- You can reassign input parameters to local variables. This popular fix forces the optimizer to make a best guess at the values likely to be used by looking at the statistics of the data being referenced, which can and does eliminate the values being taken into account. This is the old way of doing it and has been replaced by using OPTIMIZE FOR UNKNOWN.

- You can use a query hint, OPTIMIZE FOR, when you create the procedure and supply it with known good parameters that will generate a plan that works well for most of your queries. You can specify a value that generates a specific plan, or you can specify UNKNOWN to get a generic plan based on the average of the statistics.

- You can use a plan guide, which is a mechanism to get a query to behave a certain way without making modifications to the procedure. This will be covered in detail in Chapter 17.

- You can disable parameter sniffing for the server by setting trace flag 4136 to on. Understand that this beneficial behavior will be turned off for the entire server, not just one problematic query. This is potentially a highly dangerous choice to make for your system. I discuss it further in a moment.

- If you have a particular query pattern that leads to bad parameter sniffing, you can isolate the functionality by setting up two, or more, different procedures using a wrapper procedure to determine which to call. This can help you use multiple different approaches at the same time.

Each of these possible solutions comes with trade-offs that must be taken into account. If you decide to just recompile the query each time it's called, you'll have to pay the price for the additional CPU needed to recompile the query. This goes against the whole idea of trying to get plan reuse by using parameterized queries, but it could be the best solution in your circumstances. Reassigning your parameters to local variables is something of an old-school approach; the code can look quite silly.

```
ALTER PROC dbo.AddressByCity @City NVARCHAR(30)
AS
DECLARE @LocalCity NVARCHAR(30) = @City;

SELECT  a.AddressID,
        a.AddressLine1,
        AddressLine2,
        a.City,
        sp.[Name] AS StateProvinceName,
        a.PostalCode
FROM    Person.Address AS a
JOIN    Person.StateProvince AS sp
        ON a.StateProvinceID = sp.StateProvinceID
WHERE   a.City = @LocalCity;
```

Using this approach, the optimizer makes its cardinality estimates based on the density of the columns in question, not using the histogram. But it looks odd in a query. In fact, if you take this approach, I strongly suggest adding a comment in front of the variable declaration, so it's clear why you're doing this. Here's an example:

```
-- This allows the query to bypass bad parameter sniffing
```

But, with this approach you're now subject to the possibility of variable sniffing, so it's not really recommended unless you're on a SQL Server instance that is older than 2008. From SQL Server 2008 and onward, you're better off using the OPTIMIZE FOR UNKOWN query hint to do the same thing.

You can use the OPTIMIZE FOR query hint and pass a specific value. So, for example, if you wanted to be sure that the plan that was generated by the value Mentor is always used, you can do this to the query:

```
ALTER PROC dbo.AddressByCity @City NVARCHAR(30)
AS
SELECT  a.AddressID,
        a.AddressLine1,
        AddressLine2,
        a.City,
        sp.[Name] AS StateProvinceName,
        a.PostalCode
```

```
FROM    Person.Address AS a
JOIN    Person.StateProvince AS sp
        ON a.StateProvinceID = sp.StateProvinceID
WHERE   a.City = @City
OPTION (OPTIMIZE FOR (@City = 'Mentor'));
```

Now the optimizer will ignore any values passed to @City and will always use the value of Mentor. You can even see this in action if you modify the query as shown, which will remove the query from cache, and then you execute it using the parameter value of London. This will generate a new plan in cache. If you open that plan and look at the SELECT properties, you'll see evidence of the hint in Figure 16-7.

Parameter List	@City
Column	@City
Parameter Compiled Value	N'Mentor'
Parameter Runtime Value	N'London'

Figure 16-7. *Runtime and compile-time values differ*

As you can see, the optimizer did exactly as you specified and used the value Mentor to compile the plan even though you can also see that you executed the query using the value London. The problem with this approach is that data changes over time and what might have been an optimal plan for your data at point is no longer. If you choose to use the OPTIMIZE FOR hint, you need to plan to regularly reassess it.

If you choose to disable parameter sniffing entirely by using the trace flag, understand that it turns it off on the entire server. Since, most of the time, parameter sniffing is absolutely helping you, you had best be sure that you're receiving no benefits from it and the only hope of dealing with it is to turn off sniffing. This doesn't require even a server reboot, so it's immediate. The plans generated will be based on the averages of the statistics available, so the plans can be seriously suboptimal depending on your data. Before doing this, explore the possibility of using the RECOMPILE hint on your most problematic queries. You're more likely to get better plans that way even though you won't get plan reuse.

With all these possible mitigations approaches, test carefully on your systems before you decide on an approach. Each of these approaches works, but they work in ways that may be better in one circumstance than another, so it's good to know the different methods, and you can experiment with them all depending on your situation.

Finally, remember that this is driven by statistics, so if your statistics are inaccurate or out-of-date, you're more likely to get bad parameter sniffing. Reexamining your statistics maintenance routines to ensure their efficacy is frequently the single best solution.

Summary

In this chapter I outlined exactly what parameter sniffing is and how it benefits all your parameterized queries most of the time. That's important to keep in mind because when you run into bad parameter sniffing, it can seem like parameter sniffing is more danger than it's worth. I discussed how statistics and data distribution can create plans that are suboptimal for some of the data set even as they are optimal for other parts of the data. This is bad parameter sniffing at work. There are several ways to mitigate bad parameter sniffing, but each one is a trade-off, so examine them carefully to ensure you do what's best for your system.

In the next chapter, I'll talk about what happens to cause queries to recompile and what can be done about that.

CHAPTER 17

∎ ∎ ∎

Query Recompilation

Stored procedures and parameterized queries improve the reusability of an execution plan by explicitly converting the variable parts of the queries into parameters. This allows execution plans to be reused when the queries are resubmitted with the same or different values for the variable parts. Since stored procedures are mostly used to implement complex business rules, a typical stored procedure contains a complex set of SQL statements, making the price of generating the execution plan of the queries within a stored procedure a bit costly. Therefore, it is usually beneficial to reuse the existing execution plan of a stored procedure instead of generating a new plan. However, sometimes the existing plan may not be optimal, or it may not provide the best processing strategy during reuse. SQL Server resolves this condition by recompiling statements within stored procedures to generate a new execution plan. This chapter covers the following topics:

- The benefits and drawbacks of recompilation
- How to identify the statements causing recompilation
- How to analyze the causes of recompilations
- Ways to avoid recompilations when necessary

Benefits and Drawbacks of Recompilation

The recompilation of queries can be both beneficial and harmful. Sometimes, it may be beneficial to consider a new processing strategy for a query instead of reusing the existing plan, especially if the data distribution in the table (or the corresponding statistics) has changed or new indexes are added to the table. Recompiles in SQL Server 2014 are at the statement level. This increases the overall number of recompiles that can occur within a procedure, but it reduces the effects and overhead of recompiles in general. Statement-level recompiles reduce overhead because they recompile only an individual statement rather than all the statements within a procedure, whereas recompiles in SQL Server 2000 caused a procedure, in its entirety, to be recompiled over and over. Despite this smaller footprint for recompiles, it's something to be reduced and controlled as much as is practical for your situation.

To understand how the recompilation of an existing plan can sometimes be beneficial, assume you need to retrieve some information from the `Production.WorkOrder` table. The stored procedure may look like this:

```
IF (SELECT  OBJECT_ID('dbo.WorkOrder')
    ) IS NOT NULL
    DROP PROCEDURE dbo.WorkOrder;
GO
CREATE PROCEDURE dbo.WorkOrder
AS
```

```
SELECT   wo.WorkOrderID,
         wo.ProductID,
         wo.StockedQty
FROM     Production.WorkOrder AS wo
WHERE    wo.StockedQty BETWEEN 500 AND 700;
```

With the current indexes, the execution plan for the SELECT statement, which is part of the stored procedure plan, scans the index PK_WorkOrder_WorkOrderID, as shown in Figure 17-1.

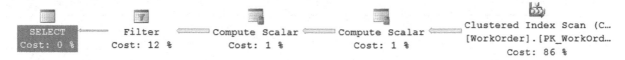

Figure 17-1. *Execution plan for the stored procedure*

This plan is saved in the procedure cache so that it can be reused when the stored procedure is reexecuted. But if a new index is added on the table as follows, then the existing plan won't be the most efficient processing strategy to execute the query.

In this case, it is beneficial to spend extra CPU cycles to recompile the stored procedure so that you generate a better execution plan.

Since index IX_Test can serve as a covering index for the SELECT statement, the cost of a bookmark lookup can be avoided by using index IX_Test instead of scanning PK_WorkOrder_ WorkOrderID. SQL Server automatically detects this change and recompiles the existing plan to consider the benefit of using the new index. This results in a new execution plan for the stored procedure (when executed), as shown in Figure 17-2.

```
CREATE INDEX IX_Test ON Production.WorkOrder(StockedQty,ProductID);
```

Figure 17-2. *New execution plan for the stored procedure*

SQL Server automatically detects the conditions that require a recompilation of the existing plan. SQL Server follows certain rules in determining when the existing plan needs to be recompiled. If a specific implementation of a query falls within the rules of recompilation (execution plan aged out, SET options changed, and so on), then the statement will be recompiled every time it meets the requirements for a recompile, and SQL Server may, or may not, generate a better execution plan. To see this in action, you'll need a different stored procedure. The following procedure returns all the rows from the WorkOrder table:

```
IF (SELECT  OBJECT_ID('dbo.WorkOrderAll')
   ) IS NOT NULL
     DROP PROCEDURE dbo.WorkOrderAll;
GO
CREATE PROCEDURE dbo.WorkOrderAll
AS
SELECT  *
FROM    Production.WorkOrder AS wo;
```

Before executing this procedure, drop the index IXTest.

```
DROP INDEX Production.WorkOrder.IX_Test;
```

When you execute this procedure, the SELECT statement returns the complete data set (all rows and columns) from the table and is therefore best served through a table scan on the table WorkOrder. As explained in Chapter 4, the processing of the SELECT statement won't benefit from a nonclustered index on any of the columns. Therefore, ideally, creating the nonclustered index (as follows) before the execution of the stored procedure shouldn't matter.

```
EXEC dbo.WorkOrderAll;
GO
CREATE INDEX IX_Test ON Production.WorkOrder(StockedQty,ProductID);
GO
EXEC dbo.WorkOrderAll; --After creation of index IX_Test
```

But the stored procedure execution after the index creation faces recompilation, as shown in the corresponding extended event output in Figure 17-3.

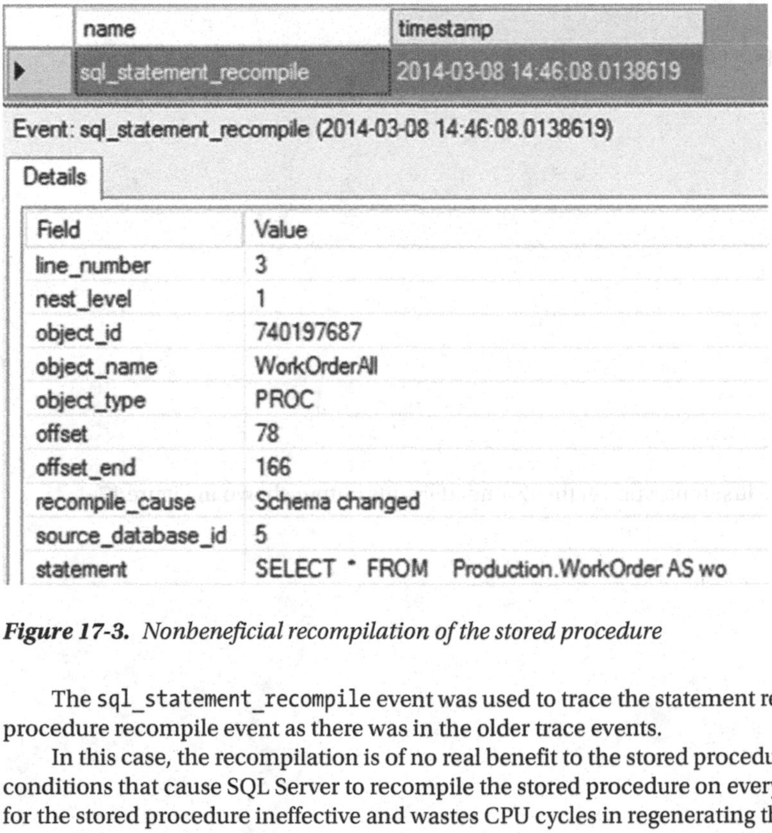

	name	timestamp
►	sql_statement_recompile	2014-03-08 14:46:08.0138619

Event: sql_statement_recompile (2014-03-08 14:46:08.0138619)

Details

Field	Value
line_number	3
nest_level	1
object_id	740197687
object_name	WorkOrderAll
object_type	PROC
offset	78
offset_end	166
recompile_cause	Schema changed
source_database_id	5
statement	SELECT * FROM Production.WorkOrder AS wo

Figure 17-3. *Nonbeneficial recompilation of the stored procedure*

The sql_statement_recompile event was used to trace the statement recompiles. There is no longer a separate procedure recompile event as there was in the older trace events.

In this case, the recompilation is of no real benefit to the stored procedure. But unfortunately, it falls within the conditions that cause SQL Server to recompile the stored procedure on every execution. This can make plan caching for the stored procedure ineffective and wastes CPU cycles in regenerating the same plan on this execution. Therefore, it is important to be aware of the conditions that cause the recompilation of queries and to make every effort to avoid those conditions when implementing stored procedures and parameterized queries that are targeted for plan reuse. I will discuss these conditions next, after identifying which statements cause SQL Server to recompile the statement in each respective case.

Identifying the Statement Causing Recompilation

SQL Server can recompile individual statements within a procedure or the entire procedure. Thus, to find the cause of recompilation, it's important to identify the SQL statement that can't reuse the existing plan.

You can use extended events to track statement recompilation. You can also use the same events to identify the stored procedure statement that caused the recompilation. Table 17-1 shows the relevant events you can use.

Table 17-1. *Events to Analyze Query Recompilation*

Events
sql_batch_completed or module_end
sql_statement_recompile
sql_batch_starting or module_start
sp_statement_completed or sql_statement_completed *(Optional)*
sp_statement_starting or sql_statement_starting *(Optional)*

Consider the following simple stored procedure:

```
IF (SELECT  OBJECT_ID('dbo.TestProc')
   ) IS NOT NULL
     DROP PROC dbo.TestProc;
GO
CREATE PROC dbo.TestProc
AS
CREATE TABLE #TempTable (C1 INT);
    INSERT  INTO #TempTable
            (C1)
    VALUES  (42);
   -- data change causes recompile
GO
```

On executing this stored procedure the first time, you get the Extended Events output shown in Figure 17-4.

```
EXEC dbo.TestProc;
```

name	timestamp
module_start	2014-03-08 15:07:15.0568210
▶ sql_statement_recompile	2014-03-08 15:07:15.0574405
module_end	2014-03-08 15:07:15.0583537

Event: sql_statement_recompile (2014-03-08 15:07:15.0574405)

Details

Field	Value
line_number	4
nest_level	1
object_id	772197801
object_name	p1
object_type	PROC
offset	104
offset_end	190
recompile_cause	Deferred compile
source_database_id	5
statement	INSERT INTO #t1 (c1) VALUES (42)

Figure 17-4. Extended Events output showing an sql_statement_recompile event from recompilation

In Figure 17-4, you can see that you have a recompilation event (sql_statement_recompile), indicating that the stored procedure went through recompilation. When a stored procedure is executed for the first time, SQL Server compiles the stored procedure and generates an execution plan, as explained in the previous chapter. By the way, you might see other statements if you're using Extended Events to follow along. Just filter or group by your database ID to make it easier to see the events you're interested in. It's always a good idea to put filters on your Extended Events sessions.

Since execution plans are maintained in volatile memory only, they get dropped when SQL Server is restarted. On the next execution of the stored procedure, after the server restart, SQL Server once again compiles the stored procedure and generates the execution plan. These compilations aren't treated as a stored procedure recompilation since a plan didn't exist in the cache for reuse. An sql_statement_recompile event indicates that a plan was already there but couldn't be reused.

■ **Note** I discuss the significance of the recompile_cause data column later in the "Analyzing Causes of Recompilation" section.

To see which statement caused the recompile, look at the statement column within the sql_statement_recompile event. It shows specifically the statement being recompiled. You can also identify the stored procedure statement causing the recompilation by using any of the various statement starting events in combination with a recompile event. If you enable Causality Tracking as part of the Extended Events session, you'll get an identifier for the start of an event and then sequence numbers of other events that are part of the same chain. Figure 17-5 shows attach_activity_id.seq for the sp_statement_starting event immediately before the sql_statement_recompile event. If you look at the recompile event, it follows as the next in sequence.

name	timestamp
module_start	2014-03-08 15:18:13.2134145
sp_statement_starting	2014-03-08 15:18:13.2134426
sp_statement_completed	2014-03-08 15:18:13.2140065
sp_statement_starting	2014-03-08 15:18:13.2140468
▶ sql_statement_recompile	2014-03-08 15:18:13.2140499
sp_statement_starting	2014-03-08 15:18:13.2144286
sp_statement_completed	2014-03-08 15:18:13.2148556
module_end	2014-03-08 15:18:13.2148798

Event: sql_statement_recompile (2014-03-08 15:18:13.2140499)

Details

Field	Value
attach_activity_id.guid	DBAC2ABF-0361-4402-AE87-34A091406CEA
attach_activity_id.seq	5
line_number	4
nest_level	1
object_id	788197858
object_name	p1
object_type	PROC
offset	104
offset_end	190
recompile_cause	Deferred compile
source_database_id	5
statement	INSERT INTO #1 (c1) VALUES (42)

Figure 17-5. Extended Events output showing an `sp_statement_starting` *event causing recompilation*

Note that after the statement recompilation, the stored procedure statement that caused the recompilation is started again to execute with the new plan. You can capture the statement within the event, correlate the events through sequence using the timestamps, or best of all, use the Causality Tracking on the extended events. Any of these can be used to track down specifically which statement is causing the recompile.

Analyzing Causes of Recompilation

To improve performance, it is important that you analyze the causes of recompilation. Often, recompilation may not be necessary, and you can avoid it to improve performance. For example, every time you go through a compile or recompile process, you're using CPU for the optimizer to get its job done. You're also moving plans in and out of memory as they go through the compile process. When a query recompiles, that query is blocked while the recompile process runs, which means frequently called queries can become major bottlenecks if they also have to go through a recompile. Knowing the different conditions that result in recompilation helps you evaluate the cause of a recompilation and determine how to avoid recompiling when it isn't necessary. Statement recompilation occurs for the following reasons:

- The schema of regular tables, temporary tables, or views referred to in the stored procedure statement have changed. Schema changes include changes to the metadata of the table or the indexes on the table.

- Bindings (such as defaults) to the columns of regular or temporary tables have changed.

- Statistics on the table indexes or columns have changed, either automatically or manually.

- An object did not exist when the stored procedure was compiled, but it was created during execution. This is called *deferred object resolution,* which is the cause of the preceding recompilation.

- SET options have changed.

- The execution plan was aged and deallocated.

- An explicit call was made to the sp_recompile system stored procedure.

- There was an explicit use of the RECOMPILE hint.

You can see these changes in Extended Events. The cause is indicated by the recompile_cause data column value for the sql_statement_recompile event, as shown in Table 17-2.

Table 17-2. *Recompile Cause Data Column Reflecting Causes of Recompilation*

Description
Schema or bindings to regular table or view changed
Statistics changed
Object did not exist in the stored procedure plan but was created during execution
SET options changed
Schema or bindings to temporary table changed
Schema or bindings of remote rowset changed
FOR BROWSE permissions changed
Query notification environment changed
MPI view changed
Cursor options changed
WITH RECOMPILE option invoked

Let's look at some of the reasons listed in Table 17-2 for recompilation in more detail and discuss what you can do to avoid them.

Schema or Bindings Changes

When the schema or bindings to a view, regular table, or temporary table change, the existing query's execution plan becomes invalid. The query must be recompiled before executing any statement that refers to a modified object. SQL Server automatically detects this situation and recompiles the stored procedure.

■ **Note** I talk about recompilation due to schema changes in more detail in the "Benefits and Drawbacks of Recompilation" section.

Statistics Changes

SQL Server keeps track of the number of changes to the table. If the number of changes exceeds the recompilation threshold (RT) value, then SQL Server automatically updates the statistics when the table is referred to in the statement, as you saw in Chapter 12. When the condition for the automatic update of statistics is detected, SQL Server automatically marks the statement for recompile, along with the statistics update.

The RT is determined by a formula that depends on the table being a permanent table or a temporary table (not a table variable) and how many rows are in the table. Table 17-3 shows the basic formula so that you can determine when you can expect to see a statement recompile because of data changes.

Table 17-3. *Formula for Determining Data Changes*

Type of Table	Formula
Permanent table	If number of rows (n) <= 500, RT = 500
	If n > 500, RT = 500 + .2 * n Or Proportional after 25,000 rows when trace flag 2371 is set
Temporary table	If n < 6, RT = 6
	If 6 <= n <= 500, RT = 500 If n > 500, RT = 500 + .2 * n Or Proportional after 25,000 rows when trace flag 2317 is set

To understand how statistics changes can cause recompilation, consider the following example. The stored procedure is executed the first time with only one row in the table. Before the second execution of the stored procedure, a large number of rows are added to the table.

■ **Note** Please ensure that the AUTO_UPDATE_STATISTICS setting for the database is ON. You can determine the AUTO_UPDATE_STATISTICS setting by executing the following query:

```
SELECT  DATABASEPROPERTYEX('AdventureWorks2012', 'IsAutoUpdateStatistics');
```

```
IF EXISTS ( SELECT   *
            FROM     sys.objects AS o
            WHERE    o.object_id = OBJECT_ID(N'dbo.NewOrderDetail')
                     AND o.type IN (N'U') )
    DROP TABLE dbo.NewOrderDetail;
GO
SELECT   *
INTO     dbo.NewOrderDetail
FROM     Sales.SalesOrderDetail;
GO
CREATE INDEX IX_NewOrders_ProductID ON dbo.NewOrderDetail (ProductID);
GO
IF EXISTS ( SELECT   *
            FROM     sys.objects
            WHERE    object_id = OBJECT_ID(N'dbo.NewOrders')
                     AND type IN (N'P',N'PC') )
    DROP PROCEDURE dbo.NewOrders;
GO
CREATE PROCEDURE dbo.NewOrders
AS
SELECT   nod.OrderQty,
         nod.CarrierTrackingNumber
FROM     dbo.NewOrderDetail nod
WHERE    nod.ProductID = 897;
GO
SET STATISTICS XML ON;
EXEC dbo.NewOrders;
SET STATISTICS XML OFF;
GO
```

Next you need to modify a number of rows before reexecuting the stored procedure.

```
UPDATE   dbo.NewOrderDetail
SET      ProductID = 897
WHERE    ProductID BETWEEN 800 AND 900;
GO
SET STATISTICS XML ON;
EXEC dbo.NewOrders;
SET STATISTICS XML OFF;
GO
```

The first time, SQL Server executes the SELECT statement of the stored procedure using an Index Seek operation, as shown in Figure 17-6.

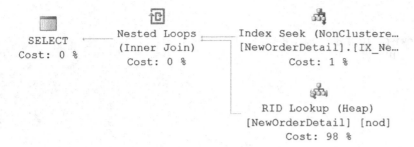

Figure 17-6. *Execution plan prior to data changes*

■ **Note**   Please ensure that the setting for the graphical execution plan is OFF; otherwise, the output of STATISTICS XML won't display.

While reexecuting the stored procedure, SQL Server automatically detects that the statistics on the index have changed. This causes a recompilation of the SELECT statement within the procedure, with the optimizer determining a better processing strategy, before executing the SELECT statement within the stored procedure, as you can see in Figure 17-7.

Figure 17-7. *Effect of statistics change on the execution plan*

Figure 17-8 shows the corresponding Extended Events output (with the auto_stats event added).

name	timestamp
module_start	2014-03-10 18:56:54.5254103
sp_statement_starting	2014-03-10 18:56:54.5254516
sql_statement_recompile	2014-03-10 18:56:54.5254754
auto_stats	2014-03-10 18:56:54.5258835
sp_statement_starting	2014-03-10 18:56:54.5267464
sp_statement_completed	2014-03-10 18:56:54.6345228

Event: sql_statement_recompile (2014-03-10 18:56:54.5254754)

Details

Field	Value
attach_activity_id.g...	BCBEE423-C74C-4D5B-853E-2A85717BD5D0
attach_activity_id.s...	3
line_number	3
nest_level	1
object_id	820197972
object_name	NewOrders
object_type	PROC
offset	72
offset_end	304
recompile_cause	Statistics changed
source_database_id	5
statement	SELECT nod.OrderQty, nod.CarrierTrackingNumber FRO...

Figure 17-8. *Effect of statistics change on the stored procedure recompilation*

In Figure 17-8, you can see that to execute the SELECT statement during the second execution of the stored procedure, a recompilation was required. From the value of recompile_cause (Statistics Changed), you can understand that the recompilation was because of the statistics change. As part of creating the new plan, the statistics are automatically updated, as indicated by the Auto Stats event, which occurred after the call for a recompile of the statement. You can also verify the automatic update of the statistics using the DBCC SHOW_STATISTICS statement, as explained in Chapter 12.

Deferred Object Resolution

Queries often dynamically create and subsequently access database objects. When such a query is executed for the first time, the first execution plan won't contain the information about the objects to be created during runtime. Thus, in the first execution plan, the processing strategy for those objects is deferred until the runtime of the query. When a DML statement (within the query) referring to one of those objects is executed, the query is recompiled to generate a new plan containing the processing strategy for the object.

Both a regular table and a local temporary table can be created within a stored procedure to hold intermediate result sets. The recompilation of the statement because of deferred object resolution behaves differently for a regular table when compared to a local temporary table, as explained in the following section.

Recompilation Because of a Regular Table

To understand the query recompilation issue by creating a regular table within the stored procedure, consider the following example:

```
IF (SELECT  OBJECT_ID('dbo.TestProc')
   ) IS NOT NULL
     DROP PROC dbo.TestProc;
GO
CREATE PROC dbo.TestProc
AS
CREATE TABLE dbo.ProcTest1 (C1 INT);  --Ensure table doesn't exist
SELECT  *
FROM    dbo.ProcTest1;   --Causes recompilation
DROP TABLE dbo.ProcTest1;
GO

EXEC dbo.TestProc;   --First execution
EXEC dbo.TestProc;   --Second execution
```

When the stored procedure is executed for the first time, an execution plan is generated before the actual execution of the stored procedure. If the table created within the stored procedure doesn't exist (as expected in the preceding code) before the stored procedure is created, then the plan won't contain the processing strategy for the SELECT statement referring to the table. Thus, to execute the SELECT statement, the statement needs to be recompiled, as shown in Figure 17-9.

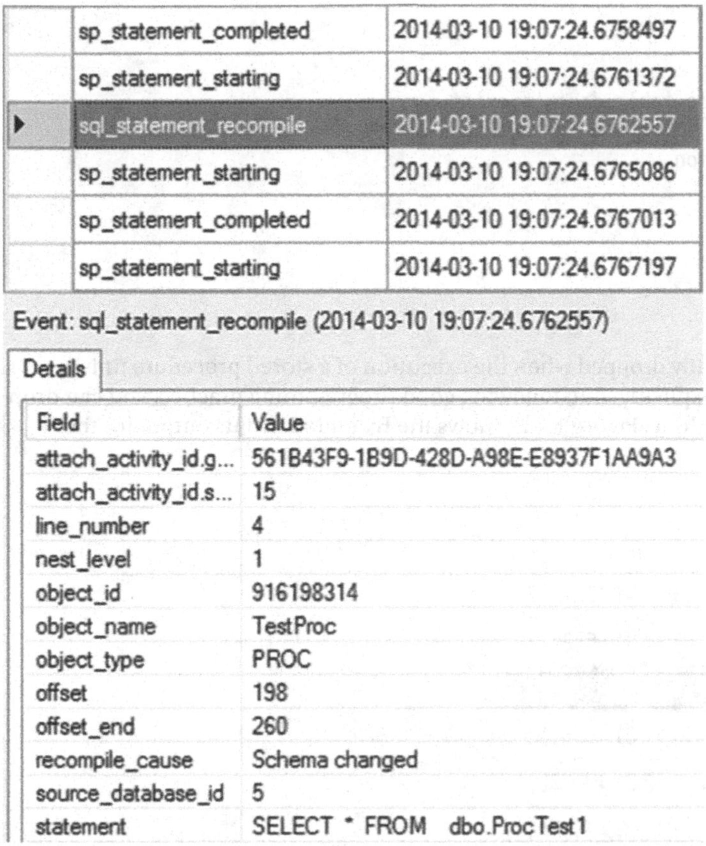

	sp_statement_completed	2014-03-10 19:07:24.6758497
	sp_statement_starting	2014-03-10 19:07:24.6761372
▶	sql_statement_recompile	2014-03-10 19:07:24.6762557
	sp_statement_starting	2014-03-10 19:07:24.6765086
	sp_statement_completed	2014-03-10 19:07:24.6767013
	sp_statement_starting	2014-03-10 19:07:24.6767197

Event: sql_statement_recompile (2014-03-10 19:07:24.6762557)

Details

Field	Value
attach_activity_id.g...	561B43F9-1B9D-428D-A98E-E8937F1AA9A3
attach_activity_id.s...	15
line_number	4
nest_level	1
object_id	916198314
object_name	TestProc
object_type	PROC
offset	198
offset_end	260
recompile_cause	Schema changed
source_database_id	5
statement	SELECT * FROM dbo.ProcTest1

Figure 17-9. *Extended Events output showing a stored procedure recompilation because of a regular table*

You can see that the SELECT statement is recompiled when it's executed the second time. Dropping the table within the stored procedure during the first execution doesn't drop the query plan saved in the plan cache. During the subsequent execution of the stored procedure, the existing plan includes the processing strategy for the table. However, because of the re-creation of the table within the stored procedure, SQL Server considers it a change to the table schema. Therefore, SQL Server recompiles the statement within the stored procedure before executing the SELECT statement during the subsequent execution of the rest of the stored procedure. The value of the recompile_clause for the corresponding sql_statement_recompile event reflects the cause of the recompilation.

Recompilation Because of a Local Temporary Table

Most of the time in the stored procedure you create local temporary tables instead of regular tables. To understand how differently the local temporary tables affect stored procedure recompilation, modify the preceding example by just replacing the regular table with a local temporary table.

```
IF (SELECT  OBJECT_ID('dbo.TestProc')
   ) IS NOT NULL
   DROP PROC dbo.TestProc;
```

```
GO
CREATE PROC dbo.TestProc
AS
CREATE TABLE #ProcTest1 (C1 INT);  --Ensure table doesn't exist
SELECT  *
FROM    #ProcTest1;    --Causes recompilation
DROP TABLE #ProcTest1;
GO

EXEC dbo.TestProc;   --First execution
EXEC dbo.TestProc;   --Second execution
```

Since a local temporary table is automatically dropped when the execution of a stored procedure finishes, it's not necessary to drop the temporary table explicitly. But, following good programming practice, you can drop the local temporary table as soon as its work is done. Figure 17-10 shows the Extended Events output for the preceding example.

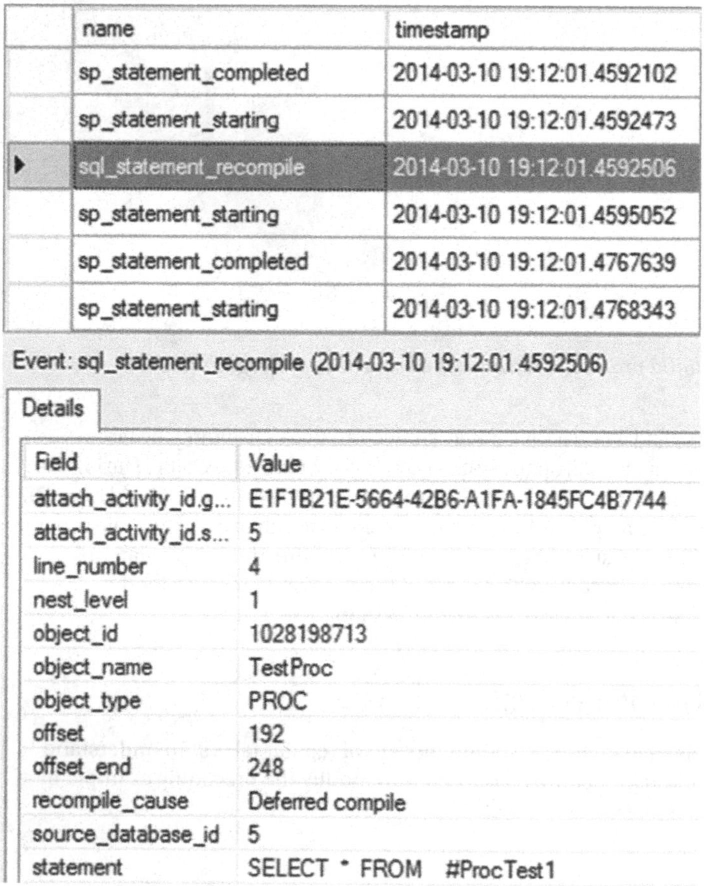

name	timestamp
sp_statement_completed	2014-03-10 19:12:01.4592102
sp_statement_starting	2014-03-10 19:12:01.4592473
sql_statement_recompile	2014-03-10 19:12:01.4592506
sp_statement_starting	2014-03-10 19:12:01.4595052
sp_statement_completed	2014-03-10 19:12:01.4767639
sp_statement_starting	2014-03-10 19:12:01.4768343

Event: sql_statement_recompile (2014-03-10 19:12:01.4592506)

Details

Field	Value
attach_activity_id.g...	E1F1B21E-5664-42B6-A1FA-1845FC4B7744
attach_activity_id.s...	5
line_number	4
nest_level	1
object_id	1028198713
object_name	TestProc
object_type	PROC
offset	192
offset_end	248
recompile_cause	Deferred compile
source_database_id	5
statement	SELECT * FROM #ProcTest1

Figure 17-10. Extended Events output showing a stored procedure recompilation because of a local temporary table

You can see that the query is recompiled when executed for the first time. The cause of the recompilation, as indicated by the corresponding `recompile_cause` value, is the same as the cause of the recompilation on a regular table. However, note that when the stored procedure is reexecuted, it isn't recompiled, unlike the case with a regular table.

The schema of a local temporary table during subsequent execution of the stored procedure remains the same as during the previous execution. A local temporary table isn't available outside the scope of the stored procedure, so its schema can't be altered in any way between multiple executions. Thus, SQL Server safely reuses the existing plan (based on the previous instance of the local temporary table) during the subsequent execution of the stored procedure and thereby avoids the recompilation.

■ **Note**   To avoid recompilation, it makes sense to hold the intermediate result sets in the stored procedure using local temporary tables, instead of using temporarily created regular tables. But, this makes sense only if you can avoid data skew, which could lead to other bad plans. In that case, the recompile might be less painful.

SET Options Changes

The execution plan of a stored procedure is dependent on the environment settings. If the environment settings are changed within a stored procedure, then SQL Server recompiles the queries on every execution. For example, consider the following code:

```
IF (SELECT  OBJECT_ID('dbo.TestProc')
    ) IS NOT NULL
      DROP PROC dbo.TestProc;
GO
CREATE PROC dbo.TestProc
AS
SELECT 'a' + NULL + 'b'; --1st
SET CONCAT_NULL_YIELDS_NULL OFF;
SELECT 'a' + NULL + 'b'; --2nd
SET ANSI_NULLS OFF;
SELECT 'a' + NULL + 'b';
 --3rd
GO
EXEC dbo.TestProc; --First execution
EXEC dbo.TestProc; --Second execution
```

Changing the SET options in the stored procedure causes SQL Server to recompile the stored procedure before executing the statement after the SET statement. Thus, this stored procedure is recompiled twice: once before executing the second SELECT statement and once before executing the third SELECT statement. The Extended Events output in Figure 17-11 shows this.

name	timestamp
module_start	2014-03-10 19:19:38.7005051
▶ sql_statement_recompile	2014-03-10 19:19:38.7005762
sql_statement_recompile	2014-03-10 19:19:38.7072542
module_end	2014-03-10 19:19:38.7073536

Event: sql_statement_recompile (2014-03-10 19:19:38.7005762)

Details

Field	Value
line_number	5
nest_level	1
object_id	1092198941
object_name	TestProc
object_type	PROC
offset	198
offset_end	244
recompile_cause	Set option change
source_database_id	5
statement	SELECT 'a' + NULL + 'b'

Figure 17-11. *Extended Events output showing a stored procedure recompilation because of a SET option change*

If the procedure were reexecuted, you wouldn't see a recompile since those are now part of the execution plans.

Since SET NOCOUNT doesn't change the environment settings, unlike the SET statements used to change the ANSI settings as shown previously, SET NOCOUNT doesn't cause stored procedure recompilation. I explain how to use SET NOCOUNT in detail in Chapter 18.

Execution Plan Aging

SQL Server manages the size of the procedure cache by maintaining the age of the execution plans in the cache, as you saw in Chapter 15. If a stored procedure is not reexecuted for a long time, the age field of the execution plan can come down to 0, and the plan can be removed from the cache because of memory pressure. When this happens and the stored procedure is reexecuted, a new plan will be generated and cached in the procedure cache. However, if there is enough memory in the system, unused plans are not removed from the cache until memory pressure increases.

Explicit Call to sp_recompile

SQL Server automatically recompiles queries when the schema changes or statistics are altered enough. It also provides the sp_recompile system stored procedure to manually mark entire stored procedures for recompilation. This stored procedure can be called on a table, view, stored procedure, or trigger. If it is called on a stored procedure or a trigger, the stored procedure or trigger is recompiled the next time it is executed. Calling sp_recompile on a table or a view marks all the stored procedures and triggers that refer to the table/view for recompilation the next time they are executed.

For example, if sp_recompile is called on table Test1, all the stored procedures and triggers that refer to table Test1 are marked for recompilation and are recompiled the next time they are executed, like so:

```
sp_recompile 'Test1';
```

You can use sp_recompile to cancel the reuse of an existing plan when executing dynamic queries with sp_executesql. As demonstrated in the previous chapter, you should not parameterize the variable parts of a query whose range of values may require different processing strategies for the query. For instance, reconsidering the corresponding example, you know that the second execution of the query reuses the plan generated for the first execution. The example is repeated here for easy reference:

```
DBCC FREEPROCCACHE;
 --Clear the procedure cache
GO
DECLARE @query NVARCHAR(MAX);
DECLARE @param NVARCHAR(MAX);
SET @query = N'SELECT     soh.SalesOrderNumber ,soh.OrderDate ,sod.OrderQty ,sod.LineTotal FROM
Sales.SalesOrderHeader AS soh
JOIN Sales.SalesOrderDetail AS sod ON soh.SalesOrderID = sod.SalesOrderID WHERE
soh.CustomerID >= @CustomerId;'
SET @param = N'@CustomerId INT';
EXEC sp_executesql @query,@param,@CustomerId = 1;
EXEC sp_executesql @query,@param,@CustomerId = 30118;
```

The second execution of the query performs an Index Scan operation on the SalesOrderHeader table to retrieve the data from the table. As explained in Chapter 8, an Index Seek operation may have been preferred on the SalesOrderHeader table for the second execution. You can achieve this by executing the sp_recompile system stored procedure on the SalesOrderHeader table as follows:

```
EXEC sp_recompile 'Sales.SalesOrderHeader'
```

Now, if the query with the second parameter value is reexecuted, the plan for the query will be recompiled as marked by the preceding sp_recompile statement. This allows SQL Server to generate an optimal plan for the second execution.

Well, there is a slight problem here: You will likely want to reexecute the first statement again. With the plan existing in the cache, SQL Server will reuse the plan (the Index Scan operation on the SalesOrderHeader table) for the first statement even though an Index Seek operation (using the index on the filter criterion column soh.CustomerID) would have been optimal. One way of avoiding this problem is to create a stored procedure for the query and use the OPTION (RECOMPILE) clause on the statement. I'll go over the various methods for controlling the recompile next.

Explicit Use of RECOMPILE

SQL Server allows stored procedures and queries to be explicitly recompiled using the RECOMPILE command in three ways: with the CREATE PROCEDURE statement, as part of the EXECUTE statement, and in a query hint. These methods decrease the effectiveness of plan reusability, so you should consider them only under the specific circumstances explained in the following sections.

RECOMPILE Clause with the CREATE PROCEDURE Statement

Sometimes the plan requirements of a stored procedure will vary as the parameter values to the stored procedure change. In such a case, reusing the plan with different parameter values may degrade the performance of the stored procedure. You can avoid this by using the RECOMPILE clause with the CREATE PROCEDURE statement. For example, for the query in the preceding section, you can create a stored procedure with the RECOMPILE clause.

```
IF (SELECT  OBJECT_ID('dbo.CustomerList')
    ) IS NOT NULL
      DROP PROC dbo.CustomerList;
GO
CREATE PROCEDURE dbo.CustomerList @CustomerId INT
    WITH RECOMPILE
AS
SELECT   soh.SalesOrderNumber,
         soh.OrderDate,
         sod.OrderQty,
         sod.LineTotal
FROM     Sales.SalesOrderHeader AS soh
JOIN     Sales.SalesOrderDetail AS sod
         ON soh.SalesOrderID = sod.SalesOrderID
WHERE    soh.CustomerID >= @CustomerId;
GO
```

The RECOMPILE clause prevents the caching of the stored procedure plan for every statement within the procedure. Every time the stored procedure is executed, new plans are generated. Therefore, if the stored procedure is executed with the soh.CustomerID value as 30118 or 1

```
EXEC CustomerList
    @CustomerId = 1;
EXEC CustomerList
    @CustomerId = 30118;
```

a new plan is generated during the individual execution, as shown in Figure 17-12.

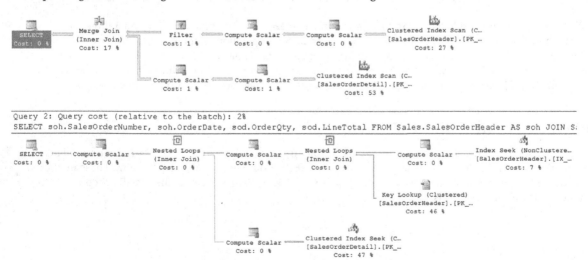

Figure 17-12. *Effect of the RECOMPILE clause used in stored procedure creation*

RECOMPILE Clause with the EXECUTE Statement

As shown previously, specific parameter values in a stored procedure may require a different plan, depending upon the nature of the values. You can take the RECOMPILE clause out of the stored procedure and use it on a case-by-case basis when you execute the stored procedure, as follows:

```
EXEC dbo.CustomerList
    @CustomerId = 1
    WITH RECOMPILE;
```

When the stored procedure is executed with the RECOMPILE clause, a new plan is generated temporarily. The new plan isn't cached, and it doesn't affect the existing plan. When the stored procedure is executed without the RECOMPILE clause, the plan is cached as usual. This provides some control over reusability of the existing plan cache rather than using the RECOMPILE clause with the CREATE PROCEDURE statement.

Since the plan for the stored procedure when executed with the RECOMPILE clause is not cached, the plan is regenerated every time the stored procedure is executed with the RECOMPILE clause. However, for better performance, instead of using RECOMPILE, you should consider creating separate stored procedures, one for each set of parameter values that requires a different plan, assuming they are easily identified and you're dealing only with a small number of possible plans.

RECOMPILE Hints to Control Individual Statements

While you can use either of the previous methods to recompile an entire procedure, this can be problematic if the procedure has multiple commands. All statements within a procedure will all be recompiled using either of the previous methods. Compile time for queries can be the most expensive part of executing some queries, so recompiles should be avoided. Because of this, a more granular approach is to isolate the recompile to just the statement that needs it. This is accomplished using the RECOMPILE query hint as follows:

```
IF (SELECT  OBJECT_ID('dbo.CustomerList')
    ) IS NOT NULL
    DROP PROC dbo.CustomerList;
GO
CREATE PROCEDURE dbo.CustomerList @CustomerId INT
AS
SELECT  soh.SalesOrderNumber,
        soh.OrderDate,
        sod.OrderQty,
        sod.LineTotal
FROM    Sales.SalesOrderHeader AS soh
JOIN    Sales.SalesOrderDetail AS sod
        ON soh.SalesOrderID = sod.SalesOrderID
WHERE   soh.CustomerID >= @CustomerId
OPTION  (RECOMPILE);
GO
```

This procedure will appear to behave the same way as the one where the RECOMPILE was applied to the entire procedure, but if you added multiple statements to this query, only the statement with the OPTION (RECOMPILE) query hint would be compiled at every execution of the procedure.

Avoiding Recompilations

Sometimes recompilation is beneficial, but at other times it is worth avoiding. If a new index is created on a column referred to in the WHERE or JOIN clause of a query, it makes sense to regenerate the execution plans of stored procedures referring to the table so they can benefit from using the index. However, if recompilation is deemed detrimental to performance, such as when it's causing blocking or using up resources such as the CPU, you can avoid it by following these implementation practices:

- Don't interleave DDL and DML statements.
- Avoid recompilation caused by statistics changes.
- Use the KEEPFIXED PLAN option.
- Disable the auto update statistics feature on the table.
- Use table variables.
- Avoid changing SET options within the stored procedure.
- Use the OPTIMIZE FOR query hint.
- Use plan guides.

Don't Interleave DDL and DML Statements

In stored procedures, DDL statements are often used to create local temporary tables and to change their schema (including adding indexes). Doing so can affect the validity of the existing plan and can cause recompilation when the stored procedure statements referring to the tables are executed. To understand how the use of DDL statements for local temporary tables can cause repetitive recompilation of the stored procedure, consider the following example:

```
IF (SELECT   OBJECT_ID('dbo.TempTable')
   ) IS NOT NULL
     DROP PROC dbo.TempTable
GO
CREATE PROC dbo.TempTable
AS
CREATE TABLE #MyTempTable (ID INT,Dsc NVARCHAR(50))
INSERT   INTO #MyTempTable
        (ID,
         Dsc)
        SELECT   pm.ProductModelID,
                 pm.[Name]
        FROM     Production.ProductModel AS pm;    --Needs 1st recompilation
SELECT   *
FROM     #MyTempTable AS mtt;
CREATE CLUSTERED INDEX iTest ON #MyTempTable (ID);
SELECT   *
FROM     #MyTempTable AS mtt; --Needs 2nd recompilation
CREATE TABLE #t2 (c1 INT);
SELECT   *
FROM     #t2;
 --Needs 3rd recompilation
GO

EXEC dbo.TempTable; --First execution
```

The stored procedure has interleaved DDL and DML statements. Figure 17-13 shows the Extended Events output of this code.

name	timestamp
module_start	2014-03-10 19:54:30.1854109
sql_statement_recompile	2014-03-10 19:54:30.1860960
sql_statement_recompile	2014-03-10 19:54:30.2038682
sql_statement_recompile	2014-03-10 19:54:30.3060383
▶ sql_statement_recompile	2014-03-10 19:54:30.3377181
module_end	2014-03-10 19:54:30.3628372

Event: sql_statement_recompile (2014-03-10 19:54:30.3377181)

Details

Field	Value
line_number	17
nest_level	1
object_id	1156199169
object_name	TempTable
object_type	PROC
offset	968
offset_end	1010
recompile_cause	Deferred compile
source_database_id	5
statement	SELECT * FROM #t2

Figure 17-13. *Extended Events output showing recompilation because of DDL and DML interleaving*

You can see that the statements are recompiled four times.

- The execution plan generated for a query when it is first executed doesn't contain any information about local temporary tables. Therefore, the first generated plan can never be used to access the temporary table using a DML statement.

- The second recompilation comes from the changes encountered in the data contained within the table as it gets loaded.

- The third recompilation is because of a schema change in the first temporary table (#MyTempTable). The creation of the index on #MyTempTable invalidates the existing plan, causing a recompilation when the table is accessed again. If this index had been created before the first recompilation, then the existing plan would have remained valid for the second SELECT statement, too. Therefore, you can avoid this recompilation by putting the CREATE INDEX DDL statement above all DML statements referring to the table.

- The fourth recompilation generates a plan to include the processing strategy for #t2. The existing plan has no information about #t2 and therefore can't be used to access #t2 using the third SELECT statement. If the CREATE TABLE DDL statement for #t2 had been placed before all the DML statements that could cause a recompilation, then the first recompilation itself would have included the information on #t2, avoiding the third recompilation.

Avoiding Recompilations Caused by Statistics Change

In the "Analyzing Causes of Recompilation" section, you saw that a change in statistics is one of the causes of recompilation. On a simple table with uniform data distribution, recompilation because of a change of statistics may generate a plan identical to the previous plan. In such situations, recompilation can be unnecessary and should be avoided if it is too costly. But, most of the time, changes in statistics need to be reflected in the execution plan. I'm just talking about situations where you have a long recompile time or excessive recompiles hitting your CPU.

You have two techniques to avoid recompilations caused by statistics change.

- Use the KEEPFIXED PLAN option.

- Disable the auto update statistics feature on the table.

Using the KEEPFIXED PLAN Option

SQL Server provides a KEEPFIXED PLAN option to avoid recompilations because of a statistics change. To understand how you can use KEEPFIXED PLAN, consider statschanges.sql with an appropriate modification to use the KEEPFIXED PLAN option.

```
--Create a small table with one row and an index
IF (SELECT  OBJECT_ID('dbo.Test1')
    ) IS NOT NULL
    DROP TABLE dbo.Test1 ;
GO
CREATE TABLE dbo.Test1 (C1 INT, C2 CHAR(50)) ;
INSERT  INTO dbo.Test1
VALUES  (1, '2') ;
CREATE NONCLUSTERED INDEX IndexOne ON dbo.Test1 (C1) ;

--Create a stored procedure referencing the previous table
IF (SELECT  OBJECT_ID('dbo.TestProc')
    ) IS NOT NULL
    DROP PROC dbo.TestProc ;
GO
CREATE PROC dbo.TestProc
AS
SELECT  *
FROM    dbo.Test1 AS t
WHERE   t.C1 = 1
OPTION  (KEEPFIXED PLAN) ;
GO


--First execution of stored procedure with 1 row in the table
EXEC dbo.TestProc ;
 --First execution

--Add many rows to the table to cause statistics change
WITH    Nums
        AS (SELECT    1 AS n
            UNION ALL
            SELECT    n + 1
            FROM      Nums
```

```
        WHERE       n < 1000
        )
INSERT  INTO dbo.Test1
        (C1,
         C2
        )
        SELECT  1,
                n
        FROM    Nums
   OPTION   (MAXRECURSION 1000) ;
GO
--Reexecute the stored procedure with a change in statistics
EXEC dbo.TestProc ; --With change in data distribution
```

Figure 17-14 shows the Extended Events output.

name	timestamp	
▶ module_start	2014-03-10 19:58:39.7450481	
module_end	2014-03-10 19:58:39.7524200	
module_start	2014-03-10 19:58:39.8940711	
module_end	2014-03-10 19:58:39.9381027	

Event: module_start (2014-03-10 19:58:39.7450481)

Details

Field	Value
line_number	3
object_id	1204199340
object_name	TestProc
object_type	P
offset	132
offset_end	332
source_database_id	5
statement	EXEC dbo.TestProc ; --First execution --Add many rows to the ...

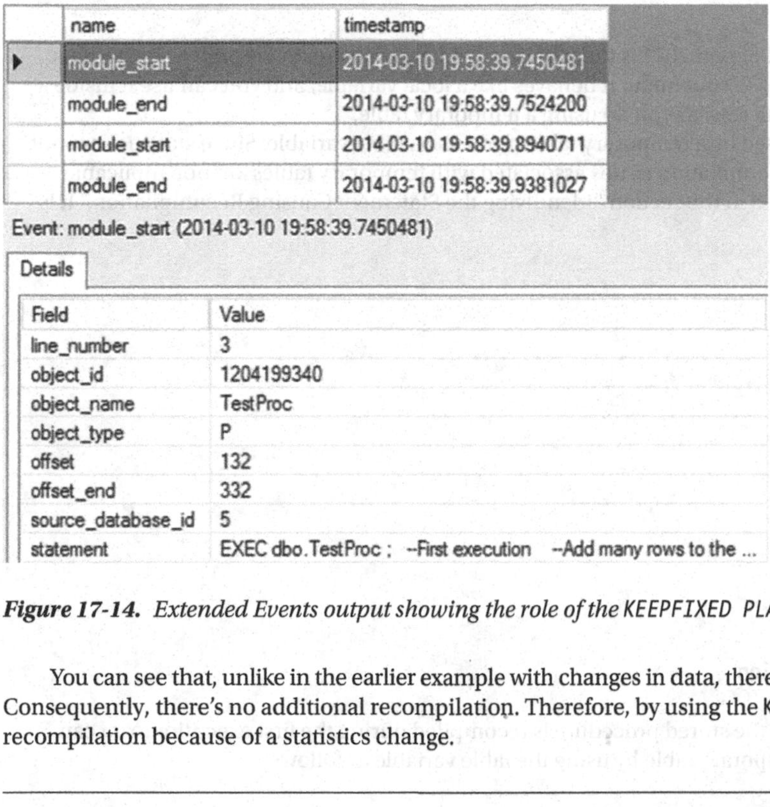

Figure 17-14. *Extended Events output showing the role of the KEEPFIXED PLAN option in reducing recompilation*

You can see that, unlike in the earlier example with changes in data, there's no auto_stats event (see Figure 17-8). Consequently, there's no additional recompilation. Therefore, by using the KEEPFIXED PLAN option, you can avoid recompilation because of a statistics change.

■ **Note** This is a potentially dangerous choice. Before you consider using this option, ensure that any new plans that would have been generated are not superior to the existing plan and that you've exhausted all other possible solutions. In most cases, recompiling queries is preferable, though potentially costly.

Disable Auto Update Statistics on the Table

You can also avoid recompilation because of a statistics update by disabling the automatic statistics update on the relevant table. For example, you can disable the auto update statistics feature on table Test1 as follows:

```
EXEC sp_autostats
    'dbo.Test1',
    'OFF' ;
```

If you disable this feature on the table before inserting the large number of rows that causes statistics change, you can avoid the recompilation because of a statistics change.

However, be cautious with this technique, since outdated statistics can adversely affect the effectiveness of the cost-based optimizer, as discussed in Chapter 12. Also, as explained in Chapter 12, if you disable the automatic update of statistics, you should have a SQL job to manually update the statistics regularly.

Using Table Variables

One of the variable types supported by SQL Server 2014 is the table variable. You can create the table variable data type like other data types by using the DECLARE statement. It behaves like a local variable, and you can use it inside a stored procedure to hold intermediate result sets, as you do using a temporary table.

You can avoid the recompilations caused by a temporary table if you use a table variable. Since statistics are not created for table variables, the different recompilation issues associated with temporary tables are not applicable to it. For instance, consider the script used in the section "Identifying the Statement Causing Recompilation." It is repeated here for your reference.

```
IF (SELECT  OBJECT_ID('dbo.TestProc')
    ) IS NOT NULL
    DROP PROC dbo.TestProc ;
GO
CREATE PROC dbo.TestProc
AS
CREATE TABLE #TempTable (C1 INT) ;
    INSERT  INTO #TempTable
            (C1)
    VALUES  (42) ;
    -- data change causes recompile
GO

EXEC dbo.TestProc ;   --First execution
```

Because of deferred object resolution, the stored procedure is recompiled during the first execution. You can avoid this recompilation caused by the temporary table by using the table variable as follows:

```
IF (SELECT  OBJECT_ID('dbo.TestProc')
    ) IS NOT NULL
    DROP PROC dbo.TestProc;
GO
CREATE PROC dbo.TestProc
AS
DECLARE @TempTable TABLE (C1 INT);
```

```
INSERT  INTO @TempTable
        (C1)
VALUES  (42);
 --Recompilation not needed
GO

EXEC dbo.TestProc; --First execution
```

Figure 17-15 shows the Extended Events output for the first execution of the stored procedure. The recompilation caused by the temporary table has been avoided by using the table variable.

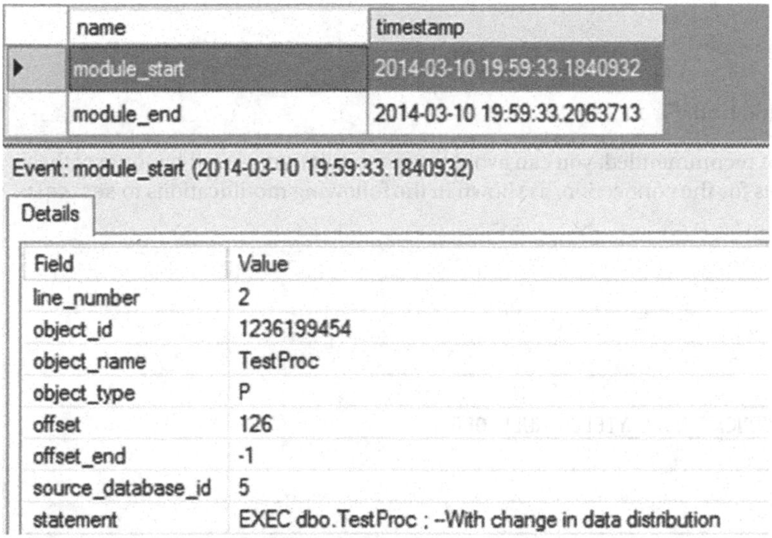

name	timestamp
module_start	2014-03-10 19:59:33.1840932
module_end	2014-03-10 19:59:33.2063713

Event: module_start (2014-03-10 19:59:33.1840932)

Details

Field	Value
line_number	2
object_id	1236199454
object_name	TestProc
object_type	P
offset	126
offset_end	-1
source_database_id	5
statement	EXEC dbo.TestProc ; --With change in data distribution

Figure 17-15. Extended Events output showing the role of a table variable in resolving recompilation

However, table variables have their limitations. The main ones are as follows:

- No DDL statement can be executed on the table variable once it is created, which means no indexes or constraints can be added to the table variable later. Constraints can be specified only as part of the table variable's DECLARE statement. Therefore, only one index can be created on a table variable, using the PRIMARY KEY or UNIQUE constraint.

- No statistics are created for table variables, which means they resolve as single-row tables in execution plans. This is not an issue when the table actually contains only a small quantity of data, approximately less than 100 rows. It becomes a major performance problem when the table variable contains more data since appropriate decisions regarding the right sorts of operations within an execution plan are completely dependent on statistics.

- The following statements are not supported on the table variables:

  - INSERT INTO TableVariable EXEC StoredProcedure

  - SELECT SelectList INTO TableVariable FROM Table

  - SET TableVariable = Value

Avoiding Changing SET Options Within a Stored Procedure

It is generally recommended that you not change the environment settings within a stored procedure and thus avoid recompilation because the SET options changed. For ANSI compatibility, it is recommended that you keep the following SET options ON:

- ARITHABORT
- CONCAT_NULL_YIELDS_NULL
- QUOTED_IDENTIFIER
- ANSI_NULLS
- ANSI_PADDINC
- ANSI_WARNINGS
- And NUMERIC_ROUNDABORT should be OFF.

Although the following approach is not recommended, you can avoid the recompilation caused by some of these SET options changes by resetting the options for the connection, as shown in the following modifications to set.sql:

```
IF (SELECT  OBJECT_ID('dbo.TestProc')
   ) IS NOT NULL
    DROP PROC dbo.TestProc
GO
CREATE PROC dbo.TestProc
AS
SELECT  'a' + NULL + 'b'; --1st SET CONCAT_NULL_YIELDS_NULL OFF

SELECT  'a' + NULL + 'b'; --2nd
SET ANSI_NULLS OFF
SELECT  'a' + NULL + 'b';
 --3rd
GO

SET CONCAT_NULL_YIELDS_NULL OFF;
SET ANSI_NULLS OFF;

EXEC dbo.TestProc;

SET CONCAT_NULL_YIELDS_NULL ON;
 --Reset to default
SET ANSI_NULLS ON;        --Reset to default
```

Figure 17-16 shows the Extended Events output.

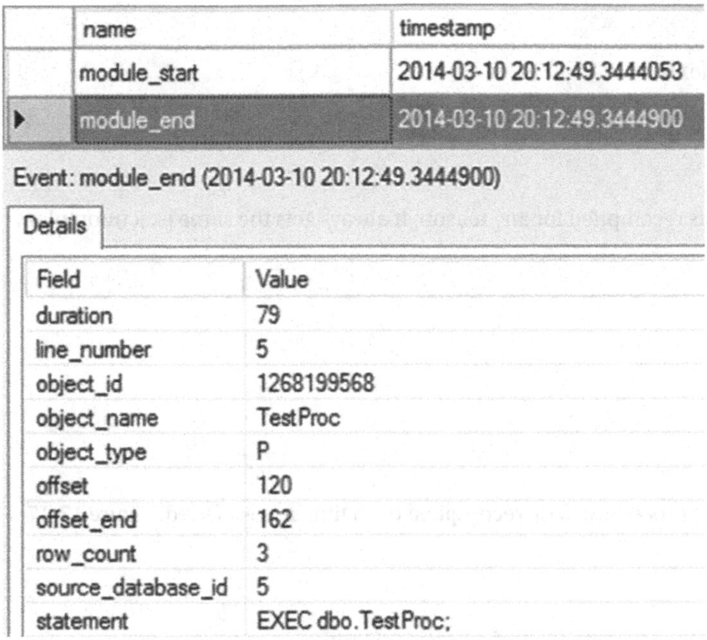

	name	timestamp
	module_start	2014-03-10 20:12:49.3444053
▶	module_end	2014-03-10 20:12:49.3444900

Event: module_end (2014-03-10 20:12:49.3444900)

Details

Field	Value
duration	79
line_number	5
object_id	1268199568
object_name	TestProc
object_type	P
offset	120
offset_end	162
row_count	3
source_database_id	5
statement	EXEC dbo.TestProc;

Figure 17-16. *Extended Events output showing effect of the ANSI SET options on stored procedure recompilation*

You can see that there were fewer recompilations when compared to the original set.sql code (Figure 17-11). Out of the SET options listed previously, the ANSI_NULLS and QUOTED_ IDENTIFIER options are saved as part of the stored procedure when it is created. Therefore, setting these options in the connection outside the stored procedure won't affect any recompilation issues; only re-creating the stored procedure can change these settings.

Using OPTIMIZE FOR Query Hint

Although you may not always be able to reduce or eliminate recompiles, using the OPTIMIZE FOR query hint can help you get the plan you want when the recompile does occur. The OPTIMIZE FOR query hint uses parameter values supplied by you to compile the plan, regardless of the values of the parameter passed in by the calling application.

For an example, examine CustomerList from earlier in the chapter. You know that if this procedure receives certain values, it will need to create a new plan. Knowing your data, you also know two more important facts: The frequency that this query will return small data sets is exceedingly small, and when this query uses the wrong plan, performance suffers. Rather than recompiling it over and over again, modify it so that it creates the plan that works best most of the time.

```
IF (SELECT  OBJECT_ID('dbo.CustomerList')
    ) IS NOT NULL
    DROP PROC dbo.CustomerList
GO
CREATE PROCEDURE dbo.CustomerList @CustomerID INT
AS
SELECT  soh.SalesOrderNumber,
        soh.OrderDate,
        sod.OrderQty,
        sod.LineTotal
```

```
FROM    Sales.SalesOrderHeader AS soh
JOIN    Sales.SalesOrderDetail AS sod
        ON soh.SalesOrderID = sod.SalesOrderID
WHERE   soh.CustomerID >= @CustomerID
OPTION  (OPTIMIZE FOR (@CustomerID = 1));
GO
```

When this query is executed the first time or is recompiled for any reason, it always gets the same execution plan. To test this, execute the procedure this way:

```
EXEC dbo.CustomerList
    @CustomerID = 7920
    WITH RECOMPILE;
EXEC dbo.CustomerList
    @CustomerID = 30118
    WITH RECOMPILE;
```

Just as earlier in the chapter, this will force the procedure to be recompiled each time it is executed. Figure 17-17 shows the resulting execution plans.

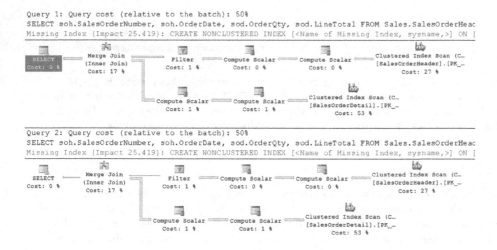

Figure 17-17. WITH RECOMPILE doesn't change identical execution plans

Unlike earlier in the chapter, recompiling the procedure now doesn't result in a new execution plan. Instead, the same plan is generated, regardless of input, because the query optimizer has received instructions to use the value supplied, @CustomerId = 1, when optimizing the query.

This can reduce the number of recompiles, and it does help you control the execution plan generated. It requires that you know your data very well. If your data changes over time, you may need to reexamine areas where the OPTIMIZE FOR query hint was used.

To see the hint in the execution plan, just look at the SELECT operator properties, as shown in Figure 17-18.

Parameter List	@CustomerID
Column	@CustomerID
Parameter Compiled Value	(1)
Parameter Runtime Value	(30118)

Figure 17-18. *The Parameter Compiled Value matches the value supplied by the query hint*

You can see that while the query was recompiled and it was given a value of 30118, because of the hint, the compiled value used was 1 as supplied by the hint.

You can specify that the query be optimized using OPTIMIZE FOR UNKOWN. This is almost the opposite of the OPTIMIZE FOR hint. The OPTIMIZE FOR hint will attempt to use the histogram, while the OPTIMIZE FOR UNKNOWN hint will use the density vector of the statistics. What you are directing the processor to do is perform the optimization based on the average of the statistics, always, and to ignore the actual values passed when the query is optimized. You can use it in combination with OPTIMIZE FOR <value>. It will optimize for the value supplied on that parameter but will use statistics on all other parameters. As was discussed in the preceding chapter, these are both mechanisms for dealing with bad parameter sniffing.

Using Plan Guides

A plan guide allows you to use query hint or other optimization techniques without having to modify the query or procedure text. This is especially useful when you have a third-party product with poorly performing procedures you need to tune but can't modify. As part of the optimization process, if a plan guide exists when a procedure is compiled or recompiled, it will use that guide to create the execution plan.

In the previous section, I showed you how using OPTIMIZE FOR would affect the execution plan created on a procedure. The following is the query from the original procedure, with no hints:

```
IF (SELECT  OBJECT_ID('dbo.CustomerList')
    ) IS NOT NULL
    DROP PROC dbo.CustomerList;
GO
IF (SELECT  OBJECT_ID('dbo. CustomerList')
    ) IS NOT NULL
    DROP PROC dbo. CustomerList;
GO
CREATE PROCEDURE dbo.CustomerList @CustomerID INT
AS
SELECT  soh.SalesOrderNumber,
        soh.OrderDate,
        sod.OrderQty,
        sod.LineTotal
FROM    Sales.SalesOrderHeader AS soh
JOIN    Sales.SalesOrderDetail AS sod
        ON soh.SalesOrderID = sod.SalesOrderID
WHERE   soh.CustomerID >= @CustomerID;
GO
```

Now assume for a moment that this query is part of a third-party application and you are not able to modify it to include OPTION (OPTIMIZE FOR). To provide it with the query hint, OPTIMIZE FOR, create a plan guide as follows:

```
sp_create_plan_guide @name = N'MyGuide',
    @stmt = N'SELECT  soh.SalesOrderNumber,
        soh.OrderDate,
        sod.OrderQty,
        sod.LineTotal
FROM    Sales.SalesOrderHeader AS soh
JOIN    Sales.SalesOrderDetail AS sod
        ON soh.SalesOrderID = sod.SalesOrderID
WHERE   soh.CustomerID >= @CustomerID;',@type = N'OBJECT',
    @module_or_batch = N'dbo.CustomerList',@params = NULL,
    @hints = N'OPTION (OPTIMIZE FOR (@CustomerID = 1))';
```

Now, when the procedure is executed with each of the different parameters, even with the RECOMPILE being forced as shown next, the OPTIMIZE FOR hint is applied. Figure 17-19 shows the resulting execution plan.

```
EXEC dbo.CustomerList
    @CustomerID = 7920
    WITH RECOMPILE;
EXEC dbo.CustomerList
    @CustomerID = 30118
    WITH RECOMPILE;
```

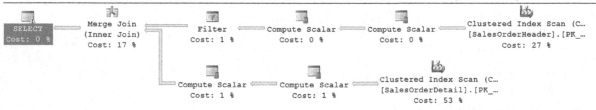

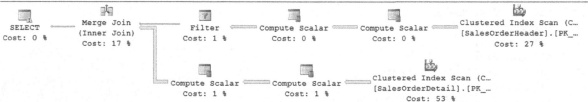

Figure 17-19. Using a plan guide to apply the OPTIMIZE FOR query hint

The results are the same as when the procedure was modified, but in this case, no modification was necessary. You can see that a plan guide was applied within the execution plan by looking at the SELECT properties again (Figure 17-20).

Parameter List	@CustomerID
Column	@CustomerID
Parameter Compiled Value	(1)
Parameter Runtime Value	(7920)
Physical Operation	
PlanGuideDB	AdventureWorks2012
PlanGuideName	MyGuide

Figure 17-20. *SELECT operator properties show the plan guide*

Various types of plan guides exist. The previous example is an *object* plan guide, which is a guide matched to a particular object in the database, in this case CustomerList. You can also create plan guides for ad hoc queries that come into your system repeatedly by creating a *SQL* plan guide that looks for particular SQL statements. Instead of a procedure, the following query gets passed to your system and needs an OPTIMIZE FOR query hint:

```
SELECT   soh.SalesOrderNumber,
         soh.OrderDate,
         sod.OrderQty,
         sod.LineTotal
FROM     Sales.SalesOrderHeader AS soh
JOIN     Sales.SalesOrderDetail AS sod
         ON soh.SalesOrderID = sod.SalesOrderID
WHERE    soh.CustomerID >=1;
```

Running this query results in the execution plan you see in Figure 17-21.

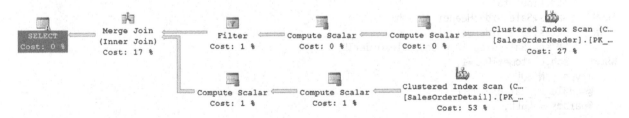

Figure 17-21. *The query uses a different execution plan from the one wanted*

To get a query plan guide, you first need to know the precise format used by the query in case parameterization, forced or simple, changes the text of the query. The text has to be precise. If your first attempt at a query plan guide looked like this:

```
EXECUTE sp_create_plan_guide
    @name = N'MyBadSQLGuide',
    @stmt = N'SELECT  soh.SalesOrderNumber,
        soh.OrderDate,
        sod.OrderQty,
        sod.LineTotal
FROM Sales.SalesOrderHeader AS soh
join Sales.SalesOrderDetail AS sod
ON soh.SalesOrderID = sod.SalesOrderID
WHERE   soh.CustomerID >= @CustomerID',
    @type = N'SQL',
    @module_or_batch = NULL,
    @params = N'@CustomerID int',
    @hints = N'OPTION  (TABLE HINT(soh,  FORCESEEK))';
```

then you'll still get the same execution plan when running the select query. This is because the query doesn't look like what was typed in for the plan guide. Several things are different, such as the spacing and the case on the JOIN statement. You can drop this bad plan guide using the T-SQL statement.

```
EXECUTE sp_control_plan_guide
    @operation = 'Drop',
    @name = N'MyBadSQLGuide';
```

Inputting the correct syntax will create a new plan.

```
EXECUTE sp_create_plan_guide
    @name = N'MyGoodSQLGuide',
    @stmt = N'SELECT  soh.SalesOrderNumber,
        soh.OrderDate,
        sod.OrderQty,
        sod.LineTotal
FROM    Sales.SalesOrderHeader AS soh
JOIN    Sales.SalesOrderDetail AS sod
        ON soh.SalesOrderID = sod.SalesOrderID
WHERE   soh.CustomerID >=1;',
    @type = N'SQL',
    @module_or_batch = NULL,
    @params = NULL,

        @hints = N'OPTION  (TABLE HINT(soh,  FORCESEEK))';
```

Now when the query is run, a completely different plan is created, as shown in Figure 17-22.

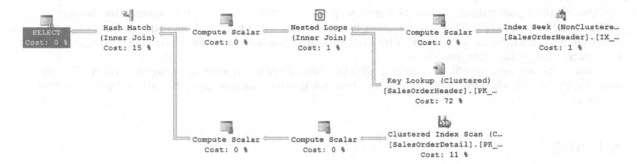

Figure 17-22. *The plan guide forces a new execution plan on the same query*

One other option exists when you have a plan in the cache that you think performs the way you want. You can capture that plan into a plan guide to ensure that the next time the query is run, the same plan is executed. You accomplish this by running sp_create_plan_ guide_from_handle.

To test it, first clear the procedure cache so you can control exactly which query plan is used.

```
DBCC FREEPROCCACHE();
```

With the procedure cache clear and the existing plan guide, MyGoodSOQLGuide, in place, rerun the query. It will use the plan guide to arrive at the execution plan displayed in Figure 17-20. To see whether this plan can be kept, first drop the plan guide that is forcing the Index Seek operation.

```
EXECUTE sp_control_plan_guide
    @operation = 'Drop',
    @name = N'MyGoodSQLGuide' ;
```

If you were to rerun the query now, it would revert to its original plan. However, right now in the plan cache, you have the plan displayed in Figure 17-20. To keep it, run the following script:

```
DECLARE @plan_handle VARBINARY(64),
    @start_offset INT ;

SELECT  @plan_handle = deqs.plan_handle,
        @start_offset = deqs.statement_start_offset
FROM    sys.dm_exec_query_stats AS deqs
CROSS APPLY sys.dm_exec_sql_text(sql_handle)
CROSS APPLY sys.dm_exec_text_query_plan(deqs.plan_handle,
                                        deqs.statement_start_offset,
                                        deqs.statement_end_offset) AS qp
WHERE   text LIKE N'SELECT  soh.SalesOrderNumber%'

EXECUTE sp_create_plan_guide_from_handle
    @name = N'ForcedPlanGuide',
    @plan_handle = @plan_handle,
    @statement_start_offset = @start_offset ;
GO
```

This creates a plan guide based on the execution plan as it currently exists in the cache. To be sure this works, clear the cache again. That way, the query has to generate a new plan. Rerun the query, and observe the execution plan. It will be the same as that displayed in Figure 17-20 because of the plan guide created using `sp_create_plan_guide_from_handle`.

Plan guides are useful mechanisms for controlling the behavior of SQL queries and stored procedures, but you should use them only when you have a thorough understanding of the execution plan, the data, and the structure of your system.

Summary

As you learned in this chapter, query recompilation can both benefit and hurt performance. Recompilations that generate better plans improve the performance of the stored procedure. However, recompilations that regenerate the same plan consume extra CPU cycles without any improvement in processing strategy. Therefore, you should look closely at recompilations to determine their usefulness. You can use Extended Events to identify which stored procedure statement caused the recompilation, and you can determine the cause from the `recompile_clause` data column value in the Extended Events output. Once you determine the cause of the recompilation, you can apply different techniques to avoid the unnecessary recompilations.

Up until now, you have seen how to benefit from proper indexing and plan caching. However, the performance benefit of these techniques depends on the way the queries are designed. The cost-based optimizer of SQL Server takes care of many of the query design issues. However, you should adopt a number of best practices while designing queries. In the next chapter, I will cover some of the common query design issues that affect performance.

■■■

## CHAPTER 18

Query Design Analysis

A database schema may include a number of performance-enhancement features such as indexes, statistics, and stored procedures. But none of these features guarantees good performance if your queries are written badly in the first place. The SQL queries may not be able to use the available indexes effectively. The structure of the SQL queries may add avoidable overhead to the query cost. Queries may be attempting to deal with data in a row-by-row fashion (or to quote Jeff Moden, Row By Agonizing Row, which is abbreviated to RBAR and pronounced "reebar") instead of in logical sets. To improve the performance of a database application, it is important to understand the cost associated with varying ways of writing a query.

In this chapter, I cover the following topics:

- Aspects of query design that affect performance

- How query designs use indexes effectively

- The role of optimizer hints on query performance

- The role of database constraints on query performance

Query Design Recommendations

When you need to run a query, you can often use many different approaches to get the same data. In many cases, the optimizer generates the same plan, irrespective of the structure of the query. However, in some situations the query structure won't allow the optimizer to select the best possible processing strategy. It is important that you are aware that this can happen and, should it occur, what you can do to avoid it.

In general, keep the following recommendations in mind to ensure the best performance:

- Operate on small result sets.

- Use indexes effectively.

- Avoid optimizer hints.

- Use domain and referential integrity.

- Avoid resource-intensive queries.

- Reduce the number of network round-trips.

- Reduce the transaction cost. (I'll cover the last three in the next chapter.)

Careful testing is essential to identify the query form that provides the best performance in a specific database environment. You should be conversant with writing and comparing different SQL query forms so you can evaluate the query form that provides the best performance in a given environment. You'll also want to be able to automate your testing.

Operating on Small Result Sets

To improve the performance of a query, limit the amount of data it operates on, including both columns and rows. Operating on a small result set reduces the amount of resources consumed by a query and increases the effectiveness of indexes. Two of the rules you should follow to limit the data set's size are as follows:

- Limit the number of columns in the select list.

- Use highly selective WHERE clauses to limit the rows returned.

It's important to note that you will be asked to return tens of thousands of rows to an OLTP system. Just because someone tells you those are the business requirements doesn't mean they are right. Human beings don't process tens of thousands of rows. Few human beings are capable of processing thousands of rows. Be prepared to push back on these requests, and be able to justify your reasons.

Limit the Number of Columns in select_list

Use a minimum set of columns in the select list of a SELECT statement. Don't use columns that are not required in the output result set. For instance, don't use SELECT * to return all columns. SELECT * statements render covered indexes ineffective, since it is usually impractical to include all columns in an index. For example, consider the following query:

```
SELECT  Name,
        TerritoryID
FROM    Sales.SalesTerritory AS st
WHERE   st.Name = 'Australia' ;
```

A covering index on the Name column (and through the clustered key, ProductID) serves the query quickly through the index itself, without accessing the clustered index. When you have STATISTICS 10 and STATISTICS TIME switched on, you get the following number of logical reads and execution time, as well as the corresponding execution plan (shown in Figure 18-1):

```
Table 'SalesTerritory'. Scan count 0, logical reads 2
CPU time = 0 ms,   elapsed time = 6 ms.
```

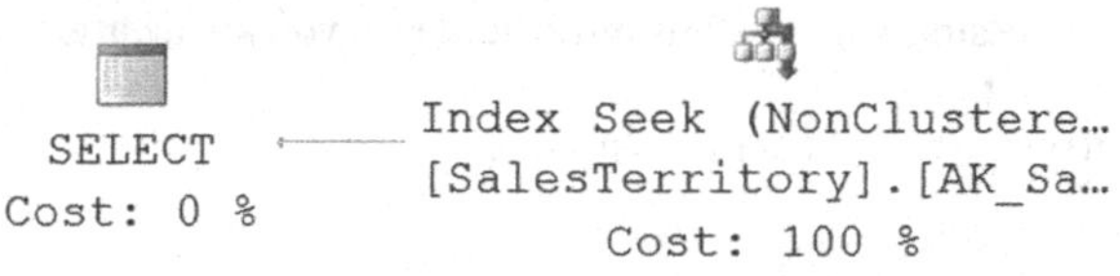

Figure 18-1. Execution plan showing the benefit of referring to a limited number of columns

If this query is modified to include all columns in the select list as follows, then the previous covering index becomes ineffective because all the columns required by this query are not included in that index:

```
SELECT  *
FROM    Sales.SalesTerritory AS st
WHERE   st.[Name] = 'Australia';
```

Subsequently, the base table (or the clustered index) containing all the columns has to be accessed, as shown next. The number of logical reads and the execution time have both increased.

```
Table 'SalesTerritory'. Scan count 0, logical reads 4
CPU time = 0 ms,   elapsed time = 20 ms
```

As shown in Figure 18-2, the fewer the columns in the select list, the better the query performance. And remember, the query we've been looking at is a simple query returning a single, small row of data, and it has doubled the number of reads and tripled the execution time. Selecting too many columns also increases data transfer across the network, further degrading performance.

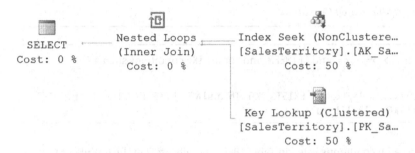

Figure 18-2. *Execution plan showing the added cost of referring to too many columns*

Use Highly Selective WHERE Clauses

As explained in Chapter 8, the selectivity of a column referred to in the WHERE and HAVING clauses governs the use of an index on the column. A request for a large number of rows from a table may not benefit from using an index, either because it can't use an index at all or, in the case of a nonclustered index, because of the overhead cost of the bookmark lookup. To ensure the use of indexes, the columns referred to in the WHERE clause should be highly selective.

Most of the time, an end user concentrates on a limited number of rows at a time. Therefore, you should design database applications to request data incrementally as the user navigates through the data. For applications that rely on a large amount of data for data analysis or reporting, consider using data analysis solutions such as Analysis Services or PowerPivot. Remember, returning huge result sets is costly, and this data is unlikely to be used in its entirety.

Using Indexes Effectively

It is extremely important to have effective indexes on database tables to improve performance. However, it is equally important to ensure that the queries are designed properly to use these indexes effectively. These are some of the query design rules you should follow to improve the use of indexes:

- Avoid nonsargable search conditions.
- Avoid arithmetic operators on the WHERE clause column.
- Avoid functions on the WHERE clause column.

I cover each of these rules in detail in the following sections.

Avoid Nonsargable Search Conditions

A *sargable* predicate in a query is one in which an index can be used. The word is a contraction of "Search ARGument ABLE." The optimizer's ability to benefit from an index depends on the selectivity of the search condition, which in turn depends on the selectivity of the column(s) referred to in the WHERE clause, all of which are referred back to the statistics on the index. The search predicate used on the column(s) in the WHERE clause determines whether an index operation on the column can be performed.

The sargable search conditions listed in Table 18-1 generally allow the optimizer to use an index on the column(s) referred to in the WHERE clause. The sargable search conditions generally allow SQL Server to seek to a row in the index and retrieve the row (or the adjacent range of rows until the search condition remains true).

Table 18-1. Common Sargable and Nonsargable Search Conditions

Type	Search Conditions
Sargable	Inclusion conditions =, >, >=, <, <=, and BETWEEN, and some LIKE conditions such as LIKE '<literal>%'
Nonsargable	Exclusion conditions <>, !=, !>, !<, NOT EXISTS, NOT IN, and NOT LIKE IN, OR, and some LIKE conditions such as LIKE '%<literal>'

On the other hand, the *nonsargable* search conditions listed in Table 18-1 generally prevent the optimizer from using an index on the column(s) referred to in the WHERE clause. The exclusion search conditions generally don't allow SQL Server to perform Index Seek operations as supported by the sargable search conditions. For example, the != condition requires scanning all the rows to identify the matching rows.

Try to implement workarounds for these nonsargable search conditions to improve performance. In some cases, it may be possible to rewrite a query to avoid a nonsargable search condition. For example, consider replacing an IN/OR search condition with a BETWEEN condition, as described in the following section.

BETWEEN vs. IN/OR

Consider the following query, which uses the search condition IN:

```
SELECT * FROM Sales.SalesOrderDetail AS sod
WHERE sod.SalesOrderID IN (51825,51826,51827,51828);
```

Another way to write the same query is to use the OR command:

```
SELECT  sod.*
FROM    Sales.SalesOrderDetail AS sod
WHERE   sod.SalesOrderID = 51825 OR
        sod.SalesOrderID = 51826 OR
        sod.SalesOrderID = 51827 OR
        sod.SalesOrderID = 51828 OR
```

You can replace either of these search condition in this query with a BETWEEN clause as follows:

```
SELECT  sod.*
FROM    Sales.SalesOrderDetail AS sod
WHERE   sod.SalesOrderID BETWEEN 51825 AND 51828;
```

All three queries return the same results. On the face of it, the execution plan of all three queries appear to be the same, as shown in Figure 18-3.

Figure 18-3. *Execution plan for a simple SELECT statement using a BETWEEN clause*

However, a closer look at the execution plans reveals the difference in their data-retrieval mechanism, as shown in Figure 18-4. The top box is the IN condition, and the bottom box is the BETWEEN condition.

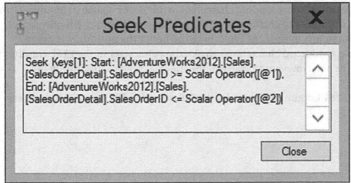

Figure 18-4. *Execution plan details for an IN condition (top) and a BETWEEN condition (bottom)*

As shown in Figure 18-4, SQL Server resolved the IN condition containing four values into four OR conditions. Accordingly, the clustered index (PKSalesTerritoryTerritoryId) is accessed four times (Scan count 4) to retrieve rows for the four IN and OR conditions, as shown in the following corresponding STATISTICS 10 output. On the other hand, the BETWEEN condition is resolved into a pair of >=and <= conditions, as shown in Figure 18-4. SQL Server accesses the clustered index only once (Scan count 1) from the first matching row until the match condition is true, as shown in the following corresponding STATISTICS 10 and QUERY TIME output.

- With the IN condition:

    ```
    Table 'SalesOrderDetail'.  Scan count 4,  logical reads 18
    CPU time = 0 ms,    elapsed time = 102 ms.
    ```

- With the BETWEEN condition:

    ```
    Table 'SalesOrderDetail'.  Scan count 1,  logical reads 6
    CPU time = 0 ms,    elapsed time = 63 ms.
    ```

Replacing the search condition IN with BETWEEN decreases the number of logical reads for this query from 18 to 6. As just shown, although all three queries use a clustered index seek on OrderID, the optimizer locates the range of rows much faster with the BETWEEN clause than with the IN clause. The same thing happens when you look at the BETWEEN condition and the OR clause. Therefore, if there is a choice between using IN/OR and the BETWEEN search condition, always choose the BETWEEN condition because it is generally much more efficient than the IN/OR condition. In fact, you should go one step further and use the combination of >=and <= instead of the BETWEEN clause only because you're making the optimizer do a little less work.

Also worth noting is that this query violates the earlier suggestion to return only a limited set of columns rather than using SELECT *.

Not every WHERE clause that uses exclusion search conditions prevents the optimizer from using the index on the column referred to in the search condition. In many cases, the SQL Server 2014 optimizer does a wonderful job of converting the exclusion search condition to a sargable search condition. To understand this, consider the following two search conditions, which I discuss in the sections that follow:

- The LIKE condition

- The !< condition vs. the >=condition

LIKE Condition

While using the LIKE search condition, try to use one or more leading characters in the WHERE clause if possible. Using leading characters in the LIKE clause allows the optimizer to convert the LIKE condition to an index-friendly search condition. The greater the number of leading characters in the LIKE condition, the better the optimizer is able to determine an effective index. Be aware that using a wildcard character as the leading character in the LIKE condition *prevents* the optimizer from performing a SEEK (or a narrow-range scan) on the index; it relies on scanning the complete table instead.

To understand this ability of the SQL Server 2014 optimizer, consider the following SELECT statement that uses the LIKE condition with a leading character:

```
SELECT  c.CurrencyCode
FROM    Sales.Currency AS c
WHERE   c.[Name] LIKE 'Ice%';
```

The SQL Server 2012 optimizer does this conversion automatically, as shown in Figure 18-5.

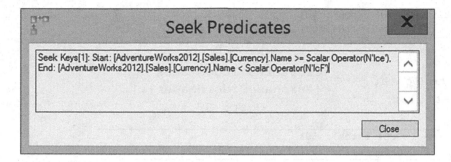

Figure 18-5. *Execution plan showing automatic conversion of a LIKE clause with a trailing % sign to an indexable search condition*

As you can see, the optimizer automatically converts the LIKE condition to an equivalent pair of >=and < conditions. You can therefore rewrite this SELECT statement to replace the LIKE condition with an indexable search condition as follows:

```
SELECT  c.CurrencyCode
FROM    Sales.Currency AS c
WHERE   c.[Name] >=N'Ice'
        AND c.[Name] < N'IcF';
```

Note that, in both cases, the number of logical reads, the execution time for the query with the LIKE condition, and the manually converted sargable search condition are all the same. Thus, if you include leading characters in the LIKE clause, the SQL Server 2014 optimizer optimizes the search condition to allow the use of indexes on the column.

!< Condition vs. >=Condition

Even though both the !< and >=search conditions retrieve the same result set, they may perform different operations internally. The >=comparison operator allows the optimizer to use an index on the column referred to in the search argument because the = part of the operator allows the optimizer to seek to a starting point in the index and access all the index rows from there onward. On the other hand, the !< operator doesn't have an = element and needs to access the column value for every row.

Or does it? As explained in Chapter 14, the SQL Server optimizer performs syntax-based optimization, before executing a query, to improve performance. This allows SQL Server to take care of the performance concern with the !< operator by converting it to >=, as shown in the execution plan in Figure 18-6 for the two following SELECT statements:

```
SELECT  *
FROM    Purchasing.PurchaseOrderHeader AS poh
WHERE   poh.PurchaseOrderID >=2975;
SELECT  *
FROM    Purchasing.PurchaseOrderHeader AS poh
WHERE   poh.PurchaseOrderID !< 2975;
```

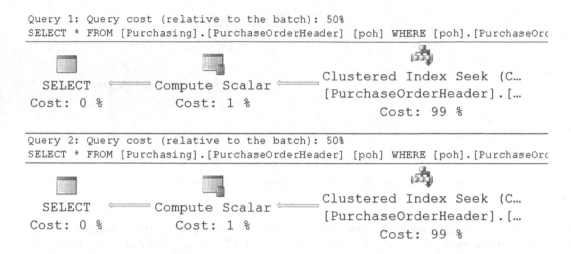

```
Query 1: Query cost (relative to the batch): 50%
SELECT * FROM [Purchasing].[PurchaseOrderHeader] [poh] WHERE [poh].[PurchaseOrc
```

```
Query 2: Query cost (relative to the batch): 50%
SELECT * FROM [Purchasing].[PurchaseOrderHeader] [poh] WHERE [poh].[PurchaseOrc
```

Figure 18-6. *Execution plan showing automatic transformation of a nonindexable !< operator to an indexable >=operator*

As you can see, the optimizer often provides you with the flexibility of writing queries in the preferred T-SQL syntax without sacrificing performance.

Although the SQL Server optimizer can automatically optimize query syntax to improve performance in many cases, you should not rely on it to do so. It is a good practice to write efficient queries in the first place.

Avoid Arithmetic Operators on the WHERE Clause Column

Using an arithmetic operator on a column in the WHERE clause can prevent the optimizer from using the index on the column. For example, consider the following SELECT statement:

```
SELECT  *
FROM    Purchasing.PurchaseOrderHeader AS poh
WHERE   poh.PurchaseOrderID * 2 = 3400;
```

A multiplication operator, *, has been applied on the column in the WHERE clause. You can avoid this on the column by rewriting the SELECT statement as follows:

```
SELECT  *
FROM    Purchasing.PurchaseOrderHeader AS poh
WHERE   poh.PurchaseOrderID = 3400 / 2;
```

The table has a clustered index on the PurchaseOrderID column. As explained in Chapter 4, an Index Seek operation on this index is suitable for this query since it returns only one row. Even though both queries return the same result set, the use of the multiplication operator on the PurchaseOrderID column in the first query prevents the optimizer from using the index on the column, as you can see in Figure 18-7.

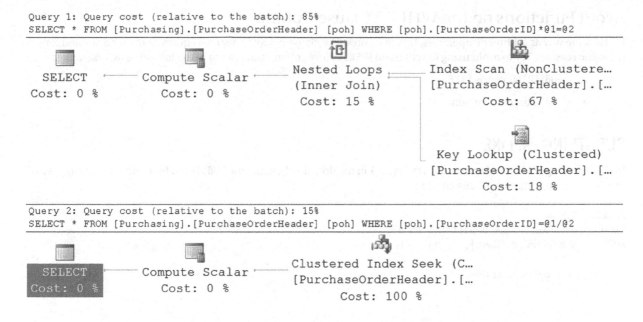

```
Query 1: Query cost (relative to the batch): 85%
SELECT * FROM [Purchasing].[PurchaseOrderHeader] [poh] WHERE [poh].[PurchaseOrderID]*@1=@2
```

```
Query 2: Query cost (relative to the batch): 15%
SELECT * FROM [Purchasing].[PurchaseOrderHeader] [poh] WHERE [poh].[PurchaseOrderID]=@1/@2
```

Figure 18-7. *Execution plan showing the detrimental effect of an arithmetic operator on a WHERE clause column*

The following are the corresponding STATISTICS IO and TIME outputs.

- With the * operator on the PurchaseOrderID column:

  Table 'PurchaseOrderHeader'. Scan count *1*, logical reads 11 CPU time = 0 ms,
  elapsed time = 61 ms.

- With no operator on the PurchaseOrderID column:

  Table 'PurchaseOrderHeader'. Scan count 0, logical reads 2 CPU time = 0 ms,
  elapsed time =27 ms.

Therefore, to use the indexes effectively and improve query performance, avoid using arithmetic operators on column(s) in the WHERE clause or JOIN criteria when that expression is expected to work with an index.

Worth noting in the queries shown in Figure 18-7, both queries were simple enough to qualify for parameterization as indicated by the @1 and @2 in the queries instead of the values supplied.

■ **Note**   For small result sets, even though an index seek is usually a better data-retrieval strategy than a table scan (or a complete clustered index scan), for small tables (in which all data rows fit on one page) a table scan can be cheaper. I explain this in more detail in Chapter 8.

Avoid Functions on the WHERE Clause Column

In the same way as arithmetic operators, functions on WHERE clause columns also hurt query performance—and for the same reasons. Try to avoid using functions on WHERE clause columns, as shown in the following two examples:

- SUBSTRING versus LIKE

- Date part comparison

SUBSTRING vs. LIKE

In the following SELECT statement (substring.sql in the download), using the SUBSTRING function prevents the use of the index on the ShipPostalCode column.

```
SELECT   d.Name
FROM     HumanResources.Department AS d
WHERE    SUBSTRING(d.[Name], 1, 1) = 'F';
```

Figure 18-8 illustrates this.

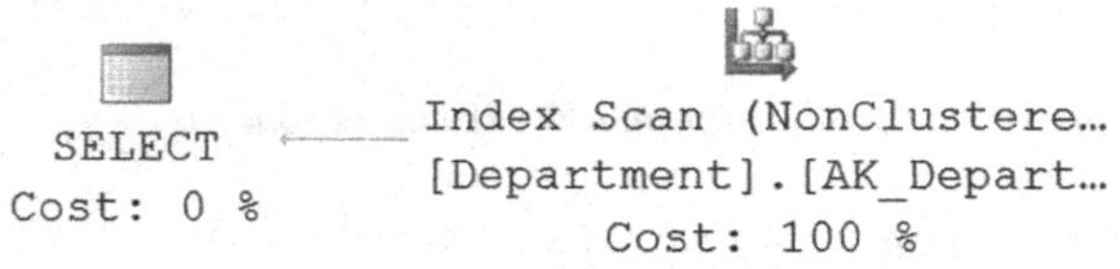

Figure 18-8. *Execution plan showing the detrimental effect of using the SUBSTRING function on a WHERE clause column*

As you can see, using the SUBSTRING function prevented the optimizer from using the index on the [Name] column. This function on the column made the optimizer use a clustered index scan. In the absence of the clustered index on the DepartmentID column, a table scan would have been performed.

You can redesign this SELECT statement to avoid the function on the column as follows:

```
SELECT   d.Name
FROM     HumanResources.Department AS d
WHERE    d.[Name] LIKE 'F%';
```

This query allows the optimizer to choose the index on the [Name] column, as shown in Figure 18-9.

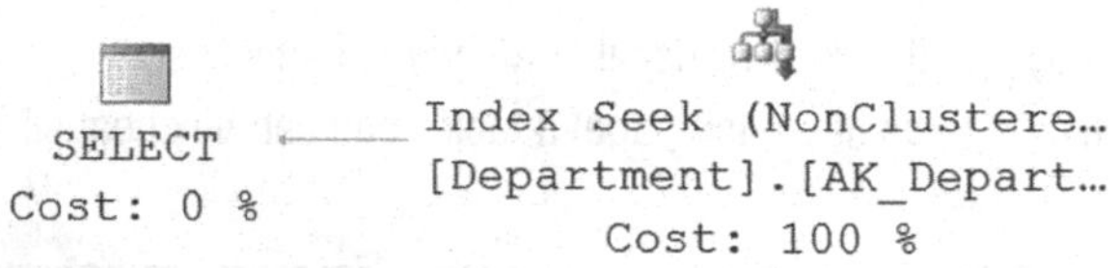

Figure 18-9. *Execution plan showing the benefit of not using the SUBSTRING function on a WHERE clause column*

Date Part Comparison

SQL Server can store date and time data as separate fields or as a combined DATETIME field that has both. Although you may need to keep date and time data together in one field, sometimes you want only the date, which usually means you have to apply a conversion function to extract the date part from the DATETIME data type. Doing this prevents the optimizer from choosing the index on the column, as shown in the following example.

First, there needs to be a good index on the DATETIME column of one of the tables. Use Sales.SalesOrderHeader and create the following index:

```
IF EXISTS ( SELECT  *
            FROM    sys.indexes
            WHERE   object_id = OBJECT_ID(N'[Sales].[SalesOrderHeader]')
                    AND name = N'IndexTest' )
    DROP INDEX IndexTest ON [Sales].[SalesOrderHeader];
GO
CREATE INDEX IndexTest ON Sales.SalesOrderHeader(OrderDate);
```

To retrieve all rows from Sales.SalesOrderHeader with OrderDate in the month of April in the year 2008, you can execute the following SELECT statement:

```
SELECT  soh.SalesOrderID,
        soh.OrderDate
FROM    Sales.SalesOrderHeader AS soh
JOIN    Sales.SalesOrderDetail AS sod
        ON soh.SalesOrderID = sod.SalesOrderID
WHERE   DATEPART(yy, soh.OrderDate) = 2008
        AND DATEPART(mm, soh.OrderDate) = 4;
```

Using the DATEPART function on the column OrderDate prevents the optimizer from properly using the index IndexTest on the column and instead causes a scan, as shown in Figure 18-10.

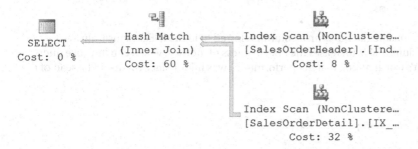

Figure 18-10. *Execution plan showing the detrimental effect of using the DATEPART function on a WHERE clause column*

This is the output of SET STATISTICS IO and TIME:

```
Table 'Worktable'. Scan count 0, logical reads 0 Table 'SalesOrderDetail'. Scan count 1, logical
reads 276 Table 'SalesOrderHeader'. Scan count 1, logical reads 73
CPU time = 15 ms,    elapsed time = 143 ms.
```

The date part comparison can be done without applying the function on the DATETIME column.

```
SELECT  soh.SalesOrderID,
        soh.OrderDate
FROM    Sales.SalesOrderHeader AS soh
JOIN    Sales.SalesOrderDetail AS sod
        ON soh.SalesOrderID = sod.SalesOrderID
WHERE   soh.OrderDate >= '2008-04-01'
        AND soh.OrderDate < '2008-05-01';
```

This allows the optimizer to properly reference the index IndexTest that was created on the DATETIME column, as shown in Figure 18-11.

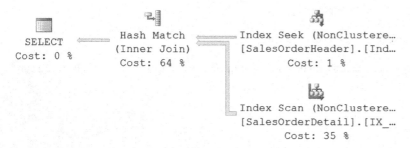

Figure 18-11. *Execution plan showing the benefit of not using the CONVERT function on a WHERE clause column*

This is the output of SET STATISTICS IO and TIME:

```
Table 'Worktable'. Scan count 0, logical reads 0
Table 'SalesOrderDetail'. Scan count 1, logical reads 276
Table 'SalesOrderHeader'. Scan count 1, logical reads 8
CPU time = 0 ms,    elapsed time = 132 ms
```

Therefore, to allow the optimizer to consider an index on a column referred to in the WHERE clause, always avoid using a function on the indexed column. This increases the effectiveness of indexes, which can improve query performance. In this instance, though, it's worth noting that the performance was minor since there's still a scan of the SalesOrderDetail table.

Be sure to drop the index created earlier.

```
DROP INDEX Sales.SalesOrderHeader.IndexTest;
```

Avoiding Optimizer Hints

SQL Server's cost-based optimizer dynamically determines the processing strategy for a query based on the current table/index structure and statistics. This dynamic behavior can be overridden using optimizer hints, taking some of the decisions away from the optimizer by instructing it to use a certain processing strategy. This makes the optimizer behavior static and doesn't allow it to dynamically update the processing strategy as the table/index structures or statistics change.

Since it is usually difficult to outsmart the optimizer, the usual recommendation is to avoid optimizer hints. Generally, it is beneficial to let the optimizer determine a cost-effective processing strategy based on the data distribution statistics, indexes, and other factors. Forcing the optimizer (with hints) to use a specific processing strategy hurts performance more often than not, as shown in the following examples for these hints:

- JOIN hint
- INDEX hint

JOIN Hint

As explained in Chapter 6, the optimizer dynamically determines a cost-effective JOIN strategy between two data sets based on the table/index structure and data. Table 18-2 presents a summary of the JOIN types supported by SQL Server 2012 for easy reference.

Table 18-2. *JOIN Types Supported by SQL Server 2014*

JOIN Type	Index on Joining Columns	Usual Size of Joining Tables	Presorted JOIN Clause
Nested loop	Inner table a must Outer table preferable	Small	Optional
Merge	Both tables a must Optimal condition: clustered or covering index on both	Large	Yes
Hash	Inner table *not* indexed	Any Optimal condition: Inner table large, outer table small	No

■ **Note** The outer table is usually the smaller of the two joining tables.

You can instruct SQL Server to use a specific JOIN type by using the JOIN hints in Table 18-3.

Table 18-3. *JOIN Hints*

JOIN Type	JOIN Hint
Nested loop	LOOP JOIN
Merge	MERGE JOIN
Hash	HASH JOIN

To understand how the use of JOIN hints can affect performance, consider the following SELECT statement:

```
SELECT s.[Name] AS StoreName,
    p.[LastName] + ', ' + p.[FirstName]
FROM   [Sales].[Store] s
JOIN   [Sales].SalesPerson AS sp
    ON s.SalesPersonID = sp.BusinessEntityID
JOIN   HumanResources.Employee AS e
    ON sp.BusinessEntityID = e.BusinessEntityID
JOIN   Person.Person AS p
    ON e.BusinessEntityID = p.BusinessEntityID;
```

Figure 18-12 shows the execution plan.

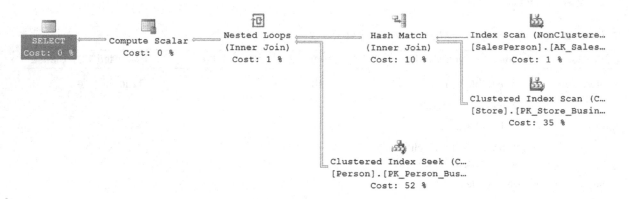

Figure 18-12. *Execution plan showing choices made by the optimizer*

As you can see, SQL Server dynamically decided to use a LOOP JOIN to add the data from the Person.Person table and to add a HASH JOIN for the Sales.Salesperson and Sales.Store tables. As demonstrated in Chapter 6, for simple queries affecting a small result set, a LOOP JOIN generally provides better performance than a HASH JOIN or MERGE JOIN. Since the number of rows coming from the Sales.Salesperson table is relatively small, it might feel like you could force the JOIN to be a LOOP like this:

```
SELECT  s.[Name] AS StoreName,
        p.[LastName] + ',   ' + p.[FirstName]
FROM    [Sales].[Store] s
JOIN    [Sales].SalesPerson AS sp
        ON s.SalesPersonID = sp.BusinessEntityID
JOIN    HumanResources.Employee AS e
        ON sp.BusinessEntityID = e.BusinessEntityID
JOIN    Person.Person AS p
        ON e.BusinessEntityID = p.BusinessEntityID
OPTION  (LOOP JOIN);
```

When this query is run, the execution plan changes, as you can see in Figure 18-13.

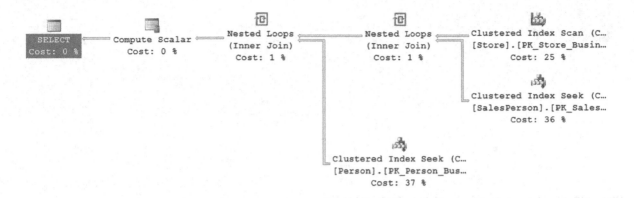

Figure 18-13. *Changes made by using the JOIN query hint*

Here are the corresponding STATISTICS IO and TIME outputs for each query.

- With no JOIN hint:

```
Table 'Person'. Scan count 0, logical reads 2155
Table 'Worktable'. Scan count 0, logical reads 0
Table 'Store'. Scan count 1, logical reads 103
Table 'SalesPerson'. Scan count 1, logical reads 2
CPU time = 0 ms, elapsed time = 48 ms.
```

- With a JOIN hint:

```
Table 'Person'. Scan count 0, logical reads 2155
Table 'SalesPerson'. Scan count 0, logical reads 1402
Table 'Store'. Scan count 1, logical reads 103
CPU time = 16 ms, elapsed time = 73 ms.
```

You can see that the query with the JOIN hint takes longer to run than the query without the hint. It also adds overhead to the CPU. And you can make this even worse. Instead of telling all hints used in the query to be a LOOP join, it is possible to target just the one you are interested in, like so:

```
SELECT    s.[Name] AS StoreName,
          p.[LastName] + ',   ' + p.[FirstName]
FROM      [Sales].[Store] s
INNER LOOP JOIN [Sales].SalesPerson AS sp
          ON s.SalesPersonID = sp.BusinessEntityID
JOIN      HumanResources.Employee AS e
          ON sp.BusinessEntityID = e.BusinessEntityID
JOIN      Person.Person AS p
          ON e.BusinessEntityID = p.BusinessEntityID ;
```

Running this query results in the execution plan shown in Figure 18-14.

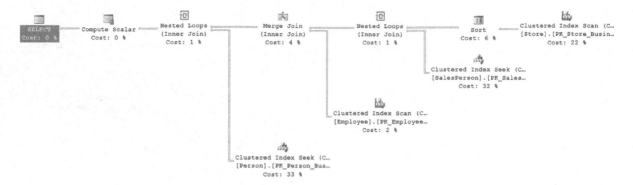

Figure 18-14. *More changes from using the LOOP join hint*

As you can see, there are now four tables referenced in the query plan. There have been four tables referenced through all the previous executions, but the optimizer was able to eliminate one table from the query through the simplification process of optimization (referred to in Chapter 8). Now the hint has forced the optimizer to make different choices than it otherwise might have and removed simplification from the process. The reads and execution time suffered as well.

```
Table 'Person'. Scan count 0, logical reads 2155
Table 'Worktable'. Scan count 0, logical reads 0
Table 'Employee'. Scan count 1, logical reads 9
Table 'SalesPerson'. Scan count 0, logical reads 1402
Table 'Store'. Scan count 1, logical reads 103
CPU time = 0 ms, elapsed time = 92 ms.
```

JOIN hints force the optimizer to ignore its own optimization strategy and use instead the strategy specified by the query. JOIN hints generally hurt query performance because of the following factors:

- Hints prevent autoparameterization.

- The optimizer is prevented from dynamically deciding the joining order of the tables.

Therefore, it makes sense to not use the JOIN hint but to instead let the optimizer dynamically determine a cost-effective processing strategy. There are exceptions of course, but the exceptions must be validated through thorough testing.

INDEX Hints

As mentioned earlier, using an arithmetic operator on a WHERE clause column prevents the optimizer from choosing the index on the column. To improve performance, you can rewrite the query without using the arithmetic operator on the WHERE clause, as shown in the corresponding example. Alternatively, you may even think of forcing the optimizer to use the index on the column with an INDEX hint (a type of optimizer hint). However, most of the time, it is better to avoid the INDEX hint and let the optimizer behave dynamically.

To understand the effect of an INDEX hint on query performance, consider the example presented in the "Avoid Arithmetic Operators on the WHERE Clause Column" section. The multiplication operator on the PurchaseOrderID column prevented the optimizer from choosing the index on the column. You can use an INDEX hint to force the optimizer to use the index on the OrderID column as follows:

```
SELECT   *
FROM     Purchasing.PurchaseOrderHeader AS poh WITH (INDEX (PK_PurchaseOrderHeader_PurchaseOrderID))
WHERE    poh.PurchaseOrderID * 2 = 3400 ;
```

Note the relative cost of using the INDEX hint in comparison to not using the INDEX hint, as shown in Figure 18-14. Also, note the difference in the number of logical reads shown in the following STATISTICS IO outputs.

- No hint (with the arithmetic operator on the WHERE clause column):

  Table 'PurchaseOrderHeader'. Scan count 1, logical reads 11

- CPU time = 0 ms, elapsed time = 61 ms.

- No hint (without the arithmetic operator on the WHERE clause column):

  Table 'PurchaseOrderHeader'. Scan count 0, logical reads 2
  CPU time = 0 ms, elapsed time = 27 ms.

- INDEX hint:

  Table 'PurchaseOrderHeader'. Scan count 1, logical reads 44
  CPU time = 0 ms, elapsed time = 83 ms.

From the relative cost of execution plans and number of logical reads, it is evident that the query with the INDEX hint actually impaired the query performance. Even though it allowed the optimizer to use the index on the PurchaseOrderID column, it did not allow the optimizer to determine the proper index-access mechanism. Consequently, the optimizer used the index scan to access just one row. In comparison, avoiding the arithmetic operator on the WHERE clause column and not using the INDEX hint allowed the optimizer not only to use the index on the PurchaseOrderID column but also to determine the proper index access mechanism: INDEX SEEK.

Therefore, in general, let the optimizer choose the best indexing strategy for the query and don't override the optimizer behavior using an INDEX hint. Also, not using INDEX hints allows the optimizer to decide the best indexing strategy dynamically as the data changes over time. Figure 18-15 shows the difference between specifying index hints and not specifying them.

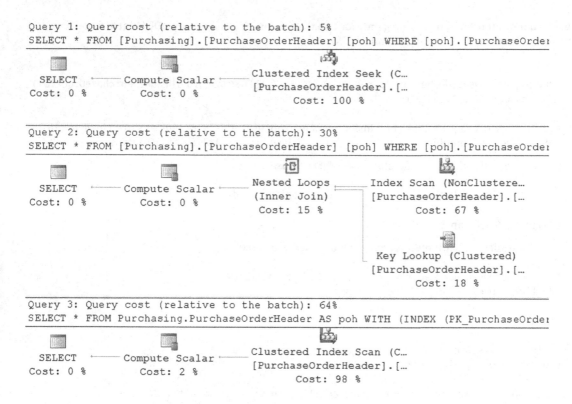

Query 1: Query cost (relative to the batch): 5%
SELECT * FROM [Purchasing].[PurchaseOrderHeader] [poh] WHERE [poh].[PurchaseOrder

SELECT   Compute Scalar   Clustered Index Seek (C...
Cost: 0 %   Cost: 0 %   [PurchaseOrderHeader].[...
                                            Cost: 100 %

Query 2: Query cost (relative to the batch): 30%
SELECT * FROM [Purchasing].[PurchaseOrderHeader] [poh] WHERE [poh].[PurchaseOrder

SELECT   Compute Scalar   Nested Loops   Index Scan (NonClustere...
Cost: 0 %   Cost: 0 %   (Inner Join)   [PurchaseOrderHeader].[...
                                   Cost: 15 %   Cost: 67 %

                                                        Key Lookup (Clustered)
                                                        [PurchaseOrderHeader].[...
                                                             Cost: 18 %

Query 3: Query cost (relative to the batch): 64%
SELECT * FROM Purchasing.PurchaseOrderHeader AS poh WITH (INDEX (PK_PurchaseOrder

SELECT   Compute Scalar   Clustered Index Scan (C...
Cost: 0 %   Cost: 2 %   [PurchaseOrderHeader].[...
                                            Cost: 98 %

Figure 18-15. *Cost of a query with and without different INDEX hints*

Using Domain and Referential Integrity

Domain and referential integrity help define and enforce valid values for a column, maintaining the integrity of the database. This is done through column/table constraints.

Since data access is usually one of the most costly operations in a query execution, avoiding redundant data access helps the optimizer reduce the query execution time. Domain and referential integrity help the SQL Server 2014 optimizer analyze valid data values without physically accessing the data, which reduces query time.

To understand how this happens, consider the following examples:

- The NOT NULL constraint

- Declarative referential integrity (DRI)

NOT NULL Constraint

The NOT NULL column constraint is used to implement domain integrity by defining the fact that a NULL value can't be entered in a particular column. SQL Server automatically enforces this fact at runtime to maintain the domain integrity for that column. Also, defining the NOT NULL column constraint helps the optimizer generate an efficient processing strategy when the ISNULL function is used on that column in a query.

To understand the performance benefit of the NOT NULL column constraint, consider the following example. These two queries are intended to return every value that does not equal 'B'. These two queries are running against similarly sized columns, each of which will require a table scan in order to return the data:

```
SELECT  p.FirstName
FROM    Person.Person AS p
WHERE   p.FirstName < 'B'
        OR p.FirstName >= 'C';


SELECT  p.MiddleName
FROM    Person.Person AS p
WHERE   p.MiddleName < 'B'
        OR p.MiddleName >= 'C';
```

The two queries use identical execution plans, as you can see in Figure 18-16.

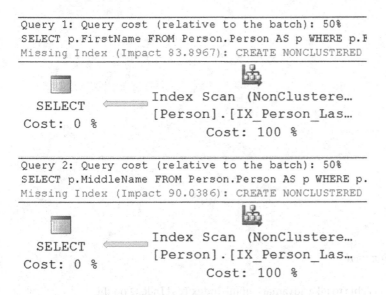

Figure 18-16. *Table scans caused by a lack of indexes*

Since the column Person.MiddleName can contain NULL, the data returned is incomplete. This is because, by definition, although a NULL value meets the necessary criteria of not being in any way equal to 'B', you can't return NULL values in this manner. An added OR clause is necessary. That would mean modifying the second query like this:

```
SELECT  p.FirstName
FROM    Person.Person AS p
WHERE   p.FirstName < 'B'
        OR p.FirstName >= 'C' ;


SELECT  p.MiddleName
FROM    Person.Person AS p
WHERE   p.MiddleName < 'B'
        OR p.MiddleName >= 'C'
        OR p.MiddleName IS NULL;
```

Also, as shown in the missing index statements in the execution plan in Figure 18-15, these two queries can benefit from having indexes created on their tables. Creating test indexes like the following should satisfy the requirements:

```
CREATE INDEX TestIndex1
ON Person.Person (MiddleName);

CREATE INDEX TestIndex2
ON Person.Person (FirstName);
```

When the queries are reexecuted, Figure 18-17 shows the resultant execution plan for the two SELECT statements.

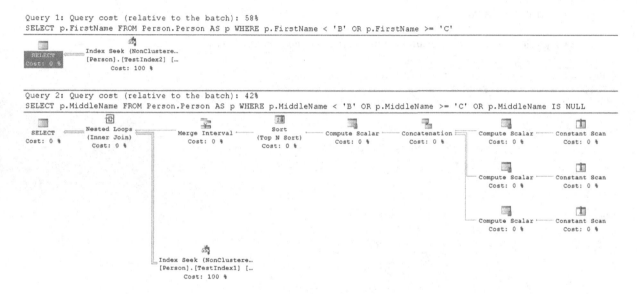

Figure 18-17. *Effect of the IS NULL option being used*

As shown in Figure 18-17, the optimizer was able to take advantage of the index TestIndex2 on the Person.FirstName column to get a nice clean Index Seek operation. Unfortunately, the requirements for processing the NULL columns were very different. The index TestIndex1 was not used in the same way. Instead, three constants were created for each of the three criteria defined within the query. These were then joined together through the Concatenation operation, sorted and merged prior to scanning the index three times through the Nested Loop operator to arrive at the result set. Although it appears, from the estimated costs in the execution plan, that this was the less costly query (42 percent compared to 58 percent), STATISTICS 10 and TIME tell the more accurate story, which is that the NULL queries were more costly.

```
Table 'Person'. Scan count 2, logical reads 66 CPU time = 0 ms, elapsed time = 126 ms.
```

vs.

```
Table 'Person'. Scan count 3, logical reads 42 CPU time = 0 ms, elapsed time = 137 ms.
```

Be sure to drop the test indexes that were created.

```
DROP INDEX TestIndex1 ON Person.Person;

DROP INDEX TestIndex2 ON Person.Person;
```

As much as possible, you should attempt to leave NULL values out of the database. However, when data is unknown, default values may not be possible. That's when NULL will come back into the design. I find NULLs to be unavoidable, but they are something to minimize as much as you can.

When it is unavoidable and you will be dealing with NULL values, keep in mind that you can use a filtered index that removes NULL values from the index, thereby improving the performance of that index. This was detailed in Chapter 7. Sparse columns offer another option to help you deal with NULL values. Sparse columns are primarily aimed at storing NULL values more efficiently and therefore reduce space—at a sacrifice in performance. This option is specifically targeted at business intelligence (BI) databases, not OLTP databases where large amounts of NULL values in fact tables are a normal part of the design.

Declarative Referential Integrity

Declarative referential integrity is used to define referential integrity between a parent table and a child table. It ensures that a record in the child table exists only if the corresponding record in the parent table exists. The only exception to this rule is that the child table can contain a NULL value for the identifier that links the rows of the child table to the rows of the parent table. For all other values of the identifier in the child, a corresponding value must exist in the parent table. In SQL Server, DRI is implemented using a PRIMARY KEY constraint on the parent table and a FOREIGN KEY constraint on the child table.

With DRI established between two tables and the foreign key columns of the child table set to NOT NULL, the SQL Server 2014 optimizer is assured that for every record in the child table, the parent table has a corresponding record. Sometimes this can help the optimizer improve performance because accessing the parent table is not necessary to verify the existence of a parent record for a corresponding child record.

To understand the performance benefit of implementing declarative referential integrity, let's consider an example. First, eliminate the referential integrity between two tables, Person.Address and Person.StateProvince, using this script:

```
IF EXISTS ( SELECT   *
            FROM     sys.foreign_keys
            WHERE    object_id = OBJECT_ID(N'[Person].[FK_Address_StateProvince_StateProvinceID]')
                     AND parent_object_id = OBJECT_ID(N'[Person].[Address]') )
    ALTER TABLE   [Person].[Address] DROP CONSTRAINT [FK_Address_StateProvince_StateProvinceID];
```

Consider the following SELECT statement:

```
SELECT  a.AddressID,
        sp.StateProvinceID
FROM    Person.Address AS a
JOIN    Person.StateProvince AS sp
        ON a.StateProvinceID = sp.StateProvinceID
WHERE   a.AddressID = 27234;
```

Note that the SELECT statement fetches the value of the StateProvinceID column from the parent table (Person.Address). If the nature of the data requires that for every product (identified by StateProvinceId) in the child table (Person.StateProvince) the parent table (Person.Address) contains a corresponding product, then you can rewrite the preceding SELECT statement as follows:

```
SELECT  a.AddressID,
        a.StateProvinceID
FROM    Person.Address AS a
JOIN    Person.StateProvince AS sp
        ON a.StateProvinceID = sp.StateProvinceID
WHERE   a.AddressID = 27234;
```

Both SELECT statements should return the same result set. Even the optimizer generates the same execution plan for both the SELECT statements, as shown in Figure 18-18.

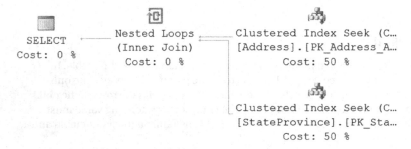

Figure 18-18. *Execution plan when DRI is not defined between the two tables*

To understand how declarative referential integrity can affect query performance, replace the FOREIGN KEY dropped earlier.

```
ALTER TABLE [Person].[Address]
WITH CHECK ADD CONSTRAINT [FK_Address_StateProvince_StateProvinceID]
FOREIGN KEY ([StateProvinceID])
REFERENCES [Person].[StateProvince] ([StateProvinceID]);
```

■ **Note**   There is now referential integrity between the tables.

Figure 18-19 shows the resultant execution plans for the two SELECT statements.

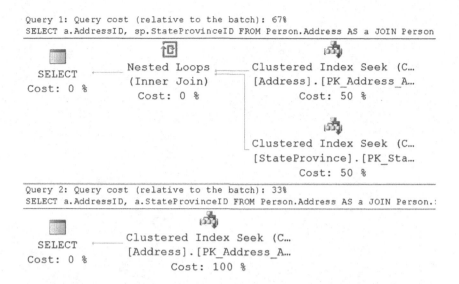

Query 1: Query cost (relative to the batch): 67%
SELECT a.AddressID, sp.StateProvinceID FROM Person.Address AS a JOIN Person

SELECT
Cost: 0 %

Nested Loops
(Inner Join)
Cost: 0 %

Clustered Index Seek (C...
[Address].[PK_Address_A...
Cost: 50 %

Clustered Index Seek (C...
[StateProvince].[PK_Sta...
Cost: 50 %

Query 2: Query cost (relative to the batch): 33%
SELECT a.AddressID, a.StateProvinceID FROM Person.Address AS a JOIN Person.:

SELECT
Cost: 0 %

Clustered Index Seek (C...
[Address].[PK_Address_A...
Cost: 100 %

Figure 18-19. *Execution plans showing the benefit of defining DRI between the two tables*

As you can see, the execution plan of the second SELECT statement is highly optimized: The Person.StateProvince table is not accessed. With the declarative referential integrity in place (and Address.StateProvince set to NOT NULL), the optimizer is assured that for every record in the child table, the parent table contains a corresponding record. Therefore, the JOIN clause between the parent and child tables is redundant in the second SELECT statement, with no other data requested from the parent table.

You probably already knew that domain and referential integrity are Good Things, but you can see that they not only ensure data integrity but also improve performance. As just illustrated, domain and referential integrity provide more choices to the optimizer to generate cost-effective execution plans and improve performance.

To achieve the performance benefit of DRI, as mentioned previously, the foreign key columns in the child table should be NOT NULL. Otherwise, there can be rows (with foreign key column values as NULL) in the child table with no representation in the parent table. That won't prevent the optimizer from accessing the primary table (Prod) in the previous query. By default—that is, if the NOT NULL attribute isn't mentioned for a column—the column can have NULL values. Considering the benefit of the NOT NULL attribute and the other benefits explained in this section, always mark the attribute of a column as NOT NULL if NULL isn't a valid value for that column.

You also must make sure you are using the WITH CHECK option when building your foreign key constraints. If the NOCHECK option is used, these are considered to be untrustworthy constraints by the optimizer and you won't realize the performance benefits that they can offer.

Summary

As discussed in this chapter, to improve the performance of a database application, it is important to ensure that SQL queries are designed properly to benefit from performance-enhancement techniques such as indexes, stored procedures, database constraints, and so on. Ensure that queries don't prevent the use of indexes. In many cases, the optimizer has the ability to generate cost-effective execution plans irrespective of query structure, but it is still a good practice to design the queries properly in the first place. Even after you design individual queries for great performance, the overall performance of a database application may not be satisfactory. It is important not only to improve the performance of individual queries but also to ensure that they don't use up the available resources on the system. The next chapter will cover how to reduce resource usage within your queries.

CHAPTER 19

■ ■ ■

Reduce Query Resource Use

In the previous chapter you focused on writing queries in such a way that they appropriately used indexes and statistics. In this chapter, you'll make sure you're writing a queries in such a way that they don't use your resources in inappropriate ways. There are ways to write queries that avoid using memory, CPU, and I/O, as well as ways to write the queries that use more of these resources than you really should. I'll go over a number of mechanisms to ensure your resources are used optimally by the queries under your control.

In this chapter, I cover the following topics:

- Query designs that are less resource-intensive
- Query designs that use the procedure cache effectively
- Query designs that reduce network overhead
- Techniques to reduce the transaction cost of a query

Avoiding Resource-Intensive Queries

Many database functionalities can be implemented using a variety of query techniques. The approach you should take is to use query techniques that are resource friendly and set-based. These are a few techniques you can use to reduce the footprint of a query:

- Avoid data type conversion.
- Use EXISTS over COUNT(*) to verify data existence.
- Use UNION ALL over UNION.
- Use indexes for aggregate and sort operations.
- Avoid local variables in a batch query.
- Be careful when naming stored procedures.

I cover these points in more detail in the next sections.

Avoid Data Type Conversion

SQL Server allows, in some instances (defined by the large table of data conversions available in Books Online), a value/constant with different but compatible data types to be compared with a column's data. SQL Server automatically converts the data from one data type to another. This process is called *implicit data type conversion*. Although useful, implicit conversion adds overhead to the query optimizer. To improve performance, use a value/constant with the same data type as that of the column to which it is compared.

To understand how implicit data type conversion affects performance, consider the following example:

```
IF EXISTS ( SELECT  *
            FROM    sys.objects
            WHERE   object_id = OBJECT_ID(N'dbo.Test1') )
    DROP TABLE  dbo.Test1;

CREATE TABLE dbo.Test1 (
Id INT IDENTITY(1,1),
MyKey VARCHAR(50),
MyValue VARCHAR(50));
CREATE UNIQUE CLUSTERED INDEX Test1PrimaryKey ON dbo.Test1  ([Id] ASC);
CREATE UNIQUE NONCLUSTERED INDEX TestIndex ON dbo.Test1 (MyKey);
GO

SELECT TOP 10000
        IDENTITY( INT,1,1 ) AS n
INTO    #Tally
FROM    Master.dbo.syscolumns sc1,
        Master.dbo.syscolumns sc2;

INSERT  INTO dbo.Test1
        (MyKey,
         MyValue)
        SELECT TOP 10000
                'UniqueKey' + CAST(n AS VARCHAR),
                'Description'
        FROM    #Tally;

DROP TABLE #Tally;

SELECT  t.MyValue
FROM    dbo.Test1 AS t
WHERE   t.MyKey = 'UniqueKey333';

SELECT  t.MyValue
FROM    dbo.Test1 AS t
WHERE   t.MyKey = N'UniqueKey333';
```

After creating the table Test1, creating a couple of indexes on it, and placing some data, two queries are defined. Both queries return the same result set. As you can see, both queries are identical except for the data type of the variable equated to the MyKey column. Since this column is VARCHAR, the first query doesn't require an implicit data type conversion. The second query uses a different data type from that of the MyKey column, requiring an implicit data type conversion and thereby adding overhead to the query performance. Figure 19-1 shows the execution plans for both queries.

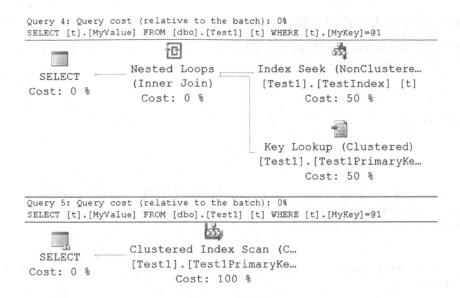

```
Query 4: Query cost (relative to the batch): 0%
SELECT [t].[MyValue] FROM [dbo].[Test1] [t] WHERE [t].[MyKey]=@1
```

SELECT
Cost: 0 %

Nested Loops
(Inner Join)
Cost: 0 %

Index Seek (NonClustere…
[Test1].[TestIndex] [t]
Cost: 50 %

Key Lookup (Clustered)
[Test1].[Test1PrimaryKe…
Cost: 50 %

```
Query 5: Query cost (relative to the batch): 0%
SELECT [t].[MyValue] FROM [dbo].[Test1] [t] WHERE [t].[MyKey]=@1
```

SELECT
Cost: 0 %

Clustered Index Scan (C…
[Test1].[Test1PrimaryKe…
Cost: 100 %

Figure 19-1. *Cost of a query with and without implicit data type conversion*

The complexity of the implicit data type conversion depends on the precedence of the data types involved in the comparison. The data type precedence rules of SQL Server specify which data type is converted to the other. Usually, the data type of lower precedence is converted to the data type of higher precedence. For example, the TINYINT data type has a lower precedence than the INT data type. For a complete list of data type precedence in SQL Server 2014, please refer to the MSDN article "Data Type Precedence" (http://bit.ly/1cN7AYc). For further information about which data type can implicitly convert to which data type, refer to the MSDN article "Data Type Conversion" (http://bit.ly/1j7kIJf).

Note the warning icon on the SELECT operator. It's letting you know that there's something questionable in this query. In this case, it's the fact that there is a data type conversion operation. The optimizer lets you know that this might negatively affect its ability to find and use an index to assist the performance of the query. This can also be a false positive. If there are conversions on columns that are not used in any of the predicates, it really doesn't matter at all that an implicit, or even an explicit, conversion has occurred.

When SQL Server compares a column value with a certain data type and a variable (or constant) with a different data type, the data type of the variable (or constant) is always converted to the data type of the column. This is done because the column value is accessed based on the implicit conversion value of the variable (or constant). Therefore, in such cases, the implicit conversion is always applied on the variable (or constant).

As you can see, implicit data type conversion adds overhead to the query performance both in terms of a poor execution plan and in added CPU cost to make the conversions. Therefore, to improve performance, always use the same data type for both expressions.

Use EXISTS over COUNT(*) to Verify Data Existence

A common database requirement is to verify whether a set of data exists. Usually you'll see this implemented using a batch of SQL queries, as follows (--count in the download):

```
DECLARE @n INT ;
SELECT  @n = COUNT(*)
FROM    Sales.SalesOrderDetail AS sod
WHERE   sod.OrderQty = 1;
IF @n > 0
    PRINT 'Record Exists';
```

Using COUNT(*) to verify the existence of data is highly resource-intensive, because COUNT(*) has to scan all the rows in a table. EXISTS merely has to scan and stop at the first record that matches the EXISTS criterion. To improve performance, use EXISTS instead of the COUNT(*) approach.

```
IF EXISTS ( SELECT  sod.*
            FROM    Sales.SalesOrderDetail AS sod
            WHERE   sod.OrderQty = 1 )
    PRINT 'Record Exists';
```

The performance benefit of the EXISTS technique over the COUNT(*) technique can be compared using the STATISTICS IO and TIME output, as well as the execution plan in Figure 19-2, as you can see from the output of running these queries.

```
Table  'SalesOrderDetail'.  Scan count 1,  logical reads 1246
CPU time = 0 ms,     elapsed time = 29 ms.
Table 'SalesOrderDetail'. Scan count 1, logical reads 3
CPU time = 0 ms,    elapsed time = 4 ms.
```

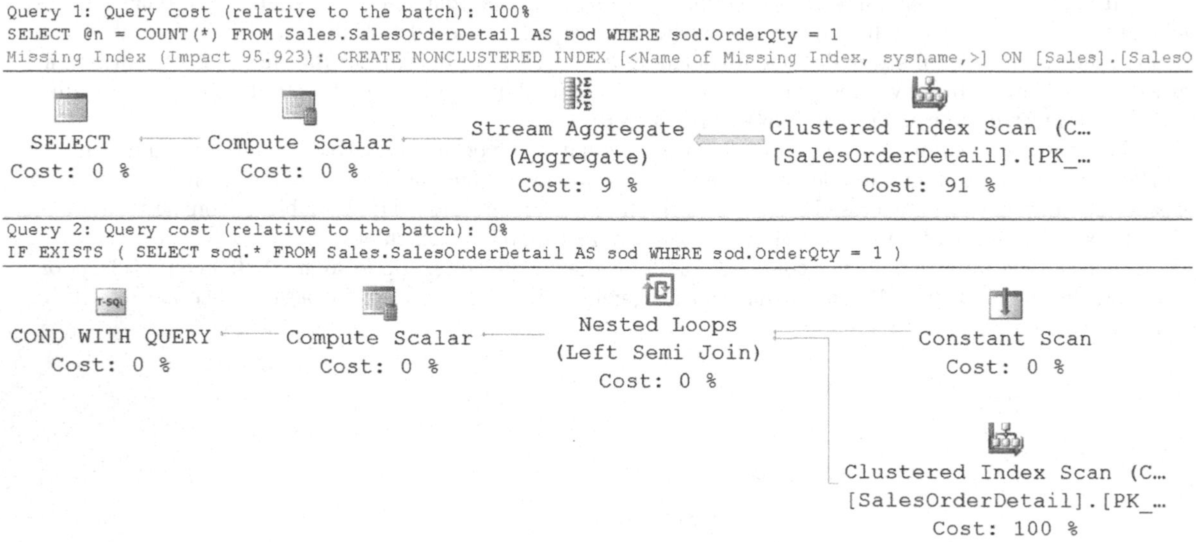

Figure 19-2. *Difference between COUNT and EXISTS*

As you can see, the EXISTS technique used only three logical reads compared to the 1,246 used by the COUNT(*) technique, and the execution time went from 29ms to 4ms. Therefore, to determine whether data exists, use the EXISTS technique.

Use UNION ALL Instead of UNION

You can concatenate the result set of multiple SELECT statements using the UNION clause as follows, as shown in Figure 19-3:

```
SELECT   *
FROM     Sales.SalesOrderDetail AS sod
WHERE    sod.ProductID = 934
UNION
SELECT   *
FROM     Sales.SalesOrderDetail AS sod
WHERE    sod.ProductID = 932;
```

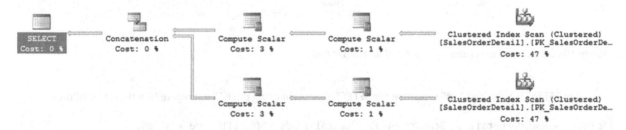

Figure 19-3. *The execution plan of the query using the UNION clause*

The UNION clause processes the result set from the two SELECT statements, removing duplicates from the final result set and effectively running DISTINCT on each query. If the result sets of the SELECT statements participating in the UNION clause are exclusive to each other or you are allowed to have duplicate rows in the final result set, then use UNION ALL instead of UNION. This avoids the overhead of detecting and removing any duplicates and therefore improves performance, as shown in Figure 19-4.

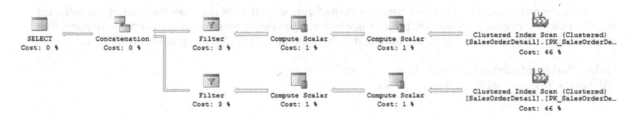

Figure 19-4. *The execution plan of the query using UNION ALL*

As you can see, in the first case (using UNION), the optimizer filtered the records completely differently in order to eliminate the duplicates while concatenating the result set of the two SELECT statements. Since the result sets are exclusive to each other, you can use UNION ALL instead of the UNION clause. Using the UNION ALL clause avoids the overhead of detecting duplicates and thereby improves performance.

Use Indexes for Aggregate and Sort Conditions

Generally, aggregate functions such as MIN and MAX benefit from indexes on the corresponding column. Without any index on the column, the optimizer has to scan the base table (or the clustered index), retrieve all the rows, and perform a stream aggregate on the group (containing all rows) to identify the MIN/MAX value, as shown in the following example (see Figure 19-5):

```
SELECT  MIN(sod.UnitPrice)
FROM    Sales.SalesOrderDetail AS sod;
```

Figure 19-5. *A scan of the entire table filtered to a single row*

The STATISTICS IO and TIME output of the SELECT statement using the MIN aggregate function is as follows:

```
Table  'SalesOrderDetail'.  Scan count 1,  logical reads 1246  CPU time = 46 ms,
elapsed time = 52 ms.
```

As shown in the STATISTICS output, the query performed more than 1,200 logical reads just to retrieve the row containing the minimum value for the UnitPrice column. You can see this represented in the execution plan in Figure 19-5. A huge fat row comes out of the Clustered Index Scan only to be filtered to a single row by the Stream Aggregate operation. If you create an index on the UnitPrice column, then the UnitPrice values will be presorted by the index in the leaf pages.

```
CREATE INDEX TestIndex ON Sales.SalesOrderDetail (UnitPrice ASC);
```

The index on the UnitPrice column improves the performance of the MIN aggregate function significantly. The optimizer can retrieve the minimum UnitPrice value by seeking to the topmost row in the index. This reduces the number of logical reads for the query, as shown in the corresponding STATISTICS output (see Figure 19-6).

```
Table  'SalesOrderDetail'.  Scan count 1,  logical reads 3
CPU time = 0 ms,    elapsed time = 20 ms.
```

Figure 19-6. *An index radically improves performance*

Similarly, creating an index on the columns referred to in an ORDER BY clause helps the optimizer organize the result set fast because the column values are prearranged in the index. The internal implementation of the GROUP BY clause also sorts the column values first because sorted column values allow the adjacent matching values to be grouped quickly. Therefore, like the ORDER BY clause, the GROUP BY clause also benefits from having the values of the columns referred to in the GROUP BY clause sorted in advance.

Avoid Local Variables in a Batch Query

Often, multiple queries are submitted together as a batch, avoiding multiple network round-trips. It's common to use local variables in a query batch to pass a value between the individual queries. However, using local variables in the WHERE clause of a query in a batch doesn't allow the optimizer to generate an efficient execution plan.

To understand how the use of a local variable in the WHERE clause of a query in a batch can affect performance, consider the following batch query (--batch):

```
DECLARE @Id INT = 1;
SELECT  pod.LineTotal,
        poh.OrderDate
FROM    Purchasing.PurchaseOrderDetail AS pod
JOIN    Purchasing.PurchaseOrderHeader AS poh
        ON poh.PurchaseOrderID = pod.PurchaseOrderID
WHERE   poh.PurchaseOrderID >= @Id;
```

Figure 19-7 shows the execution plan of this SELECT statement.

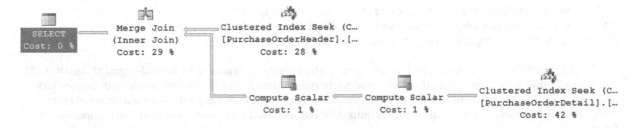

Figure 19-7. *Execution plan showing the effect of a local variable in a batch query*

As you can see, a Clustered Index Seek operation is performed to access the rows from the Purchasing.PurchaseOrderDetail table. If the SELECT statement is executed without using the local variable, by replacing the local variable value with an appropriate constant value as in the following query, the optimizer makes different choices.

```
SELECT  pod.LineTotal,
        poh.OrderDate
FROM    Purchasing.PurchaseOrderDetail AS pod
JOIN    Purchasing.PurchaseOrderHeader AS poh
        ON poh.PurchaseOrderID = pod.PurchaseOrderID
WHERE   poh.PurchaseOrderID >=1;
```

Figure 19-8 shows the result.

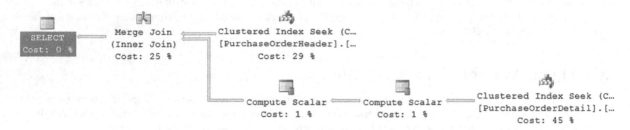

Figure 19-8. *Execution plan for the query when the local variable is not used*

Although these two approaches look identical, on closer examination, interesting differences begin to appear. Notice the estimated cost of some of the operations. For example, the Merge Join is different between Figure 19-6 and Figure 19-7; it's 29 percent in the first and 25 percent in the second. If you look at STATISTICS IO and TIME for each query, other differences appear. First, here's the information from the initial query:

```
Table  'PurchaseOrderDetail'.  Scan count 1,     logical reads 66
Table  'PurchaseOrderHeader'.  Scan count 1,     logical reads 44
CPU time = 16 ms,     elapsed time = 151 ms.
```

Then here's the second query, without the local variable:

```
Table  'PurchaseOrderDetail'.  Scan count 1,     logical reads 66
Table  'PurchaseOrderHeader'.  Scan count 1,     logical reads 44
CPU time = 0 ms,     elapsed time = 132 ms.
```

Notice that the scans and reads are the same, as might be expected of queries with near identical plans. The CPU and elapsed times are different, with the second query (the one without the local variable) consistently being a little less. Based on these facts, you may assume that the execution plan of the first query will be somewhat more costly compared to the second query. But the reality is quite different, as shown in the execution plan cost comparison in Figure 19-9.

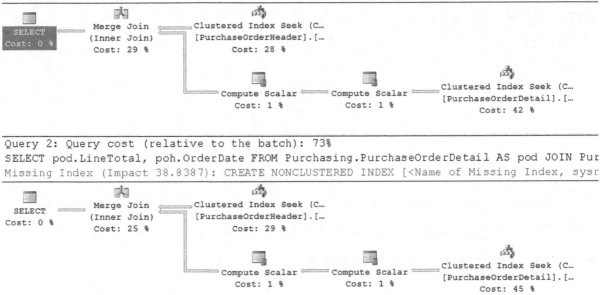

```
Query 1: Query cost (relative to the batch): 27%
SELECT pod.LineTotal, poh.OrderDate FROM Purchasing.PurchaseOrderDetail AS pod JOIN Pur
Missing Index (Impact 22.9061): CREATE NONCLUSTERED INDEX [<Name of Missing Index, sysr
```

```
Query 2: Query cost (relative to the batch): 73%
SELECT pod.LineTotal, poh.OrderDate FROM Purchasing.PurchaseOrderDetail AS pod JOIN Pur
Missing Index (Impact 38.8387): CREATE NONCLUSTERED INDEX [<Name of Missing Index, sysr
```

Figure 19-9. *Relative cost of the query with and without the use of a local variable*

From the relative cost of the two execution plans, it appears that the second query isn't cheaper than the first query. However, from the STATISTICS comparison, it appears that the second query should be cheaper than the first query. Which one should you believe: the comparison of STATISTICS or the relative cost of the execution plan? What's the source of this anomaly?

The execution plan is generated based on the optimizer's estimation of the number of rows affected for each execution step. If you take a look at the properties for the various operators in the initial execution plan for the query with the local variable (as shown in Figure 19-7), you may notice a disparity. Take a look at this in Figure 19-10.

Actual Execution Mode	Row
Actual Number of Batches	0
Actual Number of Rows	4012
Actual Rebinds	0
Actual Rewinds	0
Defined Values	[AdventureW
Description	Scanning a p
Estimated CPU Cost	0.001481
Estimated Execution Mode	Row
Estimated I/O Cost	0.0120139
Estimated Number of Executions	1
Estimated Number of Rows	1203.6

Figure 19-10. *Clustered index seek details with a local variable*

The disparity you're looking for is the Actual Number of Rows value (near the top) compared to the Estimated Number of Rows value (at the bottom). In the properties shown in Figure 19-10, there are 1,203.6 estimated rows, while the actual number is considerably higher at 4,012. If you compare this to the same operator in the second query (the one without the local variable), you may notice something else. Take a look at Figure 19-11.

Actual Execution Mode	Row
Actual Number of Batches	0
Actual Number of Rows	4012
Actual Rebinds	0
Actual Rewinds	0
Defined Values	[AdventureW
Description	Scanning a p
Estimated CPU Cost	0.0045702
Estimated Execution Mode	Row
Estimated I/O Cost	0.0334954
Estimated Number of Executions	1
Estimated Number of Rows	4012

Figure 19-11. *Clustered index seek details without a local variable*

Here you'll see that the Actual Number of Rows and Estimated Number of Rows values are the same: 4,012. From these two measures, you can see that the estimated rows for the execution steps of the first query (using a local variable in the WHERE clause) is way off the actual number of rows returned by the steps. Consequently, the execution plan cost for the first query, which is based on the estimated rows, is somewhat misleading. The incorrect estimation misguides the optimizer and causes some variations in how the query is executed. You can see this in the return times on the query, even though the number of rows returned is identical.

Any time you find such an anomaly between the relative execution plan cost and the STATISTICS output for the queries under analysis, you should verify the basis of the estimation. If the underlying facts (estimated rows) of the execution plan itself are wrong, then it is quite likely that the cost represented in the execution plan will also be wrong. But since the output of the various STATISTICS measurements shows the actual number of logical reads and the real elapsed time required to perform the query without being affected by the initial estimation, you can rely on the STATISTICS output.

Now let's return to the actual performance issue associated with using local variables in the WHERE clause. As shown in the preceding example, using the local variable as the filter criterion in the WHERE clause of a batch query doesn't allow the optimizer to determine the right indexing strategy. This happens because, during the optimization of the queries in the batch, the optimizer doesn't know the value of the variable used in the WHERE clause and can't determine the right access strategy—it knows the value of the variable only during execution. Effectively this means the optimizer had to use the density vector instead of looking up information through the histogram in the statistics.

To avoid this particular performance problem, use one of the following approaches. Don't use a local variable as a filter criterion in a batch for a query like this. A local variable is different from a parameter value, as demonstrated in Chapter 16. Create a stored procedure for the batch and execute it as follows:

```
CREATE PROCEDURE spProductDetails (@id INT)
AS
SELECT  pod.*
FROM    Purchasing.PurchaseOrderDetail AS pod
JOIN    Purchasing.PurchaseOrderHeader AS poh
        ON poh.PurchaseOrderID = pod.PurchaseOrderID
WHERE   poh.PurchaseOrderID >= @id;

GO
EXEC spProductDetails
    @id = 1;
```

The optimizer generates the same execution plan as the query that doesn't use a local variable for the ideal case. Correspondingly, the execution time is also reduced. In the case of a stored procedure, the optimizer generates the execution plan during the first execution of the stored procedure and uses the parameter value supplied to determine the right processing strategy.

This approach can backfire. The process of using the values passed to a parameter is referred to as *parameter sniffing*. Parameter sniffing occurs for all stored procedures and parameterized queries automatically. Depending on the accuracy of the statistics and the values passed to the parameters, it is possible to get a bad plan using specific values and a good plan using the sampled values that occur when you have a local variable. Testing is the only way to be sure which will work best in any given situation. However, in most circumstances, you're better off having accurate values rather than sampled ones. For more details on parameter sniffing, see Chapter 16.

Be Careful When Naming Stored Procedures

The name of a stored procedure does matter. You should not name your procedures with a prefix of sp_. Developers often prefix their stored procedures with sp_ so that they can easily identify the stored procedures. However, SQL Server assumes that any stored procedure with this exact prefix is probably a system stored procedure, whose home is in the master database. When a stored procedure with an sp_ prefix is submitted for execution, SQL Server looks for the stored procedure in the following places in the following order:

- In the master database

- In the current database based on any qualifiers provided (database name or owner)

- In the current database using dbo as the schema, if a schema is not specified

Therefore, although the user-created stored procedure prefixed with sp_ exists in the current database, the master database is checked first. This happens even when the stored procedure is qualified with the database name.

To understand the effect of prefixing sp_ to a stored procedure name, consider the following stored procedure:

```
IF EXISTS ( SELECT  *
            FROM    sys.objects
            WHERE   object_id = OBJECT_ID(N'[dbo].[sp_Dont]')
                    AND type IN (N'P', N'PC') )
    DROP PROCEDURE  [dbo].[sp_Dont]
GO
CREATE PROC [sp_Dont]
AS
PRINT 'Done!'
GO
--Add plan of sp_Dont to procedure cache
EXEC AdventureWorks2012.dbo.[sp_Dont] ;
GO
--Use the above cached plan of sp_Dont
EXEC AdventureWorks2012.dbo.[sp_Dont] ;
GO
```

The first execution of the stored procedure adds the execution plan of the stored procedure to the procedure cache. A subsequent execution of the stored procedure reuses the existing plan from the procedure cache unless a recompilation of the plan is required (the causes of stored procedure recompilation are explained in Chapter 10). Therefore, the second execution of the stored procedure spDont shown in Figure 19-12 should find a plan in the procedure cache. This is indicated by an SP:CacheHit event in the corresponding Extended Events output.

Event: sp_cache_miss (2014-03-16 13:14:31.4205172)

Details	
Field	Value
cached_text	EXEC AdventureWorks2012.dbo.[sp_Dont];
database_id	5
database_name	AdventureWorks2012
object_id	635974943
object_name	
object_type	ADHOC

Figure 19-12. *Extended Events output showing the effect of the sp_ prefix on a stored procedure name*

Note that an SP:CacheMiss event is fired before SQL Server tries to locate the plan for the stored procedure in the procedure cache. The SP:CacheMiss event is caused by SQL Server looking in the master database for the stored procedure, even though the execution of the stored procedure is properly qualified with the user database name.

This aspect of the sp_ prefix becomes more interesting when you create a stored procedure with the name of an existing system stored procedure.

```
CREATE PROC sp_addmessage @param1 NVARCHAR(25)
AS
PRINT '@param1 = '  + @param1 ;
GO


EXEC AdventureWorks2012.dbo.[sp_addmessage]   'AdventureWorks';
```

The execution of this user-defined stored procedure causes the execution of the system stored procedure sp_addmessage from the master database instead, as you can see in Figure 19-13.

```
Msg 8114, Level 16, State 5, Procedure sp_addmessage, Line 4009
Error converting data type varchar to int.
```

Figure 19-13. *Execution result for stored procedure showing the effect of the sp_ prefix on a stored procedure name*

Unfortunately, it is not possible to execute this user-defined stored procedure. You can see now why you should not prefix a user-defined stored procedure's name with sp_. Use some other naming convention.

Reducing the Number of Network Round-Trips

Database applications often execute multiple queries to implement a database operation. Besides optimizing the performance of the individual query, it is important that you optimize the performance of the batch. To reduce the overhead of multiple network round-trips, consider the following techniques:

- Execute multiple queries together.
- Use SET NOCOUNT.

Let's look at these techniques in a little more depth.

Execute Multiple Queries Together

It is preferable to submit all the queries of a set together as a batch or a stored procedure. Besides reducing the network round-trips between the database application and the server, stored procedures also provide multiple performance and administrative benefits, as described in Chapter 15. This means the code in the application needs to be able to deal with multiple result sets. It also means your T-SQL code may need to deal with XML data or other large sets of data, not single-row inserts or updates.

Use SET NOCOUNT

You need to consider one more factor when executing a batch or a stored procedure. After every query in the batch or the stored procedure is executed, the server reports the number of rows affected.

```
(<Number> row(s) affected)
```

This information is returned to the database application and adds to the network overhead. Use the T-SQL statement SET NOCOUNT to avoid this overhead.

```
SET NOCOUNT ON <SQL queries> SET NOCOUNT OFF
```

Note that the SET NOCOUNT statement doesn't cause any recompilation issue with stored procedures, unlike some SET statements, as explained in Chapter 17.

Reducing the Transaction Cost

Every action query in SQL Server is performed as an *atomic* action so that the state of a database table moves from one *consistent* state to another. SQL Server does this automatically, and it can't be disabled. If the transition from one consistent state to another requires multiple database queries, then atomicity across the multiple queries should be maintained using explicitly defined database transactions. The old and new states of every atomic action are maintained in the transaction log (on the disk) to ensure *durability,* which guarantees that the outcome of an atomic action won't be lost once it completes successfully. An atomic action during its execution is *isolated* from other database actions using database locks.

Based on the characteristics of a transaction, here are two broad recommendations to reduce the cost of the transaction:

- Reduce logging overhead.
- Reduce lock overhead.

Reduce Logging Overhead

A database query may consist of multiple data manipulation queries. If atomicity is maintained for each query separately, then a large number of disk writes are performed on the transaction log. Since disk activity is extremely slow compared to memory or CPU activity, the excessive disk activity can increase the execution time of the database functionality. For example, consider the following batch query:

```
--Create a test table
IF (SELECT  OBJECT_ID('dbo.Test1')
    ) IS NOT NULL
    DROP TABLE dbo.Test1;
GO
CREATE TABLE dbo.Test1 (C1 TINYINT);
GO

--Insert 10000 rows
DECLARE @Count INT = 1;
```

```
WHILE @Count <= 10000
    BEGIN
        INSERT  INTO dbo.Test1
                (C1)
        VALUES  (@Count % 256);
        SET @Count = @Count + 1;
    END
```

Since every execution of the INSERT statement is atomic in itself, SQL Server will write to the transaction log for every execution of the INSERTstatement.

An easy way to reduce the number of log disk writes is to include the action queries within an explicit transaction.

```
DECLARE @Count INT = 1;
DBCC SQLPERF(LOGSPACE);
BEGIN TRANSACTION
WHILE @Count <= 10000
    BEGIN
        INSERT  INTO dbo.Test1
                (C1)
        VALUES  (@Count % 256) ;
        SET @Count = @Count + 1 ;
        END
COMMIT
DBCC SQLPERF(LOGSPACE);
```

The defined transaction scope (between the BEGIN TRANSACTION and COMMIT pair of commands) expands the scope of atomicity to the multiple INSERT statements included within the transaction. This decreases the number of log disk writes and improves the performance of the database functionality. To test this theory, run the following T-SQL command before and after each of the WHILE loops.

```
DBCC SQLPERF(LOGSPACE);
```

This will show you the percentage of log space used. On running the first set of inserts on my database, the log went from 2.6 percent used to 29 percent. When running the second set of inserts, the log grew about 6 percent.

The best way is to work with sets of data rather than individual rows. A WHILE loop can be an inherently costly operation, like a cursor (more details on cursors in Chapter 22). So, running a query that avoids the WHILE loop and instead works from a set-based approach is even better.

```
DECLARE @Count INT = 1;
BEGIN TRANSACTION
WHILE @Count <= 10000
    BEGIN
        INSERT  INTO dbo.Test1
                (C1)
        VALUES  (@Count % 256);
        SET @Count = @Count + 1;
        END
COMMIT
```

Running this query with the DBCC SQLPERF() function before and after showed less than 4 percent growth of the used space within the log, and it ran in 41ms as compared to more than 2s for the WHILE loop.

One area of caution, however, is that by including too many data manipulation queries within a transaction, the duration of the transaction is increased. During that time, all other queries trying to access the resources referred to in the transaction are blocked. Rollback duration and recovery time during a restore increase because of long transactions.

Reduce Lock Overhead

By default, all four SQL statements (SELECT, INSERT, UPDATE, and DELETE) use database locks to isolate their work from that of other SQL statements. This lock management adds a performance overhead to the query. The performance of a query can be improved by requesting fewer locks. By extension, the performance of other queries are also improved because they have to wait a shorter period of time to obtain their own locks.

By default, SQL Server can provide row-level locks. For a query working on a large number of rows, requesting a row lock on all the individual rows adds a significant overhead to the lock-management process. You can reduce this lock overhead by decreasing the lock granularity, say to the page level or table level. SQL Server performs the lock escalation dynamically by taking into consideration the lock overheads. Therefore, generally, it is not necessary to manually escalate the lock level. But, if required, you can control the concurrency of a query programmatically using lock hints as follows:

```
SELECT * FROM <TableName> WITH(PAGLOCK)  --Use page level lock
```

Similarly, by default, SQL Server uses locks for SELECT statements besides those for INSERT, UPDATE, and DELETE statements. This allows the SELECT statements to read data that isn't being modified. In some cases, the data may be quite static, and it doesn't go through much modification. In such cases, you can reduce the lock overhead of the SELECT statements in one of the following ways:

- Mark the database as READONLY.

  ```
  ALTER DATABASE <DatabaseName> SET READ_ONLY
  ```

This allows users to retrieve data from the database, but it prevents them from modifying the data. The setting takes effect immediately. If occasional modifications to the database are required, then it may be temporarily converted to READWRITE mode.

```
ALTER DATABASE <DatabaseName> SET READ_WRITE
<Database modifications>
ALTER DATABASE <DatabaseName> SET READONLY
```

- Use one of the snapshot isolations.

SQL Server provides a mechanism to put versions of data into tempdb as updates are occurring, radically reducing locking overhead and blocking for read operations. You can change the isolation level of the database by using an ALTER statement.

```
ALTER DATABASE AdventureWorks2012 SET TRANSACTION ISOLATION LEVEL READ_COMMITTED_SNAPSHOT;
```

- Prevent SELECT statements from requesting any lock.

  ```
  SELECT * FROM <TableName> WITH(NOLOCK)
  ```

This prevents the SELECT statement from requesting any lock, and it is applicable to SELECT statements only. Although the NOLOCK hint can't be used directly on the tables referred to in the action queries (INSERT, UPDATE, and DELETE), it may be used on the data retrieval part of the action queries, as shown here:

```
DELETE Sales.SalesOrderDetail
FROM Sales.SalesOrderDetail sod WITH(NOLOCK)
JOIN Production.Product p WITH(NOLOCK)
ON sod.ProductID = p.ProductID
AND p.ProductID = 0;
```

Just know that this leads to dirty reads, which can cause duplicate rows or missing rows and is therefore considered to be a last resort to control locking. The best approach is to mark the database as read-only or use one of the snapshot isolation levels.

This is a huge topic, and a lot more can be said about it. I discuss the different types of lock requests and how to manage lock overhead in the next chapter. If you made any of the proposed changes to the database from this section, I recommend restoring from a backup.

Summary

As discussed in this chapter, to improve the performance of a database application, it is important to ensure that SQL queries are designed properly to benefit from performance enhancement techniques such as indexes, stored procedures, database constraints, and so on. Ensure that queries are resource friendly and don't prevent the use of indexes. In many cases, the optimizer has the ability to generate cost-effective execution plans irrespective of query structure, but it is still a good practice to design the queries properly in the first place. Even after you design individual queries for great performance, the overall performance of a database application may not be satisfactory. It is important not only to improve the performance of individual queries but also to ensure that they work well with other queries without causing serious blocking issues. In the next chapter, you will look into the different blocking aspects of a database application.

CHAPTER 20

■ ■ ■

Blocking and Blocked Processes

You would ideally like your database application to scale linearly with the number of database users and the volume of data. However, it is common to find that performance degrades as the number of users increases and as the volume of data grows. One cause for degradation, especially associated with ever-increasing scale, is blocking. In fact, database blocking is usually one of the biggest enemies of scalability for database applications.

In this chapter, I cover the following topics:

- The fundamentals of blocking in SQL Server

- The ACID properties of a transactional database

- Database lock granularity, escalation, modes, and compatibility

- ANSI isolation levels

- The effect of indexes on locking

- The information necessary to analyze blocking

- A SQL script to collect blocking information

- Resolutions and recommendations to avoid blocking

- Techniques to automate the blocking detection and information collection processes

Blocking Fundamentals

In an ideal world, every SQL query would be able to execute concurrently, without any blocking by other queries. However, in the real world, queries *do* block each other, similar to the way a car crossing through a green traffic signal at an intersection blocks other cars waiting to cross the intersection. In SQL Server, this traffic management takes the form of the *lock manager,* which controls concurrent access to a database resource to maintain data consistency. The concurrent access to a database resource is controlled across multiple database connections.

I want to make sure things are clear before moving on. Three terms are used within databases that sound the same and are interrelated but have different meanings. These are frequently confused, and people often use the terms incorrectly. These terms are *locking, blocking*, and *deadlocking*. Locking is an integral part of the process of SQL Server managing multiple sessions. When a session needs access to a piece of data, a lock of some type is placed on it. This is different from blocking, which is when one session, or thread, needs access to a piece of data and has to wait for another session's lock to clear. Finally, deadlocking is when two sessions, or threads, form what is sometimes referred to as a *deadly embrace.* They are each waiting on the other for a lock to clear. Deadlocking could also be referred to as a permanent blocking situation, but it's one that won't resolve by waiting any period of time. Deadlocking will be covered in more detail in Chapter 21. So, locks can lead to blocks, and both locks and blocks play a part in deadlocks, but these are three very distinct concepts. Please understand the differences between these terms and use them correctly. It will help in your understanding of the system, your ability to troubleshoot, and your ability to communicate with other database administrators and developers.

In SQL Server, a database connection is identified by a session ID. Connections may be from one or many applications and one or many users on those applications; as far as SQL Server is concerned, every connection is treated as a separate session. Blocking between two sessions accessing the same piece of data at the same time is a natural phenomenon in SQL Server. Whenever two sessions try to access a common database resource in conflicting ways, the lock manager ensures that the second session waits until the first session completes its work in conjunction with the management of transactions within the system. For example, a session might be modifying a table record while another session tries to delete the record. Since these two data access requests are incompatible, the second session will be blocked until the first session completes its task.

On the other hand, if the two sessions try to read a table concurrently, both requests are allowed to execute without blocking, since these data access requests are compatible with each other.

Usually, the effect of blocking on a session is quite small and doesn't affect its performance noticeably. At times, however, because of poor query and/or transaction design (or maybe bad luck), blocking can affect query performance significantly. In a database application, every effort should be made to minimize blocking and thereby increase the number of concurrent users who can use the database.

With the introduction of in-memory tables in SQL Server 2014, locking, at least for these tables, takes on whole new dimensions. I'll cover their behavior separately in Chapter 23.

Understanding Blocking

In SQL Server, a database query can execute as a logical unit of work in itself, or it can participate in a bigger logical unit of work. A bigger logical unit of work can be defined using the BEGIN TRANSACTION statement along with COMMIT and/or ROLLBACK statements. Every logical unit of work must conform to a set of four properties called *ACID* properties:

- Atomicity

- Consistency

- Isolation

- Durability

I cover these properties in the sections that follow because understanding how transactions work is fundamental to understanding blocking.

Atomicity

A logical unit of work must be *atomic*. That is, either all the actions of the logical unit of work are completed or no effect is retained. To understand the atomicity of a logical unit of work, consider the following example:

```
USE AdventureWorks2012;
GO
IF (SELECT OBJECT_ID('dbo.ProductTest')
    ) IS NOT NULL
    DROP TABLE dbo.ProductTest;
GO
CREATE TABLE dbo.ProductTest (
ProductID INT CONSTRAINT ValueEqualsOne CHECK (ProductID = 1));
GO
```

```
--All ProductIDs are added into t1 as a logical unit of work
INSERT INTO dbo.ProductTest
        SELECT p.ProductID
        FROM   Production.Product AS p;
GO
SELECT *
FROM   dbo.ProductTest; --Returns 0 rows
```

SQL Server treats the preceding INSERT statement as a logical unit of work. The CHECK constraint on column ProductID of the dbo.ProductTest table allows only the value of 1. Although the ProductID column in the Production.Product table starts with the value of 1, it also contains other values. For this reason, the INSERT statement won't add any records at all to the dbo.ProductTest table, and an error is raised because of the CHECK constraint. This atomicity is automatically ensured by SQL Server.

So far, so good. But in the case of a bigger logical unit of work, you should be aware of an interesting behavior of SQL Server. Imagine that the previous insert task consists of multiple INSERT statements. These can be combined to form a bigger logical unit of work, as follows:

```
BEGIN TRAN
 --Start:  Logical unit of work
--First:
INSERT  INTO dbo.ProductTest
        SELECT  p.ProductID
        FROM    Production.Product AS p;
--Second:
INSERT  INTO dbo.ProductTest
VALUES  (1);
COMMIT --End:  Logical unit of work
GO
```

With the dbo.ProductTest table already created in the preceding script, the BEGIN TRAN and COMMIT pair of statements defines a logical unit of work, suggesting that all the statements within the transaction should be atomic in nature. However, the default behavior of SQL Server doesn't ensure that the failure of one of the statements within a user-defined transaction scope will undo the effect of the prior statement(s). In the preceding transaction, the first INSERT statement will fail as explained earlier, whereas the second INSERT is perfectly fine. The default behavior of SQL Server allows the second INSERT statement to execute, even though the first INSERT statement fails. A SELECT statement, as shown in the following code, will return the row inserted by the second INSERT statement:

```
SELECT  *
FROM    dbo.ProductTest; --Returns a row with t1.c1 = 1
```

The atomicity of a user-defined transaction can be ensured in the following two ways:

- SET XACT_ABORT ON
- Explicit rollback

Let's look at these quickly.

SET XACT_ABORT ON

You can modify the atomicity of the INSERT task in the preceding section using the SET XACT_ ABORT ON statement:

```
SET XACT_ABORT ON;
GO
BEGIN TRAN
 --Start:  Logical unit of work
--First:
INSERT  INTO dbo.ProductTest
        SELECT  p.ProductID
        FROM    Production.Product AS p;
--Second:
INSERT  INTO dbo.ProductTest
VALUES  (1);
COMMIT
 --End:   Logical unit of work GO
SET XACT_ABORT OFF;
GO
```

The SET XACT_ABORT statement specifies whether SQL Server should automatically roll back and abort an entire transaction when a statement within the transaction fails. The failure of the first INSERT statement will automatically suspend the entire transaction, and thus the second INSERT statement will not be executed. The effect of SET XACT_ABORT is at the connection level, and it remains applicable until it is reconfigured or the connection is closed. By default, SET XACT_ABORT is OFF.

Explicit Rollback

You can also manage the atomicity of a user-defined transaction by using the TRY/CATCH error-trapping mechanism within SQL Server. If a statement within the TRY block of code generates an error, then the CATCH block of code will handle the error. If an error occurs and the CATCH block is activated, then the entire work of a user-defined transaction can be rolled back, and further statements can be prevented from execution, as follows:

```
BEGIN TRY
    BEGIN TRAN
    --Start: Logical unit of work
    --First:
    INSERT  INTO dbo.ProductTest
            SELECT  p.ProductID
            FROM    Production.Product AS p

    Second:
    INSERT  INTO dbo.ProductTest
            (ProductID)
    VALUES  (1)
    COMMIT --End: Logical unit of work
END TRY
BEGIN CATCH
    ROLLBACK
    PRINT 'An error occurred'
    RETURN
END CATCH
```

The ROLLBACK statement rolls back all the actions performed in the transaction until that point. For a detailed description of how to implement error handling in SQL Server-based applications, please refer to the MSDN Library article titled "Using TRY . . . CATCH in Transact SQL" (http://bit.ly/PNlAHF) or to the introductory article titled "SQL Server Error Handling Workbench" (http://bit.ly/1nC3VBt).

Since the atomicity property requires that either all the actions of a logical unit of work are completed or no effects are retained, SQL Server *isolates* the work of a transaction from that of others by granting it exclusive rights on the affected resources. This means the transaction can safely roll back the effect of all its actions, if required. The exclusive rights granted to a transaction on the affected resources block all other transactions (or database requests) trying to access those resources during that time period. Therefore, although atomicity is required to maintain the integrity of data, it introduces the undesirable side effect of blocking.

Consistency

A logical unit of work should cause the state of the database to travel from one *consistent* state to another. At the end of a transaction, the state of the database should be fully consistent. SQL Server always ensures that the internal state of the databases is correct and valid by automatically applying all the constraints of the affected database resources as part of the transaction. SQL Server ensures that the state of internal structures, such as data and index layout, are correct after the transaction. For instance, when the data of a table is modified, SQL Server automatically identifies all the indexes, constraints, and other dependent objects on the table and applies the necessary modifications to all the dependent database objects as part of the transaction.

The logical consistency of the data required by the business rules should be ensured by a database developer. A business rule may require changes to be applied on multiple tables. The database developer should accordingly define a logical unit of work to ensure that all the criteria of the business rules are taken care of. SQL Server provides different transaction management features that the database developer can use to ensure the logical consistency of the data.

As just explained, maintaining a consistent logical state requires the use of transactions to define the logical unit of work per the business rules. Also, to maintain a consistent physical state, SQL Server identifies and works on the dependent database objects as part of the logical unit of work. The atomicity characteristic of the logical unit of work blocks all other transactions (or database requests) trying to access the affected objects during that time period. Therefore, even though consistency is required to maintain a valid logical and physical state of the database, it also introduces the undesirable side effect of blocking.

Isolation

In a multiuser environment, more than one transaction can be executed simultaneously. These concurrent transactions should be isolated from one another so that the intermediate changes made by one transaction don't affect the data consistency of other transactions. The degree of *isolation* required by a transaction can vary. SQL Server provides different transaction isolation features to implement the degree of isolation required by a transaction.

■ **Note** Transaction isolation levels are explained later in the chapter in the "Isolation Levels" section.

The isolation requirements of a transaction operating on a database resource can block other transactions trying to access the resource. In a multiuser database environment, multiple transactions are usually executed simultaneously. It is imperative that the data modifications made by an ongoing transaction be protected from the modifications made by other transactions. For instance, suppose a transaction is in the middle of modifying a few rows in a table. During that period, to maintain database consistency, you must ensure that other transactions do not modify or delete the same rows. SQL Server logically isolates the activities of a transaction from that of others by blocking them appropriately, which allows multiple transactions to execute simultaneously without corrupting one another's work.

Excessive blocking caused by isolation can adversely affect the scalability of a database application. A transaction may inadvertently block other transactions for a long period of time, thereby hurting database concurrency. Since SQL Server manages isolation using locks, it is important to understand the locking architecture of SQL Server. This helps you analyze a blocking scenario and implement resolutions.

■ **Note** The fundamentals of database locks are explained later in the chapter in the "Capturing Blocking Information" section.

Durability

Once a transaction is completed, the changes made by the transaction should be *durable*. Even if the electrical power to the machine is tripped off immediately after the transaction is completed, the effect of all actions within the transaction should be retained. SQL Server ensures durability by keeping track of all pre- and post-images of the data under modification in a transaction log as the changes are made. Immediately after the completion of a transaction, SQL Server ensures that all the changes made by the transaction are retained—even if SQL Server, the operating system, or the hardware fails (excluding the log disk). During restart, SQL Server runs its database recovery feature, which identifies the pending changes from the transaction log for completed transactions and applies them to the database resources. This database feature is called *roll forward*.

The recovery interval period depends on the number of pending changes that need to be applied to the database resources during restart. To reduce the recovery interval period, SQL Server intermittently applies the intermediate changes made by the running transactions as configured by the recovery interval option. The recovery interval option can be configured using the spconfigure statement. The process of intermittently applying the intermediate changes is referred to as the *checkpoint* process. During restart, the recovery process identifies all uncommitted changes and removes them from the database resources by using the pre-images of the data from the transaction log.

The durability property isn't a direct cause of most blocking since it doesn't require the actions of a transaction to be isolated from those of others. But in an indirect way, it increases the duration of the blocking. Since the durability property requires saving the pre- and post-images of the data under modification to the transaction log on disk, it increases the duration of the transaction and blocking.

Introduced in SQL Server 2014 is the ability to reduce latency, the time waiting on a query to commit and write to the log, by modifying the durability behavior of a given database. You can now use delayed durability. This means that when a transaction completes, it reports immediately to the application as a successful transaction, reducing latency. But the writes to the log have not yet occurred. This may also allow for more transactions to be completed while still waiting on the system to write all the output to the transaction log. While this may increase apparent speed within the system, as well as possibly reducing contention on transaction log I/O, it's inherently a dangerous choice. This is a difficult recommendation to make. Microsoft suggests three possible situations that may make it attractive.

- *You don't care about the possible loss of some data*: Since you can be in a situation where you need to restore to a point in time from log backups, by choosing to put a database in delayed durability you may lose some data when you have to go to a restore situation.

- *You have a high degree of contention during log writes*: If you're seeing a lot of waits while transactions get written to the log, delayed durability could be a viable solution. But, you're also going to want to be tolerant of data loss, as discussed earlier.

- *You're experiencing high overall resource contention*: A lot of resource contention on the server comes down to the locks being held longer. If, you're seeing lots of contention and you're seeing long log writes or also seeing contention on the log and you have a high tolerance for data loss, this may be a viable way to help reduce the system's contention.

In other works, I recommend using delayed durability only if you meet all those criteria, with the first being the most important.

■ **Note**   Out of the four ACID properties, the `isolation` property, which is also used to ensure atomicity and consistency, is the main cause of blocking in a SQL Server database. In SQL Server, isolation is implemented using locks, as explained in the next section.

Locks

When a session executes a query, SQL Server determines the database resources that need to be accessed; and, if required, the lock manager grants different types of locks to the session. The query is blocked if another session has already been granted the locks; however, to provide both transaction isolation and concurrency, SQL Server uses different lock granularities, as explained in the sections that follow.

Lock Granularity

SQL Server databases are maintained as files on the physical disk. In the case of a traditional nondatabase file such as an Excel file on a desktop machine, the file may be written to by only one user at a time. Any attempt to write to the file by other users fails. However, unlike the limited concurrency on a nondatabase file, SQL Server allows multiple users to modify (or access) contents simultaneously, as long as they don't affect one another's data consistency. This decreases blocking and improves concurrency among the transactions.

To improve concurrency, SQL Server implements lock granularities at the following resource levels and in this order:

- Row (RID)

- Key (KEY)

- Page (PAG)

- Extent (EXT)

- Heap or B-tree (HoBT)

- Table (TAB)

- File (FIL)

- Application (APP)

- MetaData (MDT)

- Allocation Unit (AU)

- Database (DB)

Let's take a look at these lock levels in more detail.

Row-Level Lock

This lock is maintained on a single row within a table and is the lowest level of lock on a database table. When a query modifies a row in a table, an RID lock is granted to the query on the row. For example, consider the transaction on the following test table:

```
--Create a test table
IF (SELECT  OBJECT_ID('dbo.Test1')
   ) IS NOT NULL
    DROP TABLE dbo.Test1;
GO
CREATE TABLE dbo.Test1 (C1 INT);
INSERT  INTO dbo.Test1
VALUES  (1);
GO

BEGIN TRAN
DELETE  dbo.Test1
WHERE   C1 = 1;

SELECT  dtl.request_session_id,
        dtl.resource_database_id,
        dtl.resource_associated_entity_id,
        dtl.resource_type,
        dtl.resource_description,
        dtl.request_mode,
        dtl.request_status
FROM    sys.dm_tran_locks AS dtl
WHERE   dtl.request_session_id = @@SPID;
ROLLBACK
```

The dynamic management view, sys.dm_tran_locks, can be used to display the lock status. The query against sys.dm_tran_locks in Figure 20-1 shows that the DELETE statement acquired, among other locks, an exclusive RID lock on the row to be deleted.

	request_session_id	resource_database_id	resource_associated_entity_id	resource_type	resource_description	request_mode	request_status
1	52	5	0	DATABASE		S	GRANT
2	52	5	1668200993	OBJECT		IX	GRANT
3	52	5	72057594071285760	PAGE	1:23819	IX	GRANT
4	52	5	72057594071285760	RID	1:23819:0	X	GRANT

Figure 20-1. *Output from sys.dm_tran_locks showing the row-level lock granted to the DELETE statement*

■ **Note**   I explain lock modes later in the chapter in the "Lock Modes" section.

Granting an RID lock to the DELETE statement prevents other transactions from accessing the row.

The resource locked by the RID lock can be represented in the following format from the resource_description column:

```
DatabaseID:FileID:PageID:Slot(row)
```

In the output from the query against sys.dm_tran_locks in Figure 20-1, the DatabaseID is displayed separately under the resource_database_id column. The resource_description column value for the RID type represents the remaining part of the RID resource as 1:23819:0. In this case, a FileID of 1 is the primary data file, a PageID of 23819 is a page belonging to the dbo.Test1 table identified by the C1 column, and a Slot (row) of 0 represents the row position within the page. You can obtain the table name and the database name by executing the following SQL statements:

```
SELECT  OBJECT_NAME(1668200993),
        DB_NAME(5);
```

The row-level lock provides very high concurrency since blocking is restricted to the row under effect.

Key-Level Lock

This is a row lock within an index, and it is identified as a KEY lock. As you know, for a table with a clustered index, the data pages of the table and the leaf pages of the clustered index are the same. Since both of the rows are the same for a table with a clustered index, only a KEY lock is acquired on the clustered index row, or limited range of rows, while accessing the rows from the table (or the clustered index). For example, consider having a clustered index on the Test1 table.

```
CREATE CLUSTERED INDEX TestIndex ON dbo.Test1(C1);
```

Next, rerun the following code:

```
BEGIN TRAN
DELETE  dbo.Test1
WHERE   C1 = 1 ;

SELECT  dtl.request_session_id,
        dtl.resource_database_id,
        dtl.resource_associated_entity_id,
        dtl.resource_type,
        dtl.resource_description,
        dtl.request_mode,
        dtl.request_status
FROM    sys.dm_tran_locks AS dtl
WHERE   dtl.request_session_id = @@SPID ;
ROLLBACK
```

The corresponding output from sys.dm_tran_locks shows a KEY lock instead of the RID lock, as you can see in Figure 20-2.

	request_session_id	resource_database_id	resource_associated_entity_id	resource_type	resource_description	request_mode	request_status
1	52	5	0	DATABASE		S	GRANT
2	52	5	1668200993	OBJECT		IX	GRANT
3	52	5	72057594071351296	KEY	(de42f79bc795)	X	GRANT
4	52	5	72057594071351296	PAGE	1:24117	IX	GRANT

Figure 20-2. *Output from sys.dm_tran_locks showing the key-level lock granted to the DELETE statement*

When you are querying sys.dm_tran_locks, you will be able to retrieve the database identifier, resource_database_id. You can also get information about what is being locked from resource_associated_entity_id; however, to get to the particular resource (in this case, the page on the key), you have to go to the resource_description column for the value, which is 1:24117. In this case, the Index ID of 1 is the clustered index on the dbo.Test1 table. You also see the types of requests that are made: S, Sch-S, X, and so on. I cover these in more detail in the upcoming "Lock Modes" section.

■ **Note**   You'll learn about different values for the IndId column and how to determine the corresponding index name in this chapter's "Effect of Indexes on Locking" section.

Like the row-level lock, the key-level lock provides very high concurrency.

Page-Level Lock

A page-level lock is maintained on a single page within a table or an index, and it is identified as a PAG lock. When a query requests multiple rows within a page, the consistency of all the requested rows can be maintained by acquiring either RID/KEY locks on the individual rows or a PAG lock on the entire page. From the query plan, the lock manager determines the resource pressure of acquiring multiple RID/KEY locks, and if the pressure is found to be high, the lock manager requests a PAG lock instead.

The resource locked by the PAG lock may be represented in the following format in the resource_description column of sys.dm_tran_locks:

DatabaseID:FileID:PageID

The page-level lock can increase the performance of an individual query by reducing its locking overhead, but it hurts the concurrency of the database by blocking access to all the rows in the page.

Extent-Level Lock

An extent-level lock is maintained on an extent (a group of eight contiguous data or index pages), and it is identified as an EXT lock. This lock is used, for example, when an ALTER INDEX REBUILD command is executed on a table and the pages of the table may be moved from an existing extent to a new extent. During this period, the integrity of the extents is protected using EXT locks.

Heap or B-tree Lock

A heap or B-tree lock is used to describe when a lock to either type of object could be made. The target object could be an unordered heap table, a table without a clustered index, or a B-tree object, usually referring to partitions. A setting within the ALTER TABLE function allows you to exercise a level of control over how locking escalation (covered in the "Lock Escalation" section) is affected with the partitions. Because partitions can be across multiple filegroups, each one has to have its own data allocation definition. This is where the HoBT lock comes into play. It acts like a table-level lock but on a partition instead of on the table itself.

Table-Level Lock

This is the highest level of lock on a table, and it is identified as a TAB lock. A table-level lock on a table reserves access to the complete table and all its indexes.

When a query is executed, the lock manager automatically determines the locking overhead of acquiring multiple locks at the lower levels. If the resource pressure of acquiring locks at the row level or the page level is determined to be high, then the lock manager directly acquires a table-level lock for the query.

The resource locked by the TAB lock will be represented in resource_description in the following format:

DatabaseID:ObjectID

A table-level lock requires the least overhead compared to the other locks and thus improves the performance of the individual query. On the other hand, since the table-level lock blocks all write requests on the entire table (including indexes), it can significantly hurt database concurrency.

Sometimes an application feature may benefit from using a specific lock level for a table referred to in a query. For instance, if an administrative query is executed during nonpeak hours, then a table-level lock may not impact the users of the system too much; however, it can reduce the locking overhead of the query and thereby improve its performance. In such cases, a query developer may override the lock manager's lock level selection for a table referred to in the query by using locking hints.

```
SELECT * FROM <TableName> WITH(TABLOCK)
```

But, be cautious when taking control away from SQL Server like this. Test it thoroughly prior to implementation.

Database-Level Lock

A database-level lock is maintained on a database and is identified as a DB lock. When an application makes a database connection, the lock manager assigns a database-level shared lock to the corresponding session_id. This prevents a user from accidentally dropping or restoring the database while other users are connected to it.

SQL Server ensures that the locks requested at one level respect the locks granted at other levels. For instance, once a user acquires a row-level lock on a table row, another user can't acquire a lock at any other level that may affect the integrity of the row. The second user may acquire a row-level lock on other rows or a page-level lock on other pages, but an incompatible page- or table-level lock containing the row won't be granted to other users.

The level at which locks should be applied need not be specified by a user or database administrator; the lock manager determines that automatically. It generally prefers row-level and key-level locks when accessing a small number of rows to aid concurrency. However, if the locking overhead of multiple low-level locks turns out to be very high, the lock manager automatically selects an appropriate higher-level lock.

Lock Operations and Modes

Because of the variety of operations that SQL Server needs to perform, an equally large and complex set of locking mechanisms are maintained. In addition to the different types of locks, there is an escalation path to change from one type of lock to another. The following sections describe these modes and processes, as well as their uses.

Lock Escalation

When a query is executed, SQL Server determines the required lock level for the database objects referred to in the query, and it starts executing the query after acquiring the required locks. During the query execution, the lock manager keeps track of the number of locks requested by the query to determine the need to escalate the lock level from the current level to a higher level.

The lock escalation threshold is determined by SQL Server during the course of a transaction. Row locks and page locks are automatically escalated to a table lock when a transaction exceeds its threshold. After the lock level is escalated to a table-level lock, all the lower-level locks on the table are automatically released. This dynamic lock escalation feature of the lock manager optimizes the locking overhead of a query.

It is possible to establish a level of control over the locking mechanisms on a given table. For example, you can control whether lock escalation occurs. The following is the T-SQL syntax to make that change:

```
ALTER TABLE schema.table
SET (LOCK_ESCALATION = DISABLE)
```

This syntax will disable lock escalation on the table entirely (except for a few special circumstances). You can also set it to TABLE, which will cause the escalation to go to a table lock every single time. You can also set lock escalation on the table to AUTO, which will allow SQL Server to make the determination for the locking schema and any escalation necessary. If that table is partitioned, you may see the escalation change to the partition level. Again, exercise caution using these types of modifications to standard SQL Server behavior.

You also have the option to disable lock escalation on a wider basis by using trace flag 1224. This disables lock escalation based on the number of locks but leaves intact lock escalation based on memory pressure. You can also disable the memory pressure lock escalation as well as the number of locks by using trace flag 1211, but that's a dangerous choice and can lead to errors on your systems. I strongly suggest thorough testing before using either of these options.

Lock Modes

The degree of isolation required by different transactions may vary. For instance, consistency of data is not affected if two transactions read the data simultaneously; however, the consistency is affected if two transactions are allowed to modify the data simultaneously. Depending on the type of access requested, SQL Server uses different lock modes while locking resources:

- Shared (S)
- Update (U)
- Exclusive (X)
- Intent:
  - Intent Shared (IS)
  - Intent Exclusive (IX)
  - Shared with Intent Exclusive (SIX)

- Schema:

- Schema Modification (Sch-M)

- Schema Stability (Sch-S)

- Bulk Update (BU)

- Key-Range

Shared (S) Mode

Shared mode is used for read-only queries, such as a `SELECT` statement. It doesn't prevent other read-only queries from accessing the data simultaneously because the integrity of the data isn't compromised by the concurrent reads. However, concurrent data modification queries on the data are prevented to maintain data integrity. The (S) lock is held on the data until the data is read. By default, the (S) lock acquired by a `SELECT` statement is released immediately after the data is read. For example, consider the following transaction:

```
BEGIN TRAN
SELECT  *
FROM    Production.Product AS p
WHERE   p.ProductID = 1;
--Other queries
COMMIT
```

The (S) lock acquired by the `SELECT` statement is not held until the end of the transaction; instead, it is released immediately after the data is read by the `SELECT` statement under read_ committed, the default isolation level. This behavior of the (S) lock can be altered by using a higher isolation level or a lock hint.

Update (U) Mode

Update mode may be considered similar to the (S) lock, but it also includes an objective to modify the data as part of the same query. Unlike the (S) lock, the (U) lock indicates that the data is read for modification. Since the data is read with an objective to modify it, SQL Server does not allow more than one (U) lock on the data simultaneously. This rule helps maintain data integrity. Note that concurrent (S) locks on the data are allowed. The (U) lock is associated with an `UPDATE` statement, and the action of an `UPDATE` statement actually involves two intermediate steps.

1. Read the data to be modified.

2. Modify the data.

Different lock modes are used in the two intermediate steps to maximize concurrency. Instead of acquiring an exclusive right while reading the data, the first step acquires a (U) lock on the data. In the second step, the (U) lock is converted to an exclusive lock for modification. If no modification is required, then the (U) lock is released; in other words, it's not held until the end of the transaction. Consider the following example, which demonstrates the locking behavior of the `UPDATE` statement:

```
BEGIN TRANSACTION LockTran1
UPDATE  Sales.Currency
SET     Name = 'Euro'
WHERE   CurrencyCode = 'EUR';
COMMIT
```

To understand the locking behavior of the intermediate steps of the UPDATE statement, you need to obtain data from sys.dm_tran_locks at the end of each step. You can obtain the lock status after each step of the UPDATE statement by following the steps outlined next. You're going have three connections open that I'll refer to as Connection 1, Connection 2, and Connection 3. This will require three different query windows in Management Studio. You'll run the queries in the connections I list in the order that I specify to arrive at a blocking situation; the point of this is to observe those blocks as they occur. The initial query, which was listed previously, is in Connection 1:

3. Block the second step of the UPDATE statement by first executing a transaction from a second connection, Connection 2.

```
--Execute from a second connection

BEGIN TRANSACTION LockTran2
--Retain an  (S) lock on the resource
SELECT  *
FROM    Sales.Currency AS c WITH (REPEATABLEREAD)
WHERE   c.CurrencyCode = 'EUR' ;
--Allow DMVs to be executed before second step of
-- UPDATE statement is executed by transaction LockTran1
WAITFOR DELAY  '00:00:10';
COMMIT
```

The REPEATABLEREAD locking hint, running in Connection 2, allows the SELECT statement to retain the (S) lock on the resource.

4. While the transaction LockTran2 is executing, execute the UPDATE transaction, updatelock, from the first connection (repeated here for clarity), Connection 1.

```
BEGIN TRANSACTION LockTran1
UPDATE  Sales.Currency
SET     Name = 'Euro'
WHERE   CurrencyCode = 'EUR';
-- NOTE: We're not committing yet
--COMMIT
```

5. While the UPDATE statement is blocked, query the sys.dm_tran_locks DMV from a third connection, Connection 3, as follows:

```
SELECT  dtl.request_session_id,
        dtl.resource_database_id,
        dtl.resource_associated_entity_id,
        dtl.resource_type,
        dtl.resource_description,
        dtl.request_mode,
        dtl.request_status
FROM    sys.dm_tran_locks AS dtl
ORDER BY dtl.request_session_id;
```

The output from sys.dm_tran_locks in Connection 3 will provide the lock status after the first step of the UPDATE statement since the lock conversion to an exclusive (X) lock by the UPDATE statement is blocked by the SELECT statement.

6. The lock status after the second step of the UPDATE statement will be provided by rerunning the query against sys.dm_tran_locks in Connection 3.

Next, let's look at the lock status provided by sys.dm_tran_locks as you go through the individual steps of the UPDATE statement.

- Figure 20-3 shows the lock status after step 1 of the UPDATE statement (obtained from the output from sys.dm_tran_locks executed on the third connection, Connection 3, as explained previously).

	request_session_id	resource_database_id	resource_associated_entity_id	resource_type	resource_description	request_mode	request_status
1	51	5	0	DATABASE		S	GRANT
2	51	5	72057594044612608	PAGE	1:865	IS	GRANT
3	51	5	72057594044612608	KEY	(0d881dadfc5c)	S	GRANT
4	51	5	933578364	OBJECT		IS	GRANT
5	52	5	0	DATABASE		S	GRANT
6	53	5	72057594044612608	PAGE	1:865	IX	GRANT
7	53	5	0	DATABASE		S	GRANT
8	53	5	72057594044612608	KEY	(0d881dadfc5c)	X	CONVERT
9	53	5	933578364	OBJECT		IX	GRANT
10	53	5	72057594044612608	KEY	(0d881dadfc5c)	U	GRANT
11	54	5	0	DATABASE		S	GRANT

Figure 20-3. *Output from sys.dm_tran_locks showing the lock conversion state of an UPDATE statement*

■ **Note** The order of these rows is not that important. I've ordered by session_id in order to group the locks from each query.

- Figure 20-4 shows the lock status after step 2 of the UPDATE statement.

	request_session_id	resource_database_id	resource_associated_entity_id	resource_type	resource_description	request_mode	request_status
1	51	5	0	DATABASE		S	GRANT
2	52	5	0	DATABASE		S	GRANT
3	53	5	72057594044612608	PAGE	1:865	IX	GRANT
4	53	5	72057594044612608	KEY	(0d881dadfc5c)	X	GRANT
5	53	5	933578364	OBJECT		IX	GRANT
6	53	5	0	DATABASE		S	GRANT
7	54	5	0	DATABASE		S	GRANT

Figure 20-4. *Output from sys.dm_tran_locks showing the final lock status held by the UPDATE statement*

From the `sys.dm_tran_locks` output after the first step of the UPDATE statement, you can note the following:

- A (U) lock is granted to the SPID on the data row.

- A conversion to an (X) lock on the data row is requested.

From the output of `sys.dm_tran_locks` after the second step of the UPDATE statement, you can see that the UPDATE statement holds only an (X) lock on the data row. Essentially, the (U) lock on the data row is converted to an (X) lock.

By not acquiring an exclusive lock at the first step, an UPDATE statement allows other transactions to read the data using the SELECT statement during that period. This is possible because (U) and (S) locks are compatible with each other. This increases database concurrency.

■ **Note** I discuss lock compatibility among different lock modes later in this chapter.

You may be curious to learn why a (U) lock is used instead of an (S) lock in the first step of the UPDATE statement. To understand the drawback of using an (S) lock instead of a (U) lock in the first step of the UPDATE statement, let's break the UPDATE statement into two steps.

1. Read the data to be modified using an (S) lock instead of a (U) lock.

2. Modify the data by acquiring an (X) lock.

Consider the following code:

```
BEGIN TRAN
--1.Read data to be modified using (S)lock instead of (U)lock.
--    Retain the (S)lock using REPEATABLEREAD locking hint, since
--    the original (U)lock is retained until the conversion to
--    (X)lock.
SELECT  *
FROM    Sales.Currency AS c WITH (REPEATABLEREAD)
WHERE   c.CurrencyCode = 'EUR' ;
--Allow another equivalent update action to start concurrently
WAITFOR DELAY '00:00:10' ;

--2. Modify the data by acquiring (X)lock
UPDATE  Sales.Currency WITH (XLOCK)
SET     Name = 'EURO'
WHERE   CurrencyCode = 'EUR' ;
COMMIT
```

If this transaction is executed from two connections simultaneously, then it causes a deadlock, as follows:

```
Msg 1205, Level 13, State 51, Line 13
Transaction (Process ID 58) was deadlocked on lock resources with another process and has been
chosen as the deadlock victim. Rerun the transaction.
```

Both transactions read the data to be modified using an (S) lock and then request an (X) lock for modification. When the first transaction attempts the conversion to the (X) lock, it is blocked by the (S) lock held by the second transaction. Similarly, when the second transaction attempts the conversion from (S) lock to the (X) lock, it is blocked by the (S) lock held by the first transaction, which in turn is blocked by the second transaction. This causes a circular block—and therefore, a deadlock.

■ **Note**   Deadlocks are covered in more detail in Chapter 21.

To avoid this typical deadlock, the UPDATE statement uses a (U) lock instead of an (S) lock at its first intermediate step. Unlike an (S) lock, a (U) lock doesn't allow another (U) lock on the same resource simultaneously. This forces the second concurrent UPDATE statement to wait until the first UPDATE statement completes.

Exclusive (X) Mode

Exclusive mode provides an exclusive right on a database resource for modification by data manipulation queries such as INSERT, UPDATE, and DELETE. It prevents other concurrent transactions from accessing the resource under modification. Both the INSERT and DELETE statements acquire (X) locks at the very beginning of their execution. As explained earlier, the UPDATE statement converts to the (X) lock after the data to be modified is read. The (X) locks granted in a transaction are held until the end of the transaction.

The (X) lock serves two purposes.

- It prevents other transactions from accessing the resource under modification so that they see a value either before or after the modification, not a value undergoing modification.

- It allows the transaction modifying the resource to safely roll back to the original value before modification, if needed, since no other transaction is allowed to modify the resource simultaneously.

Intent Shared (IS), Intent Exclusive (IX and Shared with Intent Exclusive (SIX) Modes

Intent Shared, Intent Exclusive, and Shared with Intent Exclusive locks indicate that the query intends to grab a corresponding (S) or (X) lock at a lower lock level. For example, consider the following transaction on the Sales.Currency table:

```
BEGIN TRAN
DELETE   Sales.Currency
WHERE    CurrencyCode = 'ALL';

SELECT   tl.request_session_id,
         tl.resource_database_id,
         tl.resource_associated_entity_id,
         tl.resource_type,
         tl.resource_description,
         tl.request_mode,
         tl.request_status
FROM     sys.dm_tran_locks tl;

ROLLBACK TRAN
```

Figure 20-5 shows the output from sys.dm_tran_locks.

413

	request_session_id	resource_database_id	resource_associated_entity_id	resource_type	resource_description	request_mode	request_status
1	52	5	0	DATABASE		S	GRANT
2	52	5	72057594049855488	KEY	(f9b93c451603)	X	GRANT
3	52	5	72057594044612608	PAGE	1:865	IX	GRANT
4	52	5	72057594049855488	PAGE	1:9270	IX	GRANT
5	52	5	72057594044612608	KEY	(cadf591d32de)	X	GRANT
6	52	5	933578364	OBJECT		IX	GRANT

Figure 20-5. *Output from sys.dm_tran_locks showing the intent locks granted at higher levels*

The (IX) lock at the table level (PAGE) indicates that the DELETE statement intends to acquire an (X) lock at a page, row, or key level. Similarly, the (IX) lock at the page level (PAGE) indicates that the query intends to acquire an (X) lock on a row in the page. The (IX) locks at the higher levels prevent another transaction from acquiring an incompatible lock on the table or on the page containing the row.

Flagging the intent lock—(IS) or (IX)—at a corresponding higher level by a transaction, while holding the lock at a lower level, prevents other transactions from acquiring an incompatible lock at the higher level. If the intent locks were not used, then a transaction trying to acquire a lock at a higher level would have to scan through the lower levels to detect the presence of lower-level locks. While the intent lock at the higher levels indicates the presence of a lower level lock, the locking overhead of acquiring a lock at a higher level is optimized. The intent locks granted to a transaction are held until the end of the transaction.

Only a single (SIX) lock can be placed on a given resource at once. This prevents updates made by other transactions. Other transactions can place (IS) locks on the lower-level resources while the (SIX) lock is in place.

Furthermore, there can be a combination of locks requested (or acquired) at a certain level and the intention of having a lock (or locks) at a lower level. For example, there can be (SIU) and (UIX) lock combinations indicating that an (S) or a (U) lock has been acquired at the corresponding level and that (U) or (X) lock(s) are intended at a lower level.

Schema Modification (Sch-M) and Schema Stability (Sch-S) Modes

Schema Modification and Schema Stability locks are acquired on a table by SQL statements that depend on the schema of the table. A DDL statement, working on the schema of a table, acquires an (Sch-M) lock on the table and prevents other transactions from accessing the table. An (Sch-S) lock is acquired for database activities that depend on the schema but do not modify the schema, such as a query compilation. It prevents an (Sch-M) lock on the table, but it allows other locks to be granted on the table.

Since, on a production database, schema modifications are infrequent, (Sch-M) locks don't usually become a blocking issue. And because (Sch-S) locks don't block other locks except (Sch-M) locks, concurrency is generally not affected by (Sch-S) locks either.

Bulk Update (BU) Mode

The Bulk Update lock mode is unique to bulk load operations. These operations are the older-style bcp (bulk copy), the BULK INSERT statement, and inserts from the OPENROWSET using the BULK option. As a mechanism for speeding up these processes, you can provide a TABLOCK hint or set the option on the table for it to lock on bulk load. The key to (BU) locking mode is that it will allow multiple bulk operations against the table being locked but prevent other operations while the bulk process is running.

Key-range Mode

The Key-Range mode is applicable only while the isolation level is set to Serializable (you'll learn more about transaction isolation levels in the later "Isolation Levels" section). The Key-Range locks are applied to a series, or range, of key values that will be used repeatedly while the transaction is open. Locking a range during a serializable transaction ensures that other rows are not inserted within the range, possibly changing result sets within the transaction. The range can be locked using the other lock modes, making this more like a combined locking mode rather than a distinctively separate locking mode. For the Key-Range lock mode to work, an index must be used to define the values within the range.

Lock Compatibility

SQL Server provides isolation to a transaction by preventing other transactions from accessing the same resource in an incompatible way. However, if a transaction attempts a compatible task on the same resource, then, to increase concurrency, it won't be blocked by the first transaction. SQL Server ensures this kind of selective blocking by preventing a transaction from acquiring an incompatible lock on a resource held by another transaction. For example, an (S) lock acquired on a resource by a transaction allows other transactions to acquire an (S) lock on the same resource. However, an (Sch-M) lock on a resource by a transaction prevents other transactions from acquiring any lock on that resource.

Isolation Levels

The lock modes explained in the previous section help a transaction protect its data consistency from other concurrent transactions. The degree of data protection or isolation a transaction gets depends, not only on the lock modes but also on the isolation level of the transaction. This level influences the behavior of the lock modes. For example, by default an (S) lock is released immediately after the data is read; it isn't held until the end of the transaction. This behavior may not be suitable for some application functionality. In such cases, you can configure the isolation level of the transaction to achieve the desired degree of isolation.

SQL Server implements six isolation levels, four of them as defined by ISO:

- Read Uncommitted
- Read Committed
- Repeatable Read
- Serializable

Two other isolation levels provide row versioning, which is a mechanism whereby a version of the row is created as part of data manipulation queries. This extra version of the row allows read queries to access the data without acquiring locks against it. The extra two isolation levels are as follows:

- Read Committed Snapshot (actually part of the Read Committed isolation)
- Snapshot

The four ISO isolation levels are listed in increasing order of degree of isolation. You can configure them at either the connection or query level by using the SET TRANSACTION ISOLATION LEVEL statement or the locking hints, respectively. The isolation level configuration at the connection level remains effective until the isolation level is reconfigured using the SET statement or until the connection is closed. All the isolation levels are explained in the sections that follow.

Read Uncommitted

Read Uncommitted is the lowest of the four isolation levels, and it allows SELECT statements to read data without requesting an (S) lock. Since an (S) lock is not requested by a SELECT statement, it neither blocks nor is blocked by the (X) lock. It allows a SELECT statement to read data while the data is under modification. This kind of data read is called a *dirty read*.

Assume you have an application in which the amount of data modification is extremely minimal and that your application doesn't require much in the way of accuracy from the SELECT statement it issues to read data. In this case, you can use the Read Uncommitted isolation level to avoid having some other data modification activity block the SELECT statement.

You can use the following SET statement to configure the isolation level of a database connection to the Read Uncommitted isolation level:

```
SET TRANSACTION ISOLATION LEVEL READ UNCOMMITTED
```

You can also achieve this degree of isolation on a query basis using the NOLOCK locking hint.

```
SELECT  *
FROM    Production.Product AS p WITH (NOLOCK);
```

The effect of the locking hint remains applicable for the query and doesn't change the isolation level of the connection.

The Read Uncommitted isolation level avoids the blocking caused by a SELECT statement, but you should not use it if the transaction depends on the accuracy of the data read by the SELECT statement or if the transaction cannot withstand a concurrent change of data by another transaction.

It's important to understand what is meant by a dirty read. Lots of people think this means that, while a field is being updated from Tusa to Tulsa, a query can still read the previous value or even the updated value, prior to the commit. Although that is true, much more egregious data problems could occur. Since no locks are placed while reading the data, indexes may be split. This can result in extra or missing rows of data returned to the query. To be clear, using Read Uncommitted in any environment where data manipulation as well as data reads are occurring can result in unanticipated behaviors. The intention of this isolation level is for systems primarily focused on reporting and business intelligence, not online transaction processing.

Read Committed

The Read Committed isolation level prevents the dirty read caused by the Read Uncommitted isolation level. This means that (S) locks are requested by the SELECT statements at this isolation level. This is the default isolation level of SQL Server. If needed, you can change the isolation level of a connection to Read Committed by using the following SET statement:

```
SET TRANSACTION ISOLATION LEVEL READ COMMITTED
```

The Read Committed isolation level is good for most cases, but since the (S) lock acquired by the SELECT statement isn't held until the end of the transaction, it can cause nonrepeatable read or phantom read issues, as explained in the sections that follow.

The behavior of the Read Committed isolation level can be changed by the READ_COMMITTED_SNAPSHOT database option. When this is set to ON, row versioning is used by data manipulation transactions. This places an extra load on tempdb because previous versions of the rows being changed are stored there while the transaction is uncommitted. This allows other transactions to access data for reads without having to place locks on the data, which can improve the speed and efficiency of all the queries in the system without resulting in the issues generated by page splits with NOLOCK or READ UNCOMMITTED.

Next, modify the AdventureWorks2012 database so that READ_COMMITTED_SNAPSHOT is turned on.

```
ALTER DATABASE AdventureWorks2012
SET READ_COMMITTED_SNAPSHOT ON;
```

Now imagine a business situation. The first connection and transaction will be pulling data from the Production.Product table, acquiring the color of a particular item.

```
BEGIN TRANSACTION;
SELECT  p.Color
FROM    Production.Product AS p
WHERE   p.ProductID = 711;
```

A second connection is made with a new transaction that will be modifying the color of the same item.

```
BEGIN TRANSACTION ;
UPDATE  Production.Product
SET     Color = 'Coyote'
WHERE   ProductID = 711;
SELECT  p.Color
FROM    Production.Product AS p
WHERE   p.ProductID = 711;
```

Running the SELECT statement after updating the color, you can see that the color was updated. But if you switch back to the first connection and rerun the original SELECT statement (don't run the BEGIN TRAN statement again), you'll still see the color as Blue. Switch back to the second connection and finish the transaction.

```
COMMIT TRANSACTION;
```

Switching again to the first transaction, commit that transaction, and then rerun the original SELECT statement. You'll see the new color updated for the item, Coyote. You can reset the isolation level on AdventureWorks2012 before continuing.

```
ALTER DATABASE AdventureWorks2012
SET READ_COMMITTED_SNAPSHOT OFF;
```

■ **Note** If the tempdb is filled, data modification using row versioning will continue to succeed, but reads may fail since the versioned row will not be available. If you enable any type of row versioning isolation within your database, you must take extra care to maintain free space within tempdb.

Repeatable Read

The Repeatable Read isolation level allows a SELECT statement to retain its (S) lock until the end of the transaction, thereby preventing other transactions from modifying the data during that time. Database functionality may implement a logical decision inside a transaction based on the data read by a SELECT statement within the transaction. If the outcome of the decision is dependent on the data read by the SELECT statement, then you should consider preventing modification of the data by other concurrent transactions. For example, consider the following two transactions:

- *Normalize the price for* ProductID = 1: For ProductID = 1, if Price > 10, then decrease the price by 10.

- *Apply a discount*: For products with Price > 10, apply a discount of 40 percent.

Now consider the following test table:

```
IF (SELECT  OBJECT_ID('dbo.MyProduct')
    ) IS NOT NULL
DROP TABLE dbo.MyProduct ;
GO
CREATE TABLE dbo.MyProduct
    (ProductID INT,
     Price MONEY
    ) ;
INSERT  INTO dbo.MyProduct
VALUES  (1, 15.0) ;
```

You can write the two transactions like this:

```
DECLARE @Price INT ;
BEGIN TRAN NormailizePrice
SELECT  @Price = mp.Price
FROM    dbo.MyProduct AS mp
WHERE   mp.ProductID = 1 ;
/*Allow transaction 2 to execute*/
WAITFOR DELAY '00:00:10' ;
IF @Price > 10
    UPDATE  dbo.MyProduct
    SET     Price = Price - 10
    WHERE   ProductID = 1 ;
COMMIT

--Transaction 2 from Connection 2
BEGIN TRAN ApplyDiscount
UPDATE  dbo.MyProduct
SET     Price = Price * 0.6 --Discount = 40%
WHERE   Price > 10 ;
COMMIT
```

On the surface, the preceding transactions may look good, and yes, they do work in a single-user environment. But in a multiuser environment, where multiple transactions can be executed concurrently, you have a problem here!

To figure out the problem, let's execute the two transactions from different connections in the following order:

1. Start transaction 1 first.

2. Start transaction 2 within ten seconds of the start of transaction 1.

As you may have guessed, at the end of the transactions, the new price of the product (with ProductID = 1) will be -1.0. Ouch—it appears that you're ready to go out of business!

The problem occurs because transaction 2 is allowed to modify the data while transaction 1 has finished reading the data and is about to make a decision on it. Transaction 1 requires a higher degree of isolation than that provided by the default isolation level (Read Committed).

As a solution, you want to prevent transaction 2 from modifying the data while transaction 1 is working on it. In other words, provide transaction 1 with the ability to read the data again later in the transaction without being modified by others. This feature is called *repeatable read*. Considering the context, the implementation of the solution is probably obvious. After re-creating the sample table, you can write this:

```
SET TRANSACTION ISOLATION LEVEL REPEATABLE READ ;
GO
--Transaction 1 from Connection 1
DECLARE @Price INT ;
BEGIN TRAN NormalizePrice
SELECT  @Price = Price
FROM    dbo.MyProduct AS mp
WHERE   mp.ProductID = 1 ;
/*Allow transaction 2 to execute*/
WAITFOR DELAY  '00:00:10' ;
IF @Price > 10
    UPDATE  dbo.MyProduct
    SET     Price = Price - 10
    WHERE   ProductID = 1 ;
COMMIT
GO
SET TRANSACTION ISOLATION LEVEL READ COMMITTED --Back to default
GO
```

Increasing the isolation level of transaction 1 to Repeatable Read will prevent transaction 2 from modifying the data during the execution of transaction 1. Consequently, you won't have an inconsistency in the price of the product. Since the intention isn't to release the (S) lock acquired by the SELECT statement until the end of the transaction, the effect of setting the isolation level to Repeatable Read can also be implemented at the query level using the lock hint.

```
DECLARE @Price INT ;
BEGIN TRAN NormalizePrice
SELECT  @Price = Price
FROM    dbo.MyProduct AS mp WITH (REPEATABLEREAD)
WHERE   mp.ProductID = 1 ;
/*Allow transaction 2 to execute*/
WAITFOR DELAY  '00:00:10'
IF @Price > 10
    UPDATE  dbo.MyProduct
    SET     Price = Price - 10
    WHERE   ProductID = 1 ;
COMMIT
```

This solution prevents the data inconsistency of MyProduct.Price, but it introduces another problem to this scenario. On observing the result of transaction 2, you realize that it could cause a deadlock. Therefore, although the preceding solution prevented the data inconsistency, it is not a complete solution. Looking closely at the effect of the Repeatable Read isolation level on the transactions, you see that it introduced the typical deadlock issue avoided by the internal implementation of an UPDATE statement, as explained previously. The SELECT statement acquired and retained an (S) lock instead of a (U) lock, even though it intended to modify the data later within the transaction. The (S) lock allowed transaction 2 to acquire a (U) lock, but it blocked the (U) lock's conversion to an (X) lock. The attempt of transaction 1 to acquire a (U) lock on the data at a later stage caused a circular block, resulting in a deadlock.

To prevent the deadlock and still avoid data corruption, you can use an equivalent strategy as adopted by the internal implementation of the UPDATE statement. Thus, instead of requesting an (S) lock, transaction 1 can request a (U) lock by using an UPDLOCK locking hint when executing the SELECT statement.

```
DECLARE @Price INT ;
BEGIN TRAN NormalizePrice
SELECT  @Price = Price
FROM    dbo.MyProduct AS mp WITH (UPDLOCK)
WHERE   mp.ProductID = 1 ;
/*Allow transaction 2 to execute*/
WAITFOR DELAY  '00:00:10'
IF @Price > 10
    UPDATE  dbo.MyProduct
    SET     Price = Price - 10
    WHERE   ProductID = 1 ;
COMMIT
```

This solution prevents both data inconsistency and the possibility of the deadlock. If the increase of the isolation level to Repeatable Read had not introduced the typical deadlock, then it would have done the job. Since there is a chance of a deadlock occurring because of the retention of an (S) lock until the end of a transaction, it is usually preferable to grab a (U) lock instead of holding the (S) lock, as just illustrated.

Serializable

Serializable is the highest of the six isolation levels. Instead of acquiring a lock only on the row to be accessed, the Serializable isolation level acquires a range lock on the row and the next row in the order of the data set requested. For instance, a SELECT statement executed at the Serializable isolation level acquires a (RangeS-S) lock on the row to be accessed and the next row in the order. This prevents the addition of rows by other transactions in the data set operated on by the first transaction, and it protects the first transaction from finding new rows in its data set within its transaction scope. Finding new rows in a data set within a transaction is also called a *phantom read*.

To understand the need for a Serializable isolation level, let's consider an example. Suppose a group (with GroupID = 10) in a company has a fund of $100 to be distributed among the employees in the group as a bonus. The fund balance after the bonus payment should be $0. Consider the following test table:

```
IF (SELECT  OBJECT_ID('dbo.MyEmployees')
   ) IS NOT NULL
    DROP TABLE dbo.MyEmployees ;
GO
CREATE TABLE dbo.MyEmployees
    (EmployeeID INT,
     GroupID INT,
     Salary MONEY
     ) ;
CREATE CLUSTERED INDEX i1 ON dbo.MyEmployees  (GroupID) ;

--Employee 1 in group 10
INSERT  INTO dbo.MyEmployees
VALUES  (1,10,1000),
```

```
--Employee 2 in group 10
        (2,10,1000),
--Employees 3 & 4 in different groups
        (3,20,1000),
        (4,9,1000);
```

The preceding business functionality may be implemented as follows:

```
DECLARE @Fund MONEY = 100,
    @Bonus MONEY,
    @NumberOfEmployees INT;

BEGIN TRAN PayBonus
SELECT  @NumberOfEmployees = COUNT(*)
FROM    dbo.MyEmployees
WHERE   GroupID = 10;

/*Allow transaction 2 to execute*/
WAITFOR DELAY '00:00:10';

IF @NumberOfEmployees > 0
    BEGIN
        SET @Bonus = @Fund / @NumberOfEmployees;
        UPDATE  dbo.MyEmployees
        SET     Salary = Salary + @Bonus
        WHERE   GroupID = 10;
        PRINT 'Fund balance =
' + CAST((@Fund - (@@ROWCOUNT * @Bonus)) AS VARCHAR(6)) + '   $';
    END
COMMIT
```

You'll see the returned value as a fund balance of $0 since the updates complete successfully. The PayBonus transaction works well in a single-user environment. However, in a multiuser environment, there is a problem.

Consider another transaction that adds a new employee to GroupID = 10 as follows and is executed concurrently (immediately after the start of the PayBonus transaction) from a second connection:

```
BEGIN TRAN NewEmployee
INSERT  INTO MyEmployees
VALUES  (5, 10, 1000);
COMMIT
```

The fund balance after the PayBonus transaction will be -$50! Although the new employee may like it, the group fund will be in the red. This causes an inconsistency in the logical state of the data.

To prevent this data inconsistency, the addition of the new employee to the group (or data set) under operation should be blocked. Of the five isolation levels discussed, only Snapshot isolation can provide a similar functionality, since the transaction has to be protected not only on the existing data but also from the entry of new data in the data set. The Serializable isolation level can provide this kind of isolation by acquiring a range lock on the affected row and the next row in the order determined by the MyEmployees.il index on the GroupID column. Thus, the data inconsistency of the PayBonus transaction can be prevented by setting the transaction isolation level to Serializable.

Remember to re-create the table first.

```
SET TRANSACTION ISOLATION LEVEL SERIALIZABLE;
GO
DECLARE @Fund MONEY = 100,
    @Bonus MONEY,
    @NumberOfEmployees INT;

BEGIN TRAN PayBonus
SELECT  @NumberOfEmployees = COUNT(*)
FROM    dbo.MyEmployees
WHERE   GroupID = 10;

/*Allow transaction 2 to execute*/
WAITFOR DELAY  '00:00:10';
IF @NumberOfEmployees > 0
    BEGIN
        SET @Bonus = @Fund / @NumberOfEmployees;
        UPDATE  dbo.MyEmployees
        SET     Salary = Salary + @Bonus
        WHERE   GroupID = 10;

        PRINT 'Fund balance =
' + CAST((@Fund - (@@ROWCOUNT * @Bonus)) AS VARCHAR(6)) + '    $';
    END
COMMIT
GO
--Back to default
SET TRANSACTION ISOLATION LEVEL READ COMMITTED ;
GO
```

The effect of the Serializable isolation level can also be achieved at the query level by using the HOLDLOCK locking hint on the SELECT statement, as shown here:

```
DECLARE @Fund MONEY = 100,
    @Bonus MONEY,
    @NumberOfEmployees INT ;

BEGIN TRAN PayBonus
SELECT  @NumberOfEmployees = COUNT(*)
FROM    dbo.MyEmployees WITH (HOLDLOCK)
WHERE   GroupID = 10 ;

/*Allow transaction 2 to execute*/
WAITFOR DELAY  '00:00:10' ;

IF @NumberOfEmployees > 0
    BEGIN
        SET @Bonus = @Fund / @NumberOfEmployees
        UPDATE  dbo.MyEmployees
        SET     Salary = Salary + @Bonus
        WHERE   GroupID = 10 ;
```

```
      PRINT 'Fund balance = ' + CAST((@Fund - (@@ROWCOUNT * @Bonus)) AS VARCHAR(6)) + '   $' ;
   END
COMMIT
```

You can observe the range locks acquired by the PayBonus transaction by querying sys.dm_tran_locks from another connection while the PayBonus transaction is executing, as shown in Figure 20-6.

	request_session_id	resource_database_id	resource_associated_entity_id	resource_type	resource_description	request_mode	request_status
1	54	5	0	DATABASE		S	GRANT
2	53	5	0	DATABASE		S	GRANT
3	52	5	0	DATABASE		S	GRANT
4	52	5	72057594071678976	KEY	(fca1e333d991)	RangeS-S	GRANT
5	52	5	72057594071678976	KEY	(1c95cdbc1d2d)	RangeS-S	GRANT
6	53	5	72057594071678976	PAGE	1:24272	IX	GRANT
7	52	5	72057594071678976	PAGE	1:24272	IS	GRANT
8	52	5	72057594071678976	KEY	(241332e1ddb0)	RangeS-S	GRANT
9	53	5	2020202247	OBJECT		IX	GRANT
10	52	5	2020202247	OBJECT		IS	GRANT
11	52	5	72057594071678976	KEY	(69c872e07e60)	RangeS-S	GRANT
12	53	5	72057594071678976	KEY	(69c872e07e60)	RangeI-N	WAIT

Figure 20-6. *Output from sys.dm_tran_locks showing range locks granted to the serializable transaction*

The output of sys.dm_tran_locks shows that shared-range (RangeS-S) locks are acquired on three index rows: the first employee in GroupID = 10, the second employee in GroupID = 10, and the third employee in GroupID = 20. These range locks prevent the entry of any new employee in GroupID = 10.

The range locks just shown introduce a few interesting side effects.

- No new employee with a GroupID between 10 and 20 can be added during this period. For instance, an attempt to add a new employee with a GroupID of 15 will be blocked by the PayBonus transaction.

  ```
  BEGIN TRAN NewEmployee
  INSERT  INTO dbo.MyEmployees
  VALUES  (6, 15, 1000);
  COMMIT
  ```

- If the data set of the PayBonus transaction turns out to be the last set in the existing data ordered by the index, then the range lock required on the row, after the last one in the data set, is acquired on the last possible data value in the table.

  To understand this behavior, let's delete the employees with a GroupID > 10 to make the GroupID = 10 data set the last data set in the clustered index (or table).

  ```
  DELETE  dbo.MyEmployees
  WHERE   GroupID > 10;
  ```

Run the updated bonus and newemployee again. Figure 20-7 shows the resultant output of sys.dm_tran_locks for the PayBonus transaction.

	request_session_id	resource_database_id	resource_associated_entity_id	resource_type	resource_description	request_mode	request_status
1	54	5	0	DATABASE		S	GRANT
2	53	5	0	DATABASE		S	GRANT
3	52	5	0	DATABASE		S	GRANT
4	52	5	720057594071678976	KEY	(ffffffffffff)	RangeS-S	GRANT
5	53	5	720057594071678976	KEY	(ffffffffffff)	RangeI-N	WAIT
6	52	5	720057594071678976	KEY	(e5d9a62bf821)	RangeS-S	GRANT
7	52	5	720057594071678976	KEY	(fca1e333d991)	RangeS-S	GRANT
8	52	5	720057594071678976	KEY	(1c95cdbc1d2d)	RangeS-S	GRANT
9	53	5	720057594071678976	PAGE	1:24272	IX	GRANT
10	52	5	720057594071678976	PAGE	1:24272	IS	GRANT
11	52	5	720057594071678976	KEY	(241332e1ddb0)	RangeS-S	GRANT
12	53	5	2020202247	OBJECT		IX	GRANT
13	52	5	2020202247	OBJECT		IS	GRANT

Figure 20-7. Output from sys.dm_tran_locks showing extended range locks granted to the serializable transaction

The range lock on the last possible row (KEY = ffffffffffff) in the clustered index, as shown in Figure 20-7, will block the addition of employees with all GroupIDs greater than or equal to 10. You know that the lock is on the last row, not because it's displayed in a visible fashion in the output of sys.dm_tran_locks but because you cleaned out everything up to that row previously. For example, an attempt to add a new employee with GroupID = 999 will be blocked by the PayBonus transaction.

```
BEGIN TRAN NewEmployee
INSERT  INTO dbo.MyEmployees
VALUES  (7, 999, 1000);
COMMIT
```

Guess what will happen if the table doesn't have an index on the GroupID column (in other words, the column in the WHERE clause)? While you're thinking, I'll re-create the table with the clustered index on a different column.

```
IF (SELECT  OBJECT_ID('dbo.MyEmployees')
    ) IS NOT NULL
     DROP TABLE dbo.MyEmployees;
GO
CREATE TABLE dbo.MyEmployees
    (EmployeeID INT,
     GroupID INT,
     Salary MONEY
    );
CREATE CLUSTERED INDEX i1 ON dbo.MyEmployees  (EmployeeID);

--Employee 1 in group 10
INSERT  INTO dbo.MyEmployees
VALUES  (1,10,1000),
--Employee 2 in group 10
        (2,10,1000),
--Employees 3 & 4 in different groups
        (3,20,1000),
        (4,9,1000);
```

Now rerun the updated bonus query and the new employee query. Figure 20-8 shows the resultant output of sys.dm_tran_locks for the PayBonus transaction.

	request_session_id	resource_database_id	resource_associated_entity_id	resource_type	resource_description	request_mode	request_status
1	54	5	0	DATABASE		S	GRANT
2	53	5	0	DATABASE		S	GRANT
3	52	5	0	DATABASE		S	GRANT
4	52	5	72057594071678976	KEY	(ffffffffffff)	RangeS-S	GRANT
5	53	5	72057594071678976	KEY	(ffffffffffff)	RangeI-N	WAIT
6	52	5	72057594071678976	KEY	(e5d9a62bf821)	RangeS-S	GRANT
7	52	5	72057594071678976	KEY	(ddfc91a29454)	RangeS-S	GRANT
8	52	5	72057594071678976	KEY	(fca1e333d991)	RangeS-S	GRANT
9	52	5	72057594071678976	KEY	(1c95cdbc1d2d)	RangeS-S	GRANT
10	53	5	72057594071678976	PAGE	1:24272	IX	GRANT
11	52	5	72057594071678976	PAGE	1:24272	IS	GRANT
12	52	5	72057594071678976	KEY	(241332e1ddb0)	RangeS-S	GRANT
13	53	5	2020202247	OBJECT		IX	GRANT
14	52	5	2020202247	OBJECT		IS	GRANT

Figure 20-8. *Output from sys.dm_tran_locks showing range locks granted to the serializable transaction with no index on the WHERE clause column*

Once again, the range lock on the last possible row (KEY = ffffffffffff) in the new clustered index, as shown in Figure 20-8, will block the addition of any new row to the table. I will discuss the reason behind this extensive locking later in the chapter in the "Effect of Indexes on the Serializable Isolation Level" section.

As you've seen, the Serializable isolation level not only holds the share locks until the end of the transaction like the Repeatable Read isolation level but also prevents any new row from appearing in the data set by holding range locks. Because this increased blocking can hurt database concurrency, you should avoid the Serializable isolation level. If you have to use Serializable, then be sure you have good indexes and queries in place to optimize performance in order to minimize the size and length of your transactions.

Snapshot

Snapshot isolation is the second of the row-versioning isolation levels available in SQL Server since SQL Server 2005. Unlike Read Committed Snapshot isolation, Snapshot isolation requires an explicit call to SET TRANSACTION ISOLATION LEVEL at the start of the transaction. It also requires setting the isolation level on the database. Snapshot isolation is meant as a more stringent isolation level than the Read Committed Snapshot isolation. Snapshot isolation will attempt to put an exclusive lock on the data it intends to modify. If that data already has a lock on it, the snapshot transaction will fail. It provides transaction-level read consistency, which makes it more applicable to financial-type systems than Read Committed Snapshot.

Effect of Indexes on Locking

Indexes affect the locking behavior on a table. On a table with no indexes, the lock granularities are RID, PAG (on the page containing the RID), and TAB. Adding indexes to the table affects the resources to be locked. For example, consider the following test table with no indexes:

```
IF (SELECT  OBJECT_ID('dbo.Test1')
    ) IS NOT NULL
    DROP TABLE dbo.Test1;
GO
```

```
CREATE TABLE dbo.Test1 (C1 INT, C2 DATETIME);

INSERT  INTO dbo.Test1
VALUES  (1, GETDATE());
```

Next, observe the locking behavior on the table for the transaction (--indexlock in the download).

```
BEGIN TRAN LockBehavior
UPDATE  dbo.Test1 WITH (REPEATABLEREAD)  --Hold all acquired locks
SET     C2 = GETDATE()
WHERE   C1 = 1 ;
--Observe lock behavior from another connection
WAITFOR DELAY  '00:00:10' ;
COMMIT
```

Figure 20-9 shows the output of sys.dm_tran_locks applicable to the test table.

	request_session_id	resource_database_id	resource_associated_entity_id	resource_type	resource_description	request_mode	request_status
1	51	5	0	DATABASE		S	GRANT
2	52	5	0	DATABASE		S	GRANT
3	52	5	72057594071744512	RID	1:24274:0	X	GRANT
4	52	5	72057594071744512	PAGE	1:24274	IX	GRANT
5	52	5	2036202304	OBJECT		IX	GRANT

Figure 20-9. *Output from sys.dm_tran_locks showing the locks granted on a table with no index*

The following locks are acquired by the transaction:

- An (IX) lock on the table
- An (IX) lock on the page containing the data row
- An (X) lock on the data row within the table

When the resource_type is an object, the resource_associated_entity_id column value in sys.dm_tran_locks indicates the objectid of the object on which the lock is placed. You can obtain the specific object name on which the lock is acquired from the sys.object system table, as follows:

```
SELECT OBJECT_NAME(<object_id>);
```

The effect of the index on the locking behavior of the table varies with the type of index on the WHERE clause column. The difference arises from the fact that the leaf pages of the nonclustered and clustered indexes have a different relationship with the data pages of the table. Let's look into the effect of these indexes on the locking behavior of the table.

Effect of a Nonclustered Index

Because the leaf pages of the nonclustered index are separate from the data pages of the table, the resources associated with the nonclustered index are also protected from corruption. SQL Server automatically ensures this. To see this in action, create a nonclustered index on the test table.

```
CREATE NONCLUSTERED INDEX iTest ON dbo.Test1(C1);
```

On running the LockBehavior transaction again and querying sys.dm_ tran_locks from a separate connection, you get the result shown in Figure 20-10.

	request_session_id	resource_database_id	resource_associated_entity_id	resource_type	resource_description	request_mode	request_status
1	51	5	0	DATABASE		S	GRANT
2	52	5	0	DATABASE		S	GRANT
3	52	5	72057594071744512	RID	1:24274:0	X	GRANT
4	52	5	72057594071810048	PAGE	1:24283	IU	GRANT
5	52	5	72057594071744512	PAGE	1:24274	IX	GRANT
6	52	5	2036202304	OBJECT		IX	GRANT
7	52	5	72057594071810048	KEY	(58ca6fb4eef9)	U	GRANT

Figure 20-10. *Output from sys.dm_tran_locks showing the effect of a nonclustered index on locking behavior*

The following locks are acquired by the transaction:

- An (IU) lock on the page containing the nonclustered index row
- A (U) lock on the nonclustered index row within the index page
- An (IX) lock on the table
- An (IX) lock on the page containing the data row
- An (X) lock on the data row within the data page

Note that only the row-level and page-level locks are directly associated with the nonclustered index. The next higher level of lock granularity for the nonclustered index is the table-level lock on the corresponding table.

Thus, nonclustered indexes introduce an additional locking overhead on the table. You can avoid the locking overhead on the index by using the ALLOW_ROW_LOCKS and ALLOW_PAGE_LOCKS options in ALTER INDEX. Understand, though, that this is a trade-off that could involve a loss of performance, and it requires careful testing to ensure it doesn't negatively impact your system.

```
ALTER INDEX iTest ON dbo.Test1
    SET (ALLOW_ROW_LOCKS = OFF ,ALLOW_PAGE_LOCKS= OFF);

BEGIN TRAN LockBehavior
UPDATE  dbo.Test1 WITH (REPEATABLEREAD)  --Hold all acquired locks
SET     C2 = GETDATE()
WHERE   C1 = 1;

--Observe lock behavior using sys.dm_tran_locks
--from another connection
WAITFOR DELAY  '00:00:10';
COMMIT

ALTER INDEX iTest ON dbo.Test1
    SET (ALLOW_ROW_LOCKS = ON ,ALLOW_PAGE_LOCKS= ON);
```

You can use these options when working with an index to enable/disable the KEY locks and PAG locks on the index. Disabling just the KEY lock causes the lowest lock granularity on the index to be the PAG lock. Configuring lock granularity on the index remains effective until it is reconfigured.

■ **Note**   Modifying locks like this should be a last resort after many other options have been tried. This could cause significant locking overhead that would seriously impact the performance of the system.

Figure 20-11 displays the output of sys.dm_tran_locks executed from a separate connection.

	request_session_id	resource_database_id	resource_associated_entity_id	resource_type	resource_description	request_mode	request_status
1	51	5	0	DATABASE		S	GRANT
2	52	5	0	DATABASE		S	GRANT
3	52	5	2036202304	OBJECT		X	GRANT

Figure 20-11. Output from sys.dm_tran_locks showing the effect of sp_index option on lock granularity

The only lock acquired by the transaction on the test table is an (X) lock on the table.

You can see from the new locking behavior that disabling the KEY lock escalates lock granularity to the table level. This will block every concurrent access to the table or to the indexes on the table; consequently, it can seriously hurt the database concurrency. However, if a nonclustered index becomes a point of contention in a blocking scenario, then it may be beneficial to disable the PAG locks on the index, thereby allowing only KEY locks on the index.

■ **Note**   Using this option can have serious side effects. You should use it only as a last resort.

Effect of a Clustered Index

Since for a clustered index the leaf pages of the index and the data pages of the table are the same, the clustered index can be used to avoid the overhead of locking additional pages (leaf pages) and rows introduced by a nonclustered index. To understand the locking overhead associated with a clustered index, convert the preceding nonclustered index to a clustered index.

```
CREATE CLUSTERED INDEX iTest ON dbo.Test1(C1) WITH DROP_EXISTING;
```

If you run the locking script again and query sys.dm_tran_locks in a different connection, you should see the resultant output for the LockBehavior transaction on iTest shown in Figure 20-12.

	request_session_id	resource_database_id	resource_associated_entity_id	resource_type	resource_description	request_mode	request_status
1	51	5	0	DATABASE		S	GRANT
2	52	5	0	DATABASE		S	GRANT
3	52	5	72057594071941120	KEY	(de42f79bc795)	X	GRANT
4	52	5	72057594071941120	PAGE	1:24291	IX	GRANT
5	52	5	2036202304	OBJECT		IX	GRANT

Figure 20-12. Output from sys.dm_tran_locks showing the effect of a clustered index on locking behavior

The following locks are acquired by the transaction:

- An (IX) lock on the table
- An (IX) lock on the page containing the clustered index row
- An (X) lock on the clustered index row within the table or clustered index

The locks on the clustered index row and the leaf page are actually the locks on the data row and data page, too, since the data pages and the leaf pages are the same. Thus, the clustered index reduced the locking overhead on the table compared to the nonclustered index.

Reduced locking overhead of a clustered index is another benefit of using a clustered index over a heap.

Effect of Indexes on the Serializable Isolation Level

Indexes play a significant role in determining the amount of blocking caused by the Serializable isolation level. The availability of an index on the WHERE clause column (that causes the data set to be locked) allows SQL Server to determine the order of the rows to be locked. For instance, consider the example used in the section on the Serializable isolation level. The SELECT statement uses a filter on the GroupID column to form its data set, like so:

```
DECLARE @NumberOfEmployees INT;
SELECT  @NumberOfEmployees = COUNT(*)
FROM    dbo.MyEmployees WITH (HOLDLOCK)
WHERE   GroupID = 10;
```

A clustered index is available on the GroupID column, allowing SQL Server to acquire a (RangeS-S) lock on the row to be accessed and the next row in the correct order.

If the index on the GroupID column is removed, then SQL Server cannot determine the rows on which the range locks should be acquired since the order of the rows is no longer guaranteed. Consequently, the SELECT statement acquires an (IS) lock at the table level instead of acquiring lower-granularity locks at the row level, as shown in Figure 20-13.

	request_session_id	resource_database_id	resource_associated_entity_id	resource_type	resource_description	request_mode	request_status
9	52	5	720575940716789976	PAGE	1:24272	IS	GRANT

Figure 20-13. *Output from sys.dm_tran_locks showing the locks granted to a SELECT statement with no index on the WHERE clause column*

By failing to have an index on the filter column, you significantly increase the degree of blocking caused by the Serializable isolation level. This is another good reason to have an index on the WHERE clause columns.

Capturing Blocking Information

Although blocking is necessary to isolate a transaction from other concurrent transactions, sometimes it may rise to excessive levels, adversely affecting database concurrency. In the simplest blocking scenario, the lock acquired by a session on a resource blocks another session requesting an incompatible lock on the resource. To improve concurrency, it is important to analyze the cause of blocking and apply the appropriate resolution.

In a blocking scenario, you need the following information to have a clear understanding of the cause of the blocking:

- *The connection information of the blocking and blocked sessions:* You can obtain this information from the sys.dm_os_waiting_tasks dynamic management view or the sp_who2 system stored procedure.

- *The lock information of the blocking and blocked sessions:* You can obtain this information from the sys.dm_tran_locks DMO.

- *The SQL statements last executed by the blocking and blocked sessions:* You can use the sys.dm_exec_requests DMV combined with sys.dm_exec_sql_text and sys.dm_exec_queryplan or Extended Events to obtain this information.

You can also obtain the following information from SQL Server Management Studio by running the Activity Monitor. The Processes page provides connection information of all SPIDs. This shows blocked SPIDS, the process blocking them, and the head of any blocking chain with details on how long the process has been running, its SPID, and other information. It is possible to put Extended Events to work using the blocking report to gather a lot of the same information. For immediate checks on locking, use the DMOs; for extended monitoring and historical tracking, you'll want to use Extended Events. You can find more on this in the "Extended Events and the blocked_ process_report Event" section.

To provide more power and flexibility to the process of collecting blocking information, a SQL Server administrator can use SQL scripts to provide the relevant information listed here.

Capturing Blocking Information with SQL

To arrive at enough information about blocked and blocking processes, you can bring several dynamic management views into play. This query will show information necessary to identify blocked processes based on those that are waiting. You can easily add filtering to access only those processes blocked for a certain period of time or only within certain databases, among other options.

```
SELECT  dtl.request_session_id AS WaitingSessionID,
        der.blocking_session_id AS BlockingSessionID,
        dowt.resource_description,
        der.wait_type,
        dowt.wait_duration_ms,
        DB_NAME(dtl.resource_database_id) AS DatabaseName,
        dtl.resource_associated_entity_id AS WaitingAssociatedEntity,
        dtl.resource_type AS WaitingResourceType,
        dtl.request_type AS WaitingRequestType,
        dest.[text] AS WaitingTSql,
        dtlbl.request_type BlockingRequestType,
        destbl.[text] AS BlockingTsql
FROM    sys.dm_tran_locks AS dtl
JOIN    sys.dm_os_waiting_tasks AS dowt
        ON dtl.lock_owner_address = dowt.resource_address
JOIN    sys.dm_exec_requests AS der
        ON der.session_id = dtl.request_session_id
CROSS APPLY sys.dm_exec_sql_text(der.sql_handle) AS dest
LEFT JOIN sys.dm_exec_requests derbl
        ON derbl.session_id = dowt.blocking_session_id
OUTER APPLY sys.dm_exec_sql_text(derbl.sql_handle) AS destbl
LEFT JOIN sys.dm_tran_locks AS dtlbl
        ON derbl.session_id = dtlbl.request_session_id;
```

To understand how to analyze a blocking scenario and the relevant information provided by the blocker script, consider the following example. First, create a test table.

```
IF (SELECT  OBJECT_ID('dbo.BlockTest')
    ) IS NOT NULL
    DROP TABLE dbo.BlockTest;
GO

CREATE TABLE dbo.BlockTest
    (C1 INT,
     C2 INT,
     C3 DATETIME
    );

INSERT  INTO dbo.BlockTest
VALUES  (11, 12, GETDATE()),
        (21, 22, GETDATE());
```

Now open three connections and run the following two queries concurrently. Once you run them, use the blocker script in the third connection. Execute the following code in one connection:

```
BEGIN TRAN User1
UPDATE  dbo.BlockTest
SET     C3 = GETDATE();
```

Next, execute this code while the User1 transaction is executing:

```
BEGIN TRAN User2
SELECT  C2
FROM    dbo.BlockTest
WHERE   C1 = 11;
COMMIT
```

This creates a simple blocking scenario where the User1 transaction blocks the User2 transaction.

The output of the blocker script provides information immediately useful to begin resolving blocking issues. First, you can identify the specific session information, including the session ID of both the blocking and waiting sessions. You get an immediate resource description from the waiting resource, the wait type, and the length of time in milliseconds that the process has been waiting. It's that value that allows you to provide a filter to eliminate short-term blocks, which are part of normal processing.

The database name is supplied because blocking can occur anywhere in the system, not just in AdventureWorks2012. You'll want to identify it where it occurs. The resources and types from the basic locking information are retrieved for the waiting process.

The blocking request type is displayed, and both the waiting T-SQL and blocking T-SQL, if available, are displayed. Once you have the object where the block is occurring, having the T-SQL so that you can understand exactly where and how the process is either blocking or being blocked is a vital part of the process of eliminating or reducing the amount of blocking. All this information is available from one simple query. Figure 20-14 shows the sample output from the earlier blocked process.

	WaitingSessionID	BlockingSessionID	resource_description	wait_type	wait_duration_ms	DatabaseName	WaitingAssociatedEntity	WaitingResourceType	WaitingRequestType	WaitingTSql
1	66	65	ridlock fileid=1 pageid=30689 dbid=5 id=lock1a1f...	LCK_M_S	7281	AdventureWorks2012	72057594069516288	RID	LOCK	BEGIN TRAN User2 SELECT C2 FROM dbo.BlockT...

Figure 20-14. *Output from the blocker script*

Be sure to go back to Connection 1 and commit or roll back the transaction.

Extended Events and the blocked_process_report Event

Extended Events provide an event called blocked_process_report. This event works off the blocked process threshold that you need to provide to the system configuration. This script sets the threshold to five seconds:

```
EXEC sp_configure 'show advanced option', '1';
RECONFIGURE;
EXEC sp_configure
    'blocked process threshold',
    5;
RECONFIGURE;
```

This would normally be a very low value in most systems. If you have an established performance service level agreement (SLA), you could use that as the threshold. Once the value is set, you can configure alerts so that e-mails, tweets, or instant messages are sent if any process is blocked longer than the value you set. It also acts as a trigger for the extended event.

To set up a session that captures the blocked_process_report, first open the Extended Events session properties window. (Although you should use scripts to set up this event in a production environment, I'll show how to use the GUI.) Provide the session with a name and then navigate to the Events page. Type **block** into the Event library text box, which will find the blocked_process_report event. Select that event by clicking the right arrow. You should see something similar to Figure 20-15.

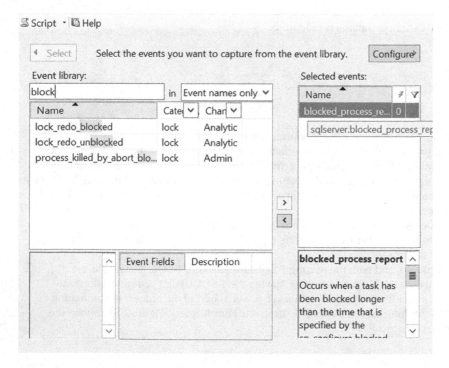

Figure 20-15. The blocked process report event selected in the Extended Events window

The event fields are all preselected for you. If you still have the queries running from the previous section that created the block, all you need to do now is click the Run button to capture the event. Otherwise, go back to Listings 20-1 and 20-2 and run them in two different connections. After the blocked process threshold is passed, you'll see the event fire . . . and fire. It will fire every five seconds if that's how you've configured it and you're leaving the connections running from Listings 20-1 and 20-2. The output in the live data stream looks like Figure 20-16.

Field	Value
blocked_process	<blocked-process-report monitorLoop="29133"> <blocked-proc...
database_id	5
database_name	AdventureWorks2012
duration	5331000
index_id	0
lock_mode	S
object_id	0
resource_owner_type	LOCK
transaction_id	255377

Figure 20-16. *Output from the blocked_process_report event*

Some of the information is self-explanatory; to get into the details, you need to look at the XML generated in the blocked_process field.

```
<blocked-process-report monitorLoop="29133">
<blocked-process>
 <process id="process26911b848" taskpriority="0" logused="0" waitresource="RID: 5:1:24292:0"
waittime="5331" ownerId="255377" transactionname="User2" lasttranstarted="2014-03-26T20:31:40.427"
XDES="0x26b386d70" lockMode="S" schedulerid="1" kpid="2340" status="suspended" spid="55"
sbid="0" ecid="0" priority="0" trancount="1" lastbatchstarted="2014-03-26T20:31:40.427"
lastbatchcompleted="2014-03-26T20:31:40.423" lastattention="1900-01-01T00:00:00.423"
clientapp="Microsoft SQL Server Management Studio - Query" hostname="WIN-TUTJRM1T45J" hostpid="2324"
loginname="WIN-TUTJRM1T45J\Administrator" isolationlevel="read committed (2)" xactid="255377"
currentdb="5" lockTimeout="4294967295" clientoption1="671098976" clientoption2="390200">
   <executionStack>
    <frame line="2" stmtstart="24" stmtend="118" sqlhandle="0x02000000ccf3e6045e680885750c3f36d7cc54
9d8ff01368000000000000000000000000000000000000000000" />
    <frame line="2" stmtstart="36" stmtend="134" sqlhandle="0x0200000063e12d309fa7874804b7b56c7be7be
ecf2a0255b00000000000000000000000000000000000000000" />
   </executionStack>
   <inputbuf>
BEGIN TRAN User2
SELECT  C2
FROM    dbo.BlockTest
WHERE   C1 = 11;
COMMIT   </inputbuf>
  </process>
 </blocked-process>
```

```
<blocking-process>
  <process status="sleeping" spid="52" sbid="0" ecid="0" priority="0" trancount="1"
lastbatchstarted="2014-03-26T20:31:36.567" lastbatchcompleted="2014-03-26T20:31:36.567"
lastattention="1900-01-01T00:00:00.567" clientapp="Microsoft SQL Server Management Studio -
Query" hostname="WIN-TUTJRM1T45J" hostpid="2324" loginname="WIN-TUTJRM1T45J\Administrator"
isolationlevel="read committed (2)" xactid="255368" currentdb="5" lockTimeout="4294967295"
clientoption1="671098976" clientoption2="390200">
    <executionStack />
    <inputbuf>
SET STATISTICS IO OFF SET STATISTICS TIME OFF    </inputbuf>
  </process>
</blocking-process>
</blocked-process-report>
```

The elements are clear if you look through this XML. <blocked-process> shows information about the process that was blocked, including familiar information such as the session ID (labeled with the old-fashioned SPID here), the database ID, and so on. You can see the query in the <inputbuf> element. Details such as the lockMode are available within the <process> element. Note that the XML doesn't include some of the other information that you can easily get from T-SQL queries, such as the query string of the blocked and waiting processes. But with the SPID available, you can get them from the cache, if available, or you can combine the Blocked Process report with other events such as rpc_starting to show the query information. However, doing so will add to the overhead of using those events long term within your database. If you know you have a blocking problem, this can be part of a short-term monitoring project to capture the necessary blocking information.

Blocking Resolutions

Once you've analyzed the cause of a block, the next step is to determine any possible resolutions. Here are a few techniques you can use to do this:

- Optimize the queries executed by blocking and blocked SPIDs.

- Decrease the isolation level.

- Partition the contended data.

- Use a covering index on the contended data.

■ **Note**   A detailed list of recommendations to avoid blocking appears later in the chapter in the "Recommendations to Reduce Blocking" section.

To understand these resolution techniques, let's apply them in turn to the preceding blocking scenario.

Optimize the Queries

Optimizing the queries executed by the blocking and blocked processes helps reduce the blocking duration. In the blocking scenario, the queries executed by the processes participating in the blocking are as follows:

- Blocking process:

```
BEGIN TRAN User1
UPDATE  dbo.BlockTest
SET     C3 = GETDATE();
```

- Blocked process:

```
BEGIN TRAN User2
SELECT  C2
FROM    dbo.BlockTest
WHERE   C1 = 11;
COMMIT
```

Next, let's analyze the individual SQL statements executed by the blocking and blocked SPIDs to optimize their performance.

- The UPDATE statement of the blocking SPID accesses the data without a WHERE clause. This makes the query inherently costly on a large table. If possible, break the action of the UPDATE statement into multiple batches using appropriate WHERE clauses. Remember to try to use set-based operations such as a TOP statement to limit the rows. If the individual UPDATE statements of the batch are executed in separate transactions, then fewer locks will be held on the resource within one transaction and for shorter time periods. This could also help reduce or avoid lock escalation.

- The SELECT statement executed by the blocked SPID has a WHERE clause on the C1 column. From the index structure on the test table, you can see that there is no index on this column. To optimize the SELECT statement, you could create a clustered index on the C1 column:

```
CREATE CLUSTERED INDEX i1 ON dbo.BlockTest(C1);
```

■ **Note**   Since the example table fits within one page, adding the clustered index won't make much difference to the query performance. However, as the number of rows in the table increases, the beneficial effect of the index will become more pronounced.

Optimizing the queries reduces the duration for which the locks are held by the processes. The query optimization reduces the impact of blocking, but it doesn't prevent the blocking completely. However, as long as the optimized queries execute within acceptable performance limits, a small amount of blocking may be ignored.

Decrease the Isolation Level

Another approach to resolve blocking can be to use a lower isolation level, if possible. The SELECT statement of the User2 transaction gets blocked while requesting an (S) lock on the data row. The isolation level of this transaction can be mitigated by taking advantage of SNAPSHOT isolation level Read Committed Snapshot so that the (S) lock is not requested by the SELECT statement. The Read Committed Snapshot isolation level can be configured for the connection using the SET statement.

```
SET TRANSACTION ISOLATION LEVEL READ COMMITTED SNAPSHOT;
GO
BEGIN TRAN User2
SELECT  C2
FROM    dbo.BlockTest
WHERE   C1 = 11;
COMMIT
GO
--Back to default
SET TRANSACTION ISOLATION LEVEL READ COMMITTED;
GO
```

This example shows the utility of reducing the isolation level. Using this SNAPSHOT isolation is radically preferred over using any of the methods that produce dirty reads that could lead to incorrect data or missing or extra rows.

Partition the Contended Data

When dealing with large data sets or data that can be discretely stored, it is possible to apply table partitioning to the data. Partitioned data is split horizontally, that is, by certain values (such as splitting sales data up by month, for example). This allows the transactions to execute concurrently on the individual partitions, without blocking each other. These separate partitions are treated as a single unit for querying, updating, and inserting; only the storage and access are separated by SQL Server. It should be noted that partitioning is available only in the Developer and Enterprise editions of SQL Server.

In the preceding blocking scenario, the data could be separated by date. This would entail setting up multiple filegroups if you're concerned with performance (or just put everything on PRIMARY if you're worried about management) and splitting the data per a defined rule. Once the UPDATE statement gets a WHERE clause, then it and the original SELECT statement will be able to execute concurrently on two separate partitions. This does require that the WHERE clause filters only on the partition key column. As soon as you get other conditions in the mix, you're unlikely to benefit from partition elimination, which means performance could be much worse, not better.

■ **Note** Partitioning, if done properly, can improve both performance and concurrency on large data sets. But, partitioning is primarily a data management solution, not a performance tuning option.

In a blocking scenario, you should analyze whether the query of the blocking or the blocked process can be fully satisfied using a covering index. If the query of one of the processes can be satisfied using a covering index, then it will prevent the process from requesting locks on the contended resource. Also, if the other process doesn't need a lock on the covering index (to maintain data integrity), then both processes will be able to execute concurrently without blocking each other.

For instance, in the preceding blocking scenario, the SELECT statement by the blocked process can be fully satisfied by a covering index on the C1 and C2 columns.

```
CREATE NONCLUSTERED INDEX iAvoidBlocking ON dbo.BlockTest(C1,  C2) ;
```

The transaction of the blocking process need not acquire a lock on the covering index since it accesses only the C3 column of the table. The covering index will allow the SELECT statement to get the values for the C1 and C2 columns without accessing the base table. Thus, the SELECT statement of the blocked process can acquire an (S) lock on the covering-index row without being blocked by the (X) lock on the data row acquired by the blocking process. This allows both transactions to execute concurrently without any blocking.

Consider a covering index as a mechanism to "duplicate" part of the table data in which consistency is automatically maintained by SQL Server. This covering index, if mostly read-only, can allow some transactions to be served from the "duplicate" data while the base table (and other indexes) can continue to serve other transactions. The trade-offs to this approach are the need for additional storage and the potential for additional overhead during data modification.

Recommendations to Reduce Blocking

Single-user performance and the ability to scale with multiple users are both important for a database application. In a multiuser environment, it is important to ensure that the database operations don't hold database resources for a long time. This allows the database to support a large number of operations (or database users) concurrently without serious performance degradation. The following is a list of tips to reduce/avoid database blocking:

- Keep transactions short.
  - Perform the minimum steps/logic within a transaction.
  - Do not perform costly external activity within a transaction, such as sending an acknowledgment e-mail or performing activities driven by the end user.
- Optimize queries.
  - Create indexes as required to ensure optimal performance of the queries within the system.
  - Avoid a clustered index on frequently updated columns. Updates to clustered index key columns require locks on the clustered index and all nonclustered indexes (since their row locator contains the clustered index key).
  - Consider using a covering index to serve the blocked SELECT statements.
  - Consider partitioning a contended table.
- Use query timeouts or a resource governor to control runaway queries. For more on the resource governor, consult Books Online: http://bit.ly/1jiPhfS.
  - Avoid losing control over the scope of the transactions because of poor error-handling routines or application logic.
  - Use SET XACTABORT ON to avoid a transaction being left open on an error condition within the transaction.
  - Execute the following SQL statement from a client error handler (TRY/CATCH) after executing a SQL batch or stored procedure containing a transaction.

    ```
    IF @@TRANCOUNT > 0 ROLLBACK
    ```
- Use the lowest isolation level required.
  - Consider using row versioning, one of the SNAPSHOT isolation levels, to help reduce contention.

Automation to Detect and Collect Blocking Information

In addition to capturing information using extended events, you can automate the process of detecting a blocking condition and collecting the relevant information using SQL Server Agent. SQL Server provides the Performance Monitor counters shown in Table 20-1 to track the amount of wait time.

Table 20-1. *Performance Monitor Counters*

Object	Counter	Instance	Description
SQLServer:Locks (For SOL Server named instance MSSOL$<InstanceName>:Locks)	Average Wait Time(ms)	_Total	Average amount of wait time for each lock that resulted in a wait
	Lock Wait Time (ms)	_Total	Total wait time for locks in the last second

You can create a combination of SQL Server alerts and jobs to automate the following process:

1. Determine when the average amount of wait time exceeds an acceptable amount of blocking using the Average Wait Time (ms) counter. Based on your preferences, you can use the Lock Wait Time (ms) counter instead.

2. Once you've established the minimum wait, set Blocked Process Threshold. When the average wait time exceeds the limit, notify the SQL Server DBA of the blocking situation through e-mail.

3. Automatically collect the blocking information using the blocker script or a trace that relies on the Blocked Process report for a certain period of time.

To set up the Blocked Process report to run automatically, first create the SQL Server job, called Blocking Analysis, so that it can be used by the SQL Server alert you'll create later. You can create this SQL Server job from SQL Server Management Studio to collect blocking information by following these steps:

1. Generate an extended events script (as detailed in Chapter 6) using the blocked_process_report event.

2. Run the script to create the session on the server, but don't start it yet.

3. In Management Studio, expand the server by selecting <ServerName> ➤ SQL Server Agent ➤ Jobs. Finally, right-click and select New Job.

4. On the General page of the New Job dialog box, enter the job name and other details.

5. On the Steps page, click New and enter the command to start and stop the session through T-SQL, as shown in Figure 20-17.

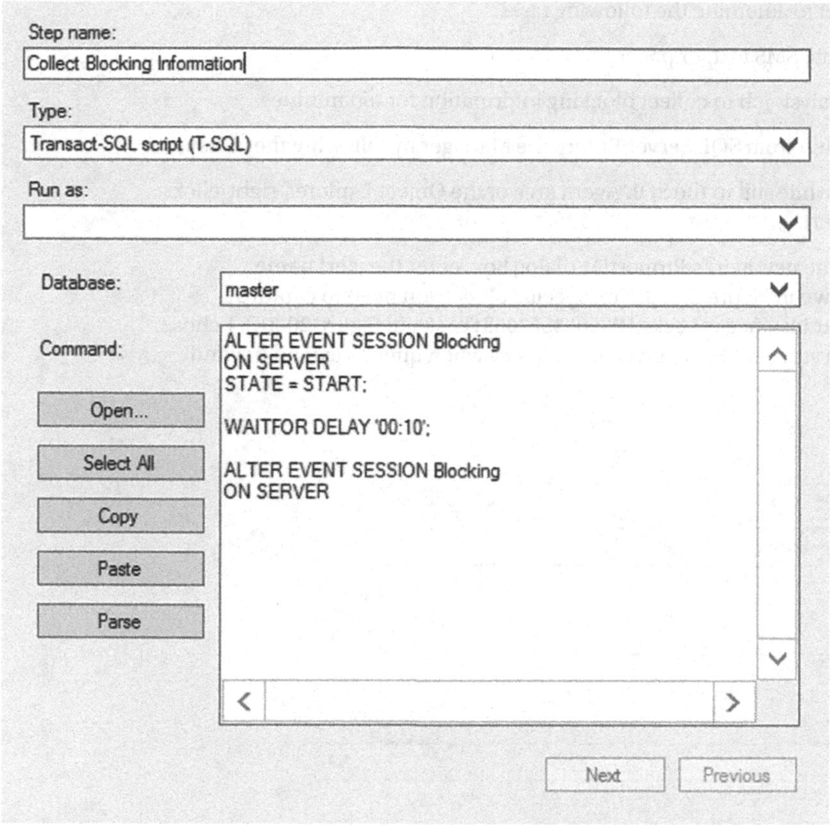

Figure 20-17. *Entering the command to run the blocker script*

You can do this using the following command:

```
ALTER EVENT SESSION Blocking
ON SERVER
STATE = START;

WAITFOR DELAY '00:10';

ALTER EVENT SESSION Blocking
ON SERVER
STATE = STOP;
```

The output of the session is determined by how you defined the target or targets when you created it.

1. Return to the New Job dialog box by clicking OK.

2. Click OK to create the SQL Server job. The SQL Server job will be created with an enabled and runnable state to collect blocking information for ten minutes using the trace script.

You can create a SQL Server alert to automate the following tasks:

- Inform the DBA via e-mail, SMS text, or pager.

- Execute the Blocking Analysis job to collect blocking information for ten minutes.

You can create the SQL Server alert from SQL Server Enterprise Manager by following these steps:

1. In Management Studio, while still in the SQL Agent area of the Object Explorer, right-click Alerts and select New Alert.

2. On the General page of the new alert's Properties dialog box, enter the alert name and other details, as shown in Figure 20-18. The specific object you need to capture information from for your instance is Locks (MSSQL$GF2008:Locks in Figure 20-18). I chose 500ms as an example of a stringent SLA that wants to know when queries extend beyond that value.

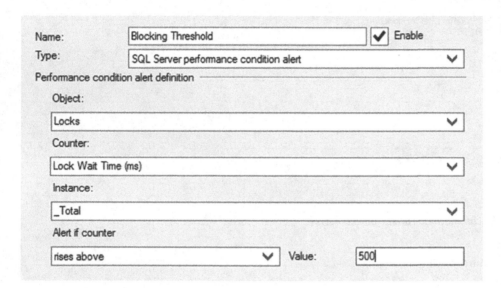

Figure 20-18. *Entering the alert name and other details*

1. On the Response page, define the response you think appropriate, such as alerting an operator.

2. Return to the new alert's Properties dialog box by clicking OK.

3. On the Response page, enter the remaining information shown in Figure 20-19.

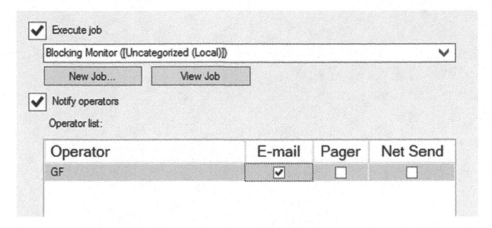

Figure 20-19. *Entering the actions to be performed when the alert is triggered*

 4. The Blocking Analysis job is selected to automatically collect the blocking information.

 5. Once you've finished entering all the information, click OK to create the SQL Server alert. The SQL Server alert will be created in the enabled state to perform the intended tasks.

 6. Ensure that the SQL Server Agent is running.

Together, the SQL Server alert and the job will automate the blocking detection and the information collection process. This automatic collection of the blocking information will ensure that a good amount of the blocking information will be available whenever the system gets into a massive blocking state.

Summary

Even though blocking is inevitable and is in fact essential to maintain isolation among transactions, it can sometimes adversely affect database concurrency. In a multiuser database application, you must minimize blocking among concurrent transactions.

SQL Server provides different techniques to avoid/reduce blocking, and a database application should take advantage of these techniques to scale linearly as the number of database users increases. When an application faces a high degree of blocking, you can collect the relevant blocking information using various tools to understand the root cause of the blocking. The next step is to use an appropriate technique to either avoid or reduce blocking.

Blocking can not only hurt concurrency but lead to an abrupt termination of a database request in the case of mutual blocking between processes or even within a process. We will cover this event, known as a *deadlock*, in the next chapter.

CHAPTER 21

∎ ∎ ∎

Causes and Solutions for Deadlocks

In the preceding chapter, I discussed how blocking works. Blocking is the primary cause of poor performance. It can lead to a special situation referred to as a *deadlock*, which in turn means that deadlocks are fundamentally a performance problem. When a deadlock occurs between two or more transactions, SQL Server allows one transaction to complete and terminates the other transaction, rolling back the transaction. SQL Server then returns an error to the corresponding application, notifying the user that he has been chosen as a deadlock victim. This leaves the application with only two options: resubmit the transaction or apologize to the end user. To successfully complete a transaction and avoid the apologies, it is important to understand what might cause a deadlock and the ways to handle a deadlock.

In this chapter, I cover the following topics:

- Deadlock fundamentals

- Error handling to catch a deadlock

- Ways to analyze the cause of a deadlock

- Techniques to resolve a deadlock

Deadlock Fundamentals

A *deadlock* is a special blocking scenario in which two processes get blocked by each other. Each process, while holding its own resources, attempts to access a resource that is locked by the other process. This will lead to a blocking scenario known as a *deadly embrace,* as illustrated in Figure 21-1.

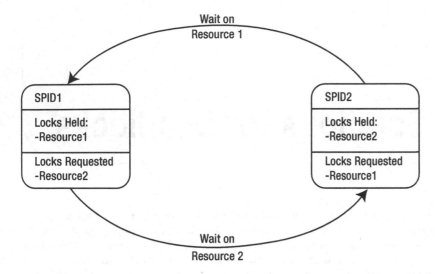

Figure 21-1. *A deadlock scenario*

Deadlocks also frequently occur when two processes attempt to escalate their locking mechanisms on the same resource. In this case, each of the two processes has a shared lock on a resource, such as an RID, and each attempts to promote the lock from shared to exclusive; however, neither can do so until the other releases its shared lock. This too leads to one of the processes being chosen as a deadlock victim.

Finally, it is possible for a single process to get a deadlock during parallel operations. During parallel operations, it's possible for a thread to be holding a lock on one resource, A, while waiting for another resource, B; at the same time, another thread can have a lock on B while waiting for A. This is as much a deadlock situation as when multiple processes are involved, but instead involving multiple threads from one process. This is a rare event, but it is possible.

Deadlocks are an especially nasty type of blocking because a deadlock cannot resolve on its own, even if given an unlimited period of time. A deadlock requires an external process to break the circular blocking.

SQL Server has a deadlock detection routine, called a *lock monitor*, that regularly checks for the presence of deadlocks in SQL Server. Once a deadlock condition is detected, SQL Server selects one of the sessions participating in the deadlock as a *victim* to break the circular blocking. The victim is usually the process with the lowest estimated cost since this implies that process will be the easiest one for SQL Server to roll back. This operation involves withdrawing all the resources held by the victim session. SQL Server does so by rolling back the uncommitted transaction of the session picked as a victim.

Choosing the Deadlock Victim

SQL Server determines the session to be a deadlock victim by evaluating the cost of undoing the transaction of the participating sessions, and it selects the one with the least estimated cost. You can exercise some control over the session to be chosen as a victim by setting the deadlock priority of its connection to LOW.

```
SET DEADLOCK_PRIORITY LOW;
```

This steers SQL Server toward choosing this particular session as a victim in the event of a deadlock. You can reset the deadlock priority of the connection to its normal value by executing the following SET statement:

```
SET DEADLOCK_PRIORITY NORMAL;
```

The SET statement allows you to mark a session as a HIGH deadlock priority, too. This won't prevent deadlocks on a given session, but it will reduce the likelihood of a given session being picked as the victim. You can even set the priority level to a number value from –10 for the lowest priority or to 10 for the highest.

■ **Caution**   Setting the deadlock priority is not something that should be applied promiscuously. You could accidently set the priority on a report that causes mission-critical processes to be chosen as a victim. Careful testing is necessary with this setting.

In the event of a tie, one of the processes is chosen as a victim and rolled back as if it had the least cost. Some processes are invulnerable to being picked as a deadlock victim. These processes are marked as such and will never be chosen as a deadlock victim. The most common example that I've seen occurs when processes are already involved in a rollback.

Using Error Handling to Catch a Deadlock

When SQL Server chooses a session as a victim, it raises an error with the error number. You can use the TRY/CATCH construct within T-SQL to handle the error. SQL Server ensures the consistency of the database by automatically rolling back the transaction of the victim session. The rollback ensures that the session is returned to the same state it was in before the start of its transaction. On determining a deadlock situation in the error handler, it is possible to attempt to restart the transaction within T-SQL a number of times before returning the error to the application.

Take the following T-SQL statement as an example of one method for handling a deadlock error:

```
DECLARE @retry AS TINYINT = 1,
    @retrymax AS TINYINT = 2,
    @retrycount AS TINYINT = 0;
WHILE @retry = 1
    AND @retrycount <= @retrymax
    BEGIN
        SET @retry = 0;

        BEGIN TRY
            UPDATE   HumanResources.Employee
            SET      LoginID = '54321'
            WHERE    BusinessEntityID = 100;
        END TRY
        BEGIN CATCH
            IF (ERROR_NUMBER() = 1205)
                BEGIN
                    SET @retrycount = @retrycount + 1;
                    SET @retry = 1;
                END
        END CATCH
    END
```

The TRY/CATCH methodology allows you to capture errors. You can then check the error number using the ERROR_NUMBER() function to determine whether you have a deadlock. Once a deadlock is established, it's possible to try restarting the transaction a set number of times—two, in this case. Using error trapping will help your application deal with intermittent or occasional deadlocks, but the best approach is to analyze the cause of the deadlock and resolve it, if possible.

Deadlock Analysis

You can sometimes prevent a deadlock from happening by analyzing the causes. You need the following information to do this:

- The sessions participating in the deadlock
- The resources involved in the deadlock
- The queries executed by the sessions

Collecting Deadlock Information

You have four ways to collect the deadlock information.

- Use Extended Events
- Set trace flag 1222
- Set trace flag 1204
- Use trace events

Trace flags are used to customize certain SQL Server behavior such as, in this case, generating the deadlock information. But, they're an older way to capture this information. Within SQL Server, on every instance since 2008, there is an Extended Events session called system_health. This session runs automatically, and one of the events it gathers by default is the deadlock graph. This is the easiest way to get immediate access to deadlock information without having to modify your server in any way.

However, system_health is only good for spot checks. And since it uses the ring_buffer to capture data, unless you're looking at it immediately after experiencing a deadlock, you may find that the information is missing. If you need to gather information for longer periods of time and ensure that you capture as many events as possible, Extended Events provides several ways to gather the deadlock information. This is probably the best method you can apply to your server for collecting deadlock information. You can use these options:

- Lock_deadlock: Displays basic information about a deadlock occurrence
- Lock_deadlock_chain: Captures information from each participant in a deadlock
- Xml_deadlock_report: Displays an XML deadlock graph with the cause of the deadlock

The deadlock graph generates XML output. After Extended Events captures the deadlock event, you can view the deadlock graph within SSMS either through the event viewer or by opening the XML file if you output your event results there. While similar information is displayed in all three events, for basic deadlock information, the easiest to understand is the xml_deadlock_report. When monitoring for deadlocks, I recommend also capturing the lock_deadlock_chain so that you have more detailed information about the individual sessions involved in the deadlock if you need it.

You can open the deadlock graph in Management Studio. You can search the XML, but the deadlock graph generated from the XML works almost like an execution plan for deadlocks, as shown in Figure 21-2.

Figure 21-2. *A deadlock graph as displayed in the Profiler*

I'll show you how to use this in the "Analyzing the Deadlock" section later in this chapter.

The two trace flags that generate deadlock information can be used individually or together to generate different sets of information. Usually people will prefer to run one or the other because they write a lot of information into the error log of SQL Server. The trace flags write the information gathered into the log file on the server where the deadlock event occurred. Trace flag 1222 provides the most detailed information on the deadlock.

Trace flag 1204 provides detailed deadlock information that helps you analyze the cause of a deadlock. It sorts the information by each of the nodes involved in the deadlock. Trace flag 1222 also provides detailed deadlock information, but it breaks the information down differently. Trace flag 1222 sorts the information by resource and processes, and it provides even more information. Both sets of data will be discussed in the "Analyzing the Deadlock" section.

The DBCC TRACEON statement is used to turn on (or enable) the trace flags. A trace flag remains enabled until it is disabled using the DBCC TRACEOFF statement. If the server is restarted, this trace flag will be cleared. You can determine the status of a trace flag using the DBCC TRACESTATUS statement. Setting both of the deadlock trace flags looks like this:

```
DBCC TRACEON (1222, -1);
DBCC TRACEON (1204, -1);
```

To ensure that the trace flags are always set, it is possible to make them part of the SQL Server startup in the SQL Server Configuration Manager by following these steps:

1. Open the Properties dialog box of the instance of SQL Server.

2. Switch to the Startup Parameters tab of the Properties dialog box, as shown in Figure 21-3.

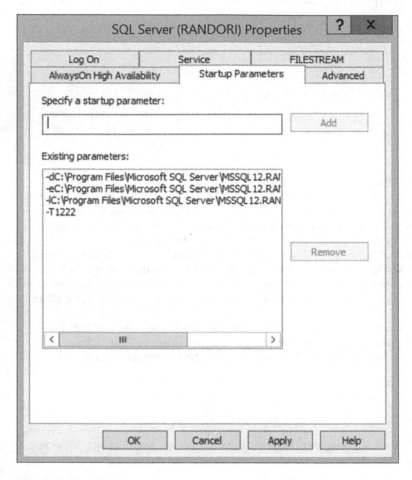

Figure 21-3. A SQL Server instance's Properties dialog box showing the Startup Parameters tab

3. Type **-T1222** in the "Specify a startup parameter" text box, and click Add to add trace flag 1222.

4. Click the OK button to close all the dialog boxes.

These trace flag settings will be in effect after you restart your SQL Server instance.

Analyzing the Deadlock

To analyze the cause of a deadlock, let's consider a straightforward little example. First, make sure you've turned on the deadlock trace flag 1222 and created an Extended Events session that uses the xml_deadlock_report event. I'm using both methods for demonstration purposes. You would normally need only one method to capture deadlock information.

In one connection, execute this script:

```
BEGIN TRAN
UPDATE  Purchasing.PurchaseOrderHeader
SET     Freight = Freight * 0.9 -- 10% discount on shipping
WHERE   PurchaseOrderID = 1255;
```

In a second connection, execute this script:

```
BEGIN TRANSACTION
UPDATE  Purchasing.PurchaseOrderDetail
SET     OrderQty = 4
WHERE   ProductID = 448
        AND PurchaseOrderID = 1255;
```

Each of these scripts opens a transaction and manipulates data, but neither commits or rolls back the transaction. Switch back to the first transaction and run this additional query:

```
UPDATE  Purchasing.PurchaseOrderDetail
SET     OrderQty = 2
WHERE   ProductID = 448
        AND PurchaseOrderID = 1255;
```

Unfortunately, after possibly a few seconds, the first connection faces a deadlock.

```
Msg 1205, Level 13, State 51, Line 1
Transaction (Process ID 52) was deadlocked on lock resources with another process and has been
chosen as the deadlock victim. Rerun the transaction.
```

Any idea what's wrong here?

Let's analyze the deadlock by first examining the deadlock graph collected through the trace event. There is a separate tab in the Event explorer window for the xml_deadlock_report event. Opening that tab will show you the deadlock graph (see Figure 21-4).

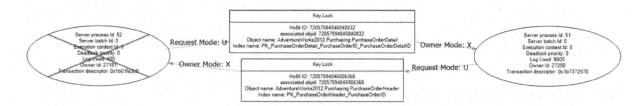

Figure 21-4. *A deadlock graph displayed in the Profiler tool*

From the deadlock graph displayed in Figure 21-4, it's fairly clear that two processes were involved: session 51 and session 52. Session 52, the one with the big *X* crossing it out (blue on the deadlock graph screen), was chosen as the deadlock victim. Two different keys were in question. The top key was owned by session 51, as indicated by the arrow pointing to the session object, named Owner Mode, and marked with an X for exclusive. Session 52 was attempting to request the same key for an update. The other key was owned by session 54 with session 51 requesting an update, indicated by the U. You can see the exact HoBt ID, object ID, object name, and index name for the objects in question for the deadlock. For a classic, simple deadlock like this, you have most of the information you need. The last piece would be the queries running from each process. These would need to be captured using a different extended event.

This visual representation of the deadlock can do the job. However, you may need to drill down into the underlying XML to really understand exactly where deadlocks occurred, what processes caused them, and which objects were involved. If you open that XML file directly from the extended event value, you can find a lot more information available than the simple set displayed for you in the graphical deadlock graph. Take a look at Figure 21-5.

```
<deadlock>
  <victim-list>
    <victimProcess id="process1ae136108" />
  </victim-list>
  <process-list>
    <process id="process1ae136108" taskpriority="0" logused="400" waitresource="KEY: 5:720575940468408
      <executionStack>
        <frame procname="adhoc" line="1" stmtend="240" sqlhandle="0x02000000d0c7f31a30fb1ad425c34357fe8e
unknown        </frame>
        <frame procname="adhoc" line="1" stmtend="240" sqlhandle="0x0200000078e11002bcaae2b31f94099f8a7a
unknown        </frame>
      </executionStack>
      <inputbuf>
UPDATE    Purchasing.PurchaseOrderDetail
SET       OrderQty = 2
WHERE     ProductID = 448
          AND PurchaseOrderID = 1255 ;    </inputbuf>
  </process>
    <process id="process1ae137088" taskpriority="0" logused="9800" waitresource="KEY: 5:72057594046906
      <executionStack>
        <frame procname="AdventureWorks2012.Purchasing.uPurchaseOrderDetail" line="39" stmtstart="2732"
UPDATE [Purchasing].[PurchaseOrderHeader]
              SET [Purchasing].[PurchaseOrderHeader].[SubTotal] =
                  (SELECT SUM([Purchasing].[PurchaseOrderDetail].[LineTotal])
                     FROM [Purchasing].[PurchaseOrderDetail]
                    WHERE [Purchasing].[PurchaseOrderHeader].[PurchaseOrderID]
                       = [Purchasing].[PurchaseOrderDetail].[PurchaseOrderID])
              WHERE [Purchasing].[PurchaseOrderHeader].[PurchaseOrderID]
                 IN (SELECT inserted.[PurchaseOrderID] FROM inserted     </frame>
        <frame procname="adhoc" line="2" stmtstart="24" stmtend="264" sqlhandle="0x02000000d0c7f31a30fb1
unknown        </frame>
        <frame procname="adhoc" line="2" stmtstart="24" stmtend="264" sqlhandle="0x02000000d2e9d200d0704
unknown        </frame>
      </executionStack>
```

Figure 21-5. *The XML information that defines the deadlock graph*

If you look through this, you can see some of the information on display in the deadlock graph, but you also see a whole lot more. For example, part of this deadlock actually involves code that I did not write or execute as part of the example. There's a trigger on the table called uPurchaseOrderDetail. You can also see the code I used to generate the deadlock. All this information can help you identify exactly which pieces of code lead to the deadlock. You also get information such as the sqlhandle, which you can then use in combination with DMOs to pull statements and execution plans out of cache. Because the plan is created before the query is run, it will be available for you even for the queries that were chosen as the deadlock victim.

It's worth taking some time to explore this XML in a little more detail. Table 21-1 shows some of the elements from the extended event and the information it represents.

Table 21-1. *XML Deadlock Graph Data*

Entry in Log	Description
`<deadlock>` `<victim-list>`	The beginning of the deadlock information. It starts laying out the victim processes.
`<victimProcess id="processf4ced868" />`	Physical memory address of the process picked to be the deadlock victim.
`<process-list>`	Processes that define the deadlock victim. There may be more than one.
`<process id="processf4ced868" taskpriority="0" logused="400" waitresource="KEY: 9:72057594046775296 (4ab5f0d47ad5)" waittime="1718" ownerId="20008" transactionname="user_transaction" lasttranstarted="2012-01-18T17:41:50.553" XDES="0xfd04d078" lockMode="U" schedulerid="2" kpid="4404" status="suspended" spid="52" sbid="0" ecid="0" priority="0" trancount="2" lastbatchstarted="2012-01-18T17:42:12.090" lastbatchcompleted="2012-01-18T17:42:12.087" lastattention="1900-01-01T00:00:00.087" clientapp="Microsoft SQL Server Management Studio - Query" hostname="DOJO" hostpid="2376" loginname="NEVERNEVER\grant" isolationlevel="read committed (2)" xactid="20008" currentdb="9" lockTimeout="4294967295" clientoption1="671096864" clientoption2="128056">`	All the information about the session picked as the deadlock victim. Note the highlighted isolation level, which is a key for helping identify the root cause of a deadlock.
`<executionStack>`	T-SQL that was being executed.
`<frame procname="adhoc" line="1" stmtstart="44" sqlhandle="0x02000000e3586a2a82447 915dba3de497a09b2eed9643a840000 00000000000000000000 0000000000000000">` `update Purchasing . PurchaseOrderDetail set OrderQty = @0 where ProductID = @1 and PurchaseOrderID = @2 </frame>`	The type of query being executed, in this case ad hoc. Note the sqlhandle. You can use this with sys.dm_exec_query_plan to see the execution plan. This is followed by the T-SQL statement.

`<frame procname="adhoc" line="1" sqlhandle="0x020000001bdbe9296e 67741f7b4604aee8b9093427da296a00 00000000000000000000 0000000000000000">`
`UPDATE   Purchasing.PurchaseOrderDetail`
`SET      OrderQty = 4`
`WHERE    ProductID = 448`
`AND PurchaseOrderID = 1255 ;   </frame>`
	The next statement in the batch.

`UPDATE Purchasing.PurchaseOrderDetail SET OrderQty = 4 WHERE   ProductID = 448 AND PurchaseOrderID = 1255 ;`	The query with values.

(continued)

Table 21-1. (*continued*)

Entry in Log	Description

`<inputbuf>`
`UPDATE  Purchasing.PurchaseOrderDetail`
`SET     OrderQty = 4`
`WHERE   ProductID = 448`
`AND PurchaseOrderID = 1255 ;   </inputbuf>`
	The statements for the current batch. This is followed by the query showing the precise values used by the statement defined earlier. They were substituted as parameters as simple parameterization.

`<process id="processf4ecf498" taskpriority="0"`
`logused="10896" waitresource="KEY:`
`9:72057594046840832 (4bc08edebc6b)" waittime="7851"`
`ownerId="21222" transactionname="user_transaction"`
`lasttranstarted="2012-01-18T17:42:05.957"`
`XDES="0xf682cd28" lockMode="U" schedulerid="2"`
`kpid="4944" status="suspended" spid="55"`
`sbid="0" ecid="0" priority="0" trancount="2"`
`lastbatchstarted="2012-01-18T17:42:05.957"`
`lastbatchcompleted="2012-01-18T17:42:05.957"`
`lastattention="1900-01-01T00:00:00.957"`
`clientapp="Microsoft SQL Server Management`
`Studio - Query" hostname="DOJO" hostpid="2376"`
`loginname="NEVERNEVER\grant" isolationlevel="read`
`committed (2)" xactid="21222" currentdb="9"`
`lockTimeout="4294967295" clientoption1="673327200"`
`clientoption2="390200">`
	The next process in the deadlock. In this case, this is the process that succeeded. Sometimes you can see a different order in the output of the graph.

`<executionStack>`
`<frame procname="`**`AdventureWorks2008R2.Purchasing.`**
`uPurchaseOrderDetail``" line="39" stmtstart="2732"`
`stmtend="3864" sqlhandle="0x0300090076146e6c1`
`6a11f01c69d00000000000000000000 000000000000000000000`
`0000000000000000000">`
`UPDATE [Purchasing].[PurchaseOrderHeader]`
`SET [Purchasing].[PurchaseOrderHeader].[SubTotal] =`
`(SELECT SUM([Purchasing].[PurchaseOrderDetail].`
`[LineTotal])`
`FROM [Purchasing].[PurchaseOrderDetail]`
`WHERE [Purchasing].[PurchaseOrderHeader].`
`[PurchaseOrderID]`
`= [Purchasing].[PurchaseOrderDetail].`
`[PurchaseOrderID])`
`WHERE [Purchasing].[PurchaseOrderHeader].`
`[PurchaseOrderID]`
`IN (SELECT inserted.[PurchaseOrderID] FROM`
`inserted);    </frame>`
	Note the procname value, AdventureWorks2008R2. Purchasing.uPurchaseOrderDetail. This is a trigger fired and running the following code.

(*continued*)

Table 21-1. (*continued*)

Entry in Log	Description

`<frame procname="adhoc" line="2" stmtstart="44" sqlhandle="0x02000000e3586a2a82 447915dba3de497a09b2eed9643a8 4000000000000000000000 00000000000000000">`
 	
`update Purchasing . PurchaseOrderDetail set OrderQty = @0 where ProductID = @1 and PurchaseOrderID = @2 </frame>`
	The ad hoc code defined in the listings being run. You can see the autoparameterization at work on it again.

`<frame procname="adhoc" line="2" stmtstart="38" sqlhandle="0x02000000178f4e2824eef6 8b5abf0096b085df45a8cbe9d9000000000 000000000000000 000000000000000">`
 	
`UPDATE  Purchasing.PurchaseOrderDetail`
`SET     OrderQty = 2`
`WHERE   ProductID = 448`
`AND PurchaseOrderID = 1255 ;    </frame>`
	The definition of the T-SQL.

`<inputbuf>`
`BEGIN TRANSACTION`
`UPDATE  Purchasing.PurchaseOrderDetail`
`SET     OrderQty = 2`
`WHERE   ProductID = 448`
`AND PurchaseOrderID = 1255 ;    </inputbuf>`
	T-SQL, including the actual values. This would be the cause of firing the trigger.

`</process-list>`
`<resource-list>`
`<keylock hobtid="72057594046775296" dbid="9" objectname="AdventureWorks2008R2.Purchasing. PurchaseOrderDetail" indexname="1" id="lockf98b8c00" mode="X" associatedObjectId="72057594046775296">`
`<owner-list>`
`<owner id="processf4ecf498" mode="X" />`
`</owner-list>`
`<waiter-list>`
`<waiter id="processf4ced868" mode="U" requestType="wait" />`
`</waiter-list>`
`</keylock>`
	The objects that caused the conflict. Within this is the definition of the primary key from the `Purchasing.PurchaseOrderDetail` table. You can see which process from the earlier code owned which resource. You can also see the information defining the processes that were waiting. This is everything you need to discern where the issue exists.

(*continued*)

Table 21-1. (*continued*)

Entry in Log	Description
<keylock hobtid="72057594046840832" dbid="9" objectname="AdventureWorks2008R2.Purchasing. PurchaseOrderHeader" indexname="1" id="lockf98b8800" mode="X" associatedObjectId="72057594046840832"> <owner-list> <owner id="processf4ced868" mode="X" /> </owner-list> <waiter-list> <waiter id="processf4ecf498" mode="U" requestType="wait" /> </waiter-list> </keylock> </resource-list> </deadlock>	

This information is a bit more difficult to read through than the clean set of data provided by the graphical deadlock graph. However, it is a similar set of information, just more detailed. You can see, highlighted in bold near the bottom, the definition of one of the keys associated with the deadlock. You can also see, just before it, that the text of the execution plans is available through extended event XML output, unlike the deadlock graph. In this case, you are much more likely to have everything you need to isolate the cause of the deadlock.

The information gathered by trace flag 1222 is almost identical to the XML data in every regard. The main differences are the formatting and location. The output from 1222 is located in the SQL Server error log, and it's in text format instead of nice, clean XML. The information collected by trace flag 1204 is completely different from either of the other two sets of data and doesn't provide nearly as much detail. Trace flag 1204 is also much more difficult to interpret. For all these reasons, I suggest you stick to using Extended Events if you can—or trace flag 1222 if you can't—to capture deadlock data. You also have the system_health session that captures a number of events by default, including deadlocks. It's a great resource if you are unprepared for capturing this information. Just remember that it keeps only four 5MB files online. As these fill, the data in the oldest file is lost. Depending on the number of transactions in your system and the number of deadlocks or other events that could fill these files, you may have only recent data available. Further, as mentioned earlier, since the system_health session uses the ring buffer to capture events, you can expect substantial event loss, so your deadlock events could go missing.

This example demonstrated a classic circular reference. Although not immediately obvious, the deadlock was caused by a trigger on the Purchasing.PurchaseOrderDetail table. When Quantity is updated on the Purchasing.PurchaseOrderDetail table, it attempts to update the Purchasing.PurchaseOrderHeader table. When the first two queries are run, each within an open transaction, it's just a blocking situation. The second query is waiting on the first to clear so that it can also update the Purchasing.PurchaseOrderHeader table. But when the third query (that is, the second within the first transaction) is introduced, a circular reference is created. The only way to resolve it is to kill one of the processes.

Before proceeding, be sure to roll back any open transactions.

Here's the obvious question at this stage: Can you avoid this deadlock? If the answer is "yes," then how?

Avoiding Deadlocks

The methods for avoiding a deadlock scenario depend upon the nature of the deadlock. The following are some of the techniques you can use to avoid a deadlock:

- Access resources in the same physical order.

- Decrease the number of resources accessed.

- Minimize lock contention.

Accessing Resources in the Same Physical Order

One of the most commonly adopted techniques for avoiding a deadlock is to ensure that every transaction accesses the resources in the same physical order. For instance, suppose that two transactions need to access two resources. If each transaction accesses the resources in the same physical order, then the first transaction will successfully acquire locks on the resources without being blocked by the second transaction. The second transaction will be blocked by the first while trying to acquire a lock on the first resource. This will cause a typical blocking scenario without leading to a circular blocking and a deadlock.

If the resources are not accessed in the same physical order (as demonstrated in the earlier deadlock analysis example), this can cause a circular blocking between the two transactions.

- Transaction 1:

- Access Resource 1

- Access Resource 2

- Transaction 2:

- Access Resource 2

- Access Resource 1

In the current deadlock scenario, the following resources are involved in the deadlock:

- Resource 1, hobtid=72057594046578688: This is the index row within index PK_ PurchaseOrderDetail_PurchaseOrderId_PurchaseOrderDetailId on the Purchasing.PurchaseOrderDetail table.

- Resource 2, hobtid=72057594046644224: This is the row within clustered index PK_PurchaseOrderHeader_PurchaseOrderId on the Purchasing.PurchaseOrderHeader table.

Both sessions attempt to access the resource; unfortunately, the order in which they access the key is different.

It's common with some of the generated code produced by tools such as nHibernate and Entity Framework to see objects being referenced in a different order in different queries. You'll have to work with your development team to see that type of issue eliminated within the generated code.

Decreasing the Number of Resources Accessed

A deadlock involves at least two resources. A session holds the first resource and then requests the second resource. The other session holds the second resource and requests the first resource. If you can prevent the sessions (or at least one of them) from accessing one of the resources involved in the deadlock, then you can prevent the deadlock. You can achieve this by redesigning the application, which is a solution highly resisted by developers late in the project. However, you can consider using the following features of SQL Server without changing the application design:

- Convert a nonclustered index to a clustered index.

- Use a covering index for a SELECT statement.

Convert a Nonclustered Index to a Clustered Index

As you know, the leaf pages of a nonclustered index are separate from the data pages of the heap or the clustered index. Therefore, a nonclustered index takes two locks: one for the base (either the cluster or the heap) and one for the nonclustered index. However, in the case of a clustered index, the leaf pages of the index and the data pages of the table are the same; it requires one lock, and that one lock protects both the clustered index and the table because the leaf pages and the data pages are the same. This decreases the number of resources to be accessed by the same query, compared to a nonclustered index. But, it is completely dependent on this being an appropriate clustered index. There's nothing magical about the clustered index that simply applying it to any column would help. You still need to assess whether it's appropriate.

Use a Covering Index for a SELECT Statement

You can also use a covering index to decrease the number of resources accessed by a SELECT statement. Since a SELECT statement can get everything from the covering index itself, it doesn't need to access the base table. Otherwise, the SELECT statement needs to access both the index and the base table to retrieve all the required column values. Using a covering index stops the SELECT statement from accessing the base table, leaving the base table free to be locked by another session.

Minimizing Lock Contention

You can also resolve a deadlock by avoiding the lock request on one of the contended resources. You can do this when the resource is accessed only for reading data. Modifying a resource will always acquire an exclusive (X) lock on the resource to maintain the consistency of the resource; therefore, in a deadlock situation, identify the resource accesses that are read-only and try to avoid their corresponding lock requests by using the dirty read feature, if possible. You can use the following techniques to avoid the lock request on a contended resource:

- Implement row versioning.

- Decrease the isolation level.

- Use locking hints.

Implement Row Versioning

Instead of attempting to prevent access to resources using a more stringent locking scheme, you could implement row versioning through the READ_COMMITTED_SNAPSHOT isolation level or through the SNAPSHOT isolation level. The row versioning isolation levels are used to reduce blocking, as outlined in Chapter 20. Because they reduce blocking, which is the root cause of deadlocks, they can also help with deadlocks. By introducing READ_COMMITTED_SNAPSHOT with the following T-SQL, you can have a version of the rows available in tempdb, thus potentially eliminating the contention caused by the lock in the preceding deadlock scenario:

```
ALTER DATABASE AdventureWorks2012
SET READ_COMMITTED_SNAPSHOT ON;
```

This will allow any necessary reads without causing lock contention since the reads are on a different version of the data. There is overhead associated with row versioning, especially in tempdb and when marshaling data from multiple resources instead of just the table or indexes used in the query. But that trade-off of increased tempdb overhead versus the benefit of reduced deadlocking and increased concurrency may be worth the cost.

Decrease the Isolation Level

Sometimes the (S) lock requested by a SELECT statement contributes to the formation of circular blocking. You can avoid this type of circular blocking by reducing the isolation level of the transaction containing the SELECT statement to READ UNCOMMITTED. This will allow the SELECT statement to read the data without requesting an (S) lock and thereby avoid the circular blocking. However, reading uncommitted data carries with it a serious issue by returning bad data to the client. You need to be in dire straits to consider this as a method of eliminating your deadlocks.

Also check to see whether the connections are setting themselves to be SERIALIZABLE. Sometimes online connection string generators will include this option, and developers will use it completely by accident. MSDTC will use serializable by default, but it can be changed.

Use Locking Hints

I absolutely do not recommend this approach. However, you can potentially resolve the deadlock presented in the preceding technique using the following locking hints:

- NOLOCK

- READUNCOMMITTED

Like the READ UNCOMMITTED isolation level, the NOLOCK or READUNCOMMITTED locking hint will avoid the (S) locks requested by a given session, thereby preventing the formation of circular blocking.

The effect of the locking hint is at a query level and is limited to the table (and its indexes) on which it is applied. The NOLOCK and READUNCOMMITTED locking hints are allowed only in SELECT statements and the data selection part of the INSERT, DELETE, and UPDATE statements.

The resolution techniques of minimizing lock contention introduce the side effect of a dirty read, which may not be acceptable in every transaction. A dirty read can involve missing rows or extra rows because of page splits and rearranging pages. Therefore, use these resolution techniques only in situations in which a low quality of data is acceptable.

Summary

As you learned in this chapter, a deadlock is the result of conflicting blocking between processes and is reported to an application with the error number 1205. You can analyze the cause of a deadlock by collecting the deadlock information using various resources, but the extended event Xml_deadlock_report is probably the best.

You can use a number of techniques to avoid a deadlock; which technique is applicable depends upon the type of queries executed by the participating sessions, the locks held and requested on the involved resources, and the business rules governing the degree of isolation required. Generally, you can resolve a deadlock by reconfiguring the indexes and the transaction isolation levels. However, at times you may need to redesign the application or automatically reexecute the transaction on a deadlock. Just remember, at its core, deadlocks are a performance problem and anything you can do to make the queries run faster will help to mitigate, if not eliminate, deadlocks in your queries.

In the next chapter, I cover the performance aspects of cursors and how to optimize the cost overhead of using cursors.

CHAPTER 22

■ ■ ■

Row-by-Row Processing

It is common to find database applications that use cursors to process one row at a time. Developers tend to think about processing data in a row-by-row fashion. Oracle even uses something called *cursors* as a high-speed data access mechanism. But cursors in SQL Server are different. Because data manipulation through a cursor in SQL Server incurs significant additional overhead, database applications should avoid using cursors. T-SQL and SQL Server are designed to work best with sets of data, not one row at a time. Jeff Moden famously termed this type of processing RBAR (pronounced, ree-bar), meaning row by agonizing row. However, if a cursor must be used, then use a cursor with the least cost.

In this chapter, I cover the following topics:

- The fundamentals of cursors

- A cost analysis of different characteristics of cursors

- The benefits and drawbacks of a default result set over cursors

- Recommendations to minimize the cost overhead of cursors

Cursor Fundamentals

When a query is executed by an application, SQL Server returns a set of data consisting of rows. Generally, applications can't process multiple rows together; instead, they process one row at a time by walking through the result set returned by SQL Server. This functionality is provided by a *cursor*, which is a mechanism to work with one row at a time out of a multirow result set.

T-SQL cursor processing usually involves the following steps:

1. Declare the cursor to associate it with a SELECT statement and define the characteristics of the cursor.

2. Open the cursor to access the result set returned by the SELECT statement.

3. Retrieve a row from the cursor. Optionally, modify the row through the cursor.

4. Once all the rows in the result set are processed, close the cursor and release the resources assigned to the cursor.

You can create cursors using T-SQL statements or the data access layers used to connect to SQL Server. Cursors created using data access layers are commonly referred to as *client* cursors. Cursors written in T-SQL are referred to as *server* cursors. The following is an example of a server cursor processing of query results from a table:

```
--Associate a SELECT statement to a cursor and define the
--cursor's characteristics
USE AdventureWorks2012;
GO
SET NOCOUNT ON
DECLARE MyCursor CURSOR /*<cursor characteristics>*/
FOR
SELECT   adt.AddressTypeID,
         adt.Name,
         adt.ModifiedDate
FROM     Person.AddressType adt;

--Open the cursor to access the result set returned by the
--SELECT statement
OPEN MyCursor;

--Retrieve one row at a time from the result set returned by
--the SELECT statement
DECLARE @AddressTypeId INT,
    @Name VARCHAR(50),
    @ModifiedDate DATETIME;

FETCH NEXT FROM MyCursor INTO @AddressTypeId,@Name,@ModifiedDate;

WHILE @@FETCH_STATUS = 0
    BEGIN
        PRINT 'NAME =   ' + @Name;

--Optionally, modify the row through the cursor
        UPDATE   Person.AddressType
        SET      Name = Name + 'z'
        WHERE CURRENT OF MyCursor;

        FETCH NEXT FROM MyCursor
            INTO @AddressTypeId,@Name,@ModifiedDate;
    END

--Close the cursor and release all resources assigned to the
--cursor
CLOSE MyCursor;
DEALLOCATE MyCursor;
```

Part of the overhead of the cursor depends on the cursor characteristics. The characteristics of the cursors provided by SQL Server and the data access layers can be broadly classified into three categories.

- *Cursor location:* Defines the location of the cursor creation

- *Cursor concurrency:* Defines the degree of isolation and synchronization of a cursor with the underlying content

- *Cursor type:* Defines the specific characteristics of a cursor

Before looking at the costs of cursors, I'll take a few pages to introduce the various characteristics of cursors. You can undo the changes to the Person.AddressType table with this query:

```
UPDATE   Person.AddressType
SET      [Name] = LEFT([Name], LEN([Name]) - 1);
```

Cursor Location

Based on the location of its creation, a cursor can be classified into one of two categories.

- Client-side cursors

- Server-side cursors

The T-SQL cursors are always created on SQL Server. However, the database API cursors can be created on either the client or server side.

Client-Side Cursors

As its name signifies, a *client-side cursor is* created on the machine running the application, whether the app is a service, a data access layer, or the front end for the user. It has the following characteristics:

- It is created on the client machine.

- The cursor metadata is maintained on the client machine.

- It is created using the data access layers.

- It works against most of the data access layers (OLEDB providers and ODBC drivers).

- It can be a forward-only or static cursor.

■ **Note**   Cursor types, including forward-only and static cursor types, are described later in the chapter in the "Cursor Types" section.

Server-Side Cursors

A *server-side cursor* is created on the SQL Server machine. It has the following characteristics:

- It is created on the server machine.

- The cursor metadata is maintained on the server machine.

- It is created using either data access layers or T-SQL statements.

- A server-side cursor created using T-SQL statements is tightly integrated with SQL Server.

- It can be any type of cursor. (Cursor types are explained later in the chapter.)

■ **Note**   The cost comparison between client-side and server-side cursors is covered later in the chapter in the "Cost Comparison on Cursor Type" section.

Cursor Concurrency

Depending on the required degree of isolation and synchronization with the underlying content, cursors can be classified into the following concurrency models:

- *Read-only.* A nonupdatable cursor

- *Optimistic.* An updatable cursor that uses the optimistic concurrency model (no locks retained on the underlying data rows)

- *Scroll locks:* An updatable cursor that holds a lock on any data row to be updated

Read-Only

A read-only cursor is nonupdatable; no locks are held on the base tables. While fetching a cursor row, whether an (S) lock will be acquired on the underlying row depends upon the isolation level of the connection and any locking hints used in the SELECT statement for the cursor. However, once the row is fetched, by default the locks are released. The following T-SQL statement creates a read-only T-SQL cursor:

```
DECLARE MyCursor CURSOR READ_ONLY
FOR
SELECT  adt.Name
FROM    Person.AddressType AS adt
WHERE   adt.AddressTypeID = 1;
```

The lowest-level locking overhead makes the read-only type of cursor faster and safer. Just remember that you cannot manipulate data through the read-only cursor, which is the sacrifice you make for performance.

Optimistic

The optimistic with values concurrency model makes a cursor updatable. No locks are held on the underlying data. The factors governing whether an (S) lock will be acquired on the underlying row are the same as for a read-only cursor.

The optimistic concurrency model uses row versioning to determine whether a row has been modified since it was read into the cursor, instead of locking the row while it is read into the cursor. Version-based optimistic concurrency requires a ROWVERSION column (this was formerly a TIMESTAMP data type) in the underlying user table on which the cursor is created. The ROWVERSION data type is a binary number that indicates the relative sequence of modifications on a row. Each time a row with a ROWVERSION column is modified, SQL Server stores the current value of the global ROWVERSION value, @@DBTS, in the ROWVERSION column; it then increments the @@DBTS value.

Before applying a modification through the optimistic cursor, SQL Server determines whether the current ROWVERSION column value for the row matches the ROWVERSION column value for the row when it was read into the cursor. The underlying row is modified only if the ROWVERSION values match, indicating that the row hasn't been modified by another user in the meantime. Otherwise, an error is raised. In case of an error, first refresh the cursor with the updated data.

If the underlying table doesn't contain a ROWVERSION column, then the cursor defaults to value-based optimistic concurrency, which requires matching the current value of the row with the value when the row was read into the cursor. The version-based concurrency control is more efficient than the value-based concurrency control since it requires less processing to determine the modification of the underlying row. Therefore, for the best performance of a cursor with the optimistic concurrency model, ensure that the underlying table has a ROWVERSION column.

The following T-SQL statement creates an optimistic T-SQL cursor:

```
DECLARE MyCursor CURSOR OPTIMISTIC
FOR
SELECT  adt.Name
FROM    Person.AddressType AS adt
WHERE   adt.AddressTypeID = 1;
```

A cursor with scroll locks concurrency holds a (U) lock on the underlying row until another cursor row is fetched or the cursor is closed. This prevents other users from modifying the underlying row when the cursor fetches it. The scroll locks concurrency model makes the cursor updatable.

The following T-SQL statement creates a T-SQL cursor with the scroll locks concurrency model:

```
DECLARE MyCursor CURSOR SCROLL_LOCKS
FOR
SELECT  adt.Name
FROM    Person.AddressType AS adt
WHERE   adt.AddressTypeID = 1;
```

Since locks are held on a row being referenced (until another cursor row is fetched or the cursor is closed), it blocks all the other users trying to modify the row during that period. This hurts database concurrency.

Cursor Types

Cursors can be classified into the following four types:

- Forward-only cursors

- Static cursors

- Keyset-driven cursors

- Dynamic cursors

Let's take a closer look at these four types in the sections that follow.

Forward-Only Cursors

These are the characteristics of forward-only cursors:

- They operate directly on the base tables.

- Rows from the underlying tables are usually not retrieved until the cursor rows are fetched using the cursor FETCH operation. However, the database API forward-only cursor type, with the following additional characteristics, retrieves all the rows from the underlying table first:

- Client-side cursor location

- Server-side cursor location and read-only cursor concurrency.

- They support forward scrolling only (FETCH NEXT) through the cursor.

- They allow all changes (INSERT, UPDATE, and DELETE) through the cursor. Also, these cursors reflect all changes made to the underlying tables.

The forward-only characteristic is implemented differently by the database API cursors and the T-SQL cursor. The data access layers implement the forward-only cursor characteristic as one of the four previously listed cursor types. But the T-SQL cursor doesn't implement the forward-only cursor characteristic as a cursor type; rather, it implements it as a property that defines the scrollable behavior of the cursor. Thus, for a T-SQL cursor, the forward-only characteristic can be used to define the scrollable behavior of one of the remaining three cursor types.

A forward-only cursor with a read-only property can be created using a fast forward statement. The T-SQL syntax provides a specific cursor type option, FAST_FORWARD, to create a fast-forward-only cursor. The nickname for the FAST_FORWARD cursor is the *fire hose* because it is the fastest way to move data through a cursor and because all the information flows one way. However, don't be surprised when the "firehose" is still not as fast as traditional set-based operations. The following T-SQL statement creates a fast-forward-only T-SQL cursor:

```
DECLARE MyCursor CURSOR FAST_FORWARD
FOR
SELECT  adt.Name
FROM    Person.AddressType AS adt
WHERE   adt.AddressTypeID = 1;
```

The FAST_FORWARD property specifies a forward-only, read-only cursor with performance optimizations enabled.

Static Cursors

These are the characteristics of static cursors:

- They create a snapshot of cursor results in the tempdb database when the cursor is opened. Thereafter, static cursors operate on the snapshot in the tempdb database.

- Data is retrieved from the underlying tables when the cursor is opened.

- Static cursors support all scrolling options: FETCH FIRST, FETCH NEXT, FETCH PRIOR, FETCH LAST, FETCH ABSOLUTE n, and FETCH RELATIVE n.

- Static cursors are always read-only; data modifications are not allowed through static cursors. Also, changes (INSERT, UPDATE, and DELETE) made to the underlying tables are not reflected in the cursor.

The following T-SQL statement creates a static T-SQL cursor:

```
DECLARE MyCursor CURSOR STATIC
FOR
SELECT  adt.Name
FROM    Person.AddressType AS adt
WHERE   adt.AddressTypeID = 1;
```

Some tests show that a static cursor can perform as well as—and sometimes faster than—a forward-only cursor. Be sure to test this behavior on your own system.

Keyset-Driven Cursors

These are the characteristics of keyset-driven cursors:

- Keyset cursors are controlled by a set of unique identifiers (or keys) known as a *keyset.* The keyset is built from a set of columns that uniquely identify the rows in the result set.

- These cursors create the keyset of rows in the tempdb database when the cursor is opened.

- Membership of rows in the cursor is limited to the keyset of rows created in the tempdb database when the cursor is opened.

- On fetching a cursor row, the database engine first looks at the keyset of rows in tempdb and then navigates to the corresponding data row in the underlying tables to retrieve the remaining columns.

- They support all scrolling options.

- Keyset cursors allow all changes through the cursor. An INSERT performed outside the cursor is not reflected in the cursor, since the membership of rows in the cursor is limited to the keyset of rows created in the tempdb database on opening the cursor. An INSERT through the cursor appears at the end of the cursor. A DELETE performed on the underlying tables raises an error when the cursor navigation reaches the deleted row. An UPDATE on the nonkeyset columns of the underlying tables is reflected in the cursor. An UPDATE on the keyset columns is treated like a DELETE of an old key value and the INSERT of a new key value. If a change disqualifies a row for membership or affects the order of a row, then the row does not disappear or move unless the cursor is closed and reopened.

The following T-SQL statement creates a keyset-driven T-SQL cursor:

```
DECLARE MyCursor CURSOR KEYSET
FOR
SELECT  adt.Name
FROM    Person.AddressType AS adt
WHERE   adt.AddressTypeID = 1;
```

Dynamic Cursors

These are the characteristics of dynamic cursors:

- Dynamic cursors operate directly on the base tables.

- The membership of rows in the cursor is not fixed, since they operate directly on the base tables.

- As with forward-only cursors, rows from the underlying tables are not retrieved until the cursor rows are fetched using a cursor FETCH operation.

- Dynamic cursors support all scrolling options except FETCH ABSOLUTE n, since the membership of rows in the cursor is not fixed.

- These cursors allow all changes through the cursor. Also, all changes made to the underlying tables are reflected in the cursor.

- Dynamic cursors don't support all properties and methods implemented by the database API cursors. Properties such as AbsolutePosition, Bookmark, and RecordCount, as well as methods such as clone and Resync, are not supported by dynamic cursors. Instead, they are supported by keyset-driven cursors.

The following T-SQL statement creates a dynamic T-SQL cursor:

```
DECLARE MyCursor CURSOR DYNAMIC
FOR
SELECT   adt.Name
FROM     Person.AddressType AS adt
WHERE    adt.AddressTypeID = 1;
```

The dynamic cursor is absolutely the slowest possible cursor to use in all situations. It takes more locks and holds them longer, which radically increases its poor performance. Take this into account when designing your system.

Cursor Cost Comparison

Now that you've seen the different cursor flavors, let's look at their costs. If you must use a cursor, you should always use the lightest-weight cursor that meets the requirements of your application. The cost comparisons among the different characteristics of the cursors are detailed next.

Cost Comparison on Cursor Location

The client-side and server-side cursors have their own cost benefits and overhead, as explained in the sections that follow.

Client-Side Cursors

Client-side cursors have the following cost benefits compared to server-side cursors:

- *Higher scalability:* Since the cursor metadata is maintained on the individual client machines connected to the server, the overhead of maintaining the cursor metadata is taken up by the client machines. Consequently, the ability to serve a larger number of users is not limited by the server resources.

- *Fewer network round-trips:* Since the result set returned by the SELECT statement is passed to the client where the cursor is maintained, extra network round-trips to the server are not required while retrieving rows from the cursor.

- *Faster scrolling:* Since the cursor is maintained locally on the client machine, it's faster to walk through the rows of the cursor.

- *Highly portable:* Since the cursor is implemented using data access layers, it works across a large range of databases: SQL Server, Oracle, Sybase, and so forth.

Client-side cursors have the following cost overhead or drawbacks:

- *Higher pressure on client resources:* Since the cursor is managed at the client side, it increases pressure on the client resources. But it may not be all that bad, considering that most of the time the client applications are web applications and scaling out web applications (or web servers) is quite easy using standard load-balancing solutions. On the other hand, scaling out a transactional SQL Server database is still an art!

- *Support for limited cursor types:* Dynamic and keyset-driven cursors are not supported.

- *Only one active cursor-based statement on one connection:* As many rows of the result set as the client network can buffer are arranged in the form of network packets and sent to the client application. Therefore, until all the cursor's rows are fetched by the application, the database connection remains busy, pushing the rows to the client. During this period, other cursor-based statements cannot use the connection. This is negated by taking advantage of multiple active result sets (MARS), which would allow a connection to have a second active cursor.

Server-Side Cursors

Server-side cursors have the following cost benefits:

- *Multiple active cursor-based statements on one connection:* While using server-side cursors, no results are left outstanding on the connection between the cursor operations. This frees the connection, allowing the use of multiple cursor-based statements on one connection at the same time. In the case of client-side cursors, as explained previously, the connection remains busy until all the cursor rows are fetched by the application. This means they cannot be used simultaneously by multiple cursor-based statements.

- *Row processing near the data:* If the row processing involves joining with other tables and a considerable amount of set operations, then it is advantageous to perform the row processing near the data using a server-side cursor.

- *Less pressure on client resources:* It reduces pressure on the client resources. But this may not be that desirable because, if the server resources are maxed out (instead of the client resources), then it will require scaling out the database, which is a difficult proposition.

- *Support for all cursor types:* Client-side cursors have limitations on which types of cursors can be supported. There are no limits on the server-side cursors.

Server-side cursors have the following cost overhead or disadvantages:

- *Lower scalability:* They make the server less scalable since server resources are consumed to manage the cursor.

- *More network round-trips:* They increase network round-trips if the cursor row processing is done in the client application. The number of network round-trips can be optimized by processing the cursor rows in the stored procedure or by using the cache size feature of the data access layer.

- *Less portable:* Server-side cursors implemented using T-SQL cursors are not readily portable to other databases because the syntax of the database code managing the cursor is different across databases.

Cost Comparison on Cursor Concurrency

As expected, cursors with a higher concurrency model create the least amount of blocking in the database and support higher scalability, as explained in the following sections.

Read-Only

The read-only concurrency model provides the following cost benefits:

- *Lowest locking overhead:* The read-only concurrency model introduces the least locking and synchronization overhead on the database. Since (S) locks are not held on the underlying row after a cursor row is fetched, other users are not blocked from accessing the row. Furthermore, the (S) lock acquired on the underlying row while fetching the cursor row can be avoided by using the NO_LOCK locking hint in the SELECT statement of the cursor, but only if you don't care about what kind of data you get back because of dirty reads.

- *Highest concurrency:* Since additional locks are not held on the underlying rows, the read-only cursor doesn't block other users from accessing the underlying tables. The shared lock is still acquired.

The main drawback of the read-only cursor is as follows:

- *Nonupdatable:* The content of underlying tables cannot be modified through the cursor.

Optimistic

The optimistic concurrency model provides the following benefits:

- *Low locking overhead:* Similar to the read-only model, the optimistic concurrency model doesn't hold an (S) lock on the cursor row after the row is fetched. To further improve concurrency, the NOLOCK locking hint can also be used, as in the case of the read-only concurrency model. But, please know that NOLOCK can absolutely lead to incorrect data or missing or extra rows, so its use requires careful planning. Modification through the cursor to an underlying row requires exclusive rights on the row as required by an action query.

- *High concurrency:* Since only a shared lock is used on the underlying rows, the cursor doesn't block other users from accessing the underlying tables. But the modification through the cursor to an underlying row will block other users from accessing the row during the modification.

The following examples detail the cost overhead of the optimistic concurrency model:

- *Row versioning:* Since the optimistic concurrency model allows the cursor to be updatable, an additional cost is incurred to ensure that the current underlying row is first compared (using either version-based or value-based concurrency control) with the original cursor row fetched before applying a modification through the cursor. This prevents the modification through the cursor from accidentally overwriting the modification made by another user after the cursor row is fetched.

- *Concurrency control without a* ROWVERSION *column:* As explained previously, a ROWVERSION column in the underlying table allows the cursor to perform an efficient version-based concurrency control. In case the underlying table doesn't contain a ROWVERSION column, the cursor resorts to value-based concurrency control, which requires matching the current value of the row to the value when the row was read into the cursor. This increases the cost of the concurrency control. Both forms of concurrency control will cause additional overhead in the TEMPDB.

Scroll Locks

The major benefit of the scroll locks concurrency model is as follows:

- *Simple concurrency control:* By locking the underlying row corresponding to the last fetched row from the cursor, the cursor assures that the underlying row can't be modified by another user. This eliminates the versioning overhead of optimistic locking. Also, since the row cannot be modified by another user, the application is relieved from checking for a row-mismatch error.

The scroll locks concurrency model incurs the following cost overhead:

- *Highest locking overhead:* The scroll locks concurrency model introduces a pessimistic locking characteristic. A (U) lock is held on the last cursor row fetched, until another cursor row is fetched or the cursor is closed.

- *Lowest concurrency:* Since a (U) lock is held on the underlying row, all other users requesting a (U) or an (X) lock on the underlying row will be blocked. This can significantly hurt concurrency. Therefore, please avoid using this cursor concurrency model unless absolutely necessary.

Cost Comparison on Cursor Type

Each of the basic four cursor types mentioned in the "Cursor Fundamentals" section earlier in the chapter incurs a different cost overhead on the server. Choosing an incorrect cursor type can hurt database performance. Besides the four basic cursor types, a fast-forward-only cursor (a variation of the forward-only cursor) is provided to enhance performance. The cost overhead of these cursor types is explained in the sections that follow.

Forward-Only Cursors

These are the cost benefits of forward-only cursors:

- *Lower cursor open cost than static and keyset-driven cursors:* Since the cursor rows are not retrieved from the underlying tables and are not copied into the tempdb database during cursor open, the forward-only T-SQL cursor opens quickly. Similarly, the forward-only, server-side API cursors with optimistic/scroll locks concurrency also open quickly since they do not retrieve the rows during cursor open.

- *Lower scroll overhead:* Since only FETCH NEXT can be performed on this cursor type, it requires less overhead to support different scroll operations.

- *Lower impact on the* tempdb *database than static and keyset-driven cursors:* Since the forward-only T-SQL cursor doesn't copy the rows from the underlying tables into the tempdb database, no additional pressure is created on the database.

The forward-only cursor type has the following drawbacks:

- *Lower concurrency.* Every time a cursor row is fetched, the corresponding underlying row is accessed with a lock request depending on the cursor concurrency model (as noted earlier in the discussion about concurrency). It can block other users from accessing the resource.

- *No backward scrolling.* Applications requiring two-way scrolling can't use this cursor type. But if the applications are designed properly, then it isn't difficult to live without backward scrolling.

Fast-Forward-Only Cursor

The fast-forward-only cursor is the fastest and least expensive cursor type. This forward-only and read-only cursor is specially optimized for performance. Because of this, you should always prefer it to the other SQL Server cursor types.

Furthermore, the data access layer provides a fast-forward-only cursor on the client side. That type of cursor uses a so-called default result set to make cursor overhead almost disappear.

■ **Note** The default result set is explained later in the chapter in the "Default Result Set" section.

Static Cursors

These are the cost benefits of static cursors:

- *Lower fetch cost than other cursor types:* Since a snapshot is created in the tempdb database from the underlying rows on opening the cursor, the cursor row fetch is targeted to the snapshot instead of the underlying rows. This avoids the lock overhead that would otherwise be required to fetch the cursor rows.

- *No blocking on underlying rows:* Since the snapshot is created in the tempdb database, other users trying to access the underlying rows are not blocked.

On the downside, the static cursor has the following cost overhead:

- *Higher open cost than other cursor types:* The cursor open operation of the static cursor is slower than that of other cursor types, since all the rows of the result set have to be retrieved from the underlying tables and the snapshot has to be created in the tempdb database during the cursor open.

- *Higher impact on* tempdb *than other cursor types:* There can be significant impact on server resources for creating, populating, and cleaning up the snapshot in the tempdb database.

Keyset-Driven Cursors

These are the cost benefits of keyset-driven cursors:

- *Lower open cost than the static cursor:* Since only the keyset, not the complete snapshot, is created in the tempdb database, the keyset-driven cursor opens faster than the static cursor. SQL Server populates the keyset of a large keyset-driven cursor asynchronously, which shortens the time between when the cursor is opened and when the first cursor row is fetched.

- *Lower impact on* tempdb *than that with the static cursor:* Because the keyset-driven cursor is smaller, it uses less space in tempdb.

The cost overhead of keyset-driven cursors is as follows:

- *Higher open cost than forward-only and dynamic cursors:* Populating the keyset in the tempdb database makes the cursor open operation of the keyset-driven cursor costlier than that of forward-only (with the exceptions mentioned earlier) and dynamic cursors.

- *Higher fetch cost than other cursor types:* For every cursor row fetch, the key in the keyset has to be accessed first, and then the corresponding underlying row in the user database can be accessed. Accessing both the tempdb and the user database for every cursor row fetch makes the fetch operation costlier than that of other cursor types.

- *Higher impact on* tempdb *than forward-only and dynamic cursors:* Creating, populating, and cleaning up the keyset in tempdb impacts server resources.

- *Higher lock overhead and blocking than the static cursor:* Since row fetch from the cursor retrieves rows from the underlying table, it acquires an (S) lock on the underlying row (unless the NOLOCK locking hint is used) during the row fetch operation.

Dynamic Cursor

The dynamic cursor has the following cost benefits:

- *Lower open cost than static and keyset-driven cursors:* Since the cursor is opened directly on the underlying rows without copying anything to the tempdb database, the dynamic cursor opens faster than the static and keyset-driven cursors.

- *Lower impact on* tempdb *than static and keyset-driven cursors:* Since nothing is copied into tempdb, the dynamic cursor places far less strain on tempdb than the other cursor types.

The dynamic cursor has the following cost overhead:

- *Higher lock overhead and blocking than the static cursor:* Every cursor row fetch in a dynamic cursor requeries the underlying tables involved in the SELECT statement of the cursor. The dynamic fetches are generally expensive because the original select condition might have to be reexecuted.

Default Result Set

The default cursor type for the data access layers (ADO, OLEDB, and ODBC) is forward-only and read-only. The default cursor type created by the data access layers isn't a true cursor, but a stream of data from the server to the client, generally referred to as the *default result set* or fast-forward-only cursor (created by the data access layer). In ADO.NET, the DataReader control has the forward-only and read-only properties, and it can be considered as the default result set in the ADO.NET environment. SQL Server uses this type of result set processing under the following conditions:

- The application, using the data access layers (ADO, OLEDB, ODBC), leaves all the cursor characteristics at the default settings, which requests a forward-only and read-only cursor.

- The application executes a SELECT statement instead of executing a DECLARE CURSOR statement.

■ **Note**   Because SQL Server is designed to work with sets of data, not to walk through records one by one, the default result set is always faster than any other type of cursor.

The only request sent from the client to SQL Server is the SQL statement associated with the default cursor. SQL Server executes the query, organizes the rows of the result set in network packets (filling the packets as best it can), and then sends the packets to the client. These network packets are cached in the network buffers of the client. SQL Server sends as many rows of the result set to the client as the client-network buffers can cache. As the client application requests one row at a time, the data access layer on the client machine pulls the row from the client-network buffers and transfers it to the client application.

The following sections outline the benefits and drawbacks of the default result set.

Benefits

The default result set is generally the best and most efficient way of returning rows from SQL Server for the following reasons:

- *Minimum network round-trips between the client and SQL Server:* Since the result set returned by SQL Server is cached in the client-network buffers, the client doesn't have to make a request across the network to get the individual rows. SQL Server puts most of the rows that it can in the network buffer and sends to the client as much as the client-network buffer can cache.

- *Minimum server overhead:* Since SQL Server doesn't have to store data on the server, this reduces server resource utilization.

Multiple Active Result Sets

SQL Server 2005 introduced the concept of multiple active result sets, wherein a single connection can have more than one batch running at any given moment. In prior versions, a single result set had to be processed or closed out prior to submitting the next request. MARS allows multiple requests to be submitted at the same time through the same connection. MARS is enabled on SQL Server all the time. It is not enabled by a connection unless that connection explicitly calls for it. Transactions must be handled at the client level and have to be explicitly declared and committed or rolled back. With MARS in action, if a transaction is not committed on a given statement and the connection is closed, all other transactions that were part of that single connection will be rolled back. MARS is enabled through application connection properties.

Drawbacks

While there are advantages to the default result set, there are drawbacks as well. Using the default result set requires some special conditions for maximum performance:

- *It doesn't support all properties and methods:* Properties such as AbsolutePosition, Bookmark, and RecordCount, as well as methods such as Clone, MoveLast, MovePrevious, and Resync, are not supported.

- *Locks may be held on the underlying resource:* SQL Server sends as many rows of the result set to the client as the client-network buffers can cache. If the size of the result set is large, then the client-network buffers may not be able to receive all the rows. SQL Server then holds a lock on the next page of the underlying tables, which has not been sent to the client.

To demonstrate these concepts, consider the following test table:

```
USE AdventureWorks2012;
GO
IF (SELECT  OBJECT_ID('dbo.Test1')
    ) IS NOT NULL
    DROP TABLE dbo.Test1;
GO

CREATE TABLE dbo.Test1 (C1 INT, C2 CHAR(996));

CREATE CLUSTERED INDEX Test1Index ON dbo.Test1 (C1);

INSERT  INTO dbo.Test1
VALUES  (1, '1') ,
        (2, '2');
GO
```

Now consider this PowerShell script, which accesses the rows of the test table using ADO with OLEDB and the default cursor type for the database API cursor (ADODB.Recordset object) as follows:

```
$AdoConn = New-Object -comobject ADODB.Connection
$AdoRecordset = New-Object -comobject ADODB.Recordset

$AdoConn.Open("Provider= SQLOLEDB; Data Source=DOJO\RANDORI; Initial Catalog=AdventureWorks2012;
Integrated Security=SSPI")
$AdoRecordset.Open("SELECT * FROM dbo.Test1", $AdoConn)

do {
    $C1 = $AdoRecordset.Fields.Item("C1").Value
    $C2 = $AdoRecordset.Fields.Item("C2").Value
    Write-Output "C1 = $C1 and C2 = $C2"
    $AdoRecordset.MoveNext()
    } until     ($AdoRecordset.EOF -eq $True)
$AdoRecordset.Close()
$AdoConn.Close()
```

This is not how you normally access databases from PowerShell, but it does show how a client-side cursor operates. Note that the table has two rows with the size of each row equal to 1,000 bytes (=4 bytes for INT + 996 bytes for CHAR(996)) without considering the internal overhead. Therefore, the size of the complete result set returned by the SELECT statement is approximately 2,000 bytes (= 2 x 1,000 bytes).

On execution of the cursor open statement ($AdoRecordset.Open()), a default result set is created on the client machine running the code. The default result set holds as many rows as the client-network buffer can cache.

Since the size of the result set is small enough to be cached by the client-network buffer, all the cursor rows are cached on the client machine during the cursor open statement itself, without retaining any lock on the dbo.Test1 table. You can verify the lock status for the connection using the sys.dm_tran_locks dynamic management view. During the complete cursor operation, the only request from the client to SQL Server is the SELECT statement associated to the cursor, as shown in the Extended Events output in Figure 22-1.

Event: sql_batch_completed (2014-04-04 19:12:45.3182959)

Details

Field	Value
batch_text	SELECT * FROM dbo.Test1
cpu_time	0
duration	65
logical_reads	2
physical_reads	0
query_hash	0
result	OK
row_count	2
session_id	54
writes	0

Figure 22-1. *Profiler trace output showing database requests made by the default result set*

To find out the effect of a large result set on the default result set processing, let's add some more rows to the test table.

```
SELECT TOP 100000
        IDENTITY( INT,1,1 ) AS n
INTO    #Tally
FROM    Master.dbo.syscolumns sc1,
        Master.dbo.syscolumns sc2;

INSERT INTO dbo.Test1
        (C1, C2)
SELECT  n,
        n
FROM    #Tally AS t;
GO
```

The additional rows generated by this example increase the size of the result set considerably. Depending on the size of the client-network buffer, only part of the result set can be cached. On execution of the Ado.Recordset.Open statement, the default result set on the client machine will get part of the result set, with SQL Server waiting on the other end of the network to send the remaining rows.

On my machine during this period, the locks shown in Figure 22-2 are held on the underlying Test1 table as obtained from the output of sys.dm_tran_locks.

	request_session...	resource_databas...	resource_associated_entit...	resource_ty...	resource_descrip...	request_m...	request_stat...
6	54	5	160719625	OBJECT		IS	GRANT
7	54	5	72057594072137728	PAGE	1:40150	S	GRANT

Figure 22-2. *sys.dm_tran_locks output showing the locks held by the default result set while processing the large result set*

The (IS) lock on the table will block other users trying to acquire an (X) lock. To minimize the blocking issue, follow these recommendations:

- Process all rows of the default result set immediately.

- Keep the result set small. As demonstrated in the example, if the size of the result set is small, then the default result set will be able to read all the rows during the cursor open operation itself.

Cursor Overhead

When implementing cursor-centric functionality in an application, you have two choices. You can use either a T-SQL cursor or a database API cursor. Because of the differences between the internal implementation of a T-SQL cursor and a database API cursor, the load created by these cursors on SQL Server is different. The impact of these cursors on the database also depends on the different characteristics of the cursors, such as location, concurrency, and type. You can use Extended Events to analyze the load generated by the T-SQL and database API cursors. The standard events for monitoring queries are, of course, going to be useful. There are also a number of events under the category of *cursor*. The most useful of these events includes the following:

- cursor_open

- cursor_close

- cursor_execute

- cursor_prepare

The other events are useful as well, but you'll need them only when you're attempting to troubleshoot specific issues. Even the optimization options for these cursors are different. Let's analyze the overhead of these cursors one by one.

Analyzing Overhead with T-SQL Cursors

The T-SQL cursors implemented using T-SQL statements are always executed on SQL Server because they need the SQL Server engine to process their T-SQL statements. You can use a combination of the cursor characteristics explained previously to reduce the overhead of these cursors. As mentioned earlier, the most lightweight T-SQL cursor is the one created, not with the default settings but by manipulating the settings to arrive at the forward-only read-only cursor. That still leaves the T-SQL statements used to implement the cursor operations to be processed by SQL Server. The complete load of the cursor is supported by SQL Server without any help from the client machine. Suppose an application requirement results in the following list of tasks that must be supported:

- Identify all products (from the Production.WorkOrder table) that have been scrapped.

- For each scrapped product, determine the money lost, where the money lost per product equals the units in stock times the unit price of the product.

- Calculate the total loss.

- Based on the total loss, determine the business status.

The FOR EACH phrase in the second point suggests that these application tasks could be served by a cursor. However, a FOR, WHILE, cursor, or any other kind of processing of this type can be dangerous within SQL Server. Let's see how it works with a cursor. You can implement this application requirement using a T-SQL cursor as follows:

```
IF (SELECT  OBJECT_ID('dbo.TotalLoss_CursorBased')
   ) IS NOT NULL
     DROP PROC dbo.TotalLoss_CursorBased;
GO

CREATE PROC dbo.TotalLoss_CursorBased
AS --Declare a T-SQL cursor with default settings, i.e., fast
--forward-only to retrieve products that have been discarded
DECLARE ScrappedProducts CURSOR
FOR
SELECT  p.ProductID,
        wo.ScrappedQty,
        p.ListPrice
FROM    Production.WorkOrder AS wo
JOIN    Production.ScrapReason AS sr
        ON wo.ScrapReasonID = sr.ScrapReasonID
JOIN    Production.Product AS p
        ON wo.ProductID = p.ProductID;

--Open the cursor to process one product at a time
OPEN ScrappedProducts;

DECLARE @MoneyLostPerProduct MONEY = 0,
    @TotalLoss MONEY = 0;
```

```
--Calculate money lost per product by processing one product
--at a time
DECLARE @ProductId INT,
    @UnitsScrapped SMALLINT,
    @ListPrice MONEY;

FETCH NEXT FROM ScrappedProducts INTO @ProductId,@UnitsScrapped,@ListPrice;

WHILE @@FETCH_STATUS = 0
    BEGIN
        SET @MoneyLostPerProduct = @UnitsScrapped * @ListPrice; --Calculate total loss
        SET @TotalLoss = @TotalLoss + @MoneyLostPerProduct;

        FETCH NEXT FROM ScrappedProducts INTO @ProductId,@UnitsScrapped,
            @ListPrice;
    END

--Determine status
IF (@TotalLoss > 5000)
    SELECT 'We are bankrupt!' AS Status;
ELSE
    SELECT 'We are safe!' AS Status;
--Close the cursor and release all resources assigned to the cursor
CLOSE ScrappedProducts;
DEALLOCATE ScrappedProducts;
GO
```

The stored procedure can be executed as follows, but you should execute it twice to take advantage of plan caching (see Figure 22-3):

```
EXEC dbo.TotalLoss_CursorBased;
```

name	timestamp
sp_statement_completed	2014-04-07 16:38:43.734...
sp_statement_completed	2014-04-07 16:38:43.740...
sp_statement_completed	2014-04-07 16:38:43.740...
sp_statement_completed	2014-04-07 16:38:43.740...
sp_statement_completed	2014-04-07 16:38:43.740...
sp_statement_completed	2014-04-07 16:38:43.755...
sp_statement_completed	2014-04-07 16:38:43.755...
sp_statement_completed	2014-04-07 16:38:43.755...
sp_statement_completed	2014-04-07 16:38:43.755...
sp_statement_completed	2014-04-07 16:38:43.776...
sp_statement_completed	2014-04-07 16:38:43.776...
sp_statement_completed	2014-04-07 16:38:43.776...
sp_statement_completed	2014-04-07 16:38:43.776...
sp_statement_completed	2014-04-07 16:38:43.776...
sp_statement_completed	2014-04-07 16:38:43.776...
sp_statement_completed	2014-04-07 16:38:43.776...
sp_statement_completed	2014-04-07 16:38:43.776...

Event: sp_statement_completed (2014-04-07 16:38:43.7764980)

Details

Field	Value
cpu_time	0
duration	1
last_row_count	1
line_number	30
logical_reads	0
nest_level	1
object_id	496720822
object_name	TotalLoss_CursorBased
object_type	PROC
offset	1706
offset_end	1752
physical_reads	0
row_count	0
source_database_id	5
statement	WHILE @@FETCH_STATUS = 0
writes	0

Figure 22-3. *Extended Events output showing some of the total cost of the data processing using a T-SQL cursor*

As you can see in Figure 22-3, lots of statements are executed on SQL Server. Essentially, all the SQL statements within the stored procedure are executed on SQL Server, with the statements in the WHILE loop executed several times (one for each row returned by the cursor's SELECT statement).

The total number of logical reads performed by the stored procedure is 8,788 (indicated by the last sql_batch_completed event). Well, is it high or low? Considering the fact that the Production.Products table has only 6,196 pages and the Production.WorkOrder table has only 926, it's surely not low. You can determine the number of pages allocated to these tables by querying the dynamic management view, sys.dm_db_index_physical_stats.

```
SELECT  SUM(page_count)
FROM    sys.dm_db_index_physical_stats(DB_ID(N'AdventureWorks2012'),
            OBJECT_ID('Production.WorkOrder'),
            DEFAULT, DEFAULT, DEFAULT);
```

■ **Note** The sys.dm_db_index_physical_stats DMV is explained in detail in Chapter 13.

In most cases, you can avoid cursor operations by rewriting the functionality using SQL queries, concentrating on set-based methods of accessing the data. For example, you can rewrite the preceding stored procedure using SQL queries (instead of the cursor operations) as follows (nocursor.sql in the download):

```
IF (SELECT  OBJECT_ID('dbo.TotalLoss')
    ) IS NOT NULL
    DROP PROC dbo.TotalLoss;
GO
CREATE PROC dbo.TotalLoss
AS
SELECT  CASE  --Determine status based on following computation
            WHEN SUM(MoneyLostPerProduct) > 5000 THEN 'We are bankrupt!'
            ELSE 'We are safe!'
        END AS Status
FROM    (--Calculate total money lost for all discarded products
         SELECT SUM(wo.ScrappedQty * p.ListPrice) AS MoneyLostPerProduct
         FROM    Production.WorkOrder AS wo
         JOIN    Production.ScrapReason AS sr
             ON wo.ScrapReasonID = sr.ScrapReasonID
         JOIN    Production.Product AS p
             ON wo.ProductID = p.ProductID
         GROUP BY p.ProductID
        ) DiscardedProducts;
GO
```

In this stored procedure, the aggregation functions of SQL Server are used to compute the money lost per product and the total loss. The CASE statement is used to determine the business status based on the total loss incurred. The stored procedure can be executed as follows; but again, you should execute it twice, so you can see the results of plan caching:

```
EXEC dbo.TotalLoss;
```

Figure 22-4 shows the corresponding Extended Events output.

Event: sql_batch_completed (2014-04-07 16:47:53.9774097)

Field	Value
batch_text	EXEC dbo.TotalLoss;
cpu_time	31000
duration	75671
logical_reads	597
physical_reads	12
result	OK
row_count	1
writes	0

Figure 22-4. *Profiler trace output showing the total cost of the data processing using an equivalent SELECT statement*

In Figure 22-4, you can see that the second execution of the stored procedure, which reuses the existing plan, uses a total of 597 logical reads. However, you can see a result even more important than the reads: the CPU time used drops from 156 milliseconds in the first query to 31 milliseconds in Figure 22-4, and the duration falls from 682ms to 75ms. Using SQL queries instead of the cursor operations made the execution nine times faster.

Therefore, for better performance, it is almost always recommended that you use set-based operations in SQL queries instead of T-SQL cursors.

Cursor Recommendations

An ineffective use of cursors can degrade the application performance by introducing extra network round-trips and load on server resources. To keep the cursor cost low, try to follow these recommendations:

- Use set-based SQL statements over T-SQL cursors, since SQL Server is designed to work with sets of data.

- Use the least expensive cursor.

- When using SQL Server cursors, use the FAST FORWARD cursor type.

- When using the API cursors implemented by ADO, OLEDB, or ODBC, use the default cursor type, which is generally referred to as the *default result set*.

- When using ADO.NET, use the DataReader object.

- Minimize impact on server resources.

- Use a client-side cursor for API cursors.

- Do not perform actions on the underlying tables through the cursor.

- Always deallocate the cursor as soon as possible. This helps free resources, especially in tempdb.

- Redesign the cursor's SELECT statement (or the application) to return the minimum set of rows and columns.

- Avoid T-SQL cursors entirely by rewriting the logic of the cursor as set-based statements, which are generally more efficient than cursors.

- Use a ROWVERSION column for dynamic cursors to benefit from the efficient, version-based concurrency control instead of relying upon the value-based technique.

- Minimize impact on tempdb.

- Minimize resource contention in tempdb by avoiding the static and keyset-driven cursor types.

- Static and key-set cursors put additional load on tempdb, so take that into account if you must use them, or avoid them if your tempdb is under stress.

- Minimize blocking.

- Use the default result set, fast-forward-only cursor, or static cursor.

- Process all cursor rows as quickly as possible.

- Avoid scroll locks or pessimistic locking.

- Minimize network round-trips while using API cursors.

- Use the CacheSize property of ADO to fetch multiple rows in one round-trip.

- Use client-side cursors.

- Use disconnected record sets.

Summary

As you learned in this chapter, a cursor is the natural extension to the result set returned by SQL Server, enabling the calling application to process one row of data at a time. Cursors add a cost overhead to application performance and impact the server resources.

You should always be looking for ways to avoid cursors. Set-based solutions work better in almost all cases. However, if a cursor operation is mandated, then choose the best combination of cursor location, concurrency, type, and cache size characteristics to minimize the cost overhead of the cursor.

In the next chapter, we explore the special functionality introduced with in-memory tables, natively compiled procedures, and the other aspects of Hekaton in SQL Server 2014.

■ ■ ■

## CHAPTER 23

Memory-Optimized OLTP Tables and Procedures

One of the principal needs for online transaction processing (OLTP) systems is to get as much speed as possible out of the system. With this in mind, in SQL Server 2014, Microsoft introduced a new set of functionality focused around making OLTP systems as fast as possible. These are the memory-optimized technologies of in-memory tables and natively compiled stored procedures. This set of enterprise-only features is meant for high-end, transaction-intensive, OLTP-focused systems. The memory-optimized technologies are another tool in the toolbox of query tuning, but they are a highly specialized tool, applicable only to certain applications. Be cautious in adopting this new technology. That said, on the right system with the right kind of memory, I am talking about blazing-fast speed.

In this chapter, I cover the following topics:

- The basics of how in-memory tables work

- Improving performance by natively compiling stored procedures

- The benefits and drawbacks of natively compiled procedures and in-memory OLTP tables

- Recommendations for when to use in-memory OLTP tables

In-Memory OLTP Fundamentals

At the core of it all, you can tune your queries to run incredibly fast. But, no matter how fast you make them run, to a degree you're limited by some of the architectural issues within modern computers. Typically, the number-one bottleneck is the storage system. Whether you're still looking at spinning platters or you've moved on to some type of SSD or similar technology, the disks are still the slowest aspect of the system. This means for reads or writes, you have to wait. But memory is fast, and with the new 64-bit operating systems, it can be plentiful. So, if you have tables that you can move completely into memory, you can radically improve the speed. That's part of what in-memory OLTP tables are all about: moving the data access, both reads and writes, into memory and off the disk.

But Microsoft did more than that. It recognized that while the disk was slow, another aspect of the system slowing things down was how queries were compiled, stored, and accessed, as well as how the data was accessed and managed through the transaction system. So, Microsoft made a series of changes there as well. The primary one was changing from a pessimistic approach to transactions. The existing product forces all transactions to get written to the transaction log before allowing the data changes to get flushed to disk. This creates a bottleneck in the processing of transactions. So, instead of pessimism about whether a transaction will successfully complete, Microsoft took an optimistic approach that most of the time, transactions will complete. Further, instead of having a blocking situation where one transaction has to finish updating data before the next can access it or update it, Microsoft versioned the data. It has now eliminated a major point of contention within the system and radically reduced blocking, and all this is in memory, so it's even faster.

Microsoft then took all this another step further. Instead of the pessimistic approach to memory latches that prevent more than one process from accessing a page to write to it, Microsoft extended the optimistic approach to memory management as well. Now, with versioning, in-memory tables work off a model that is "eventually" consistent with a conflict resolution process that will roll back a transaction but never block one transaction by another. This has the potential to lead to some data loss, but it makes everything within the data access layer fast.

Finally, as you've seen throughout the rest of the book, a major part of query tuning is figuring out how to work with the query optimizer to get a good execution plan and then have that plan reused multiple times. This can also be an intensive and slow process. SQL Server 2014 introduces the concept of natively compiled stored procedures. These are literally T-SQL code compiled down to DLLs and made part of the SQL Server OS. This compile process is costly and shouldn't be used for just any old query. The principal idea is to spend time and effort compiling a procedure to native code and then get to use that procedure millions of times at a radically improved speed.

All this technology comes together to create new functionality that you can use by itself or in combination with existing table structures and standard T-SQL. In fact, you can treat in-memory tables much the same way as you treat normal SQL Server tables and still realize some performance improvements. But, you can't just do this anywhere. There are some fairly specific requirements for taking advantage of in-memory OLTP tables and procedures.

System Requirements

The most important system requirement for the in-memory technology is that you must be running the Enterprise version of SQL Server 2014 in order to get access to it (although it works within the Developer edition too). You must meet a few other standard requirements before you can even consider whether memory-optimized tables are a possibility.

- A modern 64-bit processor
- Twice the amount of free disk storage for the data you intend to put into memory
- Lots of memory

Obviously, for most systems, the key is lots of memory. You need to have enough memory for the operating system and SQL Server to function normally. Then you still need to have memory for all the non-memory-optimized requirements of your system including the data cache. Finally, you're going to add, on top of all that, memory for your memory-optimized tables. If you're not looking at a fairly large system, with a minimum of 64GB memory, I don't suggest even considering this as an option. Smaller systems are just not going to provide enough storage in memory to make this worth the time, effort, and added licensing costs.

Basic Setup

In addition to the hardware requirements, you have to do additional work on your database to enable in-memory tables. I'll start with a new database to illustrate.

```
CREATE DATABASE InMemoryTest ON PRIMARY
    (NAME = N'InMemoryTest_Data',
    FILENAME = N'D:\Data\InMemoryTest_Data.mdf',
    SIZE = 5GB)
LOG ON
    (NAME = N'InMemoryTest_Log',
    FILENAME = N'L:\Log\InMemoryTest_Log.ldf');
```

For the in-memory tables to maintain durability, they must write to disk as well as to memory since memory goes away with the power. Durability (part of the ACID properties of a relational dataset) means that once a transaction commits, it stays committed. You can have a durable in-memory table or a nondurable table. With a nondurable table, you may have committed transactions, but you could still lose that data, which is different from how standard tables work within SQL Server. The most commonly known uses for data that isn't durable are things such as session state or time-sensitive information such as an electronic shopping cart. Anyway, in-memory storage is not the same as the usual storage within your standard relational tables. So, a separate file group and files must be created. To do this, you can just alter the database, shown here:

```
ALTER DATABASE InMemoryTest
    ADD FILEGROUP InMemoryTest_InMemoryData
    CONTAINS MEMORY_OPTIMIZED_DATA;
ALTER DATABASE InMemoryTest
    ADD FILE (NAME='InMemoryTest_InMemoryData',
    FILENAME ='D:\Data\InMemoryTest_InMemoryData.ndf')
    TO FILEGROUP InMemoryTest_InMemoryData;
```

I would have simply altered the AdventureWorks2012 database that you've been experimenting with, but another consideration for in-memory optimized tables is that you can't remove the special filegroup once it's created. You can only ever drop the database. That's why I'll just experiment with a separate database. It's safer.

There are some limitations to features available to a database using in-memory OLTP.

- DBCC CHECKDB: You can run consistency checks, but the memory-optimized tables will be skipped. You'll get an error if you attempt to run DBCC CHECKTABLE.

- AUTO_CLOSE: This is not supported.

- DATABASE SNAPSHOT: This is not supported.

- ATTACH_REBUILD_LOG: This is also not supported.

Once these modifications are complete, you can now begin to create in-memory tables in your system.

Create Tables

Once the database setup is complete, you now have the capability to create tables that will be memory optimized as described earlier. The actual syntax is quite straightforward. I'm going to replicate, as much as I can, the Person.Address table from AdventureWorks2012.

```
USE DATABASE InMemoryTest;
GO
CREATE TABLE dbo.Address
    (
    AddressID INT IDENTITY(1, 1)
                NOT NULL
                PRIMARY KEY NONCLUSTERED HASH WITH (BUCKET_COUNT = 50000),
    AddressLine1 NVARCHAR(60) NOT NULL,
    AddressLine2 NVARCHAR(60) NULL,
    City NVARCHAR(30) NOT NULL,
    StateProvinceID INT NOT NULL,
    PostalCode NVARCHAR(15) NOT NULL,
    --[SpatialLocation geography NULL,
    --rowguid uniqueidentifier ROWGUIDCOL  NOT NULL CONSTRAINT DF_Address_rowguid  DEFAULT
(newid()),
    ModifiedDate DATETIME
        NOT NULL
```

```
        CONSTRAINT DF_Address_ModifiedDate DEFAULT (GETDATE())
)
WITH (
        MEMORY_OPTIMIZED=
        ON,
        DURABILITY =
        SCHEMA_AND_DATA);
```

This creates a durable table in the memory of the system using the disk space you defined to retain a durable copy of the data, ensuring that you won't lose data in the event of a power loss. It has a primary key that is an IDENTITY value just like with a regular SQL Server table (although, to use IDENTITY instead of SEQUENCE, you will be surrendering the capability to set the definition to anything except (1,1) in this version of SQL Server). But, the index definition is not clustered. Instead it's NON-CLUSTERED HASH. I'll talk about indexing and things like the BUCKET_COUNT in the next section. You'll also note that I had to comment out two columns, SpatialLocation and rowguid. These are using data types not available with in-memory tables. Finally, the WITH statement lets SQL Server know where to place this table by defining MEMORY_OPTIMIZED=ON. You can make an even faster table by modifying the WITH clause to make the DURABILITY=SCHEMA_ONLY. This allows data loss but makes the table even faster since nothing gets written to disk.

There are a number of unsupported data types that could prevent you from taking advantage of in-memory tables.

- XML

- ROWVERSION

- SQL_VARIANT

- HIERARCHYID

- DATETIMEOFFSET

- GEOGRAPHY/GEOMETRY

- User-defined data types

- LOB, which includes text and ntext as well as all the MAX types of varchar and binary

In addition to data types, you will run into other limitations. I'll talk about the index requirements in the "In-Memory Indexes" section. You can't create a foreign key reference to an in-memory table. This means all referential integrity will have to come from the coding side of the application.

Once a table is created in-memory, you can access it just like normal. If I were to run a query against it now, it wouldn't return any rows, but it would function.

```
SELECT  a.AddressID
FROM    dbo.Address AS a
WHERE   a.AddressID = 42;
```

So, to experiment with some actual data in the database, go ahead and load the information stored in Person.Address in AdventureWorks into the new table that's stored in-memory in this new database.

```
CREATE TABLE dbo.AddressStaging(
    AddressLine1 nvarchar(60) NOT NULL,
    AddressLine2 nvarchar(60) NULL,
    City nvarchar(30) NOT NULL,
    StateProvinceID int NOT NULL,
    PostalCode nvarchar(15) NOT NULL
);
```

```
INSERT   dbo.AddressStaging
         (AddressLine1,
          AddressLine2,
          City,
          StateProvinceID,
          PostalCode
         )
SELECT   a.AddressLine1,
         a.AddressLine2,
         a.City,
         a.StateProvinceID,
         a.PostalCode
FROM     AdventureWorks2012.Person.Address AS a;

INSERT   dbo.Address
         (AddressLine1,
          AddressLine2,
          City,
          StateProvinceID,
          PostalCode
         )
SELECT   a.AddressLine1,
         a.AddressLine2,
         a.City,
         a.StateProvinceID,
         a.PostalCode
FROM     dbo.AddressStaging AS a;

DROP TABLE dbo.AddressStaging;
```

You can't combine an in-memory table in a cross-database query, so I had to load the 19,000 rows into a staging table and then load them into the in-memory table. This is not meant to be part of the examples for performance, but it's worth nothing that it took nearly 850ms to insert the data into the standard table and only 2ms to load the same data into the in-memory table on my system.

But, with the data in place, I can rerun the query and actually see results, as shown in Figure 23-1.

	AddressID
1	42

Figure 23-1. *The first query results from an in-memory table*

Granted, this is not terribly exciting. So, in order to have something meaningful to work with, I'm going to create a couple of other tables so that you can see some more query behavior on display.

```
CREATE TABLE dbo.StateProvince(
    StateProvinceID int IDENTITY(1,1) NOT NULL PRIMARY KEY NONCLUSTERED HASH WITH (BUCKET_
COUNT=10000),
    StateProvinceCode nchar(3) COLLATE Latin1_General_100_BIN2
 NOT NULL,
```

```
      CountryRegionCode nvarchar(3) NOT NULL,
      Name VARCHAR(50) NOT NULL,
      TerritoryID int NOT NULL,
      ModifiedDate datetime NOT NULL CONSTRAINT DF_StateProvince_ModifiedDate  DEFAULT (getdate())
) WITH (MEMORY_OPTIMIZED=ON);

CREATE TABLE dbo.CountryRegion(
    CountryRegionCode nvarchar(3) NOT NULL,
    Name VARCHAR(50) NOT NULL,
    ModifiedDate datetime NOT NULL CONSTRAINT DF_CountryRegion_ModifiedDate  DEFAULT (getdate()),
 CONSTRAINT PK_CountryRegion_CountryRegionCode PRIMARY KEY CLUSTERED
(
    CountryRegionCode ASC
));
```

That's an additional memory-optimized table and a standard table. I'll also load data into these so you can make more interesting queries.

```
SELECT  sp.StateProvinceCode,
        sp.CountryRegionCode,
        sp.Name,
        sp.TerritoryID
INTO    dbo.StateProvinceStaging
FROM    AdventureWorks2012.Person.StateProvince AS sp;

INSERT  dbo.StateProvince
        (StateProvinceCode,
         CountryRegionCode,
         Name,
         TerritoryID
         )
SELECT  stateprovincecode,
        countryregioncode,
        name,
        territoryid
FROM    dbo.stateprovincestaging;

DROP TABLE dbo.StateProvinceStaging;

INSERT  dbo.countryregion
        (countryregioncode,
         name
         )
        SELECT  cr.CountryRegionCode,
                cr.Name
        FROM    AdventureWorks2012.Person.CountryRegion AS cr;
```

With the data loaded, the following query returns a single row and has an execution plan that looks like Figure 23-2:

```
SELECT  a.AddressLine1,
        a.City,
        a.PostalCode,
        sp.Name AS StateProvinceName,
        cr.Name AS CountryName
FROM    dbo.Address AS a
        JOIN dbo.StateProvince AS sp
        ON sp.StateProvinceID = a.StateProvinceID
        JOIN dbo.CountryRegion cr
        ON cr.CountryRegionCode = sp.CountryRegionCode
WHERE a.AddressID = 42;
```

Figure 23-2. *An execution plan showing both in-memory and standard tables*

As you can see, it's entirely possible to get a normal execution plan even when using in-memory tables. The operators are even the same. In this case, you have three different index seek operations. Two of them are against the nonclustered hash indexes you created with the in-memory tables, and the other is a standard clustered index seek against the standard table.

The principal performance enhancements come from the lack of locking and latching allowing massive inserts and updates while simultaneously allowing for querying. But, the queries do run faster as well. The previous query resulted in the following execution time and reads:

```
Table 'CountryRegion'. Scan count 0, logical reads 2
CPU time = 0 ms,  elapsed time = 19 ms.
```

Running a similar query against the AdventureWorks2012 database results in this behavior:

```
Table 'CountryRegion'. Scan count 0, logical reads 2
Table 'StateProvince'. Scan count 0, logical reads 2
Table 'Address'. Scan count 0, logical reads 2
CPU time = 0 ms,  elapsed time = 154 ms.
```

While it's clear that the execution times are much better with the in-memory table, what's not clear is how the reads are dealt with. But, since I'm talking about reading from the in-memory storage and not either pages in memory or pages on the disk but the hash index instead, things are completely different in terms of measuring performance.

You won't be using all the same measures as before but will instead rely on execution time. Even if you capture the metrics through extended events, you're not going to see the same types of values as shown in Figure 23-3; however, the reads in this case are a measure of the activity of the system, so you can anticipate that higher values mean more access to the data and lower values mean less.

Field	Value
batch_text	SELECT a.AddressLine1, a.City, a.PostalCode, ...
cpu_time	0
duration	42274
logical_reads	2
physical_reads	0
query_hash	0
result	OK
row_count	1
writes	0

Figure 23-3. *The Extended Events output of the SELECT query using in-memory tables shows duration, not reads*

With the tables in place and proof of improved performance both for inserts and for selects, let's talk about the indexes that you can use with in-memory tables and how they're different from standard indexes.

In-Memory Indexes

An in-memory table can have up to eight indexes created on it at one time. But, every memory-optimized table must have at least one index. The index defined by the primary key counts. A durable table must have a primary key. There are two basic index types that you can create: the nonclustered hash index that you used previously and the nonclustered index. But these indexes are not the type of indexes that are created with standard tables. First, they're maintained in-memory in the same way the in-memory tables are. Second, the same rules apply about durability of the indexes as the in-memory tables.

Hash Index

A hash index is not a balanced-tree index that's just stored in memory. Instead, the hash index uses a predefined hash bucket, or table, and hash values of the key to provide a mechanism for retrieving the data of a table. SQL Server has a hash function that will always result in a constant hash value for the inputs provided. This means for a given key value, you'll always have the same hash value. You can store multiple copies of the hash value in the hash bucket. Having a hash value to retrieve a point lookup, a single row, makes for an extremely efficient operation, that is, as long as you don't run into lots of hash collisions. This is when you have multiple values stored at the same location.

This means the key to getting the hash index right is getting the right distribution of values across buckets. You do this by defining the bucket count for the index. For the first table I created, dbo.Address, I set a bucket count of 50,000. There are 19,000 rows currently in the table. So, with a bucket count of 50,000, I ensure that I have plenty of storage for the existing set of values, and I provide a healthy growth overhead. You need to set the bucket count so that it's big enough without being too big. If the bucket count is too small, you'll be storing lots of data within a bucket and seriously impact the ability of the system to efficiently retrieve the data. In short, it's best to have your bucket be too big. If you look at Figure 23-4, you can see this laid out in a different way.

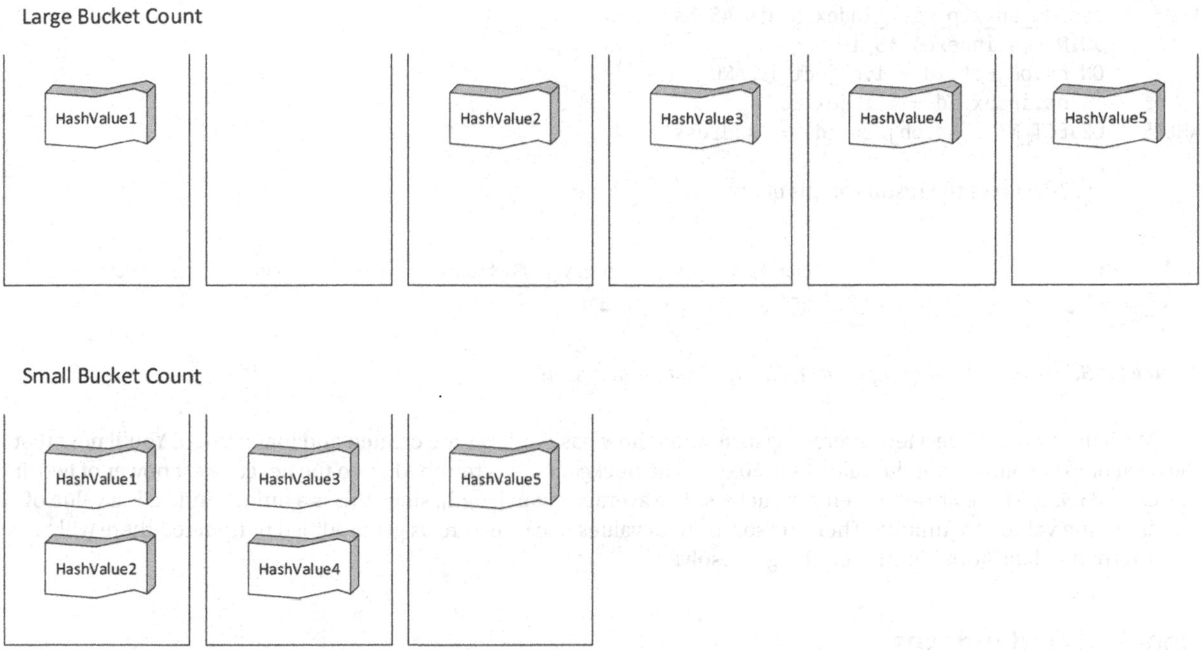

Large Bucket Count

Small Bucket Count

Figure 23-4. *Hash values in lots of buckets and few buckets*

The first set of buckets has what is called a *shallow distribution*, which is few hash values distributed across a lot of buckets. This is a more optimal storage plan. Some buckets may be empty as you can see, but the lookup speed is fast because each bucket contains a single value. The second set of buckets shows a small bucket count, or a *deep distribution*. This is more hash values in a given bucket, requiring a scan within the bucket to identify individual hash values.

Microsoft's recommendation on bucket count is go between one to two times the quantity of the number of rows in the table. But, since you can't alter in-memory tables, you also need to take into account projected growth. If you think your in-memory table is likely to grow three times as large over the next three to six months, you may want to expand the size of your bucket count. The only problem you'll encounter with an oversized bucket count is that scans will take longer, so you'll be allocating more memory. But, if your queries are likely to lead to scans, you really shouldn't be using the nonclustered hash index. Instead, just go to the nonclustered index.

You also need to worry about how many values can be returned by the hash value. Unique indexes and primary keys are prime candidates for using the hash index because they're always unique. Microsoft's recommendation is that if, on average, you're going to see more than five values for any one hash value, you should move away from the nonclustered hash index and use the nonclustered index instead. This is because the hash bucket simply acts as a pointer to the first row that is stored in that bucket. Then, if duplicate or additional values are stored in the bucket, the first row points to the next row, and each subsequent row points to the row following it. This can turn point lookups into scanning operations, again radically hurting performance. This is why going with a small number of duplicates, less than five, or unique values work best with hash indexes.

To see the distribution of your index within the hash table, you can use sys.dm_db_xtp_hash_index_stats.

```
SELECT  i.name AS 'index name',
        hs.total_bucket_count,
        hs.empty_bucket_count,
        hs.avg_chain_length,
        hs.max_chain_length
```

```
FROM    sys.dm_db_xtp_hash_index_stats AS hs
        JOIN sys.indexes AS i
        ON hs.object_id = i.object_id AND
           hs.index_id = i.index_id
WHERE   OBJECT_NAME(hs.object_id) = 'Address';
```

Figure 23-5 shows the results of this query.

index name	total_bucket_count	empty_bucket_count	avg_chain_length	max_chain_length
PK_Address_091C2A1A15112ECE	65536	48652	1	5

Figure 23-5. *Results of querying sys.dm_db_xtp_hash_index_stats*

With this you can see a few interesting facts about how hash indexes are created and maintained. You'll note that the total bucket count is not the value I set, 50,000. The bucket count is rounded up to the next closest power of two, in this case, 65,536. There are 48,652 empty buckets. The average chain length, since this is a unique index, is a value of 1 because the values are unique. There are some chain values because as rows get modified or updated there will be versions of the data stored until everything is resolved.

Nonclustered Indexes

The nonclustered indexes are basically just like regular indexes except that they're stored in-memory along with the data to assist in data retrieval. They also have pointers to the storage location of the data similar to how a nonclustered index behaves with a heap table. One interesting difference between an in-memory nonclustered index and a standard nonclustered index is that SQL Server can't retrieve the data in reverse order from the in-memory index. Other behavior seems close to the same as standard indexes.

To see the nonclustered index in action, let's take this query:

```
SELECT  a.AddressLine1,
        a.City,
        a.PostalCode,
        sp.Name AS StateProvinceName,
        cr.Name AS CountryName
FROM    dbo.Address AS a
        JOIN dbo.StateProvince AS sp
        ON sp.StateProvinceID = a.StateProvinceID
        JOIN dbo.CountryRegion AS cr
        ON cr.CountryRegionCode = sp.CountryRegionCode
WHERE   a.City = 'Walla Walla';
```

Currently the performance looks like this:

```
Table 'CountryRegion'. Scan count 1, logical reads 4
CPU time = 16 ms,  elapsed time = 118 ms.
```

Figure 23-6 shows the execution plan.

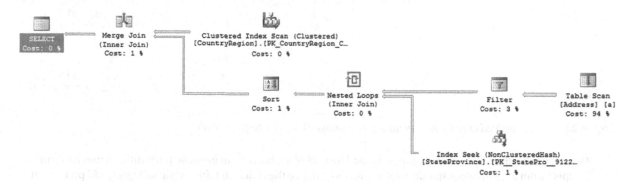

Figure 23-6. *Query results in an execution plan that has table scans*

While an in-memory table scan is certainly going to be faster than the same scan on a table stored on disk, it's still not a good situation. Plus considering the extra work resulting from the Filter operation and the Sort operation in order to satisfy the Merge Join that the optimizer felt it needed, this is a problematic query. So, you should add an index to the table to speed it up.

But, you can't just run CREATE INDEX on the dbo.Address table. Instead, you'll have to drop the table, re-create it, and then reload it with data. The table creation script now looks like this:

```
CREATE TABLE dbo.Address(
    AddressID int IDENTITY(1,1) NOT NULL PRIMARY KEY NONCLUSTERED HASH WITH (BUCKET_COUNT=50000),
    AddressLine1 nvarchar(60) NOT NULL,
    AddressLine2 nvarchar(60) NULL,
    City nvarchar(30) COLLATE Latin1_General_100_BIN2 NOT NULL,
    StateProvinceID int NOT NULL,
    PostalCode nvarchar(15) NOT NULL,
    ModifiedDate datetime NOT NULL CONSTRAINT DF_Address_ModifiedDate  DEFAULT (getdate()),
    INDEX nci NONCLUSTERED (City)
) WITH (MEMORY_OPTIMIZED=ON);
```

Please note that I had to add a collation to the City column in order to create the index. This is because indexes on character columns within in-memory databases support only *_BIN2 collations. You either need to change the entire collation of your database or set the collation on a spot basis as I did earlier.

After reloading the data into the newly created table, you can try the query again. This time it ran in 15ms on my system, much faster than it ran previously. Figure 23-7 shows the execution plan.

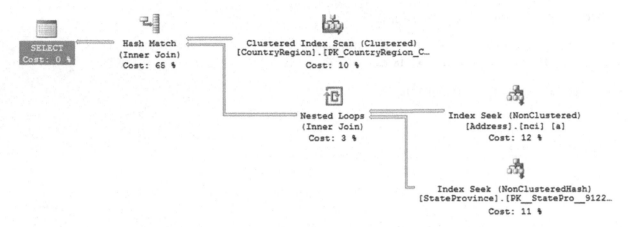

Figure 23-7. An improved execution plan taking advantage of nonclustered indexes

As you can see, the nonclustered index was used instead of a table scan to improve performance much as you would expect from an index on a standard table. However, unlike the standard table, while this query did pull columns that were not part of nonclustered index, no key lookup was required to retrieve the data from the in-memory table because each index points directly to the storage location, in memory, of the data necessary. This is yet another, small, but important improvement over how standard tables behave.

Index Maintenance

There are many fundamental differences between how indexes get created with in-memory tables when compared to standard tables. But index maintenance is still something you have to take into account. In-memory indexes maintain statistics that will need to be updated. You'll also want information about the in-memory indexes such as whether they're being accessed using scans or seeks. While the desire to track all this is the same, the mechanisms for doing so are different.

You can't actually see the statistics on in-memory indexes. You can run DBCC SHOW_STATISTICS against the index, but the output looks like Figure 23-8.

	Name	Updated	Rows	Rows Sampled	Steps	Density	Average key length	String Index	Filter Expression	Unfiltered Rows
1	nci	NULL	NULL	NULL	NULL	NULL	NULL	NULL	NULL	NULL

All density	Average Length	Columns

RANGE_HI_KEY	RANGE_ROWS	EQ_ROWS	DISTINCT_RANGE_ROWS	AVG_RANGE_ROWS

Figure 23-8. The empty output of statistics on an in-memory index

This means there is no way to look at the statistics of the in-memory indexes. However, those statistics will still get out-of-date as your data changes. What's more, they're not automatically updated with data changes regardless of the settings on your systems. So, you have to plan on running the updates yourself. You can use `sp_updatestats`. The 2014 version of the procedure is completely aware of in-memory indexes and their differences. You can also use `UPDATE STATISTICS`, but you must use `FULLSCAN` or `RESAMPLE` along with `NORECOMPUTE` as follows:

```
UPDATE STATISTICS dbo.Address WITH FULLSCAN, NORECOMPUTE;
```

If you don't use this syntax, it appears that you're attempting to alter the statistics on the in-memory table, and you can't do that. You'll be presented with a pretty clear error.

```
Msg 41346, Level 16, State 2, Line 1
CREATE and UPDATE STATISTICS for memory optimized tables requires the WITH FULLSCAN or RESAMPLE and
the NORECOMPUTE options. The WHERE clause is not supported.
```

Defining the sampling as either `FULLSCAN` or `RESAMPLE` and then letting it know that you're not attempting to turn on automatic update by using `NORECOMPUTE`, the statistics will get updated. You'll need to do this in a regular schedule based on the volatility of your data, but there's no clear way at this point to observe the statistics themselves.

In-memory indexes aren't accessed from disk, so there is no fragmentation you need to worry about these indexes, eliminating the need to defragment them.

Natively Compiled Stored Procedures

Just getting the table into memory and radically reducing the locking contention with the optimistic approaches results in fairly impressive performance improvements. But to really make things move quickly, you can also implement the new feature of compiling stored procedures into a DLL that runs within the SQL Server executable. This really makes the performance scream. The syntax is straightforward. This is how you could take the query from before and compile it:

```
CREATE PROC dbo.AddressDetails @City NVARCHAR(30)
    WITH NATIVE_COMPILATION,
        SCHEMABINDING,
        EXECUTE AS OWNER
AS
    BEGIN ATOMIC
WITH (TRANSACTION ISOLATION LEVEL = SNAPSHOT, LANGUAGE = N'us_english')
        SELECT  a.AddressLine1,
                a.City,
                a.PostalCode,
                sp.Name AS StateProvinceName,
                cr.Name AS CountryName
        FROM    dbo.Address AS a
                JOIN dbo.StateProvince AS sp
                ON sp.StateProvinceID = a.StateProvinceID
                JOIN dbo.CountryRegion AS cr
                ON cr.CountryRegionCode = sp.CountryRegionCode
        WHERE   a.City = @City;
    END
```

Unfortunately, if you attempt to run this query definition as currently defined, you'll receive the following error:

```
Msg 10775, Level 16, State 1, Procedure AddressDetails, Line 5530
Object 'dbo.CountryRegion' is not a memory optimized table and cannot be accessed from a natively
compiled stored procedure.
```

While you can query a mix of in-memory and standard tables, you can create only natively compiled stored procedures against in-memory tables. I'm going to use the same methods shown previously to load the dbo.CountryRegion table into memory and then run the script again. This time it will compile successfully. If you then execute the query using @City = 'Walla Walla' as before, the execution time won't even register inside SSMS. You have to capture the event through Extended Events, as shown in Figure 23-9.

Field	Value
batch_text	EXEC dbo.AddressDetails @City = N'Walla Walla';
cpu_time	0
duration	448
logical_reads	0
physical_reads	0
result	OK
row_count	0
writes	0

Figure 23-9. *Extended Events showing the execution time of a natively compiled procedure*

The execution time there is not in milliseconds but microseconds. So, the query execution time has gone from the native run time of 154ms down to the in-memory run time of 15ms and then finally less than ½ of one millisecond. That's a pretty hefty performance improvement.

But, there are restrictions. As was already noted, you have to be referencing only in-memory tables. The parameter values assigned to the procedures cannot accept NULL values. If you choose to set a parameter to NOT NULL, you must also supply an initial value. Otherwise, all parameters are required. You must enforce schema binding with the underlying tables. Finally, you need to have the procedures exist with an ATOMIC BLOCK. An atomic blocks require that all statements within the transaction succeed or all statements within the transaction will be rolled back.

Here are another couple of interesting points about the natively compiled procedures. You can retrieve only an estimated execution plan, not an actual plan. If you turn on actual plans in SSMS and then execute the query, nothing appears. But, if you request an estimated plan, you can retrieve one. Figure 23-10 shows the estimated plan for the procedure created earlier.

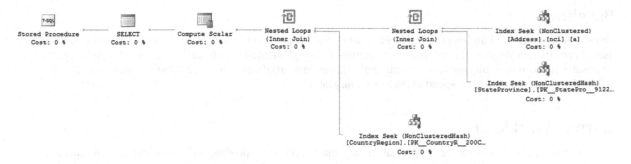

Figure 23-10. *Estimated execution plan for a natively compiled procedure*

You'll note that it looks largely like a regular execution plan, but there are quite a few differences behind the scenes. If you click the SELECT operator, you don't have nearly as many properties. Compare the two sets of data from the compiled stored procedure shown earlier and the properties of the regular query run earlier in Figure 23-11.

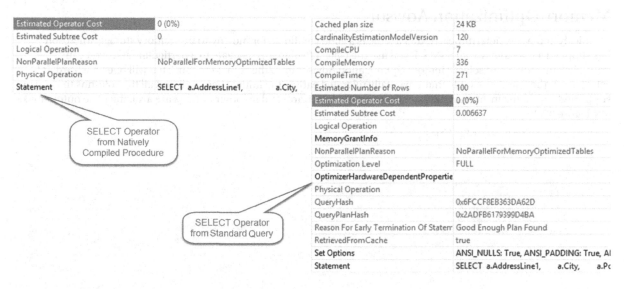

Figure 23-11. *SELECT operator properties from two different execution plans*

Much of the information you would expect to see is gone because the natively compiled procedures just don't operate in the same way as the other queries. The use of execution plans to determine the behavior of these queries is absolutely as valuable here as it was with standard queries, but the internals are going to be different.

Recommendations

While the in-memory tables and natively compiled procedures can result in radical improvements in performance within SQL Server, you're still going to want to evaluate whether their use is warranted in your situation. The limits imposed on the behavior of these new objects means they are not going to be useful in all circumstances. Further, because of the requirements on both hardware and on the need for an enterprise-level installation of SQL Server, many just won't be able to implement these new objects and their behavior. To determine whether your workload is a good candidate for the use of these new objects, you can do a number of things.

Baselines

You should already be planning on establishing a performance baseline of your system by gathering various metrics using Performance Monitor, the dynamic management objects, Extended Events, and all the other tools at your disposal. Once you have the baseline, you can make determinations if your workload is likely to benefit from the reduced locking and increased speed of the in-memory tables.

Correct Workload

This technology is called in-memory OLTP tables for a reason. If you are dealing with a system that is primarily read focused, has only nightly or intermittent loads, or has a very low level of online transaction processing as its workload, the in-memory tables and natively compiled procedures are unlikely to be a major benefit for you. If you're dealing with a lot of latency in your system, the in-memory tables could be a good solution. Microsoft has outlined several other potentially beneficial workloads that you could consider using in-memory tables and natively compiled procedures; see Books Online (`http://bit.ly/1r6dmKY`).

Memory Optimization Advisor

To quickly and easily determine whether a table is a good candidate for moving to in-memory storage, Microsoft has supplied a new tool within SSMS. If you use the Object Explorer to navigate to a particular table, you can right-click that table and select Memory Optimization Advisor from the context menu. That will open a wizard. If I select the `Person.Address` table that I manually migrated earlier, the initial check will find all the columns that are not supported within the in-memory table. That will stop the wizard, and no other options are available. The output looks like Figure 23-12.

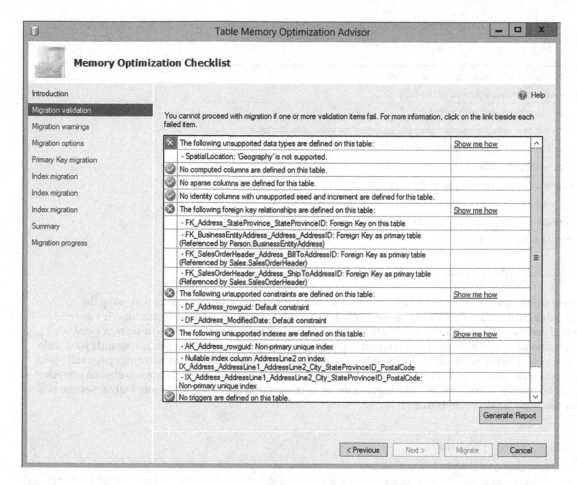

Figure 23-12. *Table Memory Optimization Advisor showing all the unsupported data types*

That means this table, as currently structured, would not be a candidate for moving to in-memory storage. So that you can see a clean run-through of the tool, I'll create a clean copy of the table in the InMemoryTest database created earlier, shown here:

```
USE InMemoryTest;
GO

CREATE TABLE dbo.AddressStaging
    (
    AddressID INT NOT NULL
                IDENTITY(1, 1)
                PRIMARY KEY,
    AddressLine1 NVARCHAR(60) NOT NULL,
    AddressLine2 NVARCHAR(60) NULL,
    City NVARCHAR(30) NOT NULL,
    StateProvinceID INT NOT NULL,
    PostalCode NVARCHAR(15) NOT NULL
    );
```

Now, running the Memory Optimization Advisor has completely different results in the first step, as shown in Figure 23-13.

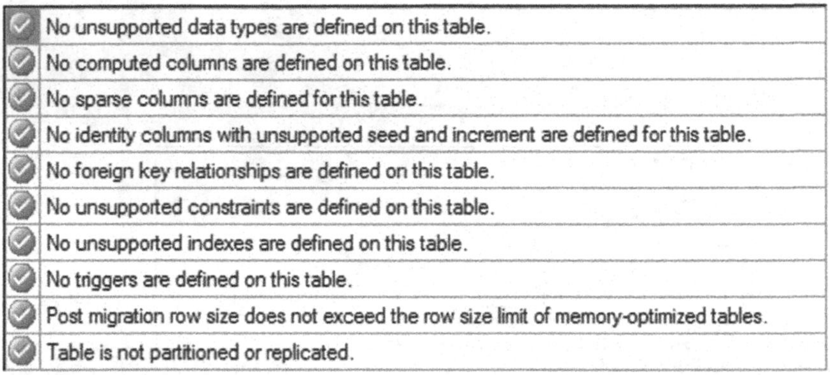

✓	No unsupported data types are defined on this table.
✓	No computed columns are defined on this table.
✓	No sparse columns are defined for this table.
✓	No identity columns with unsupported seed and increment are defined for this table.
✓	No foreign key relationships are defined on this table.
✓	No unsupported constraints are defined on this table.
✓	No unsupported indexes are defined on this table.
✓	No triggers are defined on this table.
✓	Post migration row size does not exceed the row size limit of memory-optimized tables.
✓	Table is not partitioned or replicated.

Figure 23-13. Successful first check of the Memory Optimization Advisor

The next step in the wizard shows a fairly standard set of warnings about the differences that using the in-memory tables will cause in your T-SQL as well as links to further reading about these limitations. It's a useful reminder that you may have to address your code should you choose to migrate this table to in-memory storage.

You can stop there and click the Report button to generate a report of the check that was run against your table. Or, you can use the wizard to actually move the table into memory. Clicking Next from the Warnings page will open an Options page where you can determine how the table will be migrated into memory. You get to choose what the old table will be named. It assumes you'll be keeping the table name the same for the in-memory table. Several other options are available, as shown in Figure 23-14.

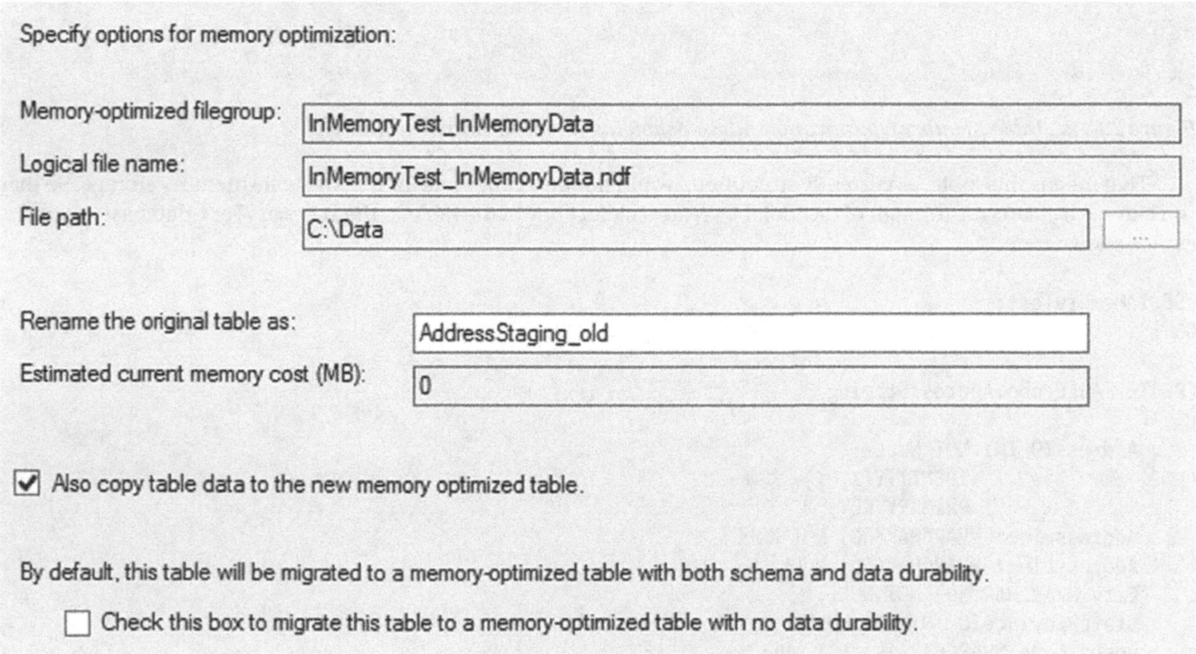

Specify options for memory optimization:

Memory-optimized filegroup:	InMemoryTest_InMemoryData
Logical file name:	InMemoryTest_InMemoryData.ndf
File path:	C:\Data

Rename the original table as:	AddressStaging_old
Estimated current memory cost (MB):	0

☑ Also copy table data to the new memory optimized table.

By default, this table will be migrated to a memory-optimized table with both schema and data durability.

☐ Check this box to migrate this table to a memory-optimized table with no data durability.

Figure 23-14. Setting the options for migrating the standard table to in-memory

Clicking Next you get to determine how you're going to create the primary key for the table. You get to supply it with a name. Then you have to choose if you're going with a nonclustered hash or a nonclustered index. If you choose the nonclustered hash, you will have to provide a bucket count. Figure 23-15 shows how I configured the key in much the same way as I did it earlier using T-SQL.

Please choose the appropriate conversion for this primary key:

	Column	Type	Collation
✔	AddressID	int	

Select a new name for this primary key: | AddressStaging_primaryKey

Select the type of this primary key:

◉ Use NONCLUSTERED HASH index

A NONCLUSTERED HASH index provides the most benefit for point lookups. It provides no discernible benefit if a query is running a Range scan.

Bucket Count: | 50000|

The Bucket Count of a NONCLUSTERED HASH index is the number of buckets in the hash table. It is recommended to set the fill factor to 50 to 60% if the table requires a lot of space for growth. Bucket Count will be rounded up to the nearest power of two.

○ Use NONCLUSTERED index

A NONCLUSTERED index provides the most benefit for range predicates and ORDER BY clauses. NONCLUSTERED indexes are unidirectional. It provides no benefit for ORDER BY clauses with orders different from the index.

Sort column and order:

Column	Sort Order

Figure 23-15. Choosing the configuration of the primary key of the new in-memory table

Clicking Next will show you a summary of the choices you have made and enable a button at the bottom of the screen to immediately migrate the table. It will migrate the table, renaming the old table however it was told to, and it will migrate the data if you chose that option. The output of a successful migration looks like Figure 23-16.

	Action	Result
✓	Renaming the original table.	Passed
	New name:AddressStaging_old	
✓	Creating the memory-optimized table in the database.	Passed
	Adding index:AddressStaging_primaryKey	
✓	Copying data from the original table to the new memory-optimized table.	Passed

Figure 23-16. *A successful in-memory table migration using the wizard*

The Memory Optimization Advisor can then identify which tables can physically be moved into memory and can do that work for you. But, it doesn't have the judgment to know which tables should be moved into memory. You're still going to have to think that through on your own.

Native Compilation Advisor

Similar in function to the Memory Optimization Advisor, the Native Compilation Advisor can be run against an existing stored procedure to determine whether it can be compiled natively. However, it's much simpler in function than the prior wizard. To show it in action, I'm going create two different procedures, shown here:

```
CREATE PROCEDURE dbo.FailWizard (@City NVARCHAR(30))
AS
    SELECT   a.AddressLine1,
             a.City,
             a.PostalCode,
             sp.Name AS StateProvinceName,
             cr.Name AS CountryName
    FROM     dbo.Address AS a
             JOIN dbo.StateProvince AS sp
             ON sp.StateProvinceID = a.StateProvinceID
             JOIN dbo.CountryRegion AS cr WITH ( NOLOCK)
             ON cr.CountryRegionCode = sp.CountryRegionCode
    WHERE    a.City = @City;
GO

CREATE PROCEDURE dbo.PassWizard (@City NVARCHAR(30))
AS
    SELECT   a.AddressLine1,
             a.City,
             a.PostalCode,
             sp.Name AS StateProvinceName,
             cr.Name AS CountryName
    FROM     dbo.Address AS a
             JOIN dbo.StateProvince AS sp
             ON sp.StateProvinceID = a.StateProvinceID
             JOIN dbo.CountryRegion AS cr
             ON cr.CountryRegionCode = sp.CountryRegionCode
    WHERE    a.City = @City;
GO
```

The first procedure includes a NOLOCK hint that can't be run against in-memory tables. The second procedure is just a repeat of the procedure you've been working with throughout this chapter. After executing the script to create both procedures, I can access the Native Compilation Advisor by right-clicking the stored procedure dbo.FailWizard and selecting Native Compilation Advisor from the context menu. After getting past the wizard start screen, the first step identifies a problem with the procedure, as shown in Figure 23-17.

(i)   To enable native compilation for this stored procedure, all tables accessed by this stored procedure must be memory-optimized tables.

	Action	Result
✖	Validating the stored procedure	One or more unsupported Transact-SQL elements exist in the stored procedure. Click Next to see a full list of unsupported elements.

Figure 23-17. *The Native Compilation Advisor has identified inappropriate T-SQL syntax*

Pay special attention to the note at the top of Figure 23-17. It states that all tables must be memory-optimized tables in order to natively compile the procedure. But, that check is not part of the Native Compilation Advisor checks.

Clicking Next as prompted, you can then see the problem that was identified by the wizard, as shown in Figure 23-18.

The following is a list of Transact-SQL elements in your stored procedure that are not supported within native compilation. In order to enable native compilation for this stored procedure, you must resolve all items in this list.

Some assistance for resolving these items are offered in this link.

Transact-SQL Element	Occurrences in the Stored Procedure	Start Line
NOLOCK	NOLOCK	9

Figure 23-18. *The problem with the code is identified by the Native Compilation Advisor*

The wizard shows the problematic T-SQL, and it shows the line on which that T-SQL occurs. That's all that's provided by this wizard. If I run the same check against the other procedure, dbo.WizardPass, it just reports that there are not any improper T-SQL statements. There is no additional action to compile the procedure for me. To get the procedure to compile, it will be necessary to add the additional functionality as defined earlier in this chapter. Except for this syntax check, there is no other help for natively compiling stored procedures.

Summary

This chapter introduced the concepts of in-memory tables and natively compiled stored procedures. These are high-end methods for achieving potentially massive performance enhancements. There are, however, a lot of limitations on implementing these new objects on a wide scale. You will need to have the Enterprise version of SQL Server and a machine with enough memory to support the additional load. You're also going to want to carefully test your data and load prior to committing to this approach in a production environment. But, if you do need to make your OLTP systems perform faster than ever before, this is a viable technology.

The next chapter shows you how to set up the ability to automate the testing of your performance using Distributed Replay.

CHAPTER 24

▪ ▪ ▪

Database Performance Testing

Knowing how to identify performance issues and knowing how to fix them are great skills to have. The problem, though, is that you need to be able to demonstrate that the improvements you make are real improvements. While you can, and should, capture the performance metrics before and after you tune a query or add an index, the best way to be sure you're looking at measurable improvement is to put the changes you make to work. Testing means more than simply running a query a few times and then putting it into your production system with your fingers crossed. You need to have a systematic way to validate performance improvements using the full panoply of queries that are run against your system in a realistic manner. Introduced with the 2012 version, SQL Server provides such a mechanism through its Distributed Replay tool.

Distributed Replay works with information generated from the SQL Profiler and the trace events created by it. Trace events capture information in a somewhat similar fashion to the Extended Events tool, but trace events are an older (and somewhat less capable) mechanism for capturing events within the system. Prior to the release of SQL Server 2012, you could use SQL Server's Profiler tool to replay captured events using a server-side trace. This worked, but the process was extremely limited. For example, the tool could be run only on a single machine, and it dealt with the playback mechanism—a single-threaded process that ran in a serial fashion, rather than what happens in reality. Microsoft has added the capability to run from multiple machines in a parallel fashion to SQL Server. Until Microsoft makes a mechanism to use Distributed Replay through Extended Events output, you'll still be using the trace events for some of your performance testing.

Distributed Replay is not a widely adopted tool. Most people just skip the idea of implementing repeatable tests entirely. Others may go with some third-party tools that provide a little more functionality. I strongly recommend you do some form of testing to ensure your tuning efforts are resulting in positive impact on your systems that you can accurately measure.

This chapter covers the following topics:

- The concepts of database testing
- How to create a server-side trace
- Using Distributed Replay for database testing

Database Performance Testing

The general approach to database performance and load testing is pretty simple. You need to capture the calls against a production system under normal load and then be able to play that load over and over again against a test system. This enables you to directly measure the changes in performance caused by changes to your code or structures. Unfortunately, accomplishing this in the real world is not as simple as it sounds.

To start with, you can't simply capture the recording of queries. Instead, you must first ensure that you can restore your production database to a moment in time on a test system. Specifically, you need to be able to restore to exactly the point at which you start recording the transactions on the system because if you restore to any other point, you might have different data or even different structures. This will cause the playback mechanism to generate errors instead of useful information. This means, to start with, you must have a database that is in Full Recovery mode so that you can take regular full backups as well as log backups in order to restore to a specific point in time when your testing will start.

Once you establish the ability to restore to the appropriate time, you will need to configure your query capture mechanism—a server-side trace definition generated by Profiler, in this case. The playback mechanism will define exactly which events you'll need to capture. You'll want to set up your capture process so that it impacts your system as little as possible.

Next, you'll have to deal with the large amounts of data captured by the trace. Depending on how big your system is, you may have a large number of transactions over a short period of time. All that data has to be stored and managed, and there will be many files.

You can set up this process on a single machine; however, to really see the benefits, you'll want to set up multiple machines to support the playback capabilities of the Distributed Replay tool. This means you'll need to have these machines available to you as part of your testing process. Unfortunately, with all editions except Enterprise, you can have only a single client, so take that into account as you set up your test environment.

When you have all these various parts in place, you can begin testing. Of course, this leads to a new question: What exactly are you doing with your database testing?

A Repeatable Process

As explained in Chapter 1, performance tuning your system is an iterative process that you may have to go through on multiple occasions to get your performance to where you need it to be and keep it there. Since businesses change over time, so will your data distribution, your applications, your data structures, and all the code supporting it. Because of all this, one of the most important things you can do for testing is to create a process that you can run over and over again.

The primary reason you need to create a repeatable testing process is because you can't always be sure that the methods outlined in the preceding chapters of this book will work well in every situation. This doubt means you need to be able to validate that the changes you have made have resulted in a positive improvement in performance. If not, you need to be able to remove any changes you've made, make a new set of changes, and then repeat the tests, repeating this process iteratively. You may find that you'll need to repeat the entire tuning cycle until you've met your goals for this round.

Because of the iterative nature of this process, you absolutely need to concentrate on automating it as much as possible. This is where the Distributed Replay tool comes into the picture.

Distributed Replay

The Distributed Replay tool consists of three pieces of architecture.

- *Distributed Replay Controller*: This service manages the processes of the Distributed Replay system.

- *Distributed Replay Administrator*: This is an interface to allow you to control the Distributed Replay Controller and the Distributed Replace process.

- *Distributed Replay Client*: This is an interface that runs on one or more machines (up to 16) to make all the calls to your database server.

You can install all three components onto one machine; however, the ideal approach is to have the controller on one machine and then have one or more client machines that are completely separated from the controller so that each of these machines is handling only some of the transactions you'll be making against the test machine. Only for the purposes of illustration, I have all the components running on a single instance.

Begin by installing the Distributed Replay Controller service onto a machine. There is no interface for the Distributed Replay utility. Instead, you'll use XML configuration files to take control of the different parts of the Distributed Replay architecture. You can use the distributed playback for various tasks, such as basic query playback, server-side cursors, or prepared server statements. Since I'm primarily covering query tuning, I'm focus on the queries and prepared server statements (also known as *parameterized queries*). This defines a particular set of events that must be captured. I'll cover how to do that in the next section.

Once the information is captured in a trace file, you will have to run that file through the preprocess event using the Distributed Replay Controller. This modifies the basic trace data into a different format that can be used to distribute to the various Distributed Replay Client machines. You can then fire off a replay process. The reformatted data is sent to the clients, which in turn will create queries to run against the target server. You can capture another trace output from the client machines to see exactly which calls they made, as well as the I/O and CPU of those calls. Presumably you'll also set up standard monitoring on the target server in order to see how the load you are generating impacts that server.

When you go to run the system against your server, you can choose one of two types of playback: Synchronization mode or Stress mode. In Synchronization mode, you will get an exact copy of the original playback, although you can affect the amount of idle time on the system. This is good for precise performance tuning because it helps you understand how the system is working, especially if you're making changes to structures, indexes, or T-SQL code. Stress mode doesn't run in any particular order, except within a single connection, where queries will be streamed in the correct order. In this case, the calls are made as fast as the client machines can make them—in any order—as fast as the server can receive them. In short, it performs a stress test. This is useful for testing database designs or hardware installations.

Capturing Data with the Server-Side Trace

Using trace events to capture data is similar to capturing query executions with Extended Events. To support the Distributed Replay process, you'll need to capture some specific events and specific columns for those events. If you want to build your own trace events, you need to go after the events listed in Table 24-1.

Table 24-1. *Events to Capture*

Events	Columns
Prepare SQL	Event Class
Exec Prepared SQL	EventSequence
SQL:BatchStarting	TextData
SQL:BatchCompleted	Application Name
RPC:Starting	LoginName
RPC:Completed	DatabaseName
RPC Output Parameter	Database ID
Audit Login	HostName
Audit Logout	Binary Data
Existing Connection	SPID
Server-side Cursor	Start Time
Server-side prepared SQL	EndTime
	IsSystem

You have two options for setting up these events. First, you can use T-SQL to set up a server-side trace. Second, you can use an external tool called Profiler. While Profiler can connect directly to your SQL Server instance, I strongly recommend against using this tool to capture data. Profiler is best used as a way to supply a template for performing the capture. You should use T-SQL to generate the actual server-side trace.

On a test or development machine, open Profiler and select TSQL_Replay from the Template list, as shown in Figure 24-1.

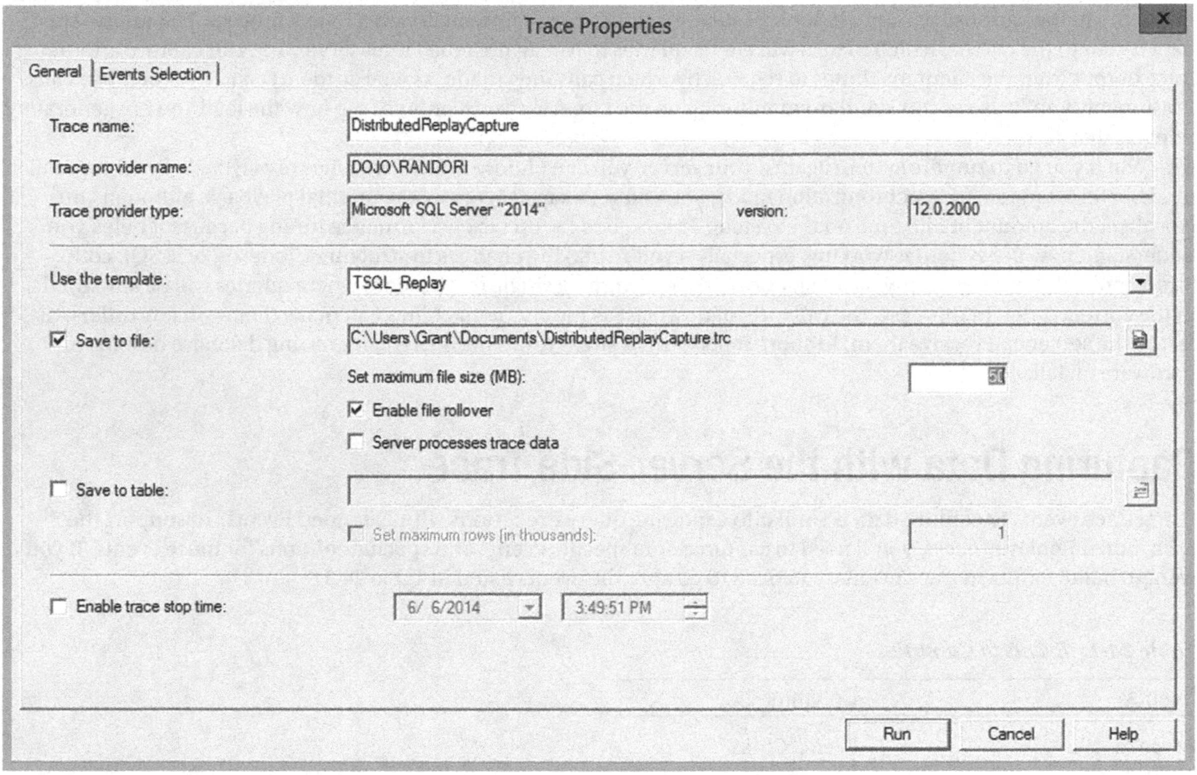

Figure 24-1. *The Distributed Replay trace template*

Since you need a file for Distributed Replay, you'll want to save the output of the trace to file. It's the best way to set up a server-side trace anyway, so this works out. You'll want to output to a location that has sufficient space. Depending on the number of transactions you have to support with your system, trace files can be extremely large. Also, it's a good idea to put a limit on the size of the files and allow them to roll over, creating new files as needed. You'll have more files to deal with, but the operating system can actually deal with a larger number of smaller files for writes better than it can deal with a single large file. I've found this to be true because of two things. First, with a smaller file size, you get a quicker rollover, which means the previous file is available for processing if you need to load it into a table or copy it to another server. Second, in my experience, it generally takes longer for writes to occur with simple log files because the size of such files gets very large. I also suggest defining a stop time for the trace process; again, this helps ensure you don't fill the drive you've designated for storing the trace data.

Since this is a template, the events and columns have already been selected for you. You can validate the events and columns to ensure you are getting exactly what you need by clicking the Events Selection tab. Figure 24-2 shows some of the events and columns, all of which are predefined for you.

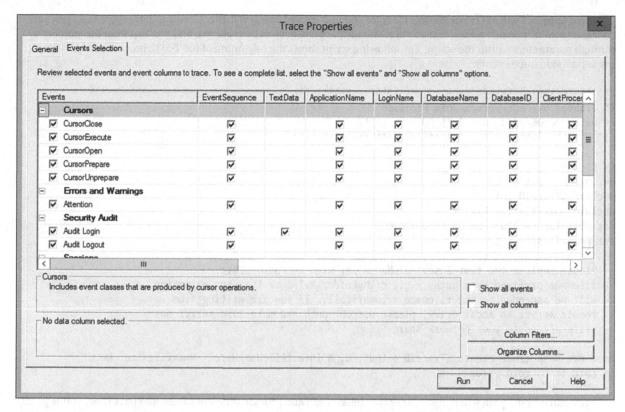

Figure 24-2. *The T-SQL_Replay template events and columns*

This template is generic, so it includes the full list of events, including all the cursor events. You can edit it by clicking boxes to deselect events; however, I do not recommend removing anything other than the cursor events, if you're going to remove any.

I started this template connected to a test server instead of a production machine because once you've set it up appropriately, you have to start the trace by clicking Run. I wouldn't do that on a production system. On a test system, however, you can watch the screen to ensure you're getting the events you think you should. It will display the events, as well as capture them to a file. When you're satisfied that it's correct, you can pause the trace. Next, click the File menu and then select Export ➤ Script Trace Definition. Finally, select For SQL Server 2005 – 2014 (see Figure 24-3).

For SQL Server 2005 - 2014...	Script Trace Definition	▶
For SQL Trace Collection Set...	Extract SQL Server Events	▶
For Analysis Services 2005 - 2014...	Extract SQL Server Analysis Services Events	▶

Figure 24-3. *The menu selection to output the trace definition*

This template will allow you to save the trace you just created as a T-SQL file. Once you have the T-SQL, you can configure it to run on any server that you like. The file path will have to be replaced, and you can reset the stop time through parameters within the script. The following script shows the beginning of the T-SQL process used to set up the server-side trace events:

```
/*****************************************************/
/* Created by: SQL Server 2014 Profiler        */
/* Date: 06/06/2014  02:58:35 PM         */
/*****************************************************/

-- Create a Queue
declare @rc int
declare @TraceID int
declare @maxfilesize bigint
set @DateTime = '2014-06-06 16:00:20.000'
set @maxfilesize = 50

-- Please replace the text InsertFileNameHere, with an appropriate
-- filename prefixed by a path, e.g., c:\MyFolder\MyTrace. The .trc extension
-- will be appended to the filename automatically. If you are writing from
-- remote server to local drive, please use UNC path and make sure server has
-- write access to your network share

exec @rc = sp_trace_create @TraceID output, 0, N'InsertFileNameHere', @maxfilesize, NULL
if (@rc != 0) goto error
```

You can edit the path where it says InsertFileNameHere and provide different values for @DateTime. At this point, your script can be run on any SQL Server 2014 server.

The amount of information you collect really depends on what kind of test you want to run. For a standard performance test, it's probably a good idea to collect at least one hour's worth of information; however, you wouldn't want to capture more than two to three hours of data in most circumstances. Plus, it can't be emphasized enough, trace events are not as lightweight as extended events, so the longer you capture data, the more you're negatively impacting your production server. Capturing more than that would entail managing a lot more data, and it would mean you were planning on running your tests for a long time.

Before you capture the data, you do need to think about where you're going to run your tests. Let's assume you're not worried about disk space and that you don't need to protect legally audited data (if you have those issues, you'll need to address them separately). If your database is not in Full Recovery mode, then you can't use the log backups to restore it to a point in time. If this is the case, I strongly recommend running a database backup as part of starting the trace data collection. The reason for this is that you need the database to be in the same condition it's in when you start recording transactions. If it's not, you may get a larger number of errors, which could seriously change the way your performance tests run. For example, attempting to select or modify data that doesn't exist will impact the I/O and CPU measured in your tests. If your database remains in the same state that it was at or near the beginning of your trace, then you should few, if any, errors.

With a copy of the database ready to go and a set of trace data, you're ready to run the Distributed Replay tool.

Distributed Replay for Database Testing

Assuming you used the Distributed Replay template to capture your trace information, you should be ready to start processing the files. As noted earlier, the first step is to convert the trace file into a different format, one that can be split up among multiple client machines for playback. But there is more to it than simply running the executable against your file. You also need to make some decisions about how you want the Distributed Replay to run; you make those decisions when you preprocess the trace file.

The decisions are fairly straightforward. First, you need to decide whether you're going to replay system processes along with the user processes. Unless you're dealing with the potential of specific system issues, I suggest setting this value to No. This is also the default value. Second, you need to decide how you want to deal with idle time. You can use the actual values for how often calls were made to the database; or, you can put in a value, measured in seconds, to limit the wait time to no more than that value. It really depends on what type of playback you're going to run. Assuming you use Synchronization mode playback, the mode best suited for straight performance measurement, it's a good idea to eliminate idle time by setting the value to something low, such as three to five seconds.

If you choose to use the default values, you don't need to modify the configuration file. But if you've chosen to include the system calls or to change the idle time, then you'll need to change the configuration file, DReplay.Exe.Preprocess.config. It's a simple XML configuration file. The one I'm using looks like this:

```xml
<?xml version="1.0" encoding="utf-8"?>
<Options>
<PreprocessModifiers>
<IncSystemSession>No</IncSystemSession>
<MaxIdleTime>2</MaxIdleTime>
</PreprocessModifiers>
</Options>
```

I've made only one change, adjusting MaxIdleTime to limit any down period during the playback.

Before you run the preprocessing, make sure have installed the DRController and that the DReplay service is running on your system. If so, you'll just need to call DReplay.exe to execute the preprocessing.

```
dreplay preprocess –i c:\data\dr.trc -d c:\DRProcess
```

In the preceding code, you can see that dreplay runs the preprocess event. The input file was supplied by the –i parameter, and a folder to hold the output was supplied through the –d parameter. The trace files will be processed, and the output will go to the folder specified. The output will look something like Figure 24-4.

```
c:\Program Files (x86)\Microsoft SQL Server\110\Tools\Binn>dreplay preprocess -d
 c:\data -i C:\Data\DR.trc -m dojo
2012-02-02 21:33:28:459 Info DReplay       Preprocessing pass 1 of 2 in progress.
2012-02-02 21:33:29:432 Info DReplay       Preprocessing pass 1 of 2 completed.
2012-02-02 21:33:29:433 Info DReplay       Preprocessing pass 2 of 2 in progress.
2012-02-02 21:33:29:434 Info DReplay       Preprocessing pass 2 of 2 completed.
2012-02-02 21:33:29:437 Info DReplay       365 replayable events written to interme
diate file in c:\data.
2012-02-02 21:33:29:438 Info DReplay       Elapsed time: 0 day(s), 0 hour(s), 0 min
ute(s), 1 second(s).
```

Figure 24-4. *Output from the preprocessing steps of Distributed Replay*

With the preprocessing complete, you're ready to move ahead with running the Distributed Replay process. Before you do so, however, you need to make sure you have one or more client systems ready to go.

Configuring the Client

The client machines will have to be configured to work with the Distributed Replay controller. Begin by installing your clients to the different machines. For illustration purposes only, I'm running everything on a single machine; however, the setup is no different if you use multiple machines. You need to configure the client to work with a controller, and a client can work with only one controller at a time. You also need to have space on the system for two items. First, you need a location for working files that are overwritten at each replay. Second, you need room for trace file output from the client if you want to collect execution data from that client. You also get to decide on the logging level of the client process. All of this is set in another XML configuration file, DReplayClient.config. Here is my configuration:

```
<Options>
<Controller>DOJO</Controller>
<WorkingDirectory>C:\DRClientWork\</WorkingDirectory>
<ResultDirectory>C:\DRClientOutput\</ResultDirectory>
<LoggingLevel>CRITICAL</LoggingLevel>
</Options>
```

The directories and logging level are clear. I also had to point the client to the server where the Distributed Replay service is running. No other settings are required for multiple clients to work; you just need to be sure they're going to the right controller system.

Running the Distributed Tests

So far you have configured everything and captured the data. Next, you need to go back to the command line to run things from the Dreplay.exe executable. Most of the control is accomplished through the configuration files, so there is little input required in the executable. You invoke the tests using the following command:

```
Dreplay replay -d c:\data -w DOJO
```

You need to feed in the location of the output from the preprocessing, which means you need to list the client machines that are taking part in a comma-delimited list. The output from the execution would look something like Figure 24-5.

```
c:\Program Files (x86)\Microsoft SQL Server\110\Tools\Binn>dreplay replay -d c:\
data -w DOJO
2012-02-02 21:39:24:046 Info DReplay      Dispatching in progress.
2012-02-02 21:39:24:052 Info DReplay      0 events have been dispatched.
2012-02-02 21:39:25:751 Info DReplay      Dispatching has completed.
2012-02-02 21:39:25:752 Info DReplay      365 events dispatched in total.
2012-02-02 21:39:25:754 Info DReplay      Elapsed time: 0 day(s), 0 hour(s), 0 min
ute(s), 1 second(s).
2012-02-02 21:39:25:755 Info DReplay      Event replay in progress.
2012-02-02 21:39:55:761 Info DReplay      DOJO: 244 events replayed, 151 events su
cceeded (pass rate 61.88 %).
2012-02-02 21:39:55:762 Info DReplay      244 events (66.84 %) have been replayed.
 Estimated time remaining: 15 second(s).
2012-02-02 21:40:22:751 Info DReplay      Event replay has completed.
2012-02-02 21:40:22:753 Info DReplay      365 events (100 %) have been replayed in
 total. Pass rate 50.13 %.
2012-02-02 21:40:22:754 Info DReplay      Elapsed time: 0 day(s), 0 hour(s), 0 min
ute(s), 58 second(s).
```

Figure 24-5. The output from running DReplay.exe

As you can see, 365 events were captured, but only 244 events were replayed. Of those, only 151 events actually succeeded. In this case, you might need to establish what information might exist about why some of the events failed. To do so, simply reconfigure the tests and run them again. The whole idea behind having a repeatable testing process is that you can run it over and over. The preceding example represents a light load run against my local copy of AdventureWorks2012, captured over about five minutes. However, I configured the limits on idle time, so the replay completes in only 58 seconds.

From here, you can reconfigure the tests, reset the database, and run the tests over and over again, as needed. Note that changing the configuration files will require you to restart the associated services to ensure that the changes are implemented with the next set of tests.

When running these tests, it's a good idea to use the types of performance data collection I talked about in Chapters 2 through 6. This helps you ensure that you can see exactly how well—or how badly—your tests are performing.

Conclusion

With the inclusion of the Distributed Replay utilities, SQL Server now gives you the ability to perform load and function testing against your databases. You accomplish this by capturing your code in a simple manner with a server-side trace. If you plan to take advantage of this feature, however, be sure to validate that the changes you make to queries based on the principles put forward in this book actually work and will help improve the performance of your system. You should also make sure you reset the database to avoid errors as much as possible.

CHAPTER 25

■ ■ ■

Database Workload Optimization

So far, you have learned about a number of aspects that can affect query performance, such as the tools that you can use to analyze query performance and the optimization techniques you can use to improve query performance. Next, you will learn how to apply this information to analyze, troubleshoot, and optimize the performance of a database workload. I'll walk you through a tuning process, including possibly going down a bad path or two, so bear with me as we navigate the process.

In this chapter, I cover the following topics:

- The characteristics of a database workload

- The steps involved in database workload optimization

- How to identify costly queries in the workload

- How to measure the baseline resource use and performance of costly queries

- How to analyze factors that affect the performance of costly queries

- How to apply techniques to optimize costly queries

- How to analyze the effects of query optimization on the overall workload

Workload Optimization Fundamentals

Optimizing a database workload often fits the 80/20 rule: 80 percent of the workload consumes about 20 percent of server resources. Trying to optimize the performance of the majority of the workload is usually not very productive. So, the first step in workload optimization is to find the 20 percent of the workload that consumes 80 percent of the server resources.

Optimizing the workload requires a set of tools to measure the resource consumption and response time of the different parts of the workload. As you saw in Chapters 4 and 5, SQL Server provides a set of tools and utilities to analyze the performance of a database workload and individual queries.

In addition to using these tools, it is important to know how you can use different techniques to optimize a workload. The most important aspect of workload optimization to remember is that not every optimization technique is guaranteed to work on every performance problem. Many optimization techniques are specific to certain database application designs and database environments. Therefore, for each optimization technique, you need to measure the performance of each part of the workload (that is, each individual query) before and after you apply an optimization technique. After this, you need to measure the impact of the optimization on the complete workload using the testing techniques outlined in Chapter 24.

It is not unusual to find that an optimization technique has little effect—or even a negative effect—on the other parts of the workload, thereby hurting the overall performance of the workload. For instance, a nonclustered index added to optimize a SELECT statement can hurt the performance of UPDATE statements that modify the value of the indexed column. The UPDATE statements have to update index rows in addition to the data rows. However, as demonstrated in Chapter 6, sometimes indexes can improve the performance of action queries, too. Therefore, improving the performance of a particular query could benefit or hurt the performance of the overall workload. As usual, your best course of action is to validate any assumptions through testing.

Workload Optimization Steps

The process of optimizing a database workload follows a specific series of steps. As part of this process, you will use the set of optimization techniques presented in previous chapters. Since every performance problem is a new challenge, you can use a different set of optimization techniques for troubleshooting different performance problems. Just remember that the first step is always to ensure that the server is well configured and operating within acceptable limits, as defined in Chapters 2 and 3.

To understand the query optimization process, you will simulate a sample workload using a set of queries. These are the optimization steps you will follow as you optimize the sample workload:

1. Capture the workload.

2. Analyze the workload.

3. Identify the costliest/most frequently called/longest-running query.

4. Quantify the baseline resource use of the costliest query.

5. Determine the overall resource use.

6. Compile detailed information on resource use.

7. Analyze and optimize external factors.

8. Analyze the use of indexes.

9. Analyze the batch-level options used by the application.

10. Analyze the effectiveness of statistics.

11. Assess the need for defragmentation.

12. Analyze the internal behavior of the costliest query.

13. Analyze the query execution plan.

14. Identify the costly operators in the execution plan.

15. Analyze the effectiveness of the processing strategy.

16. Optimize the costliest query.

17. Analyze the effects of the changes on database workload.

18. Iterate through multiple optimization phases.

As explained in Chapter 1, performance tuning is an iterative process. Therefore, you should iterate through the performance optimization steps multiple times until you achieve the desired application performance targets. After a certain period of time, you will need to repeat the process to address the impact on the workload caused by data and database changes.

Sample Workload

To troubleshoot SQL Server performance, you need to know the SQL workload that is executed on the server. You can then analyze the workload to identify causes of poor performance and applicable optimization steps. Ideally, you should capture the workload on the SQL Server facing the performance problems. In this chapter, you will use a set of queries to simulate a sample workload so that you can follow the optimization steps listed in the previous section. The sample workload you'll use consists of a combination of good and bad queries.

■ **Note**　I recommend you restore a clean copy of the AdventureWorks2012 database so that any artifacts left over from previous chapters are completely removed.

The simple test workload is simulated by the following set of sample stored procedures; you execute them using the second script on the AdventureWorks2012 database:

```
USE AdventureWorks2012;
GO


CREATE PROCEDURE dbo.ShoppingCart
    @ShoppingCartId VARCHAR(50)
AS
--provides the output from the shopping cart including the line total
SELECT  sci.Quantity,
        p.ListPrice,
        p.ListPrice * sci.Quantity AS LineTotal,
        p.[Name]
FROM    Sales.ShoppingCartItem AS sci
JOIN    Production.Product AS p
        ON sci.ProductID = p.ProductID
WHERE   sci.ShoppingCartID = @ShoppingCartId;
GO


CREATE PROCEDURE dbo.ProductBySalesOrder @SalesOrderID INT
AS
/*provides a list of products from a particular sales order,
and provides line ordering by modified date but ordered
by product name*/

SELECT  ROW_NUMBER() OVER (ORDER BY sod.ModifiedDate) AS LineNumber,
        p.[Name],
        sod.LineTotal
FROM    Sales.SalesOrderHeader AS soh
JOIN    Sales.SalesOrderDetail AS sod
        ON soh.SalesOrderID = sod.SalesOrderID
JOIN    Production.Product AS p
        ON sod.ProductID = p.ProductID
WHERE   soh.SalesOrderID = @SalesOrderID
ORDER BY p.[Name] ASC;
GO
```

```
CREATE PROCEDURE dbo.PersonByFirstName
    @FirstName NVARCHAR(50)
AS
--gets anyone by first name from the Person table
SELECT  p.BusinessEntityID,
        p.Title,
        p.LastName,
        p.FirstName,
        p.PersonType
FROM    Person.Person AS p
WHERE   p.FirstName = @FirstName;
GO


CREATE PROCEDURE dbo.ProductTransactionsSinceDate
    @LatestDate DATETIME,
    @ProductName NVARCHAR(50)
AS
--Gets the latest transaction against
--all products that have a transaction
SELECT  p.Name,
        th.ReferenceOrderID,
        th.ReferenceOrderLineID,
        th.TransactionType,
        th.Quantity
FROM    Production.Product AS p
JOIN    Production.TransactionHistory AS th
        ON p.ProductID = th.ProductID AND
           th.TransactionID = (SELECT TOP (1)
                                        th2.TransactionID
                               FROM     Production.TransactionHistory th2
                               WHERE    th2.ProductID = p.ProductID
                               ORDER BY th2.TransactionID DESC
                              )
WHERE   th.TransactionDate > @LatestDate AND
        p.Name LIKE @ProductName;
GO


ALTER PROCEDURE dbo.PurchaseOrderBySalesPersonName
    @LastName NVARCHAR(50),
    @VendorID INT = NULL
AS
    SELECT  poh.PurchaseOrderID,
            poh.OrderDate,
            pod.LineTotal,
            p.[Name] AS ProductName,
            e.JobTitle,
            per.LastName + ', ' + per.FirstName AS SalesPerson,
            poh.VendorID
```

```
    FROM    Purchasing.PurchaseOrderHeader AS poh
            JOIN Purchasing.PurchaseOrderDetail AS pod
            ON poh.PurchaseOrderID = pod.PurchaseOrderID
            JOIN Production.Product AS p
            ON pod.ProductID = p.ProductID
            JOIN HumanResources.Employee AS e
            ON poh.EmployeeID = e.BusinessEntityID
            JOIN Person.Person AS per
            ON e.BusinessEntityID = per.BusinessEntityID
    WHERE   per.LastName LIKE @LastName AND
            poh.VendorID = COALESCE(@VendorID, poh.VendorID)
    ORDER BY per.LastName,
            per.FirstName;
GO
```

Once these procedures are created, you can execute them using the following scripts:

```
EXEC dbo.PurchaseOrderBySalesPersonName
    @LastName = 'Hill%';
GO
EXEC dbo.ShoppingCart
    @ShoppingCartID = '20621';
GO
EXEC dbo.ProductBySalesOrder
    @SalesOrderID = 43867;
GO
EXEC dbo.PersonByFirstName
    @FirstName = 'Gretchen';
GO
EXEC dbo.ProductTransactionsSinceDate
    @LatestDate = '9/1/2004',
    @ProductName = 'Hex Nut%';
GO
EXEC dbo.PurchaseOrderBySalesPersonName
    @LastName = 'Hill%',
    @VendorID = 1496;
GO
```

This is an extremely simplistic workload that just illustrates the process. You're going to see hundreds and thousands of additional calls in a typical system. As simple as it is, however, this sample workload consists of the different types of queries you usually execute on SQL Server.

- Queries using aggregate functions

- Point queries that retrieve only one row or a small number of rows

- Queries joining multiple tables

- Queries retrieving a narrow range of rows

- Queries performing additional result set processing, such as providing a sorted output

The first optimization step is to identify the worst-performing queries, as explained in the next section.

Capturing the Workload

As a part of the diagnostic-data collection step, you must define an Extended Events session to capture the workload on the database server. You can use the tools and methods recommended in Chapter 6 to do this. Table 25-1 lists the specific events you should use to measure how resource intensive the queries are.

Table 25-1. *Events to Capture Information About Costly Queries*

Category	Event
Execution	rpc_completed
	sql_batch_completed

As explained in Chapter 6, for production databases it is recommended that you capture the output of the Extended Events session to a file. Here are a couple significant advantages to capturing output to a file:

- Since you intend to analyze the SQL queries once the workload is captured, you do not need to display the SQL queries while capturing them.

- Running the session through SSMS doesn't provide a flexible timing control over the tracing process.

Let's look at the timing control more closely. Assume you want to start capturing events at 11 p.m. and record the SQL workload for 24 hours. You can define an Extended Events session using the GUI or T-SQL. However, you don't have to start the process until you're ready. This means you can create commands in SQL Agent or with some other scheduling tool to start and stop the process with the ALTER EVENT SESSION command.

```
ALTER EVENT SESSION <sessionname>
ON SERVER
STATE = <start/stop>;
```

For this example, I've put a filter on the session to capture events only from the AdventureWorks2012 database. The file will capture queries against only that database, reducing the amount of information I need to deal with. This may be a good choice for your systems, too. While extended events can be very low cost, especially when compared to the older trace events, they are not free. Good filtering should always be applied to ensure minimum impact.

Analyzing the Workload

Once the workload is captured in a file, you can analyze the workload either by browsing through the data using SSMS or by importing the content of the output file into a database table.

SSMS provides the following two methods for analyzing the content of the file, both of which are relatively straightforward:

- *Sort the output on a data column by right-clicking to select a sort order or to group by a particular column*: You may want to select columns from the Details tab and use the "Show column in table" command to move them up. Once there, you can issue grouping and sorting commands on that column.

- *Rearrange the output to a selective list of columns and events*: You can change the output displayed through SSMS by right-clicking the table and selecting Pick Columns from the context menu. This lets you do more than simply pick and choose columns; it also lets you combine them into new columns.

Unfortunately, using SSMS provides limited ways of analyzing the Extended Events output. For instance, consider a query that is executed frequently. Instead of looking at the cost of only the individual execution of the query, you should also try to determine the cumulative cost of repeatedly executing the query within a fixed period of time. Although the individual execution of the query may not be that costly, the query may be executed so many times that even a little optimization may make a big difference. SSMS is not powerful enough to help analyze the workload in such advanced ways. So, while you can group by the batch_text column, the differences in parameter values mean you'll see different groupings of the same stored procedure call. If all your queries were stored procedures, you could capture the object_id and then group on that. But most systems have at least some ad hoc queries, if not a lot ad hoc queries, so that may not be workable. For in-depth analysis of the workload, you must import the content of the trace file into a database table. The output from the session puts most of the important data into an XML field, so you'll want to query it as you load the data as follows:

```
IF (SELECT  OBJECT_ID('dbo.ExEvents')
    ) IS NOT NULL
    DROP TABLE dbo.ExEvents;
GO
WITH    xEvents
            AS (SELECT   object_name AS xEventName,
                CAST (event_data AS XML) AS xEventData
          FROM       sys.fn_xe_file_target_read_file('C:\Data\MSSQL11.RANDORI\MSSQL\Log\
QueryMetrics*.xel',
                                    NULL, NULL, NULL)
            )
SELECT  xEventName,
        xEventData.value('(/event/data[@name=''duration'']/value)[1]',
                         'bigint') Duration,
        xEventData.value('(/event/data[@name=''physical_reads'']/value)[1]',
                         'bigint') PhysicalReads,
        xEventData.value('(/event/data[@name=''logical_reads'']/value)[1]',
                         'bigint') LogicalReads,
        xEventData.value('(/event/data[@name=''cpu_time'']/value)[1]',
                         'bigint') CpuTime,
        CASE xEventName
            WHEN 'sql_batch_completed'
            THEN xEventData.value('(/event/data[@name=''batch_text'']/value)[1]',
                         'varchar(max)')
            WHEN 'rpc_completed'
            THEN xEventData.value('(/event/data[@name=''statement'']/value)[1]',
                         'varchar(max)')
        END AS SQLText,
        xEventData.value('(/event/data[@name=''query_plan_hash'']/value)[1]',
                         'binary(8)') QueryPlanHash
INTO    dbo.ExEvents
FROM    xEvents;
```

You need to substitute your own path and file name for <ExEventsFileName>. Once you have the content in a table, you can use SQL queries to analyze the workload. For example, to find the slowest queries, you can execute this SQL query:

```
SELECT  *
FROM    dbo.ExEvents AS ee
ORDER BY ee.Duration DESC;
```

The preceding query will show the single costliest query, and it is adequate for the tests you're running in this chapter. You may also want to run a query like this on a production system; however, it's more likely you'll want to work from aggregations of data, as in this example:

```
SELECT  ee.SQLText,
        SUM(Duration) AS SumDuration,
        AVG(Duration) AS AvgDuration,
        COUNT(Duration) AS CountDuration
FROM    dbo.ExEvents AS ee
GROUP BY ee.SQLText;
```

Executing this query lets you order things by the fields you're most interested in—say, CountDuration to get the most frequently called procedure or SumDuration to get the procedure that runs for the longest cumulative amount of time. You need a method to remove or replace parameters and parameter values. This is necessary in order to aggregate based on just the procedure name or just the text of the query without the parameters or parameter values (since these will be constantly changing).

Another mechanism is to simply query the cache to see the costliest queries through there. It is easier than setting up Extended Events. Further, you'll probably capture most of the bad queries most of the time. Because of this, if you're just getting started with query tuning your system for the first time, you may want to skip setting up trace events to identify the costliest queries. However, I've found that as time goes on and you begin to quantify your systems behaviors, you're going to want the kind of detailed data that using Extended Events provides.

The objective of analyzing the workload is to identify the costliest query (or costly queries in general); the next section covers how to do this.

Identifying the Costliest Query

As just explained, you can use SSMS or the query technique to identify costly queries for different criteria. The queries in the workload can be sorted on the CPU, Reads, or Writes column to identify the costliest query, as discussed in Chapter 3. You can also use aggregate functions to arrive at the cumulative cost, as well as individual costs. In a production system, knowing the procedure that is accumulating the longest run times, the most CPU usage, or the largest number of reads and writes is frequently more useful than simply identifying the query that had the highest numbers one time.

Since the total number of reads usually outnumbers the total number of writes by at least seven to eight times for even the heaviest OLTP database, sorting the queries on the Reads column usually identifies more bad queries than sorting on the Writes column (but you should always test this on your systems). It's also worth looking at the queries that simply take the longest to execute. As outlined in Chapter 5, you can capture wait states with Performance Monitor and view those along with a given query to help identify why a particular query is taking a long time to run. Each system is different. In general, I approach the most frequently called procedures first; then the longest-running; and finally, those with the most reads. Of course, performance tuning is an iterative process, so you will need to reexamine each category on a regular basis.

To analyze the sample workload for the worst-performing queries, you need to know how costly the queries are in terms of duration or reads. Since these values are known only after the query completes its execution, you are mainly interested in the completed events. (The rationale behind using completed events for performance analysis is explained in detail in Chapter 6.)

For presentation purposes, open the trace file in SSMS. Figure 25-1 shows the captured trace output after moving several columns to the grid.

name	timestamp	batch_text	cpu_time	duration	logical_reads
sql_batch_completed	2014-06-12 17:35:23.1000401	EXEC dbo.PurchaseOrderBySalesPersonName @LastName = 'Hill%';	31000	175110	7570
sql_batch_completed	2014-06-12 17:35:23.1106493	EXEC dbo.ShoppingCart @ShoppingCartID = '20621';	0	755	6
sql_batch_completed	2014-06-12 17:35:23.1206846	EXEC dbo.ProductBySalesOrder @SalesOrderID = 43867;	0	1287	43
sql_batch_completed	2014-06-12 17:35:23.1331570	EXEC dbo.PersonByFirstName @FirstName = 'Gretchen';	0	1755	111
sql_batch_completed	2014-06-12 17:35:23.1447002	EXEC dbo.ProductTransactionsSinceDate @LatestDate = '9/1/2004', @ProductName = '...	0	1540	117
sql_batch_completed	2014-06-12 17:35:23.2442898	EXEC dbo.PurchaseOrderBySalesPersonName @LastName = 'Hill%', @VendorID = 1496;	16000	5066	179

Figure 25-1. *Extended Events session output showing the SQL workload*

The worst-performing query in terms of duration is also one of the worst in terms of CPU usage and reads. That procedure, dbo.PurchaseOrderBySalesPersonName, is highlighted in Figure 25-1 (you may have different values, but this query is likely to be the worst-performing query or at least one of the worst). The query inside that procedure is presented here for easy reference:

```
SELECT    poh.PurchaseOrderID,
          poh.OrderDate,
          pod.LineTotal,
          p.[Name] AS ProductName,
          e.JobTitle,
          per.LastName + ', ' + per.FirstName AS SalesPerson,
          poh.VendorID
FROM      Purchasing.PurchaseOrderHeader AS poh
          JOIN Purchasing.PurchaseOrderDetail AS pod
          ON poh.PurchaseOrderID = pod.PurchaseOrderID
          JOIN Production.Product AS p
          ON pod.ProductID = p.ProductID
          JOIN HumanResources.Employee AS e
          ON poh.EmployeeID = e.BusinessEntityID
          JOIN Person.Person AS per
          ON e.BusinessEntityID = per.BusinessEntityID
WHERE     per.LastName LIKE @LastName AND
          poh.VendorID = COALESCE(@VendorID, poh.VendorID)
ORDER BY per.LastName,
          per.FirstName;
```

Another method open to you if you can't run Extended Events is to use the sys.dm_exec_query_stats DMO. This will provide you with aggregate information about all the queries currently in cache. It's a fast way to identify the most frequently called, longest-running, and most resource-intensive procedures. It brings along the added benefit of being able to quickly join to other DMOs to pull out the execution plan and other interesting information.

Once you've identified the worst-performing query, the next optimization step is to determine the resources consumed by the query.

Determining the Baseline Resource Use of the Costliest Query

The current resource use of the worst-performing query can be considered as a baseline figure before you apply any optimization techniques. You may apply different optimization techniques to the query, and you can compare the resultant resource use of the query with the baseline figure to determine the effectiveness of a given optimization technique. The resource use of a query can be presented in two categories:

- Overall resource use
- Detailed resource use

Overall Resource Use

The overall resource use of the query provides a gross figure for the amount of hardware resources consumed by the worst-performing query. You can compare the resource use of an optimized query to the overall resource use of a nonoptimized query to ensure the overall effectiveness of the performance techniques you've applied.

You can determine the overall resource use of the query from the workload trace. You'll use the first call of the procedure since it displays the worst behavior. Table 25-2 shows the overall use of the query from the trace in Figure 25-1. One point, the durations in the table are in milliseconds, while the values in Figure 25-1 are in microseconds. Remember to take this into account when working with Extended Events.

Table 25-2. *Data Columns Representing the Amount of Resources Used by a Query*

Data Column	Value	Description
LogicalReads	7570	Number of logical reads performed by the query. If a page is not found in memory, then a logical read for the page will require a physical read from the disk to fetch the page to the memory first.
Writes	0	Number of pages modified by the query.
CPU	31 ms	How long the CPU was used by the query.
Duration	175.1 ms	The time it took SQL Server to process this query from compilation to returning the result set.

■ **Note**   In your environment, you may have different figures for the preceding data columns. Irrespective of the data columns' absolute values, it's important to keep track of these values so that you can compare them with the corresponding values later.

Detailed Resource Use

You can break down the overall resource use of the query to locate bottlenecks on the different database tables accessed by the query. This detailed resource use helps you determine which table accesses are the most problematic. Understanding the wait states in your system will help you identify where you need to focus your tuning. A rough rule of thumb can be to simply look at duration; however, duration can be affected by so many factors that it's an imperfect measure, at best. In this case, I'll spend time on all three: CPU usage, reads, and duration. Reads are a popular measure of performance, but they can be as problematic to look at in isolation as duration. This is why I spend time on all the values.

As you saw in Chapter 6, you can obtain the number of reads performed on the individual tables accessed by a given query from the STATISTICS IO output for that query. You can also set the STATISTICS TIME option to get the basic execution time and CPU time for the query, including its compile time. You can obtain this output by reexecuting the query with the SET statements as follows (or by selecting the Set Statistics IO check box in the query window):

```
--not to be run in production
DBCC FREEPROCCACHE();
DBCC DROPCLEANBUFFERS;
GO
```

```
SET STATISTICS TIME ON;
GO
SET STATISTICS IO ON;
GO
EXEC dbo.PurchaseOrderBySalesPersonName @LastName = 'Hill%';
GO
SET STATISTICS TIME OFF;
GO
SET STATISTICS IO OFF;
GO
```

To simulate the same first-time run shown in Figure 25-1, clean out the data stored in memory using DBCC DROPCLEANBUFFERS (not to be run on a production system) and remove the procedure from cache by running DBCC FREEPROCCACHE (also not to be run on a production system).

The STATISTICS output for the worst-performing query looks like this:

```
DBCC execution completed. If DBCC printed error messages, contact your system administrator.
DBCC execution completed. If DBCC printed error messages, contact your system administrator.
SQL Server parse and compile time:
   CPU time = 1 ms, elapsed time = 1 ms.

 SQL Server Execution Times:
   CPU time = 0 ms, elapsed time = 0 ms.
SQL Server parse and compile time:
   CPU time = 0 ms, elapsed time = 0 ms.
SQL Server parse and compile time:
   CPU time = 0 ms, elapsed time = 128 ms.

(1496 row(s) affected)
Table 'Employee'. Scan count 0, logical reads 2992, physical reads 2, read-ahead reads 0, lob
logical reads 0, lob physical reads 0, lob read-ahead reads 0.
Table 'Product'. Scan count 0, logical reads 2992, physical reads 3, read-ahead reads 0, lob logical
reads 0, lob physical reads 0, lob read-ahead reads 0.
Table 'PurchaseOrderDetail'. Scan count 763, logical reads 1539, physical reads 8, read-ahead reads
0, lob logical reads 0, lob physical reads 0, lob read-ahead reads 0.
Table 'Workfile'. Scan count 0, logical reads 0, physical reads 0, read-ahead reads 0, lob logical
reads 0, lob physical reads 0, lob read-ahead reads 0.
Table 'Worktable'. Scan count 0, logical reads 0, physical reads 0, read-ahead reads 0, lob logical
reads 0, lob physical reads 0, lob read-ahead reads 0.
Table 'PurchaseOrderHeader'. Scan count 1, logical reads 44, physical reads 1, read-ahead reads 42,
lob logical reads 0, lob physical reads 0, lob read-ahead reads 0.
Table 'Person'. Scan count 1, logical reads 3, physical reads 1, read-ahead reads 8, lob logical
reads 0, lob physical reads 0, lob read-ahead reads 0.

 SQL Server Execution Times:
   CPU time = 62 ms,  elapsed time = 1313 ms.

 SQL Server Execution Times:
   CPU time = 62 ms,  elapsed time = 1442 ms.
SQL Server parse and compile time:
   CPU time = 0 ms, elapsed time = 0 ms.
```

Table 25-3 summarizes the output of STATISTICS IO.

Table 25-3. *Breaking Down the Output from STATISTICS IO*

Table	Logical Reads
Person.Employee	2,992
Production.Product	2,992
Purchasing.PurchaseOrderDetail	1,539
Purchasing.PurchaseOrderHeader	44
Person.Person	3

Usually, the sum of the reads from the individual tables referred to in a query will be less than the total number of reads performed by the query. This is because additional pages have to be read to access internal database objects, such as sysobjects, syscolumns, and sysindexes.

Table 25-4 summarizes the output of STATISTICS TIME.

Table 25-4. *Breaking down the Output from STATISTICS TIME*

Event	Duration	CPU
Compile	128 ms	0 ms
Execution	1313 ms	62 ms
Completion	1442 ms	62 ms

Don't use the logical reads in isolation from the execution times. You need to take all the measures into account when determining poorly performing queries. Conversely, don't assume that the execution time is a perfect measure, either. Resource contention plays a big part in execution time, so you'll see some variation in this measure. Use both values, but use them with a full understanding that either in isolation may not be an accurate reflection of reality.

Once the worst-performing query has been identified and its resource use has been measured, the next optimization step is to determine the factors that are affecting the performance of the query. However, before you do this, you should check to see whether any factors external to the query might be causing that poor performance.

Analyzing and Optimizing External Factors

In addition to factors such as query design and indexing, external factors can affect query performance. Thus, before diving into the execution plan of the query, you should analyze and optimize the major external factors that can affect query performance. Here are some of those external factors:

- The connection options used by the application
- The statistics of the database objects accessed by the query
- The fragmentation of the database objects accessed by the query

Analyzing the Connection Options Used by the Application

When making a connection to SQL Server, various options, such as ANSI_NULL or CONCAT_NULL_YIELDS_NULL, can be set differently than the defaults for the server or the database. However, changing these settings per connection can lead to recompiles of stored procedures, causing slower behavior. Also, some options, such as ARITHABORT, must be set to ON when dealing with indexed views and certain other specialized indexes. If they are not, you can get poor performance or even errors in the code. For example, setting ANSI_WARNINGS to OFF will cause the optimizer to ignore indexed views and indexed computed columns when generating the execution plan. You can use the output from Extended Events to see this information. The options_text column contains the settings used by the connection in the login event and in the existing_connection event, as shown in Figure 25-2.

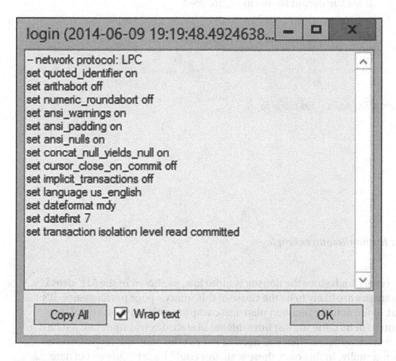

Figure 25-2. *An existing connection showing the batch-level options*

This column does more than display the batch-level options; it also lets you check the transaction isolation level. You can also get these settings from the properties of the first operator in an execution plan.

I recommend using the ANSI standard settings, in which you set the following options to ON: ANSI_NULLS, ANSI_NULL_DFLT_ON, ANSI_PADDING, ANSI_WARNINGS, CURSOR_CLOSE_ON_COMMIT, IMPLICIT_TRANSACTIONS, and QUOTED_IDENTIFIER. You can use the single command SET ANSI_DEFAULTS ON to set them all to ON at the same time.

Analyzing the Effectiveness of Statistics

The statistics of the database objects referred to in the query are one of the key pieces of information that the query optimizer uses to decide upon certain execution plans. As explained in Chapter 12, the optimizer generates the execution plan for a query based on the statistics of the objects referred to in the query. The optimizer looks at the statistics of the database objects referred to in the query and estimates the number of rows affected. In this way, it determines the processing strategy for the query. If a database object's statistics are not accurate, then the optimizer may generate an inefficient execution plan for the query.

As explained in Chapter 12, you can check the statistics of a table and its indexes using DBCC SHOW_STATISTICS. There are five tables referenced in this query: Purchasing.PurchaseOrderHeader, Purchasing.PurchaseOrderDetail, Person.Employee, Person.Person, and Production.Product. You must know which indexes are in use by the query to get the statistics information about them. You can determine this when you look at the execution plan. For now, I'll check the statistics on the primary key of the HumanResources.Employee table since it had the most reads. Now run the following query:

```
DBCC SHOW_STATISTICS('HumanResources.Employee',
'PK_Employee_BusinessEntityID');
```

When the preceding query completes, you'll see the output shown in Figure 25-3.

	Name	Updated	Rows	Rows Sampled	Steps	Density	Average key length	String Index	Filter Expression	Unfiltered Rows
1	PK_Employee_BusinessEntityID	Mar 14 2012 1:14PM	290	290	146	1	4	NO	NULL	290

	All density	Average Length	Columns	
1	0.003448276	4	BusinessEntityID	

	RANGE_HI_KEY	RANGE_ROWS	EQ_ROWS	DISTINCT_RANGE_ROWS	AVG_RANGE_ROWS
1	1	0	1	0	1
2	3	1	1	1	1
3	4	0	1	0	1
4	6	1	1	1	1
5	8	1	1	1	1
6	10	1	1	1	1
7	12	1	1	1	1
8	14	1	1	1	1
^	16	1	1	1	1

Figure 25-3. *SHOW_STATISTICS output for HumanResources.Employee*

You can see the selectivity on the index is very high since the density is quite low, as shown in the All density column. In this instance, it's doubtful that statistics are likely to be the cause of this query's poor performance. It's probably a good idea, where possible, to look at the actual execution plan and compare estimated vs. actual rows there. You can also check the Updated column to determine the last time this set of statistics was updated. If it has been more than a few days since the statistics were updated, then you need to check your statistics maintenance plan, and you should update these statistics manually. In this case, these statistics could be seriously out of date considering the data provided.

Analyzing the Need for Defragmentation

As explained in Chapter 13, a fragmented table increases the number of pages to be accessed by a query performing a scan, which adversely affects performance. However, fragmentation is frequently not an issue for point queries. For this reason, you should ensure that the database objects referred to in the query are not too fragmented.

You can determine the fragmentation of the five tables accessed by the worst-performing query by running a query against sys.dm_db_index_physical_stats. Begin by running the query against the HumanResources.Employee table.

```
SELECT  s.avg_fragmentation_in_percent,
        s.fragment_count,
        s.page_count,
        s.avg_page_space_used_in_percent,
        s.record_count,
```

```
        s.avg_record_size_in_bytes,
        s.index_id
FROM    sys.dm_db_index_physical_stats(DB_ID('AdventureWorks2012'),
                        OBJECT_ID(N'HumanResources.Employee'),
                        NULL, NULL, 'Sampled') AS s
WHERE   s.record_count > 0
ORDER BY s.index_id;
```

Figure 25-4 shows the output of this query.

	avg_fragmentation_in_percent	fragment_count	page_count	avg_page_space_used_in_percent	record_count	avg_record_size_in_bytes	index_id
1	0	1	7	91.1645416357796	290	176.158	1
2	0	1	1	60.4892512972572	290	14.889	2
3	0	1	1	67.6550531257722	290	16.889	3
4	66.6666666666667	3	3	70.1672102792192	290	56.772	5
5	50	2	2	56.6963182604398	290	29.662	6
6	0	1	1	93.1307141092167	290	24	7

Figure 25-4. *The index fragmentation of the HumanResources.Employee table*

If you run the same query for the other four tables (in order Purchasing.PurchaseOrderHeader, Purchasing.PurchaseOrderDetail, Production.Product, and Person.Person), the output will look like Figure 25-5.

	avg_fragmentation_in_percent	fragment_count	page_count	avg_page_space_used_in_percent	record_count	avg_record_size_in_bytes	index_id
1	0	1	42	99.110452186805	4012	82	1
2	28.5714285714286	3	7	99.110452186805	4012	12	2
3	28.5714285714286	3	7	99.110452186805	4012	12	3

	avg_fragmentation_in_percent	fragment_count	page_count	avg_page_space_used_in_percent	record_count	avg_record_size_in_bytes	index_id
1	0	1	64	99.0089201877934	8845	56	1
2	15	4	20	98.32592043489	8845	16	2

	avg_fragmentation_in_percent	fragment_count	page_count	avg_page_space_used_in_percent	record_count	avg_record_size_in_bytes	index_id
1	15.3846153846154	4	13	92.7999876451693	504	191.793	1
2	50	2	2	94.6009389671361	504	28.392	2
3	75	4	4	79.0832715591796	504	48.817	3
4	50	2	2	80.9241413392637	504	24	4

	avg_fragmentation_in_percent	fragment_count	page_count	avg_page_space_used_in_percent	record_count	avg_record_size_in_bytes	index_id
1	0.183727034120735	164	3810	85.6470595502842	19972	1320.83	1
2	6.60377358490566	9	106	96.3203607610576	19972	39.388	2
3	0	2	65	98.6755621447986	19972	24	3
4	0	1	3	68.2151470224858	195	82.974	256000
5	0.0464900046490005	50	2151	99.6140597973808	301696	55.499	256001
6	0.504322766570605	84	1388	99.4144304423029	301696	35.028	256002
7	1.07913669064748	98	1390	99.2713615023474	301696	35.028	256003
8	1.0806916426513	70	1388	99.4144304423029	301696	35.028	256004

Figure 25-5. *The index fragmentation for the four tables in the problem query*

The fragmentation of the Purchasing.PurchaseOrderHeader table is extremely light: 28 percent. Meanwhile, the avg_page_space_used_in_percent is greater than 90 percent for many of the indexes. When you take into account the number of pages for the indexes on the table (42 or less), you're very unlikely to get an improvement in performance by defragging the index (assuming you can), as detailed in Chapter 13.

The same can be said of Purchasing.PurchaseOrderDetail, which has very low fragmentation and a low page count. Production.Product has slightly higher degrees of fragmentation; but again, the page count is very low, so defragging the index is not likely to help much. Person.Employee has one index with **66** percent fragmentation; once again, however, it's only on three pages. Finally, Person.Person has almost no fragmentation to speak of.

Here's an experiment to try as part of the iterative performance-tuning process. Run the index defragmentation script supplied in Chapter 13 (and repeated here).

```
DECLARE @DBName NVARCHAR(255),
    @TableName NVARCHAR(255),
    @SchemaName NVARCHAR(255),
    @IndexName NVARCHAR(255),
    @PctFrag DECIMAL,
    @Defrag NVARCHAR(MAX)

IF EXISTS ( SELECT  *
            FROM    sys.objects
            WHERE   object_id = OBJECT_ID(N'#Frag') )
    DROP TABLE #Frag;
CREATE TABLE #Frag
    (
    DBName NVARCHAR(255),
    TableName NVARCHAR(255),
    SchemaName NVARCHAR(255),
    IndexName NVARCHAR(255),
    AvgFragment DECIMAL
    )
EXEC sys.sp_MSforeachdb 'INSERT INTO #Frag ( DBName, TableName, SchemaName, IndexName, AvgFragment )
SELECT    ''?''  AS DBName ,t.Name AS TableName ,sc.Name AS SchemaName ,i.name AS IndexName ,s.avg_
fragmentation_in_percent FROM       ?.sys.dm_db_index_physical_stats(DB_ID(''?''), NULL, NULL,
NULL,  ''Sampled'') AS s JOIN ?.sys.indexes i ON s.Object_Id = i.Object_id
AND s.Index_id = i.Index_id JOIN ?.sys.tables t ON i.Object_id = t.Object_Id JOIN ?.sys.schemas sc
ON t.schema_id = sc.SCHEMA_ID

WHERE s.avg_fragmentation_in_percent > 20
AND t.TYPE = ''U''
AND s.page_count > 8
ORDER BY TableName,IndexName';

DECLARE cList CURSOR
FOR
    SELECT  *
    FROM    #Frag
```

```
OPEN cList;
FETCH NEXT FROM cList
INTO @DBName, @TableName, @SchemaName, @IndexName, @PctFrag;

WHILE @@FETCH_STATUS = 0
    BEGIN
        IF @PctFrag BETWEEN 20.0 AND 40.0
            BEGIN
                SET @Defrag = N'ALTER INDEX ' + @IndexName + ' ON ' + @DBName +
                    '.' + @SchemaName + '.' + @TableName + ' REORGANIZE';
                EXEC sp_executesql @Defrag;
                PRINT 'Reorganize index: ' + @DBName + '.' + @SchemaName + '.' +
                    @TableName + '.' + @IndexName;
            END
        ELSE
            IF @PctFrag > 40.0
                BEGIN
                    SET @Defrag = N'ALTER INDEX ' + @IndexName + ' ON ' +
                        @DBName + '.' + @SchemaName + '.' + @TableName +
                        ' REBUILD';
                    EXEC sp_executesql @Defrag;
                    PRINT 'Rebuild index: ' + @DBName + '.' + @SchemaName +
                        '.' + @TableName + '.' + @IndexName;
                END
        FETCH NEXT FROM cList
INTO @DBName, @TableName, @SchemaName, @IndexName, @PctFrag;
    END
CLOSE cList;
DEALLOCATE cList;
DROP TABLE #Frag;
GO
```

After defragging the indexes on the database, rerun the query against sys.dm_db_index_ physicalstats for all five tables. This will let you determine the changes in the index defragmentation, if any (see Figure 25-6).

	avg_fragmentation_in_percent	fragment_count	page_count	avg_page_space_used_in_percent	record_count	avg_record_size_in_bytes	index_id
1	0	1	7	91.1645416357796	290	176.158	1
2	0	1	1	60.4892512972572	290	14.889	2
3	0	1	1	67.6550531257722	290	16.889	3
4	66.6666666666667	3	3	70.1672102792192	290	56.772	5
5	50	2	2	56.6963182604398	290	29.662	6
6	0	1	1	93.1307141092167	290	24	7

	avg_fragmentation_in_percent	fragment_count	page_count	avg_page_space_used_in_percent	record_count	avg_record_size_in_bytes	index_id
1	0	1	42	99.110452186805	4012	82	1
2	28.5714285714286	3	7	99.110452186805	4012	12	2
3	28.5714285714286	3	7	99.110452186805	4012	12	3

	avg_fragmentation_in_percent	fragment_count	page_count	avg_page_space_used_in_percent	record_count	avg_record_size_in_bytes	index_id
1	0	1	64	99.0089201877934	8845	56	1
2	15	4	20	98.32592043489	8845	16	2

	avg_fragmentation_in_percent	fragment_count	page_count	avg_page_space_used_in_percent	record_count	avg_record_size_in_bytes	index_id
1	15.3846153846154	4	13	92.7999876451693	504	191.793	1
2	50	2	2	94.6009389671361	504	28.392	2
3	75	4	4	79.0832715591796	504	48.817	3
4	50	2	2	80.9241413392637	504	24	4

	avg_fragmentation_in_percent	fragment_count	page_count	avg_page_space_used_in_percent	record_count	avg_record_size_in_bytes	index_id
1	0.183727034120735	164	3810	85.6470595502842	19972	1320.83	1
2	6.60377358490566	9	106	96.3203607610576	19972	39.388	2
3	0	2	65	98.6755621447986	19972	24	3
4	0	1	3	68.2151470224858	195	82.974	256000
5	0.0464900046490005	50	2151	99.6140597973808	301696	55.499	256001
6	0.504322766570605	84	1388	99.4144304423029	301696	35.028	256002
7	1.07913669064748	98	1390	99.2713615023474	301696	35.028	256003
8	1.0806916426513	70	1388	99.4144304423029	301696	35.028	256004

Figure 25-6. *The index fragmentation of the various tables after rebuilding indexes*

As you can see in Figure 25-6, the fragmentation was not reduced at all in any of the indexes in the tables used by the poorest-performing query. In most cases, this is because the number of pages is so small that defragmentation just isn't possible. In general, I wouldn't even bother defragmenting an index with fewer than 100 pages. The recommendation from Microsoft is to wait until 1,000 pages before defragmenting.

Once you've analyzed the external factors that can affect the performance of a query and resolved the nonoptimal ones, you should analyze internal factors, such as improper indexing and query design.

Analyzing the Internal Behavior of the Costliest Query

Now that the statistics are up-to-date, you can analyze the processing strategy for the query chosen by the optimizer to determine the internal factors affecting the query's performance. Analyzing the internal factors that can affect query performance involves these steps:

- Analyzing the query execution plan
- Identifying the costly steps in the execution plan
- Analyzing the effectiveness of the processing strategy

Analyzing the Query Execution Plan

To see the execution plan, click the Show Actual Execution Plan button to enable it and then run stored procedure. Be sure you're doing these types of tests on a nonproduction system. For more details on reading execution plans, check out my book *SQL Server Execution Plans* (Red Gate Publishing, 2013). Figure 25-7 shows the graphical execution plan of the worst-performing query.

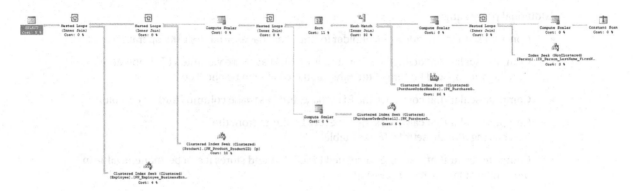

Figure 25-7. *The actual execution plan of the worst-performing query*

The graphic of this plan is somewhat difficult to read. I'll break down a few of the interesting details in case you're not following along with code. Reading execution plans was explained in Chapter 15. You could observe the following from this execution plan:

- SELECT properties:

  - Optimization Level: Full

  - Reason for Early Termination: Good enough plan found

- Data access:

  - Index seek on nonclustered index, Person.IX_Person_LastName_FirstName_MiddleName

  - Clustered index scan on, PurchaseOrderHeader.PK_PruchaseOrderHeader_PurchaseOrderID

  - Clustered index seek on PurchaseOrderDetail.PK_PurchaseOrderDetail_PurchaseOrderDetailID

  - Index seek on clustered index, Product.PK_Product_ProductID

  - Index seek on clustered index Employee.PK_Employee_BusinessEntityID

- Join strategy:

  - Nested loop join between the constant scan and Person.Person table with the Person.Person table as the outer table

  - Nested loop join between the output of the previous join and Purchasing.PurchaseOrderHeader with the Purchasing.PurchaseOrderHeader table as the outer table

- Nested loop join between the output of the previous join and the `Purchasing.PurchaseOrderDetail` table that was also the outer table

- Nested loop join between the output of the previous join and the `Production.Product` table with `Production.Product` as the outer table

- Nested loop join between the previous join and the `HumanResources.Employee` table with the `HumanResource.Employee` table as the outer table

- Additional processing:

  - Constant scan to provide a placeholder for the `@LastName` variable's `LIKE` operation

  - Compute scalar that defined the constructs of the `@LastName` variable's `LIKE` operation, showing the top and bottom of the range and the value to be checked

  - Compute scalar that combines the `FirstName` and `LastName` columns into a new column

  - Compute scalar that calculates the `LineTotal` column from the `Purchasing.PurchaseOrderDetail` table

  - Compute scalar that takes the calculated `LineTotal` and stores it as a permanent value in the result set for further processing

All this information is available by browsing the details of the operators exposed in the properties sheet from the graphical execution plan.

Identifying the Costly Steps in the Execution Plan

Once you understand the execution plan of the query, the next step is to identify the steps estimated as the most costly in the execution plan. Although these costs are estimated and don't reflect reality in any way, they are the only numbers you will receive that measure the function of the plan, so identifying, understanding, and possibly addressing the most costly operations can result in massive performance benefit. You can see that the following are the two costliest steps:

- *Costly step 1*: The clustered index scan on the `Purchasing.PurchaseOrderHeader` table is 36 percent.

- *Costly step 2*: The hash match join operation is 32 percent.

The next optimization step is to analyze the costliest steps so you can determine whether these steps can be optimized through techniques such as redesigning the query or indexes.

Analyzing the Processing Strategy

While the optimizer completed optimizing the plan, which you know because the reason for early termination of the optimization process was "Good Enough Plan Found," that doesn't mean there are not tuning opportunities in the query and structure. You can begin evaluating it by following the traditional steps.

Costly step 1 is a clustered index scan. Scans are not necessarily a problem. They're just an indication that a full scan of the object in question, in this case the entire table, was less costly than the alternatives to retrieve the information needed by the query.

Costly step 2 is the hash match join operation of the query. This again is not necessarily a problem. But, sometimes, a hash match is an indication of bad or missing indexes, or queries that can't make use of the existing indexes, so they are frequently an area that needs work. At least, that's frequently the case for OLTP systems. For large data warehouse systems, a hash match may be ideal for dealing with the types of queries you'll see there.

■ **Tip** At times you may find that no improvements can be made to the costliest step in a processing strategy. In that case, concentrate on the next costliest step to identify the problem. If none of the steps can be optimized further, then move on to the next costliest query in the workload. You may need to consider changing the database design or the construction of the query.

Optimizing the Costliest Query

Once you've diagnosed the queries with costly steps, the next stage is to implement the necessary corrections to reduce the cost of these steps.

The corrective actions for a problematic step can have one or more alternative solutions. For example, should you create a new index or structure the query differently? In such cases, you should prioritize the solutions based on their expected effectiveness and the amount of work required. For example, if a narrow index can more or less do the job, then it is usually better to prioritize that over changes to code that might lead to business testing. Making changes to code may also be the less intrusive approach. You need to evaluate each situation within the business and application construct you have.

Apply the solutions individually in the order of their expected benefit, and measure their individual effect on the query performance. Finally, you can apply the solution (or solutions) that provides the greatest performance improvement to correct the problematic step. Sometimes, it may be evident that the best solution will hurt other queries in the workload. For example, a new index on a large number of columns can hurt the performance of action queries. However, since that's not always true, it's better to determine the effect of such optimization techniques on the complete workload through testing. If a particular solution hurts the overall performance of the workload, choose the next best solution while keeping an eye on the overall performance of the workload.

Modifying the Code

The costliest operation in the query is a clustered index scan of the PurchaseOrderHeader table. The first thing you need to do is understand if the clustered index scan is necessary for the query and data returned or may be there because of the code or even because another index or a different index structure could work better. To begin to understand why you're getting a clustered index scan, you should look at the properties of the scan operation. Since you're getting a scan, you also need to look to the code to ensure it's sargable. Specifically you're interested in the Predicate property, as shown in Figure 25-8.

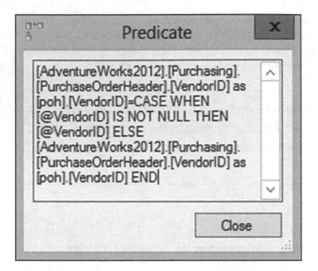

Figure 25-8. *The predicate of the clustered index scan*

This is a calculation. There is an existing index on the VendorID column of the PurchaseOrderTable that might be of use to this query, but because you're using a COALESCE statement to filter values, a scan of the entire table is necessary to retrieve the information. The COALESCE operator is basically a way to take into account that a given value might be NULL and, if it is NULL, to provide an alternate value, possibly several alternate values. However, it's a function, and a function against a column within a WHERE clause, the JOIN criteria, or a HAVING clause is likely to lead to scans, so you need to get rid of the function. Because of this function, you can't simply add or modify the index because you'd still end up with a scan. You could try rewriting the query with an OR clause like this:

```
...WHERE    per.LastName LIKE @LastName AND
        poh.VendorID = @VendorID
        OR poh.VendorID = poh.VendorID...
```

But logically, that's not the same as the COALESCE operation. Instead, it's substituting one part of the WHERE clause for another, not just using the OR construct. So, you could rewrite the entire stored procedure definition like this:

```
ALTER PROCEDURE dbo.PurchaseOrderBySalesPersonName
    @LastName NVARCHAR(50),
    @VendorID INT = NULL
AS
IF @VendorID IS NULL
BEGIN
SELECT  poh.PurchaseOrderID,
        poh.OrderDate,
        pod.LineTotal,
        p.[Name] AS ProductName,
        e.JobTitle,
        per.LastName + ', ' + per.FirstName AS SalesPerson,
        poh.VendorID
```

```
FROM    Purchasing.PurchaseOrderHeader AS poh
        JOIN Purchasing.PurchaseOrderDetail AS pod
        ON poh.PurchaseOrderID = pod.PurchaseOrderID
        JOIN Production.Product AS p
        ON pod.ProductID = p.ProductID
        JOIN HumanResources.Employee AS e
        ON poh.EmployeeID = e.BusinessEntityID
        JOIN Person.Person AS per
        ON e.BusinessEntityID = per.BusinessEntityID
WHERE   per.LastName LIKE @LastName
ORDER BY per.LastName,
        per.FirstName;

END
ELSE
BEGIN
SELECT  poh.PurchaseOrderID,
        poh.OrderDate,
        pod.LineTotal,
        p.[Name] AS ProductName,
        e.JobTitle,
        per.LastName + ', ' + per.FirstName AS SalesPerson,
        poh.VendorID
FROM    Purchasing.PurchaseOrderHeader AS poh
        JOIN Purchasing.PurchaseOrderDetail AS pod
        ON poh.PurchaseOrderID = pod.PurchaseOrderID
        JOIN Production.Product AS p
        ON pod.ProductID = p.ProductID
        JOIN HumanResources.Employee AS e
        ON poh.EmployeeID = e.BusinessEntityID
        JOIN Person.Person AS per
        ON e.BusinessEntityID = per.BusinessEntityID
WHERE   per.LastName LIKE @LastName AND
        poh.VendorID = @VendorID
ORDER BY per.LastName,
        per.FirstName;

END
GO
```

Using the IF construct breaks the queries in two. Running it with the same set of parameters resulted in a change in execution time from 1313ms to 267ms, which is a fairly strong improvement. The reads on Purchasing.PurchaseOrderHeader went up from 44 to 87, which may not be good. But the Purchasing.PurchaseOrderDetail reads went down from 1,539 to 763. Between the reduction in reads and the reduction in performance time, we're looking at a good solution, possibly. The execution plan is certainly different, as shown in Figure 25-9.

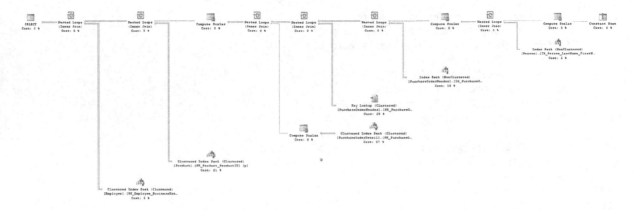

Figure 25-9. *New execution plan after breaking apart the query*

The two costliest operators are now gone. There are no more scan operations, and all the join operations are now loop joins. But, a new data access operation has been added. You're now seeing a key lookup operation, as described in Chapter 11, so you have more tuning opportunities.

Fixing the Key Lookup Operation

Now that you know you have a key lookup, you need to determine whether any of the methods for addressing it suggested in Chapter 11 can be applied. First, you need to know what columns are being retrieved in the operation. This means accessing the properties of the key lookup operator. The properties show the VendorID and OrderDate columns. This means you only need to add those columns to the leaf pages of the index through the INCLUDE part of the nonclustered index. You can modify that index as follows:

```
CREATE NONCLUSTERED INDEX [IX_PurchaseOrderHeader_EmployeeID] ON [Purchasing].[PurchaseOrderHeader]
(
    [EmployeeID] ASC
)
INCLUDE (VendorID, OrderDate)
WITH DROP_EXISTING;
```

Applying this index results in a change in the execution plan and a modification in the performance. The previous structure and code resulted in 267ms. With this new index in place, the query execution time dropped to 56ms. The execution plan is now completely different, as shown in Figure 25-10.

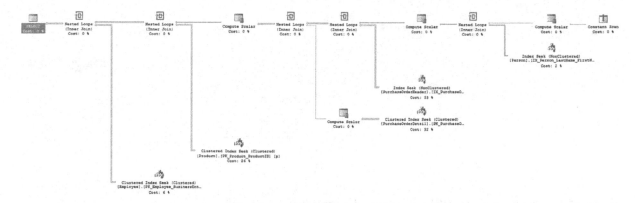

Figure 25-10. *New execution plan after modifying the index*

At this point there are nothing but nested loop joins and index seeks. There's not even a sort operation any more despite the ORDER BY statement in the query. This is because the output of the index seek against the Person table is Ordered. In short, you're largely in good shape as far as this query goes, but there were two queries in the procedure now.

Tuning the Second Query

Eliminating the COALESCE allowed you to use existing indexes, but in doing this you effectively created two paths through your query. Because you've explored the first path only because you have used only the single parameter, you've been ignoring the second query. Let's modify the test script to see how the second path through the query will work.

```
DBCC FREEPROCCACHE();
DBCC DROPCLEANBUFFERS;
GO
SET STATISTICS TIME ON;
GO
SET STATISTICS IO ON;
GO
EXEC dbo.PurchaseOrderBySalesPersonName @LastName = 'Hill%',
    @VendorID = 1496;
GO
SET STATISTICS TIME OFF;
GO
SET STATISTICS IO OFF;
GO
```

Running this query results in a different execution plan entirely, as you can see in Figure 25-11.

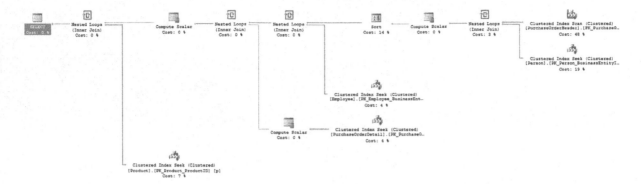

Figure 25-11. *Execution plan for the other query in the procedure*

This new query has different behaviors because of the differences in the query. The main issue here is a clustered index scan against the PurchaseOrderHeader table. You're seeing a scan despite that there is an index on VendorID. Again, you can look to see what the output of the operator includes. This time, it's more than just two columns: OrderDate, EmployeeID, PurchaseOrderID. These are not very large columns, but they will add to the size of the index. You'll need to evaluate whether this increase in index size is worth the performance benefits of the elimination of the scan of the index. I'm going to go ahead and try it by modifying the index as follows:

```
CREATE NONCLUSTERED INDEX IX_PurchaseOrderHeader_VendorID ON Purchasing.PurchaseOrderHeader
(
VendorID ASC
)
INCLUDE(OrderDate,EmployeeID,PurchaseOrderID)
WITH DROP_EXISTING;
GO
```

Prior to applying the index, the execution time was around 340ms. After applying the index, the execution time dropped to 154ms. The execution plan now looks like Figure 25-12.

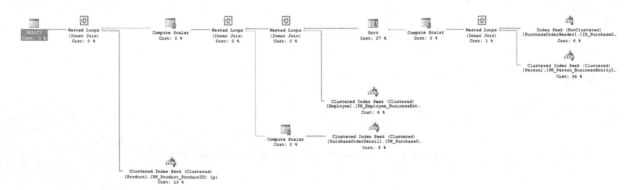

Figure 25-12. *The second execution plan after modifying the index*

The new execution plan consists of index seeks and nested loops joins. There is a sort operator, the second costliest in the plan, ordering the data by LastName and FirstName. Getting this to be taken care of by the retrieval process might help to improve performance, but I've had a fairly successful tuning to this point, so I'll leave it as is for now.

One additional consideration should be made for the split query. When the optimizer processes a query like this, both statements will be optimized for the parameter values passed in. Because of this, you may see bad execution plans, especially for the second query that uses the VendorID for filtering, because of parameter sniffing gone bad. To avoid that situation, one additional tuning effort should be made.

Creating a Wrapper Procedure

Because you've created two paths within the procedure in order to accommodate the different mechanisms of querying the data, you have the potential for getting bad parameter sniffing because both paths will be compiled, regardless of the parameters passed. One mechanism around this is to run the procedure you have into a wrapper procedure. But first, you have to create two new procedures, one for each query like this:

```
CREATE PROCEDURE dbo.PurchaseOrderByLastName @LastName NVARCHAR(50)
AS
    SELECT  poh.PurchaseOrderID,
            poh.OrderDate,
            pod.LineTotal,
            p.[Name] AS ProductName,
            e.JobTitle,
            per.LastName + ', ' + per.FirstName AS SalesPerson,
            poh.VendorID
    FROM    Purchasing.PurchaseOrderHeader AS poh
            JOIN Purchasing.PurchaseOrderDetail AS pod
            ON poh.PurchaseOrderID = pod.PurchaseOrderID
            JOIN Production.Product AS p
            ON pod.ProductID = p.ProductID
            JOIN HumanResources.Employee AS e
            ON poh.EmployeeID = e.BusinessEntityID
            JOIN Person.Person AS per
            ON e.BusinessEntityID = per.BusinessEntityID
    WHERE   per.LastName LIKE @LastName
    ORDER BY per.LastName,
            per.FirstName;
GO


CREATE PROCEDURE dbo.PurchaseOrderByLastNameVendor
    @LastName NVARCHAR(50),
    @VendorID INT
AS
    SELECT  poh.PurchaseOrderID,
            poh.OrderDate,
            pod.LineTotal,
            p.[Name] AS ProductName,
            e.JobTitle,
            per.LastName + ', ' + per.FirstName AS SalesPerson,
            poh.VendorID
```

```
FROM    Purchasing.PurchaseOrderHeader AS poh
        JOIN Purchasing.PurchaseOrderDetail AS pod
        ON poh.PurchaseOrderID = pod.PurchaseOrderID
        JOIN Production.Product AS p
        ON pod.ProductID = p.ProductID
        JOIN HumanResources.Employee AS e
        ON poh.EmployeeID = e.BusinessEntityID
        JOIN Person.Person AS per
        ON e.BusinessEntityID = per.BusinessEntityID
WHERE   per.LastName LIKE @LastName AND
        poh.VendorID = @VendorID
ORDER BY per.LastName,
        per.FirstName;
GO
```

Then you have to modify the existing procedure so that it looks like this:

```
ALTER PROCEDURE dbo.PurchaseOrderBySalesPersonName
    @LastName NVARCHAR(50),
    @VendorID INT = NULL
AS
    IF @VendorID IS NULL
        BEGIN
            EXEC dbo.PurchaseOrderByLastName @LastName
        END
    ELSE
        BEGIN
            EXEC dbo.PurchaseOrderByLastNameVendor @LastName, @VendorID
        END
GO
```

With that in place, regardless of the code path chosen, the first time these queries are called, each procedure will get its own unique execution plan, avoiding bad parameter sniffing. And, this won't negatively impact performance time. If I run both the queries now the results are approximately the same.

Taking the performance from 1313ms to 56ms or 154ms is a pretty good reduction in execution time. If this query were called hundreds of times in a minute, that level of reduction would be quite serious indeed. But, you should always go back and assess the impact on the overall database workload.

Analyzing the Effect on Database Workload

Once you've optimized the worst-performing query, you must ensure that it doesn't hurt the performance of the other queries; otherwise, your work will have been in vain.

To analyze the resultant performance of the overall workload, you need to use the techniques outlined in Chapter 15. For the purposes of this small test, reexecute the complete workload and capture extended events in order to record the overall performance.

■ **Tip** For proper comparison with the original extended events, please ensure that the graphical execution plan is off.

Figure 25-13 shows the corresponding trace output captured.

name	timestamp	batch_text	cpu_time	duration	logical_reads
sql_batch_completed	2014-06-13 18:37:44.3462379	EXEC dbo.PurchaseOrderBySalesPersonName @LastName = 'Hill%';	31000	78825	7747
sql_batch_completed	2014-06-13 18:37:44.4965000	EXEC dbo.ShoppingCart @ShoppingCartID = '20621';	0	115899	8
sql_batch_completed	2014-06-13 18:37:44.5462441	EXEC dbo.ProductBySalesOrder @SalesOrderID = 43867;	0	30504	45
sql_batch_completed	2014-06-13 18:37:44.7240866	EXEC dbo.PersonByFirstName @FirstName = 'Gretchen';	0	128867	113
sql_batch_completed	2014-06-13 18:37:44.7613258	EXEC dbo.ProductTransactionsSinceDate @LatestDate = '9/1/2004', @ProductName = '...	0	19430	119
sql_batch_completed	2014-06-13 18:37:44.8063391	EXEC dbo.PurchaseOrderBySalesPersonName @LastName = 'Hill%', @VendorID = 1496;	0	19400	289

Figure 25-13. *The Extended Events output showing the effect of optimizing the costliest query on the complete workload*

From this trace, Table 25-5 summarizes the resource use and the response time (in other words, Duration) of the query under consideration.

Table 25-5. *Resource Usage and Response Time of the Optimized Query Before and After Optimization*

Column	Before Optimization	After Optimization
Reads	1901	289
Writes	0	0
CPU	16 ms	0 ms
Duration	1313 ms	19.4 ms

■ **Note** The absolute values are less important than the relative difference between the Before Optimization and the corresponding After Optimization values. The relative differences between the values indicate the improvement in performance.

It's possible that the optimization of the worst-performing query may hurt the performance of some other query in the workload. However, as long as the overall performance of the workload is improved, you can retain the optimizations performed on the query. In this case, the other queries were not impacted. But now, there is a query that takes longer than the others. It too might need optimization, and the whole process starts again.

Iterating Through Optimization Phases

An important point to remember is that you need to iterate through the optimization steps multiple times. In each iteration, you can identify one or more poorly performing queries and optimize the query or queries to improve the performance of the overall workload. You must continue iterating through the optimization steps until you achieve adequate performance or meet your service-level agreement (SLA).

Besides analyzing the workload for resource-intensive queries, you must also analyze the workload for error conditions. For example, if you try to insert duplicate rows into a table with a column protected by the unique constraint, SQL Server will reject the new rows and report an error condition to the application. Although the data was not entered into the table and no useful work was performed, valuable resources were used to determine that the data was invalid and must be rejected.

To identify the error conditions caused by database requests, you will need to include the following in your Extended Events session (alternatively, you can create a new session that looks for these events in the errors or warnings category):

- error_reported
- execution_warning
- hash_warning
- missing_column_statistics
- missing_join_predicate
- sort_warning

For example, consider the following SQL queries:

```
INSERT  INTO Purchasing.PurchaseOrderDetail
        (PurchaseOrderID,
         DueDate,
         OrderQty,
         ProductID,
         UnitPrice,
         ReceivedQty,
         RejectedQty,
         ModifiedDate
        )
VALUES  (1066,
         '1/1/2009',
         1,
         42,
         98.6,
         5,
         4,
         '1/1/2009'
        ) ;
GO

SELECT  p.[Name],
        psc.[Name]
FROM    Production.Product AS p,
        Production.ProductSubCategory AS psc ;
GO
```

Figure 25-14 shows the corresponding session output.

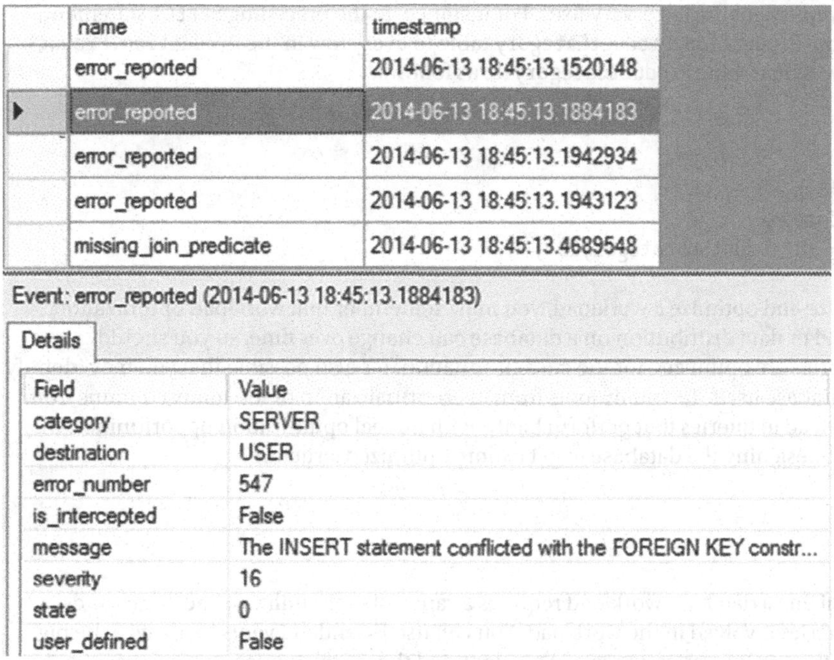

name	timestamp
error_reported	2014-06-13 18:45:13.1520148
error_reported	2014-06-13 18:45:13.1884183
error_reported	2014-06-13 18:45:13.1942934
error_reported	2014-06-13 18:45:13.1943123
missing_join_predicate	2014-06-13 18:45:13.4689548

Event: error_reported (2014-06-13 18:45:13.1884183)

Details

Field	Value
category	SERVER
destination	USER
error_number	547
is_intercepted	False
message	The INSERT statement conflicted with the FOREIGN KEY constr...
severity	16
state	0
user_defined	False

Figure 25-14. *Extended Events output showing errors raised by a SQL workload*

From the Extended Events output in Figure 25-14, you can see that the two errors I intentionally generated occurred.

- error_reported

- missing_join_predicate

The error_reported error was caused by the INSERT statement, which tried to insert data that did not pass the referential integrity check; namely, it attempted to insert ProductId = 42 when there is no such value in the Production.Product table. From the error_number column, you can see that the error number is 547. The message column shows the full description for the error. It's worth noting, though, that error_reported can be quite chatty with lots of data returned and not all of it useful.

The second type of error, missing_join_predicate, is caused by the SELECT statement.

```
SELECT    p.[Name]
    ,c.[Name]
FROM        Production.Product AS p
    ,Production.ProductSubCategory AS c;
GO
```

If you take a closer look at the SELECT statement, you will see that the query does not specify a JOIN clause between the two tables. A missing join predicate between the tables usually leads to an inaccurate result set and a costly query plan. This is what is known as a *Cartesian join,* which leads to a *Cartesian product,* where every row from one table is combined with every row from the other table. You must identify the queries causing such events in the

Errors and Warnings section and implement the necessary fixes. For instance, in the preceding SELECT statement, you should not join every row from the Production.ProductCategory table to every row in the Production.Product table—you must join only the rows with matching ProductCategoryID, as follows:

```
SELECT p.[Name]
    ,c.[Name]
FROM       Production.Product AS p
    JOIN Production.ProductSubCategory AS c
    ON p.ProductSubcategoryID = c.ProductSubcategoryID ;
```

Even after you thoroughly analyze and optimize a workload, you must remember that workload optimization is not a one-off process. The workload or data distribution on a database can change over time, so you should periodically check whether your queries are optimized for the current situation. It's also possible that you may identify shortcomings in the design of the database itself. Too many joins from overnormalization or too many columns from improper denormalization can both lead to queries that perform badly, with no real optimization opportunities. In this case, you will need to consider redesigning the database to get a more optimized structure.

Summary

As you learned in this chapter, optimizing a database workload requires a range of tools, utilities, and commands to analyze different aspects of the queries involved in the workload. You can use Extended Events to analyze the big picture of the workload and identify the costly queries. Once you've identified the costly queries, you can use the query window and various SQL commands to troubleshoot the problems associated with the costly queries. Based on the problems detected with the costly queries, you can apply one or more sets of optimization techniques to improve the query performance. The optimization of the costly queries should improve the overall performance of the workload; if this does not happen, you should roll back the change or changes.

In the next chapter, I summarize the performance-related best practices in a nutshell. You'll be able to use this information as a quick and easy-to-read reference.

■ ■ ■

## CHAPTER 26

SQL Server Optimization Checklist

If you have read through the previous 25 chapters of this book, then you understand the major aspects involved in performance optimization. You also understand that it is a challenging and ongoing activity.

What I hope to do in this chapter is to provide a performance-monitoring checklist that can serve as a quick reference for database developers and DBAs when in the field. The idea is similar to the notion of tear-off cards of best practices. This chapter does not cover everything, but it does summarize, in one place, some of the major tuning activities that can have a quick and demonstrable impact on the performance of your SQL Server systems. I have categorized these checklist items into the following sections:

- Database design
- Configuration settings
- Database administration
- Database backup
- Query design

Each section contains a number of optimization recommendations and techniques. Where appropriate, each section also cross-references specific chapters in this book that provide more detailed information.

Database Design

Database design is a broad topic, and it can't be given due justice in a small section in this query tuning book; nevertheless, I advise you to keep an eye on the following design aspects to ensure that you pay attention to database performance from an early stage:

- Balancing under- and overnormalization
- Benefiting from using entity-integrity constraints
- Benefiting from using domain and referential integrity constraints
- Adopting index-design best practices
- Avoiding the use of the sp_ prefix for stored procedure names
- Minimizing the use of triggers
- Considering putting tables into in-memory storage

Balancing Under- and Overnormalization

When designing a database, you have the following two extreme options:

- Save the complete data in a single, flat table with little to no normalization.
- Save the data in fine-grained tables by exploding every attribute into its own table and thus allowing every attribute to save an unlimited number of multiple values.

Don't get me wrong. There are excellent places where you can put NoSQL-style databases to work using an ID-value pair mechanism for storage and even retrieval. But, there is a need for relational storage. Reasonable normalization enhances database performance. The presence of wide tables with a large number of columns is usually a characteristic of an undernormalized database. *Undernormalization* causes excessive repetition of data, which can lead to improper results and often hurts query performance. For example, in an ordering system, you can keep a customer's profile and all the orders placed by the customer in a single table, as shown in Table 26-1.

Table 26-1. *Original Customers Table*

CustID	Name	Address	Phone	OrderDt	ShippingAddress
100	Liu Hong	Boise, ID, USA	123-456-7890	08-Jul-04	Boise, ID, USA
100	Liu Hong	Boise, ID, USA	123-456-7890	10-Jul-04	Austin, TX, USA

Keeping the customer profile and the order information together in a single table will repeat the customer profile in every order placed by the customer, making the rows in the table very wide. Consequently, fewer customer profiles can be saved in one data page. For a query interested in a range of customer profiles (not their order information), more pages have to be read compared to a design in which customer profiles are kept in a separate table. Also, with every bit of data in one large table, you're going to see a lot more locking and concurrency issues since more people are going to access the same data out of the same page or row much more frequently. This is especially true because you'll be storing fewer rows of data on each page because they're wider. To avoid the performance impact of undernormalization, you must normalize the two logical entities (for example, customer profile and orders), which have a one-to-many type of relationship, into separate tables, as shown in Tables 26-2 and 26-3.

Table 26-2. *New Customers Table*

CustID	Name	Address	Phone
100	Liu Hong	Boise, ID, USA	123-456-7890

Table 26-3. *Orders Table*

CustID	OrderDt	ShippingAddress
100	08-Jul-04	Boise, ID, USA
100	10-Jul-04	Austin, TX, USA

Yes, there are further normalization opportunities possible with these tables; however, that's up to you, working with your business, to determine whether they're needed.

Similarly, overnormalization is not good for query performance. *Overnormalization* causes excessive joins across too many narrow tables. Misestimations on cardinality in one table can seriously impact a large number of others as they get joined. Although a 20-table join can perform perfectly fine and a 2-table join can be a problem, a good rule of thumb is to more closely examine a query when it exceeds 8 to 12 tables in the join criteria. That is not to say that anything below that number is good and anything above that is bad; however, this number of joins should act as a flag for evaluation. To fetch any useful content from the database, a database developer has to join a large number of tables in the SQL queries. For example, if you create separate tables for a customer name, address, and phone number, then you will have to join at least three tables to retrieve the customer information. If the data (for example, the customer name and address) has a one-to-one type of relationship and is usually accessed together by the queries, then normalizing the data into separate tables can hurt query performance.

Benefiting from Entity-Integrity Constraints

Data integrity is essential to ensuring the quality of data in the database. An essential component of data integrity is *entity integrity,* which defines a row as a unique entity for a particular table; that is, every row in a table must be uniquely identifiable. The column or columns serving as the unique row identifier for a table must be represented as the primary key of the table.

Sometimes, a table may contain an additional column (or columns) that also can be used to uniquely identify a row in the table. For example, an Employee table may have the EmployeeID and SocialSecurityNumber columns. The EmployeeID column serves as the unique row identifier, and it can be defined as the *primary key*. Similarly, the SocialSecurityNumber column can be defined as the *alternate key*. In SQL Server, alternate keys can be defined using unique constraints, which are essentially the younger siblings to primary keys. In fact, both the unique constraint and the primary key constraint use unique indexes behind the scenes.

It's worth noting that there is honest disagreement regarding the use of a natural key (for example, the SocialSecurityNumber column in the previous example) or an artificial key (for example, the EmployeeID column). I've seen both designs succeed, but each approach has strengths and weaknesses. Rather than suggest one over the other, I'll provide you with a couple of reasons to use both and some of the costs associated with each and thereby avoid the religious argument. An identity column is usually an INT or a BIGINT, which makes it narrow and easy to index, improving performance. Also, separating the value of the primary key from any business knowledge is considered good design in some circles. One of the drawbacks of this approach is that the numbers sometimes acquire business meaning, which should never happen. Another thing to keep in mind is that you have to create a unique constraint for the alternate keys to prevent the creation of multiple rows where none should exist. This increases the amount of information you have to store and maintain. Natural keys provide a clear, human-readable, primary key that has true business meaning. They tend to be wider fields—sometimes very wide—making them less efficient inside indexes. Also, sometimes the data may change, which has a profound trickle-down effect within your database and your enterprise.

Let me just reiterate that either approach can work well and that each provides plenty of opportunities for tuning. Either approach, properly applied and maintained, will protect the integrity of your data.

Besides maintaining data integrity, unique indexes—the primary vehicle for entity-integrity constraints—help the optimizer generate efficient execution plans. SQL Server can often search through a unique index faster than it can search through a nonunique index. This is because each row in a unique index is unique; and, once a row is found, SQL Server does not have to look any further for other matching rows (the optimizer is aware of this fact). If a column is used in sort (or GROUP BY or DISTINCT) operations, consider defining a unique constraint on the column (using a unique index) because columns with a unique constraint generally sort faster than ones with no unique constraint.

To understand the performance benefit of entity-integrity or unique constraints, consider an example. Assume you want to modify the existing unique index on the Production.Product table.

```
CREATE   NONCLUSTERED INDEX [AK_Product_Name]
ON [Production].[Product]  ([Name] ASC) WITH (
DROP_EXISTING = ON)
ON   [PRIMARY];
GO
```

The nonclustered index does not include the UNIQUE constraint. Therefore, although the [Name] column contains unique values, the absence of the UNIQUE constraint from the nonclustered index does not provide this information to the optimizer in advance. Now, let's consider the performance impact of the UNIQUE constraint (or a missing UNIQUE constraint) on the following SELECT statement:

```
SELECT DISTINCT
        (p.[Name])
FROM    Production.Product AS p;
```

Figure 26-1 shows the execution plan of this SELECT statement.

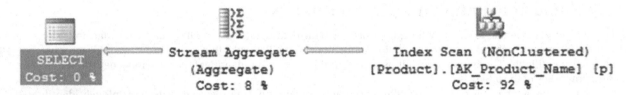

Figure 26-1. *An execution plan with no UNIQUE constraint on the [Name] column*

From the execution plan, you can see that the nonclustered AK_ProductName index is used to retrieve the data, and then a Stream Aggregate operation is performed on the data to group the data on the [Name] column so that the duplicate [Name] values can be removed from the final result set. Note that the Stream Aggregate operation would not have been required if the optimizer had been told in advance about the uniqueness of the [Name] column. You can accomplish this by defining the nonclustered index with a UNIQUE constraint, as follows:

```
CREATE UNIQUE NONCLUSTERED INDEX [AK_Product_Name]
ON [Production].[Product]([Name] ASC)
WITH (
DROP_EXISTING = ON)
ON   [PRIMARY];
GO
```

Figure 26-2 shows the new execution plan of the SELECT statement.

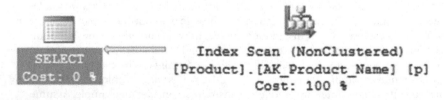

Figure 26-2. *An execution plan with a UNIQUE constraint on the [Name] column*

In general, the entity-integrity constraints (in other words, primary keys and unique constraints) provide useful information to the optimizer about the expected results, assisting the optimizer in generating efficient execution plans. Of note is the fact that sys.dm_db_index_usage_stats doesn't show when a constraint check has been run against the index that defines the unique constraint.

Benefiting from Domain and Referential Integrity Constraints

The other two important components of data integrity are *domain integrity* and *referential integrity*. Domain integrity for a column can be enforced by restricting the data type of the column, defining the format of the input data, and limiting the range of acceptable values for the column. SQL Server provides the following features to implement the domain integrity: data types, FOREIGN KEY constraints, CHECK constraints, DEFAULT definitions, and NOT NULL definitions. If an application requires that the values for a data column be restricted to a range of values, then this business rule can be implemented either in the application code or in the database schema. Implementing such a business rule in the database using domain constraints (such as the CHECK constraint) usually helps the optimizer generate efficient execution plans.

To understand the performance benefit of domain integrity, consider this example:

```
--Create two test tables
IF (SELECT  OBJECT_ID('dbo.Test1')
   ) IS NOT NULL
     DROP TABLE dbo.Test1;
GO
CREATE TABLE dbo.Test1 (
    C1 INT,
    C2 INT CHECK (C2 BETWEEN 10 AND 20)
    ) ;
INSERT  INTO dbo.Test1
VALUES  (11, 12);
GO
IF (SELECT  OBJECT_ID('dbo.Test2')
   ) IS NOT NULL
     DROP TABLE dbo.Test2;
GO
CREATE TABLE dbo.Test2 (C1 INT, C2 INT);
INSERT  INTO dbo.Test2
VALUES  (101, 102);
```

Now execute the following two SELECT statements:

```
SELECT  T1.C1,
        T1.C2,
        T2.C2
FROM    dbo.Test1 AS T1
JOIN    dbo.Test2 AS T2
        ON T1.C1 = T2.C2 AND
           T1.C2 = 20;
GO
SELECT  T1.C1,
        T1.C2,
        T2.C2
FROM    dbo.Test1 AS T1
JOIN    dbo.Test2 AS T2
        ON T1.C1 = T2.C2 AND
           T1.C2 = 30;
```

The two SELECT statements appear to be the same, except for the predicate values (20 in the first statement and 30 in the second). Although the two SELECT statements have the same form, the optimizer treats them differently because of the CHECK constraint on the T1.C2 column, as shown in the execution plan in Figure 26-3.

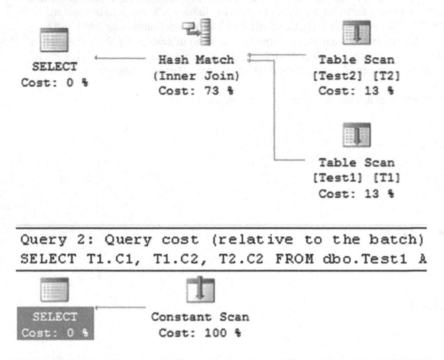

Query 2: Query cost (relative to the batch)
SELECT T1.C1, T1.C2, T2.C2 FROM dbo.Test1 A

Figure 26-3. Execution plans with predicate values within and outside the CHECK constraint boundaries

From the execution plan, you can see that, for the first query (with T1.C2 = 20), the optimizer accesses the data from both tables. For the second query (with T1.C2 = 30), the optimizer understands from the corresponding CHECK constraint on the column T1.C2 that the column can't contain any value outside the range of 10 to 20. Thus, the optimizer doesn't even access the data from the tables. Consequently, the relative estimated cost of the second query is 0 percent.

I explained the performance advantage of referential integrity in detail in the "Declarative Referential Integrity" section of Chapter 18.

Therefore, you should use domain and referential constraints not only to implement data integrity but also to facilitate the optimizer in generating efficient query plans. To understand other performance benefits of domain and referential integrity, please refer to the "Using Domain and Referential Integrity" section of Chapter 18.

Adopting Index-Design Best Practices

The most common optimization recommendation—and frequently one of the biggest contributors to good performance—is to implement the correct indexes for the database workload. Indexes are unlike tables, which are used to store data and can be designed even without knowing the queries thoroughly (as long as the tables properly represent the business entities). Instead, indexes must be designed by reviewing the database queries thoroughly. Except in common and obvious cases, such as primary keys and unique indexes, please don't fall into the trap of designing indexes without knowing the queries. Even for primary keys and unique indexes, I advise you to validate the applicability of those indexes as you start designing the database queries. Considering the importance of indexes for database performance, you must be careful when designing indexes.

Although the performance aspect of indexes is explained in detail in Chapters 8, 11, and 12, I'll reiterate a short list of recommendations for easy reference here:

- Choose narrow columns for indexes.

- Ensure that the selectivity of the data in the candidate column is very high (that is, the column must have a large number of unique values).

- Prefer columns with the integer data type (or variants of the integer data type). Also, avoid indexes on columns with string data types such as VARCHAR.

- Consider listing columns having higher selectivity first in a multicolumn index.

- Use the INCLUDE list in an index as a way to make an index cover the index key structure without changing that structure. Do this by adding columns to the key, which enables you to avoid expensive lookup operations.

- When deciding which columns to index, pay extra attention to the queries' WHERE clauses and JOIN criteria columns and HAVING clause. These can serve as the entry points into the tables, especially if a WHERE clause criterion on a column filters the data on a highly selective value or constant. Such a clause can make the column a prime candidate for an index.

- When choosing the type of an index (clustered or nonclustered), keep in mind the advantages and disadvantages of clustered and nonclustered index types.

Be extra careful when designing a clustered index because every nonclustered index on the table depends on the clustered index. Therefore, follow these recommendations when designing and implementing clustered indexes:

- Keep the clustered indexes as narrow as possible. You don't want to widen all your nonclustered indexes by having a wide clustered index.

- Create the clustered index first and then create the nonclustered indexes on the table.

- If required, rebuild a clustered index in a single step using the DROP_EXISTING = {ON|OFF} command in the CREATE INDEX command. You don't want to rebuild all the nonclustered indexes on the table twice: once when the clustered index is dropped and again when the clustered index is re-created.

- Do not create a clustered index on a frequently updated column. If you do so, the nonclustered indexes on the table will create additional load by remaining in sync with the clustered index key values.

- Where applicable, such as when you need aggregations across large data sets, consider using columnstore indexes.

To keep track of the indexes you've created and determine others that you need to create, you should take advantage of the dynamic management views that SQL Server 2014 makes available to you. By checking the data in sys.dm_db_index_usage_stats on a regular basis—say once a week or so—you can determine which of your indexes are actually being used and which are redundant. Indexes that are not contributing to your queries to help you improve performance are just a drain on the system. They require both more disk space and additional I/O to maintain the data inside the index as the data in the table changes. On the other hand, querying sys.dm_db_missing_indexes_details will show potential indexes deemed missing by the system and even suggest INCLUDE columns. You can access the DMV sys.dm_db_missing_indexes_groups_ stats to see aggregate information about the number of times queries are called that could have benefited from a particular group of indexes. Just remember to test these suggestions thoroughly and don't assume that they will be correct. All these suggestions are just that: suggestions. All these tips can be combined to give you an optimal method for maintaining the indexes in your system over the long term.

Avoiding the Use of the sp_ Prefix for Stored Procedure Names

As a rule, don't use the sp_ prefix for user stored procedures since SQL Server assumes that stored procedures with the sp_ prefix are system stored procedures, and these are supposed to be in the master database. Using sp or usp as the prefix for user stored procedures is quite common. This is neither a major performance hit nor a major problem, but why court trouble? The performance hit of the sp_ prefix is explained in detail in the "Be Careful Naming Stored Procedures" section of Chapter 19. Getting rid of prefixes entirely is a fine way to go. You have plenty of space for descriptive object names. There is no need for odd abbreviations that don't add to the functional definition of the queries.

Minimizing the Use of Triggers

Triggers provide an attractive method for automating behavior within the database. Since they fire as data is manipulated by other processes (regardless of the processes), triggers can be used to ensure certain functions are run as the data changes. That same functionality makes them dangerous since they are not immediately visible to the developer or DBA working on a system. They must be taken into account when designing queries and when troubleshooting performance problems. Because they carry a somewhat hidden cost, triggers should be considered carefully. Before using a trigger, make sure that the only way to solve the problem presented is with a trigger. If you do use a trigger, document that fact in as many places as you can to ensure that the existence of the trigger is taken into account by other developers and DBAs.

Consider Putting Tables into In-Memory Storage

While there are a large number of limitations on the new in-memory storage mechanisms, the performance benefits are high. If you have a high volume OLTP system and you're seeing lots of contention on I/O, especially around latches, the in-memory storage is a viable option. You may also want to explore using in-memory storage for table variables to help enhance their performance. If you have data that doesn't have to persist, you can even create the table in-memory using the SCHEMA_ONLY durability option. All these methods lead to significant performance benefits. But remember, you must have the memory available to support these options. There's nothing magic here. You're enhancing performance by throwing significant amounts of memory, and therefore money, at the problem. You also have to be running the Enterprise version of SQL Server to make this work.

Configuration Settings

Here's a checklist of the server and database configurations settings that have a big impact on database performance:

- Memory configuration options
- Cost threshold for parallelism
- Max degree of parallelism
- Optimize for ad hoc workloads
- Blocked process threshold
- Database file layout
- Database compression

I cover these settings in more detail in the sections that follow.

Memory Configuration Options

As explained in the "SQL Server Memory Management" section of Chapter 2, it is strongly recommended that the max server memory setting be configured to a nondefault value determined by the system configuration. These memory configurations of SQL Server are explained in detail in the "Memory Bottleneck Analysis" and "Memory Bottleneck Resolutions" sections of Chapter 2.

Cost Threshold for Parallelism

On systems with multiple processors, the parallel execution of queries is possible. The default value for parallelism is 5. This represents a cost estimate by the optimizer of a five-second execution on the query. In most circumstances, I've found this value to be too low; in other words, a higher threshold for parallelism results in better performance. Testing on your system will help you determine the appropriate value. Suggesting a value for this can be considered somewhat dangerous, but I'm going to do it anyway. I'd begin testing with a value of 35 and see where things go from there.

Max Degree of Parallelism

When a system has multiple processors available, by default SQL Server will use all of them during parallel executions. To better control the load on the machine, you may find it useful to limit the number of processors used by parallel executions. Further, you may need to set the affinity so that certain processors are reserved for the operating system and other services running alongside SQL Server. OLTP systems may receive a benefit from disabling parallelism entirely. Try increasing the cost threshold for parallelism first because, even in OLTP systems, there are queries that will benefit from parallel execution. You may also explore the possibility of using the Resource Governor to control some workloads.

Optimize for Ad Hoc Workloads

If the primary calls being made to your system come in as ad hoc or dynamic SQL instead of through well-defined stored procedures or parameterized queries, such as you might find in some of the implementation of object relational mapping (ORM) software, then turning on the optimize for ad hoc workloads setting will reduce the consumption of procedure cache because plan stubs are created for initial query calls instead of full execution plans. This is covered in detail in Chapter 17.

Blocked Process Threshold

The blocked process threshold setting defines in seconds when a blocked process report is fired. When a query runs and exceeds the threshold, the report is fired. An alert, which can be used to send an e-mail or a text message, is also fired. Testing an individual system determines what value to set this to. You can monitor for this using events within traces defined by SQL Profiler.

Database File Layout

For easy reference, the following are the best practices you should consider when laying out database files:

- Place the data and transaction log files of a user database on different disks. This allows the transaction log disk head to progress sequentially without being moved randomly by the nonsequential I/Os commonly used for the data files.

- Placing the transaction log on a dedicated disk also enhances data protection. If a database disk fails, you will be able to save the completed transactions until the point of failure by performing a backup of the transaction log. By using this last transaction log backup during the recovery process, you will be able to recover the database up to the point of failure. This is known as *point-in-time recovery*.

- Avoid RAID 5 for transaction logs because, for every write request, RAID 5 disk arrays incur twice the number of disk I/Os compared to RAID 1 or 10.

- You may choose RAID 5 for data files, since even in a heavy OLTP system, the number of read requests is usually seven to eight times the number of write requests. Also, for read requests the performance of RAID 5 is similar to that of RAID 1 and RAID 10 with an equal number of total disks.

- Look into moving to a more modern disk subsystem like SSD or FusionIO.

For a detailed understanding of database file layout and RAID subsystems, please refer to the "Disk Bottleneck Resolutions" section of Chapter 3.

Database Compression

SQL Server has supplied data compression since 2008 with the Enterprise and Developer editions of the product. This can provide a great benefit in space used and in performance as more data gets stored on a page. These benefits come at the cost of added overhead in the CPU and memory of the system; however, the benefits usually far outweigh the costs. Take this into account as you implement compression.

Database Administration

For your reference, here is a short list of the performance-related database administrative activities that you should perform on a regular basis as part of the process of managing your database server:

- Keep the statistics up-to-date.

- Maintain a minimum amount of index defragmentation.

- Avoid automatic database functions such as AUTOCLOSE or AUTOSHRINK.

- Minimize the overhead of SQL tracing.

In the following sections, I cover the preceding activities in more detail.

■ **Note** For a detailed explanation of SQL Server 2014 administration needs and methods, please refer to the Microsoft SQL Server Books Online article "Database Engine Features and Tasks" (http://bit.ly/SIlz8d).

Keep the Statistics Up-to-Date

The performance impact of database statistics is explained in detail in Chapter 12; however, this short list will serve as a quick and easy reference for keeping your statistics up-to-date:

- Allow SQL Server to automatically maintain the statistics of the data distribution in the tables by using the default settings for the configuration parameters AUTO_CREATE_ STATISTICS and AUTO_UPDATE_STATISTICS.

- As a proactive measure, you can programmatically update the statistics of every database object on a regular basis as you determine it is needed and supported within your system. This practice partly protects your database from having outdated statistics in case the auto update statistics feature fails to provide a satisfactory result. In Chapter 12, I illustrate how to set up a SQL Server job to programmatically update the statistics on a regular basis.

- Remember that you also have the ability to update the statistics in an asynchronous fashion. This reduces the contention on stats as they're being updated; thus, if you have a system with fairly constant access, you can use this method to update the statistics more frequently.

■ **Note** Please ensure that the statistics update job is scheduled before the completion of the index defragmentation job, as explained later in this chapter.

Maintain a Minimum Amount of Index Defragmentation

The following best practices will help you maintain a minimum amount of index defragmentation:

- Defragment a database on a regular basis during nonpeak hours.

- On a regular basis, determine the level of fragmentation on your indexes; then, based on that fragmentation, either rebuild the index or defrag the index by executing the defragmentation queries outlined in Chapter 13.

- Remember that very small tables don't need to be defragmented at all.

- Different rules may apply for very large databases when it comes to defragmenting indexes.

- If you have indexes that are only ever used for single seek operations, then fragmentation doesn't impact performance.

Avoid Database Functions Such As AUTO_CLOSE or AUTO_SHRINK

AUTO_CLOSE cleanly shuts down a database and frees all its resources when the last user connection is closed. This means all data and queries in the cache are automatically flushed. When the next connection comes in, not only does the database have to restart but all the data has to be reloaded into the cache. Also, stored procedures and the other queries have to be recompiled. That's an extremely expensive operation for most database systems. Leave AUTO_CLOSE set to the default of OFF.

AUTO_SHRINK periodically shrinks the size of the database. It can shrink the data files and, when in Simple Recovery mode, the log files. While doing this, it can block other processes, seriously slowing down your system. More often than not, file growth is also set to occur automatically on systems with AUTO_SHRINK enabled, so your system will be slowed down yet again when the data or log files have to grow. Further, you're going to see the physical file storage get fragmented at the operating system level, seriously impacting performance. Set your database sizes to an appropriate size, and monitor them for growth needs. If you must grow them automatically, do so by physical increments, not by percentages.

Database Backup

Database backup is a broad topic and can't be given due justice in this query optimization book. Nevertheless, I suggest that when it comes to database performance, you be attentive to the following aspects of your database backup process:

- Differential and transaction log backup frequency

- Backup distribution

- Backup compression

The next sections go into more detail on these suggestions.

Incremental and Transaction Log Backup Frequency

For an OLTP database, it is mandatory that the database be backed up regularly so that, in case of a failure, the database can be restored on a different server. For large databases, the full database backup usually takes a long time, so full backups cannot be performed often. Consequently, full backups are performed at widespread time intervals, with incremental backups and transaction log backups scheduled more frequently between two consecutive full backups. With the frequent incremental and transaction log backups set in place, if a database fails completely, the database can be restored up to a point in time.

Differential backups can be used to reduce the overhead of a full backup by backing up only the data that has changed since the last full backup. Because this is potentially much faster, it will cause less of a slowdown on the production system. Each situation is unique, so you need to find the method that works best for you. As a general rule, I recommend taking a weekly full backup and then daily differential backups. From there, you can determine the needs of your transaction log backups.

Frequently backing up of the transaction log adds a small amount of overhead to the server, especially during peak hours.

For most businesses, the acceptable amount of data loss (in terms of time) usually takes precedence over conserving the log-disk space or providing ideal database performance. Therefore, you must take into account the acceptable amount of data loss when scheduling the transaction log backup, as opposed to randomly setting the backup schedule to a low-time interval.

Backup Scheduling Distribution

When multiple databases need to be backed up, you must ensure that all full backups are not scheduled at the same time so that the hardware resources are not hit at the same time. If the backup process involves backing up the databases to a central SAN disk array, then the full backups from all the database servers must be distributed across the backup time window so that the central backup infrastructure doesn't get slammed by too many backup requests at the same time. Flooding the central infrastructure with a great deal of backup requests at the same time forces the components of the infrastructure to spend a significant part of their resources just managing the excessive number of requests. This mismanaged use of the resources increases the backup durations significantly, causing the full backups to continue during peak hours and thus affecting the performance of the user requests.

To minimize the impact of the full backup process on database performance, you must first determine the nonpeak hours when full backups can be scheduled and then distribute the full backups across the nonpeak time window, as follows:

1. Identify the number of databases that must be backed up.

2. Prioritize the databases in order of their importance to the business.

3. Determine the nonpeak hours when the full database backups can be scheduled.

4. Calculate the time interval between two consecutive full backups as follows:
   Time interval = (Total backup time window) / (Number of full backups).

5. Schedule the full backups in order of the database priorities, with the first backup starting at the start time of the backup window and subsequent backups spread uniformly at the time intervals calculated in the preceding equation.

This uniform distribution of the full backups will ensure that the backup infrastructure is not flooded with too many backup requests at the same time, thereby reducing the impact of the full backups on the database performance.

Backup Compression

For relatively large databases, the backup durations and backup file sizes usually become an issue. Long backup durations make it difficult to complete the backups within the administrative time windows and thus start affecting the end user's experience. The large size of the backup files makes space management for the backup files quite challenging, and it increases the pressure on the network when the backups are performed across the network to a central backup infrastructure. Compression also acts to speed up the backup process since fewer writes to the disk are needed.

The recommended way to optimize the backup duration, the backup file size, and the resultant network pressure is to use *backup compression*. SQL Server 2008R2 SP1 and greater allows for backup compression for the Standard edition and better.

Query Design

Here's a list of the performance-related best practices you should follow when designing the database queries:

- Use the command SET NOCOUNT ON.
- Explicitly define the owner of an object.
- Avoid *nonsargable* search conditions.
- Avoid arithmetic operators and functions on WHERE clause columns.
- Avoid optimizer hints.
- Stay away from nesting views.
- Ensure there are no implicit data type conversions.
- Minimize logging overhead.
- Adopt best practices for reusing execution plans.
- Adopt best practices for database transactions.
- Eliminate or reduce the overhead of database cursors.
- Natively compile stored procedures.

I further detail each best practice in the following sections.

Use the Command SET NOCOUNT ON

As a rule, always use the command SET NOCOUNT ON as the first statement in stored procedures, triggers, and other batch queries. This enables you to avoid the network overhead associated with the return of the number of rows affected after every execution of a SQL statement. The command SET NOCOUNT is explained in detail in the "Use SET NOCOUNT" section of Chapter 19.

Explicitly Define the Owner of an Object

As a performance best practice, always qualify a database object with its owner to avoid the runtime cost required to verify the owner of the object. The performance benefit of explicitly qualifying the owner of a database object is explained in detail in the "Do Not Allow Implicit Resolution of Objects in Queries" section of Chapter 15.

Avoid Nonsargable Search Conditions

Be vigilant when defining the search conditions in your query. If the search condition on a column used in the WHERE clause prevents the optimizer from effectively using the index on that column, then the execution cost for the query will be high in spite of the presence of the correct index. The performance impact of nonsargable search conditions is explained in detail in the corresponding section of Chapter 18.

Additionally, please be careful when about providing too much flexibility on search capabilities. If you define an application feature such as "retrieve all products with product name ending in caps," then you will have queries scanning the complete table (or the clustered index). As you know, scanning a multimillion-row table will hurt your database performance. Unless you use an index hint, you won't be able to benefit from the index on that column. However, using an index hint overrides the decisions of the query optimizer, so it's generally not recommended that you use index hints either (see Chapter 18 for more information). To understand the performance impact of such a business rule, consider the following SELECT statement:

```
SELECT   p.*
FROM     Production.Product AS p
WHERE    p.[Name] LIKE '%Caps';
```

In Figure 26-4, you can see that the execution plan used the index on the [Name] column, but it had to perform a scan instead of a seek. Since an index on a column with character data types (such as CHAR and VARCHAR) sorts the data values for the column on the leading-end characters, using a leading % in the LIKE condition doesn't allow a seek operation into the index. The matching rows may be distributed throughout the index rows, making the index ineffective for the search condition and thereby hurting the performance of the query.

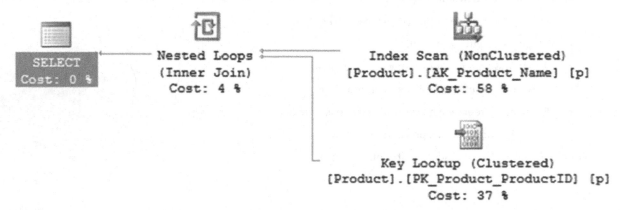

Figure 26-4. An execution plan showing a clustered index scan caused by a nonsargable LIKE clause

Avoid Arithmetic Expressions on the WHERE Clause Column

Always try to avoid using arithmetic operators and functions on columns in the WHERE and JOIN clauses. Using operators and functions on columns prevents the use of indexes on those columns. The performance impact of using arithmetic operators on WHERE clause columns is explained in detail in the "Avoid Arithmetic Operators on the WHERE Clause Column" section of Chapter 18, and the impact of using functions is explained in detail in the "Avoid Functions on the WHERE Clause Column" section of the same chapter.

To see this in action, consider the following queries:

```
SELECT  soh.SalesOrderNumber
FROM    Sales.SalesOrderHeader AS soh
WHERE   'SO5' = LEFT(SalesOrderNumber, 3);

SELECT  soh.SalesOrderNumber
FROM    Sales.SalesOrderHeader AS soh
WHERE   SalesOrderNumber LIKE 'SO5%';
```

These queries basically implement the same logic: they check SalesOrderNumber to see whether it is equal to SO5. However, the first query performs a function on the SalesOrderNumber column, while the second uses a LIKE clause to check for the same data. Figure 26-5 shows the resulting execution plans.

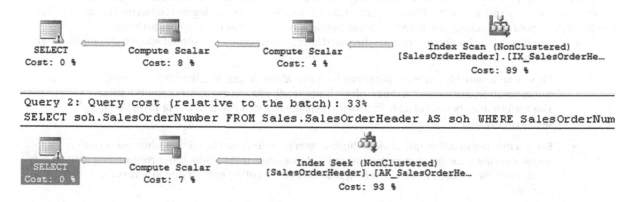

Figure 26-5. *Execution plans showing a function that prevents index use*

As you can see in Figure 26-5, the first query forces an Index Scan operation, while the second is able to perform a nice, clean Index Seek. These examples demonstrate clearly why you should avoid functions and operators on WHERE clause columns.

The warning you see in the plans relates to the implicit conversion occurring within the calculated columns in the SalesOrderHeader table.

Avoid Optimizer Hints

As a rule, avoid the use of optimizer hints, such as index hints and join hints, because they overrule the decision-making process of the optimizer. In most cases, the optimizer is smart enough to generate efficient execution plans, and it works the best without any optimizer hint imposed on it. The same applies to plan guides. Forcing a plan will help in rare circumstances, but it's usually better to rely on the optimizer to make good choices. For a detailed understanding of the performance impact of optimizer hints, please refer to the "Avoiding Optimizer Hints" section of Chapter 18.

Stay Away from Nesting Views

A nested view exists when one view calls another view, which calls more views, and so on. This can lead to confusing code for two reasons. First, the views are masking the operations being performed. Second, the query may be simple, but the execution plan and subsequent operations by the SQL engine can be complex and expensive. This occurs because the optimizer doesn't have time to simplify the query, eliminating tables and columns it doesn't need; instead, the optimizer assumes that all tables and columns are needed. The same rule applies to nesting user-defined functions.

Ensure No Implicit Data Type Conversions

When you create variables in a query, be sure those variables are of the same data type as the columns that they will be used to compare against. Even though SQL Server can and will convert, for example, a VARCHAR to a DATE, that implicit conversion can prevent indexes from being used. You have to be just as careful in situations like table joins so that the primary key data type of one table matches the foreign key of the table being joined. You may occasionally see a warning in the execution plan to help you with this, but you can't count on this.

Minimize Logging Overhead

SQL Server maintains the old and new states of every atomic action (or transaction) in the transaction log to ensure database consistency and durability. This can place tremendous pressure on the log disk, often making the log disk a point of contention. Therefore, to improve database performance, you must try to optimize the transaction log overhead. In addition to the hardware solutions discussed later in the chapter, you should adopt the following query-design best practices:

- Choose table variables over temporary tables for small result sets, less than 20 to 50 rows, where possible. Remember: If the result set is not small, you can encounter serious issues. The performance benefit of table variables is explained in detail in the "Using Table Variables" section of Chapter 17.

- Batch a number of action queries in a single transaction. You must be careful when using this option because if too many rows are affected within a single transaction, the corresponding database objects will be locked for a long time, blocking all other users trying to access the objects.

- Reduce the amount of logging of certain operations by using the Bulk Logged recovery model. This rule applies primarily when dealing with large-scale data manipulation. You also will use minimal logging when Bulk Logged is enabled, and you use the WRITE clause of the UPDATE statement or drop or create indexes.

Adopt Best Practices for Reusing Execution Plans

The best practices for optimizing the cost of plan generation can be broadly classified into these two categories:

- Caching execution plans effectively
- Minimizing recompilation of execution plans

Caching Execution Plans Effectively

You must ensure that the execution plans for your queries are not only cached but reused often. Do so by adopting the following best practices:

- Avoid executing queries as nonparameterized, ad hoc queries. Instead, parameterize the variable parts of a query and submit the parameterized query using a stored procedure or the spexecutesql system stored procedure.

- If you must use lots of ad hoc queries, enable the Optimize for Ad Hoc Workload option, which will create a plan stub instead of a full plan the first time a query is called. This radically reduces the amount of procedure cache used.

- Use the same environment settings (such as ANSI NULLS) in every connection that executes the same parameterized queries. This is important because the execution plan for a query is dependent on the environment settings of the connection.

- As explained earlier in the "Explicitly Define the Owner of an Object" section, explicitly qualify the owner of the objects when accessing them in your queries.

The preceding aspects of plan caching are explained in detail in Chapter 16.

Minimizing Recompilation of Execution Plans

To minimize the cost of generating execution plans for queries, you must ensure that the plans in the cache are not invalidated or recompiled for reasons that are under your control. The following recommended best practices minimize the recompilation of stored procedure plans:

- Do not interleave DDL and DML statements in your stored procedures. You should put all the DDL statements at the top of the stored procedures.

- In a stored procedure, avoid using temporary tables that are created outside the stored procedure.

- Prefer table variables over temporary tables for small data sets.

- Do not change the ANSI SET options within a stored procedure.

- If you really can't avoid a recompilation, then identify the stored procedure statement that is causing the recompilation, and execute it through the sp_execute_sql system stored procedure.

The causes of stored procedure recompilation and the recommended solutions are explained in detail in Chapter 17.

Adopt Best Practices for Database Transactions

The more effectively you design your queries for concurrency, the faster the queries will be able to complete without blocking one another. Consider the following recommendations while designing the transactions in your queries:

- Keep the scope of the transactions as short as possible. In a transaction, include only the statements that must be committed together for data consistency.

- Prevent the possibility of transactions being left open because of poor error-handling routines or application logic. Do so using the following techniques:

  - Use SET XACTABORT ON to ensure that a transaction is aborted or rolled back on an error condition within the transaction.

  - After executing a stored procedure or a batch of queries containing a transaction from a client code, always check for an open transaction and then roll back any open transactions using the following SQL statement:

    ```
    IF @@TRANCOUNT > 0 ROLLBACK
    ```

- Use the lowest level of transaction isolation required to maintain data consistency as determined by your application requirements. The amount of isolation provided by the Read Committed isolation level, the default isolation level, is sufficient most of the time. If excessive locking is occurring, consider using the Read Committed Snapshot isolation level.

The impact of transactions on database performance is explained in detail in Chapter 19.

Eliminate or Reduce the Overhead of Database Cursors

Since SQL Server is designed to work with sets of data, processing multiple rows using DML statements is generally much faster than processing the rows one by one using database cursors. If you find yourself using lots of cursors, reexamine the logic to see whether there are ways you can eliminate the cursors. If you must use a database cursor, then use the database cursor with the least overhead: the FASTFORWARD cursor type (generally referred to as the *fast-forward-only cursor*). You can also use the equivalent DataReader object in ADO.NET.

The performance overhead of database cursors is explained in detail in Chapter 22.

Natively Compile Stored Procedures

In situations where you're accessing only in-memory tables, you have one additional performance enhancement open to you, which is to compile your stored procedures into a DLL that runs within the SQL Server executable. As was shown in Chapter 23, this has fairly radical performance implications. Just be sure that you call the procedures in the correct fashion passing parameters by ordinal position rather than by parameter name. Although this feels like you're breaking a best practice, it leads to better performance of the compiled procedure.

Summary

Performance optimization is an ongoing process. It requires continual attention to database and query characteristics that affect performance. The goal of this chapter was to provide you with a checklist of these characteristics to serve as a quick and easy reference during the development and maintenance phases of your database applications.

Index

■ E

■ K

■ L

Get the eBook for only $10!

Now you can take the weightless companion with you anywhere, anytime. Your purchase of this book entitles you to 3 electronic versions for only $10.

This Apress title will prove so indispensible that you'll want to carry it with you everywhere, which is why we are offering the eBook in 3 formats for only $10 if you have already purchased the print book.

Convenient and fully searchable, the PDF version enables you to easily find and copy code—or perform examples by quickly toggling between instructions and applications. The MOBI format is ideal for your Kindle, while the ePUB can be utilized on a variety of mobile devices.

Go to www.apress.com/promo/tendollars to purchase your companion eBook.